WOMEN IN THE WORLD'S LEGAL PROFESSIONS

Oñati International Series in Law and Society
A SERIES PUBLISHED FOR THE OÑATI INSTITUTE
FOR THE SOCIOLOGY OF LAW

General Editors

William LF Felstiner   Eve Darian-Smith

Board of General Editors

Johannes Feest   Peter Fitzpatrick
Hazel Genn   Eliane Junqueira
Hubert Rottleuthner   Ronen Shamir

Titles in this Series

Social Dynamics of Crime and Control: New Theories for a World in Transition
Edited by Susanne Karstedt and Kai-D Bussmann

Criminal Policy in Transition
Edited by Penny Green and Andrew Rutherford

Making Law for Families
Edited by Mavis Maclean

Poverty and the Law
Edited by Peter Robson and Asbjørn Kjønstad

Adapting Legal Cultures
Edited by David Nelken and Johannes Feest

Rethinking Law, Society and Governance: Foucault's Bequest
Edited by Gary Wickham and George Pavlich

Rules and Networks
Edited by Richard Appelbaum, William LF Felstiner and Volkmar Gessner

Women in the World's Legal Professions

Edited by

ULRIKE SCHULTZ

and

GISELA SHAW

Oñati International Series in Law and Society

A SERIES PUBLISHED FOR THE OÑATI INSTITUTE
FOR THE SOCIOLOGY OF LAW

·HART·
PUBLISHING

OXFORD – PORTLAND OREGON
2003

Hart Publishing
Oxford and Portland, Oregon

Published in North America (US and Canada) by
Hart Publishing c/o
International Specialized Book Services
5804 NE Hassalo Street
Portland, Oregon
97213-3644
USA

Hart Publishing is a specialist legal publisher based in Oxford, England.
To order further copies of this book or to request a list of other
publications please write to:

Hart Publishing, Salter's Boatyard, Folly Bridge,
Abingdon Road, Oxford OX1 4LB
Telephone: +44 (0)1865 245533 or Fax: +44 (0)1865 794882
e-mail: mail@hartpub.co.uk
WEBSITE: http//www.hartpub.co.uk

British Library Cataloguing in Publication Data
Data Available
ISBN 1–84113–319–1 (cloth)
1–84113–320–5 (paper)

Typeset by Hope Services (Abingdon) Ltd.
Printed and bound in Great Britain on acid-free paper by
Biddles Ltd, www.biddles.co.uk

Contents

Preface

The origins of this anthology on women in the legal profession can be traced back well over a decade. It was in the early 1980s that I, Ulrike Schultz, joined an international working group on the legal profession, convened by Rick Abel and Philip Lewis. Three years later (July 1984) I attended their conference on the legal profession at the Rockefeller Foundation Centre in Bellagio on Lake Como, where a number of participants presented national reports on the situation of the legal profession in their respective countries. Methodological and theoretical tools for comparison and evaluation were suggested and developed. Market control theory and the professional project were magic notions pervading the discussion, uniting some, dividing others.

In most of the national reports, the situation of women lawyers was barely referred to. No one had as yet given the matter much thought, although the numbers of women studying at law schools and being admitted to the bar were rising in most countries (with the notable exception of Japan, the Islamic states and a number of other countries characterised by a strongly traditional social order). Only one of the leisurely evening meetings under the big tree on the terrace of Villa Serbelloni was devoted to the subject. There, in a relaxed atmosphere, it occurred to participants that this might be one of the salient issues affecting future developments in the legal profession.

At that time just one monograph had been published on women in the legal profession, namely Cynthia Fuchs Epstein's *Women in Law* (1981). Having compiled and analysed the findings of the papers presented at Bellagio, Carrie Menkel-Meadow created the first comparative and comprehensive picture of women in the legal profession from a cross-cultural and cross-national perspective. Her report was published in 1989 in the third volume of Abel's and Lewis' *Lawyers in Society*, a work which itself arose out of the Bellagio conference. Cynthia Fuchs Epstein had focused on the questions why women's entry into the legal profession had occurred so late and so reluctantly and what, once they had arrived, had impeded their career progress. She had scrutinised techniques and strategies of exclusion and on the basis of her research findings had developed the notion of the 'glass ceiling'. Carrie Menkel-Meadow approached her subject with different questions in mind. Given the undeniable rise in women's share in the legal profession, would their presence change the profession or would the profession change them? Put slightly differently: would women lawyers, in the longer run, turn out to be winners or losers? and: would their participation benefit or damage the profession in terms of status, reputation, income, quality of work etc? Agreeing with Carol Gilligan's (1981) views, Menkel-Meadow took an essential psychological difference between the two sexes as given. In

1985 I began to set up a training programme on 'Women and Law' ('Frauen im Recht') for my university, the FernUniversität Hagen, Germany, aiming to compile and structure any available data concerning women's issues in law and concepts of women's rights in Germany. Drawing on Carrie Menkel-Meadow's categories and grid for description and evaluation, I produced a teaching unit on 'Women in the Legal Profession in Germany'. In 1989 I met Carrie in Aix-en-Provence in France at a conference of the Legal Profession Group which had continued working on international and comparative issues. It was at this juncture that it was decided to try and organise a 'Women in the Legal Profession' project along the lines of the Abel/Lewis venture (Abel and Lewis 1988a, 1988b, 1989). The first step was to draft a research agenda and to mobilise potential collaborators. At the large international joint meeting of socio-legal associations in Amsterdam in 1991, feminism in socio-legal work had become a major topic, and a first session on women in the legal profession was held. In 1994 at the biannual meeting of the Legal Profession Group in Rouen in France, the existence of a women's working group co-ordinated by myself was formally sanctioned.

There followed for me a busy period of setting up a network of interested colleagues (most but not all of them female) and of (mainly electronic) correspondence, leading up to the writing and presenting of conference papers: at the big socio-legal conference in Glasgow and the meeting of the Legal Profession Group in Peyresq in France (both 1996); at the biannual meeting of the Research Committee for the Sociology of Law in Antwerp (1997) where, at a plenary session, a synthesis of work done so far was presented; and at the meeting of the Legal Profession Group at the International Institute for the Sociology of Law (IISL) in Oñati, Spain (1998), where, in recognition of the significance of the group's work, the Women in the Legal Profession panel was invited to occupy the opening session.

By the time plans for this book began to take shape, I had met my future collaborator in this venture—Gisela Shaw, Professor of German Studies in Bristol, England. As a team, we have been able to bring to this truly interdisciplinary and international project a range of mutually complementary expertise, skills and personal strengths, not to mention encouragement and support for each other.

The project reached its peak at a specially designed conference/workshop on Women in the Legal Profession at the IISL in Oñati, Spain, in July 1999, when most of the papers in this volume had their first public airing. Contributors who were unable to attend presented their papers at the subsequent meeting of the Legal Profession Group in Peyresq, France (July 2000).

Some of our authors turned to the subject afresh simply because it inspired them. Others had been compiling data and preparing their papers over a number of years. There are contributors who had already published in the field, including books on women in the legal profession, and who were therefore able to draw on considerable expertise and data. All articles were written specially for this collection, most of them with a comparative perspective in mind, resulting in an up-to-date and comprehensive picture of women in the legal profession in a whole range of countries.

The project is truly transdisciplinary. Except for Gisela Shaw (a philosopher come Germanist), authors divide evenly into lawyers and sociologists. All ranks of the academic hierarchy are represented. Some are specialists in feminist subjects, such as Harriet Silius and Malgorzata Fuszara both of whom head a women's study programme in their respective universities. Most (22 out of 25) are female, but our Group circulation lists and attendance at the 1999 Oñati workshop reflect a wider cross-gender interest. It is intriguing to reflect on the fact that at the seminal Bellagio meeting in 1984, of the 27 participants only five were women. But these five have remained committed to their work on the legal profession, amongst them three contributors to this volume (Anne Boigeol, Georgina Murray, and Ulrike Schultz).

As can be expected in the context of women's projects, time management has been a particularly important factor as writing often adds yet another burden to contributors' already considerable workload (most of the authors are mothers). All the more reason to celebrate our joint achievement. Another hurdle to overcome has been language. For only fourteen of our authors is English their mother-tongue. This helps to explain not only a slight over-representation of Anglo-American perspectives, but also the occasional idiosyncratic use of the English language on the part of those valiantly struggling with the foreign idiom.

Different generations of women are represented amongst the authors, the youngest being in her late twenties and the oldest having celebrated her sixtieth birthday. This has further enriched the overall picture presented as differing ages reflect differing experiences and patterns of exposure to discrimination and rejection.[1]

Producing a work of this kind is, by its very nature, not only a protracted but also a complex operation. This has also meant that successful completion presupposed availability of advice, assistance and practical support from a whole host of colleagues, friends and helpers, too numerous to thank here individually. We are particularly grateful to the IISL at Oñati and its staff for providing the venue and structural framework for our very intensive and fruitful 1999 meeting. Successive Institute Directors Pierre Guibentif, Jacek Kurszewski and Bill Felstiner, the latter also Chair of the Legal Profession Group and a friend and adviser of long standing, have done a great deal to facilitate the project's successful completion. Invaluable organisational support was provided by Malen Gordoa Mendizabal, while José Antonio Azpiazu added a regional flavour to the conference programme with his talk on the history of

---

[1] Unfortunately, Carmen Luisa Roche from Venezuela was prevented by serious illness from completing her contribution for this volume. It will now appear in a special issue of the *International Journal of the Legal Profession* dedicated to the subject of women in the legal profession. This issue will also contain an agenda for further research in this area and will signal a slight shift of focus from women to gender.

women in the Basque country and his expert guidance through the art and archi-
tectural treasures of Oñati. Final editorial work was expertly carried out by
Sandra Hansen at the FernUniversität.

Ulrike Schultz and Gisela Shaw

REFERENCES

Abel, Richard and Phillip Lewis (eds). 1988–1989. *Lawyers in Society*. Vol. 1: *The
    Common Law World*. Vol. 2: *The Civil Law World*. Vol. 3: *Comparative Theories*.
    Berkeley: University of California Press.
Epstein, Cynthia Fuchs. 1981. *Women in Law*. Garden City/New York: Basic Book
    Publishers.
Menkel-Meadow, Carrie. 1989. Feminization of the Legal Profession: The Comparative
    Sociology of Women Lawyers, in Abel, Richard and Phillip Lewis (eds). 1989.
    Lawyers in Society. Vol. 3: *Comparative Theories*. Berkeley: University of California
    Press, 196–255.

List of Contributors

Bryna Bogoch is a Senior Lecturer in the Department of Political Studies and the Department of Interdisciplinary Social Science Studies, Bar Ilan University, Ramat Gan, Israel. She was principal researcher of a study on gender bias in the Israeli courts, supported by the Ford Foundation.

Anne Boigeol is a researcher at the Institut d'histoire du temps présent at the Centre National de la Recherche Scientifique (CNRS) in Paris.

Joan Brockman is a professor at the School of Criminology, Simon Fraser University, Burnaby, British Columbia, Canada.

William LF Felstiner is Distinguished Research Professor of Law, Cardiff University, and Scientific Director, International Institute for the Sociology of Law, Oñati, Spain.

Malgorzata Fuszara is an assistant professor, Director of the Institute of Applied Social Sciences, and Head of the Centre for Socio-Legal Studies on the Situation of Women and of the Gender Studies Programme at the University of Warsaw, Poland.

Leny E de Groot-van Leuwen is associate professor of sociology of law at the University of Nijmegen, The Netherlands.

Rosemary Hunter is professor and Dean of law and former Director of the Socio-Legal Research Centre at Griffith University, Brisbane, Australia.

Heleen FP Ietswaart is professor of feminist jurisprudence at the Erasmus University, Rotterdam, The Netherlands.

Eliane Junqueira is professor of sociology of law at the Pontifícia Universidade Católica do Rio de Janeiro, Brazil, and Director of the Instituto Direito e Sociedade.

Yuriko Kaminaga is professor of law at the Senshu University, Japan.

Fiona Kay is associate professor of sociology at the Queen's University, Kingston, Ontario, Canada.

Haesook Kim is associate professor of sociology at Long Island University, New York, USA.

Allan Lind is the Finch Distinguished Professor of Business Administration at Duke University, USA.

Kate Malleson is a senior lecturer in law at the London School of Economics, UK.

Lynn Mather is professor of law and political science and Director of the Baldy Center for Law and Social Policy at the University at Buffalo, USA. Formerly the Nelson A. Rockefeller Chair of Government at Dartmouth College, USA, she was also President of the Law & Society Association.

Clare McGlynn is a reader in the Department of Law, University of Durham, UK; she previously taught at the University of Newcastle upon Tyne, UK, and as visiting associate professor at Stockholm University (1999–2000).

Mary Jane Mossman is professor of law at Osgoode Hall Law School of York University in Toronto, Canada, and has been a visiting scholar at the Universities of Sydney (Australia), Kobe (Japan), Columbia (USA), and Aix Marseilles (France).

Georgina Murray is a senior lecturer in humanities at Griffith University, Brisbane, Queensland, Australia.

Vittorio Olgiati is a qualified lawyer and associate professor in the faculty of sociology at the University of Urbino, Italy.

Nils Olsen was until recently a visiting lecturer in the Department of Psychology at the University of North Carolina at Chapel Hill, USA.

Ben Pettit is a lawyer and currently studying for a PhD in political science at the University of California at Santa Barbara, USA.

Deborah L Rhode is professor of law and Director of the Keck Center on the Legal Profession, Stanford University, USA, former Director of the Institute for Research on Women and Gender, former President of the Association of American Law Schools and current Chair of the American Bar Association's Commission on Women in the Profession.

Ulrike Schultz is a senior academic (*Akademische Oberrätin*) in law at the *FernUniversität* Hagen, Germany (the German distance-learning university), Head of the law faculty's Teaching and Learning Unit, and Chair of the university's Equal Opportunities Commission. She acts as a practical skills trainer for lawyers in Germany.

Gisela Shaw is professor of German studies at the University of the West of England, Bristol, UK. From 1996 to 2001 she chaired the Women in German Studies (WIGS) association in the UK.

Harriet Silius is professor of feminist studies and Director of the Institute of Women's Studies Åbo Akademi University, Finland. She is President Elect of the Association of Institutions for Feminist Education and Research in Europe (AOIFE) and a member of the external advisory group for socio-economic research to the European Commission.

Hilary Sommerlad is a solicitor and principal lecturer in law at Leeds Metropolitan University, UK. She formerly taught political studies at the University of York, UK.

Celia Wells is professor of law at Cardiff University, Wales, and founded the UK Women Law Professors Network in 1998.

Jörn Westhoff, lawyer and Japanologist, is currently working with an international law firm in Tokyo. He was admitted to the Tokyo Bar in 2001. While practising law in Düsseldorf, Germany, he also taught Japanese law at the universities of Düsseldorf and Bochum.

Introduction: Women in the World's Legal Professions: Overview and Synthesis[1]

ULRIKE SCHULTZ

1. OVERVIEW: CONTRIBUTIONS

Fifteen countries from four continents feature in this volume. It tells the story of women in the legal profession in the developed world. By the very nature of the topic, Europe is particularly well represented, including two former Socialist Bloc countries, Poland and the German Democratic Republic. We cover the situation of women in the legal profession in Australia, New Zealand, East Asia, the USA and Latin America. What remains to be written is the story of women lawyers in underdeveloped and in developing countries, including those belonging to the world of Islam. Sadly, we failed to recruit a contributor from any country on the African continent. Also, a colleague from India eventually declined the invitation to submit a paper, very possibly due to the absence of relevant data—a problem many of us encountered in one form or another. Thus very few data were available even for Spain. It is hoped that this volume will act as an incentive to colleagues to help to close the information gap.

1 Variations in Approach

The book is structured by legal cultures and by countries, thus following the pattern of Abel's and Lewis' work (Abel and Lewis 1988a, 1988b, 1989). Contributions on common law countries precede those of civil law countries, a sequence which is to reflect not any hegemonic trait in American sociology (which Europeans would regard with some suspicion), but rather the fact that a number of contributions on common law countries offer more comprehensive theoretical discussion of, in particular, Gilligan's approach, which after all was the project's starting-point (Gilligan 1981). This is not to say that some of the contributions on civil law countries do not, on their part, undertake to either support or refute Gilligan's views. But here we also find engagement with specifically European intellectuals and intellectual traditions.[2]

---

[1] I owe great thanks to Gisela Shaw for her constant support and constructive criticism in drafting this synthesis of our work. As in the context of a number of other contributions to this volume, her function has been one of language arbiter, moderator and, indeed, midwife.

[2] Cf. particularly the contributions by Anne Boigeol and Vittorio Olgiati.

Irrespective of the specific focus chosen by individual contributors, the respective national culture is implicitly always present. Approaches and styles vary, depending on authors' personalities as well as on their professional backgrounds and national cultures. A German jurist writes and argues differently from a Canadian sociologist. Some contributions are designed as opinions on particular issues (Clare McGlynn's analysis of the validity of economic arguments in favour of gender equality, or Kate Malleson's assessment of the prospects for parity in the judiciary); others apply a more narrative or a more descriptive approach (Mary Jane Mossman on the implementation of educational strategies, Ulrike Schultz on perception and construction of femininity, or Heleen Ietswaart on Dutch women lawyers' career trajectories). One presents a self-referential project drawing on autobiographical experiences of women law professors (Celia Wells). Three contributions address issues of targeted equal opportunities policies. While Clare McGlynn (England and Wales) critically investigates the validity of a business case for equality, Ulrike Schultz (Germany) analyses legal concepts of state-prescribed policies of equality and sameness, and Mary Jane Mossman (Canada) explores the value of educational strategies in reducing sex discrimination in law firms.

A number of contributions specifically set out to present and evaluate empirical data on women in the legal profession (Rosemary Hunter on Australia, Georgina Murray on New Zealand, Clare McGlynn on England and Wales, Ulrike Schultz on Germany). Amongst broad-brush accounts of the situation of women in one country's legal profession are those by Malgorzata Fuszara on Poland and Gisela Shaw on the new federal states in united Germany. They provide mutually complementary insights into the impact on the profession and, in particular, its female members of recent socio-political upheavals in Central and Eastern Europe, when a socialist order was replaced by liberal capitalism. Haesook Kim sketches the professional portrait of one South Korean woman lawyer, which reflects the close interaction between one outstanding and exemplary individual's personal achievement and the socio-political context within which it occurred, while also acting as a reminder of the dramatic (and still relative) progress made in terms of gender equality in Western societies.

The French and Brazilian contributions (Anne Boigeol and Eliane Junqueira) centre on judges, a natural approach to take in the context of a legal culture shaped by a Roman law tradition and by the institution of career judges. Analogously, contributions from the United States (Deborah Rhode, Bill Felstiner et al., Lynn Mather) and Canada (Mary Jane Mossman, Fiona Kay and Joan Brockman) foreground attorneys who, in common law countries, are the dominant group within the legal profession. Kate Malleson's analysis of the situation of women judges in England and Wales represents a revealing account of the gendered impact of a system of judicial appointments that lacks standardisation and transparency. Significant consequences for women lawyers derive from the division of the legal profession into solicitors and barristers (Australia, and England and Wales), with Germany representing the opposite end of the spectrum where all jurists undergo an essentially uniform training programme which is largely determined by judicial requirements.

2 Conceptual Frameworks

In line with a general intellectual trend away from grand theories and narratives in favour of more differentiated, less all-embracing and more strongly context-related explanatory models, contributors to this volume use theoretical under-pinnings with some caution. None of them offers wholehearted support for an essentialist position of the kind generally associated with Carol Gilligan's work and translated into feminist legal sociology by Carrie Menkel-Meadow. On the other hand, Gilligan's and Menkel-Meadow's positions frequently serve as a helpful backdrop allowing authors to define their own positions more clearly. This applies particularly to the three contributions from the United States (Deborah Rhode, William Felstiner et al., Lynn Mather). Crucial in this context is the weight attributed to contextual factors perceived to be either re-enforcing or, more likely, overlaying, concealing or even cancelling out the impact of gender. Such factors can be located at any level— global, national, local, class, profession-specific, personal etc. Also, conceptual tools drawn from a number of theoretical fields are introduced where these seem to be helpful in throwing light on the increasingly complex issue of discrimination or marginalisation of women in the legal profession.

Thus Deborah Rhode (USA) deploys the concept of diversity originating in personnel management theory to highlight the significance of factors such as ethnicity, age, class, education, competencies etc alongside gender and sex. Rosemary Hunter looks at the Australian Bar as an 'imagined community' defined by 'hegemonic masculinity' and sustained by invented traditions, where women represent the *Other* and have to find ways of either conforming to or sub-verting the dominant culture. Similarly, Anne Boigeoil (France) regards the mas-culine professional *habitus* as a key factor in defining the role of women in the field of law. Gisela Shaw (German Democratic Republic/new federal German states) explains gender inequality in both socialist and capitalist societies as a derivative form of exclusion, drawing attention to the overriding significance of political power structures and ideologies in determining the prominence or otherwise of women lawyers' marginalisation. Yuriko Kaminaga and Jörn Westhoff show convincingly the tension for women lawyers in Japan between their elite status as members of the legal profession and their inferior social rank-ing as women, the latter resulting in a pronounced lack of interest on their part in feminist issues. Vittorio Olgiati (Italy), in a subtly balanced argument, pre-sents a case study of the professional exclusion (subsequently reversed) of one early Italian female jurist, which helps to illuminate a whole range of wider issues concerning professionalisation in a specific historical legal and socio-political context. Hilary Sommerlad (England and Wales), while acknowledging the undeniable existence of a certain level of gender-based biological and cultural differences and their transformative potential in the legal sphere, does query the significance of their impact compared with sweeping developments affecting the profession as a whole (which may even lend support to and coincide with the influence brought to bear specifically by women). Fiona Kay and Jean Brockman (Canada) select facets of human capital and gender stratification theory in their discussion of the reasons for the perceived underrating of female social, cultural or human capital in law firms. And Harriet Silius, rather than pursuing her earlier theoretical approaches to defining and interpreting the situation of women jurists in Finland within the framework of a specifically Nordic gender contract, now points to comprehensive socio-economic change to explain recent developments which run counter to her own predictions made a decade or so ago.

2. COMPARING CULTURES AND COUNTRIES: PROBLEMS AND PITFALLS

Three major factors are shown to cut across and blur the boundaries of any straightforward comparative classification of women in the world's legal professions. These are: the existence of two very different legal traditions and cultures; national characteristics in the organisation and structure of the various branches of the legal profession, and national languages and their specific legal concepts and terminology.

1 Major Legal Traditions and Cultures

Not surprisingly, the most striking divide separating women in the world's legal professions is that between common law and civil law countries. Its impact on any facet of legal organisation and culture, including the situation of women within them, can hardly be overestimated. This divide not withstanding, there are also areas of overlap as well as mutual influences between these two cultural spheres, and each of them in turn encompasses a wide range of differentiations within it.

The common law tradition in its various manifestations, reflecting the sweep and impact of the British Commonwealth, is represented in this volume by studies on women lawyers in the United States of America, Canada, Australia, New Zealand, England and Wales, and Israel which also adopted English law. The civil law world, which is firmly rooted in the history of the continent of Europe, includes three streams: firstly, countries with a Romance tradition, i.e. Italy, France, Spain and Portugal, represented in this volume by studies on Italy and France; secondly, countries where Roman and Germanic elements have merged to form a new tradition, i.e. Germany and the Netherlands (this mixed culture has also decisively influenced the legal system of Poland); and thirdly, the Nordic tradition which is represented here by Finland. The legal systems of non-European countries outside the common law sphere have been variously exposed to Romance or German influence. Of the countries dealt with in this volume, Brazil has broadly followed a Romance tradition. South Korea and Japan have tended to look towards Germany, while also adapting parts of the French *Code Civil* as well as retaining a strong national tradition of their own.

2 National Characteristics

Aspects of national legal cultures that emerge as being of particular relevance to the situation of women lawyers include countries' historically grown professional structures, their judicial systems, certain legal regulations, and the social status of women. Additional factors are countries' political systems, the state of their economy, and social and political traditions. Religion comes to the fore as a major factor only in relation to one country discussed in this volume, namely Israel. As Bryna Bogoch explains, women's scope for action in religious courts in Israel continues to be severely limited. Her account highlights an urgent need to widen our awareness of the nature and impact on the situation of women in the legal profession of systems where state courts and religious courts operate side by side or, indeed, where the latter have exclusive authority as is the case in a number of Islamic states.

One very striking difference regarding the structure of legal professions, and their impact on the role and situation of women within them, is that between countries where there is a split between barristers and solicitors, i.e. between lawyers pleading in court and those focusing on client advice (England and Wales, and parts of Australia), and those where all practising lawyers are members of a unitary profession performing both functions, i.e. the continent of Europe and also the USA and Canada. As Rosemary Hunter convincingly demonstrates for Queensland in Australia, barristers continue to cultivate a traditionally male culture.

Although in Romance countries (France, Italy, Spain and Portugal) the legal profession, in line with Roman tradition, had for centuries been split into two functional groups, i.e. the *procurator/avoué* who was responsible for adherence to formal proceedings, and the *advocatus* who did the pleading, this division has today lost its practical significance and is merely mentioned in passing (France, Italy).

However, functional criteria concerning the kind of work lawyers do come into play as far as women lawyers' roles are concerned, even where practising lawyers belong to a unitary profession. In countries where advisory and transaction work has high significance in lawyers' overall portfolio, women face the problem of being pushed into the invisible functions in the backrooms (Mossman for Canada).

A further structural difference of considerable relevance to women jurists' role in civil law countries is the statutory concentration of certain functions, frequently including conveyancing, in the hands of the profession of public notary, a profession of little or no relevance in common law systems where these functions are carried out by various professions, in particular solicitors. Civil law notaries enjoy high social status and incomes and are overwhelmingly male. Revealingly, in former socialist countries where the profession had been stripped of its most important roles and relegated to the lowest level within the hierarchy of legal professions, the bulk of notaries were female.

Whatever the functional differences within the profession of practising lawyers, a dramatic rise in their overall numbers is evident in most countries discussed. This rise is largely explained by the opening up of educational opportunities and is directly (albeit not solely) related to an increase in the number of female members of the profession. The proportion of lawyers per head of the population is especially high in countries in Latin and North America with a tradition of immigration and an absence of a long-standing professional culture, but with a high regard for the law as a bonding force in a multi-ethnic society. Japan and Korea represent something of an exception in this context, as their consensus-oriented cultures have kept numbers of practising lawyers down, which in turn comprise only a tiny percentage of women.

Structural differences which impact on the role of women jurists are also a feature of the judiciaries studied. In civil law countries, judicial professions (judge and public prosecutor) are a career. Access is gained via clearly specified academic hurdles and as such has proved favourable to female applicants (France, Germany). In common law jurisdictions members of the judiciary are appointed later in life and on the basis of a selection process whose lack of transparency has only recently begun to be seriously questioned (England and Wales). Women's opportunities to join the ranks of the judiciary have been slim.

The impact of political systems on the role and position of jurists in general and female jurists in particular can best be gauged from studies of member states of the former socialist bloc (German Democratic Republic, Poland). As opportunities for individuals fighting for their rights were not seen to be in the interest of a socialist society, the number of practising lawyers was strictly limited, while judges and in particular public prosecutors had a function best compared to that of social / ideological workers. On the other hand, the small group of practising lawyers that did exist enjoyed higher prestige and incomes than any other branch of the legal profession, with the judiciary falling well behind and state notaries bringing up the rear. The percentage of women in each of these groups changed in direct proportion to their social and professional standing.

Life and career planning for women generally, including women jurists, is shown to be greatly influenced by national preferences for specific life models for women. A conservative picture emerges not only for Korea and Japan, but also for Germany and the Netherlands. Ulrike Schultz ('Perception and Construction of Femininity') shows that in Germany the housewife ideal continues to be widely accepted.[3] Heleen Ietswaart reports that Dutch women

---

[3] In what follows, the two contributions by Ulrike Schultz will be referred to as Schultz 1 ('The Status of Women Lawyers in Germany') and Schultz 2 ('Women Lawyers in Germany: Perception and Construction of Femininity').

frequently prioritise their domestic duties and therefore opt for part-time rather than full-time employment. Ideas regarding the nature of femininity, as reflected in the acceptance or otherwise of women's gainful employment generally and of women aiming for and occupying more elevated professional positions, are deeply rooted in the national subconscious and not easily reached by well-intentioned state programmes. Kaminaga and Westhoff demonstrate persuasively that in Japanese society even professionally successful women who benefit from being members of a social elite never wholly escape being associated with the socially low status of their sex.

Recognition of the dual burden of family duties and gainful employment carried by large numbers of women in all countries has led to various legislative measures (tax, social and labour legislation, regulations governing child care) being passed and intended to ease the pressure on them. These vary considerably from country to country, with women in German-speaking countries being particularly disadvantaged due to the fact that full-time schooling is still not the norm, although there exists a markedly developed body of legislation aimed to achieve equal standing of the sexes. Varying national models of equal opportunities legislation may well bring about new structural differentiations in the context of professional opportunities for women.

3 Language Barriers

The uniform use of English in this volume conceals many of these multifaceted nation-specific features. The same terms are used to refer to what often are very different phenomena—an inevitable dilemma facing any international comparison. English terms may spark off inappropriate or wrong associations. On occasion, terms that were entirely suitable were lacking in the English language, and compromises had to be found.

To give just a few obvious examples. The terms 'attorney', 'barrister' and 'solicitor' designate practising lawyers in common law countries, while the term 'advocate' tends to be used in this volume to refer to practising lawyers in civil law countries, signalling the fact that their work comprises both advisory and forensic functions and that traditionally the latter have been dominant. Correspondingly, 'advocacy' is normally used for the profession collectively. 'Jurist' in these countries is the designation for anyone qualified to work in any of the branches of the legal profession. The Anglo-American concept of a 'profession' and of 'professionalism' has been used across the board, but is intrinsically misleading with reference to countries where the notion of a liberal profession (in German: *freier Beruf*) is associated with different standards of practice and ethics than in the common law world. Similarly, the notion of the 'law firm' if used outside the Anglo-American sphere and its large law firm culture can be misleading in countries where law firms tend to be small or medium-sized.

3. SYNTHESIS OF RESULTS

1 History Shaping the Present

The history of women lawyers generally comprises little more than one century and, particularly in Europe, is closely linked with the emergence of nation states and their interest in creating uniform professional profiles. Ever since antiquity, individual female members of social elites had occasionally been allowed to perform legal functions (Olgiati), but in principle law and administration were seen to be central to state power and a male prerogative.

From the late eighteenth century, Rousseau's *Social Contract* (1762) and the French Revolution had introduced the idea of a modern civic society, but restricted its blessings to the male sex. Nor did the grand legislative projects of the nineteenth century do anything to rectify this imbalance. Rather, women were systematically denied important civic rights, and were legally subordinate to their fathers and husbands. They had no access to higher education and to the professions on the grounds that women's natural disposition made them unsuited, while eminently qualifying them for a key role in domestic life (cf. contributions on Germany and England).

It was the early women's movement's struggle for civic rights for women in the late nineteenth century that paved the way for their being allowed to choose a legal career. Another important force that helped to break down the barriers was the unstoppable progress of professionalisation, as social status lost its significance and a rational system of formal qualifications became the key to access to the professions and public office. Women soon demonstrated that they were perfectly capable of meeting these new criteria.

In most Western countries women were granted suffrage and full civic rights just before or just after World War I. This finally removed any excuse for excluding them from the legal professions without undermining the legitimacy of the state's demand for strict adherence to the law. An additional important social factor resulting in decreasing resistance against women jurists was the social, political and moral upheaval following the First World War. Egalitarian views became more acceptable and women began to be appreciated in the new social order as a valuable human resource.

Moral considerations suggesting that women ought to be granted equal rights carried relatively little weight at this time. As a general principle, full equality of both sexes took much longer to find its way into European national constitutions, as reports in this volume on France and Germany testify. And translating this principle into social reality required further tough struggles which lasted into our own time. Generally speaking, World War II and its aftermath brought about a consolidation of the drive towards full integration of women into society and the professions.

Individual contributions to this volume focus on a range of national facets of this comprehensive evolutionary process. Vittorio Olgiati uses the controversies surrounding the first admission of a woman to the Italian advocacy to highlight, on the one hand, the role of the courts in bringing this about, and on the other hand the weakening of the social and political power of the advocacy resulting from the interference of the courts. At the same time he stresses the close association between gender integration and the strengthening of professional autonomy.

Anglo-American and Australian reports reflect the crucial significance of women acquiring the legal status of 'persons' before becoming eligible for legal office, as maleness was equated with humanness and accordingly with 'persons' in the legal sense. Special legislation was needed in many countries to open the doors for women to the legal professions. In most Western states, admission of the first female jurists to the advocacy occurred at the turn of the nineteenth to the twentieth century or during the first decades of the twentieth century.

Granting women access to the legal professions was delayed even longer in countries where the move towards an industrialised economy and a modern state occurred at a later stage. Thus in Venezuela the first woman was awarded a law degree in 1936. In South Korea, it took until 1952 for the first woman to be admitted to the advocacy. A whole series of external structural factors had to coincide in this woman's life in order for this to happen: improved educational opportunities, a shift in cultural perceptions of women's nature and potential, and support by individual members of the male sex as well as by other women, in particular their mothers. There are no indications that these factors have lost much of their relevance to the present day. (Table 1)

In the countries of the Anglo-Saxon world women's first admission to the legal professions occurred at very different times, with federally organised states such as Australia and Canada presenting a mixed picture in themselves. Judiciaries proved an even higher hurdle for women to take than the bar. In England and Wales, Australia and New Zealand, where access to judicial positions is not decided by open competition on the basis of academic qualifications (as it is for instance in Germany) but judges are individually recruited from among older and especially meritorious members of the bar, it took until the 1960s and 1970s before women were appointed to county courts or high courts. Even today, the High Court of Northern Ireland does not have a single female judge.

Reports on France and Italy show a similar discrepancy between women's first access to the advocacy and to the judiciary, albeit for very different reasons.[4] While in France and Italy the first woman was admitted to the advocacy in 1900 and 1919 respectively, the corresponding dates for the judiciary were 1946 and 1963. Vittorio Olgiati argues that in Italy this was achieved by means of a specially created distinction between 'ordinary' professions and professions implying juridical public powers (the latter to be strictly reserved for men), in order to soften the impact of women having, in 1919, been awarded equal civic rights with men. This subtle, but highly effective, distinction made it possible to continue the ban on women holding positions of state power even

---

[4] This contrasts with other European countries, such as Germany, where the timing of women's first access to the advocacy and to the judiciary broadly coincided.

Table 1: Historical Milestones Marking the Entry of Women into the Legal Professions[5]

Country	First Woman Admitted to Law Faculties	First Woman Law Student Graduated	First Woman in Legal Profession		
			Lawyers	Judges	Legal Academics
USA	2nd half of 19th century; 1950 Harvard Law School	2nd half of 19th century			
Canada	1899 Northwest Territories	1892	1895–1942 (Ontario 1895, New Brunswick 1905, British Columbia 1912, Alberta/Manitoba 1915, Quebec 1942)		
Australia			1905 (Victoria) -1935 (Tasmania)	(1965 1st Supreme Court judge, 1987 first High Court judge)	
New Zealand	c. 1893	1897(1971: 1st Maori; 1982: 1st Pacific Islander)		1975	1957 1st law lecturer
UK	1873	1917	Solicitors: Scotland 1920 England 1922 Wales 1922 Barristers: 1920	1960s (County Court) 1988 1st Court of Appeal judges)	
Germany	1900–1909	1912	1922		1965 1st law professor
Netherlands			1903	1947	
Poland	1915		1925	1929	
Norway		1890			
Sweden		1897	(doctoral degree)		
Finland		1906		1930s	
France	1887	1897	1900	1946	1931 1st law professor
Italy	1876	1777	1919	1963	
Korea	1946	1951	1952		
Belgium			1921		
Denmark			1919		
Ireland			1920		
Portugal			1918		
Venezuela		1936			

[5] Additional data taken from Bevan, Stephen, Susan Hayday, Claire Callender (1993) *Women Professionals in the EC*. London: The Law Society.

when the law had granted them access to any profession, and thus to avoid the perceived risk of a destabilisation of the political system. In France, the main stumbling block for women gaining access to judicial posts had been the denial of the right to vote in national elections. It took until 1944 for this obstacle to be removed. Intriguingly, today Italy and France enjoy the highest female participation rate in their judiciaries of all countries investigated in contributions to this volume.

While gaining initial access to the legal professions was one thing, achieving equal participation for women within them proved to be quite another. Certainly, demonstrating legal skills and ability wholly in keeping with those of their male competitors was not sufficient. By the mid-1950s the number of female jurists had grown at no more than a snail's pace. Even thereafter developments were slow and it took until the 1970s / early 1980s for real change to occur.

The shift to a modern meritocratic system, most noticeably reflected in the replacement of an apprenticeship system by a system based on academic qualifications, brought women the opportunity not merely to study for a law degree but also to have a proper career in the field of law (Clare McGlynn's and Anne Boigeol's accounts for England and Wales and for France respectively). In England this only happened fairly recently. Traditionally, pupils for barristers' chambers and articled clerks for solicitors' firms were selected mainly according to social origin and status as well as (male) sex, and less according to ability. Also a certain financial investment was needed, which was harder to find for women. In Germany, too, financial considerations in the face of many years of study required for a law degree often disadvantaged women (who, it was assumed, were unlikely to prove worth the investment), a situation which only changed when, from the 1970s, student grants removed the danger of gender-based discrimination on financial grounds.

More subtle forms of discrimination survived well beyond the formal opening of access to the legal professions for women, such as the prioritisation in German public service of (male) soldiers returning from World War II and, until very recently, that of young men who had completed compulsory military service in the allocation of university places. Celibacy clauses helped to re-enforce the model of the single-earner marriage and to exclude women from public service after their marriage. Even in 1975, there existed for barristers' chambers in England a quota of a maximum of two women. In addition, as the reports show, it was not uncommon for male gate keepers to the profession to operate more informal mechanisms of exclusion, rejection, and discouragement in order to keep the uninvited intruders at bay.

2 Comparing National Professional Profiles: Quantitative Data

Broadly speaking, women today make up a sizeable share in the various branches of the legal profession, although significant differences remain. Our country reports project the following picture for practising lawyers (Table 2):

Table 2: Percentage of Women Lawyers by Country

Country	Lawyers %	Commonwealth States Solicitors %	Barristers %	Notaries %	
USA (2000)	27				
Canada (1999)	32 (Quebec 40) (1996: only 20.8 for private practitioners)			Quebec: 43	
Australia	1994/95: 24.7	1997: 28	1997: 15.8 (QCs: 6) Cat. a (QC or more than 15 years): 5 Cat. c (Juniors, fewer than 6 years): 28		
UK (1998)		34 (1997 practising: 29)	(1997 practising: 22)		
Israel (2000)	36				
Germany (2000)	24.6			*Advocate notaries* 1999:8.24	*full-time notaries* 1999:18.4 (1994:old FRG: 3; former GDR 48.6)
Netherlands (1993)	30			1994: notaries: 3 junior notaries (lower level notaries): 42	
Poland (1998)	advocates: 29.5 in-house legal advisers: 49.3			notaries: 63.3	
France (1999)	45			notaries: 12.4	
Brazil (State of Rio de Janeiro) (1995)	37.8				
Japan (1991)	5.9				
South-Korea (1998)	1.9				
New Zealand (1999)			29 (QCs: 6)		
Finland (2000)	43				

The share of female practising lawyers tends to hover somewhere between one quarter and one third, although in Brazil and France it is considerably higher. In South Korea and Japan participation rates for women are very low, which is not only due to their late entry into the profession (see Brazil for comparison and contrast) but also to the persistently applied exclusionary strategies operated in these countries (Kaminaga and Westhoff on Japan).

There is less consistency regarding the judicial field. Compared with civil law countries, common law countries—exception for Israel—continue to stand out for the tiny share of posts given over to women, obviously a consequence of selection procedures which set great store by experience, age and professional networks—all of which criteria are more easily met by male applicants. (Table 3)

Table 3: Percentage of Women in the Judiciary

Country	Judges %	Prosecutors %
USA (2000)	10–12	
Australia (1999)	federal court: 8.3 supreme courts: 9.1 high courts: 14.3 district courts: 13.9 magistrates courts: 16 family courts: 22.6	
New Zealand (1999)	7.9 high court: 14 district courts: 16	
U.K. (1999)	11.8 House of Lords: 0 Court of Appeal: 3 High Court: 8 circuit judges: 6 district judges: 14	
Israel (2000)	42 Supreme Court: 21 district courts: 36 magistrates courts: 44 rabbinical courts: 0	69 (state attorney's office)
Germany (1999)	26.31 on probation: 45.72 federal courts: 11.6	27.9
Netherlands (1995)	34 low level: 45.6 middle level: 23.3 high level: 7.4 trainees: 68	33

Table 3: (*cont.*)

Country	Judges %	Prosecutors %
Poland (2000)	63.6	
	highest courts: 22 (1997)	territorial prosecutor's
	courts of appeal: 53.1	office (lower level): 50.9
	regional courts: 58.4	prosecutor's office
	district courts: 66.2	of appeal: 36
Finland (2000)	46	27
France (2000)	54	35
	court presidents: 14.6 (2000)	chief public prosecutors: 10
Brazil (State of Rio de Janeiro) (1996)	28.1	
South Korea (1999)	6.9	1.6
Japan (1991)	5	4.2

Percentages for women in the judiciary range from very high (Poland)[6], to more or less balanced between the sexes (France), to very low (East Asia). Similar disparities exist in the gender profile of the public prosecution service. The strikingly high share of female state attorneys in Israel may be attributed to the relatively low incomes and status of public service employees.

Comparative data are less readily available for women jurists working in administration and in industry, but certain assumptions seem reasonable in the light of indirect evidence. For instance, in Canada 81 per cent of male jurists but only 63 per cent of female jurists are attorneys. The situation is not dissimilar in Finland, Germany, England and Wales, Poland and New Zealand. We can therefore assume that a greater proportion of well qualified women than men work in administration and in industry and that job security represents a criterion of some significance in their choice of profession, a development poignantly portrayed by Harriet Silius in her account of the situation in Finland.

3 Women in Legal Education

Parity in terms of numbers of male and female law students has been achieved in most countries. Indeed, in some countries, women have overtaken their male competitors (France, New Zealand). This dramatic development within the space of only a few decades (starting from a point of total exclusion) has no parallel in any other academic subject.[7]

Female jurists' academic qualifications tend to be just as good or even better than those of men (France, England and Wales), a situation that applies across most subjects. Germany presents an exception here, as women's average legal

---

[6] In keeping with the profession's low status and income under the communist regime.
[7] Schultz (1990), 324–334, discusses possible explanations in detail. Cf. also Schultz 1.

examination results do not quite come up to those of men. This is particularly significant, as these results count as a guarantee of quality and prestige and are crucial in subsequent job applications. It is not unreasonable to regard as at least a partial explanation of men's superior examination success the fact that oral examinations, which produce an important component of the overall results, are conducted mainly by male examiners and according to male standards. In these oral examinations, what counts is the candidate's general *habitus*, that is the degree to which her appearance and behaviour meet traditional expectations.[8] Not surprisingly, women experience them as an initiation test into professional conformity. Anne Boigeol's findings for France support this hypothesis, in that they confirm that women feel more at ease in written examinations where knowledge and professional competence are tested, than in oral examinations where self-presentation is of central significance.[9]

Women's motivation to study law shows similarities across national boundaries. In particular, there is a stronger emphasis on altruism (Deborah Rhode) as well as a desire to promote justice (Leny de Groot). However, neither their level of ambition nor their drop-out rate is very different from that of men.

Several studies in this volume refer to women students' contributions in class being treated with less attention and respect than those of their male colleagues, resulting in detrimental subconscious effects on their professional self-confidence. Even when formal barriers to women's access to the legal professions had been removed, mechanisms of rejection and marginalisation continued to be used in legal education, in that women were not merely disadvantaged, but found themselves humiliated and their abilities openly queried. In today's age of political correctness such strategies have been refined to take the form of subjection aimed at assimilation, and have been described elsewhere as the 'chilly climate in the law school' (Krauskopf 1994), leading to a sense of alienation (Schultz 2). (Cf. also Thornton 1998, Collier 1991)

Assimilation is achieved through mainly male tutors teaching the traditional law school curriculum, which is characterised by an ideology of masculinism and homosociality at the expense of attentiveness to feelings and personal beliefs. Little or no effort is made to unmask and discuss the patriarchal structure of the law, and female experiences and perspectives are ignored. Gender-related issues have been included in Anglo-American law school curricula, but have not yet found their way into legal studies on the continent of Europe where they have met with little sympathy.

---

[8] As § 25 of the Legal Training Act (*Juristenausbildungsgesetz, JAG*) states:
(1) The second state examination in law is to verify whether candidates (*Referendarinnen* and *Referendare*) have met the examination objectives (§ 22) and whether their subject and general knowledge and abilities, their practical skills, and *the overall impression created by their personality* [my italics, US] warrant the award of the qualification admitting them to judicial and to higher general administrative office.

[9] These results tie in with the fact that in Israel men judges seem to be less persuaded by women arguments in court.

Table 4: Percentage of Women in Legal Education

Country	Students %	Lecturers %	Professors %	Total Academic Legal Staff %
USA (2000)[10]	50		21.9	31.5
Canada				40.8
Australia (1999)	1998: 55.9	sen. lect. 33.7 lecturers 49.6 ass. lect. 61.5	prof. 15.5 ass. prof. 34.6	39.9
New Zealand) (1995)	1998: 62	68 (8 sen. lect.)	(1 dean, 2 prof., 3 ass. prof.)	28
UK (1997)	58.6	lecturers 49 readers 22	prof. 14 (but: in 69% of law schools no female prof.)	40
Germany (1997)	44	21.5 other academic staff: Wiss. Mit. 38.5 (1998)	4.7	
Netherlands (1995)	51			
Poland (1998)	53			
Finland (1989)	> 50			
France (1997)	65.2 first degree		13.6 (1998)	

Problems encountered by female law students are mirrored in those facing their female tutors. Women academics generally suffer from isolation, marginalisation, and underrating of their achievements. In law schools, their percentage share has been rising at the lower levels of the faculty hierarchy, but higher up 'glass ceilings' are a frequent phenomenon in many countries and female law professors are a very recent creation. In Germany, where law professors enjoy particularly high prestige and potentially high incomes, their numbers are still tiny.

Celia Wells, in her report on women law professors in the United Kingdom, which resulted from a first systematic investigation into this exclusive professional grouping, offers fascinating insights into the difficulties they have encountered. She concludes that these difficulties have a great deal in common with those faced by women aiming for top positions in industry. It is easier for them to get into law faculties of lower reputation. Their income is higher if they work in male-dominated faculties, but generally their market value is lower than that of male law professors. Also, incomes remain lower where the share of women is higher, and successful women frequently end up taking on less conspicuous and less profitable tasks than their male colleagues, as they invest more time and energy in improving their teaching and have less to spare for

[10] Data from Epstein (2001), 741.

purposes of enhancing their incomes and prestige through additional activities. Those who succeed match a certain personality profile aptly characterised by Margaret Thornton (1996) as ranging from 'body beautiful' to 'dutiful daughter' or 'adoring acolyte' (Wells for UK, Schultz 2 for Germany).

4 Women in Legal Practice

At first glance, the dramatic rise in female participation in all key areas of law, including legal practice, creates the impression of a success story, as if the 'woman question' had been resolved and women lawyers had made significant inroads into a previously inaccessible elitist profession. However, on closer inspection discrimination against women, however well concealed and refined and possibly subconscious, is still rife. Women lawyers tend to remain on the margins of power and privilege. Discrimination often occurs unwittingly or in the conviction that it can be rationally justified. As Deborah Rhode shows, women tend to notice acts of discrimination much more clearly than men, but both are inclined to attribute them to individual failings rather than to gender-based issues.

4.1 Practising Lawyers

4.1.1 Entering the Profession

On entering the world of legal professions, women soon find that in order for them to be successful, academic capital (which they have) needs to be complemented by social capital (regarding which men are much better placed). Indeed, the latter is of greater significance than the former (Boigeol). Entering the profession has been compared with gaining access to a hegemonic power grouping through socially institutionalised rites of passage (Olgiati). In Germany, the academic qualification is admittedly of key significance, but the social assimilation process has already occurred during women students' university studies.

More men than women succeed in gaining the training place of their choice and subsequently their first job. The fact that men enjoy greater network support and male cultural capital[11] is of prime importance in the application process (Canada, England). Women try to set up their own mentoring systems and networks, but their slight representation at the higher echelons makes this a less effective process. Japanese women face particular problems, as male applicants are often openly preferred and firms even advertise exclusively for male applicants, a practice which in Western states has been stopped through anti-discrimination regulations.

In times of a shortage of legal practitioners, women's chances improve—as was the case in England in the late 1980s and early 1990s, and is currently true of Germany in the context of large international law firms. Women generally

---

[11] Cultural capital understood as the norms, attitudes, and values explicit and implicit in law firm/organisational culture; human capital as the lawyering skills acquired through legal education and practice; social capital as the social connections, respect and reputation.

represent the labour market's reserve army: they work on insecure and often temporary contracts, under less favourable working conditions, are often overqualified for the actual job they do, and are the first to be made redundant.

International comparisons reveal significant differences in terms of the kind of law firm women find themselves in. For instance, in Germany they are more likely to be sole practitioners, in Japan it is small law firms that provide most posts for women lawyers, and in Canada women are just as likely to be practising on their own as they are to be working in large law firms.

4.1.2 Specialisation

Women tend to be less specialised than men. They are also more likely to work with individual clients from the lower and middle social strata as well as in particular female-dominated segments of the legal services market, such as family law (Mather) and a whole range of generalist fields of little prestige and financial clout (Schultz 2). In most countries the latter includes tort, in particular for damage resulting from traffic accidents. On the other hand, there are differences worth analysing. For instance, in Canada female lawyers often specialise in tax law, while in other countries fields associated with money and figures are more likely to be in male hands. Broadly speaking, men dominate commercial and property work, and women are to be found in areas of little prestige and financial gain but greater emotional labour. Characteristically, criminal lawyers in Germany tend to be male, but youth crime is dealt with by women.

The interesting question is the extent to which this distribution of labour is the outcome of self-selection, and/or results from women being encouraged or even pushed into certain areas of work which are associated with supposed feminine features such as sympathy, intuitiveness and altruism. Family law is a case in point. Women do frequently opt for it themselves in preference to other areas of law as it usually means routinised work easily fitted into a planned work schedule, requiring less technology, literature and regular updating through training. Divorce cases can be dealt with in small firms and unlike commercial cases rarely require working overtime or giving up one's weekends.

4.1.3 Career Prospects

Women represent the 'working class' of the legal services market, where the distribution of work and clients is subject to strategic planning aimed at defending one's own patch (Sommerlad). Women are more likely to be encouraged to concentrate on matters of lower visibility, profile and financial rewards (cf. Mossman's reference to 'pink files'). Men are more inclined (as well as being encouraged) to focus on work which offers greater prestige as well as better opportunities to develop legal skills and client contact and correspondence, which is important to develop a client base (Mossman: 'blue files').

Women associates are required to conform to standards derived from an exaggerated view of the ideal partner: extraordinary commitment (for instance in the form of client recruitment), creator of a comprehensive network of commercial clients, and in particular a high level of billable hours. Growing competition in the legal services market makes for ever harsher working conditions and enhances 'women's deviant or potentially deviant professional status' (Sommerlad). However, women fail to complain to avoid damaging their career chances.

Partnerships are significantly less likely to go to women than to men, particularly in the face of a continuing increase in the overall number of lawyers, which encourages the introduction of more hierarchical structures. New career stages (non-equity partner, junior partner etc.) are being introduced, which frequently results in women's promotion being restricted to the lower rungs of the career hierarchy. As Hilary Sommerlad has shown for England and Wales, men are more likely to make it to partner status, irrespective of any specific achievements (experience, specialisation, billable hours, client structure), thus lending support to the view that partnerships are based on fraternal trust and male bonding.

Although these findings largely derive from Anglo-American studies, they can easily be adapted to a civil law context in Europe. Thus Leny de Groot highlights the lack of partnership opportunities for women in the Netherlands, especially in small law firms which tend to have retained a more traditional view of the social roles of the two sexes. A Dutch study has found that promotion was more probable for men than for women. In explaining their career ambitions, both sexes mentioned family responsibilities, but for men this represented a further reason to aim for promotion, while women saw it as a reason for cutting back on their career in order to accommodate their domestic duties. Even in Poland where equality of the sexes had been part of the communist ideology, women now tend to work as employees or run small law firms for individual rather than corporate clients, and generally find it difficult to reach top positions in large law firms or companies (Fuszara).

Traditional social class structures still survive in the Anglo-American bar which is dominated by older white males from elite law schools who work in commercial law with corporate clients (Canada, USA, England and Wales, Australia, New Zealand). In a study on Chicago lawyers, Robert Nelson recently noted a shifting pattern of stratification, with ethno-religious segmentation being replaced by stratification by gender and race across and within practice contexts (Nelson et al. 2001). In continental Europe, ethnic criteria have not yet started to play a role, as immigrants such as Asians from former Dutch colonies in the Netherlands, Arabs in France, or Turks in Germany are still a marginal phenomenon amongst the ranks of the respective national advocacy.

4.1.4 Income Differentials

Low incomes are typical of women lawyers working on their own (Germany), although this cannot altogether be blamed on a self-chosen limitation of work but is also due to lack of clientele or the type of cases dealt with. Significant income and salary differentials in law firms are only partly due to differences in specialisation, age, professional experience and the size of the firm, but have to be attributed also to female commitment and productivity being held in lower esteem, i.e. to discrimination (Canada, McGlynn for England and Wales, Germany). Starting salaries for women tend to be lower than those for men (Sommerlad quotes 6.2 per cent for England and Wales), and with each move up on the career ladder the disparity increases proportionately. Average gender-based income differentials in the various countries tend to range between 10 and 35 per cent.[12] It appears that the old argument that women's incomes do not need to support a family is still alive today (Ietswaart for the Netherlands).

4.1.5 Power and Privilege: Significance of Social Capital

Although law firms continue to be dominated by a male culture, women lawyers tend not to wish to admit this to themselves or to others (MyGlynn, Sommerlad, Hunter). In fact, even those who have risen to full partnerships and higher incomes do not have the same degree of power, independence, decision-making and other authority as their male colleagues. They lack the appropriate social and cultural capital. This emerges particularly clearly from reports about large law firms and their corporate identity in England and Wales, Australia and New Zealand, and about barristers' chambers which tend to be organised on the model of fraternities. This phenomenon is less apparent in the many small and medium-sized law firms in continental Europe, where each individual lawyer sees him- or herself as a 'sole fighter' and where the emphasis on academic qualifications certifying a high level of legal skills is greater than that on human capital.

Generally speaking, women's social capital is seen to be less valuable because they have fewer contacts in male networks and participate less readily in male socialising processes such as talking sports, dining and drinking (Sommerlad). Rosemary Hunter in her study on barristers in Australia concludes that male barristers resort to a sexualised treatment of their female colleagues while simultaneously distancing themselves from them in order to re-enforce their masculinity and power. Demeaning ways of talking about them and insulting remarks about errors on their part are a regular occurrence. Women are criticised for lacking authority and self-confidence and for putting moral and consensual values above profit.

Finally, women's chances of wielding organised professional power are limited compared to those of their male colleagues. They are less likely than men to have any significant involvement in professional associations (England and Wales, Germany).

4.1.6 Professional Satisfaction

Although in 1990 one Canadian study reported that female lawyers were less satisfied than their male colleagues with a range of aspects of their work (pay,

[12] It is interesting to note that this corresponds to the Geneva International Labour Organisation's annual figures for income differentials generally between men and women in a number of countries, which in Germany amount to 30%, a little more in the USA but only 10% in Australia.

working hours, career opportunities, job security, chances to combine professional and family duties, parental leave) (Kay and Brockman), female lawyers, even if their incomes are lower, generally tend to display greater professional satisfaction than males. At least they regard themselves as privileged compared to women in less prestigious jobs, who enjoy less flexibility and less favourable working conditions. This is supported by research done in Germany, Japan, and the USA and Finland.

4.1.7 Long-Hours Culture and the Dual Burden of Profession and Family

The liberal professions have always been characterised by a philosophy of total commitment and a long-hours culture. At a time of cut-throat competition in the legal services market (Sommerlad), the time spent on work symbolises the good and successful lawyer. This means that the domestic scene needs to be left to somebody else. Women lawyers with children tend to lack both time as well as domestic support, as they still take on the bulk of family duties. Even in Finland with its long-standing and strong ideology of gender equality, women's involvement in domestic chores is three times higher than that of men and their total workload burden is accordingly higher (Silius). Men regard their professional commitment as fixed and unchangeable, while considering that of women as perfectly negotiable. Women are expected to prioritise the family and therefore have to make a choice which men are spared. The traditional gendered distribution of labour, described by Silius for Nordic countries as the old 'gender contract', continues to be in operation. Yet, compared to other women in the labour market, female jurists in many countries are privileged in that at least they are in a position to hire and finance domestic help (Japan, Germany, the Netherlands).

To ease their burden, female jurists have been found to forego a family (Kaminaga and Westhoff for Japan). In Germany, three quarters of women have children, but only half of those in higher positions, including lawyers. It is up to each individual to find her own solution to the problem.

One option open to women jurists is part-time work, frequently taken up especially in the Netherlands but also in Germany, while it is unusual in Finland and exceptional in the United States. For this option to work successfully, there must be suitable positions, which is not always the case. Frequently, those working part-time are regarded as not pulling their professional weight (also referred to as 'lawyer light') as well as having made a rational voluntary choice not to work full-time. Generally speaking, women with children are suspected of lacking full commitment. In some parts of the world—East Asia, the German-speaking part of Europe, the Netherlands—a woman's place is seen to be in the home, while this attitude is less common in Romance countries, North America and northern Europe.

4.1.8 Professional Mobility and the Revolving-Door Effect

Female lawyers have a higher mobility rate than their male colleagues, but this tends to be less upward than sideways, downward, or out. The so-called revolving-door[13] effect turns women into transient members of the profession (Canada; analysed for the USA in Donnell et al. 1998). If men leave their jobs, they do so for professional reasons, in particular for purposes of career advancement, while women are often left with no choice because they find it impossible to cope with their dual burden of job and family.[14]

4.2 Women in Other Legal Occupations

4.2.1 Women Notaries

In civil law jurisdictions public notaries hold a key position, tend to be high earners, and have been most successful as male gate-keepers. Without exception, women in all countries were allowed into the notariat late and reluctantly. In Romance countries this was helped by the profession's traditional recruitment strategies which did not rely on legal qualifications but on an apprenticeship system. Also, to this day French notaries are allowed to sell or bequeath their office to a person of their choice. All of this favours a male culture to the exclusion of women. There are clear similarities in terms of selection procedures and social status with barristers in common law jurisdictions, as applicants for the bar are also hand-picked and subsequently subjected to a process of acculturation during their pupillage. However, even in countries such as Germany where recruitment of jurists in all fields is characterised by reliance on legal qualifications, notaries have remained a strongly male-dominated profession, albeit more so for full-time than for solicitor notaries (Shaw).

By contrast, notaries in former socialist systems stood out for low pay and low social prestige and were predominantly female. As from the early 1990s, the process of economic and political transformation reversed the profession's fate and notaries acquired the high social and professional status they have traditionally held in Western Europe, the proportion of women in the profession has begun to decline—more rapidly in the new federal states of Germany due to the integration into an all-German profession (Shaw), and more gently in other former member states of the Eastern Bloc where the transition from socialism to democracy and a market economy and therefore the transformation of former state notaries to members of an independent profession has been a more gradual process. Yet in Poland, too, the proportion of female notaries has declined since 1989/90 (Fuszara).

4.2.2 Women in the Judiciary

In civil law countries women have, after slow beginnings, taken the judiciary by storm (see Table 3 above). Around half of all judges in France and Italy are female, worldwide the figure stands at around 25 per cent. As posts are allocated on the basis of academic merit, women's chances of success have been excellent. This

---

[13] Or open-door effect, cf. Fuchs Epstein (1995) .
[14] Which offers no basis for a rational choice theory.

contrasts sharply with the situation in common law countries where selection is based on a form of self-reproduction of male members of the profession, and even the removal of formal barriers some thirty years ago has not brought about equality of opportunities for men and women. The system continues to rely on patronage aimed at maintaining homogeneity amongst the group (Malleson).[15]

Women jurists in civil law countries prefer the judiciary to other fields of legal work, as it provides the advantages of public service (protection of working mothers, parental leave, a certain range of career opportunities, gender-neutral remuneration). Indeed, a degree of stagnation of salary levels may have to do with the growing female participation rate. While in France and Italy judicial work is regarded as relatively poorly paid, this does not apply to Germany (25 per cent female, rising), where judges and public prosecutors are paid according to a dedicated salary scale which compares favourably with that for public service professionals with comparable qualifications—a legacy of the 'golden' 1970s. Female judges and public prosecutors in civil law countries have had the chance of working part-time for some thirty years. In England and Wales this step was taken as late as 1997.

A study on women judges and public prosecutors in France has shown that women join the judiciary because it offers them a better chance of combining professional and family duties, while men are looking for professional challenge (Boigeol). An additional appeal of the judiciary of a general kind is that it offers a combination of various attractive features: a relatively elevated position, a moderate or at least a plannable workload, and little competitive pressure. As Eliane Junqueira has shown for Brazil, women feel that they can reach a prominent position more easily in the judiciary than in a large law firm. With certain provisos, this also applies to other civil law countries.

In civil law countries (Germany, France) women prefer the self-determined role of the judge to the work of a public prosecutor in a hierarchically structured judicial authority. Women judges tend to concentrate on family law and parent and child matters as well as on more 'general' matters of everyday significance (France, Germany, Brazil). In functional terms, therefore, the gender profile in the judiciary is not dissimilar to that in the advocacy, i.e. in both professions 'important' matters, characterised by a high degree of visibility and impact on the wider world, have remained in male hands. At least to the outside world the traditionally male image of the judiciary has been safeguarded. Anne Boigeol (France) refers to a symbolic male dominance in a feminised judiciary.

Career opportunities are limited for both women judges and women public prosecutors. The higher the position, the lower the proportion of women. This is not a generation problem which will be solved by a 'trickle-up' process

---

[15] Kate Malleson welcomes recent changes in the judicial selection process for judges in England and Wales which have sought to widen the recruitment pool but argues that existing arrangements, most particularly the consultation process, continue to favour lawyers from a very narrow education and career background. The need to be 'known' by senior judges advantages barristers educated at private schools and Oxford or Cambridge who are members of a small number of elite chambers.

(Germany, France, Kate Malleson for England and Wales). Informal qualification structures for career posts and selection mechanisms advantage the male sex. Intriguingly, in Italy feminisation has actually brought about structural change and has led to the disappearance of hierarchies. Seniority, not merit, is now crucial for promotion decisions.

In France, the judiciary has for some time suffered from a loss of image brought about by feminisation as well as by a number of other factors: standardisation of procedures as called for in a mass society, declining prestige, poor pay, lack of up-to-date facilities, unattractive office environment. Recruitment problems have resulted from young men increasingly giving preference to other more challenging fields of law, especially commercial legal practice, leaving the judicial field and its 'boredom' to women. Even female judges now express regret at the high degree of feminisation of the French judiciary.

Two measures have been introduced to halt this loss of image of the judiciary: a differentiation of professional functions to allow for some possibility of male distinctiveness (France), and the chance of a sideways move into higher positions in the judiciary (France, the Netherlands). In the Netherlands, the latter has remained almost exclusively a male choice (97per cent), while in France the proportion of women and men opting for this route has been 40 per cent and 60 per cent respectively.

Also, non-jurists have been allowed by the French government to enter the judiciary through a newly created non-traditional *concours*, thus further increasing the proportion of male judges, while the proportion of women is stagnating just above the 50 per cent mark. In sum, a new male strategy has begun to emerge aimed at increasing individuals' social capital by encouraging them to move between the judiciary, the advocacy and industry.

4.2.3 Women Jurists in Other Professional Fields

A large and ever growing number of female law graduates work outside the classical legal professions, that is in industry and in public services other than the courts. Precise statistical data allowing for comparisons do not exist (although in Germany, certain data have been produced in connection with 'equal standing' legislation). It can be assumed that in civil law countries the situation of women jurists in the public services generally is not dissimilar to that in the judiciary, and that the same goes for women in private industry in relation to private legal practice. Further research would be greatly desirable as these fields represent important occupational fields for women jurists.

4.3 Special Regulations and Measures to Protect Professional Women

The question is what impact national regulations for the advancement of women have on women lawyers. All Western countries have introduced legislation for the protection of women and as a means of compensating them for the disadvantages they suffer through family duties (family and medical leave acts, pension benefits for caring work etc). In recent years, additional legislative and other measures have been introduced to promote women in the labour market: equal opportunities programmes (England), *parité* policies (France), quota systems (Germany). Affirmative action programmes are most in evidence in the Anglo-American world. In continental Europe measures of this kind tend to focus on public service, therefore also covering women in the judiciary, the public prosecution service and public administration. Although such measures are enforceable in court, German women jurists, for instance, have rarely taken advantage of this opportunity for fear of stigmatisation. Also, heated debates about 'equal standing' legislation for the private sector in Germany have gone on for years, but have so far failed to produce any tangible results.

While public authorities in Germany have to submit women's promotion programmes, and their implementation is jealously guarded by a network of specially appointed officers, the professional associations of advocates here as elsewhere in the civil law world would never envisage special measures of this kind. Female advocates with employee status enjoy a certain degree of protection through the existence of general regulations in labour and social law relating to the protection of mothers, parental leave and part-time work. But it is doubtful how much use is actually made of them (irrespective of clauses expressly forbidding women's employment after giving birth). In professional codes gender issues receive no mention.

In common law countries, lawyers' organisations have equal opportunities programmes which may compensate for the absence of relevant legislative measures. In Canada, the abolition of gender discrimination and sexual harassment has been enshrined in the professional code of the Canadian Bar Association since 1993. In the same year, a Gender Equality Task Force was set up, there are 'safe counsels' ready to advise female lawyers on issues of equality and discrimination, and gender education programmes are conducted in large Canadian law firms (Mossman). In 1995, the Law Society of England and Wales on its part drew up an anti-discrimination programme.

The question is what help such legislation and other relevant measures and programmes are to women. Developments in Germany over the last decade have shown that equal standing policies have indeed borne fruit in that they have kept the issue alive in public awareness and have encouraged women to exchange their experiences and to set up their own networks. The same applies to northern European countries. However, ultimately only modest change has been brought about, and it has been counteracted by new male strategies aiming to preserve functional stratification (as noted above for the French judiciary).

Male support for the women lawyers' cause is not necessarily an altruistic move, as is shown by Clare McGlynn's analysis of the pros and cons of a 'business case for equality' propagated by the Law Society of England and Wales in the late 1980s in support of its anti-discrimination programme. She concludes that the Law Society's argument that equal wages and a fair system of measuring and evaluating women lawyers' human capital leads to greater economic prosperity of the law firm was flawed in that it was merely intended to help fill a gap in the legal labour market at that time. Any such measures are ultimately bound to collide with the cost-benefit orientated managerial decision-making in law firms.

Also, and more importantly, any state interference of this kind is readily criticised as interventionalism and is not looked upon kindly by national bars which tend to have a liberal political bias. Nor is there any socio-political agreement on the merits of equal opportunities and equal standing regulations, which are often regarded as no more than a necessary evil that will eventually pass. Ironically, discrimination against men has recently become a topic attracting quite some interest. What is really needed is the will to bring about change.

Does this mean that gender training or gender education programmes of the kind conducted by Mary Jane Mossman for Canadian law firms, which focus on moral and ethical aspects, are ultimately more effective? She herself has decided that they are not, as they ask for symbolic compliance which helps avoid discrimination law suits while the profession continues to re-enforce gender inequality. Clare McGlynn (England and Wales) concludes that mere persuasion to introduce voluntary self-regulatory measures in this area is bound to fail. We therefore need to ask ourselves whether the strategy of insisting on legal responsibility and accountability chosen by northern European countries and Germany, irrespective of its only limited effect, is perhaps the only way of bringing about real improvement.

4.4 Provisional Conclusions

Not surprisingly in an age of globalisation and internationalisation where national political, social and economic trends frequently coincide or at least impact on each other, our international comparison of the situation of women jurists has brought out a range of similarities and parallels. In continental Europe this has often been described (and criticised) as 'Americanisation'.

We have noted that due to the continuing gendered division of labour between the sexes in the family, female jurists work harder but stand fewer chances of professional success. There are intentional and unintentional mechanisms that produce professional hierarchies and persistent social forces that cause gender discrepancies. To name but a few: conscious and unconscious stereotyping (men as breadwinners while women work to meet the bill for the child-minder); the effects and notions of motherhood and even of femininity as damaging to professional commitment and efficiency; structural barriers in selection procedures and workplace arrangements; a male symbolic order based on homo-social bonding; male networks and style of working; a 'hegemonic masculinity' with a fixation on male cultural capital as opposed to women's human capital. All this leaves women with either no choice at all or with choices taken under pressure, thus belying rational choice theory.

It has been shown that legislative as well as voluntary measures to reduce discrimination against women (and gender stratification) have met with no more than limited success. Two forms of segregation persist: firstly, vertical segregation in a hierarchical order where women are pushed into the low ranks and male gate-keeping mechanisms force them either to conform or to create their own niches outside the traditional order (Silius); or, secondly, horizontal segregation allocating men and women to different fields.

5 What Change Through the Arrival of Women on the Legal Scene?

Yet, our reports also demonstrate that the entry of women into the legal profession has brought about real change. Which takes us back to the seminal question which originally sparked off the decision to initiate a project on 'Women in the Legal Profession', i.e.: does the legal profession change women? or: do women change the legal profession, in the sense that their participation benefits or damages the profession in terms of status, reputation, income, quality of work etc?

It is these questions which we initially set out to answer.

Couched in this generalised form, the questions are based on the inaccurate assumption that there is such a thing as 'the' woman jurist. In fact, our research has shown that women lawyers′ life realities and professional ambitions are far too complex, diverse, and contextually divergent to be subsumed under any one category. In other words, there cannot be any simple and straightforward answers to our questions, but merely answers of matching complexity and diversity. To arrive at these, careful and detailed studies are required of changes that have occurred in any of the fields of legal practice. All we can aim for here is tentative answers based on the results presented in the reports.

5.1 Conforming to Male Rules: Does the Profession Change Women?

The first question is a fairly simple one to answer. Ulrike Schultz deals with it in detail (Schultz 2). Irrespective of all the changes that have taken place in the legal profession, traditional male structures have survived intact. As has become amply evident from contributions to this volume, overt as well as indirect discrimination against female members of the profession has remained a fact of life, placing the latter in danger of being regarded as deviant and weak professionals (Sommerlad). Under these circumstances, one of the obvious responses open to women is to assert their achievement and commitment by conforming to the male culture as best they can, in order to acquire and display the expected cultural capital. Rosemary Hunter concludes that women barristers in Queensland, Australia, are faced with the choice of becoming honorary men or otherwise resigning themselves to an existence on the margins of the profession. Anne Boigeol (France) and Eliane Junqueira (Brazil) describe women judges' attempts at projecting the image of asexual beings, thus counteracting their

---

[16] A self-imposed severe and formal dress code is one means of avoiding being noted as different (Junqueira), although conformity easily runs the risk of being regarded as excessive and therefore counterproductive (Schultz 2).

male colleagues' attempts at sexualising them.[16] On the other hand, Anne Boigeol also records a gradual diminishing of this tendency among the French judiciary as feminisation progresses. Overall, the younger generation of women judges and prosecutors in civil law countries seem to find themselves under less pressure to conform to the male model of behaviour than their counterparts in the common law world, although some pressure still persists.

Acceptance of the need to conform to the legal world they have joined can be regarded as part of women's professional contract.[17] Women are prepared for it during their legal training at law school where strong pressure is exerted on them to conform to the traditional masculine culture (Schultz 1). Deborah Rhode notes the irony of the fact that having for centuries been excluded from the legal profession on the grounds of their being intrinsically different from men, women are now expected to be the same as men, to fit into established structures which, however, are not designed to accommodate them. And yet if they do conceal their own sex and try to conform, their otherness, Rosemary Hunter argues, is simultaneously and continually re-enforced, while if they don't, marginalisation is a serious danger. Like Hunter, Ulrike Schultz (Schultz 2) has found that women who aim at assimilation may meet with the accusation of being rather masculine and hard, and run the risk of penalties. In other words, women can't win. Their dilemma leads them to devise two different gender identities for themselves, one for private and one for public consumption. The question arises whether and to what extent they can sustain this schizophrenic role.

Of course, not every woman is faced with the same demands for conformity, as national, institutional and corporate cultures vary. However, it is intriguing to find that coercion against women jurists to assimilate themselves to the prevailing male culture is by no means limited to national cultures that are openly masculine, such as that of Brazil where, as Eliane Junqueira reports, women lawyers suffer discrimination from their professional partners as well as clients. Western countries, which pride themselves of being egalitarian and postmodern, are by no means beyond reproach in this respect either.

Therefore the answer to our question is: yes, women are changed through the professional acculturation processes, they are definitely influenced in their *habitus*, their behaviour—though in varying degrees, depending on their will to adapt and their handling of the pressure for conformity and the field they work in.

5.2 Women and Structural Change in the Profession

The second question—in what way and how far do women influence the profession?—is far more complex and will form the subject of the remaining

---

[17] Cf. Harriet Silius (1992), also: Harriet Silius, Gender Contract of Women Lawyers. The Case of Finland. Paper presented in 1992 at the Third European Conference of the Working Group on the Legal Profession, Aix-en-Provence. According to Silius, a woman jurist's professional contract comprises two parts: a work contract aimed at creating, maintaining and reproducing existing power and hierarchical structures, and a caring contract, obliging women to carry the burden of domestic work but also entitling them to a reduction of overtime work or to working part-time.

part of this synthesis. It requires us to look at the major tendencies for change in the profession and the role women play in it.

Two developments over recent decades, reflected over and over again in contributions to this volume, have brought about structural change in the legal profession. On the one hand, a dramatic increase in the number of practising lawyers, on the other hand the commercialisation of legal practice. Both have been crucial in shaping the role and situation of women in today's legal profession.

5.2.1 Women's Share in the Increase of Lawyers

Compared to the relative stability in terms of numbers in professions where appointments are made on the basis of need (judiciaries as well as notariats in civil law countries), a veritable numerical explosion has occurred in the profession of legal practitioners where no such restrictions to access exist. To take the example of Germany, the country with the largest judiciary: while in the 1950s the number of practising lawyers was roughly equivalent to that of judges (13,000 *Rechtsanwälte* (1950) compared to 17,000 judges (1955)) with a population per capita rate of about 3,500 lawyers, by 1980 the number of lawyers (36,000) had grown to double that of judges (17,500). By 1990 it had trebled (57,000 lawyers), and in 2002 the number of lawyers had risen to roughly 116,300 compared to some 21,000 judges, i.e. a proportion of five to one.[18] There is now on average one lawyer for every 800 inhabitants. Women make up 27 per cent in the German advocacy, but account for 40 per cent of the rise in numbers newly admitted to the profession.

How to evaluate this contribution in terms of mere numbers? Is there any justification for attributing to this influx of women any possible consequences such as growing and intensified competition, an erosion of professional ethics, or a stratification of income levels? Or are these changes which would have happened anyway due to economic pressure in capitalist systems and the effects of modernisation and globalisation?

5.2.2 Exposure to Market Forces

While structural change has been almost non-existent and technological change has been slow as far as the working environment of judges and notaries is concerned, the work of practising lawyers has undergone revolutionary developments. Most strikingly, the rise of the large law firm and an accompanying loss of ground on the part of solo practitioners and small law firms have created two separate hemispheres, each with its own structures, identities, ideologies as well as ethics. The homogeneity of the legal profession has suffered serious erosion. This process of fracturing appears to be unstoppable. It is the inevitable outcome of law firms' exposure to market forces and lawyers' having to respond to demands of powerful clients in industry, as the profession is undergoing a

---

[18] The rise in the number of German judges from 17,000 to 21,000 is attributable to the impact of German unification.

transformation from a liberal profession proud of its ethical stance to an entrepreneurial one working on purely commercial principles. In law firms this
results in a process of hierarchisation, with fewer positions at the top of the
pyramid and a broadening of its base. All in all there has been a blurring of
professional contours in the course of these modernisation processes.

The degree to which this transformation has progressed so far varies considerably from country to country. In Germany, only 10 per cent of the legal profession work in large law firms and the traditional role model has broadly retained
its validity. In England and Wales, on the other hand, commercialisation has
made the gentlemanly profession a thing of the past, as calculating rationality
replaces altruistic and ethical values, and corporate managerialism determines all
aspects of a law firm's culture. Hilary Sommerlad's detailed study bears witness
to this. But our studies also make it clear that rather than being the agents behind
this process, women have taken on the roles of victims or passive bystanders.

5.3 Differences After All: Female Lawyering?

So there remains the question of the qualitative impact of women lawyers on
legal work. Do women 'rewrite the rules'?[19] What about 'women's other voice',
to use Carol Gilligan's memorable phrase? What about distinctively feminine
forms of legal practice? Is there no such a thing? And if there is, how can we
define the difference which sets it aside from the established abstract and
masculine culture of law and legal practice?

Gilligan's work is embedded in feminist thinking of the 1980s, which pro-
mulgated the view that there are differences between men and women and that
'women's way of being' is potentially suited to promote a more moral and a
more humane form of modernisation of society.[20] Today this approach is often
dismissed as 'essentialism'. A number of contributions to this volume focus on
the issue of a female ethic of care versus a male ethic of justice, some of them
using empirical studies arguing against the existence of any significant differences between male and female jurists' working styles and results (Felstiner et
al., de Groot).

5.3.1 Perception of Femininity

Both male and female jurists have confirmed perceptions of differences between
their own attitude to work and behaviour and that of members of the other sex
(Schultz 2, Ietswaart, Sommerlad). But one can sense a certain reluctance to
make too much of any feminine features like intuitiveness, empathy, emotionality, sensitivity, context-relatedness etc, as these used to be the basis for declar-
ing women unfit for the profession. Nor are they features which are typically

---

[19] Cf. Mona Harrington. *Women Lawyers: Rewriting the Rules*, New York: A A Knopf, 1994
[20] It is of interest to note that contemporary personnel management theory supports this view
when highlighting certain feminine qualities as being of particular significance for successful management of the future, even when measured by standards of efficiency, effectiveness and economy.

associated with professional success. Sommerlad draws attention to a general perception that male lawyers are inclined to be strong, powerful, aggressive, with a sense of logic, and resistant to emotional issues. However, the fact that feminine or 'soft' skills are increasingly valued in certain entrepreneurial contexts (not least in personnel management) has raised feminist hopes that cultivating these skills might improve the professional culture if not in law firms then at least in the judiciary (Schultz 2).

5.3.2 Lawyering outcomes

Judging   The question poses itself in how far these 'typically female' qualities can affect legal work—a question of particular significance in a judicial context. After all, there is a certain incompatibility between these qualities and the requirements of objectivity and justice. Nor are those seeking justice free from gender-based prejudices with reference to judges of either sex. The issue is addressed most clearly in reports about female judges in Brazil and France, but is also touched on in other contributions. In France, female judges are suspected of being more repressive than men. Studies for Germany, Poland and Brazil have found only isolated cases of gender-specific approaches to the judicial task which tended to be influenced by personal experience and situations. In criminal trials, female judges occasionally showed greater empathy with male offenders in assessing their personality—a factor of relevance to the punishment finally imposed. The only exception were cases of rape and violence, where some measure of identification with the victim can be assumed. But the opposite has been found to be true for Israel. Here Bryna Bogoch notes that women judges imposed lower sentences for sexual offences than for bodily harm offences and interprets this as indicating that there was no special sympathy on the part of the women judges for the victims of rape and sexual assault.

In maintenance cases female judges have been observed to be more inclined than male judges to find against housewives, as presumably they apply their own personal standards as professional women (Poland, Brazil). On the other hand, examples of prejudice in favour of or against women influencing male judges' verdicts are not hard to find either (an argument of considerable significance in the early women's movement's campaign in favour of female jurists).

Of particular interest in this context is Bryna Bogoch's study of linguistic interaction in Israeli courts in various scenarios involving judges, attorneys and witnesses of both sexes. She found that male communications addressed to women, whichever side they came from or were addressed to, reflected a desire to project power and hierarchical status. But even female utterances if addressed to women were phrased with less respect for the addressees' dignity than those addressed to men. All this had serious and very tangible results: sentences were higher where defendants were represented by a woman rather than a man, but lower if prosecutors were female rather than male. Bogoch concludes that none of this provides evidence to support Gilligan's theory of women's 'different voice', but merely reflects the still tenuous position of women in the judiciary where their competence is consistently questioned and their confidence undermined, making gender the interpretive framework within which lawyers' actions and the persuasiveness of their case is assessed.

Other studies emphasise minor gender-related differences in working styles and behaviours. Eliane Junqueira reports that female judges in Brazil tend to pay greater attention to detail with regard to the facts of the proceedings and the final reasoning for their judgment, and that their style of delivering decisions may also differ from that of their male colleagues.[21] They are perceived to be inclined to take greater responsibility for their work, get more emotionally involved, show more concern for improving the working atmosphere, and have greater consideration for colleagues of inferior status (cf. also Schultz 2).

Leny de Groot refers to her study where she concluded that male and female judges, when invited to predict the outcome of a case, did not differ regarding the accuracy or otherwise of their predictions, but that the latter were more likely to learn from their mistakes.

In sum then, gender-specific features can be shown to exist in terms of judges' behaviours and working styles, but in most countries there is not sufficient hard evidence to prove that they affect the actual outcome of particular cases.

Lawyers' work   As for female practising lawyers and their particular style of negotiation, Bryna Bogoch points to a small-scale study carried out in Israel which discovered that they were occasionally willing to acknowledge the legitimacy of clients' emotional concerns rather than maintaining neutral detachment throughout. However, they did so having noted expressly their departure from their normal professional role. Clients of women lawyers on their part reported that they experienced greater respect, concern and responsiveness than from male lawyers.

These findings might be seen as contradicting results recorded by William Felstiner et al.[22] Their study—a comprehensive US-wide survey of clients acting as individuals—had not shown any significant client perceptions of gender-specific behavioural features on the part of male and female lawyers. Both sexes were described by clients as friendly, confident, polite, organised, trustworthy, and fair, a set of attributes which according to Menkel-Meadow (1989) are more likely to be attributed to women.[23] Yet it is conceivable that the difference between Felstiner's and Bogoch's findings can be explained by each of them applying a different approach to the problem, the former inquiring into clients'

---

[21] Frances Raday (1996) provides impressive illustrations of female judges' emotional rhetoric.

[22] It is interesting to note that in this study only 13 per cent of the clients responding had chosen a woman lawyer, a proportion that is significantly lower than women's average membership in the profession. On the other hand, Mather (like Bogoch) recorded in her American study an above-average share of women lawyers involved in family matters.

[23] This lends support to Robert Rosen's view presented in 1999 at a workshop at the International Institute for the Sociology of Law in Oñati, Spain, that the ethic of care and emotional labour have always been at the heart of lawyers' relationships towards their clients.

absolute views of male and female lawyers they had consulted, while the latter analysed various parties' behaviour on a comparative basis. Looking at it in this way, it would be legitimate to conclude that representatives of both sexes were perceived to do their job well (Felstiner et al.), but that women lawyers might have done so even better than men (Bogoch).

Ulrike Schultz, in informal face-to-face discussions with female lawyers working in small law firms in Germany, found support for Bogoch's views, in that they did perceive their own working style to be different from that of male lawyers. They described themselves as more generous with their time, taking less notice of cost-benefit criteria, being more concerned with maintaining good relations with their clients, and investing greater emotional labour in their dealings with them.

Are women lawyers perhaps more ethical than male lawyers? Data collected in the Netherlands suggest that women are less likely to be involved in disciplinary complaints than men (de Groot), which fits in with criminological statistics showing a significantly lower crime rate (approx. 20 per cent) on the part of women than of men.[24]

Finally, a study by Lynn Mather based on interviews with divorce lawyers in two American states showed up both similarities and differences between female and male lawyers' behaviour towards their clients. Confirming Bogoch's findings for Israel, Mather notes women lawyers' perceptions of greater concern for and more careful listening to their clients in the context of family matters. On the other hand, she also records both male and female lawyers' preference for peaceful settlements, which contrasts with theories based on Gilligan's work which regard men as typically inclined to look for adversarial solutions and therefore make the Anglo-American system in general appear more masculine in character. Lynn Mather is keen to assert that her results need to be evaluated in the context of social, economic and legal forces and that gender is just one, albeit an important, factor determining attorneys' work. She argues that any perceived differences between female and male lawyers need to be interpreted as the result of a multi-faceted interaction with other contextual factors.

6 A Women Lawyers' Project

Our investigations lead us to conclude that women lawyers' primary motivation is a sense of obligation towards their professional role which encourages them to adapt to existing norms. This process of integration has largely been completed by the time they finish their legal training. Stepping outside that predetermined framework would require a bold decision on their parts. The first condition for women finding and articulating a voice of their own would be a further increase in numbers. Bryna Bogoch rightly argues that only when

[24] However, feminist criminologists by no means agree on whether this is due to women being 'better' or to the fact that their specific forms of offending have simply not been captured by criminal law regulations.

women feel secure in their professional position can they consider adopting their own style of lawyering. But then, as the example of the French judiciary teaches us, not even numbers are sufficient if women jurists' position as such is still contested. Quantitative feminisation does not automatically equate with feminisation in the sense of demasculinisation, or a change of gendered practices in legal work and culture or in the profession itself. In the 1980s, the 'critical mass' required was put at about one third. It now seems that women would rather need an uncontested majority to create a new majority culture.

6.1 Project Lost?

Where does all this leave us? It seems clear that for the time being there is insufficient evidence to justify the assumption of one common women's project or even of one clearly definable and localisable women's culture in legal practice. Women in the various branches of the legal profession do not speak with one voice. The need to perform professionally encourages women to aim for a levelling out of attributes and behaviour that might set them apart from their male colleagues—but not all of these nor all to the same degree. This makes for a fragmentation of their own group. There are complex patterns of identity, such as the cool and tough female lawyer and the motherly woman judge concerned with individuals' welfare, or vice versa, or variants of the two. Femininity and motherliness with ethic of care alone cannot appropriately conceptualise the effects of the increasing numbers of women in legal professions. This suggests that it is, indeed, important to contextualise gender issues by including such aspects as class, ethnicity, age and sexual orientation which create diversity. Thus Hilary Sommerlad has repeatedly pointed out the fragmentation of the legal field into specialisms and the significance of different working environments within it. But there is something unsatisfactory about this emphasis on contextual factors as it ultimately makes for a denial of the existence of the influence of gender and in particular of femininity. Seen in this light, the female lawyer remains an unknown creature.

Many legal feminists would regard it as regrettable if there were no such thing as a women lawyers' project. Members of the second women's movement were agreed on the need to seek a different, a better way out of a world which had traditionally been shaped by men. They wanted women to become visible in society, male power monopolies to be broken up, and female counter-visions of the world to be translated into reality. To achieve this, it was necessary to critique the status quo and to draw on female knowledge and female experience.

Rhode speaks of a vision of professions enriched with female experience, but on the basis of feminist commitment rather than biological categories. This aim has been lost sight of, if not before then at the point when women ceased to be the focus of feminist attention and made way to gender; when—a popular move in today's social sciences—gender was hastily deconstructed, and gender policies performed a change of paradigm towards gender mainstreaming. Female jurists in particular appear to be mainly concerned with acquiring a share in the profession's prestige and power rather than with choosing a 'third way', that is a morally based gender-specific reform of the legal professions and their culture.

Celia Wells deplores this as a voluntary surrender of something precious. The process of commercialisation and growing managerialism has brought about the opposite of feminist visions. It is conceivable that looked at realistically women were and are unable to offer any resistance. Any serious threat to a male professional project of acquiring market control has thus been diverted.

6.2 Subliminal Change

Even if we have been unable to establish a collective women's way or a common women's voice, this does not mean to say that women have not left their mark on the profession, thus adding colour to the uniformity of brotherhoods. As individuals they practise caring and motherliness in their respective professional contexts.[25] This does have an impact even if this impact is not easily measured or quantified. Besides, some would hesitate to discuss any such impact which at the turn of the millennium has come to be associated with old-fashioned values.

Sommerlad identifies a strengthening of the feminine element in the wake of a consumer revolution which reinforces expectations of more developed 'soft skills'. Boigeol describes a move to a more 'feminine model' of administering justice, with both men and women having become more feminine in their approach to legal justice compared with the past when the profession was strictly dominated by men and service obligations carried little weight.

Even if women jurists have failed to achieve any clearly defined change in their working environments, they have at least succeeded in softening the rigid contours of the life model of the male breadwinner and in bringing about a flexibilisation of workplace structures. And there is another undeniable fact: women have changed the very tool of lawyers' work—they have changed the law. They have enforced legislative measures which take into account modern notions of equality, equal rights and (now) equal standing, and have created the legislative base for women's participation in all social functions and in the exercise of power. Important questions remain: do women have an impact on the public image of the profession? can today's progressive loss of formal social procedures and the growing emphasis on subjectivity be attributed to the participation of women? analogously, is the accompanying loss of formality in legal work attributable to the influence of women jurists? and, crucially, will these in turn encourage a creeping process of deprofessionalisation? (Schultz 2)

---

[25] Silius distinguishes between three kinds of motherliness: paternal motherliness towards clients (to enforce ethics and morality); sisterly motherliness towards colleagues; and social motherliness towards those who are weaker.

7 What Way Forward for Women Lawyers?

What solutions are open to women in the future, in the face of the dilemma that, although formally equally qualified as men, they fail to meet with the same professional success as well as having to accommodate in their lives the dual burden of private and professional duties? Predictions are difficult to make.

The professions, as we have seen, are exposed to market forces. This includes public service, previously a sheltered area but now increasingly subject to the management criteria of private industry, resulting in a fracturing of traditional structures. Identity and ideology in the professions have become objects of critical scrutiny, and it is worth reminding ourselves that women are but one agent in the complex process of social change.

The report on Finland by Harriet Silius highlights the problems inherent in any attempt to predict the professional future of women in the legal professions. It is not inconceivable that developments in Finland might represent a prototype, an indication of things to come on a wider scale. Harriet Silius deconstructs the results of her own comprehensive study on women in the legal profession in Finland carried out a decade ago. She then predicted a steady increase in the number of women in the public sector and in particular in the judiciary. Ten years later, her prediction had been proved wrong, indeed, the opposite was happening: women were leaving the public in favour of the private sector. Even more surprisingly, they were not moving into law firms (where their share has remained roughly stable), but into the non-classical legal fields, such as insurance, commerce, and banking.

Harriet Silius considers the reshaping of gendering processes, and their increasing complexity. She has found decreasing income discrepancies between the sexes but growing income differentials among women themselves. By way of explanation, she refers us to broader economic trends captured in more general theories of employment discrimination, human capital and feminism. There are the loss of jobs through rationalisation of public services and their general devaluation, the effects of the old exclusionary strategies, the younger generation's lack of desire to follow in their mothers' footsteps and take on the burden of conforming, and their preference for moving into areas of work where acceptance is more likely and discrimination can be avoided. This might be one solution for an obviously growing number of women jurists who are looking for sufficient income as well as the chance of combining family and profession without being threatened by total exhaustion.

Whatever the answer, there can be no doubt that, for the time being, the old social patterns are still with us: an obituary in the *Daily Express* (7 May 2002) for Michael Kerr, a well-known English judge and Queen's Council, was entitled, 'A Legal Titan with a Tireless Sense of Duty'. Readers learnt that his wife had 'given' him a son and a daughter—no mention of the fact that she herself is a solicitor of some repute and that these are their joint children. The notions of masculinity and femininity informing this obituary could not be less ambiguous. Is it conceivable that one day a statement of this kind might be applied to a woman? And are we therefore perhaps looking at no more than the final stirrings of an order now passed?

REFERENCES

Abel, Richard and Phillip Lewis (eds). 1988–1989. *Lawyers in Society*. Vol. 1: *The Common Law World*. Vol. 2: *The Civil Law World*. Vol. 3: *Comparative Theories*. Berkeley: University of California Press.

——, 1995. *Lawyers in Society. An Overview*. Berkeley: University of California Press.

Collier, Richard. 1999. Masculinism, Law and Law Teaching. *International Journal of the Sociology of Law* 19, 427–451.

Donnell, Cathlin, Joyce Sterling and Nancy Reichman. 1998. *Gender Penalties: The Results of the Careers and Compensation Project*. Colorado Women's Bar Association.

Epstein, Cynthia Fuchs, Robert Saute, Bonnie Oglensky and Martha Gever. 1995. Glass ceilings and open doors: Women's advancement in the legal profession. *Fordham Law Review,* 200–360.

Epstein, Cynthia Fuchs. 2001. Women in the Legal Profession at the Turn of the Twenty-First Century: Assessing Glass Ceilings and Open Doors. *Kansas Law Review*, 39, 733–760.

Gilligan, Carol. 1981. *In A Different Voice: Psychological Theory and Women's Development*. Cambridge, Mass.: Harvard University Press.

Krauskopf, Joan. 1994. 'Touching the Elefant': Perceptions of Gender Issues in Nine Law Schools. *Journal of Legal Education* 44, 311–340.

Menkel-Meadow, Carrie. 1985. Portia In A Different Voice: Speculation on a Women's Lawyering Process, 1 *Berkeley Women's Law Journal* 39.

——, 1987. Excluded Voices: New Voices in the Legal Profession. Making New Voices in the Law, 42 *University of Miami Law Review* 701.

——, 1988. Feminist Legal Theory, Critical Legal Studies and Legal Education or the 'Fem-Crits' Go to Law School, 38 *Journal of Legal Education* 61.

Nelson, Robert, Rebecca Sandfur and John Heinz. 2001. Inequalities of Ethnicity, Gender, and Race and the Transformation of an Urban Legal Profession: Chicago Lawyers 1975–1995, paper presented at the Law and Society Meeting, Budapest, July 5, 2001.

Raday, Frances. 1996. Women in Law in Israel: A Study of the Relationship between Professional Integration and Feminism. *Georgia State University Law Review* 12, 525–552.

Rosen, Robert. 2003. "You are too emotional to be a lawyer!": Talcott Parsons, Legal Ethics, and the Misuse of both Affective Neutrality and Role-Distance. *International Journal of the Legal Profession,* forthcoming.

Silius, Harriet. 1992. *Contracted Femininity. The Case of Women Lawyers in Finland*. Abo: Abo Academy Press. (Finnish original title: Den kringgärdade kvinnligheten. Att vara kvinnlig jurist i Finland. English summary provided).

Thornton, Margaret. 1996. *Dissonance and Distrust. Women in the Legal Profession*. Melbourne: Oxford University Press.

——, 1998. *Technocentrism in the Law School*. Osgoode Hall Law Journal 36, 369–398.

PART 1

Women Lawyers in the Common Law World

1

Gender and the Profession: An American Perspective

DEBORAH L RHODE[1]

Abstract

This article provides an overview of two central questions concerning the American bar: how gender structures professional roles and how gender affects access to professional opportunities. Discussion begins by evaluating claims that women approach their legal career from a distinctive perspective, and that their values may foster more humane, less hierarchical structures for professional life. Analysis of relevant research underscores the risks associated with oversimplifying and overclaiming gender differences. Context matters greatly in eliciting characteristics traditionally associated with women, and other factors, such as race and ethnicity, may be equally important. Research on professional opportunities finds that despite women's increasing representation and influence in the profession, the 'woman problem' has not been solved and a major problem is the lack of acknowledgement that there remains in fact a problem. The article summarises major barriers such as unconscious stereotypes and inflexible workplace structures and identifies promising strategies for reform.

1 INTRODUCTION

IN COMMENTING ON women's admission to Harvard Law School in 1950, then Dean Erwin Griswold reassured anxious alums that this development was not 'very important or very significant.' 'Most of us,' he noted,

> have seen women from time to time in our lives and have managed to survive the shock. I think we can take it, and I doubt that it will change the character of the School or even its atmosphere to any detectable extent.' (Griswold 1950)

Such perceptions remain common. In one representative survey, less than half of the male attorneys (compared with three-quarters of females) believed that

---

[1] Ideas expressed in this essay appear in different form in others of my publications (1994, 1996, 1997).

women's entry would have major consequences for the profession (Winter 1983: 1384, 1388).

Such perceptions are not without irony. For centuries, women were excluded from the professions on the assumption that they were different; once admitted, the assumption typically was that they were the same. By and large, women have been expected to practise within established structures; those structures have not sufficiently changed to accommodate women.

This essay is part of a broader feminist effort to alter such patterns. In many respects, the very existence of such efforts is a testament to partial progress. When I entered law school a quarter century ago, issues concerning women were noticeable largely for their absence. I had no courses from or about women. And what seems especially striking to me now is that it never seemed striking to me then. It was simply the way law—and life—were. I, and many of my female classmates, just felt grateful to have gained admission, particularly since many male students and professors seemed clearly uncomfortable when we were around. And as a prominent Washington practitioner, Sol Linowitz, ruefully recalls, 'it never occurred to [these men] to wonder whether the women felt uncomfortable' (Linowitz 1994: 6).

That question is, at least, now on the agenda. Over the last quarter century, sensitivity to gender bias has increased dramatically, as has women's representation in the legal profession. Female attorneys now account for about 45 per cent of new entrants to the American bar. But ironically enough, this partial progress has created its own obstacles to further reform. Women's growing opportunities are often taken as evidence that the 'woman problem' has been solved. But the recent accumulation of judicial, bar, and scholarly studies on gender raises concerns about both the structure of professional roles and the inequality of professional opportunities. In exploring those issues, the following discussion makes clear how values traditionally associated with women remain undervalued in lawyers' daily lives.

2 PROFESSIONAL ROLES

2.1 Theoretical Frameworks

For those interested in gender and the professions, a central issue is whether women approach their occupational role from a distinctive perspective. One important strand of feminist theory, popularised by Carol Gilligan, argues that women tend to reason in a 'different voice': they are less likely than men to privilege abstract rights over concrete relationships, and are more attentive to values of care, connection and context. Building on this relational approach, some feminists argue that women bring a distinctive perspective to professional roles, and that their values may foster more humane, less hierarchical structures for professional life. (Gilligan 1982; Harrington 1993: 251; Jack and Jack 1989:

56–58; Cahn 1992: 1039, 1045; Menkel-Meadow 1985: 39, 55; Spelman 1988; Fuchs Epstein 1988; Greeno and Maccoby 1986; Larrabee 1993; Deaux 1984, 1990; Molm and Hedley 1992; Shibley Hyde 1990) Other feminists, including Catharine MacKinnon, have emphasised women's subordination as a source of women's distinctive interests and concerns (1989, 1985).

Claims about gender difference in the profession draw on a variety of narrative accounts and empirical research. For example, some small-scale studies find that women rank competitiveness as less desirable than do men (Lipman-Blumen 1992: 183, 200–01); that women in certain decision-making contexts are more inclined than men to prefer collaborative, interactive leadership styles (Yancey Martin 1990: 184; Rosener 1990, 120); and that women professionals are more likely to value interpersonal client relationships (Menkel-Meadow 1989: 227–28), public service work (Menkel-Meadow 1989: 226, 228),[2] and empathetic reasoning processes Jack & Jack 1989: 56–58; Menkel-Meadow 1985: 55).

The strength of such analyses lies in their demand that values traditionally associated with women be valued and that we focus on transforming social institutions, not just assimilating women within them. Yet efforts to claim an authentic female voice illustrate the difficulty with theorising from experience without homogenising it. To divide the world solely along gender lines is to ignore the ways in which biological status is experienced differently by different groups under different circumstances. There is no 'generic woman' (Spelman 1988: 114, 117), and relational feminism has not sufficiently acknowledged variations across culture, class, race, ethnicity, age, and sexual orientation (Fuchs Epstein 1988: 185; Greeno and Maccoby 1986: 312–16; Larrabee 1993). Nor have relational frameworks addressed the contextual forces that lead the same women to vary in their expression of 'women's' values and characteristics in different social circumstances.

The celebration of gender difference risks not only oversimplifying, but also overclaiming. Recent research raises substantial questions about how different women's voice in fact is. Psychological surveys generally find few attributes on which the sexes consistently vary. (Eagly 1987: 31; Maccoby 1990: 513, 513–15; Deaux and Major 1990: 89) Even for these attributes, gender typically accounts for only about five per cent of the variance. (Eagly 1987: 115; Molm and Hedley 1992: 1, 6; Deaux 1984: 105, 110–11; Shibley 1990: 55, 64–68) The similarities between men and women are far greater than the disparities, and small statistical distinctions do not support sweeping sex-based dichotomies. Most empirical studies of moral development or altruistic behavior do not find significant gender distinctions. (For altruism see Kohn 1990: 82; Tavris 1992: 63–67; for moral behavior see Epstein 1988: 76–77; Greeno and Maccoby 1986: 315) Nor does related research on managerial behavior reveal the consistent sex-linked

[2] Indicating that women lawyers are more likely to cite social service as a reason for entering the profession and for entering legal aid, public interest and government service work.

variations that relational feminism would suggest. (Epstein 1988: 173–184; Forisha 1981: 23; Mendelson Freeman 1990; Moss Kanter 1982: 234, 236–45) Employees who confront similar occupational pressures have similar responses. (England and Farkas 1986: 137–41; Epstein 1988: 179–81; Gomez-Mejia 1983: 492, 495)

What emerges from these and related studies is the importance of context in eliciting traits traditionally associated with women. (England and Farkas 1986: 137–41; Epstein 1988: 130–61; Molm and Hedley 1992: 6–8; Tavris 1992: 290–96; Tavris 1991: 150, 150–51, 154–56, 159–60)[3] Changes in the gender composition and social expectations of a particular professional setting significantly affect the likelihood that 'feminine' attributes will be expressed. A representative case in point involves female judges. Surveys of judicial decision-making reflect no consistent gender differences even in areas involving women's rights or sentencing for violent crimes against women (Gruhl *et al* 1981, 308, 319–20[4]; Walker and Barrow 1985: 596, 607[5]). Yet all-female judicial associations display greater sensitivity to traditionally female values than their male-dominated counterparts. Programmes for women judges often focus on issues such as combating bias, accommodating family concerns in courthouse administration, and ensuring more empathetic treatment of vulnerable witnesses. (Heilbrun and Resnik 1990: 1913, 1948–50) Similarly, feminist political groups and all-female law firms generally have established less hierarchical, more participatory structures than comparable male-dominated institutions. (Fuchs Epstein 1993: 131–61)

Taken together, these divergent findings on sex-based difference underscore the need for greater contextual analysis. To that end, some strains of feminist jurisprudence have sought to recognise difference without universalising its content. Drawing on postmodern and pragmatic traditions, these frameworks emphasise multiple sources of identity and avoid abstract, acontextual theory. Both postmodern and pragmatic approaches to difference recognise that women's voice speaks in more than one register; its expression depends heavily on the social circumstances and cross-cutting affiliations of the speaker, including not only gender but class, race, ethnicity, age and sexual orientation. (see eg Fraser and Nicholson 1990: 13, 35; Grant 1993: 107, 124, 160–63; Bartlett 1990: 89, 884; Harris 1990: 581, 585; Radin 1990: 1699, 1707)

Such approaches can also recognise the strategic costs as well as values in asserting a 'woman's point of view.' Emphasising males' interest in abstract principles and females' concern for interpersonal relationships reinforces long-standing stereotypes that have restricted opportunities for both sexes. However feminist in inspiration, any dualistic world view is readily appropriated for non-

---

[3] Comments of Cynthia Fuchs Epstein, Jane Mansbridge and Jeffrey A Sonnenfeld.
[4] Finding no gender difference among judges, except for female judges' greater propensity to sentence female offenders to prison.
[5] Finding no significant male/female difference on issues of criminal law and women's rights.

feminist objectives. For example, as the analysis of gender bias below suggests, professional women too often find that emphasis on their distinctive capacities and needs reinforces structures that are separate but not equal.

A more effective strategy is neither to exaggerate nor deny gender differences. We can avoid sweeping claims about woman's essential nature, while noting that particular groups of women under particular social conditions practice their professions based on different expectations and experiences than men. We also can observe that values traditionally associated with women—care, cooperation, context—have been undervalued in traditionally male-dominated professions, and that their absence impoverishes the lives of both sexes. In short, we can advocate visions of professionalism that resonate with women's experiences, but on the basis of feminist commitments, not biological categories.

2.2 The Morality of Role

Although women by no means share a single view of lawyer's appropriate role, they do express some common concerns and values that challenge conventional views. The traditional approach to professional responsibility builds on a concept of role-differentiated morality that departs from ordinary personal morality. (Montaigne; quoted in Curtis 1951: 20) The prevailing assumption is that individuals' ability to assert legal rights rests on having lawyers who defend, not judge, their clients. (For critical accounts of this coventional view, see Luban 1988; Rhode 1985: 589, 589–659; Wasserstrom 1975: 1, 1–24) Fulfilling professional responsibilities may require actions that run counter to individuals' personal values.

From a feminist perspective, this traditional concept of role-differentiated morality is unsatisfying in several respects. At the most fundamental level, feminists join other critics in questioning the distinction between ordinary morality and role morality. As they note, 'no one is ever an abstract moral agent.' (MacIntyre 1978: 37) Individuals always function within relationships and make ethical choices in view of their particular responsibilities as parents, friends, spouses, employees and so forth. Ordinary morality, no less than role morality, assumes that individuals 'in different circumstances and with different abilities have different obligations.' (Held 1984: 60, 67)

A related criticism is that traditional concepts of role do not advance analysis about what those different obligations entail. All too often, lawyers deny personal accountability for professional acts on the ground that their role as loyal advocate demands it. Yet this strategy attempts to avoid responsibility even as it is exercised. The choice to defer to a particular concept of role is itself a moral choice and needs to be justified as such. Conventional approaches to professional ethics fail to provide adequate justifications. By encouraging deference to abstract role-based norms, these approaches devalue the contextual and relational dimensions that are central to feminist theory and that should be central to ethical analysis. The result is to impoverish both personal and professional identity.

Under conventional understandings of role morality, attorneys are expected to act as neutral partisans who represent their clients zealously within the bounds of the law. (Model Code of Professional Responsibility DR 4 –101, DR 7–101, EC 7–1 1980; Model Rules of Professional Conduct, Rule 1.2, 1992) Although lawyers may not assist fraudulent, harassing or illegal conduct, they are given wide latitude to protect client interests at the expense of broader societal concerns. For example, they may present evidence that they reasonably believe to be inaccurate or misleading as long as they do not know it to be false; they may withhold material information that the other side fails to discover; they may invoke technical defences to defeat rightful claims; and they may remain silent about a client's wrongful conduct even when disclosure would prevent substantial financial harm or physical risk to innocent parties. (Frankel 1980: 25–29; Rhode and Luban 1992: 221–56; Rhode 1994b: 665, 667–76)

The rationale for this morally neutral advocacy rests on two primary lines of argument. The first invokes utilitarian, instrumental reasoning. It assumes that the most effective way to achieve justice is through the competitive clash of two zealous adversaries, and that their effectiveness depends on trusting relationships with clients. On this view, an adversarial system will function fairly only if individuals have full confidence in the loyalty and confidentiality of their advocates.

From feminists' standpoint, this conventional justification for the advocate's role is too abstract and acontextual to yield morally satisfying outcomes. The assumption that truth or fairness necessarily results from adversarial clashes is neither self-evident nor supported by empirical evidence. It is not the way most professions or most legal systems pursue knowledge. (Luban 1988: 67–103; Frankel 1975: 1031, 1036–37) Moreover, the conventional paradigm presupposes a fair contest between combatants with roughly equal resources, capacities, and incentives. Such equality is all too infrequent in a society that tolerates vast disparities in wealth, renders most legal proceedings enormously expensive and allocates civil legal assistance largely through market mechanisms. (Galanter 1974: 95, 97–114; Rhode 1985: 595–605)

In response to such criticisms, defenders of partisan norms rely on an alternative rights-based justification. On this view, respect for clients' individual autonomy implies respect for their legal entitlements and requires undivided loyalty from their legal advisers. By absolving attorneys from accountability for their clients' acts, the traditional advocacy role encourages representation of those most in need of ethical counselling and those most vulnerable to public prejudice or state oppression. Any alternative system, it is argued, would threaten rule by an oligarchy of lawyers. (Pepper 1986: 613, 629–30; for a critical perspective, see Wasserstrom 1975)

Feminists join other critics in raising two central objections to this rights-based defence of neutral partisanship. The first is that it collapses legal and moral entitlements. It assumes that society benefits by allowing clients to pursue whatever objectives the law permits. Yet conduct that is harmful to the public interest in general or to subordinate groups in particular sometimes remains legal. For example, prohibitions may appear too difficult or costly to enforce, or decision-makers may be uninformed, overworked or vulnerable to interest-group pressures. In such contexts, lawyers may have no particular moral expertise, but they at least have a more disinterested perspective than clients on the ethical dimensions of certain practices. For attorneys to accept moral responsibility is not necessarily to impose it. Unless the lawyer is the last in town (or the functional equivalent for indigent clients), his or her refusal of the neutral partisan role does not preempt representation. It simply imposes on clients the psychological and financial cost of finding alternative counsel (Luban 1988: 166; Rhode 1985: 621–26).

A second problem with rights-based justifications for partisanship is that they fail to explain why rights of clients should trump those of all other individuals whose interests are inadequately represented. For feminists, that failure is most apparent when it threatens the welfare of disadvantaged groups including women, or of especially vulnerable third parties, such as children in divorce cases, or consumers of hazardous products. In such circumstances, partisanship on behalf of corporate profits inadequately serves values of care and connection. Case histories of the Dalkon Shield and asbestos litigation, as well as less politicised financial scandals, illustrate the human misery and social costs that can accompany unqualified advocacy (Brodeur 1985: 184; Perry and Dawson 1985; Rhode 1991: 29; Rhode 1994b: 617–26).

Finally, the submersion of self into role carries a price not only for the public in general, but for lawyers in particular. The detachment of personal and professional ethics often encourages an 'uncritical, uncommitted state of mind,' a 'deep moral skepticism', or a loss of sensitivity to the social costs of legal strategies (Postema 1980: 63, 77–80).

From most feminists' perspective, a preferable alternative would break down the boundary between personal and professional ethics and situate legal decision-making in a social context. In essence, lawyers should accept direct moral accountability for their professional acts. Attorneys' actions should not depend on a reflexive retreat into role; rather, individuals need to consider how the purposes of that role can best be served within a particular context. In some instances, those purposes call for deference to collectively determined legal and ethical rules. But such deference is justifiable only if the rules themselves allow room to take account of all the morally relevant factors in a given situation. So, for example, lawyers need to evaluate the rationale for zealous partisanship not by reference to some abstract model of an equal adversarial contest before a neutral tribunal. Instead, they need to consider a realistic social and economic landscape in which legal rights and resources may be unevenly distributed, applicable laws may be unjustly skewed, and the vast majority of cases settle without ever reaching an impartial decision-maker (Luban 1988; Postema 1980: 81–89; Rhode 1985: 617–26).

So too, lawyers need to consider how professional choices affect professional opportunities. The values of care, connection, and context that should inform lawyers' roles should also shape the structure of their professional workplaces.

3   PROFESSIONAL OPPORTUNITIES

Paradoxically enough, women's increasing representation and influence in the profession has recreated the 'woman problem' in different form. The central contemporary problem is the denial that there is in fact a serious problem. The prevailing assumption is that barriers have come down, women have moved up, and full equality is just around the corner. Recent surveys find that only one-quarter to one-third of men report observing gender bias in the profession, although two-thirds to three-quarters of women indicate that they personally have experienced it (Gellis 1991: 941, 971; Rhode 1994a: 39, 64–65). Even those men who perceive such bias often discount its significance. As practitioners in one Texas study put it, 'Women should grow up and stop whining.' And 'of all the problems we have as lawyers, gender discrimination [is] low on the list of important ones' (State Bar of Texas 1994; Norwood and Molina 1992: 50, 51).

To him, perhaps. But a wide array of recent studies on gender bias leaves a different impression. Taken together, they expose the fallacies in the American bar's prevailing myths of meritocracy. These myths rest on two dominant assumptions: (1) that female lawyers are already achieving close to proportionate representation in almost all professional contexts; and (2) that any lingering disparities are attributable to women's own 'different' choices and capabilities.

3.1 Myths of Opportunity

A common assumption, repeatedly echoed in gender bias studies, is that 'women's advancement is only a matter of time.[F]orcing the situation is not [necessary or] helpful' (Fuchs Epstein *et al*. 1995: 291, 356–57). Yet if time alone is viewed as the answer, American lawyers are in for a very long wait. Women now account for about 45 per cent of law students and almost 25 per cent of the bar, but only about 20 per cent of general counsels and tenured law school faculty, 13 per cent of large law firm partners, 10 to 12 per cent of judges, and 10 per cent of law school deans. (Rhode forthcoming: 5–8, 11, 16) Such under-representation cannot be explained simply by disparities in the pool of eligible candidates. Virtually all gender bias studies have found substantial disparities in promotion and pay among male and female lawyers with comparable positions, experience and qualifications. In general, they suggest that women are about half as likely as men to achieve partnership status, and reveal pay gaps ranging from 10 to 35 per cent (Fuchs Epstein *et al*. 1995: 359; American Bar Association Young Lawyers Division 1991: 63; Rhode forthcoming: 10; Bortnick 1998: 3).

What limited data are available for women of colour reveal even greater under-representation, particularly in positions with the highest salaries and status (American Bar Association 1995; American Bar Association Multicultural Attorney's Network 1994).

Given these patterns, what accounts for many attorneys' failure to perceive significant gender bias? Part of the problem involves their restrictive definitions of discrimination. To many lawyers, discrimination implies overt intentional prejudice. The professional workplaces they inhabit produce few clear examples. Most attorneys who harbour conscious racist or sexist attitudes have the sense not to share them openly. Moreover, because most employment decisions are subjective and confidential, clear proof of bias is hard to come by. Discrimination claims involving lawyers are expensive to litigate in both personal and financial terms. Plaintiffs risk having all their deficiencies publicly aired, and the rare individual who wins in court may lose in life. As one Chicago practitioner put it, an attorney who sues for discrimination 'may never eat lunch in this town again' (Barrett 1998: 59).

Less egregious conduct may pass unnoticed among those who don't need to notice because it doesn't affect their lives. And much of what they do see—demeaning assumptions, inadvertent slights, petty sexual harassment, condescending labels ('little lady,' 'lawyerette,' 'Taco Bell')—will seem like isolated instances, not institutionalised patterns (Judicial Council of California Advisory Committee 1996: 424; Rhode 1994a: 64). But the legal landscape looks different to attorneys who are on the receiving end of repeated forms of bias, however unintended. The black woman partner of a Chicago firm sees patterns when she is mistaken for a stenographer at *every* deposition she has attended (American Bar Association Multicultural Women Attorney's Network 1994: 41). For lawyers with these experiences, the problem has less to do with intentional discrimination than with unconscious stereotypes, unacknowledged preferences, and workplace policies that are neutral in form but not in practice.

Both psychological research and empirical surveys underscore the lingering influence of gender and racial stereotypes. Women and minorities do not enjoy the same presumption of competence as their white male colleagues. Traditionally disfavoured groups find that their mistakes are more readily noticed and their achievements more often attributed to luck or special treatment (Rhode 1997: 145; Hall and Nelson 1998: 688, 691). For some racial minorities, longstanding myths of intellectual inferiority, coupled with lower average grades and test scores, make these stereotypes particularly difficult to overcome (Rhode forthcoming; Bar Association of San Francisco 1996: 14–15; Wilkins and Gulati 1996: 501, 570). So too, the mismatch between characteristics traditionally associated with women and those typically associated with professional success leave female lawyers in a longstanding double bind. They are faulted as too 'passive' or too 'pushy,' too 'feminine' or not feminine enough. What is assertive in a man is abrasive in a woman (Rhode 1997: 67; Morrison 1994: 54, 61–62).

12   *Deborah L. Rhode*

Gender inequalities also reflect other gender stereotypes, such as the assumption that women with young children are likely to be insufficiently committed to their careers. These preconceptions often distort performance evaluations and eventually become self-fulfilling prophesies. As cognitive psychological research consistently demonstrates, individuals generally want to believe that they live in a 'just world', in which people by and large get what they deserve and deserve what they get (Lerner 1980: vii–viii; Rhode 1997: 9; Hamilton Krieger 1995: 1161). To hold on to such beliefs, people often selectively perceive or retain information that confirms initial biases and that justifies unequal outcomes. So, for example, attorneys will tend to remember the times that mothers leave early, not the occasions where they stay late. So too, when supervising lawyers doubt that a woman will make the sacrifices necessary to become a partner, they frequently fail to provide her with the experience, support and client contact that are essential to that achievement.

A related problem involves the reluctance that some male clients and attorneys still feel in working closely with women, or including them in informal networks where mentoring and rainmaking occur. As one participant in the United States Labor Department's Glass Ceilings study noted, 'what's important [in organisations] is comfort, chemistry . . . and collaborations.' (Federal Glass Ceiling Commission 1995) Such comfort levels are more difficult to sustain among those who look differently on important dimensions such as gender, race, ethnicity, disability and sexual orientation. Many women of colour report being treated as outsiders by white practitioners, and as potential competitors by non-white men (American Bar Association Multicultural Women's Network 1999). Lesbians are routinely hazed, isolated and denied professional opportunities. They, like Linowitz's classmates, often make others feel 'uncomfortable' and this is viewed as their, and not their colleagues', problem (Los Angeles County Bar Association 1995: 295, 444–49, 471). Even in jurisdictions that prohibit discrimination on the basis of sexual preference, noncompliance is widespread and sometimes quite explicit. A recent bar association survey in Los Angeles, which bans discrimination against gays and lesbians, produced responses like '[D]on't have any; don't want any.' (ibid, 312) Almost 40 per cent of surveyed practitioners reported witnessing or experiencing discrimination based on sexual orientation (*ibid*, 297).

White men are, of course, not the only group responsible for these patterns of prejudice; women can be perpetrators as well as targets of bias. As recent reports make clear, legal workplaces still have what sociologists once labelled 'Queen Bees'—women who believe that they managed without special help, so why can't everyone else (Wilson Schaef 1981: 44; Epstein *et al.* 1995: 408[6];

---

[6] Noting that some older women consider their younger colleagues to be 'naive' in failing to 'accept the fact that being a high powered lawyer is hard work and basically incompatible with a part-time schedule'.

Harvard Women's Law Association 1995: 18–19[7]). Some senior women also lack the time or influence to provide effective assistance to younger colleagues. Others worry that they risk professional opportunities even for trying. The experience of one African American member of a glass ceiling audit team is all too common. After pointing out her own legal department's failure to abide by equal opportunity standards, she learned that her superiors viewed such can-dour as 'poor judgment'. Their message was, in effect, '[W]e're not really com-fortable with what you're saying and we don't want [to work with] people who make us uncomfortable.' (American Bar Association Committee on the Status of Women 1995: 3)

As a result of such patterns, women often remain outside of the informal net-works of support that can be crucial for professional advancement. Pointing out this exclusion can compound the problem, which creates another double bind for female attorneys. When many vote with their feet, they confirm the percep-tion that women simply do not make the same career choices as their male colleagues. This perception then encourages unequal treatment of women and perpetuates the stereotypes that underlie such treatment.

3.2 Myths of Choice

Women's choices also figure prominently in a second common explanation for persistent gender inequalities. Many lawyers assume that women have different family priorities than men and that these personal commitments exact a profes-sional price. Although there is some truth to this view, it provides neither a com-plete explanation nor an adequate justification for prevailing gender inequalities. Women's different preferences cannot account for the extent of their underrepresentation. Recent surveys find that only about four per cent of female associates have part-time or flexible schedules, and that substantial gen-der disparities persist among lawyers in similar full-time positions (American Bar Association Committee on Women in the Profession 1990: 17; Part-Time Lawyering 1996: 11).

It is, of course, true that women express greater dissatisfaction with current workplace structures than men, and are disproportionately likely to opt out of positions with the greatest demands on time, travel and unpredictable sched-ules. Yet such patterns are not simply a function of 'natural' preferences. Women's career sacrifices are attributable not just to women's choices but to men's choices as well. Male spouses' failure to shoulder equal family responsi-bilities and male colleagues' failure to support alternative working arrange-ments are also responsible.

---

[7] Quoting Baker & Botts associates who find that most female partners do not 'care to relate to younger [women]' and are not receptive to accommodating family needs because these partners 'sac-rificed to get where they are' and believe others should do the same.

Employed women spend about twice as much time on domestic chores as do employed men, and not always by choice (Schor 1991: 36–38; South and Spitze 1994: 337). Female attorneys with significant family commitments tend to have partners, husbands or former husbands with equally demanding careers. These men frequently view their own professional obligations as fixed and women's as negotiable. Rather than accept an equal division of household tasks, many partners manage not to notice when their tasks need to be done, or they mismanage key parts of the job. To avoid a culture of complaints about family obligations, professional women often pick up the pieces that their partners do not even realise have been dropped (Rhode 1997: 7; Hochschild and Machung 1989: 259).

The problem is not only that many men are reluctant to make career sacrifices, but also that those who attempt to do so encounter too much resistance. Colleagues who are reluctant to accommodate mothers often have even less tolerance for fathers. A common attitude among prominent male lawyers has been, 'I have a family. I didn't get time off to do that. Why should you?' (Epstein *et al.* 1995: 409)

Ironically enough, managing attorneys sometimes invoke these refusals to accommodate male lawyers' family commitments as evidence that gender bias is not a problem in their workplaces. After all, women are more likely than men to receive 'special' treatment concerning family leaves and reduced schedules. But that response misses a central part of the problem at issue. Discrimination against men with family commitments also discriminates against women. It reaffirms traditional stereotypes, discourages male attorneys from assuming an equal division of household responsibilities, and requires their partners, who may also be lawyers, to pay a professional price.

The limits of current family-related policies pose increasing difficulties in a legal workplace marked by increasing hourly demands. Over the last quarter century, the average billable hours for American lawyers have grown from between 1200 to 1500 to between 1800 to 2000. What has not changed is the number of hours in the day. To charge honestly at those levels, given standard amounts of non-billable office time, requires 60 hour weeks and demands can be even greater in the large elite firms (Rhode forthcoming; Schlitz 1998: 871, 888–896). A willingness to work sweatshop hours functions as a proxy for commitment and those with competing family demands often drop by the wayside or are relegated to second class status. Unsurprisingly, most women lawyers feel that they have insufficient time for themselves and their families (Sells 1994a, 1994b).

In short, women lawyers face lingering double standards and double binds. Working mothers are held to higher standards than working fathers and are often criticised for being insufficiently committed, either as parents or professionals. Those who seem willing to sacrifice family needs to workplace demands appear lacking as mothers. Those who want extended leave and reduced schedules appear lacking as lawyers. These mixed messages leave many women with the uncomfortable sense that whatever they are doing, they should be doing something else. As long as work/family conflicts remain primarily 'women's issues', they are unlikely to receive adequate attention in decision-making structures dominated by men.

3.3 Alternative Structures

Responses to these problems follow directly from the diagnoses. One set of strategies involves improving policies concerning sexual harassment, hiring, retention and mentoring, as well as family leave and part-time work. Many bar associations and gender bias commissions have developed model proposals and training programmes that can be adapted for most workplace contexts (American Bar Association Committee on Women in the Profession 1990; Hecht Schafran 1990: 181, 199–204). More can be done to include gender-related issues in law school curricula and continuing legal education programmes for the practising bar.[8]

Yet many of these proposals remain controversial, particularly those that appear to involve preferential treatment for white women. As critics note, these women have not suffered the same history of economic and educational deprivation as minorities, and are no longer significantly under-represented in the profession's hiring pool. Singling out female attorneys for 'special assistance' can also reinforce the very assumption of inferiority that feminists seek to challenge. Even when women perform effectively, if their presence can be attributed to affirmative action, their performance can be devalued.

Yet while the price of special solicitude should not be underestimated, neither should the cost of inaction. Preferential treatment risks stigmatising underrepresented groups, but the fact of under-representation is stigmatising as well. Perceptions of inferiority predated affirmative action and would persist without it. In assessing the price of preference, the most relevant question is always, compared to what? When asked how they feel about gaining an advantage because they are women, many attorneys note that it feels better than being denied one because you're a woman. In contexts where equality in form is insufficient to secure equality in fact, preferential treatment generally is worth the cost. To reach a social order in which wealth, power, and status are not distributed by gender, we must first dispel the stereotypes contributing to this distribution. Affirmative action is often crucial to that effort. Only by insuring a critical mass of professional women in positions of influence can we counter the patterns that perpetuate inequality (Rhode 1997: 161–173).

Moreover, many of the policies that are most critical for reducing gender disadvantages need not be gender specific. Men as well as women can benefit from

---

[8] For example, California's continuing legal education requirement includes coverage of bias, and such coverage is increasingly part of major legal ethics casebooks. See Gillers 1998; Rhode & Luban 1992: 969–71; Rhode 1998: 50–56.

adequate parental and part-time policies, and from complaint structures that do not victimise victims who complain about harassment or homophobia.

Yet, while many bar leaders agree in principle, they often prove unenthusiastic in practice. For example, when asked why more legal employers don't allow attorneys to opt for reduced hours in exchange for reduced salaries, managing partners frequently respond that the costs are prohibitive. Clients reportedly want total availability. Flexible or reduced workloads cost money. Getting additional lawyers up to speed, adjusting to reduced schedules and paying extra overheads are expensive. But so too are the failures to make such accommodations. The inadequacy of time for family and personal needs is one of the leading causes not only of glass ceilings but of lawyers' exceptionally high rates of job dissatisfaction, stress and related problems such as depression and substance abuse (Schlitz 1998: 888–896; Rhode forthcoming; American Bar Association Young Lawyers Division 1991: 54; Herrmann 1991: 1[9]; Sells 1994a, 1994b).[10] In many institutions, the pressure to bill extended hours preempts the pro bono public service that attorneys often rank as their most satisfying professional experiences. The average pro bono commitment for the American bar is less than a half an hour a week, and many lawyers cannot find time for the public interest causes that led them to enter law in the first instance (Rhode 1999: 2415).

In the long run, an unwillingness to accommodate family need and pro bono commitments takes a toll on the bottom line. Employers who provide opportunities for flexible hours generally find gains in efficiency, morale, recruitment, and retention (Schor 1991; American Bar Association Committee on Women in the Profession 1990; Menkel-Meadow 1994: 621, 658–59). A growing number of large firms and corporations have managed to create 'family friendly' policies without apparent financial sacrifice (Harvard Women's Law Association 1995: 7). Even if there is some price to pay for gender equality, can the legal profession, which is the nation's second most highly paid occupation, and which will soon be almost half female, really not afford the cost? American lawyers have long been leaders in the national struggle for gender equality. The challenge remaining is to confront the problems in their own profession and to translate egalitarian commitments into workplace reorganisation.

Throughout the nineteenth century, anti-feminists based much of their opposition to women professionals on assumptions about women's difference. As one state judge explained when excluding female candidates from the bar, the 'peculiar qualities of womanhood, its gentle graces, its quick sensibility, its tender susceptibility' were surely not qualifications for 'forensic strife.' (in *re Goodell*, 39 Wis 232, 245 [1875]). Ironically enough, these are the same sensibilities that many contemporary female lawyers hope will transform the professional culture. Yet unlike their predecessors, these latest invocations of difference need not rest on

---

[9] Reporting survey findings that lawyers top the list of professionals likely to suffer major depression.

[10] For estimates suggesting that the percentage of lawyers with substance abuse problems is twice the national average, see Morris 1994: A27.

some exaggerated perception of woman's essential nature. Rather, these aspirations can be grounded in values traditionally associated with women, and commitments necessary to secure their equality.

For centuries, as Virginia Woolf observed, women were spectators at the 'procession of educated men' (Woolf 1938: 62–63). From the sidelines, women watched as men marched. Now that the obstacles to membership have broken down, women can ask some fundamental questions. On what terms should they join the parade? 'Above all, where is it taking us, the procession of educated men?' (*ibid*) The challenge for contemporary lawyers is to refocus attention on these issues. With a critical mass of new members in the profession comes an opportunity to rethink its traditional destinations.

4 REFERENCES

American Bar Association Committee on Women in the Profession. 1990. *Lawyers and Balanced Lives: A Guide to Drafting and Implementing Workplace Policies for Lawyers*. Part II. Chicago: ABA.

American Bar Association Committee on Women in the Profession. 1995. *Women in the Law: A Look at the Numbers*. 17 Chicago: ABA.

American Bar Association Committee on the Status of Women. Summer 1995. *Greener Pastures, Perspectives*. Chicago: ABA.

American Bar Association Multicultural Women Attorneys' Network. 1994. *The Burdens of Both, the Privileges of Neither*. Chicago: ABA.

American Bar Association Multicultural Women's Network, Commission on Opportunities for Minorities in the Profession. 1999. *Miles to Go: Progress of Minorities in the Profession*. Chicago: ABA.

American Bar Association Young Lawyers Division. 1991. *The State of the Legal Profession 1990*. Chicago: ABA.

Bar Association of San Francisco. 1996. *Goals 95 Report: Goals and Timetables for Minority Hiring and Advancement*.

Barrett, Paul M. 1998. *The Good Black*. New York: Dutton.

Bartlett, Katharine T. 1990. Feminist Legal Methods. *Harvard Law Review* 103; 829–888.

Bortnick, V Scott. 1998. Surveys of Women Lawyers Show Inequities. In Pay, Partnership. *S. F. Daily Journal*, 25 Aug, p 3.

Brodeur, Paul. 1985. *Outrageous Misconduct: The Asbestos Industry on Trial*. New York: Pantheon Books.

OPM Leasong Sources, Inc. 1988. In *The Social Responsibility of Lawyers*, edited by Heymann, Phillip, and Lance Liebman, Westbury, NY: Foundation Press.

Cahn, Naomi. 1992. Styles of Lawyering. *Hastings Law Journal* 43; 1039–1069.

Curtis, Charles P. 1951. The Ethics of Advocacy. *Stanford Law Review* 4. 3ff.

Deaux, Kay. 1984. From Individual Differences to Social Categories: Analysis of a Decade's Research on Gender. *American Psychologist* 39; 105ff.

Deaux, Kay, and Brenda Major. 1990. A Social-Psychological Model of Gender in Rhode, Deborah L (ed) *Theoretical Perspectives on Sexual Difference*. New Haven: Yale University Press.

Eagly, Alice H. 1987. *Sex Differences in Social Behavior: A Social-Role Interpretation.* Hillsdale, NJ: Erlbaum Associates.

England, Paula, and George Farkas. 1986. *Households, Employment, and Gender: A Social, Economic, and Demographic View.* New York: Aldine Pub Co.

Epstein, Cynthia Fuchs. 1988. *Deceptive Distinctions: Sex, Gender, and the Social Order.* New Haven: Yale University Press; New York: Russell Sage Foundation.

Epstein, Cynthia Fuchs. 1993. 2nd edn *Women in Law.* Urbana: University of Illinois Press.

Epstein, Cynthia Fuchs. *et al.* 1995. Glass Ceilings and Open Doors: Women's Advancement in the Legal Profession. *Fordham Law Review* (64) 2; 291ff.

Federal Glass Ceiling Commission. 1995. *Good For Business: Making Full Use of the Nation's Human Capital.* 28. Washington DC: USGPO.

Forisha, Barbara. 1981. The Inside and the Outsider: Women in Organisations in Forisha, Barbara L and Barbara H Goldman (eds) *Outsiders on the Inside: Women and Organisations.* Englewood Cliffs, NJ: Prentice Hall.

Frankel, Marvin E. 1975. The Search for Truth: An Umpireal View. *University of Pennsylvania Law Review.* 123 [New York]: Association of the Bar of the City of New York, 1975 [c1974] (also published as book).

Frankel, Marvin E. 1980. *Partisan Justice.* New York: Hill and Wang.

Fraser, Nancy, and Linda J Nicholson. 1990. Social Criticism Without Philosophy: An Encounter Between Feminism and Postmodernism in Nicholson, Linda J (ed) *Feminism/Postmodernism.* New York: Routledge.

Galanter, Marc. 1974. Why the 'Haves' Come Out Ahead: Speculations on the Limits of Legal Change. *Law & Society Review* (9) 1; 95ff.

Gellis, Ann J. 1991. Great Expectations: Women in the Legal Profession, A Commentary on State Studies. *Indiana Law Review* 66; 941ff.

Gillers, Stephen. 1998. *Regulation of Lawyers: Problems of Law and Ethics.* New York: Aspen Law & Business.

Gilligan, Carol. 1982. *In a Different Voice: Psychological Theory and Women's Development.* Cambridge, Mass.: Harvard University Press.

Gomez-Mejia, Luis R. 1983. Sex Differences During Occupational Socialisation. *Academic Management Journal* 26; *In re Goodell,* 39 Wisc 232 (1875).

Grant, Judith. 1993. *Fundamental Feminism: Contesting the Core Concepts of Feminist Theory.* New York: Routledge.

Greeno, Catherine G, and Eleanor E Maccoby. 1986. How Different is the Different Voice'? *11 Signs* 310–16.

Griswold, Erwin. 1950. Developments at the Law School. *Harvard Law School Year Book* 10. Cambridge, Mass.: Year Book Committee of Phillips Brooks House Association of Harvard University.

Gruhl, John *et al.* 1981. Women as Policymakers: The Case of Trial Judges. *American Journal of Political Science* (25) 2; 308ff.

Hall, Kathleen E, and Robert L Nelson. 1998. Gender Inequality in Law: Problems of Structure and Agency in Recent Studies of Gender in Anglo-American Legal Professions. *Law & Society Inquiry* 23.

Harrington, Mona. 1993. *Women Lawyers: Rewriting the Rules.* New York: A A Knopf.

Harris, Angela. 1990. Race and Essentialism in Feminist Legal Theory. *Stanford Law Review* (42) 3; 581ff.

Harvard Women's Law Association. 1995. *Presumed Equal: What America's Top Women Lawyers Really Think About Their Firms.* Franklin Lakes, NJ: Career Press.

Heilbrun, Carolyn, and Judith Resnik. 1990. Convergences: Law, Literature, and Feminism. *Yale Law Journal* 99.

Held, Virginia. 1984. The Division of Moral Labor and the Role of the Lawyer in Luban, David (ed) *The Good Lawyer: Lawyers' Roles and Lawyers' Ethics.* Place: Publisher, 1984.

Herrmann, Andrew. 1991. Depressing News For Lawyers. *Chicago Sunday Times* 13 Sept at 1.

Hochschild, Arlie with Ann Machung. 1989. *The Second Shift: Working Parents and the Revolution at Home.* New York: Viking.

Jack, Rand, and Dana Crowely Jack. 1989. *Moral Vision and Professional Decisions: The Changing Values of Women and Men Lawyers.* Cambridge (UK)/(New York: Cambridge University Press.

Judicial Council of California Advisory Committee on Gender Bias in the Courts. 1996. Achieving Justice for Women and Men in the California Courts. *Final Report.*

Kohn, Alfie. 1990. *The Brighter Side of Human Nature: Altruism and Empathy in Everyday Life.* New York: Basic Books.

Krieger, Linda. 1995. The Content of Our Categories: A Cognitive Bias Approach to Discrimination and Equal Employment Opportunity. *Stanford Law Review* (47) 6; 1161ff.

Larrabee, Mary Jeanne (ed). 1993. *An Ethic of Care: Feminist and Interdisciplinary Perspectives.* New York: Routledge.

Lerner, Melvin. 1980. *The Belief in a Just World.* New York: Plenum Press.

Linowitz, Sol M, and Martin Mayer. 1994. *The Betrayed Profession.* New York: C Scribener's Sons.

Lipman-Blumen, Jean. 1992. Connective Leadership: Female Leadership Styles in the 21st-Century Workplace. *Social Perspectives* 35.

Los Angeles County Bar Association Ad Hoc Committee on Sexual Orientation Bias. 1995. The Los Angeles County Bar Association Report on Sexual Orientation Bias, reprinted in *S. Cal. Rev. L. & Women's Stud.* 4.

Luban, David. 1988. *Lawyers and Justice.* Princeton, N.J.: Princeton University Press.

Maccoby, Eleanor E. 1990. Gender and Relationships: A Developmental Account. *45 American Psychologist* 45; 513ff.

MacIntyre, Alisdair. 1978. What Has Ethics to Learn from Medical Ethics? *Phil. Exchange* 2.

MacKinnon, Catharine. 1985. Feminist Discourse, Moral Values, and the Law—A Conversation. *Buffalo Law Review* 34; 11 (comments of Catharine MacKinnon.

MacKinnon, Catharine. 1989. *Feminism Unmodified: Discourses on Life and Law.* Cambridge, Mass.: Harvard University Press, (1987 according to Library of Congress).

Mendelson Freeman, Sue Joan. 1990. *Managing Lives: Corporate Women and Social Change.* Amherst: University of Massachusetts Press.

Menkel-Meadow, Carrie. 1985. Portia in a Different Voice: Speculations on a Women's Lawyering Process. *Berkeley Women's Law Journal* 1; 39–63.

Menkel-Meadow, Carrie. 1989. Feminisation of the Legal Profession in Abel, Richard L, and Philip SC Lewis (eds) *Lawyers in Society: Comparative Theories* Vol 3. Berkeley: Unversity of California Press.

Menkel-Meadow, Carrie. 1994. Culture Clash in the Quality of Life in the Law: Changes in the Economic Diversification and Organisation of Lawyering. *Case W. Res. L. Rev.* 44.

Molm, Linda D, and Mark Hedley. 1992. Gender, Power and Social Exchange in Ridgeway, Cecelia B (ed) *Gender Interaction and Inequality*. New York: Springer-Verlag.

Morris, Anne Fahy. 1994. 'Justifiable Paranoia' Afflicts Lawyers, Psychologist Says'. *LA Times*, 1 May at A 27.

Morrison, Ann M. 1994. *Breaking the Glass Ceiling: can women reach the top of America's largest corporations?*. Reading, Mass.: Addison-Wesley Pub Co.

Moss Kanter, Rosabeth. 1982. The Impact of Hierarchical Structures on the Work Behavior of Women and Men in Kahn-Hut, Rachel *et al* (eds) *Women and Work: Problems and Perspectives*. New York: Oxford University Press.

Norwood, Diane F, and Arlette Molina. 1992. Sex Discrimination in the Profession: 1990 Survey Results Reported. *Tex. B. J.*, Jan.

Part-Time Lawyering, Partner's Rep, Jan 1996.

Pepper, Stephen L. 1986. The Lawyer's Amoral Ethical Role: A Defense, A Problem, and Some Possibilities. *Am. B. Found. Res. J.*

Perry, Susan, and Jim Dawson. 1985. *Nightmare: Women and the Dalkon Shield*. New York: Macmillan.

Postema, Gerald J. 1980. Moral Responsibility in Professional Ethics. *New York University Law Review 55*.

Radin, Margaret J. 1990. The Pragmatist and the Feminist. *S. Cal. L. Rev.* (63) 6; 1699ff.

Rhode, Deborah L. 1985. Ethical Perspectives on Legal Practice. *Stan. L. Rev.* (37) 2; 589ff.

Rhode, Deborah L. 1991. An Adversarial Exchange on Adversarial Ethics: Text, Subtext and Context (Henry Brougham's Thought on Client's Protection and Legal Ethics). *Journal of Legal Education* (41) 1; 29ff.

Rhode, Deborah L. 1994a. Gender and Professional Roles. *Fordham Law Review* 63; 39–72.

Rhode, Deborah L. 1994b. Institutionalising Ethics. *Case W. L. Rev.* 44.

Rhode, Deborah L. 1996. Myths of Meritocracy. *Fordham Law Review* 65.

Rhode, Deborah L. 1997. *Speaking of Sex: the Denial of Gender Inequality*. Cambridge, Mass.: Harvard University Press.

Rhode, Deborah L. 1998. *Professional Responsibility: Ethics by the Pervasive Method*. New York: Aspen Law & Business.

Rhode, Deborah L. 1999. Cultures of Commitment: Pro Bono for Lawyers and Law Students. (67) 5; 2415ff.

Rhode, Deborah L. Lawyers. (forthcoming).

Rhode, Deborah L, and David Luban. 1992. *Legal Ethics*. Westbury, NY: Foundation-Press.

Rosener, Judith B. 1990. Ways Women Lead. *Harvard Business Review* Nov–Dec (68) 6; 119ff.

Schafran, Lynn. 1990. Gender and Justice: Florida and the Nation. *Florida Law Review* 42.

Schlitz, Patrick. 1998. On Being a Happy, Healthy Member of an Unhappy, Unhealthy, and Unethical Profession. *Vavid. L. Rev. 58*.

Schor, Juliet B. 1991. *The Overworked American. The Unexpected Decline of Leisure*. New York: Basic Books.

Sells, Benjamin. 1994a. Stressed Out Lawyers. *S.F. Daily J.*, 25 May.

Sells, Benjamin. 1994b. Counsel on the Verge of a Nervous Breakdown. *S.F. Daily J.*, 25 May.

Shibley Hyde, Janet. 1990. Meta-Analysis and the Psychology of Gender Differences. *Signs* 16.

Simon, William. 1978. The Ideology of Advocacy: Procedural Justice and Professional Ethics. *Wis. L. Rev.* 29, 29ff.

South, Scott J, and Glenna Spitze. 1994. Housework in Marital and Nonmarital Households. *American Sociological Review* (59) 3, 327ff.

Spelman, Elizabeth V. 1988. *Inessential Woman: Problems of Exclusion in Feminist Thought*. Boston: Beacon Press.

State Bar of Texas. 1994. *Gender Bias Task Force. Final Report* 25.

Tavris, Carol. 1991. Ways Men and Women Lead. *Harvard Business Review* 69.

Tavris, Carol. 1992. *The Mismeasure of Woman*. New York: Simon & Schuster.

Walker, Thomas G, and Deborah J Barrow. 1985. The Diversification of the Federal Bench: Policy and Process Ramifications. *J. Pol.* (47) 2; 596ff.

Wasserstrom, Richard. 1975. Lawyers as Professionals: Some Moral Issues. *Hum. Rts.* 5; 1–24.

Wilkins, David, and G Mitu Gulati. 1996. Why Are There So Few Black Lawyers in Corporate Law Firms? An Institutional Analysis. *California Law Review* 94.

Schaef, Anne. 1981. *Women's Reality*. Minneapolis: Winston Press.

Winter, Bill. 1983. Survey: Women Lawyers Work Harder, Are Paid Less, But They're Happy. *A.B.A. J.* 69.

Woolf, Virginia. 1938. *Three Guineas*. New York: Harcourt, Brace and Company.

Yancey Martin, Patricia. 1990. Rethinking Feminist Organisations. *Gender & Society* 4.

2

The Effect of Lawyer Gender on Client Perceptions of Lawyer Behaviour

W LF FELSTINER, B PETTIT, EA LIND, N OLSEN*

Abstract

Menkel-Meadow, relying on Gilligan, has suggested that women might practise law in ways different from men. We conducted a US-wide random telephone survey of clients acting as individuals. These clients did not perceive major differences in the behaviour of lawyers by gender. However, running contrary to the literature, we found that the common behaviour of men and women was close to the model normally prescribed for women. Finally, we compare our findings to different results reached by researchers in the UK.

1 INTRODUCTION

BETWEEN 1974 AND 1982 the view that women in general have a more relational notion of self than men was extensively explored (Noddings 1974; Miller 1976; Chodorow 1978; Dinnerstein 1978; Schaef 1981; Gilligan 1982). Gilligan's studies of the moral development of children were particularly influential. Her work was first made relevant to research on the legal profession by Menkel-Meadow, particularly through her paper *Portia in a Different Voice* (1985). Although centrally concerned with how the more relational concept of self and the consequent priority to context affects the way that women lawyers might react to and manipulate legal process (more oriented toward co-operative solutions, less aggressive and adversarial, more interested in relationships and less in rights), *Portia* also discusses the potential effects of gender on the lawyer-client relationship (57–58). It suggests that women lawyers' greater sense of empathy and altruism, and lesser inclination toward parentalism, would be translated into securing more information on more subjects, thereby giving women lawyers a better grasp of a wider range of client needs and objectives (57). Starting from the same base, Menkel-Meadow could have expanded her

* This project was funded by the American Bar Foundation. We are also grateful for the work done on pilot surveys by Lisa Torres and Jane Ward.

speculations to include the effect of the 'care perspective' on the respect, concern and responsiveness shown to clients (see Cahn 1992: 1049).

Although Menkel-Meadows' hypotheses were investigated over the next decade in various ways by various researchers (Taber *et al* 1988; Jack & Jack 1989; Cahn 1992; Turnier *et al* 1996), no clear picture of the behaviour or effect of women lawyers has emerged. This result is not at all surprising when one notes that, perhaps for heuristic reasons, the Gilligan/Menkel-Meadow perspective does not distinguish between the reality of gendered identity and expectations about it. That is, even if one found that men and women lawyers behaved differently, is the actual behaviour different or are observations of that behaviour dominated by expectations about it? Nor does that view take account of the wide attitudinal and behavioural variation that we know exists within genders.

Most research on gender differences in professional practice relies on interviews with the professionals themselves. The only recent study of gender effect that is based on data derived from clients is Bogoch's (1997) linguistic analysis of lawyer-client conversations. She concludes that lawyers' talk is influenced by role rather than gender and that marked differences in men and women lawyers occurred only in women lawyers' greater willingness to grant legitimacy to the clients' emotional concerns. We have taken the opportunity offered by data collected in a larger study to investigate whether clients of women lawyers report their experience differently from clients of men lawyers along most of the dimensions suggested by the Gilligan/Menkel-Meadow perspective. The data are drawn from a random nation-wide sample of clients acting as individuals; a sample that was itself drawn from a random nation-wide sample of the US population. Our findings do not support the Gilligan/Menkel-Meadow hypothesis; that is we find that clients do not perceive that men and women lawyers behave differently. Though substantial variation is perceived within both gender sets, the variation between sets is not statistically significant. Moreover, from the clients' perspective, the most common behaviour of both men and women lawyers appears to be that which would be attributed by Gilligan/Menkel-Meadow to women.

2 THE PROJECT

This analysis is part of a larger project investigating dysfunctional elements of lawyer-clients relations in the US—their frequency, distribution, origins and consequences. The project involves four surveys, of the general population (to find clients), clients, lawyers and, for comparative purposes, patients of doctors. This paper is based on the client survey.

Women lawyers were consulted by 13 per cent of the random, national telephone survey of clients (60 of 461). This fraction is considerably less than that of women in the profession (Galanter 1999: 1084), confirming the view that women lawyers are to be found proportionately less often in private practice than are men.

The information about these women lawyers that we currently have is that which was available to their clients. We know, then, that they are quite a bit younger than men lawyers, their clients are more likely to be women (72–57 per cent), they are more likely than men to practice by themselves (43–29 per cent), less likely to work in firms with more than 15 lawyers, more likely to be paid by someone other than their clients (reflecting the disproportionate number of women lawyers representing women in divorce cases), less likely to be paid by contingent fee and, like men lawyers, they are overwhelmingly white.

3 METHODOLOGY

To identify respondents who had used a lawyer within the previous three years we conducted a random telephone survey (random four-digit additions to existing exchanges screened to exclude those that were business or fax or modem answered) of households in the US, excepting Alaska and Hawaii (for reasons of cost and time differential). To produce the data set, a total of 9,875 calls (including call-backs) were made over a 26-month period ending in May 1999. These initial calls took about 30 seconds. The hit rate (number of households using a lawyer as a proportion of all households responding to the initial questions) was a surprising 34 per cent. In qualifying households a client interview was conducted immediately if feasible. If that was not possible, times were set to conduct interviews, and up to four attempts were made to complete them. The response rate of those eligible for the survey was 39.8 per cent, slightly above average for random call surveys (Shapland 2000: 6). There were virtually no differences in the geographic distributions between the original calls and households using lawyers or between participants and refusals among those who had used lawyers. These interviews lasted between 11 and 35 minutes. Interviewers for both surveys were undergraduate students at the University of North Carolina trained in standard interview techniques.

The number of women lawyers consulted by the clients in the survey was relatively small (60), but, in the context of the large client sample, the analysis has sufficient statistical power to detect potential differences in reactions to, and the reported actions of, men and women lawyers. For example, the statistics used to test for gender differences would have detected a moderate sized gender difference (.5 standard deviation, $f = .25$) 95 per cent of the time with the present distribution, and 100 per cent of the time with an equal distribution of attorney gender. The statistics would have detected a large gender difference 100 per cent of the time with the present sample size and gender distribution (Cohen 1988). Thus the unequal distribution of men and women lawyers hardly reduced the overall power of the statistical tests.

4 DATA ANALYSIS

There are no measurable differences in the extent to which women and men lawyers are viewed by their clients as friendly, confident, polite, organised, trustworthy or fair. There are percentage differences with respect to other behaviours by lawyer gender, but they are *not* statistically significant at the p<.05 level. On this basis, men are thought to be somewhat more leisurely, more experienced and more willing to talk about non-legal matters, while women are less evasive, listen more carefully, are more likely to let clients explain their problems as they wish, more likely to keep clients informed, more likely to answer telephone calls and letters, more willing to deal with the emotional aspects of the legal matter, more likely to treat clients with respect and to be concerned with them as people, more careful to consider the clients' views and needs, and more likely to treat a client's case as important. There are no differences in lawyer gender in the likelihood that clients would recommend the lawyer to others or use the lawyer again. Thus, the overall picture is that the great majority of both men and women lawyers are perceived to have treated these clients quite well on all the ways that we investigated.

We looked at the possibility that the impact of lawyer gender upon client evaluations was hidden by the influence of other variables likely to affect client responses. These factors were lawyer-client racial combinations (white and non-white), client gender, client status (education or income), and the areas of law for which the clients sought counsel. The logic behind each of these possibilities follows.

It is conceivable that client evaluations were to a degree determined by negative cross-race preconceptions, or that lawyers tended to treat higher status clients better than others. The literature does suggest that lawyers grant more agenda control to higher status and more powerful clients (Sarat and Felstiner 1995: 19–21). And women clients did have more education (59–31 per cent college graduates or better) and marginally more household income (21–17 per cent $75,000 or more) than men.

It is also possible that some of the difference between client perceptions of men and women lawyers was due to the fact that women lawyers have proportionately more women clients than men lawyers rather than to the lawyers' baseline behaviour. This effect may be because some proportion of lawyers believe that dealing with the emotional aspects of a legal matter is more important to women than men clients and are therefore more willing to engage in it with them. Or it could be that an apparent willingness to discuss emotional matters is simply a byproduct of women clients' greater tendency to introduce such matters into the lawyer-client agenda.

Finally, area of practice might have an effect because some areas are more hectic, adversarial and one-shot and, as a consequence, the lawyers practising in them are less likely to have good manners, open communications and liberal rules of relevance in dealing with clients. The areas of practice that we looked at are accident claims, divorce, other family matters, real estate, wills, estates, business, traffic and criminal law. There was more than a five per cent difference in area of practice by lawyer gender for personal injury and real estate (men more) and divorce and business (women more).

We controlled for the impact of each of these variables by performing ordinary least squares multiple regression models on each of the practice dimensions noted above. We found no significant correlations between lawyer gender and any of the client responses at the $p<.05$ level controlling for the effect of these other independent variables. Table 1 (attached) summarises the results of these regressions.

5 CONCLUSION

In sum, if we believe that it is socially desirable for lawyers to listen to their clients carefully, to communicate with them in a direct manner, to give them a significant role in setting the agenda for discussions, to keep them informed of the status of their legal matters, to respond promptly to their inquiries, to treat them with respect, to be concerned with them as people and to act as if their problems were important, then both men and women lawyers are doing quite well according to these 'after the fact' client reports. Though a higher proportion of women lawyers are performing at that level, the differences are small and not statistically significant.

This conclusion brings us to Sommerlad and Sanderson's exceptional book *Gender Choice and Commitment* (1998) that takes up the Gilligan question; that is how the profession has reacted to the supposedly different propensities of men and women in interpersonal relations. Sommerlad and Sanderson's male respondents, considered by them to speak for the profession, adopt what we take to be the conventional two-step argument. Men are inclined to be strong, dominant, powerful, aggressive, logical, tough and resistant to emotional issues. This macho characterisation is professionally good. Women are inclined to be vulnerable, intuitive, empathic, emotional, subjective, personal and sensitive to context. This characterisation with caring as the centerpiece is assumed to be undesirable for law practice.

The origins of this view seem to be a *post hoc* rationalisation by men solicitors of why women have not succeeded more than they have, as success is conventionally judged in the profession. It is thus a projection of what men think clients want rather than a finding directly about client preferences. On the other hand, when one looks directly at client preferences, as we do in this chapter, the results are not only more positive for women, but much less macho for men. Despite small differences, the overall picture is that the great majority of both men and women lawyers are perceived to have treated their clients with respect, to have been willing to talk about their problems in context, to have been responsive and supportive, to have listened to their views and taken them into consideration. Since the overwhelming majority of clients report that they would recommend their lawyer to others or use her or him again themselves, it is fair to conclude that our clients value many of those very traits which Sommerlad and Sanderson's respondents thought were feminine and undesirable.

Of course, we were asking different questions—they were looking at how women lawyers were treated and we were looking at how they are perceived to behave. Moreover, it is quite possible that we are looking at different populations of clients—they make heavy use of data from commercial firms because they consider them 'paradigmatic of the new approach to women solicitors' (p 156), while we excluded business organisations from our client survey. In other words, the status of 'female' values may to some extent be an artifact of our respective research strategies.

Finally, what might explain the marked lack of difference in the way that clients experience the interpersonal behaviour of men and women lawyers in the face of a not insignificant literature as well as a popular belief that men and women tend to approach problem solving differently as a matter of process as well as goals? There are several possible explanations. The first is rooted in free will at work. That is, that somewhere along the line, either in the selection of who takes up law as an occupation, how they are educated, how they are socialised to the occupation, or how they size up the behaviour that appears instrumentally effective in the occupation, women either adopt male behaviours or those women who survive in the profession are behaviourally closer to men in the first place. The second explanation is that our data are unreliable in the sense that our respondents, socialised, as we all are, to a certain set of expectations about professional behaviour, will experience lawyerly behaviour as conforming to those expectations, whatever its actuality. In this vein, expectations of lawyers as lawyers trump expectations of gendered behaviour. The third explanation is a combination of self-selection and our research design. That is, we sampled only from clients of that portion of the profession that provides services to individuals. If that domain draws disproportionately from that slice of the profession that is more oriented toward personal relations, then it is not surprising that we find men and women behaving similarly.

But the data in this paper suggest that the first and second explanations are insufficient, since the model that both men and women seem to have adopted is the feminine alternative if, in fact, either gender is to be thought to have moved away from its 'natural' approach to interpersonal relations. In other words, explanations rooted in either self-selection/socialisation or expectations based on stereotypes predict movement toward the male version, and we found the opposite. The third explanation is also suspect since it rests on the proposition that personality is a primary determinant of types of practice, while the literature (see, eg, Heinz & Laumann 1982) suggests that the dominant factor is the type of law school attended, which itself is a surrogate for many things such as class, ethnicity, university grades, and facility with standardised tests, but is not a surrogate for personality inclinations.

We are then left with the most obvious explanation of all—that the Menkel-Meadow proposition that women lawyers speak with a different and more caring voice is empirically unfounded with respect to those lawyers who counsel individual clients. That proposition may never have been correct. Lawyer behaviour may have changed over time. For instance, as the general inclination of consumers to demand that service providers pay more attention to their needs has crept into the market for legal services, men lawyers may have been motivated by prudential concerns to become more 'feminine'. Or there may be a change similar to that in doctor-patient relations where the increasing proportion of female physicians has apparently influenced the way that men practice (Roter 2001, 4). Whatever the history, we should not be surprised by the result. Sex differences in moral development, the foundations of Gilligan's theory, have not received general support. The persistence and popularity of the theory are today regarded more as a matter of gender politics than science (Mednick 1989 (collecting cites); Epstein 1988, 81–83; Colby and Damon 1987), a view supported by this research.

Table 1: Multiple Regression Results for Effect of Lawyer Gender Dummy Variable

Dependent Variables	b	Std. Error	p<	n
Item 21—Friendly	−3.38	4.7	0.48	395
Item 22—Confident	1.12	3.69	0.77	398
Item 23—Liesurely	2.73	4.01	0.5	381
Item 24—Polite	−3.08	3.67	0.41	400
Item 25—Experienced	3.26	4.01	0.42	398
Item 26—Organised	1.67	5.05	0.75	391
Item 27—Straightforward	−2.32	4.53	0.61	400
Item 28—Fair	−2.85	4.24	0.51	383
Item 29—Trustworthy	−0.99	4.7	0.84	389
Item 30—Listened	−3.94	3.64	0.29	428
Item 31—Told fees	2.16	5.28	0.69	402
Item 32—Let explain	−2.24	3.86	0.57	424
Item 33—Told promptly	−7.31	5.16	0.16	372
Item 34—Listened and followed instructions	2.07	4.98	0.68	402
Item 35—Disobeyed	−6.89	3.83	0.08	416
Item 36—Answered promptly	−3.72	4.59	0.42	419
Item 37—Kept informed	−2.43	5.15	0.64	379
Item 38—Met deadlines and kept promises	−1.65	4.48	0.72	393
Item 39—Willing to deal with emotions	−7.85	5.44	0.16	378
tem 40—Answered questions clearly	−7.11	4.11	0.09	430
Item 41—Talk about non-legal matters	2.13	6.19	0.74	362
Item 42—Treated with respect	−6.75	3.4	0.06	430
IItem 43—Tried to make dignified	1.35	7.78	0.87	426

Table 1 *cont.*

Dependent Variables	b	Std. Error	p<	n
Item 44—Paid attention to wishes	−0.19	4.32	0.97	425
Item 45—Concerned with as person	−1.79	4.83	0.72	425
Item 46—Good with forms and procedures	−1.55	4.14	0.71	399
Item 47—Kept Informed	1.69	4.79	0.73	401
Item 48—Treated with Respect	−4.48	3.62	0.22	404
Item 49—Biased against	2.34	3.23	0.48	405
Item 50—Very knowledgeable about law	−2.24	3.45	0.52	430
Item 51—Things you never told lawyer	−2.08	2.43	0.4	421
Item 52—Related well as person	−6.33	4	0.12	430
Item 53—Considered views and needs	−3.69	4.28	0.4	402
Item 54—Treated fairly	−3.67	4.12	0.38	427
Item 55—Treated as important	−0.97	4.67	0.84	428
Item 56—Willing to rely on judgement	−1.67	3.81	0.67	428
Item 76—Recommend lawyer to a friend	−1.2	5.03	0.82	428
Item 77—Use lawyer again	−5.4	5.28	0.31	426

b5 Same Race L/C + b6Client Age + b7Client Educational Level + (b8, b9, b10, b11Client Income Levels) + (b12, b13, b14, b15, b16, b17, b18, b19, b20Type of Legal Matter)

6   REFERENCES

Bogoch, Bryna. 1997. Gendered Lawyering: Difference and Dominance in Lawyer-Client Interaction. *Law & Society Review* 31; 677.

Cahn, Naomi. 1992. Styles of Lawyering. *Hastings Law Journal* 43; 1039.

Chodorow, Nancy. 1978. *The Reproduction of Mothering*. Berkeley: University of California Press.

Cohen, Jacob. 1988. *Statistical Power Analysis for the Behavioral Sciences*. Hillsdale, NJ: Lawrence Erlbaum Associates, Inc.

Colby, Anne and William Damon. 1987. Listening to a Different Voice: A Review of Gilligans *In a Different Voice* in Mary R Walsh (ed) *The Psychology of Women*. New Haven: Yale University Press.

Dinnerstein, Dorothy. 1976. *The Mermaid and the Minatour*. New York: Harper & Row.

Epstein, Cynthia F. 1988. *Deceptive Distinctions: Sex, Gender and the Social Order*. New Haven: Yale University Press.

Galanter, Marc. 1999. 'Old and in the Way': The Coming Demographic Transformation of the Legal Profession and Its Implications for the Provision of Legal Services. *Wisconsin Law Review*; 1080.

Gilligan, Carol. 1982. *In a Different Voice: Psychological Theory and Womens Development*. Cambridge: Harvard Univ Press.

Heinz, John P and Edward O Laumann. 1982. *Chicago Lawyers: The Social Structure of the Bar*. New York: Russell Sage Foundation.

Jack, Dana C and Rand Jack. 1989. *Moral Vision and Professional Decisions: The Changing Values of Women and Men Lawyers*. New York: Cambridge University Press.

Mednick, Martha T. 1989. On the Politics of Psychological Constructs. *American Psychologist* 44; 1118.

Menkel-Meadow, Carrie. 1985. Portia in a Different Voice: Speculations on a Women's Lawyering Process. *Berkeley Women's Law Journal* 1; 39.

Miller, Jean Baker. 1976. *Toward a New Psychology of Women*. London: Allen Lane.

Noddings, Nel. 1974. *Caring: A Feminine Approach to Ethics and Moral Education*. Berkeley: University of California Press.

Roter, Deborah L in *Harvard Health Letter*, May 2001. Boston: Harvard Health Publications.

Sarat, Austin and William LF Felstiner. 1995. *Divorce Lawyers and Their Clients: Power and Meaning in the Legal Process*. New York: Oxford University Press.

Schaef, Anne. 1981. *Women's Reality*. Minneapolis: Winston Press.

Shapland, Joanna. 2000. Interest in Clients: Patients, Consumers and Sharks. Paper presented at the biennial meeting of the Working Group on the Comparative Study of Legal Professions, Peyresq, France, 16–18 July 2000.

Sommerlad, Hilary and Peter Sanderson. 1998. *Gender, Choice and Commitment*. Aldershot: Ashgate.

Taber, Janet and Marguerite T Grant, Mary T Huser, Rise Norman, James Sutton, Clarence C Wong, Louise Parker, Claire Picard. 1988. Gender, Legal Education, and the Legal Profession: An Empirical Study of Stanford Law Students and Graduates, *Stanford Law Review* 40; 1209–1297.

Turnier, William J, Pamela J Conover and David Lowery. 1996. Redistributive Justice and Cultural Feminism. *American University Law Review* 45; 1275.

3

Gender in Context: Women in Family Law

LYNN MATHER

Abstract

This paper contributes to the debate on possible gender-based differences in lawyers' work style and/or approach to legal problems in the context of a rapidly increasing rate of female participation in the profession. Based on interviews with divorce lawyers in the American states of New Hampshire and Maine, this chapter identifies gender similarities and differences among divorce lawyers but subsequently places them within the context of other social, economic and legal forces. The author concludes that gender is just one—by no means unimportant—influence on attorneys' work, and any resulting differences between female and male lawyers need to be interpreted as the result of multi-faceted interaction with other contextual factors.

1 INTRODUCTION

T HE DRAMATIC INCREASE in the number of women lawyers in the United States has prompted speculation about how women might affect the legal profession. When women constituted only three per cent of lawyers, as they did in 1971 (Curran and Carson 1994: 4), they struggled simply for employment and acceptance in the male-dominated profession. However, by 1991 women comprised 21 per cent of American lawyers, and are now 45 per cent of the profession (Curran and Carson 1994: 4; Rhode in this volume). What, if any, impact have women had on legal practice? Research on women lawyers has revealed considerable sex-based discrimination in salary and promotion, sexual harassment within law firms, gender bias from judges as well as from other lawyers, and the difficulties of combining family responsibilities and a legal career (Epstein 1993; Harrington 1993; Hagan and Kay 1995). These obstacles to women's success in the profession suggest that they would have difficulty asserting any special woman's voice. Yet the notion of 'a different voice' (Gilligan 1982) in law—a caring, empathetic, conciliatory voice—remains for some commentators an attractive ideal and perhaps even an empirical reality

(Menkel-Meadow 1985, 1989, 1995; Jack and Jack 1989). Menkel-Meadow expressed this hope 18 years ago when she wrote that women entering the legal profession 'could or will alter our legal sensibilities and values' (1985: 62), and she reiterated the view a decade later (1995).

To expect that women, simply by their biological or psychological nature, would exhibit a different lawyering style than men, or perform a different lawyering role, rests on an essentialism that ignores the considerable diversity among women and the other social forces acting upon them. But, as Menkel-Meadow (1995) asks, are there differences stemming from a distinctive female socialisation or experience? Perhaps what Fineman calls 'women's gendered existence' is 'based on *experiential*, not essential differences' (Fineman 1990: 37, emphasis added). And thus women lawyers might indeed bring a different lawyering style, or approach legal problems in particular ways, as a result of their deeply ingrained habits and learned behaviours.

Critics of the difference approach, such as MacKinnon (1987), argue that it is the inequality of power between men and women that explains women's behaviour. That is, observed gender differences simply reflect underlying power differences. Thus, if women value care, it is because caregiver is the only social role they have been allowed to play (MacKinnon 1987). Mossman (1988) similarly questions whether women could ever transform the legal profession as long as they remain in the least powerful legal positions. Epstein (1989, 1990) argues that gender differences are 'deceptive distinctions' because 'they are socially imposed, regulated, and enforced, and because they are more superficial than is commonly believed' (1990: 314).

Since gender is enacted within specific social contexts, research on women lawyers should examine the particular contexts of legal practice. Different legal specialties require different skills from lawyers, and the working conditions themselves vary enormously by areas of law, nature of clients and structure of practice. Laws and lawyers' working conditions thus produce different values, ideologies, and norms—all of which emphasise different aspects of the professional legal role (Harrington 1994; Nelson and Trubek 1992). Cahn argues persuasively that 'what studying male and female styles [of lawyering] can do is open us up to appreciate the diversity in practice' (1992: 1059; and see Rhode 1994). As negotiated social constructions, gender differences are 'subject to variation according to culture, class, power, and the specific contexts in which these all interact' (Sommerlad and Sanderson 1998: 28). Consequently, contextual analysis, as Rhode suggests in an earlier chapter, will allow us to examine gender in conjunction with other political, economic, legal and social forces.

Family law, the most common legal specialty for women in the profession, provides an ideal context for research on women lawyers. Unlike corporate litigation in which women remain largely 'tokens' (Pierce 1995; Harrington 1993), family law has disproportionate representation by women. The subject matter itself—families and children—also draws ostensibly on women's expertise. It is in this legal arena, then, that we are most likely to find gender differences among lawyers—that is, if we are to find such differences at all. In this chapter I discuss women divorce lawyers in New England, drawing on statewide surveys of the New Hampshire bar, and on interviews with divorce lawyers in New Hampshire and Maine that I conducted with Craig McEwen and Richard Maiman.[1] These two neighbouring New England states each have about a million people living in small towns and a few medium-sized cities. About 60 per cent of the private legal practitioners in each of the two states work in solo law practice or in firms of two to five lawyers, the same percentage as lawyers nationwide (Curran and Carson 1994).

I begin by looking more closely at the context of family law, and the reasons lawyers reported for choosing divorce law work. Clearly, if women and men select this area of practice for different reasons, then, as Felstiner *et al* in their contribution to this volume suggest, it might be the process of self-selection that explains differences in lawyering, rather than gender. I then summarise findings from our research on gender similarity and difference among divorce lawyers. The last section analyses the gender differences among divorce lawyers in terms of the social, economic, political, and legal context of family law practice.

2 THE CONTEXT: FAMILY LAW PRACTICE

When women first entered the bar, matrimonial law was among the few areas in which women could obtain legal work. Corporate law firms routinely rejected women and during the 1960s, women lawyers were much more likely to handle divorce cases than were their male colleagues (White 1967; Epstein 1993). Both law firms and clients were more accepting of women as lawyers in cases of marital and custody conflict. The first few women who became judges were in family and juvenile law areas as well. Whether called 'matrimonial law,' 'domestic relations law,' or by the more contemporary term, 'family law,' this area of legal work was open to women lawyers. Legal specialties have their own gendered hierarchy, and family law drew on typically female attributes such as emotion, compassion and intuition (Sommerlad and Sanderson 1998: 165). Of course, matrimonial law also ranked at the bottom of legal specialties in terms of pay and prestige, and thus guaranteed that women would rarely be competing with men for legal advancement.

American law firms and government organisations have dropped their hiring barriers to women. Yet today, women lawyers remain disproportionately in family law practice. A recent statewide bar survey in New Hampshire shows that domestic relations continues to be the most common legal specialty for

[1] Our study involved 90-minute interviews in 1990–91 with 163 lawyers (one third of whom were women) and analyses of docket records on almost 7000 divorces cases in these two states over a nine-year period. Support for the project came from the National Science Foundation, Law and Social Science Program. I thank my co-authors for permission to use our data in this chapter. For further details about our research methodology, see Mather, McEwen, and Maiman (2001).

women lawyers, with 22 per cent of all women lawyers, but only six per cent of men, spending 50 per cent or more of their time practising family law (Shanelaris and Luneau 1998: 58). Even among all lawyers who handle divorce cases, women are more likely than men to specialise in this area. In our sample of 163 divorce lawyers in New Hampshire and Maine, 62 per cent of the women, but only 23 per cent of the men, reported that divorce comprised 50 per cent or more of their practice. Male lawyers in our study were more likely to handle divorce cases as part of a larger general practice, or along with several other legal specialties, in contrast to the predominantly female divorce specialists.

Both gendered and non-gendered factors explain why women attorneys gravitate toward family law work. When asked what led them to choose their legal specialty, an identical three-quarters of both male and female New Hampshire lawyers surveyed cited 'interest in duties' as the most important factor in their choice of legal work (Shanelaris and Luneau 1998: 67). Since women devote more of their legal practice to family law, these survey data do suggest that women have a greater interest in family law than men do. However, when asked in the same survey how child care responsibilities had affected their careers, 24 per cent of the female attorneys but only six per cent of the males said that their choice of a legal specialty was influenced 'a great deal' by the need to care for children (Shanelaris and Luneau 1998: 67). Divorce law work, especially in a small firm or solo practice, does not require the long hours or the night and weekend work of corporate law in large law firms. Seron and Ferris (1995) found that the women lawyers they studied in New York particularly appreciated the flexibility of small firm and solo practice in order to help balance work and family responsibilities.

Several women lawyers we interviewed in New England echoed this theme. 'I can control my time, I can control my hours,' said one woman. She explained that she finally switched out of criminal law after a murder trial forced her family to postpone a vacation. As a mother with children at home, this attorney added, 'I didn't want to have the type of practice that I couldn't discuss [with my family] or clients that perhaps I would be afraid to meet in a dark alley.' A few women practised in offices situated in their homes, and one lawyer had her young son home on school vacation during my interview with her. Other lawyers said they enjoyed divorce work because it was not a difficult area of law to practise, not something that required constant new legal research. The ability to combine a legal career with home and family life led some women to the field of divorce law.

Another practical advantage to divorce law practice (mentioned more often by men we interviewed) was the ease in attracting clients, an important consideration in a small-town law practice. Divorce is 'bread and butter work,' said one male lawyer. Or, as another said,

> In a small town practice, it's the type of practice that you really need to be involved in . . . From what I understand, one out of two married couples get divorced, and there's a demand there for the work.

Other male attorneys explained frankly, 'It's a business decision to take the [divorce] cases,' and 'It's good cash business.' Divorce work was steady business, easily available and it might also bring referrals for other types of legal work.

Lawyers who handled divorce as part of their general practice added that, although divorce work provided a ready source of clients, it was not a lucrative area of law. 'Non-payment,' said one lawyer, 'that's particularly bad in divorce cases.' Another complained that 'in divorce work, unfortunately, it is extremely difficult to get paid, because a lot of people don't have [the] money.' Several other attorneys (interestingly, all were women) also described the difficulty of earning money handling divorces, but they emphasised altruism as their motivation for entering into family law. As one said, 'I'm not out to make a million, that's not my goal in life . . . Being a lawyer is a place . . . to do the helping that needs to be done.' Another woman lawyer explained that she self-consciously focused her practice entirely on domestic relations cases (and turned away personal injury cases) because 'I don't like being a lawyer just for money.' Others spoke of choosing divorce law because of their interest in families and children, their strong desire to help empower women or their desire, as one women explained, to make 'an impact in the social fabric of society.'

Marital clients are different from other legal clients, according to the majority of our interviewees, because of the clients' highly emotional state and their difficult personal circumstances. As Sarat and Felstiner (1995) have also shown, clients in divorce are typically sad, angry, bitter, depressed, hurt or guilty. Attorneys who disliked divorce cases pointed to 'the emotional drain' of divorce work and the urgency of their clients' demands. Yet the emotional and personal nature of the work attracted other lawyers to it. As one lawyer noted, divorce law 'is not just a matter of making business judgments. You have to deal with people, you know, their personalities.' Another said, 'I have a certain empathy toward clients, especially husbands, because I went through a similar process myself.' As this last comment suggests, men as well as women lawyers said they enjoyed divorce work because of their interest in working with the human face of the law. One male attorney, for example, explained his choice of divorce work as follows:

> It's the only part of law I like and it's because it deals, it's not black and white, it deals with emotions. It allows me to personalise my involvement . . . It's much more humanistic, much [sic] more options for me to express creativity and counsel people and help emotionally.

Another attorney who herself had been divorced explained that her role as a divorce lawyer was 'not merely legal—a lot of it is teaching people *how* to be divorced.'

A final reason some attorneys gave for doing divorce work was their lack of choice in the matter. That is, the hierarchy that puts divorce cases at the bottom of a law firm's work plus a seniority principle for allocating cases often meant that the most junior lawyer in a firm would handle them. Thus, 'the low man or low woman on the pole,' as one lawyer said, does the divorce cases. In addition to seniority within a firm, gendered expectations of women attorneys—in a firm or even within a small community—also lead some women to accept divorce cases. As one woman noted, 'I think it's real tough for women not to have a considerable part of their practice in family law because people associate women lawyers with divorce.' Interestingly, only a few women we interviewed responded that they had little choice in the matter, and that it was their firm that expected them to represent divorce clients.[2]

Women lawyers we interviewed were more likely than men (64 per cent of women vs 46 per cent of men) to respond that they were content with their current proportion of divorce cases and preferred to keep it the same, while men were more likely than women to seek a decrease in the proportion of their practice devoted to divorce.[3] Since women lawyers already are handling a disproportionate share of divorce cases—and seem to be more content with these high levels—we clearly found self-selection by women into family law. To the extent that women lawyers have a greater substantive interest than men in family law issues, or more altruistic goals in lawyering, then this self-selection could explain differences in women lawyers' behaviour. But the other factors affecting women's choice of family law centred on child care considerations, flexibility of hours, the ease of this area of practice, or law firm expectations that women handle divorce—areas that do *not* translate easily into a particular female style of lawyering. Thus, self-selection alone would not explain differences between men and women in styles of divorce lawyering or in approaches to work.

3   GENDER SIMILARITIES AND DIFFERENCES

Overall we found male and female divorce lawyers generally similar in terms of their understandings of divorce work, perceptions of problems with clients and other lawyers, and ways of resolving divorce cases.[4] For example, most attorneys shared a preference for negotiating case settlements, and avoiding legal combat. Most reported recommending counselling for clients who seemed especially distraught and who were unable to focus clearly on the legal issues in their case. Most said they tried to persuade clients to avoid using the legal process as a way to enact revenge against a spouse. In these ways the norms of divorce lawyers in New Hampshire and Maine were quite typical of the divorce bar

---

[2] It could be that lawyers were reluctant to admit in interviews that divorce work was not their own choice, but that of their firm.

[3] This difference was not statistically significant (p = .08).

[4] The research conclusions and data reported throughout this section come from Mather, McEwen, and Maiman (2001). Parts of the research were also published earlier in Mather (1998); Maiman, Mather, and McEwen (1992); and Mather, Maiman, and McEwen (1996).

(Sarat and Felstiner 1995; Gilson and Mnookin 1994; Erlanger *et al* 1987). Nevertheless, we also found some differences related to gender in reports of the type of advocacy practised and in lawyers' orientation to their clients. I highlight the differences in this section because of their relevance to broader debates about gender difference and women in the legal profession.

One difference that emerged in our interviews was the more aggressive advocacy attributed to some of the women lawyers in the communities we studied. When we asked attorneys whether there were distinct types of divorce lawyers, or whether they were all pretty much alike, most responded that there were distinct types: lawyers who were 'reasonable' and others who were not. Reasonable lawyers knew the legal parameters and procedures of divorce, promoted case settlement to avoid unnecessary conflicts, were trustworthy and honest in negotiations with their peers and maintained an independent posture vis-a-vis their clients, rather than becoming hired guns for their clients.

By contrast, 'unreasonable' divorce lawyers were typically characterised by aggressive, 'Rambo-like,' 'hard-ball' advocacy on behalf of their clients. Another characterisation of the unreasonable lawyer included reliance on formal procedures to gather case information; in this view, unreasonable divorce lawyers would 'churn the files,' 'paper you to death,' or 'over-paper, over-motion, over-discover.' Unreasonable divorce lawyers also pursued their clients' goals even when these were unrealistic, rather than trying to educate the client to accept a more realistic case outcome.

When asked to describe these differences further, some said that women were disproportionately represented among the *unreasonable* divorce lawyers. 'Look at the so-called hard-nosed lawyers that we are talking about, the women would make a greater percentage,' said one attorney. Or, as another man explained,

> some of the more aggressive ones that I have dealt with I would say they have been women. I think that they have manifested less willingness to try to resolve this thing and to try to work out the differences and reach a settlement.

This aggressive advocacy style involved greater use of formal legal procedures, such as discovery through interrogatories, pretrial motions and contested hearings. It also involved painstakingly detailed settlement offers and tough-minded negotiations. For example, an older male lawyer, who had handled divorce cases for years as part of his general legal practice, commented with disgust about 'the new yuppie female lawyer' whose settlement 'demands are outrageous and unreasonable' and who creates mountains of paperwork for what should be a simple divorce case. Interestingly, some divorce lawyers studied by Sarat and Felstiner (1995: 103) also associated 'feminist' lawyering with 'unreasonable' attorney behaviour.

Women lawyers who admitted to a more aggressive advocacy style explained one difference between male lawyers and themselves as women taking family issues more seriously and caring more about the details of their clients' situations. For example, a female divorce specialist commented:

> Oftentimes, men attorneys are very willing to reach a compromise that in business would be fine. I would be lying to you if I said it wasn't a fine deal. . . . But in a divorce situation, I think it [a small amount of money] makes a big difference. I do. I think it makes a huge difference in their lives . . . Women take the divorce work a lot more seriously than men do.

Knowing the economic disparity between husbands and wives following divorce, divorce lawyers—especially those representing wives—were acutely aware of the importance of small financial differences in case settlements. But such attention to detail made 'women lawyers . . . harder to deal with than men lawyers,' as one male attorney put it. 'Men don't fool around with . . . little things,' he added. Yet a female attorney described as 'sexism . . . the view that women lawyers are Rambos in the divorce law,' and she attributed it to the fact that men care less about the specifics in divorce agreements. She said her reputation as 'a bitch' and a 'pushy lawyer' resulted from her willingness to 'fight for the details.'

Some unreasonable lawyers were said to follow their clients' wishes, acting more as a hired gun than as an independent adviser. Both women and men typically described their role as independent counsellors to their clients, educating clients about likely case outcomes and working to persuade them to accept realistic settlements. But there was a very small minority who articulated a more client-oriented perspective for decision-making. Women lawyers in this small group expressed their views in terms of a feminist goal of client empowerment. That is, especially for wives who had been controlled by their husbands throughout the marriage, the attorney for these clients should not make their decisions for them, but instead should encourage clients to assert themselves in decision making.

When confronted with clients who insisted on talking about their personal or emotional problems, most divorce lawyers said they allowed some of that discussion up to a certain point. But beyond that, they discouraged it and recommended that clients seek counselling or someone else for sympathy and emotional support. Contrary to expectations about women lawyers' greater attention to clients' emotions, we found women to be slightly *more* likely than men to report that they discouraged discussion of emotional or personal issues. This difference was not statistically significant, however. Some women explained that listening to clients' emotional outpourings would undercut their professional role as lawyers. In sociolinguistic research on lawyer-client interaction, Bogoch similarly found that women lawyers, like most men, tended to dismiss clients' emotional concerns, but that women 'had to be more explicit [than men] in proving their professional selves, especially in a profession whose image is still largely male' (Bogoch 1997: 707).

On the other hand, in answers to a question about the skills lawyers found most important in their daily divorce practice, we found a significant difference between men and women on the value they placed on 'being a sensitive listener to the client.' Women lawyers rated this skill the highest of six choices, with a mean rating of 4.5 (where 5.0 was the highest), in contrast to the 4.18 rating men gave it. There was also a much greater consensus among women respondents on the importance of client listening, in contrast to a wider range of responses by the men to this question.[5] The higher value that women attorneys gave to listening to clients is consistent with *clients'* perceptions that women lawyers listen more carefully than men do (Felstiner *et al* in this volume).

Lawyers in our interviews volunteered different reasons for the importance of listening to clients. Some valued listening because it encouraged clients' trust and helped to develop a strong lawyer-client relationship; others stressed the role listening played in providing clients with help and emotional support; still other lawyers emphasised instrumental reasons for listening, such as gleaning information about the case. Modest gender differences among these various reasons (although not statistically significant) suggest that women expressed a broader concern for clients, rather than focusing narrowly on the legal case. This finding also parallels clients' perceptions that women lawyers care more about them as people (Felstiner *et al* in this volume). Moreover, we found that men more frequently than women downplayed the importance of listening. As one male lawyer explained, since all clients 'tell you the same story anyway,' he preferred to ignore the personal details and concentrate instead on financial issues. He told his clients, 'I'm a mechanic to separate you from him or him from you. And that's my job . . . so I want to hear the economics of the situation.' His view of listening contrasted sharply with women in divorce practice who insisted on attending to 'the total needs of the client.'

Concern for clients was also expressed in some of the answers to questions about lawyer's goals, responsibilities, likes and dislikes, and the criteria they used to evaluate their success. We found that men were almost twice as likely as women to identify with a legal rights orientation, one which emphasised satisfaction in work through solving factual and legal problems, the responsibility for protecting clients' legal rights, and the enjoyment of courtroom advocacy. But women attorneys were twice as likely as men to identify with a mixed orientation, one which combined a legal-rights role with a client-focused orientation that emphasised the responsibility for helping clients move on with their lives, the satisfaction of solving 'people problems,' and the enjoyment of interpersonal contact with clients (Mather, McEwen, and Maiman 2001: 164–169).

These gender differences are not entirely consistent with expectations in the literature. That some women attorneys in family law might be more aggressive advocates, rely more on formal litigation techniques or be more stubborn, hard-nosed negotiators, flies in the face of a conciliatory female style said to prefer mediation to adjudication and to avoid legal combat. That women were generally no different than men in reporting control over their clients, and even a bit more likely than men to say they discouraged clients from discussing their

---

[5] In statistical terms, ratings by male lawyers showed a larger standard deviation (s.d. = .93) than did the ratings by female lawyers (s.d. = .59).

emotional and personal problems, does not bear out expectations of a more nurturing, attentive female style. Nevertheless, the significantly greater value women lawyers placed on the importance of 'sensitive listening' to clients lends support to notions of a women's ethic of care. Significant differences in the role orientations of men and women lend further credence to a more client-oriented approach by women lawyers, and their lesser orientation purely to legal rights.

Interestingly, a Canadian study on family law practitioners in the Vancouver area reached similar conclusions about the impact of women lawyers on family law. In their research, Hotel and Brockman (1994) found women respondents far more likely than men to describe themselves as good listeners, and empathetic with clients; yet women lawyers also expressed more difficulty in establishing professional distance from clients. Further, male divorce lawyers were more likely than women to define their success in terms of 'winning' cases (Hotel and Brockman 1994: 26), a finding consistent with our research (where men were more likely than women to express a legal rights orientation). Canadian lawyers gave a similar mix of reasons for choosing to practise family law: interest in family law issues; desire for a people-oriented practice; and pressure from law firms or expectations of others. Hotel and Brockman also report that women lawyers empathised more with the discrimination faced by wives in divorce, and articulated those concerns more forcefully. Like their New England counterparts, most Canadian respondents believed that 'the increasing number of women in the legal profession had changed or was changing the practice of family law' (Hotel and Brockman 1994: 35).

Nevertheless, gender alone does not fully explain the impact that women have had in family law. Attention to the context of work in divorce also helps to explain why this particular pattern of gender similarities and differences has emerged.

4 OTHER SOCIAL, ECONOMIC, POLITICAL AND LEGAL FORCES

Examination of lawyers in context underscores the importance of audience expectations—whether the audience is comprised of other lawyers, judges, or clients—and of lawyers' working conditions, including economic constraints, law firm culture, and the particular legal norms and processes of a given legal specialty. Certain aspects of the work contexts are themselves gendered, and individual men and women attorneys have multiple ways of reacting to the various expectations and pressures around them.

The massive influx of women into the bar occurred simultaneously with the expansion of the legal profession and its increased specialisation. Throughout the 1980s the divorce bar became more differentiated, with divorce specialists serving clients with greater economic resources, and general practice lawyers handling divorces for middle to working classes. We found that divorce specialists charged more for initial retainers and hourly fees and reported considerably more billable hours in a typical divorce case, than did the general practice lawyers (Mather, Maiman and McEwen 1996). Whereas the general practice lawyer needed to contain formal legal activity in order to minimise divorce costs, divorce specialists were responding to financial complexities in their clients' cases by bringing techniques of civil litigation into their divorce work. Specialists in family law were disproportionately women. And it was young women specialists who initiated some of the changes, such as discovery and formal motions for divorce, which so infuriated the older, general practitioners. Thus, the economics of a specialised divorce practice helps explain the lawyering style of aggressive advocacy attributed to some of the women lawyers.

Clientele resources also play a role in understanding the particular advocacy of the 'yuppie female lawyer.' Female divorce lawyers in our research disproportionately represented upper-middle class clients, while males disproportionately had a working class clientele in divorce cases. Wealthier clients have more resources to support the costs of advocacy, and they also have more complex property issues to fight about with their spouses. Thus, the nature and style of legal advocacy is shaped by clientele differences (Mather, McEwen and Maiman 2001).

Several women lawyers, when they described why they began using civil litigation techniques for divorce cases, mentioned the difficulty they faced being taken seriously by their male colleagues. Although informal communication may have worked fine for the old boy network, they said, it was disastrous for lawyers outside of the network. One woman explained her preference for formal discovery over informal sharing of case information: 'I see a lot of bad lawyering that's based on "Oh, let's be buddies." I'm not a member of the clique.' The notion of a 'clique' is not just the imaginary figment of a few paranoid women attorneys. According to a 1998 survey of the New Hampshire bar, 93 per cent of the women lawyers (and even 59 per cent of the men) believe that there is an 'old boy network' in the state bar; 83 per cent of the women (and 40 per cent of the men) say that the old boy network discriminates against female attorneys in pay, promotions, and 'level of respect' (Shanelaris and Luneau 1998: 67). Women in the survey especially complained about their treatment outside of the courtroom, eg, not being taken seriously, being ignored, inappropriate comments or sexist jokes. Reacting against hostile or demeaning treatment from their colleagues, women lawyers might then have responded with greater reliance on formal legal processes.

Constant questioning of women's abilities by their male peers may also have encouraged women to adopt a more aggressive style of advocacy, simply to prove themselves. Irwin (1998: 15) quotes Linda Dalianis, the first women Superior Court judge in New Hampshire (now a Supreme Court Justice in New Hampshire), who said, 'At the beginning of my career there was a big question mark: Can women do it? Can women be good litigators? Will they cry in the courtroom?' One way women attorneys tried to prove themselves equal to the task was by working especially hard, attending conscientiously to every detail, and becoming even more assertive and adversarial than their male colleagues—a pattern Sommerlad and Sanderson (1998), Brockman (1996), and Jack and Jack (1989) also found in their research on women in the legal profession.

Being excluded from an old boy legal network could also lead women to define their professional responsibilities more in terms of clients rather than the bar or courts. In an analysis of professional commitment, Sommerlad and Sanderson report that women solicitors in their survey tended 'to articulate a more generalised, altruistic notion of service and of commitment to the client' (1998: 221). Our finding that women divorce lawyers were half as likely as men to be oriented toward the legal community and legal rights, and more likely to include a client orientation in their approach to work, could be explained by women's altruistic reasons for choosing divorce law. But the finding could also be explained by the treatment women lawyers received from their male colleagues in the bar. A third explanation might rest in the gender differences in clienteles of male and female lawyers.

We found that women attorneys in divorce disproportionately represented wives, not husbands. Data from the case dockets for all cases in our sample between 1984 and 1988 show that 70 per cent of the clients of women lawyers were wives, but only 51 per cent of the clients of men were wives (Mather, McEwen and Maiman 2001: 208). This pattern existed regardless of lawyers' specialisation, suggesting that women clients sought out women attorneys regardless of whether they were family law specialists. In working closely with clients of their own sex, women attorneys may find they receive more respect from clients than from professional colleagues, and greater satisfaction through client work than through work with other lawyers. For these reasons, women might define their professional responsibilities more toward clients, and less toward the legal system.

Clientele differences could also influence attorneys' styles of advocacy through the nature of the issues presented in cases of wives vs husbands, especially in a no-fault legal framework. As one woman attorney commented, 'I think a lot of women seek a woman lawyer. I think that my own interest is in women's issues.' One major 'women's issue' centres on the financial difficulties women with children face in making ends meet after a divorce (Weitzman 1985). Eekelaar and Maclean (1994) summarise research on families with children showing that the economic position of wives declines, while that of husbands goes up. Through awareness of these financial disadvantages for wives, and through their experience of representing wives more than husbands, women lawyers may turn to adversarial advocacy in order to fight for their clients' every last dollar. In other words, a political agenda of helping to protect wives from the negative consequences of divorce might work in conjunction with the other factors discussed above to explain the 'yuppie female lawyer' who makes such 'outrageous demands'—in the words of her older male colleague.

5 CONCLUSION

Analysis of lawyers in the particular context of divorce law practice reveals clearly how gender is just one of many influences on attorneys in their work. Gender is not *un*important, since some significant associations between gender and legal role emerged. Yet the gender differences observed appeared to rest on the interaction between gender and various other social, political and economic factors. From their more aggressive advocacy and introduction of civil litigation techniques into divorce to their concern for listening to clients, we found women divorce lawyers disproportionately to show several distinctive traits. These traits, however, *cannot* be explained simply by gender. Gender, as a social construct, operates in a larger social context as well.

As we have seen, gender of divorce lawyers overlaps with categories of legal specialisation and the resources and gender of lawyers' client base. Further, the traits of 'the new yuppie female lawyer' present a complex and surprising mix of advocacy and caring that would not be predicted by scholars focused on gender difference. This finding, too, underlines the necessity of examining gender in context. For example, the equal numbers of women and men entering the legal profession today could transform the legal community by replacing the old boy network with a more integrated one, or even two separate networks of men and women. In either case, women lawyers may then feel less of a need to prove themselves as tough, hardball negotiators, and the particular advocacy that characterised some of the female divorce specialists may disappear. The advocacy style observed could simply have been an artifact of the first generation of women who entered the bar at that particular time. Alternatively, if it is the political and economic issues of protecting wives that has fuelled it, then legal changes in favour of wives could perhaps weaken the relation between attorneys' gender and aggressive advocacy. In short, interactions within the professional community of divorce lawyers, resources and expectations from clients, and the law itself, *all* exert powerful forces, along with gender, to shape lawyers' behaviour and values.

6 REFERENCES

Bogoch, Bryna. 1997. Gendered Lawyering: Difference and Dominance in Lawyer-Client Interaction. *Law and Society Review* 31: 677–712.

Cahn, Naomi. 1992. Styles of Lawyering. *Hastings Law Journal* 43: 1039–1069.

Curran, Barbara A and Clara N Carson. 1994. *The Lawyer Statistical Report: The U. S. Legal Profession in the 1990's.* Chicago: American Bar Foundation.

Brockman, Joan. 1996. Reluctant Adversaries in an Adversarial System. Presented at the Law and Society Association Annual Meeting, Glasgow.

Eekelaar, John and Mavis Maclean. 1994. Introduction. In *A Reader on Family Law.* New York: Oxford University Press.

Epstein, Cynthia Fuchs. 1989. On Deceptive Distinctions: What's Wrong and What's Right with the Research on Gender. *Sociological Viewpoints* 5: 1–14.

Epstein, Cynthia Fuchs. 1990. Faulty Framework: Consequences of the Difference Model for Women in the Law. *New York Law School Law Review* 35: 309–336.

Epstein, Cynthia Fuchs. 1993. *Women in Law*. 2nd ed. Urbana: University of Illinois Press.

Erlanger, Howard S *et al*. 1987. Participation and Flexibility in Informal Processes; Cautions from the Divorce Context. *Law and Society Review* 21: 585–604.

Fineman, Martha. 1990. Challenging Law, Establishing Differences: The Future of Feminist Legal Scholarship. *Florida Law Review* 42: 25–43.

Gilligan, Carol. 1982. *In A Different Voice: Psychological Theory and Women's Development*. Cambridge: Harvard University Press.

Gilson, Ronald J and Robert Mnookin. 1994. Disputing Through Agents: Cooperation and Conflict Between Lawyers in Litigation. *Columbia Law Review* 94: 509–66.

Hagan, John, and Fiona Kay. 1995. *Gender in Practice: A Study of Lawyers' Lives*. New York: Oxford University Press.

Harrington, Christine B. 1994. Outlining a Theory of Legal Practice. In *Lawyers in a Postmodern World: Translation and Transgression*, edited by M Cain and CB Harrington. New York: New York University Press.

Harrington, Mona. 1993. *Women Lawyers: Rewriting the Rules*. New York: Penguin Books.

Heinz, John and Edward Laumann. 1982. *Chicago Lawyers: The Social Structure of the Bar*. New York and Chicago: Russell Sage Foundation and American Bar Foundation.

Hotel, Carla and Joan Brockman. 1994. The Conciliatory-Adversarial Continuum in Family Law Practice. *Canadian Journal of Family Law* 12: 11–36.

Irwin, Lauren Simon. 1998. 'Gee, Mommy, I Didn't Know Boys Could Be Judges Too.' Perspectives from the Bench. *New Hampshire Bar Journal* 39: 14–19.

Jack, Rand, and Dana Cowley Jack. 1989. *Moral Vision and Professional Decisions: The Changing Values of Women and Men Lawyers*. New York: Cambridge University Press.

MacKinnon, Catherine. 1987. *Feminism Unmodified: Discourses on Life and Law*. Cambridge: Harvard University Press.

Maiman, Richard J, Lynn Mather and Craig A McEwen. 1992. Gender and Specialization in the Practice of Divorce Law. *Maine Law Review* 44: 39–61.

Mather, Lynn, Richard J Maiman and Craig A McEwen. 1996. Avocats et Divorce aux Etats-Unis: la transformation des pratiques professionelles. *Droit et Societé* 33: 341–360.

Mather, Lynn, Craig A McEwen, and Richard J Maiman. 2001. *Divorce Lawyers at Work: Varieties of Professionalism in Practice*. New York: Oxford University Press.

Menkel-Meadow, Carrie. 1985. Portia in a Different Voice: Speculations on a Women's Lawyering Process. *Berkeley Women's Law Journal* 1: 39–63.

Menkel-Meadow, Carrie. 1989. Exploring a Research Agenda of the Feminization of the Legal Profession: Theories of Gender and Social Change. *Law & Social Inquiry* 14: 289–319.

Menkel-Meadow, Carrie. 1995. Portia Redux: Another Look at Gender, Feminism, and Legal Ethics. In *Legal Ethics and Legal Practice: Contemporary Issues*, edited by S Parker and C Sampford. Oxford: Clarendon Press.

Mossman, Mary Jane. 1988. Portia's Progress: Women as Lawyers. Reflections on Past and Future. *Windsor Yearbook Access to Justice* 8: 252–266.

Nelson, Robert R and David M Trubek. 1992. Arenas of Professionalism: The Professional Ideologies of Lawyers in Context. In *Lawyers' Ideals/ Lawyers' Practices*, edited by RL Nelson, DM Trubek and RL Solomon. Ithaca, NY: Cornell University Press.

Pierce, Jennifer. 1995. *Gender Trials*. Berkeley: University of California Press.

Rhode, Deborah. 1994. Gender and Professional Roles. *Fordham Law Review* 63: 39–72.

Sarat, Austin and William LF Felstiner. 1995. *Divorce Lawyers and Their Clients: Power and Meaning in the Legal Process*. New York: Oxford University Press.

Seron, Carroll and Kerry Ferris. 1995. Negotiating Professionalism. *Work and Occupations* 22: 22–48.

Shanelaris, Catherine E and Henrietta Walsh Luneau. 1998. Ten Year Gender Survey. *New Hampshire Bar Journal* 39: 56–88.

Sommerlad, Hilary and Peter Sanderson. 1998. *Gender, Choice and Commitment: Women Solicitors in England and Wales and the Struggle for Equal Status*. Hampshire, England: Dartmouth Publishing Company.

Weitzman, Lenore. 1985. *The Divorce Revolution*. New York: Free Press.

White, J. 1967. Women in the Law. *Michigan Law Review* 65:1051–1122.

4

Barriers to Gender Equality in the Canadian Legal Establishment[1]

FIONA M KAY AND JOAN BROCKMAN

Abstract

In this paper we trace the historical exclusion of women from the legal profession in Canada. We examine women's efforts to gain entry to law practice and their progress through the last century. The battle to gain entry to this exclusive profession took place on many fronts: in the courts, government legislature, public debate and media and behind the closed doors of the law societies. After formal barriers to entry were dismantled, women continued to confront formidable barriers through overt and subtler forms of discrimination and exclusion. Today's legal profession in Canada is a contested one. Women have succeeded with large enrolments in law schools and growing representation in the profession. However, women remain on the margins of power and privilege in law practice. Our analysis of contemporary official data on the Canadian legal profession demonstrates that women are under-represented in private practice, have reduced chances for promotion and are excluded from higher echelons of authority, remuneration and status in the profession. Yet, the contemporary picture of the legal profession also reveals that women are having an important impact on the profession of law in Canada by introducing policy reforms aimed at creating a more humane legal profession.

1 INTRODUCTION

CANADA'S LEGAL PROFESSION is unusual in that both common and civil law traditions co-exist within one country. The provincial laws in Quebec operate under civil law, originating with the French settlers in the 1600s, although federal statutes, such as the Criminal Code, also apply in Quebec. Laws in 'English' Canada, that is, the regions outside Quebec, were established under British rule. In English Canada, lawyers operate as 'barristers and solicitors' although they may identify their work as primarily that of a solicitor or as a

---

[1] Originally published in (8) 2 *Feminist Legal Studies* (2000) pp. 169–198.

litigator or barrister. Law practice in Quebec consists of members of two professional organisations: the Bar of Quebec (*Barreau du Québec*) and the Board of Notaries (*Chambre des notaires du Quebec*). In Quebec, as in France, the notary plays a dual role: a legal practitioner serving clients and a public official charged with drafting deeds in notarial form (Brierley & Macdonald 1993: 60–63). Litigation and advocacy are reserved for lawyers, and only lawyers can become judges.[2] Under the *Code Civil du Quebec*, notaries have exclusive jurisdiction over mortgages, marriage contracts, wills and testaments and declaration of joint ownership (Morier 1997: 48). Under the current system of exclusive jurisdictions, notaries traditionally practise in the areas of real estate, wills and estates, marriages (but not divorces) and family mediation; while litigation (criminal law, civil litigation, divorce and so on) and advocacy are the domain of lawyers.[3]

The ten provinces and three territories (Nunavut became the third territory on 1 April 1999) in Canada have jurisdiction over the practice of law. All legislatures have created self-regulating law societies to govern the practice of law in their jurisdiction, and they have granted their respective law societies monopolies on the practice of law.[4] Some inroads into this monopoly have been made in a few provinces by paralegals, and, in British Columbia, notaries have managed to share the lawyers' monopoly in certain areas since the province joined the Confederation in 1871 (Brockman 1997a: 197–234; Brockman 1999).

Women first won entry to the Canadian legal profession in 1895, but it was not until 1942 that legal barriers directed at preventing women from practising law were removed in all provinces. The battle to gain entry to the exclusive profession of law took place on many fronts: in the courts, legislatures, public debate and media and behind the closed doors of the law societies. Once formal barriers to entry were dismantled, women still faced formidable barriers through overt and subtler forms of discrimination and exclusion. Today's legal profession in Canada is a contested one. Women have succeeded with large enrolments in law schools and growing representation in the profession. However, they remain on the margins of power and privilege in law practice. Yet, the contemporary picture of the profession suggests that women are having an important impact on the profession of law in Canada, introducing reforms aimed at producing a more humane legal profession.

The purpose of this paper is to bring together the research that has been done on women in the legal profession in Canada, including the eleven research pro-

[2] Notaries and lawyers in Quebec both attend law school, specialising in their third year. Notary students attend a fourth year leading to a master's degree in law, followed by a one-year articling period under the supervision of *la Chambre des notaires*. In contrast, after the third year of law school (bachelor's degree), the lawyer writes the Bar admission exam, followed by a six month period of articles in law firms under the supervision of *le Barreau du Québec*.

[3] As legal counsel, notaries may express opinions in all areas of law. Under the *Loi sur le notariat*, Quebec notaries are both legal advisers and public officials. As public officials, they are required to exercise neutrality and provide advice to all parties involved.

[4] Law society websites and email addresses can be found through links provided by the Federation of Law Societies of Canada=s website: http://www.flsc.ca.

jects we have conducted independently over the past 12 years.[5] We begin by tracing the historical exclusion of women from the legal profession in Canada, and then examine women's efforts to gain entry to law practice and their progress through the last century. Next, we pull together data from law societies across Canada to provide an overview to contemporary patterns of segmentation and stratification in the Canadian legal profession. We then conduct an extensive review of recent research in Canada to document women's underrepresentation in private practice, their reduced rates of promotions and their exclusion from higher echelons of authority, remuneration and status in the profession. In the final section, we provide an overview of contemporary struggles for gender equality in the Canadian legal profession, with an emphasis upon issues of systemic barriers to women's full inclusion in the profession, sexual harassment guidelines, family responsibilities and accommodations in the workplace and policy reforms initiated by the provinces' law societies and the Canadian Bar Association (CBA).[6]

2 THE HISTORICAL EXCLUSION OF WOMEN FROM THE LEGAL PROFESSION

As was the case in many other commonwealth countries, women in all but one of the Canadian provinces initially faced personnel at law societies and judges in the courts who considered them ineligible to become lawyers. However, efforts by men to exclude women from the legal profession were met by strong resistance from women, and demands made to the male legislators to amend legislation so that women could be called to the Bar were eventually successful. Racial and ethnic minorities, whether women or men, had even more difficulty gaining entrance to the Canadian legal establishment.

The first four law societies to admit women were forced to do so by provincial legislation, after they refused to admit women on the ground that they were only allowed to admit 'persons,' despite a provision in the *Interpretation Act* stating that 'words importing . . . the masculine gender . . . shall include . . . females as well as males.' Following the passage of legislation in 1891 in

---

[5] Joan has conducted two surveys in Alberta (1991), two surveys in British Columbia (1989–1990), a study involving 100 interviews in British Columbia (1993–94), and an historical analysis of women in the legal profession. Fiona has conducted one longitudinal study of Ontario lawyers (1990 and 1996), one survey of bar admission students in Ontario (1998) and two surveys of Quebec lawyers and notaries (1998, 1999). To some degree, this paper integrates our independent research projects; however, significant research has also been conducted by other Canadian scholars, as is illustrated in this compilation. For a detailed listing of research related to women and the law in Canada, see Boyd, Sheehy and Bouchard (1999).

[6] The CBA is a voluntary organisation (some law societies require membership of the CBA, others do not), with approximately 35,000 lawyers, judges, notaries, law teachers and law students from across Canada (approximately two thirds of all practising lawyers in Canada, according to the CBA's own estimates). The association has branches in each of the provinces and territories, and works through sections, committees and task forces to promote the interests of its members and effect law reform. Further information is available at the CBA website: http://www.cba.org.

Ontario, Clara Brett Martin was the first woman to be admitted to a law society in Canada in 1892. Another amendment in 1895 allowed her to be called to the bar as a barrister (Backhouse 1985: 1; Backhouse 1992: 263; Betcherman 1992: 280; Cossman & Kline 1992: 298; Pearlman 1992: 317). Following a rejection by the law society and the courts, a special Act was passed in New Brunswick allowing Mabel Penery French to be called to the bar in that province in 1905 (Yorke 1993: 3). When she later moved to British Columbia, French faced similar rejection, and, following the dismissal of her appeal by the British Columbia Court of Appeal, she lobbied the Conservative Attorney-General, William J Bowser, who was 'openly opposed to the expansion of women's rights' (Yorke 1993: 36). However, French had the support of Evelyn Farris, a strong women's advocate who had the ear of some politicians, and an Act to 'Remove the Disability of Women so far as it Relates to the Study and Practice of Law' was eventually passed, allowing French to be called to the bar in British Columbia in 1912 (Brockman 1995; Yorke 1993). In Manitoba, Melrose Sissons also had to take her cause to the provincial legislature to have it amend the Law Society Act so that she could be admitted. The legislation was amended in 1912, and she and Winnifred Wilton were the first women called to the bar in Manitoba, in 1915 (Kinnear 1992: 411).

In sharp contrast to Ontario, New Brunswick, British Columbia, and Manitoba, Ruby Clements, the first woman called in Alberta in 1915, met no public rejection by the Law Society. Neither did the first woman who articled in the Northwest Territories. Erella Alexander of Calgary was admitted to the Law Society as a student-at-law in 1899 in what was then the Northwest Territories; however, she did not complete her articles and apply for admission to the bar (Petersson 1997: 365).

The last province to pass legislation allowing the admission of women to the practice of law was Quebec in 1941, although Annie Langstaff had applied for admission as early as 1914. A single mother of an eight-year-old child, separated from her husband as to property since 1906,[7] she needed her husband's permission to carry on business, despite the fact that she did not know where he was. The Quebec Superior Court dismissed her petition, and the Court of Appeal rejected her appeal. Years later in 1941, the amendment to the Bar Act passed with 'what was in some instances almost violent opposition on the part of the members of the Bar' (Smith, Stephenson & Quijano 1973: 141; Gillett 1981; Mossman 1988: 567). Elizabeth Monk was the first woman called to the bar in Quebec, in 1942.

Although the door was slowly cracking open for women to enter law, there remained strong resistance to ethnic and cultural outsiders to the exclusively 'white' legal profession in Canada (Neallani 1992; St Lewis 1999). For example,

---

[7] Separated as to property meant she could administer but not sell her property, and was not entitled to carry on business without her husband's permission. Divorce was not open to her. Married women were not granted many contractual and civil rights in Quebec until 1964.

the legal profession in British Columbia took steps in 1918 to remain an all-white profession. Following a request by the Vancouver Law Students' Society, the Law Society passed a rule requiring applicants to be eligible to vote in provincial elections. This rule was then used to exclude those who were disenfranchised at that time (Japanese, Chinese, East Indians and Aboriginals), until the British Columbia legislature removed the barriers to voting in the late 1940s (Brockman 1995: 519–25; Tong 1996, 1998; Ferguson 1997; for a perspective in other provinces, see Backhouse 1994, 1996).

As the formal barriers to sex and race were dismantled,[8] law societies and law schools began demanding more formal education of their members. For example, in 1949, the Law Society of British Columbia required students to have a law degree prior to the required one-year articling period (Pue 1995); and, in 1950, articled students were required to serve a *continuous* year, in contrast to the previous three four-month periods spread out over three years. At the same time, the Benchers were increasing the education requirements for lawyers whilst relaxing the requirements for men who were returning from the War. Articled students with degrees could count two years overseas service towards the three years required for articles; students without degrees could count three years overseas service towards the five years required for articles (Brockman 1995: 524–25; Pue 1995: chapters 4 & 5).

Following the admission of women to the various bars in Canada, their initial numbers remained low. In 1971, women represented only 5.2 per cent of lawyers in Canada. This figure rose to 15.5 per cent in 1981, to 22.0 per cent in 1986, 29.1 per cent in 1991, and 30.6 per cent in 1996.[9] Gains remained slow through most of the twentieth century, with the most pronounced gains having taken place since the 1970s. The ratios of men to women lawyers in Canada in 1911, 1971, 1981, and 1991 were about 742:1, 20:1, 6:1, and 2.4:1, respectively (Hagan & Kay 1996: 544; Hagan 1990a: 52).

3 CONTEMPORARY PATTERNS OF INEQUALITY

In this section, we explore further women's representation in the contemporary Canadian legal profession. Table 1 displays the distribution of men and

---

[8] During the 1990s, minorities have entered the Canadian legal profession in visibly increasing numbers. The provincial law societies and the CBA have begun to study the diversification of demographics in the profession and contemporary issues of discrimination against ethnic minorities in the Canadian legal profession. For example, in 1999, the CBA released two reports by the Working Group on Racial Equality in the Legal Profession, which made 77 recommendations for improving racial equality, and eliminating systemic racism. See Canadian Bar Association (1999) and St Lewis (1999).

[9] The figures from 1971 to 1986 are taken from several reports written by Marshall (1981; 1987: 7; 1989: 13). The figures for 1991 and 1996 are taken from *Statistics Canada* (1993: 8) and *1996 Census. Statistics Canada*. The count includes all lawyers in Canada and notaries in Quebec and British Columbia.

women lawyers across Canadian provinces and territories by geographic regions. In 1996, close to 59,000 lawyers practised law in the Canadian labour force. The largest proportion of lawyers worked in central Canada (66 per cent), followed by the Western provinces (28 per cent); while 5 per cent of lawyers worked in the Maritimes and Atlantic Canada (the eastern provinces) and less than 1 per cent of lawyers practised law in the northern territories of the Yukon and Northwest. The three provinces with the largest numbers of lawyers in Canada are Ontario (40 per cent or 23,745 lawyers), Quebec (26 per cent or 15,050 lawyers), and British Columbia (14 per cent or 8,275 lawyers). Although Quebec was the last province in Canada to admit women to the legal profession, the representation of women among Quebec lawyers has grown over the last 25 years at a faster rate than elsewhere in Canada (Hagan & Kay 1996: 545) to 36.5 per cent in 1996.

Table 1: Lawyers in the Canadian Labour Force, 1996[a]

Geographic Region	Men	Women	Total	% Women
Eastern Canada				
Newfoundland	365	150	515	29.1
Prince Edward Island	125	45	170	26.5
Nova Scotia	1,015	325	1,340	24.3
New Brunswick	840	250	1,090	22.9
Central Canada				
Quebec[b]	9,560	5,490	15,050	36.5
Ontario	16,635	7,110	23,745	29.9
Western Canada				
Manitoba	1,250	395	1,645	24.0
Saskatchewan	955	330	1,285	25.5
Alberta	3,965	1,465	5,430	27.0
British Columbia[c]	5,940	2,335	8,275	28.2
Territories				
Yukon	105	40	145	27.6
Northwest Territories and Nunavut[d]	70	40	110	36.4
Canada (total)	40,835	17,985	58,820	30.6

SOURCE: 1996 Canadian Census, *Statistics Canada*.

[a] Labour force by occupation, based on the 1991 standard occupational classification and sex for Canada, Provinces Territories, and Census Metropolitan Areas, 1991 and 1996 Censuses (20% sample data).

[b] Includes lawyers (*avocats et avocates*) and notaries (*notaires*) in the province of Quebec.

[c] Includes barristers and solicitors (lawyers) and notaries. There are fewer than 200 notaries in British Columbia. The low representation of notaries is due to their numbers being fixed by statute in 1980.

[d] As of 1 April 1999 members of the Law Society of the North West Territories were 'grand-parented' into the Law Society of Nunavut (the new territory).

We canvassed the law societies of each province and territory to provide more up-to-date information on the numbers of active or practising members. These data are presented in Table 2. It is important to note that the figures in Table 1 cannot be compared directly with those of Table 2 without taking into account the different definitions and categorics employed by the official agencies. Data in Table 1 are derived from *Statistics Canada* and rely on a random sample of Canadians to report their occupation in terms of the kind of work they were doing 'during the week prior to the census, as determined by the kind of work and the description of the most important duties of the job.'[10] The 20 per cent random sample used by *Statistics Canada* allows for some error in the actual numbers arrived at, and there may be other errors in data collection and recording. In contrast, data in Table 2 are drawn from the law societies' membership records. These data may be flawed in that lawyers who are members of more than one provincial law society may be double-counted, and membership records may sometimes include lawyers who have taken a temporary absence, suspension, or are not presently residents of the province, but remain on the law society's active list.[11] These differences aside, Table 2 provides us with the most current data available on the numbers of active or practising members of law societies within each province of Canada. The largest representation of women in law practice is in Quebec. As of 1999, women represent 40 per cent of lawyers in Quebec and 43 per cent of notaries. In contrast, if we compare these figures to the provinces with the next largest number of lawyers, we see that women make up 30 per cent of Ontario's lawyers and 28 per cent of lawyers in British Columbia. In total, Canada was home to 72,761 lawyers in the spring of 1999, with women representing 32 per cent of the legal profession.

The distribution of women across sectors of the legal profession in Canada reveals that women are under-represented in the private practice of law. In Table 3 we draw on the Federation of Law Societies of Canada for available data on the distribution of lawyers across sectors of the profession. These data reveal that women represent only 26 per cent of lawyers in private practice, although they represent close to 40 per cent of lawyers working in the non-private practice of law, including: education (41 per cent), government employment (43 per cent), and corporate settings (37 per cent). Nearly half of all lawyers working in settings 'other' than these described are women (49.2 per cent). The gender difference is perhaps most striking in private practice. 81 per cent of male lawyers work in private practice compared to only 63 per cent of women (see Table 3). Women are more highly represented in government employment than men: 10 per cent of women compared with 6 per cent of men work in government settings. Meanwhile, near equivalent percentages of men

---

[10] Persons not employed during that week are asked to record their job of longest duration since January 1 of the previous year. The description is available at http://www.statcan.ca.

[11] Prior to law societies introducing inactive or non-practising membership status, it was very common for lawyers to continue paying membership fees even though they were not practising. Now that all law societies have inactive or non-practising membership categories, this is less likely.

Table 2: Active or Practising Members of Law Societies in Canada, 1999[a]

Geographic Region	Men	Women	Total	% Women
Eastern Canada				
Newfoundland	419	153	572	26.8
Prince Edward Island	147	80	227	35.2
Nova Scotia	1,151	452	1,603	28.2
New Brunswick	883	311	1,194	26.1
Central Canada				
Quebec[b]				
Lawyers	10,766	7,180	17,946	40.0
Notaries	1,855	1,374	3,229	42.6
Ontario	20,755	8,967	29,722	30.2
Western Canada				
Manitoba	1,291	408	1,699	24.0
Saskatchewan	1,095	360	1,455	24.7
Alberta	4,634	1,664	6,298	26.4
British Columbia	6,092	2,322	8,414	27.6
Territories				
Yukon	72	38	110	34.6
Northwest Territories				
and Nunavut[c]	210	82	292	28.1
Canada (total)	49,370	23,391	72,761	32.2

SOURCES (from West to East): correspondence 10 March 1999, Becky McCaffrey, Executive Director, the Law Society of the Northwest Territories; correspondence 1 March 1999, Georgina Swan, Assistant, Equity and Diversity Committee of the Law Society of British Columbia; correspondence 11 May 1999, Allison MacKenzie, The Law Society of Alberta; correspondence 1 March 1999, A Kirsten Logan, Secretary/Co-Director of Administration of the Law Society of Saskatchewan; correspondence 1 March 1999, Marilyn W Billinkoff, Deputy Chief Executive Officer of the Law Society of Manitoba; correspondence 7 May 1999, Michelle Pachecl, General Inquiry Clerk, Law Society of Upper Canada; correspondence 1 November 1998, Me Josée Deschênes, Formation continue, Direction du développement de la profession, la Chambre des notaires; correspondence 5 January 1999, Me Carole Brosseau, Recherche et législation, Barreau du Québec; correspondence 25 February 1999, Michel Carrier, Executive Director of the Law Society of New Brunswick; correspondence 31 March, 1999, Catherine Meade, Equity Officer, Nova Scotia Barristers' Society; correspondence 25 May 1999, Beverly Mills-Stetson, Secretary-Treasurer, the Law Society of Prince Edward Island; correspondence 10 March 1999, Peter Ringrose, Executive Director, The Law Society of Newfoundland.

[a] Data for this table were collected by mail, electronic-mail, and telephone correspondence with personnel at each provincial law society across Canada.

[b] Data for the province of Quebec include two categories of legal professionals: lawyers (avocats et avocates) and notaries (notaires).

[c] As of 1 April 1999 members of the Law Society of the North West Territories were 'grand-parented' into the Law Society of Nunavut (the new territory).

and women lawyers work in education and corporate settings (0.4 per cent and 1.7 per cent, respectively). In contrast, women are significantly more represented among lawyers working in alternative work settings. Close to one quarter of women lawyers work in these other settings compared with only 12 per cent of men. Among lawyers who have left the practice of law, women figure prominently. Although women represent approximately 31 per cent of lawyers in practice, they make up 39 per cent of lawyers no longer practising law. These figures do not include former practitioners who do not pay their non-practising membership fees.

Table 3: Canadian Lawyers Across Sectors of the Profession, 1995–96[a]

Sector of the Legal Profession	Men	Women	Total	% Women
Private Practice[b]	37,199 (80.6)	12,925 (62.5)	50,124 (75.0)	25.8
Education[c]	167 (0.4)	115 (0.6)	282 (0.4)	40.8
Government[d]	2,799 (6.0)	2,100 (10.2)	4,899 (7.3)	42.9
Corporate[e]	715 (1.6)	422 (2.0)	1,137 (1.7)	37.1
Other[f]	5,297 (11.5)	5,124 (24.8)	10,421 (15.6)[g]	49.2
Total	46,177	20,686	66,863	30.9
Non-practising lawyers[h]	4,824	3,104	7,928	39.2

SOURCE: *Law Societies' Statistics on Membership*, 1998 Federation of Law Societies of Canada. Date: 3 December 1998. Website: http://www.flsc.ca/English/95st-membership.htm. The percentages of men and women across sectors of the profession are indicated in brackets.

[a] Data were collected from the following provinces and current as of the following dates: British Columbia (29 January 1996), Alberta (1 January 1996), Saskatchewan (31 December 1995), Manitoba (31 December 1995), Ontario (7 January 1996), Quebec lawyers (31 January 1996), Quebec notaries (22 February 1996), New Brunswick (31 December 1995), Nova Scotia (31 December 1995), Prince Edward Island (31 December 1995), Newfoundland (31 December 1995) and Northwest and Yukon Territories (31 December 1995). Figures in parentheses represent the percentages of men and women respectively across different sized firms.

[b] Includes lawyers, resident and non-resident. Data are tabulated for lawyers in all 10 provinces and two territories.

[c] Data include British Columbia, Saskatchewan, New Manitoba, Ontario, Nova Scotia, Prince Edward Island, Northwest and Yukon Territories.

[d] Data include Quebec notaries and lawyers from British Columbia, Alberta, Saskatchewan, New Manitoba, Ontario, Quebec notaries, Nova Scotia, Prince Edward Island, Newfoundland, and Northwest and Yukon Territories.

[e] Data include British Columbia, Alberta, Saskatchewan, Manitoba, Quebec notaries, Nova Scotia, Prince Edward Island and Northwest Territories.

[f] Data include Manitoba, Ontario, Quebec (notaries and lawyers), Nova Scotia, Prince Edward Island and Northwest and Yukon Territories.

[g] An additional 496 lawyers are classified as employed in 'other' work settings in British Columbia. The distribution of men and women working in this sector were not available for this province. The percentage of women within this sector of the profession is calculated using only data for which gender distributions were available (10,421).

An analysis of gender distributions within firm settings of private practice reveals finer details in the picture of law practice in Canada. Prior research shows that the pattern of Canadian law firm growth parallels that of American firms (Daniels 1992: 807; Daniels 1993: 157), albeit on a smaller scale. Daniels' study of 48 law firms across Canada reveals that these firms grew, notwithstanding a few anomalous years, by a constant or increasing rate during the period from 1960 to 1990 (Daniels 1992: 829). In Table 4 we present national data from the Federation of Law Societies of Canada on the representation of women and men in private practice. The largest proportion of lawyers (both men and women) work in small firms of two to 10 lawyers (45 per cent) and then as sole practitioners (27 per cent), followed by large firm settings of over 51 lawyers (13 per cent). Some research suggests sole practice offers a setting where lawyers may experience a greater degree of autonomy and control of their legal work, while large law firms offer a work environment that is more bureaucratic and less subject to bias (Menkel-Meadow 1989: 213; Hagan *et al* 1991: 259). The most impressive difference is that 47 per cent of the men and only 38 per cent of the women work in firms of two to ten lawyers. The next largest difference is among sole practitioners where 30 per cent of the women, and only 26 per cent of the men are solo. This pattern of high representation of women among sole practitioners is similar to women who entered practice in the 1920s and 1930s when many women worked as sole practitioners or in association with their husband or family members.[12] The third

Table 4: Canadian Lawyers in the Private Practice of Law, 1995–96

Sector of the Legal Profession	Men	Women	Total	% Women
Sole practitioners	7,473 (26.1)	2,294 (30.4)	9,767 (27.0)	23.5
Firms of 2–10 lawyers	13,305 (46.5)	2,889 (38.3)	16,194 (44.8)	17.8
Firms of 11–25 lawyers	2,648 (9.2)	688 (9.1)	3,336 (9.2)	20.6
Firms of 26–50 lawyers	1,754 (6.1)	519 (6.9)	2,273 (6.3)	22.8
Firms of 51 + lawyers	3,455 (12.1)	1,151 (15.3)	4,606 (12.7)	25.0
Total	28,635	7,541	36,176	20.8

SOURCE: *Law Societies' Statistics on Membership*, 1998 Federation of Law Societies of Canada. Date: 3 December 1998. Website: http://www.flsc.ca/English/95st-membership.htm.

NOTE: Data were unavailable for the provinces of New Brunswick and Quebec lawyers. Data include private practitioners in British Columbia (29 January 1996), Alberta (1 January 1996), Saskatchewan (31 December 1995), Manitoba (31 December 1995), Ontario (7 January 1996), Quebec notaries (22 February 1996), Nova Scotia (31 December 1995), Prince Edward Island (31 December 1995), Newfoundland (31 December 1995) and Northwest and Yukon Territories (31 December 1995). Figures in parentheses represent the percentages of men and women respectively across differently sized firms.

[12] See Brockman (1995: 527–34). Dorothy Chunn and Joan Brockman have been studying the lives of the first 30 women called to the bar in British Columbia between 1912 and 1930, and are finding that this is the case.

largest gender difference takes place in firms of more than 50 lawyers, where 15 per cent of the women and only 12 per cent of the men work.

These data provide us with a broad sketch of contemporary patterns of segmentation in the Canadian legal profession. Women remain a minority although their representation is considerably higher in Quebec than in other provinces. Women remain under-represented in private practice and over-represented in government and among departures from the profession. Within private practice, women are more likely to work in large law firms or as sole practitioners than in small to mid-sized firm settings. Yet, there are several other important dimensions to gender inequities in the Canadian legal establishment. We now review studies of gender disparities in entry to practice, partnership, earnings, power in law practice, levels of job satisfaction and departures from the practice of law.[13]

3.1 Barriers to Entry to Practice

Women's victories in gaining access to legal education and the consent of provincial law societies to practise law have not resulted in the doors of the Canadian legal profession swinging wide open to embrace diversity and equality. Rather, research suggests that women continued to experience sexual discrimination and disadvantage in their applications for articles and initial jobs (Adam 1981). For example, an early study by Linda Dranoff in the 1970s focused on women lawyers in Toronto and their search for articles.[14] Dranoff found that 74 per cent of the respondents claimed to perceive or experience discrimination in their search for articling positions (Dranoff 1982: 177–90). A study in British Columbia in the same period by Smith, Stephenson, and Quijano also reported that women experienced greater difficulties in locating favourable articling positions (Smith *et al* 1973: 37–175). In a large-scale survey involving nearly 3,000 graduates of six Ontario law schools in the late seventies, Huxter found that 71 per cent of men, compared with 62 per cent of women, were successful in securing articling positions with the size or type of firm they preferred. Interestingly, men ranked a lack of contacts as the biggest hindrance to finding positions, while women ranked, first gender, then marital status, over contacts (Huxter 1981: 169–213).

More recently, Brockman's 1990 survey of 1,873 lawyers in British Columbia showed that nearly half of the women and 27 per cent of men reported hiring as

---

[13] We have not discussed the numerous studies that examine gender bias in law schools in Canada (see, for example, Alvi *et al* 1992: 174–214; Boyle 1986: 96–112; Mossman 1985: 213–25).

[14] Upon graduation from a three-year bachelor's degree in law, law students seek employment with law firms and other practice settings to serve an apprenticeship period of six to 12 months known as 'articles'. During this time, articling students acquire a practical knowledge of legal research and law practice under the close supervision of the firm's more experienced lawyers. In English Canada the period of articles is followed by the Bar Admissions Examination. In Quebec, the articling period follows completion of the Bar Admissions Examination.

a form of discrimination against women (Brockman 1992a: 105) and women experienced lower success at securing their preferred articling positions (Brockman 1992a: 107). A year later, in a survey of Alberta lawyers, Brockman found that one third of the women articled in the previous decade had experienced discrimination on the basis of sex during their search for articling positions (Brockman 1992b: 783). Meanwhile, a 1985 survey by Hagan of Toronto lawyers uncovered a significant gender difference in the role of social contacts in helping to secure first jobs in large law firms (Hagan & Kay 1995: 64–65). This study found that men and women were equally likely to receive and benefit from personal contacts in locating articling positions in large law firms, yet, when it came to jobs following articling, men were significantly more likely to receive assistance in securing jobs. This finding signals a source of gender stratification of lawyers that starts to build after entry to the profession and involves the use of social networks (Hagan & Kay 1995: 65). Similarly, in Quebec, a 1991 survey of lawyers in the province revealed that women experienced greater difficulty in securing their first jobs after being called to the bar and women invested on average nearly twice as much time (6 months) as men (3.5 months) in their search for initial employment (Mackaay 1991: 3; see also Barreau du Québec 1992). Finally, a national study conducted by the CBA in 1993 noted that women employed in articling positions often felt unable to complain about discrimination for fear of damaging their chances for subsequent employment (Canadian Bar Association 1993: 58).

3.2 Partnership Prospects

Although women are entering the Canadian legal profession in growing numbers, they remain under-represented in the higher echelons, even when taking into account years of experience. Mackaay's 1991 survey of Quebec lawyers reveals that, regardless of age and level of experience, women are less likely to be made partners within law firms. Among lawyers admitted to the bar between 1986 and 1991, the proportion of partners was 21 per cent for women and 28 per cent for men; for those admitted between 1981 and 1985, the figures were 53 per cent and 75 per cent respectively; and for those admitted between 1979 and 1980, 79 per cent of women and 86 per cent of men were partners (Mackaay 1991: 5). In a 1985 study of Toronto lawyers, Hagan found that both women and men are losing their proportionate shares of partnership positions in the profession, but that women are losing more than men (Hagan *et al* 1991: 239–62). Recent restructuring in the profession has seen the greatest growth at the middle and lower levels of larger firms, and women are especially likely be to represented in these work settings. Women's partnership prospects are particularly weak in smaller firms, suggesting that male-dominated smaller firms are more resistant to modifying the work roles assumed by men and women (Hagan *et al* 1991: 239). This study also suggests that women who are made partners in large firms may be restricted to partnership arrangements such as tax partners, 'non-equity' partners and junior partners (Hagan *et al* 1991: 260).

Similarly, Kay's studies of approximately 1,600 lawyers in Ontario (surveys conducted in 1990, 1996) and 700 lawyers in Quebec (studies completed in 1998 and 1999) demonstrated that, regardless of experience, field of law, billable hours, clientele responsibilities and size of firm, men are consistently more likely to attain partnership status than women (Kay & Hagan 1994: 450; Kay and Hagan *forthcoming*). And, although firms with greater representation of women have been found to be more successful in attracting and retaining institutional and corporate clients, women remain less likely to be rewarded with partnership status (Kay & Hagan 1999). Furthermore, the tremendous growth in the Canadian legal profession seems to have had a negative impact on opportunities for partnership. The profession is encountering difficulties in its efforts to absorb and provide opportunities for upward mobility to an increasing and more diverse number of entrants to law (Kay & Hagan 1994: 451). These realities may have discouraged women in their quest for or interest in partnership. A 1994 study of lawyers, called between 1986 and 1990 in British Columbia, found that only 12 per cent of the women compared with 20 per cent of the men were partners. However, what is more revealing is that a mere 18 per cent of the women, compared with 48 per cent of the men, wanted to be partners within five years (Brockman 2001: 64).

Even more troubling is recent work suggesting women associates are required to embody standards which are an exaggerated form of the 'ideal partner'. To attain partnership, women must demonstrate extraordinary work commitment, for example, by actively recruiting new clients, building a large network of corporate clientele, returning swiftly from maternity leave and continuing to bill at elevated levels, and expressing a commitment to the culture of the firm by endorsing traditional values and goals of firm lawyers (Kay & Hagan 1998: 741).

3.3 The Gap in Wages

Studies of salaries among Canadian lawyers demonstrate that substantial gender differences exist. A five-year follow-up study of the 1974 graduating class of Ontario law schools reported that women graduates earned on average about $3,000 a year less than their male counterparts (Adam & Baer 1984: 21–45). Mackaay's survey of Quebec lawyers found that across all age groups, women earned on average less than their male counterparts (1991: 3; see also Barreau du Québec 1999). Only part of the gap in wages is explained by women's lower representation in private practice, the more lucrative sector of law practice (Mackaay 1991: 5). On the other hand, Foot and Stager, analysing national data on Canadian lawyers, found a decline in the wage gap between men and women lawyers in the period from 1970 to 1980, but optimism is tempered by the fact that a sizeable component of the gender earnings differential remained unexplained, a factor they attribute to 'discrimination, differential, pay structure, and/or residual' (1989: 1017).

Other studies suggest that the wage gap between women and men cannot be explained by women's distribution across sectors of the profession, specialisation within certain areas of law, or by women's lower levels of experience or seniority. For example, Hagan's 1985 study of Toronto lawyers found that more than one quarter of the difference in earnings of men and women lawyers could conservatively be attributed to gender discrimination (Hagan 1990b: 835). Taking into account specialisation, years of experience, law school, ethnicity and employment context, there remained a significant difference in the earnings of men and women. In particular, men gained higher returns from elite education and years of experience in practice than women (1990b: 849). Kay's 1990 study of Ontario lawyers revealed not only a persistent gap between the earnings of men and women, but also an amplification of the earnings differential as lawyers climb the early stages of the career ladder. The gap in earnings remained after taking into account differences in specialisation, employment characteristics, and levels of experience (Kay & Hagan 1995: 280–309). In a 1998 study of bar admission students, Kay and colleagues found significant differences in the earnings of men and women during the articling phase (Kay *et al under review*).

3.4 Power and Privilege in Practice

Even when women lawyers have gained entry to the privileged circle of partnership and higher salaries, they may not be accorded the authority, autonomy and decision-making power of their equally senior colleagues. Research examining change in the legal profession in Ontario from 1977 to 1990 suggests that the overall hierarchical structure of law firms and the profession has remained intact, or has even intensified (Hagan & Kay 1996: 530–72). A study of Toronto lawyers provides insights into the power structure of legal practice. Hagan and his colleagues examined levels of decision-making, authority, autonomy, ownership and hierarchical position (Hagan *et al* 1988; Hagan *et al* 1991; Hagan 1990a). The results reveal that the class structure of legal practice in Toronto is dominated by older, Anglo-Saxon males with degrees from Canada's elite law schools, who practise corporate and commercial law for predominantly corporate clients (Hagan *et al* 1988: 9). Women are over-represented in the bottom ranks of lawyers, with 17 per cent of women compared with 6 per cent of men, occupying positions in the 'working class' of the profession (Hagan 1990a: 63). The contours of structural change taking place in the legal profession involve a growth of law firms with a proportionate shrinking at the top of the hierarchy of practice (lawyers as employers) and an expansion at the base of the pyramid (employed lawyers) (Hagan *et al* 1991: 259). As firms grew in size and hired lawyers as associates, the percentage of self-employed lawyers declined. One source of this change is financial, involving economies of scale associated with the sharing of overhead expenses among lawyers who no longer practise alone (Stager & Arthurs 1990: 170–71). More recent studies confirm that women continue to occupy lower positions of authority and autonomy in law practice, with fewer opportunities to participate in critical policy-making decisions or to supervise other lawyers (Brockman 1991: 18; Kay 1991: 24–31; Kay *et al* 1996: 44–5).

3.5 Job Satisfaction

Studies of job satisfaction among lawyers in Canada reveal some subtle and intriguing gender differences. For example, Brockman's study of former British Columbia lawyers shows that women reported lower levels of satisfaction than their male counterparts with remuneration, hours of work and job security in law practice (Brockman 1990: 18). In a survey of active members of the British Columbian legal profession conducted a year later, Brockman discovered that lawyers in the profession reported a similar pattern, with a greater proportion of women than men dissatisfied with earnings, employment benefits, balance with personal life, hours of work, opportunities for advancement and job security (Brockman 1991: 28). Kay's initial 1990 study of 1,600 Ontario lawyers revealed women were less satisfied than men with hours of work and parental leave arrangements. In a follow-up survey six years later, there were no significant differences in the levels of general job satisfaction reported by men and women. However, women were significantly more likely to express less satisfaction with parental leave arrangements and job security (Kay *et al* 1996: 71). Women were also more likely to apply for new jobs and to leave their existing job if a good position became available (Kay *et al* 1996: 70). In contrast, Wallace's 1991 survey of lawyers in the city of Calgary, Alberta, found that women were *more* satisfied with their pay than men, suggesting a contradiction between women's poorer work conditions (lower pay, less autonomy and reduced authority in law practice) and their levels of satisfaction (Mueller & Wallace 1996: 338–49). These studies call for research to refine assessments of job satisfaction with reference to specific aspects of employment and using a variety of measures, including: satisfaction with pay, working conditions, ability to balance family responsibilities and career demands, hours of work, work responsibilities and opportunities and perceptions of distributive justice (fairness of reward distribution).

3.6 Departures from Practice

The history of women entering the Canadian legal profession is not complete without examining the rate at which women leave the profession. In January

1990, the attrition rate for lawyers called to the bar in British Columbia between 1974 and 1988, was 22 per cent for women, and 13 per cent for men. However, the absolute number of men (523) who left during that time period was higher than the number of women (322) (Brockman 1992c: 59).[15] Similar figures exist for lawyers in Alberta. In 1991, the attrition rate for those called between 1976 and 1990 was higher for women (33 per cent) than for men (28 per cent). Again, in terms of absolute numbers, a greater number of men (1,012) than women (443) were no longer active members in 1991 (Brockman 1994: 116). Among the more commonly reported reasons for leaving law were the lack of flexibility offered by law firms, hours demanded by practice, child care commitments and the stressful nature of work. Men were substantially less likely to cite demanding hours, child care or inflexibility in work arrangements as reasons for leaving law and were more likely to mention the desire to use different skills (Brockman 1994: 116–80). Kay's 1990 study of Ontario lawyers found that women were over-represented among lawyers taking temporary absences from practice and among those having departed from the profession. Interestingly, small law firms appeared to be the least successful in retaining female lawyers (Kay 1997b). In explaining their departure from law practice, women were more likely to cite family responsibilities and general dissatisfaction with the practice of law, while men were more likely to cite improved employment opportunities (Kay 1991: 98–99; see also Kay *et al* 1996: 128–29).[16] Six years after the initial study, Kay conducted a follow-up and found that women, more often than their male colleagues, were excluded from opportunities to work on challenging and important files. This experience of being placed on the margins of firm practice significantly undermined women's trust in firm management and augmented their intent to quit the firm (Kay & Hagan *forthcoming*).

In sum, women lawyers in Canada, in both civil and common law jurisdictions of the country, experience significant hurdles in acquiring articling and opportunities for employment after bar admission, receive fewer opportunities for promotions, and are paid lower salaries than men relative to their experience and specialisation. When women do break through the 'glass ceiling' to positions of seniority and status, they are awarded less authority and autonomy than their male colleagues. Women's satisfaction with law practice is, perhaps, more of a curiosity, suggesting that women may consider different criteria in assessing the quality of their job and work setting. The outcome of their disappointment with the organisation of legal practice is that women are more likely to seek new jobs or to leave the practice of law altogether. Yet, despite these inequities confronting women in law practice, the profession shows signs of change. We turn next to consider women's impact on the legal profession in Canada through reform to the profession from within.

[15] For an earlier study of the difficulties women had finding articles, see Smith *et al* (1973: 137).
[16] For further studies of job leaving by lawyers in Canada see: Brockman (1992c; 1994); Kay (1997); Wallace (1991).

4 ONGOING STRUGGLES IN THE CANADIAN LEGAL PROFESSION

In this final section, we provide a picture of contemporary struggles for gender equality in the Canadian legal profession. Our research highlights three domains of oppression for women in law practice. First, we discuss residual forms of discrimination that persist in law practice and policy strategies that have been developed in recent years to combat these forms of gender bias. Second, we examine the issue of sexual harassment and how law societies are attempting to discourage this demeaning practice through the profession's codes of misconduct. Finally, we explore the continued inflexibility of work arrangements and the policies initiated to address systemic barriers to women's full inclusion in the legal profession.

4.1 Equality and Opportunities

Discrimination, in both overt and subtler forms, persists in the Canadian legal profession. In 1993, the CBA commissioned a Gender Equality Task Force. Their report found that law remains an unwelcoming environment for women (Canadian Bar Association 1993). The national report revealed that women perceive and experience gender bias in the legal profession. The vast majority of women lawyers confront barriers to career advancement. This is evident in the patterns of access to articles and jobs, access to areas of legal practice, work allocation, remuneration and access to partnership (Canadian Bar Association 1993: 74). For example, a survey of Quebec lawyers showed women reported discrimination in hiring, evaluation, assignment of files, promotions and salaries (Mackaay 1991: 3). In a survey of lawyers called to the bar in Saskatchewan between 1970 and 1990, 87 per cent of women and 8 per cent of men said they had experienced sexism within the legal profession (Robertson 1992: 47). Gender bias against women in the form of remuneration, hiring and unwanted teasing, jokes or comments of a sexual nature were reported by 58 per cent of women in a survey of former members of the Law Society of British Columbia. Women were also more likely than men to report bias in the assignment of files, access to clients and career advancement, including partnership and managerial positions (Brockman 1992a: 103). Access to clients was identified as an area of discrimination against women by 49 per cent of women and 25 per cent of men. In addition, 43 per cent of women and 18 per cent of men reported bias against women in the assignment of files (Brockman 1992a: 103). In Ontario, women were significantly more likely than men to report bias in hiring, assignment of files, access to clients, remuneration and opportunities to appear in court (Kay *et al* 1996: 8).

Efforts to reduce gender bias and discriminatory treatment of women in the legal profession have involved court-enforced legislation of human and civil rights and the creation of duties of non-discrimination through professional codes and rules of conduct. Canada has relied more heavily than the United States on professional self-regulation (profession codes of conduct enforced through disciplinary proceedings) and less on litigation through the courts (Hagan & Kay 1995: 188). Yet, some scholars contend that women's challenges to discrimination might better be served through highly publicised court cases (Hagan & Kay 1995 p. 189). Gupta (1993), for example, suggests that the same reasoning applied in the partnership denial cases of *Hishon* in Atlanta and *Ezold* in Philadelphia (invoking the US Civil Rights Act 1964) should be applicable using human rights legislation in Canada which prohibits discrimination on the basis of sex.[17] Partnership cases establish the illegality of grounding employment decisions in considerations of gender as well as the severity of sanctions that can be imposed on law firms found in violation of statutes (Hagan & Kay 1995: 189–90). The enactment of non-discrimination rules can hold important educational and symbolic, as well as enforcement functions. Yet, some provincial law societies have been slow to respond[18] and when policies are written the tendency is to articulate general standards as opposed to detailed black-letter rules of professional conduct (Hagan & Kay 1995: 188). Organised collectives within the profession, such as the National Association of Women and the Law in Canada (NAWL), have lobbied successfully for policy reform. In 1993, the Canadian Bar Association Task Force on Gender Equality in the Legal Profession recommended that all law societies enact non-discrimination rules in their jurisdictions and that discrimination in the profession be designated as professional misconduct. The task force also recommended that law societies encourage law firms to establish internal procedures to handle complaints about gender discrimination. The task force went one step further to recommend that law societies establish a 'safe counsel' position. A safe counsel is defined as a 'person who is able to counsel a complainant and advocate on her behalf without potential conflict of interest or interference by the person against whom the complaint is made' (Canadian Bar Association 1993: 221). Safe counsel should have independent power to investigate and to determine appropriate standards and targets for law firms to ensure that the goal of equality is achieved by the legal profession (Canadian Bar Association 1993: 221).

---

[17] *Ezold v Wolf*, 758 F Supp 303 (EDPa 1991) 56 FEP 580 (1991); *Hishon v King & Spalding*, 467 US 69(1984).

[18] In 1972 the Benchers of the Law Society of British Columbia refused to pass a rule dealing with refusals to hire women students into articling positions. The proposed rule arose from an incident in which a firm explicitly refused articles to a woman on the basis of her sex. The Law Society of British Columbia did not pass an anti-discrimination rule until 1992 (see Smith *et al* 1973: 137–75; Brockman 1997: 209–42; Hagan & Kay 1995: 189).

4.2 Sexual Harassment and Sexual Harassment Policies

Sexual harassment has been documented as a significant obstacle to women's abilities to develop their careers in the practice of law. A 1991 survey of Quebec lawyers reported that one in six women (15 per cent) perceived other women in their workplace as victims of sexual harassment and one in nine (11 per cent) reported that they themselves had been the victims of sexual harassment (Mackaay 1991a: 8; 1991b: 3). In 1990, a survey of lawyers in British Columbia found that 34 per cent of women and 10 per cent of men had observed women lawyers being subjected to unwanted sexual advances by other lawyers in the previous two years (Brockman 1992a: 129). Similar observations were made by 32 per cent of the women and 7 per cent of the men in a 1991 survey of Alberta lawyers (Brockman 1992b: 770). In interviews, in 1993–94, of lawyers called between 1986 and 1990 in British Columbia, 36 per cent of the women and 4 per cent of the men said that they had been sexually harassed in work-related situations since entering the legal profession as articling students (Brockman 2001, 14). Results of a Quebec survey showed that 15 per cent of women lawyers had been victims of sexual harassment. The principal categories of harassment were harassment by a colleague (20 per cent) and by a superior (17 per cent). The incidence of harassment by clients was much lower (3 per cent) (Barreau du Québec 1992: 21). Sexual harassment continues to be a disturbing problem in the legal profession.

In finding that sexual harassment was a form of discrimination based on sex, the Supreme Court of Canada described sexual harassment as a 'demeaning practice, one that constitutes a profound affront to the dignity of the employees forced to endure it.'[19] Sexual harassment can have profound consequences for women and affect both their work and their personal lives. In interviews conducted in 1993–94, Brockman found British Columbia lawyers described the effects of sexual harassment to include depression, embarrassment, anger, irritation and distress (Brockman 2001: 117).

In response to the numerous reports across Canada identifying sexual harassment and discrimination as barriers to women's equality in the legal profession, many of the law societies introduced rules prohibiting such behaviour and defining it as professional misconduct. Shortly after the rules were introduced in British Columbia, lawyers called between 1986 and 1990 were asked whether they thought the rules would be effective. The men were more optimistic about the rules being effective than the women, and both the women and the men were more optimistic about the rule against sexual harassment than they were about the rule against discrimination. Only 23 per cent of the women and 38 per cent of the men thought that the anti-discrimination rule would be effective, whereas 66 per cent of the women and 70 per cent of the men thought the rule against sexual harassment would be effective (Brockman 1997b: 232–34).

---

[19] *Janzen and Govereau v Platy Enterprises Ltd et al* [1989] 4 WWR 39 (SCC) at 64–65.

In 1992 Ontario's law society passed a 'Recommended Personnel Policy Regarding Employment-Related Sexual Harassment'. The policy was distributed to the managing partners of all law firms in Ontario (Law Society of Upper Canada 1994: 10). In 1994, the Law Society of Upper Canada (Ontario) passed a Rule 28 on non-discrimination. Following the introduction of Rule 28, the Law Society Equity Committee developed educational bulletins to assist members of the profession in understanding their obligations with respect to recruitment and hiring, employment with law firms, and partnership (Law Society of Upper Canada 1994: 10). Thus, policy drafting and education through distribution of guidelines is well underway. Whether these policies will have a genuine impact on improving gender inequities across various work settings remains to be seen. Much depends on the efficacy of law societies to communicate the importance of adherence to policies, the will and leadership of employers, and the sanctioning powers of law societies to enforce these new rules.

4.3 Family Responsibilities and Accommodation in the Workplace

Across Canada, women report a lack of accommodation in law practice for family commitments, a lack of flexibility to work on a part-time basis and a lack of adequate maternity leave arrangements (Brockman 1992a: 119; Brockman 1992b: 784; Canadian Bar Association 1993: 99; Kay 1991: 76; Kay *et al* 1996: 190; Kay 1997a: 198; Barreau du Québec 1992: 20–22; Hagan & Kay 1995: 99). Women lawyers with children are discriminated against through the lack of accommodation in the profession, and this results in reduced incomes and fewer opportunities for advancement (Canadian Bar Association 1993: 74).

It is important to understand the connections between hidden assumptions about the organisation of legal work and the societal roles of men and women. As Mossman points out,

> these two 'hidden' assumptions constrain the 'choices' available to women lawyers, by contrast with male lawyers, creating a gendered experience of lawyers: women lawyers make 'choices' about work and family in the context of pressures not faced by most male lawyers, 'choices' which do not occur in a neutral or equal context (Mossman 1994a: 73).

As with women in other occupations, women lawyers tend to be the ones to assume primary responsibility for the care of their children while managing full-time employment (Brockman 1992b: 761). Kay's surveys of Ontario lawyers found that women reported the proportion of responsibility borne by themselves as double the amount male lawyers reported and double the number of hours per week on child care. Women were also the ones expected to assign priority to family demands over paid work when children are in need of assistance (Kay 1997a: 207; Kay *et al* 1996: 97–99). The inequality that women experience at home may be one of the greatest barriers to women's equal participation in the paid work force (Brockman 2001: 180).

Organisational structures in Canadian law practice have offered few options by way of flexible or reduced hours or workplace family supports (Leiper 1998: 117–34; Kay 1997a: 205; Wallace 1997: 227). Alternative work schedules are available to women infrequently, and these options are even less available in private practice, especially in large law firms (Mossman, 1994b: 167). The development of alternative working patterns to accommodate family life is primarily the burden of women's individual efforts at negotiation and decision-making, with consequences for their remuneration and career advancement (Mossman 1992: 47; Mossman 1994b: 173). For example, Brockman's study of Alberta lawyers found that child care responsibilities had significantly greater effects on career decisions of women than men regarding available jobs, specialities, cases and the hours they worked (Brockman 1992b: 761).

Some progress is being made here. Law societies have produced model policies to assist law firms and other settings where lawyers work to develop personnel policies in respect of alternative work arrangements, parental responsibilities, and non-discrimination (Kay 1991: 2; Martin & Schellenberg 1995; Barreau du Québec 1996). Yet, more concrete strategies are required to better accommodate work and family demands among both women and men. Strategies include greater support for child care by employers and policymakers, improved assistance for single-parent families, enhanced leave and part-time policies, more flexible schedules for full-time practitioners, and creative solutions in the design of legal work such as 'flexiplace' and 'telecommuting' (Mossman 1994a, 1994b). These options need to be made available without 'professional risk', such as loss of employment, denial of partnership, or significant loss of income (Hagan & Kay 1995: 198). One of the more controversial recommendations of the CBA Task Force on Gender Equality in the Legal Profession was that as part of a legal duty to accommodate lawyers with family responsibilities, law firms should set reasonable targets of billable hours for women with child-rearing responsibilities, and that these reduced targets should not delay or affect eligibility for partnership nor affect normal compensation (Canadian Bar Association 1993: 99; see also, Canadian Bar Association 1995). Although these workplace supports and alternative schedules are actively discussed at legal conferences and in task force reports and scholarly publications, it remains to be seen whether these innovative practices will be adopted widely in the profession, particularly within private practice where the structure of law practice has been most impermeable as a result of rising billable hours, clientele demands and the nature of litigation.

5 CONCLUSION: REFORM AND INNOVATION IN THE CANADIAN LEGAL PROFESSION

Research reveals that women have fought a lengthy and arduous battle to gain entry to the legal profession in Canada. Although inroads have been made to

fields of law previously deemed outside women's 'nature' and to the elite echelons of the profession, women continue to be under-represented in private practice and experience, on average, reduced chances for partnership, lower salaries
and fewer opportunities to demonstrate their legal talents and skills through
positions of authority and access to high profile cases and clients. Within the
profession, women have organised associations, task forces and committees,
and their collective impact has recently led the CBA and provincial law societies
to take measures to combat gender bias and discrimination, deter sexual harassment and reduce systemic barriers in law practice, including the lack of flexible
work arrangements to accommodate women with family responsibilities. These
measures have included task forces to investigate gender bias in the profession,
policy recommendations from the CBA, disciplinary rules of professional misconduct and law society efforts through model personnel and discrimination
policies widely distributed to legal practitioners, educational bulletins and continuing education programmes.

Women have made substantial progress over the last 20 years; however, that
progress has been within extremely narrow constraints (Canadian Bar
Association 1993: 269). Considerable reform and social change remain to be
undertaken. In order to achieve the goal of gender equality, creative solutions
must be developed to dismantle barriers to women's full participation in the
legal profession. The provincial law societies and the national bar association
have a leadership role to play by encouraging innovative employment policies
and maternity and parental leave options, by monitoring parental leave policies
and retention rates for women in law firms and with other legal employers, and
publishing this information for members and students (Hagan & Kay 1995:
200). These governing bodies of the profession are also crucial to the enforcement of discrimination and sexual harassment rules of misconduct (Brockman
1997b: 238).

Another route to educational and symbolic recognition of the need for gender
equity is through the courts. The US partnership cases demonstrate the value of
court battles to establish the applicability of general statutes to the employment
of lawyers in law firms, among other settings, the importance of performance
reviews to the accountability of promotions, and the severity and certainty of
sanctions to be meted out to violators (Hagan & Kay 1995: 189–90). However,
if these duties of professional accountability and equality of women and men are
to be realised, then the leaders of the profession will need to recognise the structural conditions from which individual complaints of discrimination and gender
bias derive (Hagan & Kay 1995: 193). Court cases represent a fragmentary,
highly individual, crusader approach to equality and fail to challenge deeper
structural inequities permeating law practice. Thus, the burden of enforcement
ought to be shifted from individual complainants (either through the courts or
law society disciplinary hearings) to a collective level where law societies, law
firms and other organisational structures take on a responsibility to modify
existing work arrangements, provide improved support to lawyers with families

and restructure the terms of professional assessment to better reflect the quality and spectrum of legal work (as opposed to a fetishism over billable hours and understanding of intangible qualities that reflect 'partnership material').

Finally, individual lawyers, law firms and the broader diversity of settings where lawyers work are important players in the challenge to realise goals of gender equality in Canada's legal establishment. Through continued pressure on the governing bodies of the legal profession (law societies) and the leaders of law firms and other organisations that employ lawyers, it is possible to achieve innovative workplace arrangements to scheduling time and organisation of legal work, the creation of improved family support and effective deterrence against discriminatory practices.

6 ACKNOWLEDGEMENTS

We wish to thank Kristi J Hines for her valuable research assistance, and we greatly appreciate the co-operation of law societies across Canada in responding to our requests for contemporary data on the representation of women and men in the legal profession. An earlier version of this paper was presented at a workshop on 'Challenge to Law and Lawyers: Women in the Legal Profession' at the International Institute for the Sociology of Law, 19–21 July 1999, Oñati, Spain.

7 REFERENCES

Adam, B D. 1981. Stigma and Employability: Discrimination by Sex and Sexual Orientation in the Ontario Legal Profession. *Canadian Review of Sociology and Anthropology* 18/2, 216–221.

Adam, B D and D E Baer. 1984. The Social Mobility of Women and Men in the Ontario Legal Profession. *Canadian Review of Sociology and Anthropology* 21/1, 21–45.

Alvi, T, R Boyko, L Ma, W MacLauchlan, T Monture, Y Peters and J St Lewis. 1992. *Equality in Legal Education: Sharing a Vision, Creating the Pathways* (Special Advisory Committee to the Canadian Association of Law Teachers). Reprinted in *Queen's Law Journal* 17, 174–214.

Backhouse, C B. 1985. 'To Open the Way for Others of My Sex': Clara Brett Martin's Career as Canada's First Woman Lawyer. *Canadian Journal of Women and the Law* 1/1, 1–41.

Backhouse, C. 1992. Clara Brett Martin: Canadian Heroine or Not? *Canadian Journal of Women and the Law* 5/2, 263–279.

Backhouse, C. 1994. Racial Segregation in Canadian Legal History: Viola Desmond's Challenge, Nova Scotia, 1946. *Dalhousie Law Journal* 17/2, 299–362.

Backhouse, C. 1996. Gretta Wong Grant: Canada's First Chinese-Canadian Female Lawyer. *Windsor Yearbook of Access to Justice* 15, 3–46.

Barreau du Québec. 1992. *Les Femmes dans la Profession* (Rapport du Comité de Barreau du Québec sur les Femmes dans la Profession).

Barreau du Québec. 1996. *La Pratique du Droit au Quebec et L'Avenir de la Profession* (Un rapport présenté par le Comité du Barreau sur l'avenir de la profession avec la collaboration de Pierre Boucher et Henri Beauregard).

Barreau du Québec. 1999. *Enquête Économique Auprès des Membres. Sondage Général* 1998.

Betcherman, L. 1992. Clara Brett Martin's Anti-Semitism. *Canadian Journal of Women and the Law* 5/2, 280–297.

Boyd, S B, E Sheehy and J Bouchard. 1999. *Canadian Feminist Perspectives on Law: An Annotated Bibliography of Interdisciplinary Writings (1989–99)*. 11/1 & 2 *Canadian Journal of Women and the Law* (entire volume).

Boyle, C. 1986. Teaching Law as if Women Really Mattered, or What about the Washrooms? *Canadian Journal of Women and the Law* 2/1, 96–112.

Brierley, J E E and Macdonald, R A. 1993. *Quebec Civil Law: An Introduction to Quebec Private Law*. Toronto: Edmond Montgomery Publications, Ltd.

Brockman, J. 1990. *Encountering Barriers and/or Moving On: A Survey of Former Members of the Law Society of British Columbia* (A Report Prepared for the Law Society of British Columbia's Subcommittee on Women in the Legal Profession).

Brockman, J. 1991. *Identifying Barriers: A Survey of Members of the Law Society of British Columbia* (A Report Prepared for the Law Society of British Columbia's Subcommittee on Women in the Legal Profession).

Brockman, J. 1992a. Gender Bias in the Legal Profession: A Survey of Members of the Law Society of British Columbia. *Queen's Law Journal* 17, 91–146.

Brockman, J. 1992b. Bias in the Legal Profession: Perceptions and Experiences. *Alberta Law Review* 3/3, 747–808.

Brockman, J. 1992c. 'Resistance by the Club' to the Feminization of the Legal Profession. *Canadian Journal of Law and Society* 7/2, 47–92.

Brockman, J. 1994. Leaving the Practice of Law: The Wherefores and the Whys. *Alberta Law Review* 32(1), 116–180.

Brockman, J. 1995. Exclusionary Tactics: The History of Women and Minorities in the Legal Profession in British Columbia. In H Foster and JPS McLaren (eds), *Essays in the History of Canadian Law*. Volume VI: *British Columbia and the Yukon*. Toronto: Osgoode Society, 508–561.

Brockman, J. 1997a. 'Better to Enlist Their Support Than to Suffer Their Antagonism': The Game of Monopoly between Lawyers and Notaries In British Columbia, 1930–81. *International Journal of the Legal Profession* 4/3, 197–234.

Brockman, J. 1997b. The Use of Self-Regulation to Curb Discrimination and Sexual Harassment in the Legal Profession. *Osgoode Hall Law Journal* 35/2, 209–241.

Brockman, J. 1999. 'A Cold-Blooded Effort to Bolster Up the Legal Profession': The Battle Between Lawyers and Notaries in British Columbia, 1871–1930. *Social History* 32/64, 209–235.

Brockman, J. 2001. *Gender in the Legal Profession: Fitting or Breaking the Mould?* Vancouver: UBC Press.

Canadian Bar Association. 1993. *Touchstones for Change: Equality, Diversity and Accountability. A Report on Gender Equality in the Legal Profession*. Chair B Wilson. Ottawa: Canadian Bar Association.

Canadian Bar Association Working Group on the Legal Duty to Accommodate Lawyers with Family Responsibilities. 1995. *The Legal Duty to Accommodate Lawyers with Family Responsibilities*. Chair S Martin. Ottawa: Canadian Bar Association.

Canadian Bar Association. 1999. *The Challenge of Racial Equality: Putting Principles into Practice*, Co-chairs: J St Lewis and B Trevino. Ottawa: Canadian Bar Association.

Cossman, B and Kline, M. 1992. 'And If Not Now, When?': Feminism and Anti-Semitism Beyond Clara Brett Martin. *Canadian Journal of Women and the Law* 5/2, 298–316.

Daniels, R J. 1992. The Law Firm as an Efficient Community. *McGill Law Journal* 37, 807–841.

Daniels, R J. 1993. Growing Pains: The Why and How of Law Firm Expansion. *University of Toronto Law Journal* 43, 147–206.

Dranoff, L S. 1982. Women as Lawyers in Toronto. *Osgoode Hall Law Journal* 10, 177–190.

Ferguson, G. 1997. Ethnic and Linguistic Diversity of B C Lawyers. *Advocate* 55/6, 873–889.

Foot, D K and Stager, D A. 1989. Intertemporal Market Effect on Gender Earnings Differentials: Lawyers in Canada, 1970–1980. *Applied Economics* 21, 1011–1028.

Gillett, M. 1981. *We Walked Very Warily: A History of Women at McGill*. Montreal: Eden Press Women's Publications.

Gupta, N. 1993. Shattering the Glass Ceiling? A Review of the American Experience in Challenging Discriminatory Partnership Practices under Title VII of the US Civil Rights Act. Unpublished paper. University of Toronto of Law.

Hagan, J. 1990a. Gender and the Structural Transformation of the Legal Profession in the United States and Canada. In M T Hallinan, D M Klein and J Glass (eds), *Changes in Societal Institutions*. New York: Plenum Press, 49–70.

Hagan, J. 1990b. The Gender Stratification of Income Inequality Among Lawyers. *Social Forces* 68/3, 835–855.

Hagan, J, Huxter, M and Parker, P 1988. Class Structure and Legal Practice: Inequality and Mobility Among Toronto Lawyers. *Law and Society Review* 22/1, 501–550.

Hagan, J and Kay, F. 1995. *Gender in Practice: A Study of Lawyers' Lives*. Oxford: Oxford University Press.

Hagan, J and Kay, F. 1996. Hierarchy in Practice: The Significance of Gender in Ontario Law Firms. In Carol Wilton (ed.), *Inside the Law: Canadian Law Firms in Historical Perspective*. Toronto: University of Toronto Press.

Hagan, J, Zatz, M, Arnold, B and Kay, F. 1991. Cultural Capital, Gender, and the Structural Transformation of Legal Practice. *Law and Society Review* 25/2, 239–262.

Huxter, M T 1981. Survey of Employment Opportunities for Articling Students and Graduates of the Bar Admissions Course in Ontario. *Law Society Gazette* 15/2, 169–213.

Kay, F M. 1991. *Transition in the Ontario Legal Profession: A Survey of Lawyers Called to the Bar Between 1975–1990*. A Report to the Law Society of Upper Canada. Osgoode Hall: Toronto.

Kay, F M. 1997a. Balancing Acts: Career and Family Among Lawyers. In S. Boyd (ed.), *Challenging the Public/Private Divide: Feminism and Socio-Legal Policy*. Toronto: University of Toronto Press, 184–218.

Kay, F M. 1997b. Flight From Law: A Competing Risks Model of Departures from Law Firms. *Law and Society Review* 31/2, 301–335.

Kay, F M. Crossroads to Innovation and Diversity: The Careers of Quebec Lawyers. *Under review*.

Kay, F M, Dautovich, N and Marlor, C. 1996. *Barriers and Opportunities within Law: Women in a Changing Legal Profession*. A report to the Law Society of Upper Canada.

Kay, F M and Hagan, J. 1994. Changing Opportunities for Partnership for Men and Women Lawyers During the Transformation of the Modern Law Firm. *Osgoode Hall Law Journal* 32/3, 413–456.

Kay, F M and Hagan, J. 1995. The Persistent Glass Ceiling: Gendered Inequalities in the Earnings of Lawyers. *British Journal of Sociology* 46/2, 279–309.

Kay, F M and Hagan, J. 1998. Raising the Bar: The Gender Stratification of Law Firm Capitalization. *American Sociological Review* 63/5, 728–743.

Kay, F M and Hagan J. 1999. Cultivating Clients in the Competition for Partnership: Gender and the Organisational Restructuring of Law Firms in the 1990s. *Law and Society Review* 33(3), 101–139.

Kay, F M and Hagan, J. Building Trust: Social Capital, Distributive Justice, and Loyalty to the Firm, *forthcoming Law and Social Enquiry*.

Kay, F M, Hagan, J, and Parker, P. Crossing the Bar: A Study of Bar Admission. Students, Articles, and Legal Education. *Under review*.

Kinnear, M. 1992. That There Woman Lawyer: Women Lawyers in Manitoba 1915–1970. *Canadian Journal of Women and the Law* 5/2, 411–441.

Law Society of Upper Canada. 1994. *Bicentennial Report on Recommendations on Equity Issues in the Legal Profession*. A Report to Bicentennial Convocation. Toronto: Osgoode Hall.

Leiper, J. 1998. Women Lawyers and Their Working Arrangements: Time Crunch, Stress and Career Paths. *Canadian Journal of Law and Society* 13/2, 117–134.

Mackaay, E. 1991. *L'État de la Profession D'Avocat au Québec en 1991: Résumé des Principales Conclusions du Sondage Général des Membres du Barreau* (Un rapport au Barreau du Québec).

Marshall, K. 1981. Who Are the Professional Women? Canada: Statistics Canada, Catalogue 99–951.

Marshall, K. 1987. Women in Male Dominated Professions. *Canadian Social Trends*. Canada: Statistics Canada, 7.

Marshall, K. 1989. Women in Professional Occupations: Progress in the 1980s. *Canadian Social Trends*. Canada: Statistics Canada, 13.

Martin, S L and Schellenberg, G. 1995. *Equality of Women in the Legal Profession: A Facilitator's Manual*. Ottawa: Canadian Bar Association.

Menkel-Meadow, C. 1989. Feminization of the Legal Profession: The Comparative Sociology of Women Lawyers. In Richard L Abel and Philip S C. Lewis (eds), *Lawyers in Society: Comparative Theories*. Vol. 3. Berkeley: University of California Press.

Morier, V. 1997. Ask a General Practitioner. *National* (October 1997), 48.

Mossman, M J. 1985. 'Otherness' and the Law School: a Comment on Teaching Gender Equality. *Canadian Journal of Women and the Law* 1/1, 213–218.

Mossman, M J. 1988. 'Invisible' Constraints on Lawyering and Leadership: The Case of Women Lawyers. *Ottawa Law Review* 20/3, 567–600.

Mossman, M J. 1992. Gender Bias and the Legal Profession: Challenges and Choices. In J Brockman and D E Chunn (eds), *Investigating Gender Bias in the Law*. Toronto: Thompson Educational Publishing, Inc., 147–168.

Mossman, M J. 1994a. Lawyers and Family Life: New Directions for the 1990's (Part One). *Feminist Legal Studies* 2/1, 61–82.

Mossman, M J. 1994b. Lawyers and Family Life: New Directions for the 1990's (Part Two). *Feminist Legal Studies* 2/2, 159–182.

Mueller, C W and Wallace, J E. 1996. Justice and the Paradox of the Contented Female Worker. *Social Psychology Quarterly* 59/4, 338–349.

National Association of Women and the Law. 1993. *Brief to the Canadian Bar Association Task Force on Gender Equality*. Volume 1.

Neallani, S. 1992. Women of Colour in the Legal Profession: Facing the Familiar Barriers of Race and Sex. *Canadian Journal of Women and the Law* 5, 148–65.

Pearlman, L. 1992. Rethinking Clara Brett Martin: A Jewish Lesbian Perspective. Originally published as Through Jewish Lesbian Eyes: Rethinking Clara Brett Martin. *Canadian Journal of Women and the Law* 5/2 , 317–350.

Petersson, S. 1997. Ruby Clements and Early Women of the Alberta Bar. *Canadian Journal of Women and the Law* 9/2, 365–392.

Pue, W W. 1995. *Law School: The Story of Legal Education in British Columbia*. Vancouver: Faculty of Law, University of British Columbia.

Robertson, S. 1992. *A Study of Gender and the Legal Profession in Saskatchewan, 1990–91*. Regina: Law Society of Saskatchewan and Canadian Bar Association.

Smith, L, Stephenson, M and Quijano, G. 1973. The Legal Profession and Women: Finding Articles in British Columbia. *University of British Columbia Law Review* 8/1, 137–175.

Stager, D A A. and Arthurs, H W. 1990. *Lawyers in Canada*. Toronto: University of Toronto Press.

St. Lewis, J. 1999. *Virtual Justice: Systemic Racism and the Canadian Legal Profession*. An Independent Report by J St Lewis, Co-Chair of the Working Group on Racial Equality in the Legal Profession (Ottawa: Canadian Bar Association).

Tong, D. 1996. *Gatekeeping in Canadian Law Schools: A History of Exclusion, The Rule of 'Merit', and a Challenge to Contemporary Practices*. Unpublished LL M Thesis. Faculty of Law, University of British Columbia.

Tong, D. 1998. A History of Exclusion: The Treatment of Racial and Ethnic Minorities by the Law Society of British Columbia in Admissions to the Legal Profession. *Advocate* 56/2, 197–208.

Wallace, J E. 1991. *Why Lawyers Decide to Quit Their Jobs: A Study of Job Satisfaction and Organisational Commitment among Calgary Lawyers*. A report submitted to the Alberta Law Foundation.

Wallace, J E. 1997. It's about Time: a Study of Hours Worked and Work Spillover among Law Firm Lawyers. *Journal of Vocational Behavior* 50, 227–248.

Yorke, L K. 1993. Mabel Penery French (1881–1955): A Life Re-Created. *University of New Brunswick Law Journal* 42, 3–49.

5

Engendering the Legal Profession: the Education Strategy

MARY JANE MOSSMAN

Abstract

In 1993, the Canadian Bar Association published a major report on gender equality in the legal profession, recommending programmes of 'remedial human rights jurisprudence' to confront continuing barriers for women lawyers in Canada. Responding to this recommendation, three large law firms in Toronto requested me to design and present gender equality seminars to their partners and associate lawyers in small group settings. This paper describes the seminars, and identifies some of the challenges and constraints in this specialised context of continuing legal education. The paper also offers some reflections on gender equality education as a strategy for achieving change within the legal profession, concluding that fundamental change in the legal profession will not occur without directly confronting the powerful demands of lawyers' work.

1 INTRODUCTION

I N RECENT DECADES, there has been considerable scholarly attention paid to changes which have occurred in the structure and role of the legal profession (Larson 1977; Bledstein 1976; Abel-Smith and Stevens 1967; Derber 1982; Galanter and Palay 1991), including the major comparative project published in 1989 (Abel and Lewis 1989). Although Abel had commented that the pattern of women's entry to the profession after 1970 was 'nothing short of revolutionary' (Abel 1988), Menkel-Meadow astutely cautioned that 'whether the profession will be changed by the presence of women is a different question' (Menkel-Meadow 1989). Some scholars had earlier suggested that increasing numbers of women lawyers would per se effect change in the profession (Moss Kanter 1977 and 1978; Epstein 1968 and 1981), although some of these perceptions seem to have been tempered in more recent work (Epstein 1993).

Issues about gender equality in the legal profession have been addressed frequently in Canada in the past decade (Hagan and Kay 1995; Kay and Brockman 2000). Perhaps the most significant initiative was a 1993 report prepared by a

Task Force established by the Canadian Bar Association and chaired by former Supreme Court Justice Bertha Wilson. Its report, *Touchstones for Change: Equality, Diversity, Accountability*, documented the experiences of men and women lawyers, and the problems encountered by many women in the profession, perhaps especially by women of colour and aboriginal women. The Report made over two hundred recommendations for change, and succeeded in focusing national attention on issues about gender equality in the legal profession.

This paper focuses on one of the recommendations of the *Touchstones* Report: a suggestion that educational programmes for lawyers about gender equality would contribute to needed changes in the profession. As *Touchstones* stated:

> What is needed for the legal profession is 'remedial human rights jurisprudence' accessible to non-specialists. These messages should be repeated until they form the basis of a common understanding of our legal duties to our colleagues in the profession and beyond. . . . We must develop a culture of 'problem-solving' for our own profession. Lawyers are trained to criticize and demolish arguments. In order to achieve gender equality, we must learn how to find creative solutions for our own internal problems. (*Touchstones* 1993: 271–72)

In response to this recommendation for human rights education and the development of processes for creative problem-solving in relation to issues of gender equality, one of the largest corporate law firms in Toronto asked me to design and implement an educational programme in 1994 for all lawyers in the firm. At that time, the firm had already conducted a confidential survey about the gendered experiences of women and men in relation to a range of practice issues in the firm, and had recommended an educational programme for all its lawyers. The firm provided me with a copy of its survey report, and members of the firm assisted me in designing an educational programme to be presented to 15 to 20 lawyers in a problem-solving seminar of two and one-half hours. Between 1994 and 1997, I presented the seminar to the firm on 20 different occasions. Two other firms also requested me to present the same seminar to their lawyers, so that eventually, I presented the seminar on more than 40 occasions to groups of lawyers in three different large corporate firms in Toronto. In addition, during the same period, I presented workshops in Ontario and at the national level, under the auspices of the Canadian Bar Association, for lawyers who wished to become involved in facilitating educational programmes for the profession on issues of gender equality. As all these activities reveal, the emphasis on education for lawyers about gender equality in the years following publication of the *Touchstones* Report seemed to offer a real 'window of opportunity' in relation to the achievement of gender equality goals in the legal profession.

Yet, a fundamental question remains about whether these educational programmes were effective as strategies for achieving change in relation to gender equality goals in the legal profession. How can 'success' be measured in this context? My experience of presenting seminars to these groups of lawyers in large corporate firms provided one opportunity to examine the process of human rights education and creative problem-solving in the large firm context, as recommended by the *Touchstones* Report, and to try to assess their usefulness. This paper briefly describes the seminar programmes designed and presented to these three law firms between 1994 and 1997, and then reflects on some of the issues which surfaced in presenting them. In reflecting on these issues, I rely primarily on my own perceptions of the seminars, augmented by a number of other confidential sources of information provided by the firms. These reflections raise some important issues about two broader questions: firstly, what elements of design make educational programmes on equality issues for the legal profession really effective?; secondly and more fundamentally, what theories about the legal profession limit, or alternatively advance, the usefulness of educational programmes as strategies for achieving gender equality goals in the context of corporate legal culture in Canada?

2 THE SEMINAR ON GENDER EQUALITY FOR THREE TORONTO LAW FIRMS

The seminars were designed to provide problem-solving activities for participants (15 to 20 lawyers in each seminar) on three aspects of gender equality in corporate law practices: firstly, issues about work assignment, performance assessment and promotion criteria and procedures; secondly, issues about the work environment, including problems of sexual harassment as well as issues about collegiality and client development; and, thirdly, issues about the relationship between work and family responsibilities.

The seminar programme devoted about one third of its time to discussion of each of these three groups of issues. For each group of issues, there was a short introduction, often providing an overview of legal principles by way of overhead projection, and an opportunity for questions or initial comments from participants. Each segment then included a short video presentation[1] of some aspects of the problem, and participants were asked to consider how to define the problems and the options for solution along with their probable costs and consequences. In each segment, discussion also focused on the written problems[2] which demonstrated related, but somewhat different, aspects of the issues

---

[1] I used videos produced in the United States. One was produced by Prof Stephen Gillers at NYU Law School, entitled 'Further Adventures in Legal Ethics', and I used a segment on sexual harassment (Alexa and Leonard) and a segment on work/family responsibilities (Jane and Frank). See also Gillers 'The Case of Jane Loring-Kraft: Parent, Lawyer' (1990) 4 *Georgia Journal of Legal Ethics* 115. The second video was produced by Ginzberg Video Productions in California and was called 'All in a Day's Work'. I used excerpts relating to client and firm discussions about the staffing of a major litigation case.

[2] I used five written problems, or problem sets: (1) a junior woman partner who is excluded from an important client consultation by a senior male partner; (2) a female articling student to whom a male client makes a sexist remark while a male partner of the firm is present; (3) a woman (fifth-year) associate who is propositioned by a male client while she is attempting to be pro-active in relation to client development; in one problem outcome, her rejection of the client results in the loss of

revealed by the video problems. After a brief conclusion, the programme moved on to the next set of issues. At the end of all three segments, there was frequently time for only a brief conclusion, and participants were referred to the written materials available for them to take away from the seminar for further reference.

One of the problems involved an issue about how work is allocated in a corporate-commercial department, an issue which demonstrated the problem of 'pink files and blue files', earlier documented in the *Touchstones* Report. According to *Touchstones*, files allocated to women lawyers tend to involve 'less high profile matters, less client contact and correspondence, and reduced opportunity to develop legal skills and a client base' (*Touchstones* 1993: 87). Sometimes discussion about this issue at the seminars revealed that younger female lawyers were aware of the problem, but that it had not been recognised by male lawyers, both young and old. This situation provided a good opportunity to reinforce the idea that gender inequality often occurs without express intention, and to underline the need for firms to be vigilant about standards or accepted practices which may not always be gender-neutral in their impact on men and women lawyers in the firm. Other problem-solving in the seminars involved issues about collegiality in corporate law culture: the 'problem of playing (or not playing) golf' and its repercussions. There were also video problems and discussion about sexual harassment, and about the impact of women lawyers' disproportionate responsibilities for parenting. The discussions offered opportunities to examine the 'systemic' nature of these issues by contrast with accepted views that such problems result just from 'individual choices' (Hagan and Kay 1995).

Overall, the problems were useful in raising a number of issues about gender equality: the invisibility of some gender issues within 'normal' firm practices, the role of individual members of the firm in confronting and resolving gender equality issues, the consequences of different kinds of action or non-action and their differential impacts on firm lawyers, the need for lawyers to be responsive to concerns expressed with humour or just 'in passing' as well as those presented more directly, the need for lawyers in the firm to continue a process of creative exploration of appropriate options—and a full assessment of their costs and consequences for individual lawyers, for the firm as a whole, and for client services.

this file for the firm, and the woman associate, who has not reported the client's (mis-) behaviour, is blamed for this loss; (4) a woman associate who is not invited to golf with a senior partner and client; she is present when other junior (male) members of her litigation group are invited to the golf outing; and (5) a senior woman corporate associate who is a single parent is 'excused' by her senior male partner from regular breakfast meetings with a demanding client; however, the client then becomes 'attached' to a male associate attending the meetings and the woman associate loses the file.

3 CHALLENGES AND CONSTRAINTS

The presentation of the seminar was challenging for a number of reasons. First, it was always presented within some time constraints, and often at times when participants were either tired at the end of a long working day, or experiencing workplace emergencies. This phenomenon created major challenges in terms of keeping discussions inclusive of all participants, ensuring that important information was conveyed and reinforced, and providing a balance between offering some leeway for participants to pursue topics of interest while still ensuring that the seminar topics were all reasonably 'completed' before the seminar time ended. The dynamics of the seminar groups also created challenges because the groups always included a 'mix' of genders, ages, seniority and areas of legal expertise. This arrangement required attention to the patterns of interaction in mixed groups of male and female lawyers, and interventions from me about this issue when typical patterns of male intervention (even interruption) and female reticence occurred. It was also important to be sensitive to possible constraints on participation on the part of associates in the presence of partners who would be making decisions about their promotion to partnership.

Another challenge was the need to encourage participation from members of the seminar group in circumstances where I did not usually, at the outset, know the participants. At the beginning of the seminar, I tried to outline what would ensue, to caution that some of the problems did not have easy or obvious solutions, and to explain that one goal of the seminar was to explore the consequences of different kinds of solutions. By contrast with my experience of teaching LLB students about issues of gender equality in the legal profession, it was evident that all the participants in the law firm seminars were highly successful members of the corporate legal world—and they were often able to conceal their 'real' views so as to participate successfully in the discussions. There was also a special challenge for me in relation to a number of women lawyers who attended the seminar with very high expectations that existing problems in their firms would be solved during the seminar itself. For them, the seminar was often frustrating and disappointing because it remained focused on hypothetical, albeit often recognisable, problems. I tried to emphasise that the seminar presented an opportunity for participants to practise talking about and trying to resolve difficult, yet hypothetical, problems. This explanation probably diminished expectations on the part of some women lawyers that there would be an immediate transformation of gender practices within the firm. Yet, such an explanation also underlined the limits of the seminar as a strategy for accomplishing real change in terms of gender equality goals, and the significant power of the firm to choose whether to take up or ignore the challenges presented in the seminar.

4 RETHINKING GENDER EQUALITY EDUCATION AS A STRATEGY
FOR CHANGE

All these problems were linked to deeper structural problems which became evident along with my increasing levels of anxiety about the impact (or lack of impact) of the seminars in the firms. As an educator, I found it difficult to engage, over and over again, in the very challenging exercise of presenting these seminars with no real confidence that they would accomplish their objectives. More significantly, as with any initiatives of this kind, there was a real danger that the seminars per se could be used by firms as evidence to prove that they had addressed gender equality issues satisfactorily, and thus to justify their taking no further action. These anxieties prompted me to probe more deeply into the underlying assumptions of educational programmes about gender equality in the legal profession. What kinds of structures are needed to make such programmes effective? How can the achievement of gender goals be measured?

In my view, the fundamental problem is that, compared to many kinds of legal challenges, there is a need for fundamental rethinking of traditional firm practices to meet gender equality goals, a process which is more one of 'designing' than of 'discovering' solutions. Such a process requires the dedication of considerable time on the part of the firm and its individual lawyers. Yet, all of these lawyers faced significant, sometimes intolerable, competing demands in their busy law practices. This problem underlines the structural reality that workplace demands are primary, and the need for gender equality education something which must be 'fitted into' this reality. Thus, while it may be theoretically possible to insist that lawyers attend gender equality seminars as a matter of primary importance, and that other work responsibilities take second place, it seems unlikely that such a reordering of priorities can be readily adopted in practice without rethinking underlying values.

The priority accorded to 'work commitments' compared to 'gender equality goals' in a law firm is critical to understanding the role of educational programmes as strategies for achieving change in the legal profession. In reflecting on my experiences with these seminars in Toronto firms, I identified some of the underlying assumptions about the work of the legal profession, the role of educational programmes and the process of change within organisations. I also re-examined the *Touchstones* Report: what concept of the profession did the Report have in mind when it suggested 'remedial human rights jurisprudence' and 'creative problem-solving' as strategies for overcoming gender inequality in the profession? Did the Report understand the process of changing the legal profession as one of overcoming powerful and entrenched patterns and conflicting interests, or simply as one of gradual but necessary and inevitable change (Brockman and Chunn 1993)? And, by contrast, what other concepts of the profession and of processes of change might lead us to choose different strategies for achieving gender equality goals?

My re-examination of the *Touchstones* Report revealed that it provided admirably detailed documentation of the experiences of women lawyers in different workplace contexts: private practice, government legal departments, corporate counsel positions, the academy and administrative tribunals and the judiciary. The Report also documented women lawyers' experiences in family law practice, assessed the roles and responsibilities of law societies and voluntary legal organisations such as the CBA in relation to gender equality goals and provided a brief overview of gender equality principles in substantive law and procedure. Moreover, the Report itself stated its goal very clearly at the outset: 'The Report is about fundamental change' (*Touchstones* 1993: 9). In analysing the problems, the *Touchstones* Report adopted the requirements of Canadian law in relation to equality and non-discrimination as the basis for its recommended changes to confront problems experienced by women lawyers.

This 'legalistic' approach to the challenge of achieving gender equality in the legal profession is significant. It relies on the articulation of legal principles and their foundation in ideas of 'justice' as the basis for achieving change. In doing so, however, there appears to be little recognition in the *Touchstones* Report of the 'gaps' between statements of legal requirements and their implementation in practice, a problem which has frequently been identified in the implementation of human rights standards in other contexts (Bumiller 1988; Nelken 1981; Mossman 1990; Nelson and Bridges 1999). *Touchstones* seems to assume that recommended changes will flow from the identification of problems and delineation of legal principles applicable to them, perhaps assuming that the 'gap' problem will not occur in the legal profession context because of the profession's important responsibilities for the administration of justice. This conception of the legal profession and its essential motivation for change was addressed explicitly in Justice Wilson's Introduction which suggested that the entry of large numbers of women to the legal profession had created new demands for dramatic (even traumatic) changes in the legal profession:

> Lawyers realised that this was a time for moral and intellectual stocktaking, for taking a cold dispassionate look at where the profession was going. How was their profession faring in the larger context of society? Was it a profession they were proud to belong to? Or had it become a little tarnished over the years? . . .Were we still the moral and intellectual leaders in our communities or were we just high-priced technicians at the beck and call of the corporate elite? In sum, did the profession still warrant the description 'noble and learned'? (*Touchstones* 1993: 1).

For Justice Wilson, there was no doubt about the profession's fundamental responsibility to promote equality as a matter of justice.

Yet, although the final section of the Report acknowledged constraints on the implementation of its recommendations to achieve gender equality in the legal profession, *Touchstones* did not include a sustained analysis of the processes of change or of the barriers to change within the legal profession. In the end, the Report appeared to me to assume that the requirements of law and justice would result in the implementation of the recommended changes, and that educational programmes about human rights jurisprudence and creative problem-solving would help significantly to achieve this goal. However, the power of firms to choose whether to implement ongoing processes of change, especially in the face of very significant demands in relation to client work, creates competing challenges even for lawyers who take seriously the requirements of law and justice. It is this conflict between the demands of legal work in firms and equality goals based on law and justice which makes the provision of human rights education per se so unlikely to achieve significant change in the legal profession.

In reflecting on the limits of both individual and more systemic solutions in relation to gender equality goals in the legal profession, the absence of really effective strategies is evident (Thornton 1990). Although some scholars have suggested that women lawyers may 'equalize power' and 'rewrite the rules' (Harrington 1994: 175 and 204), it is not clear that women lawyers can engage in these actions successfully in the mainstream, as opposed to the margins, of the profession. And if the mainstream is less responsive, it will be difficult, if not impossible, to apply these strategies for change in major law firms. As other scholars who have examined lawyers' work in the context of the relationships between law and capitalism have suggested, 'lawyers' work shapes as well as reinforces the power relations in society' (Cain and Harrington 1994: 2); indeed, lawyers work effectively to 'translate' the needs of capital into legal rights. Conversely, however, these scholars have expressed doubts about lawyers' ability to challenge the goals of capital by using legal skills on behalf of a range of powerless people; law as 'transgression' is much less likely to succeed than law as 'translation'.

A focus on the *work* done by lawyers starkly reveals the power of work demands in law firms to sideline other goals such as those of gender equality. In such a context, educational seminars about gender equality provide useful information, but they cannot challenge the fundamental rationale of law practice per se. This pessimistic conclusion about the limited potential of education to achieve gender equality goals in the legal profession is captured in Margaret Thornton's apt characterisation of women as 'fringe-dwellers of the jurisprudential community.' For Thornton, the corporatism of law firm organisation renders it critical not to assume that there will be incremental change or that it will be, inevitably, progressive. According to her analysis, moreover, women lawyers who succeed in corporate law practice are unlikely to bring about significant change:

> In mainstream practice, women lawyers have all too often accepted the assumption that the effacement of the feminine is the way to 'make it in a man's world'. There is nothing potentially radical about such women because they do not wish to change any aspect of legal practice as it is . . . [As well,] the deference of such women in law to a legal culture in which the traits of the imagined masculine almost always characterize its primary actors and agents of legality makes it easier for men to assert that gender is not an issue (Thornton 1996: 290).

In this context, Thornton concluded that 'neither an increase in the number of women nor the passing of time can provide an automatic remedy' (Thornton 1996: 291). Similarly, in the context of my experiences with educational seminars for lawyers in Toronto law firms, the education strategy recommended by the *Touchstones* Report may represent only one small part of the process of achieving gender equality goals in the legal profession.

5 REFERENCES

Abel, Richard L. 1988. United States, the Contradictions of Professionalism. In *Lawyers in Society: The Common Law World*. Berkeley: University of California Press.

Abel, Richard L and Lewis, Philip S C, eds. 1989. *Lawyers in Society: Comparative Theories*. Berkeley: University of California Press.

Abel-Smith, Brian and Stevens, Robert. 1967. *Lawyers and the Courts*. London: Heineman Educational Books Ltd.

Bledstein, Burton. 1976. *The Culture of Professionalism*. New York: WW Norton & Company, Inc.

Brockman, Joan and Chunn, Dorothy, eds. 1993. *Investigating Gender Bias: Law, Courts, and the Legal Profession*. Toronto: Thompson Educational Publishing, Inc.

Bumiller, Kristin. 1988. *The Civil Rights Society: The Social Construction of Victims*. Baltimore: John Hopkins University Press.

Cain, Maureen and Harrington, Christine, 1994. *Lawyers in a Postmodern World: Translation and Transgression*. New York: New York University Press.

Derber, Charles. 1982. *Professionals as Workers*. Boston: GK Hall and Co.

Epstein, Cynthia Fuchs. 1968. *Women and Professional Careers: The Case of the Woman Lawyer*. PhD dissertation: Columbia University.

Epstein, Cynthia Fuchs. 1981. *Women in Law*. New York: Basic Books.

Epstein, Cynthia Fuchs. 1993. *Women in Law*. 2nd edition. Chicago: University of Illinois Press.

Galanter, Marc and Palay, Thomas. 1991. *Tournament of Lawyers*. Chicago: University of Chicago Press.

Hagan, John and Kay, Fiona. 1995. *Gender in Practice: A Study of Lawyers' Lives*. New York: Oxford University Press.

Harrington, Mona. 1994. *Women Lawyers: Rewriting the Rules*. New York: A A Knopf.

Kay, Fiona and Brockman, Joan. 2000. 'Barriers to Gender Equality in the Canadian Legal Establishment. *Feminist Legal Studies* 8: 2, 169.

Larson, Magali Sarfatti. 1977. *The Rise of Professionalism: A Sociological Analysis*. Berkeley: University of California Press.

Menkel-Meadow, Carrie. 1989. Feminization of the Legal Profession: The Comparative Sociology of Women Lawyers. In *Lawyers in Society: Comparative Theories*, edited by Abel and Lewis. Berkeley: University of California.

Moss-Kanter, Rosabeth. 1977. *Men and Women of the Corporation*. New York: Basic Books.

Moss-Kanter, Rosabeth. 1978. Reflections on Women and the Legal Profession: A Sociological Perspective. *Harvard Women's Law Review 1: 1*.

Mossman, Mary Jane. 1990. 'Shoulder to Shoulder': Gender and Access to Justice. *Windsor Yearbook of Access to Justice*. 10: 351–363.

Nelken, David. 1981. The 'Gap' Problem in the Sociology of Law: A Theoretical Review. *Windsor Yearbook of Access to Justice*. 1:35.

Nelson, Robert and Bridges, William. 1999. *Legalizing Gender Inequality: Courts, Markets and Unequal Pay for Women in America*. Cambridge: Cambridge University Press.

Task Force on Gender Equality in the Legal Profession. 1993. *Touchstones for Change: Equality, Diversity and Accountability*. Ottawa: Canadian Bar Association.

Thornton, Margaret. 1990. *The Liberal Promise*. Melbourne: Oxford University Press.

Thornton, Margaret. 1996. *Dissonance and Distrust: Women in the Legal Profession*. Melbourne: Oxford University Press.

6

Women in the Legal Profession: The Australian Profile

ROSEMARY HUNTER

Abstract

This chapter presents a statistical profile of women in the legal profession in Australia. It brings together data on women's representation at different periods, in various strata of the legal profession, areas of specialisation and income groups and in the judiciary, professional organisations and legal education. The chapter tracks the relationship between gender, career patterns and professional status, and concludes that while women are now a majority of law students, their male peers still face a smoother passage through the professional hierarchy.

1 STRUCTURE OF THE LEGAL PROFESSION IN AUSTRALIA

THE LEGAL PROFESSION in Australia has been largely modelled on that of England, involving a divided profession and self-regulation through the promulgation and enforcement of ethical standards.

The profession was established in the colonial period (the first half of the nineteenth century), at a time when the Australian continent was occupied by a number of independent British colonies. Those colonies federated in 1901 to form the Commonwealth of Australia, with the colonies becoming states of the federation. The legal profession continued to be organised on a state-by-state basis, with separate rules for admission to practise and separate professional bodies in each state. This remains the case, although more recently moves have been made towards mutual recognition of qualifications and a uniform national admission system.

The main division of the profession is between barristers and solicitors. Solicitors undertake transaction work and litigation paperwork, while barristers specialise in courtroom advocacy. There are many more solicitors than barristers in each jurisdiction. Most solicitors work in private law firms. The great majority of firms are small (either sole practitioners, or firms with one or two partners plus employee solicitors and paralegals). In the capital cities there are a relatively small number of large law firms, with many partners and employee solicitors, although few approaching the size of the large US firms. Solicitors may also work in the public sector (for legal agencies such as public prosecutions or government solicitors, or in other departments/agencies), as in-house counsel for private corporations, or in Community Legal Centres (which provide a broad range of advice and representation services to disadvantaged clients).

Barristers are independent practitioners working in chambers, but are organised into a fairly cohesive (formal or informal) Bar in each state. In NSW, Victoria, Queensland, Tasmania and the Australian Capital Territory there are separate professional/regulatory bodies for solicitors and barristers, while in South Australia, Western Australia and the Northern Territory there is a single body. Barristers' chambers are usually clustered around the central courts in the state capital. Bars tend to be highly hierarchical, with status associated with seniority. Successful senior barristers may be appointed as 'Queens Counsel' or 'Senior Counsel'.

In accordance with the English model, Australian judges are usually appointed from the ranks of barristers, with advocacy experience (often in commercial practice) being considered the major prerequisite for a judicial role. More recently, solicitors have been appointed in greater numbers to judicial office at lower levels in the court hierarchy (for example as magistrates and tribunal members, and also as state district court judges), however the state and federal superior courts remain the almost exclusive domain of former barristers. Until recently, too, there has been little or no formal judicial training, although some courts and the Australian Institute of Judicial Administration now offer judicial orientation courses and other (usually voluntary) training sessions.

Legal education in Australia involves approximately three years of full-time university study, plus a component of practical legal training which varies from state to state. Law is an undergraduate degree, and the majority of students take the degree in a combined programme with a generalist or other professional degree (eg Law/Arts, Law/Science, Law/Economics, Law/Engineering), which involves a total of five to six years' study. The practical training may involve either further study at a separate institution, or 'articles of clerkship' in a (usually large) law firm.

The number of legal academics has increased enormously over the last 30 years, resulting from a combination of a shift in the teaching of law from a part-time occupation undertaken by practitioners to a full-time occupation undertaken by career academics, and the opening of many new university law programmes. The Australian higher education system consists of mainly public universities (with only a few private institutions), with funding and regulation deriving largely from the federal government. Academics are not as well paid as their counterparts in the US and Canada, or as solicitors in large law firms or successful barristers. The status of academia is also somewhat below that of legal practice.

Because of the plethora of professional and regulatory bodies operating in the Australian profession, it is difficult to obtain up-to-date national statistics on all aspects of the profession. Gender breakdowns present a further difficulty, since until recently few bodies collected statistics on this basis, and some still do not. The Law Society of NSW (the solicitors' body in that state) now collects and publishes detailed information on its membership on a regular basis, but other states have not done the same. In addition, membership of some state bodies is voluntary, so membership numbers may not provide an accurate picture. There has also been only limited research on the gender dimensions of the legal profession. The following statistics reflect the paucity of available data on women in the legal profession in Australia.

2 NUMBER OF WOMEN LAWYERS/MALE LAWYERS

As Tables 1 and 2 demonstrate, the proportion of women declines as one moves up the professional hierarchy:

Table 1: Women in the Legal Profession in Australia, 1994–95

Role	Males	Male %	Females	Female %	Total
Judges & Magistrates	739	91.3	70	8.7	809
Lawyers	23358	75.3	7662	24.7	31020
Academics	496	61.0	317	39.0	813
Law Clerks	4618	37.4	7725	62.6	12343

SOURCE: Thornton (1996), 293.

Table 2: Lawyers in Practice in NSW, 1998–99

Branch	Males	Males %	Females	Female %	Total
Solicitors	9986	66.7	4980	33.3	14966
Barristers	1646	89.0	211	11.0	1857

SOURCES: Law Society of NSW (1999a); NSW Bar Association (1999)

3 SPECIALISATION OF WOMEN LAWYERS

Several of the state law societies have accreditation schemes in various practice areas. To become an accredited specialist in a given area, lawyers must have practised in that area intensively for a specified number of years, and must pass an examination and have a sample of work evaluated by senior practitioners.

Table 3: Specialisation of Women Lawyers in Victoria and NSW, 1999

Area	NSW			VIC		
	Women	Total	%	Women	Total	%
Advocacy	3	27	11.1	0	0	0
Business Law	2	138	1.4	0	97	0
Commercial Litigation	1	64	1.6	3	57	5.6
Criminal Law	22	90	24.4	19	77	24.7
Employment & Industrial Law	1	13	7.7	0	0	0
Family Law	95	237	40.1	56	161	34.8
Immigration Law	6	15	40.0	5	18	27.8
Local Govt. & Planning	4	22	18.2	6	22	27.3
Mediation	3	17	17.6	3	23	13
Personal Injury Law	70	387	18.1	13	67	19.4
Property Law	22	141	15.6	13	56	23.2
Taxation Law	1	6	1.7	0	0	0
Wills & Estates	12	34	35.3	13	47	27.7

SOURCES: Law Institute of Victoria (1999); Law Society of NSW (1999c).

Table 3 shows that women tend to specialise most in the areas of family law, immigration and wills & estates, but are greatly under-represented in the specialisations of business law, commercial litigation, employment and industrial law and taxation law.

Table 4 shows areas of practice engaged in by solicitors responding to a 1994 survey, rather than simply accredited specialists.

Table 4: Areas of Practice of Victorian and NSW Solicitors, 1994

Area	Male No	% Male Respondents	Female No	% Female Respondents
Admin/constitutional	81	7	42	4
Banking & finance	221	20	144	13
Bankruptcy/liquidation	199	18	156	14
Building & construction	120	11	68	6
Business	454	42	271	25
Criminal	205	19	128	12
Family	197	18	259	24
Intellectual property	126	12	132	12
Industrial relations	98	9	94	9
Commercial litigation	456	42	411	38
Personal injury	247	23	282	26
Planning & environment	106	10	65	6
Probate & wills	338	31	221	20
Property	422	39	305	28
Tax	119	11	49	5
Other	134	12	157	15

SOURCE: Victoria Law Foundation (1994).

According to this table, administrative/constitutional law, banking and finance, building and construction, business law, criminal law, planning and environment, probate and wills, property law, and taxation law are male-dominated areas of practice; bankruptcy/liquidation, intellectual property, industrial relations, commercial litigation and personal injury law are gender-balanced areas, while family law is the only female-dominated area. The difference between the two tables in relation to the areas of probate and wills and industrial law may be explained either by changes in practice profiles between 1994 and 1999, or different propensities for women working in those areas to obtain specialist accreditation.

4 THE JUDICIARY

Tables 5, 6 and 7 show the low proportional representation of women in the Australian judiciary, and also the tendency (as in the profession in general) for their representation to decrease, the higher the status of the court. Thus, women constitute 16 per cent of magistrates, 14 per cent of district court judges, but only 9 per cent of supreme court judges. The figures for federal courts are skewed by the relatively high proportion of women on the Family Court, and the small overall number of High Court judges. The relatively high proportion of female supreme court judges in Queensland is due to a conscious policy of appointing women to the bench pursued by the state attorney-general.

Table 5: State Superior Courts, 1999

State	Supreme Court			District Court		
	Women	Total	%	Women	Total	%
NSW	4	43	9.3	11	64	17.2
Vic	2	29	6.9	5	50	10.0
Qld	4	24	16.6	4	35	11.4
Tas	0	7	0.0	–	–	–
WA	1	16	6.3	5	20	25.0
SA	1	14	7.1	2	25	8.0
ACT	0	3	0.0	–	–	–
NT	1	7	14.3	–	–	–
TOTAL	13	143	9.1	27	194	13.9

Table 6: Federal Superior Courts, 1999

Court	Male	Female	Female %	Total
High Court	6	1	14.3	7
Federal Court	44	4	8.3	48
Family Court	41	12	22.6	53
TOTAL	91	17	15.7	108

Table 7: Magistrates Courts, 1999

State	Male	Female	Female %	Total
NSW	104	26	20.0	130
Vic	80	17	17.5	97
Qld	65	8	10.9	73
SA	31	4	11.4	35
Tas	12	1	7.7	13
WA	36	5	12.2	41
ACT	5	3	37.5	8
NT	9	1	10.0	10
TOTAL	342	65	16.0	407

SOURCE: Women Lawyers Association of NSW (1999), 17–18.

5 CHANGES OVER TIME

Table 8 shows the growth in the numbers and proportions of women in the legal profession in Australia from a very low base as recently as the mid-1970s. Between 1981 and 1991 the size of the profession doubled, but the number of women more than quadrupled.

Table 8: Women in the Legal Profession in Australia, 1947–91

Year	No Women	% Women	Total
1947	109	2.4	4576
1961	258	3.9	6636
1976	970	7.5	12909
1981	1993	11.4	17516
1986	4396	18.5	23824
1991	8971	26.3	34075

Includes judges, magistrates, barristers, solicitors and legal officers
SOURCE: Roach Anleu (1992), 164.

Tables 9, 10 and 11 show rates of increase of women's representation in different branches of the profession. The NSW figures are indicative of what has occurred in the rest of the country. It can be seen that women solicitors have accounted for most of the growth (not surprisingly, since solicitors constitute by far the largest group within the profession). Further, while the numbers and proportions of women solicitors and barristers have increased incrementally, the number and proportion of women judges has leapt markedly in the past five years.

Table 9: Solicitors in Practice in NSW, 1988–99

Year	No Women	% Women	Total
1988	1979	20.2	9808
1991	2634	23.5	11230
1994	3291	26.8	12283
1997	4099	30.6	13409
1999	4866	33.2	14643

SOURCE: Law Society of NSW (1999b).

Table 10: Barristers in Practice in NSW, 1985–98

Year	No Women	% Women	Total
1985	78	7.3	1069
1988	102	8.0	1271
1991	142	9.2	1543
1994	174	10.2	1711
1998	211	11.4	1857

SOURCE: Keys Young (1995).

Table 11: Women Judges in NSW Courts, 1970–99

Year	No Women	% Women	Total
1970	0	0.0	165
1975	1	0.6	175
1980	3	1.6	192
1985	7	3.3	211
1990	10	4.0	247
1994	20	7.5	265
1999	49	18.1	271

SOURCE: Women Lawyers Association of NSW (1999), 16.

6 LEGAL HIERARCHY

As noted earlier, and as shown in Tables 12 and 13, women remain clustered at the lower paid, lower status end of the legal professional hierarchy.

Table 12: Gender Distribution of the Legal Profession in NSW, 1995

Position	Male	Male %	Female	Female %	Total
Judges & Magistrates	250	93.3	18	6.7	268
Barristers	1498	89.7	172	10.3	1670
Solicitors	9468	72.0	3641	28.0	13109
—Partners	3197	92.3	267	7.7	3464
—Sole Practitioners	1828	85.2	318	14.8	2146
—Employees	2182	55.9	1722	44.1	3904
—Government	734	55.8	581	44.2	1315
—Corporate	729	60.3	481	39.7	1210
—Other	828	82.8	172	17.2	1000

SOURCE: Thornton (1996), 295.

At the same date (1995), close to 40 per cent of academic lawyers and 60 per cent of community lawyers were women.

Table 13: Distribution of Male and Female Solicitors in NSW, 1999

Position	% Male Solicitors	% Female Solicitors
Partner	27.9	6.8
Sole Practitioners	22.6	9.6
Employee	26.8	49.1
Government	7.9	15.0
Corporate	9.2	14.8

SOURCE: Law Society of NSW (1999b).

Women are less likely than men to be partners or sole practitioners, and more likely to be employee solicitors, or government or corporate lawyers. As explained by Israel and McDonald, 'corporate and government employers are far more likely to have equal employment policies in place and to offer more flexible work practices', such as maternity leave, part-time work and lower hours requirements (1999). Women are also less likely to face sexual harassment in those contexts.

In 1997, women constituted 16 per cent of the Victorian Bar, but only 6 per cent of Queens Counsel (nine out of a total of 152 QCs). In 1998, women constituted 11 per cent of the NSW Bar, but only 3 per cent of Senior Counsel (six out of a total of 230 SCs).

7 CAREER PATTERNS

Evidence from various surveys indicates that women are more likely than their male counterparts to drop out of the legal profession after a period in practice (often associated with the conflicting demands of child care). Systematic data on this phenomenon are more difficult to obtain.

The combination of drop-out rates and the more recent advent of substantial numbers of women in the profession result in women lawyers being on average much younger and more junior than male lawyers. Women solicitors in NSW are twice as likely as men to have been admitted to practice in the last five years; half of women solicitors but only a quarter of male solicitors are aged 35 or less (Israel and McDonald, 1999, 61). (Tables 14 and 15)

Table 14: Seniority of Solicitors in NSW, 1999

Years since admission	Male %	Female %	Total %
<= 1 year	11.7	21.8	15.1
2–3 years	7.1	14.1	9.4
4–7 years	12.3	21.3	15.3
8–14 years	21.4	26.7	23.2
15+ years	47.4	16.1	37.0

SOURCE: Law Society of NSW (1999b).

Table 15: Age of Solicitors in NSW, 1999

Age	Male %	Female %	Total %
<= 29 years	12.1	26.2	16.7
30–39 years	26.2	39.8	30.7
40–49 years	33.2	23.0	29.8
50+ years	27.4	9.0	21.3

SOURCE: Law Society of NSW (1999b).

The combination of drop-out rates and slower progress for women who remain in the profession result in markedly different patterns of advancement for women and men. Table 16 shows the relative proportions of women and men admitted to practice in particular years who had attained partnership in a law firm by 1994. In each case, women had only one third the 'success rate' of men.

Table 16: Partnerships Attained by Year of Admission in NSW, 1994

Year of Admission	% Men attained Partnership	% Women attained Partnership
1984	60	21
1989	30	9
1991	15	5

SOURCE: Keys Young (1995).

8 INCOME DIFFERENCES

In keeping with their more junior status and clustering at the lower end of the professional hierarchy, women lawyers' incomes are considerably lower on average than those of their male counterparts. (Tables 17 and 18)

Table 17: Incomes of NSW Solicitors, 1998/99

Gross Income	Male %	Female %	Total %
<=$50,000	29.9	48.1	35.7
$50,001–$75,000	22.8	27.0	24.2
$75,001–$100,000	14.0	10.6	12.0
$100,001–$150,000	14.1	6.6	11.9
$150,000+	13.2	4.0	10.6
Unknown	6.0	3.7	5.6
TOTAL	100.0	100.0	100.0

SOURCE: Law Society of NSW (1998b).

Table 18: Income of Victorian and NSW Solicitors, 1994

Gross Income	Male %	Female %
<= $30,000	8	13
$30,001–$40,000	11	24
$40,001–$50,000	22	33
$50,001–$60,000	14	12
$60,001–$80,000	12	6
$80,001–$100,000	13	6
$100,001-$150,000	19	6
Unknown	1	0
Total	100	100

SOURCE: Victoria Law Foundation (1994).

9 PART-TIME EMPLOYMENT

The majority of those working part-time in the legal profession are women. This is a considerable over-representation considering women make up less than 30 per cent of the profession overall. Opportunities for part-time employment remain limited, however, with few private law firms having formal policies or informal arrangements enabling lawyers the choice to work part-time. As noted earlier, part-time options are more likely to be available in government or corporate employment. (Table 19)

Table 19: Full-Time and Part-Time Work in the Legal Profession, 1996

Status	Men	Women	Total	Women % of Total
Full time	18624	4544	23168	19.6
Part time	629	868	1497	58.0

SOURCE: Australian Bureau of Statistics (1997), 14.

The 1998–99 NSW Practising Certificate Survey showed 490 out of 3265 women working part-time (15 per cent), compared to 339 out of 6772 men (5 per cent). The survey also sought information on the hours worked per week by those working part-time. Around half of respondents working part-time did not answer this question. Of those that did, the breakdown of hours was as follows. (Table 20)

Table 20: Hours Worked per Week by Solicitors Working Part-Time in NSW, 1998/9

Hours	Males	%	Females	%	Total	%
1–10 hrs	20	14.9	14	4.9	34	8.1
11–15 hrs	10	7.5	38	13.3	48	11.5
16–20 hrs	44	32.8	58	20.4	102	24.3
21–25 hrs	40	29.9	88	30.9	128	30.5
26–30 hrs	20	14.9	87	30.5	107	25.5
Total	134	100.0	285	100.0	419	100.0

SOURCE: Law Society of New South Wales (1998a).

It can be seen that while men working part-time were most likely to be working 16–25 hours per week, women working part-time were most likely to be working 21–30 hours per week. In other words, 'part-time' work for women lawyers may still involve a substantial time commitment to their jobs.

10 FIRST WOMEN LAWYERS TO BE ADMITTED/APPOINTED TO THE JUDICIARY

The first female supreme court Judge was Dame Roma Mitchell, appointed to the Supreme Court of South Australia in 1965. In 1976 Elizabeth Evatt became the first Chief Justice of the Family Court of Australia. In 1987 Mary Gaudron became the first, and only, woman appointed to the High Court of Australia.

Table 21: Admission of Women to Legal Practice

State	Year	Legislation
Victoria	1905	Women's Disabilities Removal Act 1903
Queensland	1915	Legal Practitioners Act 1905
South Australia	1916	Female Law Practitioners' Act 1911
New South Wales	1921	Women's Legal Status Act 1918
Western Australia	1930	Women's Legal Status Act 1923
Tasmania	1935	Legal Practitioners Act 1904

SOURCE: Thornton (1996), 292.

11 WOMEN IN LEADING POSITIONS IN PROFESSIONAL ORGANISATIONS

Women are reasonably proportionately represented on the governing bodies of the various professional organisations, although the numbers involved are quite small. (Tables 22 and 23)

Table 22: State and Territory Law Society Councils, 1999

State	No members	No women	% women	Positions held by women	Year founded
NSW	23	8	34.8	P	1842
Vic	18	5	27.8	–	1859
Qld		4			1928
SA	30	6	20.0	P, VP	1879
WA	20	10	50.0	T	
ACT	16	5	31.3	PP, S	1933
NT	14	3	21.4		1968

SOURCE: State and Territory Law Societies

P—President, PP—Past President, SVP—Senior Vice President, VP—Vice President, S—Secretary, AS—Assistant Secretary, T—Treasurer

Table 23: State and Territory Bar Association Councils, 1999

State	No members	No women	% women	Positions held by women	Year founded
NSW	21	6	28.6	SVP, S	1902
Vic	23	3	13.0	AS	1884
Qld	16	2	12.5	–	1903
Tas	13	2	15.4	–	
ACT		0	0.0	–	1964

SOURCE: State and Territory Bar Associations

12 WOMEN TEACHING LAW

Table 24 sets out the numbers and proportions of women teaching in Australian law schools in the years 1994 and 1999. It will be seen that the overall proportion of women has remained static for the past five years. There have been increases in the proportions of women at the two most senior levels, although the numbers involved remain fairly small. Women's representation at the lecturer and associate lecturer levels has remained much the same (around 50 per cent and 60 per cent respectively). During this period there have been increases in the total numbers at senior levels, but falls in the numbers of senior lecturers, lecturers and associate lecturers, reflecting a recent period of employment contraction in the higher education sector, plus a shift away from the use of associate lecturers (formerly tutors) in law teaching. The new low-status level is the 'Other' category, largely representing sessional staff, of whom almost 50 per cent are women.

Table 24: Women Teaching in Australian Law Schools, 1994–1999

Level —year	No women	Total	% women
Professor			
—1994	10	84	11.9
—1999	20	129	15.5
Associate Professor			
—1994	15	84	17.9
—1999	36	104	34.6
Senior Lecturer			
—1994	64	218	29.4
—1999	64	190	33.7
Lecturer			
—1994	146	295	49.5
—1999	120	242	49.6
Associate Lecturer			
—1994	132	82	62.1
—1999	24	39	61.5
Other			
—1994			
—1999	115	247	46.6
TOTAL			
—1994	317	813	39.0
—1999	379	951	39.9

SOURCES: JURIST (1999); Thornton (1996), 293.

13 WOMEN IN LEGAL EDUCATION

Table 25 shows that legal education is the only part of the legal profession in Australia where women are in a majority—over half of the law students in each state are female, with the national proportion at approximately 56 per cent.

Table 25: Undergraduate Law Students in Australian Universities, 1998

State	Males	Females	Total	% Females
NSW	3393	4490	7883	57.0
VIC	2310	2670	4980	53.6
QLD	2214	2730	4944	55.2
TAS	256	317	573	55.3
WA	799	978	1777	55.0
SA	659	956	1615	59.2
NT	150	212	362	58.6
ACT	692	934	1626	57.4
TOTAL	10473	13287	23760	55.9

SOURCE: Centre for Legal Education (1998), Table 2.6.

The number of female law graduates has increased from around 20 percent in the mid 1970s to around 35 per cent in the mid 1980s, reaching around 50 per cent in the late 1990s. There is no evidence (statistical or anecdotal) of any difference in success/failure rates between male and female students.

14 CONCLUSIONS

The gender profile of the Australian legal profession reflects that of many other countries, in the strong association between sex and status. Women are clustered in the lower ranks of the professional hierarchy, in lower status practice areas (particularly family law), and at the lower levels of various sections of the profession, including the courts, law firms, and academia. Correspondingly, women lawyers earn lower incomes on average than their male counterparts.

The lower status of women lawyers is in part attributable to their lower average age than male lawyers. Women have been entering the Australian legal profession in large numbers only in the last 20 years. Thus, for example, in 1999, almost half of the male solicitors in NSW had been admitted to practice for 15 years or more, while this was the case for only 16 per cent of female solicitors in the state. However age alone does not account for status. As the cohort statistics produced by Keys Young demonstrate, women who were admitted at the same time as men advance in the profession at a considerably slower rate. The Keys Young report on *Gender Bias and the Law: Women Working in the Legal Profession in NSW* (1995), Margaret Thornton's study, *Dissonance and Distrust: Women in the Legal Profession* (1996), and my own and Helen McKelvie's report on *Equality of Opportunity for Women at the Victorian Bar* (1998) documented a multitude of barriers to women's advancement, ranging from sexual harassment, to family-unfriendly working arrangements and penalties for part-time work, to masculine networking from which women are excluded. Many of these barriers are discussed in greater detail in other chapters in this volume.

The diverse regulatory structures governing the Australian profession also mean that efforts to improve the status and prospects of women lawyers will tend to be piecemeal. Further, few initiatives have yet begun to tackle the professional culture of long working hours and homosociality. It is likely, then, that the disproportionately high attrition rate of women from the legal profession will continue, and the majority of women graduating from law schools will not be reflected in the profession as a whole, or across the spectrum of legal practice, for many years to come.

15 REFERENCES

Australian Bureau of Statistics. 1997. *Legal and Accounting Services, Australia, 1995–96.* Cat. 8678.0.

Centre for Legal Education. 1998. *Australasian Legal Education Yearbook 1998.* Sydney: Centre for Legal Education.

Hunter, Rosemary and McKelvie, Helen. 1998. *Equality of Opportunity for Women at the Victorian Bar: A Report to the Victorian Bar Council.* Melbourne: Victorian Bar Council.

Israel, Susan F and McDonald, Katy. 1999. Gender Issues for the Legal Profession. *Law Society Journal*, May, 60–62.

JURIST. 1999. Website: University Law School web pages, HYPERLINK http://law.anu.edu.au/jurist/lawschls.htm. Canberra: Australian National University.

Keys Young. 1995. *Research on Gender Bias and Women Working in the Legal System: Report.* Sydney: NSW Department for Women.

Law Institute of Victoria. 1999. Website: HYPERLINK http://www.liv.asn.au/directory/specialists/ Melbourne: Law Institute of Victoria.

Law Society of New South Wales (NSW). 1998a. *Practising Certificate Survey 1998–99.* Sydney: Law Society of New South Wales.

Law Society of NSW. 1998b. *Profile of the Solicitors of New South Wales 1998.* Sydney: Law Society of NSW.

Law Society of NSW. 1999a. *Profile: Law Society Research Update.* Sydney: Law Society of NSW.

Law Society of NSW. 1999b. *Profile of the Solicitors of New South Wales 1999.* Sydney: Law Society of NSW.

Law Society of NSW. 1999c. Website: HYPERLINK http://www.lawsocnsw.asn.au/ specialists/directory/ Sydney: Law Society of NSW.

NSW Bar Association. 1999. Website: HYPERLINK http://www.fl.asn.au/ nsw_bar/about/stat101998.htm (now located at http://www.nswbar.asn.au). Sydney: NSW Bar Association.

Roach Anleu, Sharyn. 1992. Women in the Legal Profession. *Law Institute Journal* 1992: 164.

Thornton, Margaret. 1996. *Dissonance and Distrust: Women in the Legal Profession.* Melbourne: Oxford University Press.

Victoria Law Foundation. 1994. Unpublished survey data for *Facing the Future* Report. Melbourne: Victoria Law Foundation.

Women Lawyers Association of NSW. 1999. *NSW Courts' Gender Initiatives Review: Discussion Paper.* Sydney: Women Lawyers Association of NSW.

7

Women Barristers and Gender Difference

ROSEMARY HUNTER

Abstract

Barristers in Australia constitute a small, élite group, enjoying high professional status and often high incomes. This chapter discusses the ways in which barristers' distinctive culture and invented traditions involve the production and performance of hegemonic masculinity, and the implications this has for women at the Bar. While there are various ways in which women can attempt to fit into the culture, their otherness is simultaneously and continually reinforced. Nevertheless, some women have managed to disrupt the codes of hegemonic masculinity, presenting a cultural challenge that is not easily contained.

1 INTRODUCTION

T HIS PAPER ARISES from research undertaken in 1997 on the career opportunities of women barristers in the Australian state of Victoria. In most states of Australia, as in the UK, the legal profession is divided (de jure or de facto) into two branches: solicitors and barristers. Broadly, solicitors have direct contact with clients, performing transaction work and paperwork associated with litigation on the client's instructions, while barristers specialise in courtroom advocacy. If a case goes to court, particularly one of the superior state or federal courts, the solicitor will usually brief a barrister to make the necessary court appearances. Sometimes, too, barristers will be briefed at an earlier stage to provide an opinion on the state of the law and the client's prospects of success in a case. Barristers constitute a small, élite group, enjoying high professional status and often high incomes.[1] A distinguished career as a barrister is a virtual prerequisite to appointment as a judge in the superior courts (see also Malleson, this volume).

A colleague and I were commissioned by the Victorian Bar Council to undertake research to determine whether any barriers existed to the advancement of

---

[1] This is not necessarily the case in other jurisdictions (as discussed by both Murray and Malleson, this volume), but is uniformly true of the Australian states with independent Bars.

women barristers.[2] (The term 'Bar' in the Australian system refers exclusively to barristers, not to legal practitioners as a whole.) At the time of the study, women made up 15.8 per cent of barristers in Victoria, compared to 28 per cent of solicitors and over 50 per cent of law students. The study was prompted by the low number of women at the Bar, particularly in its senior ranks,[3] and anecdotal evidence of disproportionately high drop-out rates among women. We analysed court appearances over a three-month period, and conducted interviews with male and female barristers and former barristers,[4] judges, solicitors responsible for briefing and barristers' clerks.[5] We presented a report to the Bar Council which identified a range of gender-biased and discriminatory practices faced by women barristers, in areas ranging from the briefing process, the courtroom and attitudes to family responsibilities, to the general culture and organisation of the Bar, and made a series of recommendations for improving the status of women and their retention at the Bar (Hunter and McKelvie 1998).

The area that appears to present the greatest barrier to change is the culture of the Bar itself. This encompasses the structure and organisation of the Bar as a collective entity, and the day-to-day practices and interactions within

---

[2] The research was funded by the Victorian Bar Council, the Victoria Law Foundation and the International Commission of Jurists, with additional financial and administrative support provided by the Centre for Employment and Labour Relations Law, The University of Melbourne and the Justice Research Centre, Sydney.

[3] The most senior barristers are known as 'Queens Counsel' (QCs). Appointment as a QC is made by the State Attorney-General, following application and consultation with other senior barristers and judges. At the end of the study, only 6 per cent of QCs in Victoria were women: a total of only 9 women, 2 of whom were appointed during the course of the study. (See also McGlynn, 'The Status of Women Lawyers', this volume.)

[4] Twenty-five male barristers and 25 female barristers were interviewed, together with 5 male and 5 female former barristers who had left the Bar in the previous 5 years. Current barristers were selected for interview by means of a random sample drawn from the Roll of Victorian Practising Counsel, stratified by seniority (QCs, junior barristers at the Bar more than 10 years, junior barristers at the Bar 5 to 10 years, and junior barristers at the Bar less than 5 years). Former barristers were selected randomly from a list provided by the Bar Council of people who had left the Bar in the previous 5 years. However only 8 of these could be contacted. The names of the remaining 2 former barristers interviewed were provided by current members of the Bar. Each potential interviewee was sent a letter signed by the Chair of the project's Steering Committee, a Court of Appeal judge, setting out details of the research and inviting them to participate. Virtually all those invited agreed to be interviewed.

[5] Barristers' clerks perform administrative, booking agent and fee collection tasks for the barristers with whom they work. The organisation of the clerking system varies between different Bars. In some Bars, clerks are employed by the barristers on a particular floor or in a particular building of chambers. At the Victorian Bar, clerks are independent agents who make their money by taking a percentage of the fees earned by the barristers on their 'list'. They may also exercise considerable power at least in the early stages of barristers' careers by channelling work to them (or failing to do so). Each Victorian barrister belongs to one of 12 clerking lists. The lists are of varying sizes, with some primarily specialising in particular areas of law, and others housing a more general stable of barristers. Clerks also have varying reputations in terms of their ability to attract work and promote the barristers on their lists to solicitors who may want to use their services.

chambers.[6] It is significant that none of the women barristers interviewed specifically identified the structure or environment of the Bar as obstacles to their advancement, whereas from their interviews as a whole, it was clear that Bar culture has a systemically adverse impact: discouraging women from joining the Bar, undermining the authority of those who do join, and contributing to their decisions to leave. The fact that the effects of Bar culture were invisible to these women says something about its operation.

This paper discusses the ways in which the culture of the Bar involves the production and performance of particular forms of masculinity,[7] and the implications this has for women at the Bar. This analysis is connected with a set of ideas that have arisen from recent studies of nationalism—in particular, Benedict Anderson's concept (1991) of an 'imagined community', and the work of Eric Hobsbawm, Terrence Ranger and others (1993) on 'invented traditions'. The idea of the Bar as an imagined community, in which values and behaviours are transmitted by means of invented traditions, helps to explain the perceived 'naturalness' and uncontestability of the culture for women. In exploring the dimensions of masculinity produced at the Bar, this paper also provides a counterpoint to Margaret Thornton's work (1996) on the construction of the feminine as the non-rational 'other' of law, and the consequent marginalisation of women from legal practice.[8]

2 WOMEN WITHIN HEGEMONIC MASCULINITY: HONORARY BLOKES

As theorists of masculinity have noted, different kinds of masculinities are produced in different institutional settings—for example the city office, the factory, the ethnic youth club or the gay nightclub. Often, these different masculinities intersect with other aspects of identity such as age, race and class. Different masculinities may also be produced in the same institutional settings, such as a boys' school. Relations of dominance and subordination between different

---

[6] Barristers' offices are known as chambers, and are usually physically located in close proximity to each other and to the major courts. In Victoria, the overwhelming majority of barristers have their chambers in one of four buildings immediately adjacent to the Supreme and County Courts and central Magistrates Court in the capital city, Melbourne. The chambers system in Victoria does not present the same barriers to entry to the Bar as occurs in England (see McGlynn, 'The Status of Women Lawyers', this volume), and in the neighbouring state of New South Wales.

[7] Here I am following Butler (1990: 25), who argues that gender is performative in the sense of 'constituting the identity it is purported to be', hence 'gender is always a doing'. See also Collier (1995: 42).

[8] Thornton's book focuses on the socially constructed 'fictive feminine'—the ascription to women of characteristics such as passivity, dependency, docility and disorderliness—and the way in which this is invoked to deny authority to women in the public sphere. Thus, Thornton argues that rather than women becoming accepted as legal knowers as increasing numbers are 'let in' to the legal profession, they are likely to remain 'fringe dwellers of the jurisprudential community', positioned at the lower levels of the legal hierarchy, their behaviour disciplined and constrained, and their work devalued.

types of masculinity have given rise to the notion of 'hegemonic masculinity', the dominant form of masculinity in a given society (Connell 1995: 36–37; see also Collier 1995: 38, 43).

The feature of hegemonic masculinity to which feminist theorists such as Thornton have directed most attention is the association of masculinity with disembodied reason. In this, as Carol Smart (1989: 86) notes, there is an overlap between the constitution of masculinity and the constitution of law: 'doing law and being identified as masculine are congruous'. Both law and masculinity are represented as rational, authoritative, objective, abstract and principled (see also Thornton 1996: 8). This discursive correlation results in an empirical correlation:

> law is constituted as rational as are men, and men as the subjects of the discourse of masculinity come to experience themselves as rational—hence suited to a career in law (Smart 1989: 87).

Yet as Connell (1995: 181) points out (contrary to Thornton (1996)), rationality has its dangers as a legitimator of masculine domination, since modern liberal rationality supports the idea of equal opportunities for women, and hence has the potential to undermine masculine authority. Rationality dictates that women cannot be excluded simply because they are women. Our research was commissioned on the basis of this logic. Moreover, women are capable of displaying and convincing men of their rationality and technical competence (see also Sommerlad, this volume; Silius, this volume). Something more than the construct of rationality is needed to justify women's inequality at the Bar.[9]

Another element of the masculine order that provides some room for women is the way in which the sexual division of labour is played out at the Bar. Respect and success as a barrister flow from working hard for long hours, a requirement predicated on the existence of a wife at home, to manage the domestic sphere and enable the husband's focused and exclusive commitment to his work. To an extent, women barristers can assimilate to this pattern, if they do not have children, or if they completely subordinate their family to their work. Women who had managed to succeed in this way had waited until their practices were well established before having children, had taken a minimal amount of time off for childbirth, and had the children cared for by nannies or grandparents. By contrast, obvious pregnancy or emphasis on family responsibilities places women

---

[9] Atkinson and Delamont (1990: 95) distinguish two dimensions of any occupation: 'technicity' and 'indeterminacy'. 'Technicity is the explicit, rule-governed, codified part of the job' (in the case of lawyers, legal skills and knowledge), while indeterminacy is 'the "hidden curriculum" of job performance: all the tacit, implicit, unexamined ways of being a member of any occupational group' (in this instance, the performance of masculinity). They add that 'It is plausible to look for the marginal status women have held . . . as being due *not* to their lack of technical skills necessary for the jobs, but their perceived failure to behave in ways which reveal their mastery of the indeterminate' (Atkinson and Delamont 1990: 107). This notion of the informal characteristics necessary to perform a job is similar to Pierre Bourdieu's concept of 'cultural capital'. See Sommerlad and Sanderson (1998: 34–5); Sommerlad, this volume.

on the other side of the division of labour: mothers and nurturers are *not* credible barristers.

A third feature of the Bar which gives women some chance of 'fitting in' is its sense of camaraderie. Technically, barristers are independent practitioners, self-employed, and prevented by Bar rules from entering partnerships or profit sharing with other barristers. Against this, other writers have drawn attention to the literal community of the Bar—its geographical concentration, resulting in 'intensive formal and informal interaction' with other barristers (Podmore and Spencer 1982: 355), an atmosphere of 'intimate conviviality' (Cain 1976: 241), a 'tightly knit social world' (Naffine 1990: 89). The connection between this and the sexual division of labour is evident in one of our interviewees' description of the mainstream of the Bar as consisting of men 'whose whole lives [both practice and social] are at the Bar'. Similarly, a male former barrister spoke fondly of the colleagues with whom he had shared a floor of chambers:

> That's one of the things I miss. It's a bit like being in the trenches. You have had a hard day in court and . . . it's often only another barrister who will understand why you feel how you do. You swap war stories.

Yet physical proximity does not wholly explain the camaraderie of the Bar. As one of our interviewees noted, 'no one individual can get to know over a thousand plus barristers'. Our interviews also yielded widely differing experiences of and perspectives on the Bar, from barristers at different levels in the hierarchy and specialising in different kinds of work. Yet these barristers still conceived of themselves and others as part of the same entity, pointing to the Bar as an *imagined* community. As explained by Benedict Anderson (1991: 6), the members of imagined communities never meet all of their fellow members, 'but in the minds of each lives the image of their communion'. The Bar as an imagined community is sustained by invented traditions:

> 'Invented tradition' is taken to mean a set of practices, normally governed by overtly or tacitly accepted rules and of a ritual or symbolic nature, which seek to inculcate certain values and norms of behaviour by repetition, which automatically implies continuity with the past (Hobsbawm 1993: 1).

The maintenance of physical proximity with other barristers is an invented tradition in this sense. It harks back to the Inns of Court and thus suggests continuity with the long-established English Bar, as well as with the entire life of the legal profession in Victoria. Until relatively recently, Victorian barristers were required to rent chambers in one of the buildings owned by Barristers Chambers Limited (BCL) close to the central Melbourne courts. But when the rules changed, the behaviour remained the same. While barristers may now practise from any location, only a tiny minority have taken the opportunity to move out of BCL chambers. Other invented traditions underlining the community of the Bar include the 'open door policy' (the informal practice of barristers giving advice and assistance to any other barrister who walks through their door), and the ritual at the Bar's social club, The Essoign Club,[10] of members taking the nearest available seat at lunch, regardless of who is seated next to them, which provides opportunities for members from different levels and areas of practice to meet and talk.

3   WOMEN AS THE 'OTHER' OF MASCULINITY

The fraternal bonds of the Bar, however, too often tip over into exclusive homosociality, which is another marker of hegemonic masculinity (Collier 1995: 44; Buchbinder 1998: 64). As the one woman on the High Court of Australia has observed, the 'collegiate spirit and . . . ethos' of Australian Bars is 'not conducive to an atmosphere to which women easily adapt' (Gaudron 1994: 13). The Essoign Club is a prime example. One young woman observed that many of her junior male colleagues 'come to the Bar and just slip into the mould, they go to the Essoign Club, no problem'. Yet the Club was mentioned several times in interviews as a setting in which some female barristers were aware of having a 'different' status and feeling unwelcome. One senior female barrister who had found the Club 'a terrific learning tool' when she first came to the Bar twenty years ago also acknowledged that 'some [male] judges couldn't cope with women being there'. A younger female barrister saw the Club as being about the display of male egotism rather than the conveying of knowledge by older male members of the profession:

> The conversations are all about themselves and how great they are and I don't find it comfortable to be around, or very interesting.

The role of the Essoign Club in the performance of masculinity at the Bar is evidenced by the hostility faced by a group of women barristers who attempted to make the Club their own:

> Nobody bats an eye in the Essoign Club if you see a table of all males, but we still get comments if a group of women go up there and sit as a group at a table . . . There are always audible comments: 'What's the girlie club doing today, discussing cooking or knitting or gossiping?' . . . They just can't accept that a group of women might like to have lunch together, just like a group of men does.

The difference is that a group of women having lunch together subverts the masculine codes on which the Club is based.

There are many other examples of exclusive homosociality that are integral to the culture of the Bar. For example going 'on circuit' (appearing in court sittings away from the capital city) provides an intense work experience and an

---

[10] It was not clear when the Essoign Club was established, but it is probably not more than 30 years old. Note also the name of the club, which is a Law French term meaning an excuse for not appearing in court on an appointed day. Again, there is a suggestion of continuity with centuries of legal history.

important training ground, but is also an opportunity for the establishment and reinforcement of homosocial bonds. One female interviewee reported:

> If you go on circuit, as a woman, no one will bother talking to you, you don't get invited to the golf, and you don't share sexist jokes and you don't go to the pub after court and have a beer . . .

Another had a similar experience:

> They all go on circuit together and have big nights out. I went once . . . I was the only woman and I felt like a fish out of water.

Social links between barristers sharing a floor of chambers were highlighted as another potential source of women's exclusion. Interviewees noted that men tended to be 'more comfortable around other men, and on the floor they will introduce themselves more readily and offer assistance and chat more easily'. A senior male barrister admitted his lack of effort to include 'the girls in the room at the end of the hall' in the society of the floor, and to feeling guilty about it after they left, although he also commented 'perhaps girls shouldn't share a room—to get away from the concept of "the girls together" '. (As we have seen, any assembly of women is considered dangerous; never mind that this might be a survival mechanism for those women.)

Formal and informal social occasions are another part of the invented traditions of the Bar, ranging from list dinners (for members of a particular clerking list), to other Bar functions, to day-to-day lunching rituals. Whether literally or metaphorically, these occasions are widely felt to have a 'boys' club' atmosphere (see also Thornton, 1996: 166–68, 172–77), where, for example, 'after a few reds, a small number of men are quite happy to say that women shouldn't be at the Bar at all'. One interviewee described a list dinner held at the Australia Club, a men-only club, 'which as a starting point [was] pretty alienating and offensive to the women on the list'.

> The whole thing was like a male tribal bonding experience . . . it was as if there were no women present, or that's the way most of the men behaved . . . Some of the things spoken about were fairly crude . . . You feel terrible as a woman in that atmosphere and there is nothing you can do about it. It really makes being a woman at the Bar feel really strange, like you are not amongst your own kind.

This, of course, is precisely the point. The quotation neatly summarises the tension between the elements of rationality/technical competence and homosociality within hegemonic masculinity. Women may show themselves to be equally capable of the former, but are irredeemably excluded from the latter (see also McGlynn, 'Strategies for Reforming the English Solicitors Profession', this volume). Moreover, lunching and socialising have material consequences as well as symbolic content. Several barristers noted that when women are not invited out to lunch by older male barristers, they are thereby precluded from gaining access to the valuable knowledge and advice to which their male contemporaries are exposed on these occasions.

Masculine rationality has been associated by some feminist theorists with an exclusive emphasis on the mind, within a hierarchised dualism in which man stands for mind and woman stands for body. Naffine (1990: 118), for example, claims that there is nothing physical about the man of law; she contrasts the 'masculinity of the . . . legal chambers' with that of the football club. Yet according to Connell (1995), hegemonic masculinity incorporates *both* of these elements, and our research bore this out. Sports talk in particular emerged as a notable feature of masculine performances at the Bar (see also Thornton 1996: 168–72; Sommerlad and Sanderson 1998: 137). Conversations about football and other sporting events are common in and around chambers, and also in court between judges and male barristers before the commencement of proceedings. Such conversations are understood as being between men. While some of the women interviewed said they follow the football and other sports and participate in these discussions, more said they had no interest in them and often felt excluded in these contexts.[11] Legal language is also well seasoned with sporting analogies, and a broader analogy is often drawn between sporting endeavour and courtroom advocacy, in turn anchoring law and legal practice within the discourse of masculinity.

A final element of hegemonic masculinity that situates 'women' apart from 'barristers' is compulsory heterosexuality (see eg Collier 1995: 29). Within this sexual regime, men are constituted as desiring subjects and women as objects of desire.[12] Thus part of barristers' performance of masculinity is constantly to sexualise the women they encounter. A small number of female barristers and solicitors reported that some male barristers regularly make comments, or mentioned comments made, about their hair, make-up, clothes and/or general appearance. Such comments may well be intended as compliments, which makes a negative response very difficult. Nevertheless, women generally said that they would prefer to be considered as professionals whose appearance is un(re)marked.

More seriously, a few female barristers described experiences of sexual harassment. One young woman said that 'sleazy remarks' were directed at her 'relatively often'. On one occasion her male opponent asked her to sit on his lap while they finalised consent orders. She said she was especially surprised because this man was around her own age and she usually expects that that kind of treatment would come from older men. Other women said they had received unwelcome requests for dates and had had suggestive comments made in their

---

[11] Given that interviews were semi-structured, and not all interviewees addressed every issue discussed, modifiers such as 'some' and 'more' are used in preference to quantified responses. These relative terms give an idea of the balance of views or experiences, where numbers or percentages would be misleading. As an indication, however, the terms 'a few' and 'a small number' refer to 3–5 responses, the terms 'some, 'several' and 'a number' refer to 6–12 responses, while the term 'many' refers to 15 or more responses.

[12] Where this leaves gay male barristers is an interesting question. As noted later, there appears to be a sub-grouping of gay men at the Bar, but beyond this our study yielded little information.

presence. One of the clerks confirmed the environment of the Bar as one in which some male members feel free to sexually harass their female colleagues. He talked about this as a general problem with 'some fellows having a reputation for preying on young women' (see also Pagone 1996: 15).

The modernised, rational Bar Rules now include a prohibition of sexual harassment, and an internal procedure for dealing with complaints (Victorian Bar Rules 16.1). One of the barristers on the complaints panel reported, however, that it had received complaints about only a few 'very serious' matters. None of the women who related incidents of sexual harassment during the interviews had considered reporting their experiences. They said they would prefer to deal with these matters themselves at the time or 'couldn't be bothered', or did not think it was worthwhile. A male QC has made the obvious point that

> Complaint about unwanted sexual advances by a senior male in the profession may well be suppressed by a more junior female so as not to ruin her career prospects (Pagone 1996: 14).

The sexualisation of women is finally manifested in rumours and innuendo concerning the nature of their relations with male barristers and solicitors. A number of female interviewees mentioned 'there is a problem with assumptions being made about what you are doing out to lunch with an older male barrister'. A senior female barrister said that when she first came to the Bar in the 1970s,

> If I went out to lunch with a male barrister, I used to take a brief and put it on the table so that anyone who walked into the restaurant knew it was a professional lunch.

Comments from a few younger women indicate that such considerations still apply. They spoke about rumours flying around after innocent lunches with older male barristers, or after being perceived to be working 'too closely' with a particular QC. QCs often appear with a junior counsel, and this is an important potential source of both patronage and training for junior barristers. In the case of women, stories frequently circulate about sexual favours imparted for junior briefs. These constructions of women barristers within the codes of masculinity make it impossible for them to participate in social or mentoring activities in the same way as their male counterparts.

One of the sources of cohesion in imagined national communities is the identification of a national 'other'—a 'them' whom 'we' can oppose. This is usually manifested in xenophobia (against external others) and racism (against internal others) (Anderson 1991: 150). Within the imagined community of the Bar, the role of subordinated other is filled by women, who consequently face persistent sexist and misogynistic treatment, through which male barristers mutually reinforce their masculinity by distancing themselves from the feminine (Buchbinder 1998: 125). Some of these behaviours revealed in the interviews included defacement of Women Barristers Association notices posted in the lifts of chambers, sexist 'jokes' and 'bitchy criticism' undermining the achievements of women at the Bar. Female barristers reported, for example:

> If you get good work, they say it's because someone owes you a favour or you are doing favours for someone else . . . in the end that kind of thing gets you down.

> The Bar can be very hostile. There is still that stuff about if a woman asserts herself and does a good job, she is a hard-nosed bitch. If she doesn't perform well she shouldn't be there because she is not committed to the job.

> Some male barristers are particularly critical of women taking silk . . . I am very conscious that they are more critical of the women who are successful than [they are of] the men . . .

A male ex-barrister observed that some of his peers were 'very scathing' about women at the Bar, while another noted that 'at Friday night drinks there were a lot of sexist comments made about women'. As this point indicates, 'bitchy' conversations between men often taken place when there are few women in attendance, for example at the pub after work and in other predominantly male settings. The primary purpose of these conversations, then, is for men to share their views about women, rather than to share those views *with* women. The telling of sexist jokes as a performance of masculinity is underlined by the comment of one male solicitor:

> If you get six barristers milling around outside courts and they are all men, there may be some sexist remarks made then, but you would expect that at the football or anywhere else. But you probably wouldn't get the converse, a group of women barristers milling around making sexist remarks.

The appropriate feminine performance in response to sexist remarks made in their presence is difficult to gauge, and to achieve. Many women said they were comfortable with such interactions, and some said they participated in them themselves. Others spoke about having to 'have a sense of humour' or a 'thick skin'. Young women barristers and solicitors were the least willing to dismiss sexist jokes and remarks as an inevitable component of interaction at the Bar. Some spoke about strategies for dealing with situations where they felt sexist humour was being used as a 'put-down'. One young woman said she had a stock of 'anti-male jokes to fire back' where necessary. A few said 'it's important to stand up for yourself' in situations where the 'humour' is inappropriate, but not to be 'nit-picking about it' or to 'go overboard'. Given the role of sexism in sustaining the masculine identity of at least some male barristers, it is unlikely to be eradicated in the near future. Indeed as with racism, it may have a tendency to intensify in response to crises of masculinism, brought on by serious challenges to the 'traditional' gender order.

4 EDUCATION AND CONFORMITY

The reproduction of hegemonic masculinity at the Bar is achieved not just by the actions of individual barristers, but also through the Bar's structures and institutions. New members are inducted into the culture of the Bar through the compulsory Readers Course,[13] and the system of pupillage whereby every new barrister must spend their first six months at the Bar, unable to earn fees, in the chambers of a master (now known gender-neutrally as a mentor).

The Readers Course is a three-month, full-time training course, involving instruction and practice in advocacy skills and legal drafting, court attendance, and explanation of various aspects of running a practice as a barrister and the 'traditions' of the Bar. The course is primarily taught by practising members of the Bar and the bench. Most interviewees said they had 'thoroughly enjoyed' the Readers Course, however a few comments indicated that indoctrination to various gendered aspects of Bar culture was incorporated in the teaching methods and materials, such as (from the Readers Course of the early-mid 1990s) the use of gender exclusive language by 'the majority of speakers', and consistent use of hypothetical case examples involving only men. Some women also mentioned the 'matey links' between the male members of the Bar and bench that became evident in the context of their addresses during the course. At least one woman said she felt daunted by the prospect of encountering this on a daily basis in the courts.

In the Australian context, the system of pupillage is another invented tradition, operating both as a socialisation mechanism and an implied link with the English past. The master/mentor's formal role is to be a source of 'encouragement, guidance and support' for the reader at the beginning of their career at the Bar and, ideally, if the two develop a close relationship, beyond. The choice of mentor is regarded as quite important to the future prospects of a reader, as it will determine the nature and quality of practice to which they are initially exposed and the clients and solicitors they are likely to meet in the course of their time in the mentor's chambers. Mentors are sometimes able to provide their readers with work and are often the means of introduction to particular networks at the Bar.

However, there is no formal process for matching readers with mentors in appropriate fields who might be able to provide these advantages. The system (such as it is) by which prospective readers find mentors has been described as 'entirely haphazard and unstructured', and 'bordering on the mysterious' (Pagone 1996: 4). Our interviews revealed widely varying experiences and a striking overall lack of success of the mentoring system in helping to establish junior barristers in their careers. On the other hand, the system undoubtedly operates very successfully in acculturating new barristers, and for this purpose, the precise identity of the mentor is less important. Rather, it is the fact of individual mentoring that is particularly adapted to the transmission of and enforcement of compliance with the social order (Naffine 1990: 93). As noted earlier, too, male barristers are likely to have access to informal mentoring relationships

[13] For the role of compulsory state education in the construction of national communities, see Anderson (1991: 101).

developed out of shared mutual interests, to fill the gap left by the formal system. This probably explains why no moves have been made to rationalise the matching process, although the failure tends to leave women stranded in terms of their career development. Among our interviewees, twice as many women as men[14] said they had not had a mentor in the sense of a more senior person who had guided and supported them in their early years at the Bar, and the shortage of senior women makes it difficult for women to develop feminine or feminist versions of these relationships.

The established masculine order is further maintained by the structure of the Bar Council, the body which manages and administers the business and affairs of the Victorian Bar. The Council is an elected body, but the rules for election include seniority requirements which deliver a majority of positions to QCs and barristers of at least 15 years' standing. This is the section of the Bar which has the highest concentration of men.[15] Interviewees also observed that the election process is controlled by unspoken allegiances, so that 'only those in the club' should expect to be elected anyway. Membership of Bar Council subcommittees is not gained via election, but through more informal invitation and nomination, usually via the patronage of senior members. A few women barristers reported that this method of filling committee positions also makes it difficult for them to gain representation, since male members are more likely to know and feel comfortable working with other males.

Interviewees and other members of the Bar consulted during the project indicated that in recent years the Bar Council had seen a need for greater participation by female members within the committee structure, with the result that efforts had been made to invite more women to participate. Some women who had joined committees, however, described how meetings have very strict structures and are dominated by more senior participants by whom they felt intimidated and effectively silenced. One woman said of her term on a Bar committee:

> They were looking for a token woman, I was chosen as someone who wouldn't make waves . . . it was very frustrating and humiliating, disappointing . . .

Another young female barrister recounted her experience:

> I sit on a couple of committees and it is hard work . . . it's very subtle . . . They don't make eye contact . . . it took me a couple of meetings to get the courage up to have my say and there are a few people who just don't look at me . . . it's not very welcoming.

These quotations illustrate the tension between the demands of modernisation and legitimation (the perceived need to include women) and the desire to main-

---

[14] Fourteen of the 30 women barristers interviewed, but only seven of the 30 men, said they had not had a mentor at the Bar.
[15] Women make up approx. 5 per cent of Category A (QCs and barristers of at least 15 years' standing), which has 11 positions on the Council, compared to approx. 28 per cent of Category C (juniors of no more than 6 years' standing), which has 4 positions. Category B (barristers of 7 to 14 years' standing) has 6 positions.

tain masculine authority. It appears that efforts to co-opt women into the existing structure have not been entirely successful, as the Bar Council continues to receive criticism for being unrepresentative and 'out of touch'. Even one of the strongest women supporters of the status quo conceded that the current operation of the Bar Council election rules 'could well discriminate against women' so that a temporary change might be justified.

But questioning the formal power structure, while important, represents only a narrow compass of dissent. At the informal level, challenge to the exercise of masculine power is effectively constrained by another of the Bar's invented traditions, the so-called 'no dobbing rule'[16]—a generalised reluctance to complain formally about the unacceptable conduct of fellow barristers. In the English context, Helena Kennedy (1992: 41) has exposed the centrality of this norm to the imagined community of the Bar: 'for many within the profession it is an unforgivable betrayal to criticise one's brothers in law'. As noted earlier in relation to sexual harassment, both barristers and solicitors interviewed displayed a generally negative attitude to becoming involved in a formalised complaint system, preferring instead to deal with the unacceptable behaviour of other barristers themselves. Some of the younger barristers said they were actively trying to acquire the strength of character to respond directly and effectively to misbehaviour towards them, as an important part of their professional skills as a barrister. Interviewees also described the peer pressure to avoid accusing a fellow member of the profession in anything other than a spontaneous and informal setting. They spoke of real and perceived consequences of complaining, such as damage to reputation, which many emphasised as a barrister's greatest asset. In the words of one woman:

> You become worried about people commenting about you—by putting a complaint in to the Ethics Committee, you're the subject of an enormous degree of chat in the lifts. (See also Weisbrot 1990: 199.)

The negative effects of complaining may escalate if the complaint is about sexist treatment by a male colleagues. A female solicitor explained:

> You whinge about it amongst yourselves and other female colleagues but that is about as far as you get . . . If you complain, you are even more alienated and ostracised, but if you don't complain, you're acquiescing.

Women who complain are not only considered to be betraying a colleague; they also 'get labelled as a sensitive female or hysterical and unable to cope'. This was highlighted by an anecdote related by one of the male judges during the interviews. He described a situation where a male barrister had been particularly rude to a female barrister during court proceedings. The judge said he did not

---

[16] 'Dobbing' is an Australian slang term for telling tales, ie exposing or complaining about another's transgression to someone in authority.

censure the male barrister, considering that the female barrister had 'brought it on herself' by her own behaviour in making some subjective criticism of a witness. The female barrister reported her opponent to the Ethics Committee, 'which she was entitled to do' but 'a bloke wouldn't have done it . . . there are rules by which the game is played.' Thus sexist treatment of women and the no dobbing 'tradition' mutually reinforce each other in (re)producing masculine solidarity at the Bar.

The social cohesion of the Bar should not be overstated, however. Hegemonic masculinity is only hegemonic, not totalising. Several interviewees maintained they were largely unaffected by mainstream Bar culture because, as individual practitioners, they could choose to ignore it or could effectively create their own work environment amongst a small group of colleagues. Small groups were described by some female (but no male) interviewees, as providing support and a sense of place for their members. They appear to operate as 'sub-cultures', with various bases: members of the same Readers' Course; common areas of practice; proximity of chambers; or sexuality ('there's the gay group'). A few interviewees also spoke about the Bar accommodating eccentric (male) individuals who operate way outside any sub-culture and the mainstream. One female barrister said 'there are some who are completely mad'.

Yet this picture of an environment in which hegemonic masculine values coexist with sub-cultural variation and eccentricity, with individuals able to choose the degree to which they participate in the mainstream, obscures important differences in power. In terms of achieving aspirations of a 'busy practice', silk, judicial appointment, or even the confidence to continue at the Bar, acceptance within the mainstream is vital, and a sense of belonging within a small group of friends and colleagues may not be enough. This is a phenomenon that affects 'non-mainstream' men as well as women, as one male barrister with aspirations for judicial appointment attested:

> It will be more difficult for me. I don't have a big practice, I am not part of the mainstream at the Bar . . . and the informal structure of the Bar is such that you have to toe the line if you want to receive acknowledgment and support for a move onto the bench.

Thus, conformity carries with it material rewards. The decision to stand outside the mainstream is not just a choice to assert a different identity, it also has material consequences.

5 WOMEN'S SUBVERSION OF TRADITION

I have noted the role of invented traditions and the way in which their claims to antiquity (although they may be of quite recent origin) imply continuity with an idealised past (Hobsbawm 1993: 1). Such claims are evident, for example, in a female QC's admonition that there are 'good historical reasons' for many of the rules and traditions of the Bar, and one should therefore be wary of 'fiddling with' them in response to the advent of women; or in the explanation by a High Court judge that

> Any professional group which for seven hundred years has comprised solely men is bound to have inherited attitudes which may sometimes seem unwelcoming to some new entrants (Kirby 1998: 132).

On this basis, women breach tradition simply by being at the Bar. It is also arguable that their sheer presence at the Bar fundamentally alters the practices of masculinity that occur there.[17] But women barristers have been seen to transgress the traditions of the Bar in two more particular ways: by queue jumping, and by forming their own community.

As we have seen, a successful career at the Bar and progress to judicial appointment has traditionally been based upon joining the mainstream, establishing mentoring and patronage relationships with more senior barristers, and working one's way up the hierarchy with their assistance. This avenue has generally been closed to women. For instance, some of the longest serving women at the Bar were continually passed over for appointment as QCs, waiting years longer than their male contemporaries to achieve this honour, if at all. The first handful of women appointed to superior courts in Victoria were 'tried out' in lower courts first, and then promoted after proving themselves judicially competent. In the past three to four years, however, the state Attorney-General has pursued an active policy of appointing women to the bench. As part of this policy, women of unprecedentedly low seniority have been made QCs, and some have barely had time to enjoy their new status before being elevated again to the ranks of the judiciary. Female appointments to the County Court (the middle-ranking court in the state) have even been made directly from the junior Bar.

Inevitably, these appointments have attracted a great deal of criticism, primarily focused on whether they were based on 'merit'. Clearly they were not, if 'merit' is understood to be accumulated by men according to the procedure outlined above. In advancing too fast, over the heads of meritorious men, these women were the targets of a significant level of resentment.[18] Some interviewees evidently believed that the appointments process had reached an unacceptable level of reverse discrimination in favour of women, despite the numbers of women on the bench still being objectively very low. Such criticism has a disciplining effect. Women interviewees stressed that while they might aspire to become a judge, they wished to be appointed 'on merit', not because they were women. Some indicated that they might now think twice about putting themselves forward or accepting an offer, so as to avoid the degree of scrutiny to

---

[17] For a similar argument in relation to women in the medical profession, see Pringle (1998).

[18] The Bar, of course, is not the only kind of organisation in which this phenomenon occurs. Similar responses have been noted in other studies of male-dominated workplaces, eg Kanter (1977: 216–17); Cockburn (1991: 67).

which recent female appointees had been subjected. Nevertheless, these appointments have had a significant impact in displacing the exclusively masculine constitution of the senior Bar and the bench.

The Women Barristers Association (WBA) was formed in 1993. Its aims include advancing equality for women at the Bar and in the legal profession generally, and providing a professional and social network for women barristers. The group meets regularly and plays different roles for its members and within the informal structures of the Bar. It has an advocacy function in the context of publicly representing the views of female barristers on legal and other issues. In terms of a support role for its members, our interviews indicated that WBA has provided some women with a sense of place at the Bar which had previously been lacking. For example, one woman had felt as if she was the only single mother at the Bar, but has now made links with other women coping in similar situations. WBA also provides a forum for women to network and exchange relevant information about cases and practice-related issues. In other words, WBA provides a counter-community (of the face-to-face rather than imagined kind) which offers members the support and friendship that the wider, masculine community of the Bar often fails to deliver to women.

A number of male judges, QCs and other senior barristers have been very supportive of WBA. On the other hand, 'a lot of people [both women and men] felt very threatened by' WBA. Four of the female barristers interviewed volunteered the view that it is 'not necessary to have a formal organisation' and that WBA is 'divisive' and 'polarises the Bar'. How the activities of a relatively small group of women could have such a dramatic impact is difficult to conceive, until one realises that the existence of WBA is a direct challenge to the underpinnings of the imagined community of the Bar—its much vaunted collegiality. By standing apart from the general fraternity of the Bar, WBA is indeed divisive, and polarisation then occurs around attitudes to the group: one cannot remain neutral to this questioning of the masculine order. In this way, WBA is different from other established sub-groupings such as the Criminal Bar Association, which do not cause any 'gender trouble'.

The objection to WBA put forward by one woman illustrates her adherence to the Bar's (contradictory) traditions. She considered that WBA had the potential to:

> encourage recalcitrant men, of which there are a majority at the Bar, in their view that women at the Bar are different . . . we are all just barristers . . . It creates the perception that women need some sort of organisation to support them because they can't stand up for themselves . . .

This woman sought to rely on the promise that 'we are all just barristers' as protection against sexist treatment, but if such treatment did occur, the appropriate response (in accordance with the no dobbing rule) was to stand up for oneself.

The effectiveness of the masculine cultural traditions of the Bar in suppressing gender solidarity among women was further demonstrated in our interviewees' lack of consciousness of systemic discrimination against women. A range of explanations other than gender bias were suggested for why there are so few female QCs and female barristers of long standing at the Bar. Typical comments included:

> I haven't experienced any difficulties. If other people are experiencing difficulties, I don't know whether it's because they are less able or if it's for other reasons.

and, 'It's an individual profession . . . you make your own opportunities or else you may be in the wrong job' (see also Kanter 1977: 228).

For some, belief in the Bar's traditions was maintained despite experiences of its worst aspects. For example, a senior barrister said of the Bar:

> I love it, I always have. For me it is a very happy, supportive environment . . . I feel I can go to anyone and discuss anything.

During the interview she also spoke of having been sexually harassed, excluded from prestigious work because she was unable to attend the men-only social clubs where the relevant contacts were made, and subject to unjustified criticism when she was made a QC. Alternatively, senior women recounting their experiences in the 'old days' expressed a firm belief in the rationality and modernising capability of the Bar, in asserting that such problems would not be encountered by young women today or in the future.[19] Young women might have been inclined to believe this too; yet they clearly are encountering the current manifestations of masculine domination:

> I honestly thought that sexism was not an issue, until I got out into the workforce . . . I can't believe this goes on, especially in a profession that is meant to be so enlightened, intellectually superior, leading the charge for legal rights . . . but it's just so male dominated and this stuff happens.

In addition to its destabilisation of the imagined community of the Bar, WBA represents a strong voice advocating that the Bar act in an enlightened way towards women. It thus helps to expose the conflict between the rational and more tribal elements of hegemonic masculinity, and to encourage a cultural shift in order to resolve this tension.

6 CONCLUSION

I have argued that the Bar is an imagined community sustained by acculturation processes, a hierarchical power structure and invented traditions of behaviour that reproduce and reinforce hegemonic masculinity. Women are able to perform

---

[19] The tendency to ignore, deny or downplay discrimination, particularly among senior women, is the subject of another article (Hunter 2002). Briefly, these reactions seem to testify to the Bar's power to produce (self-)disciplined subjects, who conform, with whatever level of difficulty, to hegemonic behaviours and views.

some aspects of masculinity, such as rationality/technical competence, total commitment to the job and to an extent camaraderie. Other aspects, however, constitute the community of barristers as one that is exclusive of women, and that exclusion is enacted on a daily basis. Justice Catherine Branson has noted that women barristers are offered '[t]he freedom to be an honorary man, or alternatively, an outsider' (Branson 1997: 4). Different women have assumed one or other of these identities to different extents, although those who have attempted to act as honorary men may still have been considered as outsiders by their male colleagues (see also Hull and Nelson 1998: 691; Sommerlad and Sanderson 1998: 184–92).

Nevertheless, taken to their logical conclusions, the roles of both honorary men and outsiders have the potential to disrupt the codes of hegemonic masculinity, the former in the guise of newly-minted women judges, and the latter in the assertion of a separate gender identity through the Women Barristers Association. Responses to these challenges (as to the original entry of women to the Bar) will inevitably result in new mutations of hegemonic masculinity, which may perhaps concede more space for women at the Bar.

7 REFERENCES

Anderson, Benedict. 1991. Rev. Ed. *Imagined Communities: Reflections on the Origin and Spread of Nationalism*. London: Verso.

Atkinson, Paul and Delamont, Sara. 1990. Professions and Powerlessness: Female Marginality in the Learned Occupations. *Sociological Review* 30(1): 90.

Branson, The Hon. Justice Catherine. 1997. Running on the Edge. Address to the Women Lawyers Association, October 15.

Buchbinder, David. 1998. *Performance Anxieties: Re-producing Masculinity*. Sydney: Allen & Unwin.

Butler, Judith. 1990. *Gender Trouble: Feminism and the Subversion of Identity*. New York: Routledge.

Cain, Maureen. 1976. Necessarily Out of Touch: Thoughts on the Social Organisation of the Bar. In *The Sociology of Law*, edited by P Carlin. Staffordshire: University of Keele.

Cheng, Cliff, ed. 1996. *Masculinities in Organizations*. Thousand Oaks: Sage.

Cockburn, Cynthia. 1991. *In the Way of Women: Men's Resistance to Sex Equality in Organisations*. London: Macmillan.

Collier, Richard. 1995. *Masculinity, Law and the Family*. London: Routledge.

Collinson, David and Hearn, Jeff. 1996. 'Men' at 'Work': Multiple Masculinities/ Multiple Workplaces. In *Understanding Masculinities: Social Relations and Cultural Arenas*, edited by M Mac an Ghaill. Buckingham: Open University Press.

Connell, Robert W. 1995. *Masculinities*. Sydney: Allen & Unwin.

Feldthusen, Bruce. 1990. The Gender Wars: 'Where the Boys Are'. *Canadian Journal of Women and the Law* 4: 66.

Gaudron, The Hon. Justice Mary. 1994. Speech to the Women Barristers' Association Dinner, 9 June.

Hearn, Jeff. 1992. *Men in the Public Eye: The Construction and Deconstruction of Public Men and Public Patriarchies*. London: Routledge.

Hobsbawm, Eric. 1993. Introduction: Inventing Traditions. In *The Invention of Tradition*, edited by E Hobsbawm and T Ranger. Cambridge: Cambridge University Press. Original edition, 1983.

Hobsbawm, Eric and Ranger, Terrence, eds. 1993. Reprint. *The Invention of Tradition*. Cambridge: Cambridge University Press. Original edition, 1983.

Hull, Kathleen E and Nelson, Robert L. 1998. Gender Inequality in Law: Problems of Structure and Agency in Recent Studies of Gender in Anglo-American Legal Professions. *Law & Social Inquiry* 23: 681.

Hunter, Rosemary. 2002. Talking Up Equality: Women Barristers and the Denial of Discrimination. *Feminist Legal Studies* 10: 113.

Hunter, Rosemary and McKelvie, Helen. 1998. *Equality of Opportunity for Women at the Victorian Bar: A Report to the Victorian Bar Council*. Melbourne: Victorian Bar Council.

Kanter, Rosabeth Moss. 1977. *Men and Women of the Corporation*. New York: Basic Books.

Kennedy, Helena. 1992. *Eve Was Framed: Women and British Justice*. London: Vintage.

Kirby, The Hon. Justice Michael. 1998. Women Lawyers—Making a Difference. *Australian Feminist Law Journal* 10: 125.

Naffine, Ngaire. 1990. *Law and the Sexes: Explorations in Feminist Jurisprudence*. Sydney: Allen & Unwin.

Pagone, GT. 1996. Employment Practices and Awareness of Diversity. IBA Conference, Committee 11 (Discrimination and Gender Equality), Berlin, 23 October.

Parker, Andrew. 1996. Sporting Masculinities: Gender Relations and the Body. In *Understanding Masculinities: Social Relations and Cultural Arenas*, edited by M Mac an Ghaill. Buckingham: Open University Press.

Pierce, Jennifer L. 1996. Rambo Litigators: Emotional Labor in a Male-Dominated Occupation. In *Masculinities in Organizations*, edited by C Cheng. Thousand Oaks: Sage.

Podmore, David and Spencer, Anne. 1982. Women Lawyers in England: The Experience of Inequality. *Work and Occupations* 9(3): 337.

Pringle, Rosemary. 1998. *Sex and Medicine: Gender, Power and Authority in the Medical Profession*. Cambridge: Cambridge University Press.

Smart, Carol. 1989. *Feminism and the Power of Law*. London: Routledge.

Sommerlad, Hilary and Sanderson, Peter. 1998. *Gender, Choice and Commitment: Women Solicitors in England and Wales and the Struggle for Equal Status*. Aldershot: Ashgate.

Thornton, Margaret. 1996. *Dissonance and Distrust: Women in the Legal Profession*. Melbourne: Oxford University Press.

Weisbrot, David. 1990. *Australian Lawyers*. Longman Cheshire.

8

New Zealand Women Lawyers at the End of the Twentieth Century

GEORGINA MURRAY

Abstract

This chapter outlines the situation of women lawyers in the legal profession in New Zealand. The data presented and evaluated show two things: on the one hand, the quantitative as well as the qualitative position of women lawyers compared to men has improved greatly over the last two decades; on the other hand, the sheer increase in numbers and the more balanced distribution across all areas and levels of professional activity are unlikely to lead automatically to a gradual evening out of remaining gender discrimination. In other words, the 'trickle-up effect' on its own will not solve their problem.

1 INTRODUCTION[1]

C LASS HAS BECOME an unfashionable concept, particularly amongst lawyers who like to enjoy the fruits of the class system's rewards while holding on to their belief that these are entirely due to their membership of a meritocracy. This does not detract from its usefulness as an analytical tool to help to identify exploitation, as for instance in the context of women lawyers in the New Zealand legal profession.

This class, or conflict perspective, originating with Marx and Engels (1950) but subsequently effectively used by a number of sociologists of law (eg Boehringer 1977, Fraser 1978, Caine 1979, McBarnet 1984, O'Malley 1984, Hunt 1985, Rueschemeyer 1988, Johnson, Gramm & Hoass 1989) explains the role of the law in the capitalist state. The underlying assumption of conflict theory is that the law in a capitalist state is class-discriminate. Early research into the composition of the legal profession shows that the unequal class and gender distribution in capitalist societies is reflected in the composition of the legal profession (Menkel-Meadow 1988, Larson 1977). In what follows, this theory is being put to the test.

---

[1] My thanks for information and/or editing advice go to Ms Ginny Fail, Ms Deborah Hollings, Ms Pam Nuttal and Dr Tom Bramble. They are of course not responsible for any of the following.

When I began work on the New Zealand legal profession in 1982, the differences within the profession, based on class, ethnicity and gender, were both glaringly obvious and under-researched (Murray 1984). My findings then were that the New Zealand legal profession was overwhelmingly entrepreneurial rather than civic in intent and that relative to other occupational groups lawyers came from homogeneous middle-class backgrounds. However, concealed by this class homogeneity was a profession internally highly stratified and offering very unequal access to rewards. Also, women lawyers interviewed frequently identified sexist treatment from male colleagues, while non-European (Pakeha) lawyers raised the issue of racist treatment from their colleagues.

Now legal profession research is more plentiful (Gatfield 1996, Nefertari 1994, Mayhew 1992, etc), but it indicates that gender bias persists. The 1999 New Zealand Law Society data show that women lawyers' incomes have a long way to catch up with those of their male colleagues, especially in the context of partnerships in large law firms. The rationale normally offered for the relatively poor rewards for female lawyers is women's late and hesitant entry into the profession. However, neither of these arguments is going to hold water for long in view of the deluge of women pouring into the profession on the one hand and the passing of time since they first entered in large numbers on the other. But even within its own limited terms, this 'trickle-up' hypothesis remains flawed, for it does not take into account the continuing and very real discrepancies in income levels. There remains both a quantitative and a qualitative difference in the rewards and treatment of men and women in the legal profession (Gatfield 1996), a situation which is not helped by the wider social and economic climate.

What follows is, firstly, a brief set of background information on the New Zealand legal profession and the role of women lawyers within it. This is followed by a presentation and critical discussion of data on gender-based stratification within the profession that have emerged from the 1999 New Zealand Law Society conference and other sources.

2 BACKGROUND INFORMATION ON THE LEGAL PROFESSION[2]

2.1 Socio-political Environment

The political, cultural and social environment in New Zealand during the period of 1970 to 1999 was adversely affected by an unfortunate combination of, on the one hand, an uneven economic decline since the 1970s (Roper 1997), and a rigid adherence to a regime of economic liberalism since 1984 (Kelsey 1999) on

---

[2] General information on the legal profession as well as more general factual information not credited to another source is taken from the 1998 *New Zealand Yearbook* (http://www.stats.govt.nz)

the other. In the period following the 1984 setting up of David Lange's Labour government, a raft of legislation was passed in record time. This legislation promoted a deregulated financial sector, a free-floating currency, the end of tariff protection for domestic industry, privatisation of state assets and a deregulated labour market. Later Conservative governments continued to tighten economic liberal legislation further.

For the population at large this period (1984–1999) brought about considerable personal insecurity and hardship: a drop in real wages, a rapidly declining welfare state system, and a rise in social tensions between and across different ethnic groups (Easton 1999, Jesson 1999, Kelsey 1999, Roper and Rudd 1997, *New Zealand Official Yearbook* 1998). The situation has been most severe for women generally and for ethnic minority women in particular, as it entailed casualisation and low wages for women and ethnic minorities. Nationally the highest female median income, across all ages, has been lower than the lowest male median income. On the other hand, most lawyers (including women) find themselves at the élite end of the occupational spectrum and have not only escaped damage, but have even been able to exploit the situation of increasing globalisation to their advantage.

2.2 The New Zealand Legal Administration

New Zealand law operates in a post-colonial environment. Post-colonialism means in this context that the New Zealand judiciary is independent of the New Zealand government but ultimately still accountable to the Privy Council. The Privy Council is a New Zealand court that sits in Britain. Its members are eminent British judges who deliver their judgments to the British sovereign who then makes the necessary final order. The Judicature Act of 1908 and the Constitution Act of 1986 established the principle of a judiciary independent of New Zealand government but not of British judgment. Not surprisingly, the New Zealand legal system shares a number of features with other common law countries, particularly other former British colonies. As in Australia, the Governor General appoints the High Court judges. Judges at higher and lower courts may be removed from office by the Governor General on the grounds of inability or misbehaviour. They are appointed from the ranks of the two branches of the advocacy, that is barristers and solicitors, but only after at least seven years of legal practice.

The final court of appeal for New Zealanders is the Judicial Committee of the Privy Council. Below it are the Court of Appeal, the High Court and the district courts. These courts also consist of a further subset of courts—family courts (established 1980), employment courts (established 1991), environment courts (established 1991), the Maori Land Court and a Maori Appellate Court (established 1993). There are over 100 tribunals. The integration of women into the judiciary is limited: one of eight Court of Appeal judges (the Hon. Sian Elias), four of 31 permanent High Court judges, none of the five acting and temporary High Court judges, and five out of 35 family court judges (AWLA March 1998b) are female.

2.3 New Zealand Women Lawyers—Key dates

New Zealand legal 'herstory' began in 1893 when women were recognised as persons before the law. This allowed Ms Ethel Benjamin to begin her law studies at Otago University. In 1897, due to the 1896 Royal Assent legislation, Ms Benjamin was able to become the first woman law graduate in New Zealand and, indeed, in the British Empire. She was entitled to hold a legal practising certificate but was still denied access to the Supreme Court library and was not invited to the Law Society's annual dinner.

In 1900 Ms Stella Henderson became the first female applicant for a law school lecturing position. Although her male colleagues testified to her being 'admirably fitted to fill a lectureship in a University College' she was not appointed (Gatfield 1996). In 1957 Ms Shirley Smith became the first woman in New Zealand to lecture in law (at Victoria University in the capital city, Wellington). Even by 1960 there were still only 30 women in the legal profession, as compared to 2,335 men. In 1971, the first Maori woman lawyer graduated. She was Ms Georgina Te Heu Heu from the Ngati Tuwharetoa people. (In 1998 Maori made up 15 per cent of the population.) In 1982, Ms Mary Tuilotolava was the first Pacific Islander to graduate. (Pacific Islanders represent five per cent of the population.) Ms Tuilotolava is a Tongan (Tongans are 0.9 per cent of the total population). The first woman judge, Augusta Wallace, was appointed in 1975, to the District Court. At Auckland University in 1979 the first gender-critical appraisal of the law was offered in a course called *Women in the Law* which was taught by Ms Margaret Wilson and Ms Pauline Tapp. Ms Wilson went on to become the founding Professor of Law at Waikato Law School in the 1990s.

In the mid- to late 1980s there were token appointments made of women to significant legal and professional positions, be it within professional organisations or in the judiciary. Throughout the 1980s the proportion of women among the law student population grew dramatically. By 1996, 27 per cent of those holding practising certificates were women.

3 WOMEN IN THE NEW ZEALAND LEGAL PROFESSION TODAY

The results of the New Zealand Law Society's 1999 survey were presented to members for discussion at their April annual conference. These 1999 data are compared here (where appropriate) to those of a 1984 survey done for the purposes of an MA dissertation in sociology submitted to Auckland University (Murray 1984).

3.1 Gender Profile of the Legal Profession

Overall, the number of lawyers in New Zealand has grown from 14 lawyers in 1851 to 7,985 in 1998. Of the annual practising certificates issued by the New Zealand Law Society in 1998, approximately 2,555 went to women and 5,430 to men, bringing the share of women in the profession up to 32 per cent. Although this means that women still represent less than half of the legal profession, they now dominate at the stage of entry to the profession. In 1999, 826 were admitted, making their share 55 per cent.

In 1971, the profile of the New Zealand legal profession was very male dominated (1.9 per cent women), with high numbers of employed lawyers and very little legal unemployment (0.32 per cent). The average age of lawyers across the legal professions as a whole was 41.5 years, with judges and magistrates being the oldest (56.9), followed by barristers and solicitors (42.6) and other lawyers (40.9). The total number of lawyers in the 1971 sample was 2,733. (Crothers, 1984)

By 1981, this profile had changed somewhat with more women in the profession, slightly higher unemployment and a lower average age. Both samples, that of 1971 and that of 1981, are characterised by a large and growing number of private and public employees, brought about by a period of recession and a desire for job security. (Crothers, 1984)

By 1999, Law Society statistics show women lawyers still to be predominantly employees, while featuring sparsely in the high prestige areas of the legal professions. For example, women practising lawyers were more likely than men to be employed by central or local government (50 per cent) or in firms as corporate lawyers (32 per cent). Their presence was less marked in private practice (30 per cent of solicitors), but—a new development since my 1984 survey—women were gravitating towards barrister-soles (29 per cent) as an option, ie barristers not working in chambers but in their own private practice.

However, as Gatfield points out, the large number of women barrister-soles may not accurately reflect the number actually practising at the 'independent bar'. In some district law societies, the category of 'barrister' includes those barristers working in government agencies, state owned enterprises, community law centres, unions, corporations and tertiary education institutions (Gatfield 1996). Many women may also work part-time and use the barrister ticket to avoid insurance and other professional costs incurred if they chose to practise as solicitors. The figures do not record part-time workers (Hollings 1997). In total, the 1999 Law Society data show that there were 18 women lawyers in unions, 244 in government organisations, 15 in community law centres, 139 in corporate bodies, 15 in academia, and 10 in municipal local government. All of these women could be classified as barrister-soles without being dependent on solicitors' briefs.

There are still relatively few women partners in firms (14 per cent) and very few female Queens Counsel (six per cent). District courts, not being nearly as

highly regarded as the High Court, have more women (16 per cent), but somewhat surprisingly the High Court, being very highly regarded, has almost the
same percentage of women judges (14 per cent) as district courts. The Auckland
Women's Law Association complains about the relative lack of women on the
bench and suggests that there are good reasons for appointing more women
judges, particularly on the family court bench (AWLA March, 1998b). Curtis
argues in favour of more women judges in family courts because the bench is
unrepresentative of its clients (after all, 50 per cent of these lawyers' clients are
women or girls). This would help to alleviate the existing gender bias and would
introduce perspectives currently missing (Curtis 1997).

The Auckland Women Lawyer's Association argues against the assumption
that the reason for the low percentage of women judges in family courts is their
lack of experience because there are plenty of experienced women practitioners
working there. There is increasing concern that appointments are not based on
merit but (negatively) on gender (AWLA March 1998b). According to Hollings
(1997), women practitioners still suffer systematic discrimination in the courts.
'Without a doubt men and women advocates are in general perceived differently
in the courtroom by judges'. She identifies three reasons for this: firstly,
women's relatively recent entry into the legal profession; secondly, their perceived lack of authority; and thirdly, their rejection of an aggressive adversarial
stance in favour of a search for consensus ('let's discuss this and see if we can
come up with a just answer').

Women lawyers consistently appear to be over-represented in the least desirable areas of the law in relation to remuneration, intrinsic interest, and prestige.
My 1984 survey clearly showed them to be under-represented in commercial and
criminal law (Table 1).

The 1999 Law Society survey echoes these findings. Women lawyers were still
to be found mainly in work that was less well paid, relatively boring, involved

Table 1: Lawyers' Specialisms (1984)

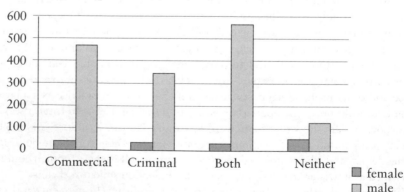

SOURCE: Murray 1984.

less client contact, and was perceived to be particularly suited to women (what Epstein (1981) calls 'blue-sky work'). Women lawyers dominated in family law (76 per cent of those practising in family law) and had a sizable share in relatively new areas, such as employment law (55 per cent), resource management law (51 per cent) and administrative law (41 per cent). Trusts and estates, the classic area of 'blue-sky work', which in the 1984 survey represented the area with the highest level of female lawyers, still had 35 per cent of women lawyers working there. Nevertheless, by 1999 the gender division into 'blue-sky work' on the one hand and commercial and related work on the other was no longer so clearly pronounced, with women holding a 35 per cent share in taxation law, 34 per cent in property law, 32 per cent in commercial law, and 32 per cent in criminal law. One area of specialisation where the proportion of women is steadily increasing is academia, where they currently hold nearly one third of law school posts.

Table 2: Distribution of Women Lawyers across Areas of Work (1999)

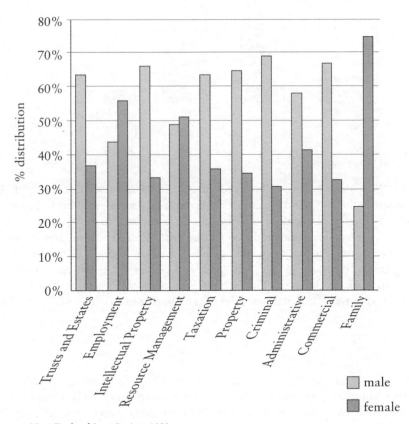

SOURCE: New Zealand Law Society 1999

These data show a more even distribution of women and men in the various areas of legal work. There remains the question whether women have become integrated as specialists or as non-specialists (the survey defines as specialists those who spend 75 per cent of their time practising in one particular area of law).

3.2 Women in Law Schools

In 1998, 62 per cent of New Zealand law students were women. Their academic achievement was good (having even exceeded men's performance in the 1984 survey) (Table 3):

Table 3: Male and Female Law Graduates' Average Academic Results (1984)

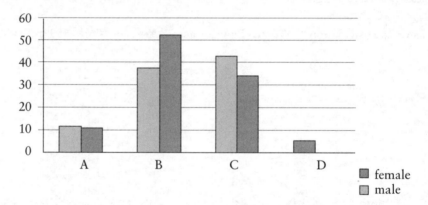

SOURCE: Murray 1984.

In 1995, women made up 28 per cent of a total of 5,935 academic law staff. As elsewhere in the New Zealand university system, they are most likely to be found in junior untenured positions (68 per cent of lecturers, associate lecturers and temporary lecturers), compared to only one dean (Professor Margaret Wilson), two professors, three associate professors and eight senior lecturers. Interestingly, Professor Wilson left Auckland University in the early 1990s to establish Waikato University Law School, where law was taught within a sociological context, in particular that relevant to Maori and women (AWLA 1997c).

4 INCOME

Women lawyers' earnings have always been below those of their male colleagues, but secrecy surrounding the topic has often prevented this from becoming public knowledge. My survey of 1984 produced some shocking results (Table 4).

Table 4: Comparative Incomes of Men and Women Lawyers in 1984 (NZ $)

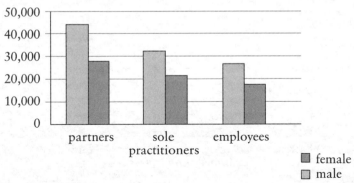

SOURCE: Murray, 1984.

The most spectacular discrepancy was that between the income of male and female partners, and the most striking similarity that between the incomes of male employees and female partners. These features have remained intact ever since, although income levels generally have increased dramatically.

A *Lawtalk* report of lawyers' incomes five years after graduating from Law School found a $6,326 difference in salaries of men and women, claiming that 'Women lawyers level peg on salary after five years' (*Lawtalk* 1997). It also noted a subsequent widening of the gender gap. According to the 1999 Law Society study findings women lawyers' earnings were well below those of male lawyers in every category other than that of employee, where salary levels generally were poor. The biggest gender-based discrepancy appeared later in lawyers' careers, most particularly in large-firm partnerships (women averaged $58,000, men $195,500).

Why do women partners in large firms continue to accept such low earnings? After all, $58,000 for women partners in large firms is only $9,000 more than male clerks get and significantly less than the average income of women partners in small firms ($82,800). Are women partners in large firms still in ignorance of their male colleagues' larger salaries? Or are they trading income for the prestige of belonging to an old established firm? Is it that women partners in large firms are such a new phenomenon that they are all still very low in terms of seniority? Or is it that most fees from partnerships come from business, and these companies do not welcome women either on their boards or as business colleagues (the latter being supported by the fact that there are few women in the world of top business in New Zealand (Murray 1990))?

Women barrister soles are the most highly paid group amongst women lawyers in New Zealand. Admittedly, they do take heavy risks going out by themselves and putting themselves at the mercy of firms to brief them, but these risks are paying off. Women barrister soles have an average annual income of $122,00, compared to male barrister soles with $149,800. But as already pointed

132   *Georgina Murray*

Table 5: Full-Time Income by Position and Gender in 1999 (NZ $)

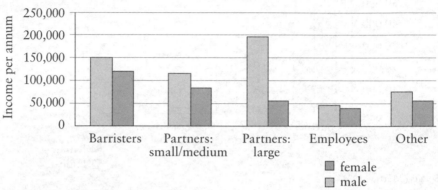

SOURCE: New Zealand Law Society 1999

out (Gatfield 1996), this could be deceptive as these women may not be dependent on solicitors' briefs but could be in a variety of forms of employment.

Judges' incomes are identical for both sexes because they are determined by the Higher Salaries Commission, under the mandate of the 1977 Higher Salaries Commission Act. A High Court judge earns $204,000, whereas a district court judge earns only $163,000. Given that professionals in New Zealand are an exclusive group of only 13 per cent of the working population and that 37 per cent of them earn less than $40,000, lawyers are very income-rich.

5 TIME SPENT IN THE PROFESSION

Women's reasons for leaving the profession remained consistent between 1984 and 1999. In the 1984 survey, two main reasons were given. The first was to have children:

> I decided that I could not cope with children and a full-time career. I decided that I would do it properly. I just retired. I saw family and the law as alternatives. (Laughs) The modern woman's dilemma. While the children are young it's not fair to them. (Interviewee 1984)

The second reason was the general unpleasantness associated with being a woman employee in a law firm:

> It makes you think that it's so unfair—so unjust. It's something that no one questions. If they did, they would not come up with the right answers. Nothing would be done about it because it's all so stacked in their favour. When one partner was asked what he thought of women in the law he said, 'What I think is not important. I have to get on with them, even if I don't like them, because one day they'll outnumber us and I want to be on their good side.' (Interviewee 1984)

In 1984, some male lawyers quite openly acknowledged their prejudice against female colleagues:

> I have seen them go through law school with children and trying to get jobs and they cannot . . . And fair enough, too. The job is demanding, not many men can do it properly, let alone women. I feel that women are not as suited as men, and women with children are not suited at all. (Interviewee 1984)

Gatfield regards the problem of discrimination as an intractable one (Gatfield 1996). She cites evidence from the Human Rights Commission that in 80 per cent of cases, women's complaints are made after they have left the job and no longer need to fear recrimination. For her the high turnover in a firm (a common phenomenon) is one of the clearest signs that sexual harassment is taking place or that there exists a glass ceiling for women lawyers. In the 1999 Law Society report, women dominated the category of those who stayed in the profession for no more than five years (46 per cent); the other end of the continuum was dominated by men, 41 per cent of whom stayed in the profession for more than 20 years.

Traditionally it has been the young vulnerable women lawyers who left the profession early (Table 6). When asked to reflect on her 40 years spent in the law, Master Anne Gambrill from the High Court bench said she had seen with dismay the high numbers of young women lawyers who left the profession soon after admission:

Table 6: Number of Years since Admission as Barrister and/or Solicitor (1999)

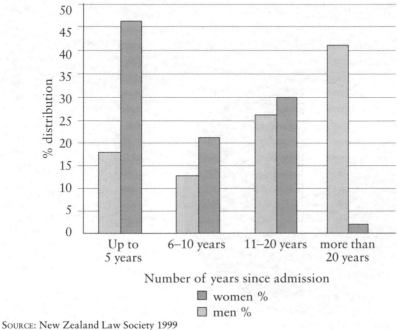

Number of years since admission
■ women %
■ men %

Source: New Zealand Law Society 1999

> I fear that, especially with the high number of graduates these days, for those who drop out or opt for long periods out of the profession, it will become increasingly hard to re-enter the profession. I think it is this fear that made me hang on through the years when it was difficult for both Chris and me to cope with practice and family (AWLA 1998c).

In the 1990s, women lawyers were no longer so much younger than male lawyers. By 1991, more than 50 per cent of women lawyers were between the ages of 30 and 49 (Gatfield 1996). This could mean at least two things: either that women were having their babies later (a factor evident in the wider population), or that even more hardened older women were leaving what they perceived to be very difficult working conditions. Thus Aitken, President of the Auckland Women's Law Association, writes about '*the working mother's dilemma*' and her own decision that '*something had to give or my children's enduring memory of their childhood would be me saying "hurry up"* '. Aitken left her South Auckland Chambers and took up a less onerous, less time-consuming position: '*I finally feel as though a sense of calm is returning to family life. I can have time with the kids where I don't feel constantly guilty*' (AWLA 1997a). Other women complain about being 'unsupported and constantly put down by (their) managing partner' (Lamb 1995).

Table 7 shows that women are considering part-time work as a serious option. It also shows that unemployment does not seem to rate as a major problem for either sex. In 1999, only 21 unemployed women lawyers were recorded. Unemployment for law graduates fell from 4 per cent in March 1991 to 2 per cent in March 1996 (*Lawtalk* 1997), while the average unemployment figure for New Zealand in 2000 is 7 per cent.

Table 7: Part-Time / Full-Time Employment for Lawyers (1999)

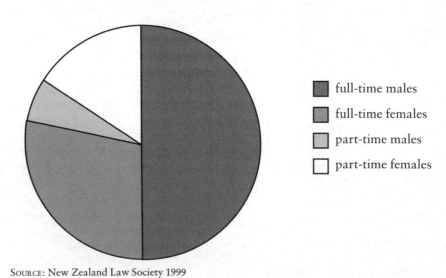

full-time males
full-time females
part-time males
part-time females

Source: New Zealand Law Society 1999

6 PROFESSIONAL ORGANISATIONS FOR WOMEN LAWYERS

In the 1980s, there was a growing awareness and public articulation of the gender bias in the legal profession. Two Law Society reports detailed this before I wrote my own in 1984 (Sargisson 1981, and Sargisson 1982). In 1984, the informal networking of Hannah Sargisson, Nancy Dolan, Rowena Lewis, Sian Elias and Margaret Wilson led to the inaugural meeting of the Women Lawyers Association (AWLA), a women-only organisation (Gatfield 1996). By May 1987, 81 per cent of Auckland women lawyers were members, with Helen Melrose as the first President. The AWLA adopted for itself the task of identifying discriminatory practices and of providing advice to women members in need. Women lawyers can belong to both their provincial law society and their society's subcommittee association for women. There are four Women's Law Society subcommittees in the major provinces—Auckland, Wellington, Canterbury and Otago. Maori women lawyers can join Hunga Roia Maori o Aotearoa (the Maori Law Society). This is a society for both sexes with women having a fairly prominent role.

7 CONCLUSION

Our evidence bears out the applicability of the conflict theory to the situation of women in the New Zealand Legal profession in that, along with women generally, they continue to represent a reserve army of labour. They are being paid less than men and are fired, rehired and casualised more easily. On the other hand, as lawyers, women lawyers are beneficiaries of the élite social status of their profession.

Even under the New Labour government women lawyers can be expected to be exposed to some degree to the adverse effects of economic liberal policy favoured by politicians from all political parties and resulting in the downsizing of public service employment opportunities which for women have always been attractive.

The 'trickle-up effect' of the growing number of women entering the legal profession is unlikely to solve the problem of women's inferior position in the profession. There are two reasons. Firstly, larger numbers of women rising up through the professional hierarchy will not remove the existing pay differential within sub-groupings. Secondly, and more seriously, conflict theory predicts that the increasing feminisation of the legal profession will result not in an improvement of the situation of women lawyers but rather in male lawyers leaving the profession in favour of more attractive fields.

Women lawyers continue to express concern about the lack of equity in the New Zealand legal profession (Hollings 1997, AWLA 1997b, AWLA 1997c, Gatfield 1996.). Thus Wilson argues, 'There are many conditions that contribute to the inequality of women. A lot of these can be addressed by child-care, better hiring practices and merit. But there is also an element called discrimination' (AWLA 1997b). For her, concerns regarding lack of equity of treatment are linked with concerns about the impact on women of the 'market paradigm' and 'a lack of vision for what is the role of law in the restructured New Zealand' (cf also Bandarage 1997).

8 REFERENCES

Abel, Richard L. 1989. *American Lawyers*, New York, Oxford University Press.

AWLA. 1997a. Presidential Profile. Emma Aitken—1998 AWLA President, *AWLA Monthly Update*, December, pp. 1–3.

AWLA. 1997b. Ursula Patel, *AWLA Monthly Update*, September/October, p. 5.

AWLA. 1997c. Profile—Professor Margaret Wilson Still Working for Women, *AWLA Monthly Update*, November, pp. 1–4.

AWLA. 1998a. Cuts to Legal Aid, *AWLA Monthly Update*, July, pp. 1–3.

AWLA. 1998b. Bench Warming—When Will We See More Family Court Judges? *AWLA Monthly Update*, March, pp. 1–3.

AWLA. 1998c. Master Gambrill Celebrates 40 Years in the Law. *AWLA Monthly Update*, April, pp. 1–3

AWLA. 1998d. Paid Paternity Leave, *AWLA Monthly Update*, October, p. 2.

AWLA. 1998e. Cathy Rodgers Is New AWLA President, *AWLA Monthly Update*, December, pp. 1–2.

Bandarage, A. 1997. *Women, Population and Global Crisis: a Political Economic Analysis*, London & New Jersey, Zed Books.

Boehringer, G. 1977. The Dialectics of Capitalist Legal Policy, *Australian Left Review*, n. 55: 51–58.

Caine, Maureen. 1979. The General Practice Lawyer and the Client: Towards a Radical Conception, *International Journal of the Sociology of Law*, n. 7, p. 331.

Crothers, C. 1984. *Statistical Profile of the Legal Profession*. Auckland University. Departmental Paper (unpubl.)

Curtis, C. 1997. *AWLA Monthly Update*, September/ October, p. 5.

Easton, Brian. 1999. *The Whimpering of the State. Policy after MMP*, Auckland University Press, Auckland.

Epstein, Cynthia. 1981. *Women in the Law*, Basic Books, New York.

Evans, W ed. 1962. *Law and Sociology: Exploratory Essays*. Glencoe, IL: Free.

Fraser, A. 1978. The Legal Theory We Need Now, *Socialist Review*, n. 40–41, pp. 147–187.

Gatfield, Jill. 1996. *Without Prejudice: Women in the Law*, Brookers Ltd, Wellington.

Hollings, Deborah. 1997. Advocacy and Gender, *AWLA Monthly Update*, May, pp. 2–4.

Hunt, Alan. 1985. The Ideology of Law: Advances and Problems in Recent Applications of the Concept of Ideology to the Analysis of the Law. *Law Sociological Review*, n. 19 (1) pp. 11–37.

Jesson, Bruce. 1999. *Only their Purpose Is Mad*, Dunmore Press, Palmerston North.

Johnson, L, Gramm, W and Hoass, D. 1989. Marx's Law of Profit: the Current State of the Controversy, *Atlantic Economic Journal*, Dec., v. 17, n. 4, pp. 55–58.

Kelsey, Jane. 1999. *Reclaiming the Future. New Zealand and the Global Economy*, Bridget Williams Books, Wellington.

Lamb, E. 1995. Interview with Ester Lamb, *AWLA Monthly Update*, October, p. 7.

Larson, Margali. 1977. *The Rise of Professionalism: A Sociological Analysis*, Berkeley: University of California Press.

Lawtalk. 1997. Report Finds Women Lawyers Level Pegging on Salary after five Years, 480, July, p. 7.

Marx, Karl and Engels, Friedrich. 1950. *Basic Writing on Politics and Philosophy*, ed L Furer, Garden City, NY: Doubleday.

Mayhew, L and Reiss, A. 1969. The Social Organisation of Legal Contracts, *American Sociological Review*, n. 34 (3), pp. 309–18.

McBarnet, Doreen. 1984. Law and Capital: The Role of the Legal Firm and the Legal Actor, *International Journal of Sociology*, n. 14, p. 231.

Menkel-Meadow, Carrie. 1989. Feminisation of the Legal Profession: The Comparative Sociology of Women Lawyers, in *Lawyers in Society*, eds Richard L Abel & Philip SC Lewis, Berkeley: University of California Press, vol. 3. pp. 196–285.

Murray, Georgina. 1984. *Sharing in the Shingles*, unpublished MA thesis, Auckland University, Auckland.

Murray, Georgina. 1990. *Corporate Capitalism in New Zealand*, unpublished PhD thesis, Auckland University, Auckland.

O'Malley, Pat. 1984. *Law, Democracy and Capitalism: A Sociology of Australian Legal Order*, Sydney, Allen and Unwin.

Nefertari, N. 1994. Dysfunction in a Law Office (Do you Recognize Anyone Here?), *Law Practice Management*, 46.

New Zealand Law Society. 1999. *Material on Women Lawyers*, Wellington, New Zealand.

New Zealand Official Yearbook. 1998. Wellington Government Printer, pp. 103, 227. Online http:/www.stats.govt.nz

Roper, Brian. 1997. New Zealand's Postwar Economic History, in Roper, B and C Rudd. 1997, pp. 3–21.

Roper, Brian and Rudd, Chris (eds). 1997. *The Political Economy of New Zealand*, Auckland: Auckland University Press.

Rueschemeyer, Dietrich. 1988. Comparing Legal Professions: A State Centered Approach, in *Lawyers in Society*, Richard L Abel & Philip SC Lewis (eds), Berkeley: University of California Press, vol. 3. pp. 289–321.

Sargisson, Hannah. 1981. *Report on Women in the Law*. Auckland Law Society Monograph.

Sargisson, Hannah. 1982. *Women in the Legal Profession*, Auckland Law Society Monograph.

Todd, A. 1997. Women Lawyers' Salaries, *Law Talk*, 508, October, p. 195.

Tremewan, L. 1997. 'Friends' wanted, *AWLA Monthly Update*, December.

9

The Status of Women Lawyers in the United Kingdom

CLARE MS McGLYNN*

Abstract

The aim of this chapter is to detail the extent of the progress made by women lawyers in the UK at the turn of the twentieth century. An account is given, largely in statistical terms, of the increasing representation of women in many fields of legal activity, together with detail of the areas in which women remain under-represented and marginalised. It is dangerous to generalise about all 'women lawyers' and to talk about the UK as a whole, but from the analysis that follows it appears that women working and studying in the law tend to be under-represented, underpaid and marginalised. More worrying is evidence of a retrenchment in some quarters, with the progress that women have been making stagnating and in some cases reversing. At the turn of the century, almost one hundred years since women were first let into the profession of law, it is not clear that the continued progress can be taken as a given.

1 INTRODUCTION

ALMOST A CENTURY after women were 'let in' to the profession of law in the United Kingdom, they generally remain marginalised, under-represented and under-paid (McGlynn 1998, Sommerlad and Sanderson 1998). It was only in 1919 that the legislature adopted the Sex Discrimination (Removal) Act which finally allowed women to practise as lawyers, overturning the common law decisions which had declared them unfit to take up public office (Sommerlad and Sanderson 1998: 51–117). The years following 1919 showed that although the formal bar to women's participation in the legal profession had been removed, informal barriers remained; and it is such informal practices which continue to limit women's opportunities. The aim of this overview is to detail the extent of the progress made by women lawyers in the

* I should like to thank Ann Sinclair for her invaluable research assistance.

UK at the turn of the twentieth century. An account is given, largely in statistical terms, of the increasing representation of women in many fields of legal activity, together with detail of the areas in which women remain under-represented and marginalised.[1]

2 THE STRUCTURE OF LEGAL EDUCATION AND THE PROFESSION

In order to place the following discussion in context, it is important to outline, albeit briefly, the structure of the English legal profession. The first stage of legal education is carried out at undergraduate level where students study for three years (full-time). Students wishing to practise law have to complete a further year of legal training after their undergraduate studies and there are separate courses for solicitors and barristers.[2]

The legal profession in England is divided into two branches, barristers and solicitors, and it is not possible to be qualified as both at the same time. Traditionally, barristers have had an exclusive right of audience in higher courts and have not normally been instructed by lay clients. Barristers are self-employed, although they often work together in 'chambers' where administrative assistance and resources are shared. Judges are traditionally drawn from the rank of barristers. Solicitors are instructed by lay clients and may instruct a barrister if required. Solicitors can operate as sole practitioners but tend to work in partnerships of other solicitors and the profession is also self-regulating. It is also possible for solicitors and barristers to work 'in-house' for companies and government, in which case they generally have the status of employees.

There are approximately 95,000 solicitors qualified in England & Wales (Cole 1998: 2) and 9,932 barristers (Bar Council 2000). In recent years, the distinctions between the two branches of the profession have reduced as each branch takes on more of the functions of the other. Thus, many solicitors conduct advocacy work in the higher courts, and many barristers give advice on non-contentious work. Increasingly, the judiciary is being drawn from the ranks of solicitors.

---

[1] The data which follow predominantly concern England & Wales, largely due to the absence of relevant data in the other jurisdictions. For example, reference to Northern Ireland can only be made because a report was published in 1999 on women solicitors in Northern Ireland. In addition, there are little data available for Scotland where the profession has all but refused to take any steps to recognise that discrimination may be a problem. The data are drawn from a wide range of sources; it is not, unfortunately, possible to refer readers to a single document or report which contains the information required as there has been no comparable quasi-governmental investigation into the status of women lawyers, as has been the case in other jurisdictions. Finally, it should be noted that England & Wales, Northern Ireland and Scotland are three separate legal jurisdictions, with their own legal systems and laws, and each with their own processes for legal training and regulation of the profession (Walker 1992, Dickson 1993, Bailey and Gunn 1996).

[2] Potential solicitors must complete the Legal Practice Course and barristers the Bar Vocational Course, both of which are one year (full-time).

3 HISTORICAL BACKGROUND: THE ENTRY OF WOMEN INTO LAW

3.1 Judicial Exclusion

The first application by a woman to be admitted as a solicitor in England was made in 1876. The application was rejected and it seems no further action was taken (Birks 1960: 276). Although it appears that at least a few women acted as legal assistants to solicitors and barristers in the years towards the end of the nineteenth century (Birks 1960: 276), it was another 30 years until a further challenge was made to the male monopoly of the law. A bill was introduced into Parliament in 1912 to enable women to become solicitors and barristers but failed to get any support (Birks 1960: 276). At around the same time, Gwyneth Bebb's application to be registered as a solicitor was rejected by the Law Society. Bebb's appeal was similarly rejected by the Court of Appeal which claimed that she was not a 'person' within the terms of the Solicitors Act 1843. Lord Justice Swinfen Eady said that it was sufficient to rest the case on the fact that 'inveterate' practice had shown that women had not been solicitors, which meant that the law is that women cannot be solicitors (*Bebb v Law Society* 1914). The common law's endorsement of custom and tradition, its tendency to look back rather than forward, was used as a justification for the continued exclusion of women (Sommerlad and Sanderson 1998; Mossman 1991: 283–300). To cap it all, the English judiciary described this exclusion as a 'privilege of the sex' (*Chorlton v Lings* 1886).

The fight for change was continued by the Committee for the Admission of Women to the Solicitors Profession (Birks 1960: 227). A private members bill was introduced in Parliament in 1914, but failed, as did a further attempt in 1917. By 1919 success was achieved with the passing of the Sex Discrimination (Removal) Act which decreed that women were, in fact, persons, and that they could hold public office. The significance of the legal struggles over the admittance of women to the legal profession can be seen not so much in the micro effect of delaying the entry of a few women by a few years, but in the ideology and culture which these struggles and their resistance reveal (Sommerlad and Sanderson 1998).

Thus, although the formal barriers to women qualifying as lawyers may have fallen in 1919, this did not mean that women were accepted into the profession. There remained a very small base from which to draw women entrants to the profession and thus it was of no surprise that there were not large numbers of women seeking admittance.

3.2 The First Women Solicitors

The first woman solicitor, Madge Easton Anderson, was admitted in Scotland in 1920. England and Wales followed shortly thereafter with Maud Crofts,

Mary Pickup and Mary Sykes being admitted in December 1922 (Jervis 1997). The first women solicitors tended to practise in the few areas which were deemed suitable, such as matrimonial and probate work, and tended to go into practice with family members. In 1923 the '1919 Club' was formed for women solicitors and the association was later renamed the Association of Women Solicitors.

The number of women solicitors hardly increased until the 1960s and 1970s (Table 1). The numbers only went into triple figures in 1973, with 222 women (13 per cent of the profession) being admitted. The increase in women solicitors resulted from the combination of a number of factors. First, there was a transformation of legal training in that a formal university education became the norm for entry into the law, rather than an apprenticeship. This assisted women whose educational qualifications were certainly of the same standard as men, and often better. In addition, the profession of the 1960s and 1970s was undergoing structural changes brought about by the greater involvement of services funded by the state which led to an increasing demand for solicitors, and the distribution of work became less reliant on networks from which women were excluded (Sommerlad 1995).

Table 1: Women and men admitted to the solicitors' profession 1923 to 1998 (Law Society 1988: 9; Cole 1998: 75; McGlynn 1998: 95)

Year	Men	Women	Total	% Women
1923	436	8	444	2
1933	580	10	590	2
1943	114	8	122	7
1953	614	35	649	5
1963	768	37	805	5
1973	1,542	222	1,764	13
1983	1,637	959	2,596	37
1986	1,521	1,204	2,725	44
1990–91	2,238	2,027	4,265	48
1991–92	2,280	2,184	4,464	48.9
1992–93	2,160	2,257	4,417	51.1
1993–94	2,281	2,520	4,801	52.5
1994–95	2,229	2,466	4,695	52.5
1995–96	2,203	2,417	4,620	52.3
1996–97	2,590	2,827	5,417	52.2
1997–98	2,784	2,901	5,685	51.0

3.3 Admitting Women to the Bar and Bench

The story of women entering the Bar is very similar to that of the solicitors' profession. The pressure for change began in the 1870s when 92 women signed a petition requesting permission to attend lectures in Lincoln's Inn (one of the four Inns of Court which play a regulatory role in the profession). Not surprisingly, the Benchers of the Inn rejected the request, not considering that a reason was needed (Kennedy 1978: 148). Thirty years later it appeared that there had been a change of heart when Gray's Inn accepted Bertha Cave in 1902. However, it turned out that this had been an oversight on the part of the Inn and they soon rectified their mistake stating that 'males, and males alone, were to be admitted to practise at the bar' (Fisher 1999: 707). Thus, as with the solicitors' profession, it was not until the passage of the 1919 Sex Discrimination (Removal) Act that women were admitted to the Bar.

Ivy Williams became the first barrister to be called to the Bar. Twenty women barristers were practising when the census in 1921 was taken, a mere 0.7 per cent of the Bar (Abel 1988: 80). Perhaps not surprisingly, of those women who were called in 1920, only 20 per cent were married, compared with 67 per cent of men (Abel 1988: 82). By 1931 the numbers had tripled to 79, 2.7 per cent of the Bar, and by 1951 there were 151 women barristers amounting to the grand total of five per cent of the Bar (Abel 1988: 80). However, this does not account for the actual number of women barristers practising. It has been estimated that only 68 women were even nominally in practice in 1957, and no more than 45 were actually practising (Abel 1988: 80).

Progress was being made, but it was 'slow and grudging' (Abel 1988: 148). As with the solicitors' profession, although formal prohibitions on women were removed in 1919, informal barriers remained. It was not until the 1960s that there were any women judges, with Elizabeth Lane being the first woman County Court judge (Kennedy 1992: 57). A few years later, she also became the first woman to sit on a High Court bench (Kennedy 1992: 57). Elizabeth Lane was also the first woman to argue an appeal before the House of Lords in 1946 (Kennedy 1992: 58). But neither of these successes brought about rapid changes. By 1968, there was only one woman on the High Court bench, one woman County Court judge and one woman QC (Abel 1988: 149). Eight years later, there were only four QCs, two High Court judges and five Circuit Judges. In 1977, there were only two women High Court Judges, and seven circuit judges, eight recorders and four QCs (Pearson and Sachs 1980: 406) These were remarkable achievements, yet 30 years later, there are only eight women High Court judges (see below).

However, even in 1976, the lack of senior women could not be accounted for in terms of the existence of only small numbers of suitably qualified women. In 1976 there were 80 women of over 15 years' call (experience) who were eligible for senior appointments, and only 17 of whom had been appointed—a proportion of 21 per cent (Kennedy 1978: 150). The proportion of men with over 15 years' call in senior positions was 53 per cent (Kennedy 1978: 150). In 1977–78, there were only two women out of 109 Benchers in Lincoln's Inn, one out of 140 in Inner Temple, two out of 142 in Middle Temple, and one out of 89 in Gray's Inn (Abel 1988: 84). By 1985, the figures of women were zero, one, two, zero, respectively (Abel 1988: 84).

It was extremely difficult for women to start their training as a barrister in the early 1970s. Studies showed that women were able to get pupillages, but it was that one step further, a tenancy in a set of chambers, which eluded them (Kennedy 1978: 151). Many chambers openly admitted to a 'no women' policy, even after the passage of the Sex Discrimination Act in 1975. However, as chambers are not partnerships and tenants are not employees, the provisions of the Sex Discrimination Act did not apply to those seeking tenancies. This situation was not remedied until the 1990 Courts and Legal Services Act. Of course, this is not to suggest that all chambers were the same. Baroness Helena Kennedy QC has told of how one set of chambers changed their 'no women' policy to 'no other women', after it admitted the daughter of the Head of Chambers (Kennedy 1978: 151).

In 1975 the Bar Council established a Special Committee on Women's Careers, disbanded shortly thereafter, and an unpublished paper of that committee recognised that a quota system was in operation in most chambers, with the maximum number of women being two. However, resistance to any change was strong. At a meeting of Heads of Chambers in 1975 which was considering the oversupply of barristers, one Head of Chambers said: 'Our prime concern must be for those young men in our chambers with wives and mortgages' (Kennedy 1978: 153).

4 THE FIRST WOMEN LAW STUDENTS AND LEGAL ACADEMICS

Although law became a subject of university study in the early part of the nineteenth century, it was not until the 1960s, with the growth in higher education generally, that numbers of law students became significant. It was also around this time that the old polytechnics, now (new) universities, began to offer law degrees, thus also contributing to an increase in the number of law students.[3]

Although the first woman was admitted to read law at University College London in 1873, it was Dorothy Bonjaree who was the first woman to be granted a degree in law in 1917 (Baker 1977: 7). Oxford did not do so until 1921 (Lawson 1968: 133), and again it was not until the 1960s that women began to enter law schools in anything like significant numbers. In 1967, women accounted for 17 per cent of law students, and this figure had risen to 39 per cent by 1978, and to 45 per cent by 1983–4 (Abel 1988: 276). These figures are similar to the entry of women into the law departments of the former polytechnics (Abel 1988: 276). It was only in the 1960s and 1970s that women began to be admitted to law schools and into the legal profession in any great numbers. This was because of the expansion in higher education, with women attending university in increasing numbers. For example, in 1963, 10,100 women entered

---

[3] The Council for National Academic Awards (CNAA) established a Legal Studies Board in 1966 which authorised law degrees for the following year.

universities, in 1993, this figure was 64,604. The number of law students also increased considerably, with 3070 in 1960–1, to 5335 in 1970–1, to 8398 in 1980–1, to just under 11,000 today (Abel 1988: 464, Cole 1998: 59).

Women were allowed to enter the law schools of the universities, although there is much anecdotal evidence that quotas were used to limit the numbers of women law students, the accepted level being about 10 to 25 per cent (Brooks 1997: 16). Although numbers of women law students were increasing, there was no concomitant increase in the number of women legal academics. There is little historical (or contemporary) data on women legal academics. It is thought that the first woman law professor was appointed in 1971 (McGlynn 1998: 62). The early 1980s saw the formation of a woman-only law teachers group, the purpose of which was to hold workshops and encourage the establishment of courses which permitted a feminist perspective (McGlynn 1998: 62).

5 WOMEN LAW STUDENTS IN THE 1990S

5.1 Law Students in the UK

The number of women law students is increasing year after year, as can be seen in Table 2. Thus, in 1997, almost two thirds of law students were women. This proportion exceeds the national average for all disciplines in which women comprise 52 per cent of students (HESA 1999: 28–29, 60–67, 238). Information on the representation of ethnic minority students, and, in particular, ethnic minority women students, is extremely difficult to find. For example, there is no information available about the comparative application and acceptance rates for ethnic minority students into law degrees (UCAS 1996: 166–171).[4] What is known is that of those who were accepted into law degrees in 1996, only one in five were from ethnic minorities, a figure which had only increased to 22.7 per cent in 1997 (Cole 1998: 60). 59 per cent of ethnic minority law students were women. These figures compare favourably with those relating to the student body as a whole (HESA 1997).

5.2 Degrees of Success

Women achieve slightly more first and upper second class law degrees than men, and are less likely to be awarded a third class degree (Table 3) (Cole 1998: 64; Lewis 1997: 69).

---

[4] Although UCAS statistics provide information on ethnicity, including a breakdown of different ethnicities and by sex, these figures are not broken down in terms of the subject matter of law.

Table 2: Applicants and acceptances for university first degree law courses in England and Wales 1994–97 (Lewis 1997: 67; Cole 1998: 61)

	Women Applics	Total Applics	Women Accept	Total Accept
For entry in:				
1987			2,631 (51.3%)	5.128
1988			2,803 (50.6%)	5,537
1989			3,048 (51.4%)	5,930
1990			3,444 (52.1%)	6,605
1991			3,782 (51.9%)	7,281
1992			4,441 (52.3)	8,444
1993			4,858 (53.0%)	9,172
1994	11,548 (54%)	21,266	4,883 (54%)	8,997
1995	11,195 (56%)	20,050	5,218 (56%)	9,382
1996	10,716 (57.6%)	18,595	5,769 (57.7%)	9,998
1997	11,332 (58.8%)	19,267	6,504 (58.6%)	11,101

Table 3: Class of law degree awarded to women in England & Wales as a percentage of the number of degrees awarded in each class, 1991–1997 (McGlynn 1998: 19)

	1991 (university)	1991 (polytechnic)	1993	1995	1996	1997
Class of degree						
First	48	58	44	51	47	51
Upper Second	52	61	53	56	56	59
Lower Second	48	50	49	51	52	52
Third/pass/other	52	47	46	40	42	50
% 2.1 & 1st				51	51	55

6   WOMEN LEGAL ACADEMICS

6.1 Women Academics Across the Disciplines

In 1997–98, 9.2 per cent of all professors in the UK were women, although as can been seen from Table 4 (HESA 1999), this figure varies from only 2 per cent in some disciplines to 20 per cent in education. Indeed, 20 higher education institutions in the UK have no women professors (AUT 1998a). (Table 4) Further evidence reveals that 29 per cent of men employed as academics are in promoted positions, compared with only 12 per cent of women (AUT 1998b). It is only when staff are under 30 years of age that there is any kind of equality, with 0.27 per cent of men and 0.33 per cent of women holding senior posts. Finally, in the

Table 4: Proportion of women professors in the UK by subject: 1997–98 (Hague 1999)

Education	20%
Languages	16%
Medicine, dentistry & health(excluding nursing)	13%
Arts (other than languages)	12%
Administrative, business & social studies (including law)	11%
Agriculture, forestry & vet. science	7%
Architecture, & planning	6%
Biological, math & physical sciences	4%
Academic services	3%
Engineering & technology	2%
Total	9.2%

management ranks of universities, there are only six women vice-chancellors (*The Independent* 1998).[5]

In addition to the under-representation of women at senior levels in UK universities, there is also evidence of substantial pay inequalities between women and men academics. Robert McNabb and Victoria Wass found that 'even after controlling for rank, age, tenure and faculty, a gender effect in the remuneration of British academics remains' (McNabb and Wass 1997: 328). The average differential between women and men's salaries was found to be 15 per cent (McNabb and Wass 1997: 334). Interestingly, McNabb and Wass' study found that women employed in more male-dominated faculties receive higher remuneration than women in less male-dominated faculties (McNabb and Wass 1997: 338). This is strongly suggestive of women not having the same 'purchase' or 'cultural capital' as men, with the effect that the more women there are in a faculty or department, the less it is valued, with lower salaries for all (Cownie 1998: 107). Final confirmation of unequal pay came in 1999 from a committee investigating the pay of academics in the UK. The Bett report discovered that full-time male academics were paid on average £4,259 a year more than their female counterparts. The gender pay gap for professors was £1,807 (*The Guardian* 1999).

The statistical evidence regarding the pay and representation of women does not, however, reveal the whole picture. Qualitative studies into the experiences of women academics have revealed a consistent picture of marginalisation effected by subtle, yet pervasive, acts of discrimination (Morley 1994, Morley and Walsh 1995, Brooks 1997, Davues *et al* 1994). Thus, the experience of women academics is that they remain largely absent from the upper echelons of universities, at all levels are on average paid less than men and often occupy a marginalised status.

---

[5] The vice-chancellor is effectively the managing executive of the university. Five of the six women vice-chancellors are at 'new' universities, that is those that were granted university status post–1992. The 'old' universities are the more traditional and research-led.

6.2 Women Legal Academics

The above data on women academics raise the question whether women academics in law schools share the same experiences. However, it is difficult to answer such a question authoritatively as there is a dearth of literature and research on women *legal* academics. The UK government body responsible for collecting higher education statistics does not collect information relating to law schools, nor is there any non-governmental organisation which takes on this task.

Thus, historical data on the representation of academic women in law schools are not available. One study did examine the working conditions of UK legal academics in 1995 (Leighton *et al* 1995)[6] which found that flexible working practices, good quality administrative support, improved financial incentives, recognition by senior staff (head of department or above) and improvements in library resources were all of greater priority to women than men (Leighton *et al* 1995: x). The authors therefore concluded that: 'Clearly, those most keenly looking to overall improvements in their work conditions and opportunities are women' (Leighton *et al* 1995: 71). Although this does not demonstrate inequality of pay or working conditions, it does suggest that research into the experiences of women legal academics may reveal a difference in expectations and rewards to those of men (Montgomery 1997: 58–71).

Table 5: Number of women and men academic staff in UK university law schools as at 1 October 1997 (McGlynn 1998: 205–242)[7]

	Men	Women	Total	% women
Dean of Faculty	27	7	34	21
Head of Department/School	60	18	78	23
Hon/visiting Professor of Law	61	10	71	14
Professor of Law	258	43	301	14
Reader in Law	70	20	90	22
Principal Lecturer in Law	105	71	176	40
Senior Lecturer in Law	453	324	777	42
Total Senior (non-professorial)	628	415	1043	40
Lecturers in Law	418	395	813	49
Total Academic Staff[8]	1,304	853	2,157	40

[6] This research was based on just over 1,000 completed questionnaires from legal academics in all sectors of higher education, 42 per cent of whom were women.

[7] Some points regarding the status of each position should be made. It should be noted that the title professor in the UK is conferred on a small number of individuals, roughly equivalent to a full/tenured professor in the US. Those who are readers/principals and some senior lecturers may be equivalent to associate professors, and lecturers/ and some senior lecturers will be broadly equivalent to assistant professors. The position of lecturer in law will normally be tenured (permanent) unless the individual is employed for a fixed term of years. Further, the position of reader in law is rare in new universities and promotion thereto is based primarily on scholarship; the position of principal lecturer in law primarily exists in new universities and is roughly equivalent to a reader in law, though criteria include administration and teaching experience; promotion to senior lecturer in

It can be seen from Table 5 that 14 per cent of law professors are women, a figure higher than the UK average for all disciplines. However, although the figure of 14 per cent compares favourably with the university sector as a whole, it remains the case that this amounts to very few women law professors. In particular, the absence of women law professors in almost two thirds of law schools raises concerns regarding the future of more junior women legal academics. Evidence from the US shows that the 'presence of a certain size core of tenured women on a faculty [equivalent to professors in the UK context] improves the likelihood that junior level women will successfully leap the tenure hurdle' (Chused 1988: 550). Moreover, in law schools with lower proportions of tenured women, the untenured women were denied tenure much more frequently and left the law schools in higher numbers than equivalent men (Chused 1988: 552). This evidence demonstrates a correlation between increasing numbers of women legal academics, especially at senior levels, and change in the law school in terms of attitudes and hiring practices.

The figures on the representation of women in the professoriate also give rise to the question why there are relatively few women, compared with men.[9] Whether it is due to women being denied the same opportunities for professional advancement as men, or whether it is due to an historically small number of women legal academics, is difficult to determine. Data were not collected on the historical representation of women in law schools, nor on patterns and methods of recruitment or promotion. Accordingly, although we know from this study that there are almost equal numbers of women and men law lecturers (Table 5), we do not know whether this is a recent or long-standing phenomenon, and thus whether or not greater numbers of women law professors could be expected.

Complacency would, however, be misguided. The study by McNabb and Wass, discussed above, examined a cohort of academics who started their careers in 1975 and remained employed in 1992. By 1992, 35 per cent of men were lecturers, compared with 57 per cent of women; 44 per cent of men were readers, compared with 35 per cent of women; and 20 per cent were professors, compared with 9 per cent of women (McNabb and Wass 1997: 340). The study concluded that unless these differences can be solely accounted for in terms of differential productivity, there is a gender element in promotions exercises. Similar comparisons may also be made with the solicitors' profession (see below).

new universities is more or less automatic, whereas in old universities it is appointed in open competition.

[8] Excludes figures for deans/heads of department (the individuals occupying such positions are included in the relevant category of staff) and honorary/visiting professors.

[9] For a detailed analysis of the situation of women law professors in England cf the contribution in this volume by Celia Wells.

Further down the academic hierarchy, the proportionate number of women increases, with 49 per cent of law lecturers being women. The higher representation of women at lecturer level can be viewed in at least two ways. First, in a more positive light, it could be suggested that although there may be under-representation of women compared to men at senior levels, this pattern of inequality is being ironed out at the junior level. This would augur well for the future representation of women. On the other hand, and more negatively, it might be concluded either that women are remaining at lecturer level, without promotion, and/or that after a number of years working in law schools women are leaving to pursue other options, perhaps as a result of the lack of opportunities or promotion prospects (Association of Commonwealth Universities nd). Overall, therefore, in 1997, women represented 40 per cent of all legal academics, although this figure does mask considerable varia-tions between law schools and hierarchies of appointment (McGlynn 1999: 83–85).

7   WOMEN SOLICITORS IN THE 1990S

7.1 The status of women solicitors

In 1998 women made up 34 per cent of solicitors holding a practising certificate, a figure which has been steadily increasing (Table 6). However, it is important to break down these figures in order to discern more clearly the patterns of representation. In 1997–98, 51 per cent of those admitted to the profession were women (Table 1). Thus, since 1983, women have comprised over one third of those being admitted to the profession and over one half since 1992–93. However, the proportion of women being admitted peaked in 1994–95 and has since then fallen back to 51 per cent (Table 1). The figures are small but significant in that they refer to a time when the proportion of women law students continues to increase year on year (Table 2).

Table 6: Solicitors who held practising certificates 1988–1998 (Cole 1998: 12)

Year	Women	Men	Total	% Women
1988	10,062	40,622	50,684	20
1990	12,683	42,051	54,734	23
1992	15,653	43,910	59,566	26
1994	18,417	45,211	63,628	29
1996	21,356	46,681	68,037	31
1998	25,439	49,633	75,072	34

Thus, one can see that at the junior levels of the profession there are many women entering and practising as solicitors. However, when one considers partnership, the figures are not so promising.[10] In 1998, 17.4 per cent of partners were women in solicitors' firms in England & Wales, a figure which had increased from 16.5 per cent in 1997 (Cole 1998: 16). To a limited extent this figure is historically understandable, however time alone does not account for the absence of women partners. For example, a 1995 study found that of those partners being made up that year, only 25 per cent were women (McGlynn and Graham 1995: 8–9; McGlynn 1995). A follow-up survey in 1997 found that 27 per cent of new partners in the largest 100 firms were women (McGlynn 1997a), and the figure remained at 27 per cent in 1999 (Law Society Gazette 1999). Thus, although there has been some welcome improvement, progress is slow.

Furthermore, many of the firms justified this low figure of new women partners by suggesting that, in time, more women would reach senior levels, as women had not been entering the profession for very many years: the 'trickle-up' theory (Sommerlad 1994: 34). However, what these figures demonstrate is that, in time, women may comprise one quarter of partnerships, but no more. Moreover, this is not a situation which is going to be solved just by time. Women have been entering the profession in almost equal numbers for a sufficient number of years to be making more of an impact at partnership level. The 'trickle-up' argument is also defeated by Law Society statistics covering all firms which show that of those solicitors with ten to 19 years of experience, 77 per cent of men are partners, compared with only 53.6 per cent of women (Cole 1998: 18). Accordingly, it must be recognised that the mere passage of time will not ensure equality for women in the solicitors' profession and this myth must be exposed.

7.2 Paying for Equality

Inequality of pay between women and men is also a serious concern in the profession. Any illusion to the contrary was shattered by the publication in 1996 of Law Society research which found that, comparing median earnings, male assistant solicitors earned £24,000, while women earned only £21,000 (McGlynn 1997b: 568–569). Even where factors such as size and location of firm, and age and length of qualification were taken into account, the difference in earnings at assistant level was £1,700. At salaried partner level men earned £37,000 compared with £32,000 for women, and at equity partner level the disparity between women and men rose to £15,000. This picture had changed little by the time of publication of figures in 1997, and indeed the gap increased in respect of the pay of assistant solicitors (to £2,340 for assistant solicitors, even taking into account the size of firm, area of work, years of experience and other

---

[10] Partners are joint owners of the firm of solicitors.

such factors) (Law Society 1997). The facts are clear: from assistant solicitor to salaried partner to equity partner, women are paid less than men.

The inequality of pay between women and men begins at the training stage. 1998 Law Society figures show that on average the starting salaries of female trainee solicitors are 4.4 per cent lower than for men, with the maximum differential being 11.3 per cent in the north of England (Cole 1998: 75). The average starting salary was £14,096 for women, compared to £14,713 for men (Cole 1998: 72). The significance of this is that it represents an *increase* in the pay gap from a difference of only 2 per cent in 1997 (Cole 1998: 74). These are particularly startling data in view of the fact that in general women graduate with better credentials than men. It confirms that it is not just qualifications that count when law firms are recruiting.

7.3 Women's Work

Women are more likely than men to practise as solicitors outside private practice. In 1998, of all solicitors in private practice, women comprised 31 per cent, compared with 43.6 per cent for all solicitors outside private practice (Cole 1998: 16). The greater proportion of women than men working outside private practice increases each year. This begins at the training stage. In 1997–98, 65 per cent of trainee solicitors in non-private practice organisations were women, an increase from 62.6 per cent in 1996–97 (Cole 1998: 58). It has been argued on a number of occasions that there are a greater proportion of women outside private practice because of the masculine culture of private practice. A woman consultant with a City firm argued that:

> There is an outpouring from law firms of the brightest and best [women], often to company legal departments, which, through sophisticated personnel and appraisal policies, are more likely to be meritocracies in which women do well (Kingsmill 1998; Equal Opportunities Commission 1999: 39).

Analysis of the allocation of the work of solicitors, and the areas of practice in which women work, is hampered by the lack of detailed research.[11] Nonetheless, one study of solicitors in private practice for 1997 found that women regularly handled fewer categories of casework than men (Cole 1997: x). In addition, personal injury and family work were relatively more important to women solicitors, and commercial property, housing law and probate work were relatively more important to men (Cole 1997: x). This perhaps results from

---

[11] However in Northern Ireland a study found that in general most respondents were involved in a large range of legal work. However, in three areas of work there were significant gender differences, namely criminal law, family law and personal injury claims. The findings showed that significantly more men than women worked over a quarter of their time on personal injury claims, 40 per cent compared to 30 per cent, and on criminal law 11 per cent compared with 5 per cent. One in five female respondents, 17 per cent, spent over a quarter of their time on family law compared with only 4 per cent of their male counterparts (Equal Opportunities Commission 1999: 23–24).

the fact that women were found to spend more time on personal injury and family work, with men spending more time on commercial affairs, residential conveyancing and crime (Cole 1997: x).

8 WOMEN BARRISTERS IN THE 1990S

8.1 Women at the Bar

The number of women being called to the Bar has increased dramatically from a paltry eight per cent in 1970 to 48 per cent in 1998 (Table 7). These statistics do not, however, paint the whole picture. Being called to the Bar is not synonymous with gaining a tenancy in chambers and practising, just as qualifying as a solicitor does not guarantee employment as a solicitor. Thus, many who are called to the Bar will not go on to practice, either through choice or the inability to gain a tenancy. It is not clear (because of a lack of statistical data) whether women and men are awarded tenancies in proportionate numbers.

Table 7: Number of women and men called to the Bar 1970–1998[12]

Year	Men	Women	% Women	Total
1970	858	77	8%	935
1975	890	112	12%	1,002
1980	617	245	28%	862
1985	663	282	30%	945
1990	507	339	40%	846
1995	599	507	46%	1,106
1996	1,034	651	39%	1,685
1997	910	698	43%	1,608
1998	795	728	48%	1,523

There is however some evidence of potentially discriminatory practices. Research commissioned by the Lord Chancellor's Department (LCD) and the Bar Council in 1992, resulting in the welcome publication of the report *Without Prejudice? Sex Equality at the Bar and in the Judiciary* (hereafter the *Without Prejudice?* research) showed that 39 per cent of women were asked in tenancy interviews about their marriage and children, compared with only 15 per cent of men. As the researchers noted, the asking of such questions is 'powerfully indicative of discriminatory practices and attitudes'. The statistical information which is available on 'squatting', that is, practising from chambers without being a full tenant, also reveals differences between the sexes. The *Without*

---

[12] Statistics provided by the Bar Council in personal communications.

Prejudice? research found that 36 per cent of women respondents had squatted, compared with only 18 per cent of men. In addition, women, on average, have to squat for a much longer period before gaining a tenancy than men. It appears therefore that women are being called to the Bar in increasing numbers, but may be continuing to experience difficulties in building a practice.

8.2 Queen's Counsel

The conferment of the title Queen's Council (QC) is a mark of distinction, signalling the achievement of senior status in the profession, and around 10 per cent of the practising Bar are QCs. To be eligible, applicants must be advocates (barristers or solicitors) who have full rights of audience. It is usual that the applicant will have been in practice for at least ten years, though in reality applicants will have between 15 and 20 years of experience. As of April 1998, there were just under 1,000 QCs of whom 73 were women, making seven per cent.

Table 8 shows that the number of women appointed QC each year is very low, with 1998 being the first year to yield double figures. The figures for 1996 and 1997 actually showed the smallest number of women appointed for some years, even though more women were applying (although the figures are small enough for a few applications to make a difference). 1998 did see an improvement, although it appears remarkable only because of the figures in 1996–7. In addition, 1998 saw the smallest number of QC appointments for many years, meaning that the percentage representation of women appears considerably higher than in earlier years. Nonetheless, the success rate for women applicants has been slightly higher than for men each year, with the exception of 1999.

Table 8: Women and men QCs 1991–1999 (LCD 1996, 1997, 1998, 1999)

	1991	1992	1993	1994	1995	1996	1997	1998	1999
Women QCs	6 (8%)	7	6	9	8	4	5	10	9
Men QCs	67	62	64	68	63	62	63	50	60
Total	73	69	70	77	71	66	68	60	69
% women applics awarded QC	25	21	16	21	19	10	12	22	20
% men applics awarded QC	17	16	15	14	14	10	12	11	12

It is often suggested that the low number of women QCs results from the historical fact that women have only been admitted to the Bar in sufficient numbers in recent years. This explanation is not, however, borne out by the facts. In 1996, of those juniors with over 15 years' call, 12 per cent were women (one in eight) (Hewson 1996: 565). Yet, at the same time, women made up only one in 15 of the QCs in private practice (Hewson 1996: 565). In 1998, 14 per cent of barristers with over 15 years' call were women (LCD 1998). Accordingly, there are many senior women barristers eligible to become QC.

9   WOMEN JUDGES[13]

No woman has ever been appointed to the UK's highest court, the House of Lords. Indeed, the very name of the supreme court, the House of *Lords*, is suggestive of exclusively male membership. The most senior woman judge in the UK is in the Court of Appeal, and there are eight women High Court judges (Table 9). This means that in the most senior judicial offices, those for whom the law making function of the judiciary is the most relevant, only six per cent of judges are women. Although this is an increase from 1.4 per cent in 1989 (Hansard Society 1990: 45), this only amounts to the appointment of seven women in 10 years. Of all the principal judicial offices (excluding tribunals), women comprise 11.8 per cent of the judges. Although there has been an improvement at the lower ends of the judicial hierarchy over recent years, particularly at the level of assistant recorder, women remain under-represented.

Table 9: Women and men judges in the UK as at 1 May 1999[14]

	Women	Men	Total	% Women
Lords of Appeal in Ordinary (House of Lords)	–	12	12	0
Lords Justices of Appeal (Court of Appeal)	1	34	35	3
High Court Judges	8	89	97	8
Circuit Judges	36	522	558	6
Recorders	78	797	875	9
Assistant Recorders	67	335	402	16
Assistant Recorders in Training	20	92	112	18
District Judges	52	326	378	14
Deputy District Judges	98	669	767	13
Stipendiary Magistrates	31	157	188	16
Total	403	3,021	3,424	11.8

10   CONCLUSIONS

It is difficult to generalise about the status of 'women lawyers', as the term comprises an extremely diverse community of lawyers in many different working environments. Furthermore, suggesting an analysis of women lawyers in the UK implies a coherence and similarity in situation across the whole of the UK which

[13] For a detailed study of women judges in England and Wales see Kate Malleson's contribution to this volume.
[14] Figures to be found at: http://www.open.gov.uk/lcd/judicial/

does not exist. Nonetheless, with those caveats in mind, it is possible to say that what is clear from the above analysis is that women working and studying in the law tend to be under-represented, underpaid and marginalised. More worrying is evidence of a retrenchment in some quarters, with the progress that women have been making stagnating and in some cases reversing. At the turn of the century, almost one hundred years since women were first let into the profession of law, it is not clear that the continued progress can be taken as a given. Constant vigilance and campaigning is required if women are to gain opportunities to pursue their professional legal careers to the extent of their choosing.

11 REFERENCES

Abel, Richard L. 1988. *The Legal Profession in England and Wales*. Oxford: Blackwell.

Association of Commonwealth Universities. nd. *Single Sex Education? Representation by Gender Amongst Staff at Commonwealth Universities*. http: //www.ACU.ac.uk/chems/surveys/women1.html.

Association of University Teachers (AUT). 1998a. Press Release, 15 May 1998.

Association of University Teachers. 1998b. *AUT Woman*. vol 45.

Bailey, S and Gunn, M. 1996. *Smith and Bailey on the Modern English Legal System*. London: Sweet & Maxwell.

Baker, JH. 1977. University College and Legal Education. *Current Legal Problems* 30; 1–13.

Bar Council. 1996. *Annual Report 1995*. London: Bar Council.

Bar Council. 2000. *1999 Annual Report*. London: General Council of the Bar.

Bebb v Law Society. [1914] Ch. 286.

Birks, Michael. 1960. *Gentlemen of the Law*. London: Stevens & Sons.

Brooks, Ann. 1997. *Academic Women*. Buckingham: Open University Press.

Chorlton v Lings. [1886] 4 LRCP 374.

Chused, R. 1998. The Hiring and Retention of Minorities and Women on American Law School Faculties. 137 *University of Pennsylvania Law Review* 537.

Cole, Bill. 1997. *Solicitors in Private Practice—Their Work and Expectations*. London: Law Society.

Cole, Bill. 1998. *Trends in the Solicitors' Profession—Annual Statistical Report*. London: Law Society.

Cownie, Fiona. 1998. Women Legal Academics: A New Research Agenda? *Journal of Law and Society* 25; 102.

Davues, Sue *et al*. 1994. *Changing the Subject—Women in Higher Education*. London: Taylor and Francis.

Dickson, D. 1993. *Legal System of Northern Ireland*. Belfast: SLS.

Equal Opportunities Commission for Northern Ireland. 1999. *A Case for Equality—Gender Equality in the Solicitors' Profession*. Belfast: EOCNI.

Fisher, David. 1999. Equal in the Law? *New Law Journal*. 706–708.

The Guardian. 1999. 4 May.

Hague, Helen. 1999. Why are only 9.2 per cent of Professors Women? *Times Higher Educational Supplement*. 28 May.

Hansard Society. 1990. *Women at the Top*. London: Hansard Society.

Higher Education Statistics Agency (HESA). 1997. Press Release 14 May.

HESA. 1997. Press Release. 9 May.

HESA. 1999. *Students in Higher Education Institutions 1997/98.* Cheltenham: HESA.

Hewson, Barbara. 1996. You've a long way to go, baby . . . *New Law Journal* 146; 565–566.

The Independent. 1998. 25 June.

Jervis, M. 1997. Working Lives of the First Four Women Solicitors to be Admitted to the Roll. *Law Society Gazette.* 17 December.

Kennedy, Helena. 1978. Women at the Bar. In *The Bar on Trial*, edited by Robert Hazell. London: Quartet Books.

Kennedy, Helena. 1992. *Eve was Framed. Women and British Justice.* London: Chatto & Windus.

Kingsmill, Denise. 1998. *Law Society Gazette.* 4 February.

Law Society Gazette. 1998. 4 February.

Law Society Gazette. 1999. 23 June.

Law Society. 1997. New Survey Reveals Continuing Inequality between Male and Female Solicitors. Press Release nd.

Lawson, F. 1968. *The Oxford Law School.* Oxford: Clarendon Press.

Leighton, Patricia *et al.* 1995. *Today's Law Teachers: Lawyers or Academics?* London: Cavendish.

Lewis, Verity. 1997. *Trends in the Solicitors Profession-Annual Statistical Report 1996.* London: Law Society.

Lord Chancellor's Department (LCD). 1996. Press Release 4 April.

LCD. 1997. Press Release 26 March.

LCD. 1998. Press Release 9 April.

LCD. 1999. Press Release 1 April.

McGlynn, Clare. 1995. Soliciting Equality—the way forward. *New Law Journal* 145; 1065–1066.

McGlynn, Clare and Graham, Caroline. 1995. *Soliciting Equality—Equality and Opportunity in the Solicitors' Profession.* London: Young Women Lawyers.

McGlynn, Clare. 1997a. Where men still rule. *The Times*, 22 April.

McGlynn, Clare. 1997b. Paying for Equality. *New Law Journal* 147; 568–569.

McGlynn, Clare. 1998. *The Women Lawyer: Making the Difference.* London: Butterworths.

McGlynn, Clare. 1999. Women, Representation and the Legal Academy. *Legal Studies* 19; 68–92.

McNabb, R and Wass, V. 1997. Male-Female Salary Differentials in British Universities. *Oxford Economic Papers* 49; 328.

Montgomery, Ann. 1997. In Law and Outlaw? In *Knowing Feminisms—on academic borders, territories and tribes.* edited by L Stanley. London: Sage.

Morley, Louise. 1994. Glass Ceiling or Iron Cage: Women in UK Academia. *Gender, Work and Organization* 1; 194.

Morley, Louise. & Walsh, Val. eds. 1995. *Feminist Academics: Creative Agents for Change.* London: Taylor & Francis.

Mossman, Mary Jane. 1991. Feminism and Legal Method in *At the Boundaries of Law—Feminism and Legal Theory*, edited by M Fineman & N Thomadsen. London: Routledge.

Pearson, Rose. & Sachs, Albie. 1980. A Critical Look at Sexism in the Legal Profession. *Modern Law Review* 43; 400–414.

Sommerlad, Hilary. 1994. The Myth of Feminisation: Women and Cultural Change in the Legal Profession. *International Journal of the Legal Profession* 1; 31–53.

Sommerlad, Hilary. 1995. Managerialism and the Legal Profession: a New Professional Paradigm. *International Journal of the Legal Profession* 2; 159.

Sommerlad, Hilary and Sanderson, Peter. 1998. *Gender, Choice and Commitment: Women Solicitors in England and Wales and the Struggle for Equal Status.* Aldershot: Ashgate.

The Times. 1998. 13 January.

UCAS. 1996. *Annual Report 1995.* Entry Cheltenham: UCAS.

Walker, D. 1992. *The Scottish Legal System.* Edinburgh: Green.

10

Strategies for Reforming the English Solicitors' Profession: An Analysis of the Business Case for Sex Equality

CLARE MS McGLYNN*

Abstract

The aim of this chapter is to analyse the likely effect of adopting the business case for sex equality as the principal strategy by which to improve the status of women solicitors. The business case suggests that employers should introduce equal opportunity measures in order to improve the profitability of their businesses. It is premised on the belief that the moral or ethical case for equality has been won, and that it is the perceived costs of introducing equal opportunity policies which act as a barrier to change. This chapter examines the key elements of the business case for equality, followed by a discussion of its development within the solicitors' profession. The chapter argues that the business case strategy is a wholly misconceived campaign and suggests that new strategies must be found, ones for which equality is the principal aim, not just a by-product of the improving economic efficiency of firms.

1 INTRODUCTION

THE MARGINALISED STATUS of women in the solicitors' profession in England and Wales is 'certainly not a feminist issue', according to Jill Whitehouse (Whitehouse 1997), formerly a partner in a City of London solicitors' firm. Rather, she continues, it is a 'real and practical problem which all firms are currently facing', the 'crux' of which is 'firmly economic'. The Law Society of England and Wales agrees. In 1995 it adopted a model anti-discrimination policy, the justification for which was contained in the first clause: 'It is good business sense for the firm to ensure that its most important resource, its staff, is used in a fair and effective way' (Law Society 1995). More

* I should like to thank Ann Sinclair for her research assistance which proved invaluable in the preparation of this essay.

particularly, the Law Society has urged solicitors' firms to introduce equal pay policies because: 'Pay equality makes good business sense. It helps keep staff turnover and loss of key skills to a minimum and avoids the expense and negative publicity of an industrial tribunal case' (Law Society 1997) The Association of Women Solicitors has supported such arguments with the plaintive cry that women are a 'vital part of the profession' which, because of 'economic reality', cannot 'afford to . . . undervalue us' (*Law Society Gazette* 1994).

This is the business case for sex equality; the argument that employers should introduce equal opportunity measures in order to improve the profitability of their businesses. It is premised on the belief that the moral or ethical case for equality has been won, and that it is the perceived costs of introducing equal opportunity policies which act as a barrier to change (Humphries and Rubery 1995: 1). The business case is the principal strategy being pursued by campaigners within the profession.

The aim of this essay is to examine the business case argument and assess its adequacy. Having briefly outlined the present status of women in the solicitors' profession in England and Wales, the essay goes on, in the second section, to examine the key elements of the business case for equality, followed by a discussion of its development within the solicitors' profession. The third section assesses the business case strategy and suggests that it is a wholly misconceived campaign. The concluding section suggests that new strategies must be found, ones for which equality is the principal aim, not just a by-product of the improving economic efficiency of firms.

2 THE STATUS OF WOMEN SOLICITORS

The context for my discussion of strategies to reform the solicitors' profession in England and Wales is the continuing under-representation and marginalised status of women solicitors (McGlynn 1998; Sommerlad and Sanderson 1998). Women have been entering law schools and the solicitors' profession in increasing numbers and by the end of the 1990s comprised more than one half of those solicitors. However, despite the high numbers of women studying law and beginning their professional careers, the representation of women within the solicitors' profession decreases rapidly further up the professional hierarchy. Thus, although more women than men are being admitted to the profession, in total women comprise only 34 per cent of practising solicitors (Cole 1998: 12). At partnership level, the most senior position in the profession, there are few women. In 1998, just over 17 per cent of partners were women in solicitors' firms in England and Wales. The numbers have been increasing over recent years, but progress is slow.[1]

[1] 17.4 per cent in 1998 up from 16.5 per cent in 1997 (Cole 1998: 15)

The under-representation of women at senior levels is often justified by reference to the historically low number of women entering the profession: the 'trickle-up' theory (Sommerlad 1994: 34).[2] However, women have been entering the profession in almost equal numbers for a sufficient number of years to be making more of an impact at partnership level. The 'trickle-up' argument is also defeated by Law Society statistics covering all firms which show that of those solicitors with 10 to 19 years of experience, 77 per cent of men are partners, compared with only just over 53 per cent of women (Cole 1998: 18). What this demonstrates is that of those men and women eligible for partnership, a man is much more likely to become a partner than a woman. Accordingly, it must be recognised that the mere passage of time will not ensure equality for women in the solicitors' profession and this myth must be exposed. Furthermore, not only are women under-represented at the senior levels of the profession, but there is evidence of inequality of pay of women and men solicitors at all levels, from a gap of £1,700 for assistant solicitors to £15,000 for equity partners (McGlynn 1997: 568–69).

3 THE BUSINESS CASE FOR SEX EQUALITY

It is in this context of continuing discrimination and marginalisation that campaigns to improve the status of women solicitors in England and Wales have continued. In recent years, momentum has gathered around a strategy which promotes the 'business case' for equality. The nature of the business case will be considered below, followed by an examination of how this strategy has been adopted within the profession.

In general, the business case for equality advocates the adoption by *employers* of equal opportunity employment policies. An improvement in the status of women is therefore dependent on the voluntary actions of employers, obviating governmental or other regulatory responsibility: a process which has been termed the 'privatisation of sex equality policy' (Forbes 1996). The business case is expounded by many organisations and institutions within the United Kingdom, including the Government,[3] the Equal Opportunities Commission (EOC)[4] and the Confederation of British Industry (CBI), the principal employers' representative organisation. It also forms the core of the organisation Opportunity 2000 (recently renamed Opportunity Now) which campaigns to improve the quality and quantity of women's employment by promoting the business case for equality (Opportunity 2000 1996).[5] Furthermore, the development of the business case

---

[2] See also the contribution by Kate Malleson in this volume who challenges the 'trickle-up' theory in the context of the judiciary.

[3] Particularly through support for the organisation Opportunity Now.

[4] Kamlesh Bahl, EOC chair for five years until 1998, placed the 'development of the business case' as one of the main accomplishments of her term of office (*The Lawyer* 1998).

[5] Members of Opportunity Now employ 25 per cent of the UK workforce and therefore represent a substantial body of employer opinion (Opportunity 2000 1996).

for equality can be viewed as part of a wider trend that seeks to justify progressive labour policy in economic terms. Thus, Simon Deakin and Frank Wilkinson have argued that establishing and maintaining high labour standards are essential to economic progress (Deakin and Wilkinson 1996). Similarly, Karl Klare has utilised economic arguments to justify workplace democracy, arguing that it is 'good for business' as part of a 'human capital strategy for economic growth' (Klare 1988: 10–13). This is part of a project whereby 'progressive labour lawyers' are attempting to 'beat economists at their own game' (Conaghan 1999: 28). Together, these various organisations, institutions and intellectual movements represent a critical mass of political weight in support of a business case for sex equality.

3.1 Key Elements of the 'Business Case for Sex Equality'

Turning to consider the business case in more detail, it assumes that the reason why there are so few senior women is largely due to the undervaluation of their human capital, that is, their skills, qualifications and experience. The consequent strategy is to persuade employers to recognise the 'true' value of their women employees by suggesting that in doing so law firms will benefit economically. For this reason, the business case privileges the economic needs of the firm, merely arguing that greater opportunities for women may be one way in which to achieve such economic gains. The goal is the improved economic efficiency of firms, with equal opportunities being one means, amongst many, of achieving such a goal.

There may be said to be three broad elements to the business case argument.[6] The first contends that the implementation and effective enforcement, at firm level, of equal opportunity policies will improve employee morale to an extent that is positively reflected in the productivity of the firm. Hence, the CBI has argued that 'effective equal opportunities policies and practices provide business with the facility to . . . increase morale at work', leading to 'sustained competitiveness' (CBI 1996: 4, 6).

The second element of the business case suggests that it makes financial sense for employers to capitalise on any investment made in their employees, that is they should make the best use of their human capital. The maximisation of women's human capital, it is argued, may involve an initial outlay of costs, but rewards will be had in terms of improved retention rates and increased efficiency. Thus, for example, a number of employers have estimated that such recruitment expenses far outweigh the costs of providing help with childcare responsibilities, or in developing suitable part-time or job-share working practices, or in changing the culture of the organisation to make it more amenable

---

[6] It should be emphasised that the business case is not a coherent philosophy as such, but a collection of ideas and propositions (Humphries and Rubery 1995).

to workers with family responsibilities (CBI 1996: 15–18; Social Justice Commission 1994: 188–191; Langdon-Down 1997).

The third aspect of the business case is directed at frightening employers into adopting and enforcing equal opportunities policies in order to obviate expensive sex discrimination claims. Although the median compensation awarded for sex discrimination claims in the UK is only £2,700 (Equal Opportunities Review 1997),[7] the publicity surrounding a number of high profile cases has portrayed a different picture. In particular, headlines such as, 'Female director wins £140,000 in equality case' (*The Independent* 1996) and '£200,000 for firewoman bullied by colleagues' (*The Times* 1997) are increasingly common. Similar headlines have appeared on a number of occasions in the legal press. Allied to the fear of substantial damages claims, this element of the business case also focuses on the cost of lost management time involved in managing and possibly defending a discrimination action, as well as the potentially negative effects of adverse publicity.

3.2 The Development of the Business Case in the Solicitors' Profession

The solicitors' profession has not been immune from broader developments in society in which the marketisation of political culture has increased. When political debate is dominated by the three 'E's of efficiency, effectiveness and economy' (Crawford 1996: 249) and where cost-benefit analyses are applied to all manner of policies, including 'human life itself' (Willets 1997: 9), it is not surprising that such values have impacted on the solicitors' profession. In such a context, it is perhaps understandable that those seeking to improve the status of women solicitors should have sought to use the tools of acceptable political rhetoric, that is the market and economics, to their own ends, by developing a business, or economic, case for equality.

The development of this strategy can be charted back to the recruitment and retention crisis in the late 1980s (Abel 1988; Galanter 1983; Flood 1996). At this time of rapid expansion of the profession, the number of women becoming solicitors was dramatically increasing, as was the number of women leaving the profession. Thus, debate on the staffing crisis took on a gender dimension as it became clear that if women continued to leave the profession, the recruitment crisis could only worsen. At this time, an influential Law Society report, *Equal in the Law*, referred to the evidence that women were leaving the profession in significant numbers and stated that 'this would be an alarming picture at any time in the history of the profession' (Law Society 1988: 12). In particular, however, the retention rate was a 'serious cause for concern' in view of the fact that 'women are making up about half of the current intake' of solicitors, and when 'there is a severe recruitment crisis which may last for several years' (Law

---

[7] Figures for 1995–96.

Society 1988: 12). Many recommendations were made in order to avert this crisis. For example, it was recommended that there should be a greater use of part-time workers who should be seen as a 'valuable and flexible resource', especially 'at a time when recruits are scarce' (Law Society 1988: 20). Accordingly, although a general concern about discrimination against women was expressed, the prime concern was with the continuation of the profession and the need to avert a recruitment crisis. This emphasis was matched in the reporting of the recommendations in the legal press. The *Solicitors Journal* headed its editorial: 'Waste of talent' (*Solicitors Journal* 1988). Subsequent articles were to take up this theme with one in 1989 beginning: 'Clued-up solicitors are already solving their recruitment crises by devising workable strategies to attract women with families back into the profession' (Allison 1989).

Having used such arguments to justify the employment of women in times of staff shortage, problems arose when the economic cycle changed and the profession faced recession in the early 1990s. Whereas women were once fêted, they were now the first in line for redundancy (Sommerlad and Sanderson 1998: 5; Sidaway 1995: 77–78; Skordaki 1996: 34). It was to economic arguments that campaigners again turned, this time to justify the continued employment of women, on the basis of securing a return on the previous investments in women. A continual theme, therefore, in the legal press in the 1990s has been the financial imperatives that demand changes in women's working conditions. One article emphasised the fact that many, now senior, women solicitors were moving firms in order to take up senior positions, including partnership, because of perceived problems in their present firms (Alcock 1998/1999). Thus, it is not surprising that a further article in 1990 claimed that the 'high cost of training a replacement for a solicitor wanting to work part-time and have a family will change working practices in the legal profession' (Staunton 1990). Ten years later the same arguments are still being made.

These themes have been further developed by the Law Society, the Association of Women Solicitors and other interested organisations. Thus, by the mid–1990s, the Law Society was coming under pressure to take some action to alleviate the discrimination against women in the profession, with discrimination and equal opportunity issues becoming a prominent feature of all Law Society events (Bawdon 1996).[8] Accordingly, in 1995 it introduced a practice rule, a code of practice and a model anti-discrimination policy, all of which are binding on all solicitors' firms. The first clause in the model anti-discrimination policy states that: 'It is good business sense for the firm to ensure that its most important resource, its staff, is used in a fair and effective way.' The measure was supported in the Law Society Council (the governing body) on the basis that firms were doing themselves a 'tremendous disservice' by failing to tap the pool of talent from women and minorities (*Solicitors Journal* 1993).

---

[8] On each occasion the emphasis has been on economics and the high cost of paying damages for discrimination and the high cost of ensuring equality of pay.

The Law Society followed this approach when in 1997 it published figures revealing the continuing inequality of pay between women and men solicitors (Law Society 1997). The then President of the Law Society and Chair of the EOC sent a joint letter to all solicitors' firms urging them to review their pay practices. This letter argued that firms should reconsider their policies for the following reasons: 'Pay equality makes good business sense. It helps keep staff turnover and loss of key skills to a minimum and avoids the expense and negative publicity of an industrial tribunal case' and goes on to warn that 'women trainee solicitors and assistant solicitors are beginning to take equal pay cases to tribunals.' It was the business case for equality which was the justification offered for reviewing the pay of male and female employees, no other reason was mentioned.

The Association of Women Solicitors (AWS) is a Law Society funded organisation which represents women solicitors and seeks ways in which to improve their status. From the late 1980s, the business case has been a crucial component of their campaigns. The AWS supported the introduction of the Law Society Practice Rule on anti-discrimination measures on the basis that women are a 'vital part of the profession' which cannot 'afford to . . . undervalue us' because of the 'economic reality' of the increasing potential for discrimination claims and unlimited damages claims being brought against firms (Willis 1994). Similarly, in 1997 the AWS argued that although 'the moral case for treating people fairly is unanswerable', the strategy was to focus on the business case since 'unless you can also present an economic argument people are not necessarily going to take any action' (Staples 1997). Most recently, the approach of the organisation was summed up in its 1999 newsletter in which it again advocated change from law firms to make work more compatible with family responsibilities by arguing that there are:

> well-documented business reasons for allowing employees to reduce their hours, including retention of experienced solicitors, reduced absenteeism, less stress, better morale. The lesson for solicitors firms is that it may not only be expensive to refuse employees a reduction in hours, but also bad for business (AWS Link 1999).

It could be said that a marker of the success of the above arguments is that they have been adopted at firm level, with clear evidence that the business case is being used as the justification for the introduction of working practices which benefit women. Thus, in 1997, the City firm Linklaters pioneered flexible partnerships, which allow partners to reduce their working time (Rice 1997). The policy was firmly based on a 'business case' with the firm stating that its priority was to ensure the retention of good lawyers in the long term (McGlynn 1998: 108–110). Policies similar to the above have recently been adopted in a number of large City firms (*The Lawyer* 1999a). In each case, the business case is the message given to the press and professional community. The managing partner of one large City firm, on the announcement of the introduction of flexible partnerships, said that the policy was introduced because 'law firms have difficulty in retaining female talent' (*The Lawyer* 1999b). The chairperson of the City of London Law Society concludes that such policy innovations have been introduced because equality is a 'bottom line issue which relates directly to profitability' (Rice 1997).

Notwithstanding the fact that the business case has invigorated debate, and encouraged the adoption of fairer employment practices amongst those employers hitherto hostile to equal opportunities, the wholesale adoption of market rhetoric to justify sex equality has profound implications, which will be considered below.

4 THE PERILS OF THE BUSINESS CASE FOR EQUALITY

Despite the potential appeal of the business case as a strategy for improving the working lives of women solicitors, primarily due to its potential support from employers, it is both flawed and unlikely to bring about the changes which campaigners seek. This is for three main reasons. First, the business case is empirically fragile and open to constant challenge. Such failings render it an inappropriate strategy on which to base a campaign to improve the status of women solicitors in the long term. Secondly, the reliance which the business case places on economic theory is misconceived and has the potential to dismantle even the most meagre advances already secured for women. Finally, the business case strategy fails to account for the real reasons behind the marginalisation of women solicitors and therefore can barely begin to bring about the changes required.

4.1 Empirical Failings

The business case is empirically based, that is, it suggests that it can be proven that economic efficiency will result from the adoption and implementation of equal opportunities policies. Although the proponents of the business case argue that studies can show that their claim is justified, many studies and rhetorical arguments are available demonstrating the opposite. For example, the first element of the business case (discussed above) suggests that employee morale, and thereby productivity, would be increased with the effective adoption and implementation of equal opportunity policies. However, it is not unreasonable to suppose that in an all-male (or predominantly male) partnership, for example, the effective implementation of equal opportunities may not improve morale. Indeed, it may significantly reduce motivation amongst the predominantly male workforce. Thus, were it to be demonstrated that any proposed changes may reduce morale, the rationale for the policies would be lost and the end goal of improved morale (the economic goal) would dictate the non-implementation of equality policies. Indeed, David Conway has argued that there is an economic justification for such sex segregation policies, in that they lead to improved morale amongst male and female workers (Conway 1998: 16–22). The business case provides no normative basis for resisting such arguments, even though they would likely lead to reduced pay rates for women. Equality would, therefore, be trumped by the business imperative of improved performance accruing from increases in morale. The business case only supports equal opportunities policies in certain contexts because the end result being sought is not sex equality, but productive efficiency.

Similar failings may be identified in relation to the second and third aspects of the business case. The second suggests that the adoption of equal opportunity measures will ensure that employers capitalise on their human resource investments. This may indeed be true in some cases. However, the focus of this element of the business case is not on the justice of the case for promoting and retaining women where their performance demands it. On the contrary, the focal point is profit maximisation, with the clear implication that where profit maximisation does not dictate fair employment practices, such policies cannot be justified. It is not inconceivable that the costs involved in introducing such policies may outweigh unspecified, future financial gains. In addition, this argument is conditional on women comprising a substantial part of any workforce, as only then will the utilisation of female resources have a financial implication. Consequently, where an employer does not, nor wishes to, employ (many) women, perhaps because they are perceived as being more costly or disruptive of the culture of the practice, the business case provides no rationale for employing women, nor does it provide any basis for condemning such discriminatory behaviour (albeit that such a decision may constitute unlawful sex discrimination).

Nor does the business case provide a cast-iron argument for encouraging employers to adopt equal opportunities policies in order to avoid discrimination claims (the third element). Despite the headline figures regarding discrimination damages awards, the reality is that the average award for damages is very low (Equal Opportunities Review 1997). Coupled with the practical reality that women are reluctant to pursue legal action, particularly in a profession which hinges on professional reputation (Sommerlad and Sanderson 1998), the possible economic costs to law firms may not be that large and may, rationally, be offset against any perceived advantages in practising discrimination (or failing to take steps to eliminate it). Furthermore, the emphasis on the possible cost of a damages claim may have the effect in the longer term of diluting the rhetorical force of the legislative regime designed to eliminate discrimination. Emphasis moves away from the morality and fairness of sex equality, to the perceived need to reduce business costs, with the effect that the legislative regime is simply seen as adding another layer of regulation to employers' businesses. It is to such potential long-term dangers that the next section turns.

4.2 Economic Analysis and the Potential Repeal of Anti-discrimination Laws

Thus far it has been argued that the business case rests on fragile foundations and is therefore open to challenge. A further concern now needs to be considered. The business case is premised on encouraging firms to do what they should already be doing, that is applying the equality legislation. It simply offers economic justifications for applying the law, taking the existence of such legislation as axiomatic. However, in privileging economic considerations, the business case opens the question of the repeal of such provisions were it to be demonstrated that the legislative framework is economically inefficient. If such a contention were to be proven, the business case would have no normative framework from which to challenge such an argument.

Richard Posner, amongst others, has argued for many years that sex discrimination legislation should be repealed on the grounds that it does not improve the 'welfare' of women (Posner 1987; Posner 1989; Epstein 1992). Posner's argument is that 'sex discrimination law has not increased, and it may even have reduced, the aggregate welfare of women' (Posner 1989: 1312). He reaches this conclusion by suggesting that it would be economically more efficient to allow employers to pay women less and discriminate against them in terms of employment opportunities. If this were allowed, Posner argues, the aggregate welfare of all women would increase by reason of the fact that the wages of men would increase and Posner contends that 'women derive a benefit from an increase in the income of a husband or other male relative' (Posner 1989: 1316). In addition, Posner suggests that the administrative costs of policing sex discrimination laws may be sufficiently high to outweigh any alternative potential benefits which the legislation might bring. Posner does recognise that there may be reasons other than economic ones why women wish to work, but economics trumps: 'the price tag for an increase in women's self-esteem, if known, might be thought to be too high by society' (Posner 1989: 1335).[9]

Posner's clear focus is on welfare and wealth as opposed to equality; a societal not individual focus. This is an approach which has been echoed in the UK. It has been argued that the interference in the 'free market' caused by anti-discrimination legislation is 'insidious' as it interferes with freedom of contract (Paul 1992), and that 'current equal opportunities legislation is causing society to produce less wealth than it would do in the absence of such legislation' (Conway 1992: 57; Conway 1998). These arguments are part of the neo-liberal tradition that conceives of almost any interference with the employment market as anathema, epitomised by Hayek who argued that the pursuit of equal opportunities is a 'wholly illusory ideal, and any attempts concretely to realise it are apt to produce a nightmare' (Hayek 1982: 85)

---

[9] Although Posner is concerned with US sex discrimination laws, his analysis can apply equally to the UK/European Union's legislative provisions on sex discrimination which are, in many respects, similar.

Notwithstanding the fact that the wholesale repeal of equality legislation is perhaps unlikely, and indeed impossible for so long as the UK remains a member of the European Union, the conduct of a debate regarding the utility of sex discrimination in economic terms opens up this question. Even if repeal is unlikely, partial repeal or resistance to any further measures is certainly possible. In moving the debate onto economic terrain, the arguments for repeal of the anti-discrimination laws, or resistance to further measures, are given a forum where they might once have been dismissed as fanciful. This is because laws and campaigns regarding sex equality have been associated more with values such as equality and justice, rather than economics. However, once a strategy is based on economics, in effect, 'support for equal opportunities becomes associated with a set of values unrelated to equality, difference, justice or diversity' (Forbes 1996: 161). Thus, although there are grounds on which to challenge Posner *et al*'s arguments (Donohue 1986; Donohue 1987; Donohue 1989), the business case strategy requires engagement with such a debate, rather than a dismissal of efficiency as being irrelevant to ideas of justice and fairness for women. In other words, emphasising the economics of sex equality legitimates the articulation of views hitherto marginalised and may eventually lead to a situation in which the existing protection of women against discrimination is reduced.

Accordingly, therefore, even were it to be the case that the cause of women's marginalisation is the undervaluation of their human capital, the adoption of this strategy is undesirable. It may bring about some positive changes in particular circumstances, as witnessed by the introduction of some flexible working policies in firms, but by relying on empirical evidence, the strategy and gains are continually open to challenge. Each woman, firm and campaigner are tasked with demonstrating an economic case for their suggestions where there may not always be one. If there is no economic justification, the cause is lost so long as the sole basis for reform is the business case for equality. The successful widespread adoption of the rationale of the business case is likely therefore to be a pyrrhic victory for women solicitors.

4.3 Failing to Confront the Real Issues

Not only is the business case misconceived for all the reasons discussed above, but also due to the fact that it fails to take into account and confront the complexity of the gendered nature of the reasons behind women's marginalised status. The recent study by Hilary Sommerlad and Peter Sanderson on the status of women solicitors in England and Wales reveals that it is not the economic cost of equality which hinders women, but a host of factors, principally the requirements of 'cultural capital', the dominance of masculinity and the assumptions regarding women's appropriate familial roles, which are the root cause of women's continued disadvantaged status (Sommerlad and Sanderson 1998).

For example, Sommerlad and Sanderson argue that the concept of 'commitment' determines the employment opportunities of many solicitors, particularly
women (Sommerlad and Sanderson 1998: 215–23). In particular, the gendered
notion of commitment works against the interests of many women who have
taken a break from their employment due to pregnancy, no matter for how short
a period of time. Thus, the taking of maternity leave is of 'iconic' significance to
the career trajectories of women, forever disabling them in the eyes of many
employers. These assumptions are based on the idea that women will necessarily choose to specialise in the home, thereby, reducing any 'commitment' to the
paid workforce. The 'problem' therefore facing women solicitors in this position, and indeed all women who may be seen to be 'potential' mothers, is the
attitudes towards pregnancy and motherhood and related cultural assumptions.
Thus, although the potential economic cost of pregnancy may be of concern to
an employer, more significant are the non-economic attitudes and cultural
assumptions. For example, the economic cost might be removed by government
or insurance, but this would not mean that pregnancy and maternity would
cease to be a 'problem'. Equally, an employer may provide adequate or even
admirable equal opportunities policies regarding pregnancy and maternity
leave, but still retain a negative perception regarding the future 'commitment'
and trustworthiness of women solicitors. The business case response is that such
an employer is failing to accord appropriate value to the human capital of its
employee. However, although such a failing may cost the employer in economic
terms, it is likely to take more than a reference to such (potential) costs to convince such an employer that different attitudes should prevail, especially as
those views are considered to be rooted in biological fact.

Similarly, in characterising the solicitors' partnership as a 'fraternal contract',
Sommerlad and Sanderson expose the nature of partnership as primarily a
brotherly relationship based on trust and homosocial bonds, not as an economic
enterprise (Sommerlad and Sanderson 1998: 119–51). Again, this is a relationship not easily disturbed by suggestions that it is uneconomic. Indeed, it may be
that partners eschew any economic justification for sharing partnership with
any, or at least many, women, preferring the 'bonds of trust', even at an economic cost. It is, thus, the demands of cultural capital, not inadequately assessed
human capital, which hinder women in the solicitors' profession. Sommerlad
and Sanderson's study shows that a vital component of the solicitors' cultural
capital is the 'ability to participate in this male culture, so that they [solicitors]
must be either male or acceptable pseudo-men' (Sommerlad and Sanderson
1998: 144). Thus, no matter what a woman's educational qualifications and
other experience, her human capital, in many cases she will lack the cultural
capital required to assist her professional career. She is not male, she will interact differently with clients and she may break the clubbable atmosphere of the
partnership or team. Even if she acquires some masculine skills, learns to play
golf, or understands the football scores, she remains pseudo-man, better than
'real woman', but not the same as 'real man'. Such are the difficulties, seemingly

indeterminate, facing women. The skills and qualifications that they require—the masculine cultural capital—cannot be acquired by learning or experience.

Thus, it is not surprising that Sommerlad and Sanderson conclude that while the 'qualifications lever may facilitate women's entry' into the profession, it will not necessarily 'assist in overcoming informal barriers, one of which is the male culture of the solicitors' world' (Sommerlad and Sanderson 1998: 144). The expected, but nonetheless significant, conclusion is that 'however excellent women's human capital, it is likely that few of them can possess appropriate cultural capital (masculinity or pseudo-masculinity being the core minimum) to be selected above associate level' (Sommerlad and Sanderson 1998: 127). Accordingly, the fact that campaigners within the profession choose to focus almost exclusively on the business case, and its attempt to ensure appropriate recognition of women's human capital, demonstrates a lack of understanding of the values of the profession and how they impact on women solicitors

Finally, the core of the business case seeks to persuade employers to adopt and implement equal opportunities policies. There is, however, little evidence that the introduction of such policies will per se end the discrimination facing women solicitors. Normatively, there is much dispute as to whether the liberal equal opportunities policy can engineer the sort of changes that would be required to grant greater opportunities to women. Margaret Thornton, for example, has argued that equal opportunities policies only aid those who conform to a stereotypical (male) career pattern, and argues that these policies simply perpetuate male hegemony, with the added disadvantage of apparent equality and universalism (Thornton 1989). This is supported by Sommerlad and Sanderson who found that despite claims by law firms that they recruit and promote on 'merit', the culture of personal bonds and cultural capital reigns supreme. It is therefore the culture, beyond the reach of anti-discrimination laws (and therefore the threat of expensive legal action), which inhibits the progress of women. The culture of personalist bonds and the familial, personal nature of partnership, subverts the potential of equal opportunity policies, let alone the 'cavalier disregard' (Sommerlad and Sanderson 1998: 121) for formal procedures and laws which Sommerlad and Sanderson found. Indeed, it is important to remember in this respect that all solicitors' firms have been required since 1995 to have an equal opportunities policy, with the Law Society's model policy applying in lieu. Although it is early days since the adoption of that measure, it does not appear that it has brought a sea-change in attitudes within law firms. Accordingly, by placing faith in the adoption and implementation of equal opportunities policies, business case advocates within the profession have failed to appreciate the culture of the law firm and the paradoxical disregard for both professional requirements and the demands of existing equality laws.

5 CONCLUSIONS

It is not clear how the business case for sex equality is going to ameliorate, let alone eradicate, the dominant cultural attitudes and traditions within the profession which Sommerlad and Sanderson uncovered. Change requires challenging the roots of such views, their foundation in biological determinism and related assumptions about the appropriate roles of women and men, and in the homosocial bonds of male networks and working practices. This first requires a recognition that it is such factors as revealed in Sommerlad and Sanderson's study which are at the root of women's marginalised status; that is, a recognition of the gendered nature of women's experiences. The continued assertion that it is the economic cost of equality that hinders women simply serves to obscure the hidden structures and attitudes which are profoundly gendered. Once recognised, strategies must be developed and adopted which acknowledge the gendered nature of the experiences of women solicitors and seek to tackle these problems directly. The business case does not do this: it simply emphasises that economic efficiency is the rightful goal of all firms and seeks to suggest ways in which this path to efficiency might be better travelled. Accordingly, it is imperative to retain a voice in which to challenge discriminatory acts, and gendered attitudes and assumptions, not just on the grounds that they may be uneconomic, but on the basis that they are unjust, unfair and have no place in a modern solicitors' profession. We must advocate reform even where there may be a financial cost.

6 REFERENCES

Abel, R L. 1988. *The Legal Profession in England and Wales*. London: Blackwell.

Alcock, M. 1998/1999. Against All Odds. *Legal Business*. Dec 1998/Jan 1999.

Allison, C. 1989. Women in the law: into the 1990s. *Solicitors Journal* 133; 1593.

Association of Women Solicitors. 1999. *AWS Link*. London: Association of Women Solicitors. January.

Bawdon, F. 1996. Sisters in Law. *Law Society Gazette*. 6 November.

Confederation of British Industry. 1996. *A Winning Strategy—The business case for equal opportunities*. London: CBI.

Cole, Bill. 1998. *Trends in the Solicitors Profession—Annual Statistical Report 1997*. London: Law Society.

Conaghan, J. 1999. Feminism and Labour Law: Contesting the Terrain in *Feminist Perspectives on Employment Law*, edited by A Morris, and T O'Donnell. London: Cavendish.

Conway, D. 1992. Do Women Benefit from Equal Opportunities Legislation? in *Equal Opportunities: A Feminist Fallacy*, edited by C Quest. London: Institute of Economic Affairs.

Conway, D. 1998. *Free-Market Feminism*. London: Institute for Economic Affairs.

Crawford, A. 1996. The Spirit of Community: Rights, Responsibilities and the Communitarian Agenda. *Journal of Law and Society* 23; 247.

Deakin, S, and Wilkinson, F. 1996. *Labour Standards—Essential to Economic and Social Progress.* London: Institute of Employment Rights.

Donohue, J. 1986. Is Title VII Efficient? *University of Pennsylvania Law Review* 134; 1411.

Donohue, J. 1987. Further Thoughts on Employment Discrimination Legislation. *University of Pennsylvania Law Review* 136; 523.

Donohue, J. 1989. Prohibiting Sex Discrimination in the Workplace: An Economic Perspective. *University of Chicago Law Review* 56; 1337.

Epstein, R. 1992. *Forbidden Grounds—The Case Against Employment Discrimination Laws.* Cambridge Mass: Harvard University Press.

Equal Opportunities Review. 1997. vol. 74.

Flood, J. 1996. Megalawyering in the global order: the cultural, social and economic transformation of global legal practice. *International Journal of the Legal Profession* 3; 169.

Forbes, I. 1996. The Privatisation of Sex Equality Policy in *Women in Politics.* edited by J Lovenduski and P Norris. Oxford: Oxford University Press.

Galanter, M. 1983. Mega-law and Mega-lawyering in the Contemporary United States in *The Sociology of the Professions*, edited by R Dingwall and P Lewis. London: Macmillan.

Hayek, F. 1982. *Law, Legislation and Liberty.* London: Routledge and Kegan Paul.

Humphries, J and Rubery, J. eds. 1995. *The Economics of Equal Opportunities.* Manchester: Equal Opportunities Commission.

The Independent. 1996. 26 March.

The Independent. 1997. 23 April.

Klare, K. 1988. Workplace Democracy and Marketplace Reconstruction. *Catholic University Law Review* 38.

Langdon-Down, G. 1997. More women equals money. *The Independent.* 23 April.

Law Society. 1988. *Equal in the Law.* London: Law Society.

Law Society. 1995. *New Anti-Discrimination Measures.* London: Law Society.

Law Society. 1997. Press Release: New Survey Reveals Continuing Inequality Between Male and Female Solicitors. 7 July.

Law Society Gazette. 1994. 9 February.

The Lawyer. 1998. 1 September.

The Lawyer. 1999a. Family demands set to affect firms' fortunes. 3 June.

The Lawyer. 1999b. 31 May.

McGlynn, C. 1997. Paying for Equality. *New Law Journal* 147; 568–569.

McGlynn, C. 1998. *The Woman Lawyer: making the difference.* London: Butterworths.

Paul, E. 1992. Fetal Protection, Women's Rights and Freedom of Contract in *Equal Opportunities: A Feminist Fallacy*, edited by C. Quest. London: Institute of Economic Affairs.

Posner, R. 1987. The Efficiency and Efficacy of Title VII. *University of Pennsylvania Law Review* 136; 153

Posner, R. 1989. An Economic Analysis of Sex Discrimination Laws. *University of Chicago Law Review* 56; 1311.

Rice, R. 1997. Female attraction. *Financial Times.* 3 June.

Sidaway, J. 1995. Gender and Status in the Private Practice Firm in *Removing the Barriers: Legal Services and the Legal Profession.* London: Law Society.

Skordaki, E. 1996. Glass slippers and glass ceilings: women in the legal profession. *International Journal of the Legal Profession* 3; 7.

Social Justice Commission. 1994. *Social Justice—Strategies for National Renewal.* London: Vintage.

Solicitors Journal. 1988. 12 February. 7 June.

Solicitors Journal. 1993. 15 October.

Sommerlad, H. 1994. The myth of feminisation: women and cultural change in the legal profession. *International Journal of the Legal Profession* 1; 31–53.

Sommerlad, H and Sanderson, P. 1998. *Gender, Choice and Commitment: women solicitors in England and Wales and the Struggle for Equal Status.* Aldershot: Ashgate.

Staples, J. 1997. in Langdon-Down, G More women equals money. *The Independent.* 23 April.

Staunton, M. 1990. Returners. *Solicitors Journal* 134; 1156.

Thornton, M. 1989. Hegemonic masculinity and the academy. *International Journal of the Sociology of Law* 17; 115.

The Times. 1997. 18 March.

Whitehouse, Jill. 1997. Glass ceilings or changing times. In *Brief*, May 10.

Willets, D. 1997. *Why Vote Conservative?* London: Penguin.

Willis, J. 1994. Defeating discrimination. *Law Society Gazette* 9 February.

11

Prospects for Parity: the Position of Women in the Judiciary in England and Wales

KATE MALLESON

Abstract

This chapter reviews the position of women in the judiciary in England and Wales. It highlights the slow progress which is being made towards numerical and functional equality and challenges the 'trickle-up' theory which is conventionally offered as an explanation for the unequal participation of women in the judiciary. Instead, it seeks to outline the limitations in the appointments process and the selection criteria which directly or indirectly disadvantage women. It argues that proactive policies which address these structural weaknesses will be required if gender equality is to be achieved in the foreseeable future.

1 INTRODUCTION

I N 2000, OVER 80 years after women were first permitted to qualify as lawyers in England and Wales, women make up approximately 12 per cent of the judiciary. For most of the period during which women have been eligible for judicial office, their limited presence on the bench has attracted relatively little comment or criticism. In recent years however, concern over the lack of diversity in the composition of the judiciary has climbed up the political agenda and is now the subject of considerable public attention and official scrutiny.[1] In response to the increasingly vocal criticisms of the system from solicitors, women lawyers and lawyers from minority ethnic backgrounds there has been a flurry of official activity on the subject. In 1996 and 1999 the Parliamentary Home Affairs Select Committee scrutinised the judicial appointments process, focusing in particular on the unrepresentative make-up of the judiciary. In 1999, the Lord Chancellor's Department commissioned research on the factors affecting the decisions of women lawyers and lawyers from

---

[1] See, for example, JUSTICE, 1992; TMS Consultants, 1992.

minority ethnic backgrounds as to whether or not to apply for judicial office in order to identify what factors hindered or encouraged applications from those under-represented groups. Most recently the Lord Chancellor appointed the retiring commissioner of public appointments, Sir Leonard Peach, to review the judicial selection criteria and processes with particular reference to issues of discrimination.[2]

In the light of the growing political importance of gender issues in the judiciary, this chapter reviews the current position of women on the bench in England and Wales, examining the way in which judges are appointed and the make-up of the pool of candidates from which they are selected. It assesses the prospects for gender parity and argues that the achievement of equality depends not just on the removal of barriers to appointment but also the construction of positive opportunity structures and a culture of 'legitimate expectation' amongst women lawyers that appointment to the judiciary represents a normal career path.

2 HISTORICAL AND COMPARATIVE TRENDS

The historical pattern of women's appointment to the bench and their promotion through the judicial ranks in England and Wales is broadly similar to that of many other common law countries where judges are recruited from amongst senior members of the legal profession and where the judiciary is a relatively small and elite cadre of high status judges. Having first gained the right of entry to the legal profession in 1919, their numbers rose amongst both barristers and solicitors very slowly. The first women judges were appointed in the County Court, the court in which less serious civil work is heard, in the 1960s but it was not until the late 1970s that the number of women lawyers entering the profession rose significantly. By the late 1980s these entrants became eligible for judicial office, resulting in a small but significant increase in the number of women in the lower ranks of the judiciary, particularly in the part-time posts of Assistant Recorder and Recorder, while for the first time a few of the earlier cohort reached the High Court.[3] This rise in the number of women judges coincided with a ten-fold increase in the overall number of judges, from approximately 300 in 1970 to just over 3,000 in 2000. The effect of this expansion was that although the overall number of women rose during this period, women as a proportion of the judiciary changed very little for most of the 1980s and 1990s.

[2] Sir Leonard Peach. December 1999. *An Independent Scrutiny of the Appointments Processes of Judges and Queen's Counsel in England and Wales* (Lord Chancellor's Department, London, 1999). The report proposed the establishment of a commissioner to overview the judicial appointments process. It attracted considerable criticism from solicitors, women lawyers groups and minority lawyers groups for not going far enough in opening up the judiciary.

[3] Barriers to practice were removed by the 1919 Sex Discrimination (Removal Act). See Clare McGlynn's chapter in this volume on 'The Status of Women Lawyers in the United Kingdom'.

Moreover, in comparison with other jurisdictions, the proportion of women judges in England and Wales remains low. A review of the gender composition of judiciaries around the world conducted in 1998 by the International Bar Association (IBA) concluded that, overall, 25 per cent of judges were women. The study revealed two general trends in gender representation. First, the existence of a broad inverse correlation between the status of judges and the proportion of women in the judiciary. Most notably, that women make up a higher proportion of judges in civil law systems compared to common law countries where the status of judges is generally higher. Second, that women are disproportionately situated at the lower end of the judicial ranks.

The position in England and Wales reflects this general pattern with the proportion of women on the bench significantly lower than most continental civil law countries but closer to other common law countries and with most women clustered in the lower ranks. The highest proportion of women is found at the first rung of the judicial ladder amongst the 469 part-time Assistant Recorders, of whom 16 per cent are women.[4] Amongst the full-time ranks, eight per cent of High Court judges, seven per cent of Circuit judges and 13 per cent of district judges are women. No woman has ever been appointed to the House of Lords but three have reached the Court of Appeal. In 1988 Lord Butler Sloss (as she was addressed until 1994) was the first woman appointed to the Court of Appeal, where she remained as the only woman for the next 11 years. This pattern appears to be shared by many other common law countries where a sole woman 'trail blazer' gains access to the upper ranks after which there is a long gap before the next woman is appointed.[5] Applying Kanter's model of representation in institutions, the distribution of women in the judiciary in England and Wales represents 'total exclusion' in the top rank and 'token presence' in the remaining ranks (up to 35 per cent). No rank has yet reached 'minority inclusion' levels of 35 per cent or over (Kanter 1977).

3 THE 'TRICKLE-UP' HYPOTHESIS

One explanation for the low proportion of women judges in common law countries such as England and Wales is that the composition of the judiciary is, to a large extent, a reflection of the make-up of the legal profession. Judges are appointed from amongst senior practitioners and the eligibility rules and selection criteria result in the exclusion of all those at the earlier stages of their career. Because women have only recently entered the profession in significant numbers

---

[4] Lord Chancellor's Department, *Judicial Appointments Annual Report, 1999–2000*, p 88.

[5] In Australia, Roma Mitchell was appointed to the South Australian Supreme Court in 1965. It was 20 years before the next woman was appointed to a state Supreme Court (Thornton 1996: 204). In the US in 1934, Florence Allen became the first woman appointed to the Federal bench where she remained alone for the next 15 years (Ginsburg and Brill 1995: 284). In South Africa there was a 26 year gap between the appointment of the first woman to the High Court bench, Loe van den Heever, and the next. (Rickards, Carmel. 1999. The Doughty Dozen *The Sunday Times*, 29 August).

they have not yet reached the stage in their careers where judicial office is a realistic option. The statutory minimum period for which candidates must have held rights of audience in certain courts before being eligible for appointment ranges from seven to 10 years depending on the judicial post. This means that most candidates would not be able to apply to the bench before their early thirties. In practice, it is very rare for a person to be appointed at that point. Job descriptions produced by the Lord Chancellor's Department set a normal minimum age of 35 for Recorders, 40 for District judges and 45 for Circuit judges. The result being that the pool of candidates are those who qualified 15 to 25 years ago amongst whom women are still under-represented in contrast to more recent entrants to the profession. In 1973 women made up 10 per cent of those called to the bar and 13 per cent of those admitted as solicitors. By 1998, these figures had risen to 37 per cent and 53 per cent respectively, while women now constitute 22 per cent of the practising bar and 29 per cent of practising solicitors. On the basis of these figures, the Lord Chancellor's Department and the judiciary argue that it is just a matter of time before women 'trickle up' onto the bench in significant numbers. Lord Mackay when Lord Chancellor summarised this position in 1994:

> Since the legal profession in this country is the base from which our judiciary is recruited, it follows that those making or recommending appointments are restricted by the nature of the members of the profession available for appointment. Over many years it had been difficult for women and members of the ethnic minorities to reach the senior ranks of the legal profession in the United Kingdom. This, I believe is in the course of changing, naturally and properly. (1994: 9).

In 1996, the then Permanent Secretary of the Lord Chancellor's Department, Sir Thomas Legg, argued in evidence to the Home Affairs Select Committee, that it was 'just a matter of time' before there were 'quite a lot of women judges'.[6] Similarly, Lord Taylor, when Lord Chief Justice, claimed that reform was imminent:

> The present imbalance between male and female, white and black in the judiciary is obvious . . . I have no doubt that the balance will be redressed in the next few years . . . Within five years I would expect to see a substantial number of appointments from both these groups. This is not just a pious hope. It will be monitored (Taylor, 1992, 9).

The 'trickle-up' hypothesis is therefore based upon an assumption that the dramatic rise in the proportion of women entering the legal profession in the last 10 years or so will naturally translate into an equivalent increase in women in the judiciary. However, by the early 1990s, doubts about the trickle-up hypothesis began to be voiced by observers of the appointments process and by many in the

---

[6] See Home Affairs Select Committee. *Report on Judicial Appointments Procedures*, vol I, para 79 (HMSO, London, 1996).

legal profession.[7] The belief, which had been widely accepted in the 1980s, that women were about to reach the top in significant numbers was increasingly re-evaluated in the light of evidence that the rate of change had been slower than anticipated. In 1992, the legal reform group JUSTICE noted that a smaller proportion of eligible women lawyers and lawyers from minority ethnic groups were being appointed to the first ranks of Assistant Recorder and Recorder than the equivalent proportion of white men.[8] Similar claims were made by the Association of Women Barristers in evidence to the Home Affairs Select Committee in 1996.[9] In the same year the Hansard Society report, *Women at the Top*, reviewed the progress of women in the judiciary since it had produced its first report in 1990. It noted the rising proportion of female High Court judges (from one per cent to seven per cent) and Assistant Recorders (from five per cent to 15 per cent) during the preceding six years. However, it found that amongst other ranks there had been very little change (McRae, 1996: 9). By 1999 this pattern of uneven change was still in evidence. The proportion of women on the Circuit bench increased from four per cent in 1989 to five per cent in 1999 while stipendiary magistrates rose from 13 to 15 per cent in the same decade.[10]

These figures, however, are of little value without a comparison with the proportion of women in the senior ranks of the legal profession from which the judges are recruited. However, whether or not women are being appointed to the judiciary in proportion to their numbers at the relevant level of seniority in the legal profession or being promoted to the higher ranks at the same rate as male judges is surprisingly difficult to determine. Despite Lord Taylor's claims that gender issues would be monitored, the statistical information needed to review the progress of women is not readily available. It is only since 1999 that the Lord Chancellor's Department has produced comprehensive statistics on the application and appointments rates according to gender so that it is not yet possible to track historical trends. Nor has there been any systematic review of the progress of a cohort of women from Assistant Recorder to the full time bench in order to assess whether they are moving up the ranks at the same rate as men. In addition, statistics produced by the Bar Council and the Law Society on the gender make-up of the profession are not gathered in a form which facilitates an analysis of the proportion of women applying and appointed compared to men at the equivalent rank of seniority.

The combined effect of such statistical limitations and uncertainties and the perception that women are making slower progress in the judiciary than was

---

[7] Similar doubts, albeit for different reasons, have been voiced regarding the reliability of the 'trickle-up' effect with respect to equality of status for women solicitors. See Clare McGlynn's chapter in this volume on 'Strategies for Reforming the English Solicitors' Profession: an Analysis of the Business Case of Sex Equality'

[8] JUSTICE, 1992: 13.

[9] Home Affairs Select Committee. *Report on Judicial Appointments Procedures*, vol II p 191 para 1.2. (HMSO, London, 1996).

[10] See Clare McGlynn, 1998: 172–73.

anticipated in the 1980s has lead to an increasing tendency to question the road to gender parity as a natural and automatic process. There is a greater awareness amongst commentators that the structural and cultural barriers to gender equality are more entrenched and complex than previously thought. During the 1990s reform groups such as JUSTICE and women lawyers' organisations have increasingly challenged the view that the under-representation of women could continue to be put down to their disproportionately small numbers in the legal profession. The IBA comparative study, for example, concluded that: 'there is a reasonable inference, from the survey results, that systematic factors may be impeding the elevation of women to the judiciary' (Tahmindjis 1998: 131). These factors are to be found in the relationship between the legal profession and the appointments process.

4 THE RECRUITMENT POOL AND SELECTION CRITERIA

There are approximately 80,000 practising solicitors and 10,000 practising barristers in England and Wales. Judicial office is, however, only a realistic option for a small percentage of these lawyers. The legal profession is a highly diversified one, and the eligibility requirements and the selection criteria narrow down the pool of qualified candidates to a small elite within the profession. Crucially, this screening process is not gender neutral. Just as the most dominant factor, that of age, disproportionately affects women since they are clustered amongst the younger cohorts of lawyers, so too other variables in the selection process have a greater negative impact on women than men.

One such factor is the different eligibility for judicial office of solicitors and barristers. Traditionally, barristers held exclusive rights of audience in the higher courts which gave them an effective monopoly over appointment to the upper ranks of the judiciary. Since 1990, lawyers in both branches have theoretically been equally eligible for judicial office provided they have held rights of audience in certain courts for certain periods or have already held certain judicial office. Under the Courts and Legal Services Act 1990 solicitors have been eligible to apply for higher rights of audience in order to appear in the higher courts. As yet, however, relatively few have been granted those rights.[11] Therefore most of the solicitors appointed to the bench are appointed to the lower ranks such as tribunal members, magistrates or district judges. Although in theory it is possible to be promoted from these ranks to the higher judiciary, in practice the career paths between the upper and lower ranks are still sharply divided. The traditional career path for the full-time upper judiciary is from the bar to Assistant Recorder, then to Recorder and then to the Circuit bench or the High Court. The highest rank which is, in practice, open to solicitors is the

---

[11] Acquiring higher rights of audience requires an applicant to take an expensive course, pass an exam and appear for a set amount of days in the lower courts.

Circuit bench. Although Circuit judges are eligible for appointment to the High Court, very few are promoted via this route and to date only one solicitor has been appointed to the High Court from the Circuit bench. Thus, in practice, the majority of solicitors remain effectively ineligible for appointment to the upper ranks. Moreover, even in relation to the lower ranks where solicitors and barristers are equally eligible, the selection criteria have been interpreted as requiring long advocacy experience, the effect of which has been to exclude a high proportion of solicitors.

The combined effect of the emphasis on advocacy in the selection process, the prioritisation of the bar and the division between the career paths of the upper and lower judiciary is disproportionately to reduce the prospects of women lawyers either being appointed to the lower ranks or being promoted to the higher ranks since women are more likely to qualify as solicitors than barristers.[12] In addition, those judges who are appointed from amongst solicitors are invariably already partners, which excludes many senior women solicitors since partnership is not equally distributed between men and women. Figures from the Law Society for 1997 showed that 88 per cent of male solicitors in private practice with 10 to 19 years of experience were partners compared with only 63 per cent of female solicitors of the same seniority.[13]

Amongst women barristers, an equivalent inhibiting factor is the selection of judges in the upper ranks from amongst Queen's Counsel (QC). Although there is no formal eligibility rule that requires senior judges to be QCs ('take Silk'), in practice, being appointed QC is generally regarded as a prerequisite for appointment. Women still make up a very small proportion of QCs—currently six per cent—a figure which has risen very little in the last decade. The Association of Women Barristers has identified the link between Silk and judicial office as 'a serious form of indirect discrimination in the present appointments system'.[14] The dominance of Silk has been paralleled by a tendency to select from certain specialisms, such as commercial law, in which women are also underrepresented. In addition, certain chambers have traditionally been regarded as 'recruiting grounds' for Silk and judicial office.[15] These too tend to be the most elite and traditional sets in which women have made slower progress.

Similar problems arise as a result of the division between employed barristers and those in private practice.[16] It has to date been assumed (though the statutory

---

[12] See *Memorandum of the Association of Women Solicitors*, Home Affairs Select Committee Report on Judicial Appointment Procedures, vol II, p 199, para 14.

[13] *Women in the Profession*, Fact Sheet Two, Law Society Annual Statistical Report 1997 (The Law Society, London).

[14] Home Affairs Select Committee Report on Judicial Appointment Procedures, vol II, p 193, para 2.9.

[15] Between 1986 and 1996 the senior judiciary was recruited exclusively from 58 of the 227 sets of barristers' chambers (Clare McGlynn 1999: 178).

[16] Most barristers are self-employed members of chambers. Employed barristers include those who work as prosecutors for the Crown Prosecution Service, or in-house advisers for government departments or companies.

position is not clear) that employed barristers are not eligible for most judicial office. This bar disproportionately affects women because a higher percentage of women than men move from private practice to the employed bar. It has been suggested that this is because women are attracted by the better maternity pay and flexible working, reduced levels of sexual discrimination, and better comparative pay levels available at the employed bar (Skordaski 1996: 22). If so, it would appear that women who move to the employed bar trade-off better working arrangements for the loss of access to judicial office.

To summarise, judges in the upper ranks have traditionally been selected from barristers in private practice from elite chambers. They have usually built up strong advocacy practices, often in commercial backgrounds and have taken Silk. Those in the lower ranks are more likely to be drawn from amongst solicitors who are partners with advocacy experience. This relatively small group excludes the majority of lawyers and disproportionately excludes women since they are more likely to be solicitors below the rank of partner, and if at the bar not to have taken Silk, to have paper practices, to work in the areas of crime and family or to be at the employed bar.

<h2 style="text-align:center">5 THE SELECTION PROCESS</h2>

Linked to these gender-specific limitations in the nature of the recruitment pool are a number of factors in the judicial selection process which similarly militate against the appointment of equal numbers of women. In particular, the lack of openness in the system and the reliance on 'soundings' as to the suitability of candidates taken from judges and senior lawyers.

Over the last 20 years or so, one of the most frequently heard criticisms of the current appointments system is that it lacks transparency and that outsiders, such as women and lawyers from minority ethnic backgrounds are disadvantaged by their lack of knowledge about or confidence in the system. In the case of women this appears to be supported by evidence that they are less likely to apply both for Silk and judicial office in comparison with men of the same level of seniority.[17] In response to criticisms of lack of openness, a significant number of changes have been introduced to the process during the last 10 years designed to increase transparency and counter the disadvantages faced by women applicants and other under-represented groups and to encourage more to apply. In 1994, for example, Lord Mackay introduced advertising for posts below the High Court and the use of annual competitions for the posts of Assistant Recorder and Recorder and the production of job descriptions for each judicial rank. Lord Irvine has built upon these reforms by extending advertising, job descriptions and formal applications to the High Court though retaining the

---

[17] See Home Affairs Select Committee. 1996. *Report on Judicial Appointments Procedures*, vol I para 57.

right to make appointments by invitation amongst those who have not applied. Appointments to the Court of Appeal and House of Lords remain by invitation only on the grounds that they are, in practice, selected from amongst High Court judges. Under Lord Mackay a system of interview panels was introduced; each panel consisting of a judge, a member of the Lord Chancellor's Department and a lay person appointed from the Advisory Committees of the Justices of the Peace by the Lord Chancellor's Department. Since 1994, all those appointed to the posts of District judge, Assistant Recorder, Recorder and Circuit judge have attended a formal interview before such a panel.

In order to encourage those without much knowledge of the day-to-day realities of judicial work to apply, a shadowing scheme has been implemented to allow potential candidates to sit with a judge in order to acquire a feel for the job. Some reforms have been specifically implemented with the needs of women in mind. Since 1997 there has been a policy of greater flexibility in part-time sitting arrangements allowing part-timers to concentrate their sittings into a shorter time. This is designed to recognise the position of candidates who have taken a career break for family reasons and so to assist them to 'catch up'. In addition, the age limit for appointment to Assistant Recorder was raised from 50 to 53 to accommodate late entrants and those who have taken career breaks.

In addition to these procedural changes, the Lord Chancellor, Lord Irvine has actively encouraged lawyers from under-represented groups to apply by writing to heads of chambers asking them to urge well-qualified women and minority barristers in their chambers to consider applying. He has also addressed women lawyers and minority lawyer group conferences, using the slogan 'don't be shy, apply!' in an attempt to dispel the belief that only certain groups were in the running for judicial office. In an address to the Minority Lawyers Conference in 1997 Lord Irvine stated:

> I will not be scattering promotions around like confetti—appointments must be made on merit. But I am determined to break down the culture of not applying because 'they'd never have me or the likes of me'.[18]

These changes have generally been welcomed and most critics would agree that the system is more open and fairer than it was 15 years ago as a result of them. They have not, however, significantly affected the heart of the process, and the subject of most criticism—the consultation process. This is often described as a system of 'secret soundings' by its critics, a term which Lord Irvine rejects on the grounds that the system cannot be said to be secret since all lawyers know it operates. However, the element of secrecy lies not in the fact of its existence, but the fact that candidates do not know who has been consulted about them and what they have said. As a result, it is argued that subjective, impressionistic or inappropriate opinions can affect a person's prospects of a judicial career without the candidate being able effectively to counter these.

---

[18] Speech to the Minority Lawyers Conference, 29 November 1997.

In practice, however, more worrying than the effect of damaging soundings, is that of no soundings. In order for the consultees to be able to comment on a candidate's abilities she or he must have appeared before them or with them in court or be known to them informally through membership of the same work or social networks. Many applicants who fail to be appointed are told this is because 'noone out there is talking for you'. Critics of the system argue that the need to be 'known' discriminates against outsiders and privileges an elite inner circle. For example, the fact that few women barristers are appointed Benchers in the Inns of Court excludes women from the informal networking which takes place amongst those running the Inns and through which barristers become known to judges.[19] The danger of the consultation system is essentially that of self-replication. Its defenders point to the generally high intellectual and moral standards of the judges appointed as evidence of the fact that merit is the over-riding criterion. This argument misses the key criticism of the system which is not so much that poor candidates are appointed but that equally good candidates who do not share the same or similar characteristics, backgrounds, views or experiences as those whose advice is sought are excluded. Outsiders are inevitably at a disadvantage in a system which relies on the opinions of insiders.

Despite the extensive reforms which have taken place in the appointments process, the continuing dependence on the consultation process has, if anything, led to intensified criticism of the appointments process through the 1990s. In 1991, a leading solicitor, Geoffrey Bindman, suggested that the consultations process might amount to indirect discrimination under the Race Relations Act and Sex Discrimination Act.[20] Lord Mackay, then Lord Chancellor, took advice from leading counsel and rejected the claim as 'wrong in law and fact'—a response which, predictably, failed to satisfy the critics of the system. In 1992, a report commissioned jointly by the Bar Council and the Lord Chancellor's Department concluded that:

> it is unlikely that the judicial appointments system offers equal access to women or fair access to promotion to women judges . . . the system depends on patronage, being noticed and being known.[21]

These criticisms were endorsed by the Association of Women Barristers in its evidence to the Home Affairs Select Committee in 1996. Similar arguments were put forward by the Law Society and the minority lawyers groups. In response to these concerns, some modification of the consultation process was undertaken by Lord Irvine. Lists of the main consultees were published and it was stated that no claim of misconduct against a candidate would be taken into account unless it was disclosed to the applicant and its maker named. Lord Irvine also

---

[19] See evidence of the Association of Women Barristers, Home Affairs Select Committee. 1996. *Report on Judicial Appointments Procedures*, vol II, p 193, para 4.6.

[20] *Law Society Gazette*, 27 February 1991.

[21] TMS Consultants, 1992 p 23, para 44.

stressed that no one person's view, however good or bad would be conclusive in a decision on appointment.

In December 1999, the Peach report on judicial appointments and Silk broadly endorsed the consultation process as 'an organised and systematic approach for collecting information.'[22] Nevertheless it acknowledged that views on the merit and legitimacy of the process were polarised as between the judiciary and many groups in the legal profession. The report proposed a number of changes which would have the effect of reducing its role and increasing the importance of referees nominated by the candidates and other means of assessment such as competence and psychometric tests and the use of One Day Assessment Centres. Predictably, these proposals have been attacked as being 'too little too late' by critics of the system.[23] The extent to which the system has lost the confidence of significant sections of the legal profession was demonstrated in October 1999 when the Law Society withdrew from the system claiming that it did not believe that the consultation process functioned fairly as between solicitors and barristers.

6 FUTURE TRENDS—OPPORTUNITY STRUCTURES AND LEGITIMATE EXPECTATIONS

There is general agreement that as the proportion of women amongst the senior ranks of the legal profession increases, the number of women in the judiciary is very likely to rise. But how far and how fast is less predictable. Assuming the continuation of the tradition of selection from amongst those lawyers who have been in practice for 15 to 25 years, a long period of inequality lies ahead before there is any realistic prospect of gender parity. In that time many factors, including those described above, may work against that outcome. There is nothing predetermined about the achievement of parity in the judiciary and experience in public and professional life over the last 80 years has demonstrated that gender transformation does not happen automatically once women achieve formal equality of access. Blair Cook has argued that equality will only be achieved if the necessary opportunity structures exist for a significant increase in women judges (1987: 155). For this to occur, she suggests that the following three conditions must be present: an increase in the overall numbers of judges, an increase in the proportion of women in the pool of candidates, and an increased willingness on the part of appointers to appoint them.

These factors are currently evident in England and Wales but there is no guarantee that they will remain so in the coming years. All three are dependent upon social, political and economic conditions which may change. If the recent

[22] Sir Leonard Peach, *An Independent Scrutiny of the Appointments Processes of Judges and Queen's Counsel in England and Wales*, Lord Chancellor's Department, 1999, p 14.
[23] See Judges' Reform must go further. *The Guardian*, 3 December 1999.

expansion in the size of the judiciary slows, and competition for judicial office intensifies, candidates from non-traditional backgrounds may lose ground. At present, the introduction of the Woolf reforms to civil justice and the Human Rights Act 1998 have increased the need for more judges. But treasury-led reductions in legal aid eligibility and the trend to encourage legal disputes to be resolved by non-court based alternative dispute resolution methods may counter this trend. Equally, the assumption of continuing political and social pressure to prioritise gender equality cannot be assumed. In South Africa, for example, despite the fact that there has been a very strong rhetoric of gender equality since the new government came to power, the increase in the numbers of women in the judiciary has been very slow and appears to have been eclipsed by the prioritisation of the appointment of non-white judges. One female judge has recently said that 'it's almost as if gender transformation has dried up'.[24] Similarly, the numbers of women judges in some of the Eastern European countries have fallen dramatically since the democratic revolution there.[25]

It may be argued that comparisons with such jurisdictions in which rapid change has occurred are inappropriate, but these examples serve as a reminder of the contingent nature of women's participation in the judiciary and public life generally. The fact that development in the UK is likely to continue to be evolutionary rather than revolutionary does not mean that equality is any less dependent on political, cultural and economic conditions. It is not hard to imagine less dramatic changes in circumstances in the UK which might undermine the move to gender parity. For example, the continuing expansion of women in the senior ranks of the legal profession, on which the appointment of women to the judiciary rests, is partially dependent on the continued promotion of working arrangements which are compatible with family commitments. More flexible arrangements which were introduced in many firms and chambers in the 1980s were partly the result of economic necessity when the economic upturn encouraged organisations to find means of retaining their qualified women lawyers. Recent research findings, however, suggest that during the recession of the early 1990s women lawyers were 'the first victims of decline' with evidence of some reversal of the trend towards 'family friendly' practices and its replacement by the 'long hours culture' (Sommerlad and Sanderson 1998: 5 and 258). The legal profession is, ultimately, no more than a disparate collection of businesses. Where economic advantage coincides with the development of conditions which promote gender equality the position of women lawyers in those businesses will be favourable. But where the two conflict, it cannot be assumed that social pressure alone will be sufficient to maintain working arrangements which do not maximise profit.

[24] The law is an ass when it comes to women. *Sunday Times*, 18 August 1999.
[25] In Moldova the number of women judges in the Supreme Court fell from 13 in 1990 to seven in 1994 while in Krygystan women made up 31 per cent of the judiciary in 1985 and eight per cent in 1995 (UNICEF 1999: 98).

Recognising that there is no 'natural' gender balance in the legal profession or the judiciary and that the move to parity is dependent on certain social, political and economic conditions requires the creation of opportunity structures which give rise to a legitimate expectation amongst women lawyers that promotion to the bench is a normal career move. Gender equality in the judiciary is therefore only possible if the career paths which women commonly pursue are on the trajectory to judicial appointment. The change required in order to bring about such opportunity structures is a profound one. It necessitates a recognition that the current appointment process did not develop as a neutral mechanism for selecting those who would make the best judges from the total possible recruitment pool. Instead, the emphasis on the bar, on advocacy, on commercial experience, on those who have Silk, those with certain practices from certain chambers is a reflection of historical power relations within the legal profession. The current path from junior barrister to QC to the bench became the opportunity structure for judicial appointment because that was the traditional career path pursued by the elite who sought judicial office and regarded it as their right. The appointments process and selection criteria adapted to the careers of those who sought judicial office not the other way around.

While 'merit' and 'competence' are the essential criteria for judicial appointment, the way in which these qualities are interpreted by selectors and demonstrated by candidates will differ greatly depending on the particular experiences and characteristics of those in the recruitment pool. The career paths of traditional appointees produce candidates with certain achievements, experiences and skills which have come to be associated with the qualifications we expect of a judge. But objectively these are not the only or, necessarily, the most appropriate qualifications. Being a Silk, having a strong advocacy practice and having acquired a tenancy in certain chambers are not essential prerequisites of being a good judge. Had solicitors emerged in the last century as the senior branch of the profession then judges would almost certainly have been appointed from amongst their ranks and advocacy would not have been accorded the pre-eminence in the selection criteria which it currently enjoys. Because women are late entrants to the legal profession they have naturally tended to occupy spaces in the interstices outside the elite career paths. Like solicitors, they have not had the power to ensure that their career paths shape the appointments processes and selection criteria.

A prerequisite of parity is that this implicit relationship between the working arrangements in the legal profession and the appointments process be made explicit. But whereas in the past this relationship has been driven by the interests of the powerful elite at the bar it must now reflect the experiences of all 90,000 lawyers so that those who have the potential to make good judges have an equal opportunity to be identified and appointed. This change is more than a mere shift of focus, it requires a reorientation of the current system. To date, the approach to change has been purely reactive. When criticisms build up, the minimum necessary reforms are introduced to alleviate pressure on the system.

Instead, what is needed is the development of an ongoing reflective process which seeks to match lawyers' working patterns, experiences and skills with a judicial appointments process which will provide opportunity structures which draw the greatest number of competent candidates into the selection process. This is a very demanding proposal because it requires an approach which recognises the need for ongoing adaptation in response to the accelerating pace of change in the legal profession. It is likely that working arrangements generally and women's participation specifically will undergo many different transformations in the coming years which will require an unprecedented degree of responsiveness from the judicial appointments process. Change will therefore need to be a natural and in-built part of the system.

It is unlikely, if not impossible, that the system in its current form could undertake this degree of reconstruction of purpose and method. For this reason, if no other, the time has come for the creation of a judicial appointments commission with full responsibility for developing the selection process. A new body is more likely to be able to reorientate the system by finding new ways of creating 'normal career paths' and 'legitimate expectations' for lawyers practising in widely different working arrangements both now and in the future.

7 CONCLUSION

Women are still a long way from parity in the judiciary in England and Wales, not just in terms of current numbers but in terms of the presence of conditions which will facilitate equality. While the proportion of women judges is likely to continue to rise, parity will not be reached unless there is a conscious decision to promote that goal. In this regard, the judiciary is no different from any other area of public life which involves power and decision-making. As UNICEF noted in its 1999 report on the participation of women in public life in Eastern Europe:

> The advancement of women to decision-making positions will not necessarily be a spontaneous outcome of political or economic reform. It requires an environment in which women are encouraged and supported in their efforts, in which women have equitable access to resources and opportunities, and in which pro-active policies and practices are pursued by governments, business and civilian institutions (UNICEF 1999: 108).

There are examples of such support and encouragement both within the legal profession and the selection process. Politically, the subject of gender equality in the judiciary is much higher on the agenda than it has ever been and the unrepresentative make-up of the judges is the subject of widespread criticism. The formal barriers which kept women out of the judiciary have been dismantled. But the opportunity structures and legitimate expectations needed for parity have not yet been constructed. The bench in England and Wales will not include equal numbers of men and women until the appointments process is reorientated to respond to the changing nature of the legal profession, and within it, the career patterns of women.

8 REFERENCES

Blair Cook, Beverley. 1987. Women Judges in the Opportunity Structure. In *Women, the Courts and Equality*, edited by L Crites and W Hepperle. Newbury Park: Sage.

Ginsburg, Ruth and Laura Brill. 1995. Women in the Federal Judiciary: Three Way Pavers and the Exhilarating Change President Carter Wrought, *Fordham Law Review*, 64; 281.

JUSTICE. 1992. *The Judiciary in England and Wales*. London: JUSTICE.

Kanter, Rosebeth. 1977. Some Effects of Proportions on Group Life: Skewed Sex Ratios and Responses to Token Women, *American Journal of Sociology*, 82; 965–990.

Mackay, Lord. 1994. *The Administration of Justice*. London: Sweet & Maxwell.

MacRae, Susan. 1996. *Women at the Top: Progress after Five Years*. London: The Hansard Society.

McGlynn, Clare. 1998. *The Woman Lawyer: Making the Difference*, London: Butterworths.

Skordaki, Eleni. 1996. Glass Slippers and Glass Ceilings: Women in the Legal Profession, *International Journal of the Legal Profession* 3, 7–42.

Sommerlad, Hilary and Peter Sanderson. 1998. *Gender, Choice and Commitment: Women Solicitors in England and Wales and the Struggle for Equal Status*, Aldershot: Ashgate.

Tahmindjis, Phillip. 1998. Women Judges: A Comparative Survey, *International Legal Practitioner*, 23; 131–134.

Taylor, Lord. 1992. *The Judiciary in the Nineties*, The Richard Dimbleby Lecture, London.

Thornton, Margaret. 1996. *Dissonance and Distrust: Women in the Legal Profession*, Melbourne: Oxford University Press.

TMS Consultants. 1992. *Without Prejudice? Sex Equality at the Bar and in the Judiciary*, London: TMS.

UNICEF. 1999. *Women in Transition: The Monee Project Regional Monitoring Report No. 6*, Florence: UNICEF.

12

Can Women Lawyer Differently?
A Perspective from the UK

HILARY SOMMERLAD

Abstract

The question of whether women can lawyer 'differently' (Menkel-Meadow 1985) remains contentious. This paper seeks to contribute to the debate in two main ways. Firstly, drawing on qualitative research into the experiences and motivations of lawyers in their work, it discusses what skills and qualities they feel are required of them, and what constraints they perceive, if any, on the way they operate. The responses provoke an analysis based in lawyers' (changing and multiple) material experiences: I consider the juridical field and, in turn, its sub-fields—constituted both by different legal specialisms and also by different working environments. Placing respondents' evidence within this context leads in turn to discussion of the pervasive influence of the public and private spheres, which continue to be critically formative, materially, ideologically and discursively, of male and female subjectivities and of the juridical field(s). Furthermore, this wider focus requires us also to examine the effect on the profession of exposure to the market, and the resulting fracturing of traditional structures, identities and ideologies, affecting the potential for further change.

> *Can women lawyer differently? Well I think you've got to start by looking at the sort of people who go into law. I mean I went into law to get away from what was a very sexist background, where the men would sit in one room and talk about male and, I thought, more interesting, things and women in another . . . so I always wanted to be with the men . . . and maybe that's the story of the sort of women who go into law. And then there's what happens to you when you train to be a lawyer. . . , and then again there's different areas of law . . . so it's complicated isn't it? (Personal Injury lawyer, white, late 30s)*

1 INTRODUCTION

A s in other jurisdictions, women's attempts to enter the professions in the UK were generally framed in terms of their equality to men (see, for instance, *Bebb v The Law Society* [1913][1]). In the judgments and propaganda campaigns which robustly countered these presumptions women were variously represented as superior morally and consequently in need of shelter from the harsh realities of the public sphere, or as unfit on grounds of excessive emotionality and irrationality, but always as essentially and irredeemably different (Gordon 1984; Sachs and Wilson 1978; Sommerlad and Sanderson 1998).

Despite the deployment of such stereotypes in order to confine women to a domestic role, 'difference feminism'[2] has also long formed a strand in women's project for public participation[3] (Banks 1981; Harrison 1978; Willis 1980; Kerber 1986; Littleton 1987; Segal 1987; Scott 1988). For instance, in her essay on professionalism and the ethic of care in Canada, Carol Baines identifies a 'maternal feminism as the underlying ideology which spurred the movement of women into the public sphere during the first wave of feminism' (1991: 37). Similarly Virginia Drachman documents the claims made by some of the pioneering women lawyers in the USA that they had 'unique values and skills' which would enrich the profession; one such woman argued that since male lawyers sacrificed principle for material reward, the role of women was to 'give the love-lit hues of Christ's teaching' (Sara Kilgore Wertman to the Equity Club 7/5/1888; cited in Drachman 1998: 77). Nevertheless during both first wave and the 'second wave feminism' of the 1970s[4], the women's movement was primarily concerned with equal opportunities[5] (Bacchi 1991). In the latter phase, despite political disagreement over issues such as the causes of women's oppression, including the role of the law[6], this entailed a strategic commitment to minimising differences between men and women (and also amongst women).

---

[1] Ch 286; see too Buckmaster in Hansard, Lords Debates XXIV, 1917, 259–61, and Grata Flos Greig (1909).

[2] Advocates of gender difference have been variously termed cultural, relational and difference feminists. In this essay I will use the term difference feminists.

[3] The conceptualisation of the law as 'male' also pre-dates second wave feminism: Georg Simmel, in essays published in 1923 spoke in these terms (cited in Gerhard 1993: 317).

[4] See Olsen (1990), Naffine (1990) and Smart (1992) for discussions of the various phases of the women's movement, and in particular the development of feminist socio-legal theory.

[5] Although it should be noted that in the UK this strategy was pursued in part in alliance with the labour movement and involved a struggle not only for equal wages but also for social provision such as health care and maternity and child welfare, and, hence, a recognition of social difference (Walby 1994: 390).

[6] For instance, the majority of women lawyers (comprising liberal feminists and those who would not describe themselves as feminist at all) broadly accepted the claims of law to be rational, objective and essentially gender-neutral, so that the primary concern was to make it live up to these claims and, correspondingly, strive for equality through assimilation (Skordaki 1996: 14; Sommerlad and Sanderson 1998: 82–3, 184–92, 260–1, 270–2). By contrast, for both radical and

This fragile consensus on gender equality and female solidarity was brought to an end by what Barrett and Phillips (1992) have described as the 'paradigm shift' of the 1980s/90s. Whilst the postmodernist conceptualisation of identity as diverse, fluid and socially constructed represented a clear challenge, the 1980s also saw the revitalisation of 'difference feminism' (Chodorow 1978; Ruddick 1989; Noddings 1984; Irigaray 1985). The empirical work of psychologist Carol Gilligan on moral development—described as an 'affirmation of female experience' (Cornell 1991: 137)—was particularly influential on this latter perspective. Gilligan's research into moral reasoning (1982) led her to conclude that women's approach to moral problems was to situate them in a web or 'network of connections'. This, she argued, resulted in a distinctive morality which she labelled the ethic of care, which, for Gilligan, represented an entirely different (and competing) approach to the requirements of others to that which had emerged from the work of her former colleague Kohlberg (1984; Gilligan 1986: 325). In Kohlberg's tests (primarily carried out with males), which he termed measures of 'justice reasoning' (Gilligan 1987: 22), moral development is equated with the development of ideas of personal autonomy, a hierarchisation of need and the universalisability of rights and obligations.

In response to critiques of her work (Kerber 1986; Williams 1989; Epstein 1991), Gilligan has stated that she did not present the care perspective as either biologically determined or 'unique to women' (1986: 327).[7] Nevertheless, her research has been seen (and used) to support suggestions both that there exists a distinctive, 'natural' (Freyer 1995: 201) female approach to moral problems, grounded in connectedness, and that this approach, even if the product of male oppression (MacKinnon: 1983), may be deployed to disrupt and reform patriarchal structures and discourses (Abrams 1991: 396; Young 1997: 159). This perspective, together with the postulate of an ethic of care 'centred around the ideal of caring (for people one knows)' (Slote 1998: 171) as an alternative to the formalism and impersonalism of the Kantian tradition embodied in the 'ethic of justice', has generated an extensive and ongoing debate amongst lawyers and legal academics over the possibility of bringing about change in the practice of law.

Some of the discussion of the potential for transformation has been situated in feminist jurisprudence. For instance there has been much work on the ways in which law disadvantages women, even (or especially) when couched in neutral terms, and, further, on how a woman's perspective is needed to shift the legal focus from one of rights to one of needs (Menkel-Meadow 1995; Freyer 1995; but see Cahn 1991; Ellmann 1993; O'Connor 1991). Thus Leslie Bender (who describes herself as a 'follower' of Carol Gilligan) argues that gender

socialist second-wave feminists the law's claims to neutrality were viewed as masking its essentially patriarchal nature (see for instance Polan 1982: 294; Rifkin 1980; MacKinnon 1983).

[7] Gilligan's work has also been criticised on methodological grounds; for example Greeno and Maccoby (1986) argue that it is not capable of supporting the assertion that the views expressed by the women she interviewed represent a different voice (and see Luria 1986).

difference theory provides a 'rich source for transforming law . . . we must supply new vocabularies, perspectives, paradigms, methodologies, and practices'. (1990: 46: see too Sherry 1986). Others have critiqued the methodologies and epistemologies of law (for instance Gerhard 1993) with the aim of transforming the production of legal knowledge and doctrines and practice by basing them in 'situated, positioned and contextualised experiences' (Bartlett 1990). There have also been specific studies of the core legal subjects (for instance see the collections of essays edited by Bottomley, 1996, and Bridgeman and Millns, 1998), and of the applicability of the ethic of care to legal education (Spigelman 1988; see too, Frug 1992), and discussion of the possibility of mainstreaming feminist legal theory (Finley 1989; Karst 1984), and of practical strategies which could expose such characteristics of the law as the reliance on male experience to define legal categories (Menkel-Meadow 1995: 37).[8]

For some socio-legal scholars Gilligan's work has also stimulated debate over whether women lawyers will adapt or assimilate to the profession or whether their participation will result in 'innovation in and transformation of the practice of law' (Menkel-Meadow 1989: 198–9; see too, Jack and Jack 1989; Kay and Hagan 1998), thus reforming the moral deficiencies of a rights-based discourse and practice.[9] Beginning with the Gilligan proposition that 'women know things differently' from white men (1995: 53), producing the 'female "ethic of care" . . . grounded in a relational, connected, contextual form of reasoning which (is) focused on people, as well as the substance of a problem' (1995: 26), Carrie Menkel-Meadow proceeds to outline the argument that this ethic is opposed to 'male moral reasoning' which is 'based on abstracted, universalistic principles applied to problematic situations to create an "ethic of justice" '. The explicit linkage of the idea of gender difference to the ethic of care then leads her to suggest that women lawyers

> may be more likely to adopt less confrontational, more mediational approaches to dispute resolution . . . women will be more sensitive to clients' needs and the interests of those who are in relation to each other, for example clients' families or employees . . . women employ less hierarchical managerial styles . . . are more likely to have social justice or altruistic motives in practising law . . . and to develop greater integration between their work and family lives (1995: 34–5).

---

[8] The insight that the 'law is male' underpins these concerns; for instance Menkel-Meadow cites Olsen: 'law is supposed to be rational, objective, abstract and principled like men; it is not supposed to be irrational, subjective, contextualised or personalized like women' (1985: 44).

[9] In the UK and Europe the debate over the question of gender difference has been notable for the fact that it has generated writing by some of the key thinkers in the field of psychoanalytic theory (for instance, Derrida, Cixous, Kristeva). However, the principal exponents of the propositions that women may 'lawyer differently', and of the desirability of practising an 'ethic of care' are North American (see for instance, Menkel-Meadow 1985, 1987, 1995; Sherry 1986; Minow 1990; West 1988; Areen 1988; Bender 1990; Fineman 1990). This chapter will be predominantly concerned with this literature, and, in particular with the work of Carrie Menkel-Meadow who has made an especially rich contribution to the debate.

She also considers the interaction of gender with existing workplace practices, speculating whether women's entry may oblige 'greedy institutions' to reevaluate the demands they make on employees (1995: 55).[10]

The question of agency is clearly central to this debate. Hull and Nelson have recently written of the need to resolve the contradiction between structure and agency in the analysis of the position of women within the legal profession (1998), and have pointed to the capacity for microprocessual analysis to uncover the way in which women's agency and subjectivity functions within the constraints imposed by the structures of professionalism. This chapter attempts to contribute to this kind of understanding in the specific context of the ethic of care as a potential source of women's agency in law. I therefore seek to take up Menkel-Meadow's proposition (hereafter the proposition) by focussing on the socio-cultural and historical context within which change—whether in the form of a distinctive female contribution or through the more gender-neutral idea of an ethic of care—would have to take place. To do this, I draw on a small scale qualitative study into the experiences and motivations of lawyers in their work,[11] to discuss the skills and qualities (including ideas of gender identity)

---

[10] In some of Menkel-Meadow's papers she briefly delineates (and contributes to) sociological work on female participation, alluding to such manifestations of a gendered configuration of the legal workplace as occupational segregation and ghettoisation (Curran 1986), exclusion from partnership (Fenning and Schnegg 1983), income differentials and long hours. Some of her work also discusses various explanations for these gender patterns, from human capital theory (Becker 1974) to 'exclusionary patriarchy' (Hartmann 1976, cited in Menkel-Meadow 1989).

[11] Two sources inform this discussion; firstly 22 lawyers (9 males and 14 females) were interviewed specifically for this chapter: Evidently with such a small sample, no claims are made for its representativeness; nevertheless an attempt was made to achieve as much variety as possible and respondents were drawn from a wide range of locations: small towns, London, decaying industrial urban centres and a regional centre. The sample comprised 1 judge (female), 1 barrister (female), 1 (female) legal manager of a multinational corporate firm and 3 law lecturers, one of whom also practised part-time. Of the practitioners, 7 were commercial lawyers and 9 worked for High Street general practices. Of these 4 (2 men, 2 women) specialised in matrimonial law, 1 (female) in child care law, 2 in Personal Injury (hereafter PI), 1 did crime, 1 immigration and 1 practised both matrimonial and PI. Interviews were semi-structured and included questions on motivations for entering law, views on the function(s) of law, on the meaning of justice, on the ways they operationalised their values/motivations, factors which facilitated/inhibited this operationalisation, the culture of their firms, of the local legal community, the nature of their work, the skills and support it required and their views of clients. Interviewees were asked to give practical examples to illustrate their more general responses. The question of gender and any effect it might have on styles and the nature of lawyering was approached obliquely and only towards the end of the interviews.

My interest in this area was originally sparked by a longitudinal study of women in the legal profession conducted for the Law Society of England and Wales, and I have also drawn on the data collected for this project. The sample comprised all female practising solicitors in West Yorkshire in 1989 and their male employers. This sample was augmented in 1995 by a follow-up questionnaire and series of interviews with respondents selected from the initial sample (Sommerlad and Sanderson 1998).

All the usual caveats concerning the limitations of qualitative data should be seen to apply to the present discussion. I draw on it is not to offer a 'true' picture which is representative of people's experience of practice as a whole. Rather, I am aiming to use practitioners' accounts to demonstrate the ways in which the context of their work can influence the way they practise. Further, given that one of my concerns is with the need to present a more nuanced understanding of both gender and the juridical field, I am aware of the difficulties of deploying the terms gender and woman as if they encompass the experience of all women. On the other hand, my data which they feel are required of them and the constraints they perceive on the way they operate. The responses provoke an analysis based in lawyers' (changing and multiple) material experiences: I therefore consider the juridical field and, in turn, its sub-fields—as constituted both by different legal specialisms and also by different working environments. Placing respondents' evidence within this context leads in turn to the pervasive influence of the division of material conditions and the symbolic order into public and private spheres, which, I argue, continue to be critically formative, materially, ideologically and discursively, of male and female subjectivities and of the juridical field(s). This wider focus then draws us into a consideration of the impact of the transformation of the profession which has taken place over the last 20 years, and which has fractured traditional structures, identities and ideologies, affecting the potential for further change.

2 THE DATA

2.1 Gender Identity

Despite widening the debate into a discussion about the possiblity of deploying an ethic of care, Menkel-Meadow and others remain committed to the view that women are the primary bearers of this alternative ethic. However this position implies that it is possible to invoke woman as a unitary, unproblematic category which somehow exists prior to and apart from the matrix of power, and, therefore, that women can enact/be that woman, or their own, individualised caring version of the category, unmediated by material circumstances or ideological frameworks. Yet one of the fundamental pillars of Menkel-Meadow's proposition rests on the currently 'masculinist' nature of the legal profession and practice, and a body of studies of women lawyers in the Western world attest to both the pressure on them to conform to its dominant (culturally male) norms, and to their subordination and ghettoisation into the least prestigious, most poorly paid, and/or 'caring' specialisms of the profession,[12] (Reskin and Roos 1990;

suggest that one of the difficulties confronting all women in the legal profession is precisely the essentialisation and reification of gender, and arguably, therefore, it remains appropriate to use the category woman whilst bearing in mind such other intersections as class, race and sexuality. Nevertheless this chapter needs to be read in the knowledge that it is written from the perspective of a white, heterosexual academic and former solicitor.

[12] The current concentration of women in these 'caring' areas, the identification of the skills they require as female, and their relative devaluation appear to indicate the political problems with the difference feminist approach. For instance the low fee-earning capacity of matrimonial law was often advanced by managing partners as one reason for its low prestige and the small numbers of female partners; conversely, the domination of the specialism by women is frequently advanced as an explanation for its low prestige. For, as equality feminists have always noted, emphasis on difference locks women into roles which are simultaneously sanctified and socially devalued, and the difference feminism position has unfortunate resonances with the judgments enunciated in the 19th century Persons cases (for instance, *Bradwell v Illinois*). Thus Wajcman argues that the assumption that women are inherently more caring and peace-loving than men is at the root of women's oppression (1991).

Hagan and Kay 1995; Thornton 1996; Kay 1997; Dixon and Seron 1995; Sommerlad and Sanderson 1998).

In considering the issue of gender identity, and also in the subsequent discussion of the different areas of legal practice, it is useful to draw on Bourdieu's concept of 'habitus'; that is the way in which social practice is enacted, intentionally yet intuitively, as a result of immersion in a field (1987). Habitus is not viewed as a product only of the constitution of a field through its orthodoxy, but also as a result of the 'doxa', or what we may term the 'common sense' of a field. As a result the 'properties' of a field, for instance, its characteristic power relations, modes of communication and social practices circumscribe the choices of actors within it. In the various legal fields therefore, not only lawyers' choices but their very identities are shaped both by such formal constraints as the rules of professional conduct, and the relevant law, and also through the internalisation of the ways of thinking and acting which are appropriate to these formal codes (miscognition). Thus Nelson and Trubek have observed that 'habitus tends to produce behaviour in individuals that reproduces the very system from which it emerged' (1992: 23).

The construction of the public sphere as a primarily economic space, detached from the social reproduction carried out in the private sphere, has produced a habitus which may be described as culturally male—because it was traditionally dominated by men both numerically and in terms of power. The public sphere therefore entailed the development of an overarching maleness, a hegemonic masculinity predicated on the sexual contract[13] (Collier 1991; 1998) (and hence the devaluation of women), involving discourse and codes which, in theory, all (professional) men could enter into—to an extent—irrespective of originating class and other variables. This point is illustrated in my study by the responses to a question about whether there was an archetypal solicitor; all those who thought there was such a beast, described a man.

When women enter this public sphere, they too must attempt to adopt this fictive identity which in turn entails—in varying degrees—acceptance of the demands of 'greedy institutions' from their hierarchical ways of working to the exclusion of the affective, and this is especially true if the woman wishes to become partner.[14] Thus the data contain many examples of women's conscious efforts to emulate a culturally male lifestyle, including male codes of behaviour, styles of dress, hours of work. For instance, in response to a question about her aspirations, one woman said: '*to maintain equity partner status by working full time plus and postponing child bearing—otherwise one is not taken seriously as a woman*' (white, City lawyer, 1994), and women repeatedly referred to the need to socialise, work the long hours, '*be better than the men*' and '*dress like the men*

---

[13] As Wendy Brown puts it: 'the sexual contract is where patriarchalism lives in the political and legal order ordinarily understood as its supersession' (1995); and see Pateman 1988) .

[14] See Kay and Hagan's discussion of factors in partnership selection; their research has led them to conclude that women lawyers have to 'model themselves on an exaggerated image of those who traditionally have been considered "suitable candidates" for partnership' (1998: 741).

in sober suits' (and see Bawdon 1994: 34; Gross 1990: 295). Other women spoke in some detail of the pressure they experienced as a result of an explicit devaluation of women, and the behaviour this evoked; for example,

> I think there is still definitely a view that women are not as strong as men. So with colleagues you always have to appear totally confident and positive—wear a smile and be a superhuman professional—and never talk about problems in your private life—that would be weak. And clients often test you out too. I've had a lot of clients say they doubt I'll be strong enough . . . recently there was a very adversarial meeting with the other side, and my own client just put me down in front of them. So I feel that I do have to try very hard—I am very tough, assertive, meticulous in preparation, to counter all of that. You have to be, because of women's reputation for weakness. (White commercial property lawyer, mid-30s, 1997)

Another woman made a similar point, but pointed too to the effects of internalising legal thinking:

> It's all about bringing the money in—lots of long hours, lots of pressure . . . conforming, playing the game, looking the part—wearing dark suits—socialising . . . otherwise you're just going to go nowhere. So I think there's L* (her name) the lawyer and then there's the other L*. So it does change you, and it does that in lots of ways . . . it has to; you can't do the job without becoming a lawyer, and that means getting trained to look at things in a certain way . . . dividing issues into categories.[15] (White insolvency practitioner, in mid-30s, 1999)

Men tended to confirm women's fears that they were still perceived as less forceful, and less effective than male lawyers; for instance:

> Clients definitely prefer males in my experience . . . often they would say that they wanted me because a woman wouldn't be strong enough especially since it was all men on the other side. And I think that's right often; male lawyers do tend to be more aggressive—in general—and I notice too that particular judges when faced with a woman on the other side would nearly always decide against her . . . (White male insolvency practitioner 1999)

These views are more consonant with the idea of woman as 'a gendered subject position' which legal discourse (along with other discourses) 'brings into being' (Smart 1992: 34), than with the Gilligan position. For Smart the construction of *woman*, who is defined above all by being caring, draws on the construction of further categories of women—the examples she gives include the female criminal, the prostitute, the bad mother. These types depend on the *idea* of woman, since this fictive figure is able to, ideologically and discursively, exclude and dehumanise other, deviant types of women: 'Thus woman has always been both kind and killing . . . virtuous and evil' (Smart 1992: 29).

This combination of conceptual instability and stereotypical representations is clearly visible in interviewees' responses; the resulting ambivalence of gen-

---

[15] These comments may be related to the critique of the ethic of care that it is not so much an alternative gendered morality as a function of education levels (Greeno and Maccoby, 1986: 312).

dered difference continually presented women with the problem of knowing 'when to hide their difference and when to assert it' (Cockburn 1991: 160). As the respondents cited above noted, failure to conform was likely to produce professional marginalisation; on the other hand, conformity generated the risk of being adjudged (and punished for being) 'too male', 'hard' or, in Smart's words 'killing' rather than 'kind'. The personnel officer of a large commercial firm summed up the dilemma posed by the feminine woman/tough lawyer dichotomy: '*if women succeed they're regarded as honorary men—but that has a penalty too because they are then seen not to be feminine enough*' (1997). The tensions generated by this dilemma surfaced in repeated criticisms (made by both women and men) of women who were felt to have gone too far in their emulation of the archetypal male solicitor;[16] for instance: '*The firm had a couple of bad experiences with two women partners—they had chips on their shoulders—very ruthless*' (female matrimonial lawyer, large commercial firm, 1994). Other women were castigated for being 'too hard', 'trying too hard', 'being surrogate men'. However, the comments of one woman illustrate Smart's point:

> Many women get the *reputation* as too hard, because they are trying to compensate, make up the ground that is lost by people assuming they are going to be soft. On the other hand, I wouldn't necessarily always agree with those evaluations. Thinking of those women . . . I don't think the same charges would ever be levelled at a man. They would never describe a man as too hard or say that he was trying to compensate . . . in fact I don't think any criticisms would be related to gender at all . . . they'd just say he was very aggressive not imply he was a freak because of his gender. (White commercial property lawyer, 1997; her emphasis)

Lawyers also pointed to a greater complexity of gender representations underlying the simple dichotomy nice woman/tough lawyer. These were the comments of one woman:

> There are two types of woman: one who joins the club. She becomes like a man . . . then there is the sex bomb. No, maybe there's three or four types. There's the nice, soft, caring woman too. Then there's the 'normal' woman, who just gets on with it. (White matrimonial lawyer, 1999).

The managing partner in a large general practice expressed similar views:

> I think there are, crudely, three types of women lawyers. There's those who are determined to get on and some of them become very dry and pushy—even more business-like and detached or whatever than the men. Others succeed by being—it's not really about being overtly sexy—that would be too cheap—but it's about playing the men . . . they use and exaggerate their femininity. So the women are either asexual, more

---

[16] Of course men are also subject to the gender regime, so that failure to conform to hegemonic masculinity is likely to lead to stigmatisation and marginalisation. For instance this was how a woman lawyer described her male colleagues who were working in what was seen as a female ghetto (with no career prospects). 'The men are generally shy and retiring types who seem to beaver away in the background . . . they are regarded as failures and a little wet.' (White support lawyer, 1999).

like the men than the men, or very feminine. And then there's the real women who aren't bothered, who have largely opted out of the race who can be more normal, more themselves. (White man, early 40s, 1999)

These categories or types emerged repeatedly in peoples' responses, exemplifying Butler's (1990) vision of gender not as fixed or natural but as a performance, a 'culturally intelligible norm', an identity stabilised as 'natural' only through the coercive 'heterosexual matrix'. Moreover, not only does the public sphere provoke forms of gender identity different to those required in the private sphere, but arguably the lawyering arena is peculiarly demanding of gender as performance. The data indicated, as Cockburn (1991: 160) has observed, that women would switch between a wide range of 'gendered performances' which related to many different variables, including legal specialism, type of firm, type of client base, whichever particular arena the lawyer was operating in at any particular moment, and the people she was interacting with. As Maccoby has argued: 'social behaviour . . . is never a function of the individual alone . . . (but) of the interaction between two or more persons. Individuals behave differently with different parties' (1990: 513); or, in the words of a white female tax lawyer: '*You behave in different ways according to who you are with. It's a game women have to play I think; I know I do it here. You conform to people's expectations; it makes life simpler.*' (1997)

Thus interpersonal behaviour is likely to be shaped by social and individual expectations. And as Greeno and Maccoby have pointed out 'women have a greater *reputation* for altruism and empathy than men, and . . . women accept its validity' (1986: 313; their emphasis). It is unsurprising therefore that, as a result of her linguistic analysis of lawyer-client conversations, Bogoch (1997) has concluded that women lawyers tended to be more willing than men to grant some legitimacy to clients' emotional concerns, and that, of my respondents, it was female matrimonial lawyers who spoke most often of clients' expectations that they would be caring. Such expectations had led one woman to give up matrimonial law:

> Clients come to you in such distress; they're always in tears or full of anger and of course you're expected to understand, empathise and so on, firstly because there's no one else to vent it all on and secondly because—usually—they've come specifically to you because you're a woman so you're supposed to understand and take it all. I hated it! (Middle aged, white female, practising law (PI) part-time, 1999)

However, for one woman, the fact that she had to adopt different personas and employ different skills depending on the situation she was in and the people she was with, was part of the attraction of the job:

> especially as a woman, I think, you have to act; sometimes hard and aggressive, sometimes soft. I don't mind, I have an aggressive streak in me. I quite enjoy it in fact. Law is basically a cabaret—it's very important to recognise that, so you have to be able to bond with people—colleagues, clients, judges, and that can involve playing a part,

being attractive and a chameleon. (Middle aged white woman, working class background, PI & family, 1997).

Similarly, despite the prevalence of such stereotypes as 'aggressive male lawyer' and 'soft women', both men and women spoke of the diversity of 'types' of lawyers, which included caring, compassionate men; for instance:

> I can think of some extremely good male family lawyers; I think it all comes down to personality and experience rather than gender. For instance—his female clients think he's wonderful, he is so empathetic. I think it's partly because he comes from a very working class background. (White female matrimonial lawyer)

These last observations lead us onto a related problem with the difference feminist position, namely that it may be criticised for precisely the binary mode of thought for which 'male' discourse is attacked; thus Smart has criticised Gilligan's stress on 'feminine values' as the antithesis of patriarchal values (1989: 72–6). Privileging the male/female division downplays other forms of differentiation, and other ways of looking at the construction of social relations (Spelman: 1988). Yet the data revealed many respondents to be more conscious of 'differences' other than their gender. For instance one woman (a white, working class lesbian) had set up a radical practice which was staffed by men and women. Although in her private life a separatist feminist she said that in her work as a practitioner she was more concerned about what she described as the class bias of the law. Similarly, a black lesbian gave an account of her feelings about the law in which she emphasised her ethnicity and class rather than her gender or sexuality:

> I did law because I had got involved in a race discrimination case; we'd tried to find a black lawyer and couldn't, so I decided to go for it. But it's been devastating for me . . . On the LPC I've now teamed up with this working class (white) woman who's also finding it really hard . . . Us outsiders are just driven out, I think, that's been my experience here—loads have left because of the crushing financial burden, but also because we don't belong. I just feel really out of it. Even at this university—I mean it's hardly a top place—most of my fellow students have either been sponsored by their work or are people who can afford to get loans or are supported by their families. I really struggled psychologically on the CPE.[17] I was the only one who came from a poor black, working class part of town—Chapeltown—and when I told people they'd always make comments. And then there is the language they use . . . and then law as a subject, just so alien, so elitist . . . It's like learning a foreign language. I learnt the law parrot fashion . . . it was like 'what is all this stuff?!

For a middle aged white woman, doing a post-graduate course in law (post-graduate diploma) ageism and class were major concerns: '*I am struck by the*

---

[17] The LPC (Legal Practice Course) is the academic stage of the vocational training to become a solicitor. CPE stands for Common Professional Examination and was the title of the one-year post-graduate course which covers the core subjects. This has now been renamed the postgraduate diploma.

sexism, but even more by the snobbery. I feel more put down by my class than my gender . . . also the ageism . . . they want attractive young people'. One Asian woman emphasised her religion and her race as vital dimensions of her gender identity:

> I feel that as an Asian woman I have a particular image; I am a religious, Muslim woman, valuing my own practices and beliefs and that means that clients know they can come in here, and they see me wearing the hijab and they know I understand—they know I can help. (Asian woman immigration lawyer, 1999).

The following comments similarly speak to the complexity of the various intersections of race, class and gender:

> There was already one black worker there when I was taken on by *(name of firm)* but he was one of them, one of the lads . . . he'd go out and get pissed with them, organise solicitors' social dos—which were all about drinking and mainly male . . . where all the bonding went on . . . I was just the backroom girl, the Asian assistant who spoke the languages . . . I think if, as an outsider, you do the law you are going to pay for it in every way, culturally you don't know where it or you is coming from—you have to lose your identity if you stick with it. I am now an outsider in my community. I play the game of going in a skirt and a blouse, though now and then I turn up in traditional clothes and get told how wonderful I look . . . It's a brotherhood, whether you're talking about Law Centres or big, commercial firms (I've worked in both), a brotherhood of male white middle class able-bodied people . . . there's solidarity up to a certain point from some white women . . . but it's limited, many are very right wing and then even some of the Asian people come from these very middle-class backgrounds and are busy assimilating. (Asian woman employment lawyer, 1997)

These remarks connect with another perspective on the ethic of care,[18] namely that the values it appears to involve are those of the excluded rather than just women. Evidently such an approach would include men whose socio-economic and political marginalisation can produce forms of relationship different to those which characterise the public sphere. Tronto (1987) considers this approach in her critique of Gilligan, in which, arguing for a degendered ethic of care, she cites Coles (1977), Gwaltney (1980) and Nobles who found that black peoples' self conception stressed 'a sense of cooperation, interdependence and collective responsiblity' (1976: 15–24, cited in Tronto 1987: 651; and see Harding 1987; Hill-Collins 1989). In other words what is described as the ethic of care could also be seen as the system of personalist relationships of reciprocity (both vertical and horizontal) which are viewed as characteristic of pre-capitalist communities (Flynn 1974; Spalding 1974). Or, similarly, it may be viewed simply as a form of morality appropriate to communitarianism (Ferguson 1984), to informal and domestic interactions where 'we should be unwilling to use 'rights' and force to obtain our moral goals' (Harding 1987:

---

[18] Menkel-Meadow implicitly acknowledges this in her comment that 'women know things differently from *white* men' (1995: 53; my emphasis).

312). This insight illuminates the importance of context in determining behaviour, leading us into the examination of the material conditions of lawyers' lives.

2.2 Legal Specialisms

In the same way that the proposition is apparently rooted in an essentialist view of women (and men), it similarly appears to be based on an essentialist and ahistorical version of legal practice. Any analysis of the potential for displacing the dominant mode of lawyering must be set in the context of discussion of the constraints on individual, or even group, agency offered by the various juridical fields, and their changing roles within the political economy. In one paper this is acknowledged by Menkel-Meadow:

> Others, like myself, are interested in exploring other explanatory variables, such as *professional context and socialization*. Thus, moral reasoning methods may be subject to greater 'switching' or plasticity depending not only on the stage of life, but also on the context in which the decisions must be made. (1995: 30; my emphasis)

Yet it is not easy to square this insight with ideas of women's transformative potential, nor is the context in which an ethic of care *could* be practised, specified. This section will therefore build on the preceding discussion of the pressures on gender identity, by considering some of the other constraints on creative, transformative lawyering posed by specific legal specialisms.

Law and legal practice are not monolithic, but highly nuanced, with, respondents claimed, different specialisms producing different styles of lawyering, a different habitus; further subdivisions within specialisms generate further differentiation:

> You can see how different child care law is from other specialisms when you have other solicitors come into it. For instance other areas of matrimonial law is mainly about ancillary stuff—money—men against women—and so that's often still very combative. And then we sometimes get dad represented by a criminal solicitor who he's always had since he was fifteen or whatever, and then you see even greater differences. Crime is extremely adversarial. So when you get lawyers getting involved who are from other specialisms you really see the differences because they're not necessarily familiar with the legal principles—for instance they don't recognise the idea of 'good enough parenting' which is what lies at the heart of child care cases—parents aren't expected to be perfect. Obviously that legal principle generates an entirely different style of practice. (White, female child care lawyer, 1999)[19]

---

[19] This interviewee went on to discuss another effect on people's behaviour: the personal bonds and shared values which can develop between lawyers from different firms who form part of the local community of lawyers, and the personalist ways of lawyering which this can generate (Griffiths 1986; Sarat and Felstiner 1995; Mather *et al* 2001).

Other lawyers endorsed the interrelationship between types of lawyer and specialism, because in the words of a (male) criminal lawyer: *'Different specialisms demand different qualities, have different norms'* (1999). Thus a PI lawyer said:

> . . . men and women having different styles of lawyering? It's hard to say because you can only make these generalisations by comparing like with like—i.e. people in the same specialisms and the same types of firms, and so on. (White, female 1999)

For the purposes of this debate therefore, we might conceptualise legal practice as comprising clusters of specialisms which may be distinguished from each other by the degree of their relationship to the private sphere. Evidently some specialisms are deeply implicated in the private sphere—most notably, matrimonial and child care which do not exclude values of caring (Mossman, 1986). While, at the other end of the spectrum, possessive individualism is central to both criminal and commercial/company law; the latter providing the central conceptual apparatus of contract, corporate personality and private property (Cain 1994). Let us begin, however, by considering the PI field which may be seen as intermediate between the hard worlds of corporate and criminal law and the caring world of matrimonial law. One (male) solicitor described this specialism as the 'gentlemanly arm of the law', one in which conciliation and co-operation was the norm; another said:

> I generally represent the victims; I often deal with the same people on the other side. It's generally quite civilised. We both—usually—know the sums we're likely to get, the moves each is likely to make, and finally we know that we're always likely to settle at the court door, or before. (White, female, mid-40s, 1999)

Nevertheless, although, as one woman said, *'I rarely have to get aggressive— though I can'*, adversarialism continues to underpin the context within which negotiation takes place. Thus one gave the following account which underlines the fact that a conciliatory approach can only work if the other side co-operates and that gender may affect the extent to which they are prepared to do this:

> I find that insurance companies try it on because I'm a woman; one is doing so now. I've tried to be reasonable, suggested a compromise rather than fight . . . .. But now they are making more difficulties . . . I feel my attempt at compromise has been abused so now I will fight them, using the law. (White woman late 20s, 1999)

Despite these comments the fact that PI work is predominantly conducted in a series of ordered steps, and often between the same personnel on each side, is likely to create dispositional traits distinct from those in other areas.

However, the nexus between the demands and functions of a field and the habitus of its practitioners is perhaps most clearly exemplified in commercial law which is most responsive to the needs of global capitalism, and furthest removed from the private sphere, and in criminal work, most directly associated with state power. Both of these fields are characterised by cultures which interviewees described as extremely, overtly 'macho' and 'hard'; though again the sub-divisions within the specialisms should not be overlooked. For instance one (female) commercial property lawyer said:

> it's a very diverse area in fact . . . a different psychology for each specialism . . . so corporate lawyers are very macho—it's the 'work through the night crap'. Commercial lawyers are more businessmen than lawyers—facilitators perhaps—and taking on the character of their different clients. Litigators are combative—always up for the argument. Insolvency people—new lads. Commercial property people are often far more conciliatory—that's quite a woman's scene now. (White female, later 30s, 1999)

Despite these nuances, a male commercial lawyer generalised in the following terms:

> commercial litigation is about game playing. Commercial lawyers use the rules of the court to score points . It's about conflict—unless it's something like commercial property, and even there. . . . its about winners and losers, so the lawyers who do it are the sort of people who are more interested in winning the game and demonstrating how clever and powerful they are, how much they earn and how long they work. It's hard and macho. (1999)

And this is how the director of legal development described her large, international firm:

> the culture here is hard, driven, unforgiving . . . and very male. I would say it's institutionalised masculinism. And as women you have to conform. In fact you are expected to do more . . . a lot more.

She went on to argue that this culture entirely precluded the possiblity of 'lawyering differently':

> There are also huge constraints. It's not just the bottom line that it's a business; rather that is its entire raison d'être; there's no room for caring. So, for instance if you were representing an insurance company which was defending an action against a hospital brought because a baby had been born quadraplegic because of negligence and they instructed you to drag it out and you knew the family desperately needed the money you would still have to do that. You would have no choice . . . As I was told when I went to work for* *(name of another corporate firm)* working in this sort of firm, in corporate law then you won't be on the side of the angels, it's all about helping the rich get richer. (White female, 1999)

Thus, although many more women are entering corporate law than before, it is clear that the constraints on creative lawyering here are very great. For instance a female tax lawyer who had practised with a large firm, but who was now an academic, said:

> I teach students to be black letter lawyers, yet in practice law isn't like that, certainly not in the corporate field. When you practise you have to be street wise, play the game, be flexible, be commercial, bring in the clients (1999).

One woman specifically addressed the question of ethics:

> I can't see how gender comes into it. First of all there is the Law Society guidelines which you have to follow—so, if there is a conflict then, ultimately, the lawyer must

put the law first, then the client and then oneself. So you are very much constrained by that, even if you didn't feel that the law was actually very ethical on a particular point.[20] But then the extent to which that is observed depends on the firm. I can think of some firms which are less than careful, even wilfully blind to ethical issues . . . we act for some very dodgy clients. (White female insolvency practitioner, multinational firm, 1999).

Another simply commented: '*You are not given brownie points for standing up for ethics . . . on the contrary, you're seen as a pain in the butt.*' (White female commercial property lawyer, 1999)

On the other hand there is evidence of two particular ways in which women's increased presence *is* making a distinctive contribution in this field, though neither are rooted in the ethic of care. Firstly in the commodification of an exaggerated 'femininity', exploiting women's ascribed cultural capital of both care and sex. This woman's account was not uncommon: '*women . . . being treated as sexual objects in law firms is especially bad in London with the big firms . . . all that corporate entertaining . . . the women are often treated as little better than—well, prostitutes really.*' (Asian academic, former corporate lawyer, 1997). I have explored this use of attractive young women in 'Practice Development' events elsewhere (Sommerlad and Sanderson, 1998), and other studies of women in service industries (and especially traditionally male dominated ones) have similarly found that women's accommodation has been accomplished by 'the implicit use of sexuality as a commercial or organisational resource by management' (Filby 1992: 25; and see Hearn and Parkin 1995). The second way is in the development of support posts which are almost exclusively occupied by women; this was the account of a professional support lawyer with a large commercial firm in London:

> I used to be in insolvency but when I had children I couldn't do the hours they demanded so now I am a support lawyer. It's a female specialism both because of the hours but also because you're like a mum really. You have to organise the department to share information and knowledge, so it's organising meetings and holding training sessions etc. and you often have to write papers for fee earners because they are too busy. Basically you're packing their bags and helping them with their homework and wishing them luck and waving them off and then greeting them on their return from their conference or whatever and listening to how magnificent they were etc etc . . . same old caring stuff. And of course completely undervalued so that often you have to remind them that you are not a paralegal or secretary. And of course because it's female, undervalued and so on, there's no career structure. (White female, 1997)

Criminal law was similarly viewed as an extremely male specialism, requiring practitioners to adopt a particular style of lawyering; for instance:

---

[20] This point is similar to that made by Baumann when he argues that law displaces or even precludes individual morality: 'individual responsibility is . . . translated . . . as the responsibility for following or breaching the socially endorsed, ethical legal rules' (1992: 29). Evidently whilst the ordinary citizen may exercise an individual responsibility which involves by-passing the law, lawyers, if they are to remain lawyers have no such choice.

Criminal lawyers, whether male or female are all, in my experience, very hands on. They swear like troopers, drink, smoke a lot, are always going off to the pub at lunch time, and are only this side of the legal line. It's a persona you have to assume to deal with criminals. (General practice lawyer, 1999)

The observations of a child care specialist of one of her colleagues who was a criminal lawyer exemplify Bourdieu's notions of habitus and bodily hexis: '*criminal lawyers have to be adversarial . . . it's like you should see B** (lawyer's name) *in court . . . she's very nice but in court an absolute bitch.*' (White female, 1999)

One lawyer compared the culture of criminal law to that of commercial law:

I shouldn't think the ethos here or in most criminal firms is any more egalitarian— maybe less because at least they've probably got anti-discrimination policies in place. And then, like them, we work extremely long hours and there's also that macho pride in doing so. Same ideas about having to be 150% committed. And I think the impetus behind these long hours is just the same—the partners are completely money oriented . . . and then of course most of the clients are male and very macho—like corporate clients! There's more women criminal lawyers now than there used to be but there's still a perception that to get on you have to be as tough as the males. And if you go into the advocates' room at the local Magistrates they're all telling dirty jokes and being fairly obnoxious . . . crude discussion of women solicitors . . . building site culture. (White man, early 40s, 1997)

Even if women are able to overcome the constraints endemic to this culture they will face problems posed by the way in which law acts, in Smart's phrase as a 'technology of gender'. These, for instance, were the views of a woman barrister on the difficulties of using the law creatively:

There are many constraints; professional ethics for one thing, the law for another. If the law says one thing and you try and argue another then you'll be in trouble; at the end of the day you've got to use the law and stereotypes to do the best for your client. (White, 40s, 1999)

Or as Hasse has argued in her discussion of the 'battered woman defence': 'zealous representation must require that the lawyer use, to her client's best advantage the very social and institutional sexism that may have driven the client to do her murderous deed' (1987: 294). Moreover, failure to do this may not only affect the outcome for the client, but also the credibility of the woman lawyer— a credibility which is, as we have already discussed, less than a man's to start with. Thus the woman barrister cited above continued her remarks by saying: '*What's more if you don't shut up about various things you are likely to be perceived ever after as a feminist, bad lawyer and so on. And that then affects the outcomes for future clients.*'

However, surely the matrimonial law field provides evidence of caring practice. As a specialism which should be concerned with conciliation rather than conflict, and which is most intimately connected with the private sphere, it has always demanded not just technical but also relational skills including—at least to some extent—emotional labour (Davis 1988; Rosenthal 1974; Sommerlad and Wall 1999)—which is of course also why it is identified as something women are 'naturally' suited to (Greeno and Maccoby, 1986). At the same time it is an area where the lawyer has traditionally had a greater discretion than other, more rule dominated specialisms, and would therefore also seem to hold out the possibility of practising transformative, creative lawyering. However, the meaning which Sarat and Felstiner identified as being produced in client-matrimonial lawyer interactions appears little different from that which characterises other areas of legal practice. In their words:

> it constructs an ideology of separate spheres, isolating emotions from other domains of human experience and disenfranchising affective life in legal affairs. Then . . . it subordinates rule systems to personalistic inclinations and resources. And third, it produces a picture of law as inexorably adversarial and opportunistic rather than fair and just' (1995: 151; and see Griffiths, 1986).

These conclusions are consonant with how one matrimonial lawyer, who described herself as a socialist, lesbian feminist, discussed her clients' expectations of care, and the problems in meeting these:

> You want to give clients a voice but that voice has to come within the law so that justice can be done and you translate what they are saying so that it comes within the ambit of the law . . . if it doesn't then it's hopeless. So I am dealing with the law primarily rather than the emotions. My job is being a lawyer, a technician if you like, someone who deals with the rules, not a social worker or a counsellor; I'm not qualified to give emotional support. I will say—I present myself I suppose as a split personality—there's J* *(her own name)*, someone who is friendly, who you can talk to, but I quickly get rid of J*, after she's made the clients feel at home and I move onto being the legal adviser. (White, early 40s, 1999)

This woman's approach to the job, and her concerns, were endorsed by another matrimonial lawyer:

> They come to you expecting care, and I will listen and empathise as part of putting them at their ease, letting them tell their story. But after that you don't have either the time or the resources really.[21] (White female, late 30s, 1997)

On the other hand, despite these comments, in England and Wales there clearly *is* a move in matrimonial law (and in civil litigation generally) away from adversarialism. Another female matrimonial specialist spoke favourably of these developments, and also supported the need for empathy in her work; however, although she believed in gender difference she did not attribute the changes to the influence of women:

---

[21] The accounts by this respondent and the previous solicitor of how they deal with clients fit with the findings of Griffiths' research into the behaviour of Dutch divorce lawyers (1986; and see Sarat and Felstiner 1995).

to do this work you must establish trust, respect . . . you have to make a relationship with the client . . . I think that is sometimes easier for a woman; we often do get requests for a woman solicitor . . . because often the details are so very personal and intimate . . . I think there is an archetypal male lawyer . . . pompous, aggressive . . . I've worked with many of them. On the other hand I know some extremely good male family lawyers . . . I think they are generally the men who have a heavy feminine side to them. I wonder if that is the way to express it; I suppose I just mean they are genuinely caring, able to listen and sympathise . . . On the other hand you do need other skills too. In negotiations you need to be detached and objective and strong, and if necessary aggressive . . . but I think that is getting less necessary. Things are changing. When I first came into law that was the normal style but now we have the SFLA[22] guidelines and when Woolf comes in it will change things even more. We're increasingly going down the road of mediation, the emphasis is on co-operation, consensual agreements in the interest of the child. Why? I think it's to do with wider changes in society, the demand for greater accountability, less respect for the profession, the influence of Europe; also to do with costs, changes in the judiciary. I don't see it as much to do with the increased numbers of female lawyers.

However the anxieties expressed by the two previous respondents, that too much emphasis on the caring, counselling side of their role could be harmful and, implicitly, detract from their primary role as advocates are echoed by some commentators on the field. For instance Neale and Smart wonder whether the solicitor's traditional role is not being undermined (with potentially negative results, especially for the poor and/or socially disadvantaged client) by the ideological framework of the reforms and the current drive to mediation (1997; and see Zander 1997), and this perspective leads us into another concern with the proposition. For Menkel-Meadow the ethic of care would involve caring not just for one's client but for others involved in that client's problem; this is consonant with Gilligan's point about relatedness. However this approach would appear to ignore the forms of class and patriarchal power which are embodied in the law, and for this reason matrimonial lawyers who described themselves as feminists were hostile to obligatory mediation. The following comments exemplify their objections:

> The new Family Law Act is horrendous—the idea of mediation[23] when the parties are so unequal . . . I believe in justice. What we want is proper justice as of right; making law act up to its liberal principles . . . justice with a vengeance . . . I believe in rights. (White female academic and legal activist, 1999)

[22] As this respondent says, both of the initiatives she refers to (The Solicitors Family Law Association (SFLA) guidelines and Woolf) represent attempts to bring about a cultural shift in legal practice in the direction advocated by Menkel-Meadow (not that either owe any debt to her proposition). The SFLA, formed in 1982 as a response to criticisms of family law practitioners of their adversarial ethos and disregard for the interests of the child, is viewed, in conjunction with the 1989 Children Act, as having encouraged the emergence of a 'new cadre of "good" conciliatory lawyers' (Neale and Smart 1997: 380). The guidelines she refers to set out appropriate behaviour and emphasise conciliation. 'Woolf' refers to the reports by Lord Woolf which identified 'cost, delay and complexity' as the 'key problems facing civil justice today' (1995: 7). The proposed solutions (now enshrined in law) include increased judicial case management.
[23] And see Grillo 1991.

Nevertheless, despite the concerns expressed above by some about aspects of the changes which are taking place in some fields, other changes may be identified which can be both positively welcomed and attributed to the action of women. For instance, an activist in the areas of domestic violence and women's rights considered that not only had there been some major changes in the law as it affects women but also that some of these could be directly attributed to the work of women lawyers. She cited the example of lesbian parenting, saying:

> It is very much the work of women lawyers who have changed the picture here. Cases were fought out on a common law basis, using the law creatively, fighting it on the principles. (Middle-aged white academic lawyer, 1999)

However she went on to remark that the amount of change that could be brought about from *within* the profession, by women lawyers was strictly limited, and that in general she thought it was often the work of women outside the law which produced effects. This viewpoint was endorsed by a radical barrister, who commented:

> I think that often I am most powerful and creative in my contributions to campaigns outside the law; when I am actually acting professionally there are so many constraints. For instance professional ethics, the nature of the law—if the law says one thing and you try and argue another, then if you don't shut up you'll be in trouble . . . you have to play by the book, act the part. (White female, 40s, 1999)

She then went on to discuss how, like her criminal colleagues, she was also limited in what she could do by the need to utilise existing gender stereotypes in order to secure the best result for female clients:

> Above all you are, of course, constrained by your duty to your client. Ironically the whole issue can get particularly difficult when you are doing lesbian parenting cases . . . Obviously you must try and win, so you'll say grow your hair, just a bit of lipstick, leave off the black leather jacket.

Other feminists working in this area indicated that they felt similarly obliged to play upon female stereotypes; for instance:

> I'd lie to you if I said I don't sometimes play the gender card of kids are better with mum, relying on the prejudices of the judge . . . time and again dad can play the money card so I have to play the TLC card, so I'm endlessly shoring up the stereotype of the loving, natural mother . . . that's what my clients want, they want their children, and who am I to challenge that? (White child care lawyer, 1999)[24]

Finally, one might ask what legal specialisms would be appropriate for the exercise of relational, caring lawyering for those involved other than the client? For instance, would it be caring in PI cases against insurance companies to care for the other side? This was precisely the difficulty which one respondent had with the proposition:

---

[24] This woman stated that she felt an increasing need to emphasise what she called the tender loving care (TLC) gender card, as, in Boyd's word the ideology of motherhood has 'waned' (1996: 497).

Caring for others . . . but you have a professional duty to your client! And what about criminal clients? Do you care for the CPS, the state? What about victims of domestic violence? It's preposterous, simple minded. (White male, late 40s, 1999)

While a well known radical criminal specialist said,

one of the main problems with the criminal law has been the extent to which lawyers have been cosy with the police, with colleagues, with the CPS. A good criminal lawyer must be extremely combative and, in my view, aggressive (White female, 50s, 1999)

Indeed it was precisely those respondents who sought to lawyer creatively, who had gone into the law with a social/political agenda who had most difficulty with the proposition. Thus a housing lawyer said:

For me it was a political decision, going into the law . . . the law is all about power. Clients' needs arise out of their poverty and powerlessness and I offer them a degree of leverage so that they can realise the rights they have in theory, against people far more powerful than themselves. I am here to fight. (White male, 40s, 1999)

A group of low paid female workers explained that what they wanted was for their lawyer to fight for them because they were:

looking for justice . . . it's not the money . . . it's the principle. We've worked for that company for years and been tret like dirt and now at least they'll have to stop and think for a moment. Now we have someone to stand up for us. (1997)

Others argued that even the concept of care for the client was difficult because of its potentially oppressive quality (Baumann 1992: 103); for instance:

I don't know about care. I always think that care and control are the two sides of one coin. Care can't co-exist without control. Personally I prefer justice . . . caring can be so patronising.[25] (White matrimonial solicitor, 1999)

Similarly, a (black, male) housing lawyer said:

As a radical lawyer one of the things I'm trying to do is empower my clients, give them back some respect. That means that although I'm compassionate and friendly and not hierarchical I'm also quite technical and professional. It seems to me very wrong to encourage a dependent relationship given the power I have as a professional. (1999; and see Ellman 1993: 2703; Cahn 1991: 4)

2.3 Different Firms, Different Jobs

The juridical field is further complicated in that it is comprised not just of specialisms, but also of individual firms with their own cultures which impose their

[25] The view that care is patronising points to another difficulty with the ethic. Precisely because care is situated and interpersonal, it is entirely subjective, and culturally specific: what one person may consider caring another may experience entirely differently, and I have come across illustrations of this in research with clients (Sommerlad and Wall 1999). Whereas some clients of a particular solicitor would 'bond' with that solicitor and find her empathetic, others would not get on with her at all.

own constraints on individualism and creative lawyering. White, in an analysis which has many parallels with that of Bourdieu, characterises professional markets as 'self-reproducing social structures among specific cliques of firms and other actors who evolve roles from observations of each other's behaviour' (1981: 518). Markets for expert knowledge are not structured as mass markets, but as arenas specialising in craft product/individual personal service entailing small numbers of producers, the membership of which is dependent on trust and order (Granovetter 1985).

On the other hand, at first sight, this diversity of institutional forms would appear to offer potential for 'creative lawyering'. However Boon and Flood note that despite the complexity of professional organisation the normative structures of the wider profession renders firms 'occasionally resistant to concerns of economy and efficiency' (1998: 623). As a result, male lawyers might be favoured because they 'fitted' even if this apparently flew in the face of economic rationality, and this formative characteristic of these markets evidently acts as a severe restraint on non-conformity.[26] Consequently, respondents who claimed to have entered the law with a political or social agenda commented on the need to find a niche.

A woman PI lawyer described a personal journey to find the right niche which had ended with her founding her own practice:

> I trained in the centre of London in a very male dominated environment. Then I moved to a High Street firm—very nice, but very traditional, very male again. Then I came to a big commercial firm in L* and I was appalled by the racist, chauvinist and sexist culture. Institutionalised sexual harassment. The first week the litigation partner made a pass at me. All very macho—you had to be in by 7 and still there 9. Then I came to this town, to a High Street general practice. It had more women, including female partners, but a really arrogant atmosphere; it's a well known practice so they just seemed to treat clients with contempt. So in the end I set up by myself; now I'm my own boss, and what I'm trying to create is a happy relaxed culture which gets away from the old hierarchical thing. (1999)

These comments also touch on the need to qualify any idea of creative lawyering by the position of the person involved. At any particular time, the ability to engage in/abstain from/reshape particular exchanges depends on bargaining power of the individual vis-a-vis others (Duxbury 1990; Cockburn 1983). The

---

[26] Reputation in these markets is therefore highly important (Hagan and Kay 1995; Sommerlad and Sanderson 1998); entering this world, let alone succeeding in it, is related not only to an individual's human capital but also to her cultural capital, and, as was clear in the opening discussion of gender identity and the archetypal solicitor, it is precisely women's 'difference' which results in the ascription of a different, generally less valuable cultural capital to women. This in turn may either result in women's exclusion from certain markets, or their relegation to subordinate positions, and/or, as noted above, in the exploitation of such 'womanly' qualities as care, or of their sexuality. This point also highlights the fact that the professional world is one which is characterised by precisely the sort of intimate relationships and connectedness which Menkel-Meadow views as a distinctive female quality. Except that it is a connectedness which is largely between men, and/or controlled by men.

scope for different lawyering (and the desire?) is likely to depend not just on the firm and the specialism but also on whether the woman is a partner, a trainee, an associate with no or good chances of promotion, a part-time returner, and, to return to the wider question of the importance of other saliencies, black, Asian British, disabled, 'attractive', old or young, childless or with grown up children. Thus the female Director of Legal Development cited in the previous section said:

> There is no choice if you work for this sort of firm. You have to accept the work which is given you—and that's especially so for women because they are generally in the more junior positions.

However, even when you are discussing women who have reached extremely powerful positions, they appear to be constrained. A female barrister commented:

> The women we have who are judges don't make a lot of difference. Maybe because it is so difficult for them to get there, they are concerned about their position. They are highly visible, they won't go out on a limb and are more timid than some of the men.

This perspective was corroborated by the reflections of an Asian part-time Adjudicator for the Immigration Appellate Authorities on the constraints on her freedom to judge:

> I came into the law to serve my community and with ideas of justice, but I now find this very difficult. Justice has two meanings for me; first of all there is what I call clinical justice, justice in accordance with the law . . . but my perception of justice is where you exercise moral judgments. It's about bending the law to achieve a moral and truly just outcome; it's about equity. But in practice I cannot do this when I adjudicate. I have no discretion. I can make recommendations but that is all and I have to be very careful about doing that because the Secretary of State is not required to take any notice of these and is highly unlikely ever to do so if I make them too often. And now we have a Secretary of State who is pandering to a media scare about immigration, and accusing us of being too lenient. So there is very little scope. (1999)

2.4 Changes in the Field: Cutbacks and Commercialisation

The interviewee last cited pointed to the political climate as a factor affecting her exercise of discretion. This point underlines the need to place this debate in the wider socio-economic/political context. Menkel-Meadow's question turns on what is the appropriate value rationality of the profession, and it could be argued that the ethic of care is another way of expressing the service ideal. Yet many of the changes which are currently affecting the legal profession are resulting in a shift from the ideal of an altruistic value rationality to an explicitly calculative rationality (Sommerlad 1996; 1999: 52–3; 2001). Evidently, as I have already discussed, some developments are in the direction of greater conciliation. On the other hand, other changes are likely to undermine the potential for anyone—male or female, junior or senior—to lawyer either creatively or caringly. The exposure of the profession to the full market is resulting in an ever increasing pressure on costs—in all sectors, and its colonisation by the forces of managerialism and entrepreneurialism. Thus several critics of the reforms which have been carried out in the public sector, including the legal aid branch of the legal profession, have focussed on the accounting logic which, it is argued, is colonising service delivery (Larner 1997) and eroding the ethical value rationality of the public sector professional.[27] For instance Laughlin and Broadbent cite Andre Gorz in support of their argument that the caring dimensions of professional work will be marginalised by considerations of efficiency (1994: 162).

This new emphasis on commercialism is further stimulated by the low rates of legal aid fees and the standardisation involved in franchising and contracting, whilst many commentators are similarly concerned about the advent of conditional fee arrangements (Shapland *et al* 1998; Yarrow 1998). The comments of a partner at a 'radical'[28] firm on the effects of the legal aid reforms and low fees on his firm point to the stimulus they have given to the processes of bureaucratisation and stratification (Sommerlad 1999; 2001):

> Increasingly our primary goal has to be to keep the franchise—and get a contract. And that is changing a lot of things. We used to practise in a very old fashioned way. You did whatever was necessary for the client, regardless of whether you got paid or not, and people had a lot of autonomy. Nowadays we have to control practitioners much more closely, work far more to a template. The top priority nowadays has to be our survival financially as a small business . . . you look at the cash flow. It's getting worse and it is very constraining. (1999)

This depiction both of increased control over individual lawyer's work and the problems in delivering the most basic legal service, let alone individualised care, surfaced repeatedly in lawyers' accounts; for instance this was how a criminal (radical) lawyer described his approach to his work, and its effects:

> I believe in continuity of care, not using runners, not processing clients, doing that extra research, scrutinising the evidence. The trouble is there's no time and money now. The future is the legal aid factory, get them in, churn them out. (1999)

---

[27] The legal aid reform programme forms part of a wider process of public sector reconstruction, which has become known as the New Public Management (NPM) (Hood 1991; Sommerlad and Wall 1999: 45–59). NPM is directly relevant to the possibility of introducing an ethic of care into lawyering; connected to the resurgence of economic liberalism, with its commitment to the liberty of individuals and belief in the benefits of the de-regulated market, it has involved the displacement of the citizen by the categories of 'consumer' and 'taxpayer' (Barron and Scott 1991) and of the 'social by economic concerns' (Burchell 1993). Its application to the legal aid sector has taken the form of franchising (see Sherr, Moorhead and Paterson 1994), and, in 1999, contracting in which, it has been argued, the motif of 'value for money' will take precedence over access to justice and care (Sommerlad & Wall 1999; and see Power 1997; Freedland 1994) and may signal the demise of the radical or 'political' lawyer (Sommerlad, 2001).

[28] This was how he termed his firm; it was a firm founded by people expressly committed to serving the community and, using McConville *et al*'s typology (1994), could alternatively be described as a 'political' firm.

Similar objections to the proposition occurred in the comments of other legal aid lawyers, including matrimonial specialists (some of which are alluded to above). Given that women (and of course children) are often either financially dependent or at least poorer than their male partners, they are frequently legally aided, and financial cutbacks in legal aid, together with pressure towards standard fees has severely weakened the extent to which lawyers can act creatively or even in a particularly caring fashion. For instance a male matrimonial lawyer stated that he would find it increasingly difficult to do legally aided work:

> The cuts in legal aid are really impacting now and as a result firms like mine may say no more legal aid work at all; or, if we do carry on, the partnership is likely to demand that the work is fed down to paralegals. I mean I get £60 an hour for legal aid work and my private charge out rate is £140 . . . (1999)

Commentators on the corporate world describe a similar transformation of professionalism, reflected in the increasing dominance of commercial and entrepreneurial criteria, which are displacing a professionalism based on (even if only nominally) ethical, technical professionalism (Hanlon 1997; Oligiati 1995: 172) A female commercial lawyer related the changes specifically to the question of ethics:

> I've worked with some truly good and great lawyers who are very ethical—and caring. I remember once we were up against a litigant in person and it was clear he didn't know what he was doing so my partner arranged to meet him at the court and sat with him for an hour before the hearing, explaining to him how he should do the application, what documents to file and so on. He said afterwards that that was what being an officer of the court involved and that it didn't hurt us. That firm had a Conflicts and Ethics Panel. But things are changing. One problem is that the law is very ageist at the moment—it's now a young man's game—long hours with lots of pressure and you're rated now almost entirely on the amount of money you bring in . . . saying no to a client who suggests certain courses of action which may be rather unethical doesn't fit with this scenario. (1999)

The dynamics of change in the profession therefore appear to be leading practice away from the possibility of assimilating an ethic of care, and towards a more universal calculus where only those aspects of practice which can be measured, counted and priced have a place.

3 CONCLUSION

I have not intended, in this chapter, to imply that differences between women as a group and men as a group do not exist; clearly there exist both biological and cultural differences. Moreover, it appears evident that the opening up of the legal profession to formally excluded groups is likely to contribute to the process of change in the way in which law is practised. Some developments in the UK in both substantive law and legal practice do in fact offer support for the notion of the transformative potential of women lawyers: for instance in the areas of domestic violence, and the work on the defence of provocation. For several decades now there have been radical solicitors' practices and barristers chambers in the UK with an explicit social agenda of using law creatively, to empower women.[29] At the same time there have been very great changes in the profession involving what one commentator describes as a shift from status to contract (Paterson 1996), and an increased emphasis on co-operation and negotiation. Furthermore, there is a growing emphasis on the importance of the client voice, and in my most recent research (Sommerlad and Wall 1999) empathy and care figured prominently in clients' statements of what they wanted from their solicitors, and more clients of women indicated that they felt they received this sort of service than did those of men.[30] Moreover, the majority of solicitors, also identified empathy as a vital component of their relationship with the client, and many spoke of discarding the hierarchical parent-child approach deemed to be characteristic of traditional lawyering, in favour of a partnership which empowered the client. Yet it must be questioned how many of these changes can be attributed to the entry of women, and if they can, to what extent they can be so attributed. Also I have identified other professional developments which are definitely linked to the entry of women but which are less positive, such as an accentuation of hegemonic masculinity which is in turn linked to the exploitation of women's sexual capital, and the ongoing development of niches of legal practice which are 'naturalised' as female and where women play a 'maternal' caring role.

Further problems may be identified with the difference feminist position and the care perspective, which it has not been possible to explore in this chapter. One such problem is that it is not always clear to what extent the debate centres on the general possibilities of using law creatively, in a more caring, and what is termed contextual way, and to what extent it centres on women, as a distinct category, with distinct qualities, being able to act as (in Cynthia Cockburn's words) paradigm breakers. When we consider the ethic of care separately from the issue of gender, various difficulties arise; for instance it may be argued that care is a practice rather than an 'ethic', and as such whether or not behaviour will be experienced as 'caring' is wholly subjective, and, further, that its nominalisation as care may well depend on the gender of both the caregiver and the recipient of care, rather than the substance of the behaviour. Moreover, supporters of the proposition seem to neglect both the power dimensions of the lawyer/client relationship (Ellmann 1993: 2696–703), and the problems inherent in the personalism and particularism which the care perspective is explicitly encouraging.[31] In short, there appears to be a tendency to treat the ethic of care

[29] Although I argue elsewhere that such firms are finding it increasingly difficult to operate (Sommerlad, 2001).
[30] But see the contribution by Felstiner *et al* to this volume whose research in the USA has led to very different conclusions.
[31] And see Cynthia Ward's discussion of difference feminism which she concludes may leave us 'without a rich defense of egalitarianism' (1997: 99).

(and indeed morality in general) as a unitary and unproblematic domain. It may be similarly argued that the historical, dynamic and problematic character of the common law and rights is largely neglected in the debate (see, for instance, Kingdom 1991); an alternative reading of the law sees it as the law 'of particularity' (Detmold 1997), or as flexible and relational (Daly 1989). On the other hand, if our view of the law stresses its constitutive relationship with capital and patriarchy, then, to adapt Maureen Cain's analysis of the difficulties of using the law for 'downsiders', merely different activation of existing discourses and procedures will be ineffective (1994); wider socio-economic and political change is essential. Yet proponents of the proposition largely fail to consider the socio-political context in which any discussion of the possibilities of making changes to law and legal practice must be situated.

The main objective of this chapter, however, has been to address what I see as the proposition's undertheorised approach to gender and, relatedly, the neglect of the material conditions which shape the habitus of the field(s). Wilkins claims that:

> the divergent realities of practising lawyers preclude the formation of a (unified) culture . . . Lawyers who represent large corporations are different from those who represent individuals. Plaintiffs' lawyers are different from defendants' lawyers. Lawyers in large cities are different from lawyers who primarily negotiate or provide office counselling. (1990: 468)

I would argue that the picture is further complicated because different firms, organisations, locations and specialisms all have their own networks, norms, codes and trajectories (and see Mather *et al* 2001). For instance solicitors spoke of the very great changes which have occurred within insolvency practice over the last 20 years, and I have discussed some of the developments in matrimonial law. To offer another example, the fortunes of two large, neighbouring towns from which several of the respondents were drawn have changed dramatically in recent years; whilst one (L*) has become the UK's 'second legal capital' and is home to several multinational firms, the other (B*) has sunk into a decaying provincialism with the result that lawyers from its booming neighbour appeared to be resented; thus a female matrimonial lawyer from L* recounted how she had been refused an order by a registrar with the words *'that may be how you do things in L *, Miss *, but I am afraid that here in B* we are rather old-fashioned, so there is no use reciting precedent and procedure at me'*. And, finally, as I have just noted, this complex picture must be situated within the wider socio-economic and political context, so that the very great changes which have overtaken legal practice in recent years are considered. The proponents of women as transformers of the law generally neglect these complexities;[32] rather the proposition is rooted in a gynotopia, and as such belongs to a

---

[32] This criticism of difference feminism is aimed specifically at Menkel-Meadow's proposition; I am aware that some of the studies which have applied it to other fields do not suffer from the same weaknesses (see for instance Sevenhuijsen, 1998).

longstanding, reactionary tradition which embraces such diverse currents as 19th century misogynist judges to chiliastic religious thinkers (see Hobsbawm 1998: 143–6).

4 REFERENCES

Cases
Bradwell v Illinois, 16 Wall. 130 (1873).
Bebb v. The Law Society (1913) 109 LT Rep 36.

Statutes
1989 Children Act.

Books and Articles
Abrams, K. 1991. Feminist Lawyering and Legal Method, *Law and Social Inquiry*, 15: 373.
Areen, J. 1988. A need for caring, *Michigan Law Review*, 86: 1067–82.
Bacchi, CL. 1996. *The Politics of Affirmative Action: 'Women', Equality and Category Politics*, London: Sage.
Baines, C. 1991. The Professional and an ethic of care in *Women's caring: Feminist Perspectives on Social Welfare*, edited by Baines, CP Evans and S Neysmith. Toronto: McClelland & Stewart.
Banks, O. 1981. *Faces of Feminism: A study of feminism as a social movement*, Oxford: Martin Robertson.
Barrett, M and A. Phillips (eds). 1992. *Destabilizing Theory: contemporary feminist debates*, Cambridge: Polity Press.
Barron, A and Scott, C. 1991. The Citizen's Charter Programme. *The Modern Law Review*, 55, 524–46.
Bartlett, K. 1990. Feminist Legal Methods: *Harvard Law Review*, 103: 829–910.
Bauman, Z. 1992. *Postmodern Ethics*, Oxford: Blackwell.
Bawdon, F. 1994. The lore of legal fashion. *The Times*, 27 September, 34.
Becker, G. 1974. A theory of marriage, in *Economics of the Family, Marriage, Children and Human Capital*. edited by Theodore Schultz, Chicago, University of Chicago Press.
Bender, L. 1990. From Gender Difference to Feminist Solidarity: using Carol Gilligan and an ethic of care in law, *Vermont Law Review*, 15, 1 : 1–48.
Bogoch, B. 1997. Gendered Lawyering: Difference and Dominance in Lawyer-Client Interaction, *Law and Society Review*, 31: 677–712.
Boon, A and Flood, J. 1998. Trials of Strength: The reconfiguration of litigation as a contested terrain, *Law & Society Review* 33, 3, 595–636.
Bottomley, A. (ed.) 1996. *Feminist Perspectives on the Foundational Subjects of Law*, London: Cavendish.
Bourdieu, P. 1987. The force of law; toward a sociology of the juridical field, *Hastings Law Journal*, 38: 805–52.
Boyd, S. 1996. Is there an ideology of motherhood in (post)modern child custody law? *Social and Legal Studies*, 5, 4: 495–521.

Bridgeman, J and Millns, S. (eds). 1998. *Feminist Perspectives on Law: Law's engagement with the female body*, London: Sweet & Maxwell .

Brown, W. 1995. *States of Injury: Power and Freedom in late modernity*, Princeton, NJ: Princeton University Press.

Burchell, G. 1993. Liberal government and techniques of the self. *Economy and Society*, 22: 267–82.

Butler, J. 1990. *Gender Trouble: Feminism and the subversion of identity*. London: Routledge.

Cain, M. 1994. The symbol traders, in *Lawyers in a Postmodern World*, edited by M Cain & C Harrington. New York: New York University Press.

Cahn, N. 1991. Defining Feminist Litigation, *Harvard Women's Law Journal*, 14,1: 1–20.

Chodorow, NJ. 1978. *The Reproduction of Mothering: psychoanalysis and the sociology of gender*, Berkeley: University of California Press.

Cockburn, C. 1983. *Brothers: male dominance and technological change*, London: Pluto Press.

Cockburn, C. 1991. *In the Way of Women: men's resistance to sex equality in organisations*. Basingstoke: Macmillan.

Coles, R. 1977. *Eskimos, Chicanos, Indians*, Boston: Little, Brown & Co.

Collier, R. 1991. Masculinism, Law and Law Teaching, *International Journal of the Sociology of Law*, 19: 427–51.

Collier, R. 1998. (Un)sexy bodies: the making of professional legal masculinities, in *Legal Feminisms: theory and practice*, edited by C McGlynn, Aldershot: Ashgate, Dartmouth.

Cornell, D. 1991. *Beyond Accommodation: Ethical Feminism, Deconstruction and the Law*, New York and London: Routledge.

Curran, BA. 1986. American Lawyers in the 1980s: A profession in transition, *Law and Society Review*, 20, 19–52.

Daly, K. 1989. Criminal Justice Ideologies and Practices in Different Voices: some feminist questions about justice, *International Journal of the Sociology of Law*, 17: 1–18.

Davis, G. 1988. *Partisans and Mediators*. Oxford: Clarendon Press.

Detmold, M. 1997. The common law as embodiment, *in Sexing the Subject of Law*, edited by N Naffine and R Owens, Sydney: Sweet & Maxwell.

Dixon, J and Seron, C. 1995. Stratification in the Legal Profession: sex, sector and salary, *Law and Society Review*, 29,3: 381–412.

Drachman, V. 1998. *Sisters in Law: Women Lawyers in Modern American History*, Cambridge, Masssachusetts: Harvard University Press.

Duxbury, N. 1990. Robert Hale and the Economy of Legal Force, *The Modern Law Review*, 53, 4: 421–44.

Ellmann, S. 1993. The Ethic of Care as an Ethic for Lawyers, *The Georgetown Law Journal*, 81, 7: 2665–726.

Epstein, CF. 1991, Faulty Framework: consequences of the difference model for women in the law, *New York Law School Law Review*, 35, 2: 309–36.

Fegan, E. 1996. Ideology after Discourse: a reconceptualisation for feminist analyses of the law, *Journal of Law and Society*, 27, 2: 173–9.

Fenning, L and Schnegg, P. 1983. The status of women in L.A.'s biggest firms, *Los Angeles Lawyers* 27 November, p 6.

Ferguson, K. 1984. *The Feminist Case against Bureaucracy*, Philadelphia: Temple University Press.

Filby, MP. 1992. The figures, the personality and the bums: service work and sexuality, *Work, Employment and Society*, 6, 1: 23–42.

Fineman, MA. 1990. Challenging law, establishing differences: the future of feminist legal scholarship, *Florida Law Review*, 42: 25–4.

Fineman, MA and Thomadsen, NW. 1991. *At the Boundaries of Law: Feminism and Legal Theory*, London : Routledge, Chapman and Hall.

Finley, L. 1989. Breaking Women's Silence in Law: the dilemma of the gendered nature of legal reasoning, *Notre Dame Law Review* 64: 886–910.

Flynn, P. 1974. Class, clientelism and coercion: some mechansims of internal dependency and control, *The Journal of Commonwealth and Comparative Politics*, XII, 2: 133–56.

Freedland, M. 1994. Government by contract and public law. *Public Law*, Spring: 86–105.

Freyer, JA. 1995, Women litigators in search of a care-oriented judicial system, *Journal of Gender and the Law*, 4: 199–218.

Frug, MJ. 1992. *Postmodern Legal Feminism*, New York and London: Routledge.

Gerhard, U. 1993. Women's Experiences of Injustice: some methodological problems and empirical findings of legal research, *Social and Legal Studies*, 2: 303–21.

Gilligan, C. 1982. *In a Different Voice*, Cambridge, Mass: Harvard University Press.

Gilligan, C. 1986. Reply by Carol Gilligan, *SIGNS*, 11, 2: 324–33.

Gilligan, C. 1987. Moral Orientation and Moral Development, in *Women and Moral Theory*, edited by E Feder Kittay & DT Meyers, Rowman and Littlefield, USA.

Glasser, C. 1990. The Legal Profession in the 1990s—Images of Change, *Legal Studies*, 10, 1: 1–11.

Gordon, WH. 1984. The right of women to graduate in medicine—Scottish judicial attitudes in the nineteenth century, *The Journal of Legal History*, 5, 2: 136–51.

Granovetter, N. 1985. Economic Action and Social Structure: the problem of embeddedness, *American Journal of Sociology*, 91; 481–510.

Greeno, C and Maccoby, E. 1986. How different is the 'Different Voice'?, *SIGNS*, 11: 310–16.

Greig, Grata Flos. 1909. The law as a profession for women, *Commonwealth Law Review*, 6: 145–54.

Griffiths, J. 1986. What do Dutch lawyers actually do in divorce cases? *Law and Society Review*, 20,1: 135–75.

Grillo, T. 1991. The Mediation Alternative: process dangers for women, *Yale Law Journal*, 100, 8: 1545–1610.

Gross, K. 1990. Foreword: She's my lawyer and she's a woman, *New York Law School Law Review*, 35, 2: 293–307.

Gwaltney, JL. 1980. *Drylongso: a self-portrait of Black America*, New York: Random House.

Hagan, J and Kay, F. 1995. *Gender in Practice: a study of lawyers' lives*, New York: Oxford University Press.

Hanlon, G. 1997. A profession in transition? Lawyers, the market and signifcant others, *Modern Law Review*, 60: 798–823.

Harding, S. 1987, The Curious Coincidence of Feminine and African Moralities: challenges for feminist theory in *Women and Moral Theory*, edited by E Feder Kittay and DT Meyers, Rowman and Littlefield, USA.

Harrison, B. 1978. *Separate Spheres: The opposition to women's suffrage in Britain*, London: Croom Helm.

Hasse, L. 1987. Legalizing gender-specific values, in *Women and Moral Theory*, edited by E Feder Kittay and DT Meyers, Rowman and Littlefield, USA.

Haywood, C and Mac an Ghaill, M. 1997. 'A Man in the Making': sexual masculinities within changing training cultures, *The Sociological Review*, 45, 4: 576–90.

Hearn, J and Parkin, W. 1995. *'Sex' at 'Work': the power and paradox of organisation sexuality*, London: Harvester Wheatsheaf.

Hill-Collins, P. 1989. The social construction of black feminist thought, *SIGNS*, 14, 4, 745–75.

Hill-Collins, P. 1991. *Black Feminist Theory: Knowledge, Consciousness and the Politics of Employment*, London: Routledge.

Hobsbawm, E. 1998. Man and Woman: Images on the Left, in *Uncommon People: Resistance, Rebellion and Jazz*, edited by E Hobsbawm, London, Abacus.

Hood, C. 1991. A public management for all seasons, *Public Administration*, 69: 3–19.

Hull, K and Nelson, R. 1998. Gender Inequality in Law: Problems of structure and agency in recent studies of gender in Anglo-American legal professions, *Law and Society Inquiry*, 681–705.

Irigaray, L. 1985. *This sex which is not one*, translated by C. Porter and C. Burke, New York, Cornell University Press.

Jack, R and Jack, DC. 1989. Women Lawyers: Archetype and alternatives, *Fordham Law Review*, 57: 935–9.

Karst, K. 1984. Woman's constitution, *Duke Law Journal*, 3: 447–507.

Kay, FM. 1997. Flight from Law: A competing risks model of departures from law firms, *Law and Society Review*, 31, 2: 301–35.

Kay, FM. and Hagan, J. 1998. Raising the bar: the gender stratification of law-firm capital, *American Sociological Review*, 63: 728–43.

Kerber, L. 1986. Some cautionary words for historians, *SIGNS* 11: 304–10.

Kingdom, E. 1991. *What's Wrong with Rights? Problems for Feminist Politics of Law*. Edinburgh: Edinburgh University Press.

Kohlberg, L. 1984. *The Psychology of Moral Development*, San Francisco, Calif: Harper & Row.

Larner, W. 1997. The Legacy of the Social: market governance and the consumer, *Economy and Society*, 26, 3: 373–99.

Laughlin, R and Broadbent, J. 1994. The managerial reform of health and education in the UK: value for money or a devaluing process, *The Political Quarterly*, 65: 152–67.

Littleton, C. 1987. Equality and feminist legal theory, *University of Pittsburgh Law Review*, 48, 4: 1043–59.

Luria, Z. 1986. A methodological critique. *SIGNS*, 11, 2:316–21.

Maccoby, E. 1990. Gender and relationships: a developmental account, *American Psychologist*, 45: 513–20.

MacKinnon, C. 1983. Feminism, Marxism, Method and the State: toward feminist jurisprudence, *SIGNS*, 8: 635–58.

Mather, L, McEwen, C & Maiman, R. 2001. *Divorce Lawyers at Work: varieties of professionalism in practice*, Oxford: Oxford University Press.

McConville, M, Hodgson, J, Bridges, L and Pavlovic, A. 1994. *Standing Accused: The organisation and practices of criminal defence lawyers in Britain*, Oxford: Clarendon Press.

Menkel-Meadow, C. 1985. Portia in a different voice: speculation on women's lawyering process, *Berkeley Women's Law Journal*, 1, 1: 39–63.

Menkel-Meadow, C. 1987. Excluded voices: new voices in the legal profession: making new voices in the law, *University of Miami Law Review*, 42, 7: 29–53.

Menkel-Meadow, C. 1989. Feminisation of the legal profession: the comparative sociology of women lawyers, in *Lawyers in Society: comparative theories* (vol 3), edited by RL Abel and PSC Lewis, Berkeley: University of California Press.

Menkel-Meadow, C. 1995. Portia Redux: another look at gender, feminism and legal ethics, in *Legal Ethics and Legal Practice: Contemporary Issues*, edited by S Parker and C Sampford, Oxford: Clarendon Press.

Minow, M. 1990. *Making all the difference*. New York: Cornell University Press.

Mossman, MJ. 1986. Feminism and Legal Method: The difference it makes, *Australian Journal of Law and Society*, 3, 283–300 .

Naffine, N. 1990. *Law and the Sexes: explorations in feminist jurisprudence*, Sydney: Unwin Hyman.

Naffine, N and Owens, R. 1997. Sexing law, in *Sexing the subject of law*, edited by N Naffine and R Owens, Sydney: Sweet & Maxwell.

Neale, B and Smart, C. 1997. 'Good' and 'bad' lawyers? Struggling in the shadow of the new law, *Journal of Social Welfare and Family Law*, 19, 4: 377–402.

Nelson, R and Trubek, D. 1992. New problems and new paradigms in studies of the legal profession, in *Lawyers' Ideals/Lawyers' Practices*, edited by R Nelson and D Trubek and R Solomon, New York, Cornell University Press.

Noddings, N. 1984. *Caring: A feminine approach to ethics and moral education*, Berkeley: University of California Press.

O'Connor, SD. 1991. Portia's progress, *New York University Law Review*, 6: 1546–58.

Olgiati, V. 1995. Process and policy of legal professionalization in Europe: the deconstruction of a normative order, in *Professional Competition and Professional Power: Lawyers, Accountants and the Social Construction of Markets*, edited by Y Dezalay and D Sugarman, London: Routledge.

Olsen, F. 1990. Feminism and Critical Legal Theory: an American perspective, *International Journal of the Sociology of Law*, 18: 199–215.

Pateman, C. 1988. *The Sexual Contract*, Oxford, Polity Press.

Paterson, A. 1996. Professionalism and the legal services market, *International Journal of the Legal Profession*, 3, 1/2: 139–68.

Polan, D. 1982. Toward a theory of law and patriarchy, in *The Politics of Law: A progressive critique*, edited by D Kairys, New York: Pantheon .

Porter, H. 1997. Smashing the glass ceiling, *The Guardian*, 26 May, 2–9.

Power, M. 1997. *The Audit Society*, Oxford: Oxford University Press.

Reskin, B and Roos, P. 1990. *Women and men at work*, Thousand Oaks California: Pine Forge Press.

Rifkin, J. 1980. Towards a theory of law and patriarchy, *Harvard Women's Law Journal*, 3, 1: 83–95.

Rosenthal, DE. 1974. *Lawyer and client: who's in charge?* New York, Russell Sage Foundation.

Ruddick, S. 1989. *Maternal thinking: towards a politics of peace*, Boston: Beacon Press.

Sachs, A and JH. Wilson. 1978. *Sexism and the Law*. London: Martin Robertson.

Sarat, A and Felstiner, WLF. 1995. *Divorce lawyers and their clients: power and meaning in the legal process*, New York: Oxford University Press.

Segal, L. 1987. *Is the future female? Troubled thoughts on contemporary feminism*, London: Virago.

Sevenhuijsen, S. 1998. *Citizenship and the Ethics of Care: feminist considerations on justice, morality and politics*, London: Routledge.

Scott, J. 1988. *Gender and the Politics of History*, New York.

Shapland, J, Otterburn, A, Canwell, N, Corre, C and Hagger, L. 1998. *Affording Civil Justice*, London: Law Society Research Study, no. 29.

Sherr, A, Moorhead, R and Paterson, A. 1994. Assessing the quality of legal work: measuring process, *International Journal of the Legal Profession*, 1, 2: 135–58.

Sherry, S. 1986. Civic virtue and the feminine voice in constitutional adjudication, *Virginia Law Review*, 72: 543–616.

Skordaki, E. 1996. Glass slippers and glass ceilings: women in the legal profession, *International Journal of the Legal Profession*, 3, 2: 7–43.

Slote, M. 1998. The Justice of Caring, *Social Philosophy and Policy*, 15, 1: 171–95.

Smart, C. 1989. *Feminism and the Power of Law*. London: Routledge.

Smart, C. 1992. The Woman of Legal Discourse, *Social and Legal Studies*, 1: 29–44.

Sommerlad, H. 1996. Criminal Legal Aid Reforms and the Restructuring of Legal Professionalism, in *Access to Criminal Justice,* edited by R Young and D Wall, London: Blackstone Press.

Sommerlad, H. 1999. The implementation of quality initiatives and the New Public Management in the legal aid sector in England and Wales: bureaucratisation, stratification and surveillance, *International Journal of the Legal Profession*, 6, 3: 311–343.

Sommerlad, H and PJ Sanderson. 1998, *Gender, Choice and Commitment: Women Solicitors in England and Wales and the Struggle for Equal Status*, Aldershot: Ashgate, Dartmouth.

Sommerlad, H and Wall, D. 1999. *Legally aided clients and their solicitors: qualitative perspectives on quality and legal aid*, London: Law Society Research Study no. 34.

Sommerlad, H. 2001. 'I've lost the plot': an everyday story of political legal aid lawyers, *Journal of Law & Society*, 28, 2 .

Spalding, K. 1974. *De Indio a Campesino: cambios en la estructura social del Peru colonial*, Lima: Instituto de estudios Peruanos ediciones.

Spelman, E. 1988. *Inessential woman: problems of exclusion in feminist thought*, Boston: Beacon Press.

Spigelman, P. 1988. Integrating doctrine, theory and practice in the Law School curriculum: the logic of Jake's ladder in the context of Amy's web, *Journal of Legal Education*, 38:243–70.

Thornton, M. 1996. *Dissonance and Distrust: Women in the Legal Profession*, Melbourne: Oxford University Press.

Tronto, J. 1987. Beyond gender difference to a theory of care, *SIGNS*, 12, 4: 644–63.

Wajcman, J. 1991. *Feminism Confronts Technology*. Cambridge: Polity Press.

Wacjman, J. 1999.The domestic basis for the managerial career, *The Sociological Review*, 44, 4: 609–29.

Walby, S. 1994. Is citizenship gendered? *Sociology*, 28,2: 379–95.

Ward, C. 1997. On difference and equality, *Legal Theory*, 3, 1: 65–99.

West, R. 1988. Jurisprudence and Gender, *University of Chicago Law Review*, 55: 1–72.

White, HC. 1981.Where do markets come from? *American Journal of Sociology*, 87: 517–47.

Wilkins, DB. 1990. Legal Realism for Lawyers, *Harvard Law Review*, 104: 468–524.

Williams, J. 1989. Deconstructing Gender, *Michigan Law Review*, 87, 797–845.

Willis, S. 1980. Homes are divine workshops, in *Women, class and history: feminist perspectives on Australia, 1788–1978*, edited by E Windschuttle: Fontana/Collins.

Woolf, LJ. 1995. *Access to Justice: Interim Report to the Lord Chancellor on the civil justice system in England and Wales*, Woolf Inquiry Team, London.

Yarrow, S. 1998. *The price of success: Lawyers, clients and conditional fees*, London: Policy Studies Institute.

Young, IM. 1997. Unruly categories: a critique of Nancy Fraser's Dual System Theory, *New Left Review*, March/April: 147–65.

Zander, M. 1997. The Woolf report: forwards or backwards for the new Lord Chancellor, *Civil Justice Quarterly*, 16: 208–27.

13

The Remains of the Day: The Women Law Professors Project

CELIA WELLS

Abstract

This chapter charts the background to a research study of women law professors in the UK. This project aims to tease out the experiences of senior women in law schools in their efforts to negotiate or transcend gender in their work within a male-dominated professional environment. I explain why I embarked on the study and discuss some broad observations from the research findings.[1]

1 INTRODUCTION

I HAVE BORROWED FROM Kazuo Ishiguro the elegant title to his novel *The Remains of the Day*,[2] in order to express the idea that women law professors occupy a remaining or end position in relation to a host of historical, political, cultural and professional processes, progressions and, perhaps, regressions. In a comment which can be adapted to apply to women academics, Hull and Nelson (1998: 681) write:

> Women lawyers stand at the intersection of three major transformations in modern society: changes in the gender composition of traditionally male occupations, changes in the social organization of professional firms [for which substitute higher education] . . . , and changes in the role of law as a vehicle for redressing social inequality.

The paper falls into five sections dealing with the project, with women in university law schools, with equal opportunities debates, and with women in senior management. In this introductory section I explain the context in which women law teachers work in the UK. I am sensitive to the fact that the organisation and structures of education provision differ between countries and attempt to

---

[1] This research was funded by the Cardiff Law School Research Committee and by the Society of Public Teachers of Law. Of the many people who have contributed to this paper, I wish to thank in particular Helen Wright and Oliver Quick for their research assistance and Bill Felstiner for his help with the pilot interviews. I am indebted also to Bob Lee and Derek Morgan without whose support this work would never have been completed.
[2] Faber and Faber 1989.

explain some of the particularities of the UK university system. For example, what is coveted and difficult in the UK is to be appointed to a post in the first place but having achieved that, tenure (or a version of it) is attained far more often than not. Promotion to senior levels is where the academic funnel begins to operate in its most marked form.

A striking characteristic of equal opportunities debates in the UK higher education sector is how far behind they are compared with those in North America (and elsewhere). UK university teachers have only recently begun to examine who they are; it is as though we are discovering patterns and practices with which others have been familiar for two decades or more. (On UK higher education generally see Becher 1989, Halsey 1995, Trow 1994, Hearn 1999; on women see Morley and Walsh 1996, Morley 1999, Brooks, 1997; on senior academics David and Woodward 1998; on law, Collier 1998, McGlynn 1999, Cownie 1998) This is a serious omission not least because university academics play central roles in preparing students for professional responsibilities and, perhaps more importantly, in advancing their civic education. Universities exercise significant powers of selection, licensing and gatekeeping, and 'they greatly influence and control definitions of knowledge and much, though not all, of the ideological machinery of the state and of society.' (Lie, Malik and Harris 1994: 4) Many studies of the rise of women in professional work and changing perceptions of their roles reveal that women are concentrated in the less well-paid and lower status jobs. Within the university sector, women are concentrated in library, administrative and clerical posts, while women in academic positions are disproportionately on fixed-term contracts, and found at junior rather than senior levels. There is clear evidence that women of all ranks in universities are paid less than their male counterparts. (McNabb and Wass 1997, Bett Report 1999).

The term professor has a specific meaning in the UK system denoting the top of the academic career pyramid. The hierarchy begins with lecturer, a career grade in its own right and effectively tenured after the first three years in post. Most staff expect to progress at least to the level of senior lecturer. Before promotion to the rank and title of professor, it is common to spend anything between five and 15 years at the lecturer grade and another three to ten at the senior lecturer grade.[3] Many professors are promoted in their early forties, although a few are considerably younger especially if they come through the external appointment route. An intermediate status between senior lecturer and professor, that of reader, is recognised in many universities.[4] Promotion is generally based on research record but teaching and administration may also play a part. Management roles in many universities are generally confined to the

---

[3] In post-1992 ('new') universities senior lecturer is equivalent to a grade B lecturer in the old universities.

[4] In some institutions the reader status is equivalent to senior lecturer the distinction being the emphasis on scholarly research for the former.

professorial level. Each stage of promotion is important in terms both of status recognition and salary enhancement.

There are more men than women in academic positions in UK law schools by a ratio of about 60 to 40. There are more men than women in senior positions (senior lecturer and above) by a proportion of about 70 to 30. There are more men at the professorial level by a factor of 83 to 17. In 2000 there was a total of 55 women law professors. This amounts to fewer than one woman professor for every law school in the UK. Nearly 60 per cent of law schools in the UK have never had a female professor. The same percentage of schools has never had a female head of school.[5] (McGlynn 1999; Wells 2001b) Overall women law professors are likely to find themselves in a minority in most of their professional activities within their academic departments, within their institutions and in the wider world of their subject associations. Unlike women entering the academic profession now, most women law professors will have spent their entire careers in this kind of isolated position.

2 THE RESEARCH PROJECT

My aim was to collect quantitative and qualitative data on the population of women law professors in the UK with the objectives of: establishing a body of knowledge about the factors which women who have been promoted to chairs associate with their success; achieving an understanding of the experiences of successful women in the academic profession; and advancing our knowledge of the perceptions of senior women of their roles within and beyond the law school, particularly in management. This project realises a singular opportunity. Because there have been few studies in the UK of the academic profession in general, fewer of legal academics, and none specifically of senior women in law departments, the results of this project may have an impact on career development, promotion and equal opportunities policies within higher education generally, in university law schools and in professional legal education and practice. Academic lawyers are in a powerful position to influence the development and implementation of anti-discrimination legislation. At the same time female academics often carry a disproportionate burden in highlighting examples of poor institutional practices and procedures. The present cohort of women law professors encompasses women who have been professors for between one and 15 years, some of whom have studied and worked in a number of institutions. The range of their experiences and perceptions of gender in their careers is a valuable resource.

---

[5] Complete accuracy is not possible. There are no centrally collected statistics on law schools. Law forms only a part of a cost centre, the categorisation used by Higher Educational Statistics Agency.

In most institutions law is self-contained; even where it is organised within a faculty law often does not identify itself clearly as a social science, or a humanities subject, and in some universities it is situated in a business faculty. Law is taught in all types of institutional settings, including 'new' and 'old' universities, and at the undergraduate,[6] postgraduate, professional education and continuing education level. Women professors in one discipline are likely to share an understanding of the values relevant to promotion. And apart from the obvious point that disciplines have their own cultures, there are some specific claims we can make about legal education, although our experiences in the university may not be qualitatively different from those of women in other disciplines, nor may what we represent to students in general be very different. One is that we represent a distinct relational group for the legal profession. The law degree is not the only route to professional qualification but it nonetheless has the closest relationship with the legal profession of all university degrees. A second reason is to do with the power of law. Law operates in a social, economic and political context, it does not operate in a vacuum. Law reflects, reinforces and recreates as well as generates political ideas. Legal academics play a role in that legal and political culture. A further argument is that the image of the ideal law professor is an exaggerated version of images of the ideal professor. Law, like the academy, is associated with values of rationality, objectivity and neutrality. Since there is plenty of evidence that women are, in any case, perceived as less competent and authoritative than men in many work situations, and that this becomes more acute for women in professional roles, these (assumed) legal values contribute to what might be thought a *double* jeopardy for women teachers of *law*. (Farley 1996: 334)

The methodology draws on a rich tradition of oral history now supplemented by autobiographical feminism. (Soothill 1999,[7] Overall 1998) I used questionnaires, including a self-report section, and a selection of semi-structured interviews.[8] Both the questionnaires (which included personal questions about health as well as an opportunity to be more discursive in the self-report section) and the interviews had the potential to stir up sensitive and possibly painful experiences. (Morley 1999: 22) One person described the interview as cathartic saying that it changed her life 'to a quite scary extent'. Another said in returning her questionnaire that the comments seem 'a bit raw' but that is 'how I felt'. As well as the need to be sensitive to the effects of the research process itself, there was the additional fact that I knew many of my subjects. There was therefore both a general and specific issue about anonymity. The fact that I know many of the women did not deter those who participated from doing so but of course may have affected what they said. 'Ethical questions about social and

---

[6] 'New' universities generally are more orientated towards teaching than research.

[7] Tony Parker's work anthologised in Soothill (1999) is a fine example. His methodology is discussed in Smith (1999).

[8] 33 questionnaire responses were received from 49 sent out. I have additionally interviewed 12 women. No-one refused an invitation to be interviewed.

professional boundaries' cannot be simply ignored. (Morley: 1999, 12–13) This leads to more general methodological issues in relation to qualitative data.

Care has to be taken with what it means to set out to 'discover' women's experiences. It is important to realise that there is not a reality to find. (Miller and Glassner 1997)

> Experiences are not just out there in the subjectivities of women, waiting for the empathic and egalitarian feminist researcher, in a dialogue, to stimulate their straightforward expression and subsequently 'mirror' them in research publications. (Alvesson and Billing 1997: 35)

Experiences are often vague, ambiguous, contradictory and above all constructed. Social worlds are not static and the interview can be seen as an interaction in which the interviewer and interview subject 'create and construct narrative versions of the social world.' (Miller and Glassner 1997: 99) Social distance was not such a problem in this study as I shared a professional identity with my subjects. However, this is not to deny that the interview process 'fractures the stories being told.' (Miller and Glassner: 101).

3 UNIVERSITIES AND LAW MEET WOMEN

The project was clearly self-referential and grounded in subjective experiences. This essay combines some of my own experiences with a preliminary analysis of the data from the project. The combination of personal reflection[9] and material from the project gives this section a rather fluid structure. Finding a key to unravel the relationship between agency, structure and culture is one of the most intractable challenges in any feminist research. Individuals respond differently both to the demands of domestic and professional roles and to the myriad different constructions placed upon their behaviour. The more I thought about it, the more the project integrated itself in a review of my life. Many of the things I am writing about are part of my history but many are part of my present. Equality legislation and my career have coincided almost exactly. The Equal Pay Act 1970 and the Sex Discrimination Act of 1975 were going through Parliament while I was a student. As someone studying law you might have hoped for a more realistic set of expectations on my part. I suppose we all thought differently in those welfare, carefree just-after-graduating-days of the early 1970s.[10] This was the time of student protests, when the words 'university' and 'management' had hardly met, let alone become engaged or consummated as a couple. It was also a time of generous grants to cover living expenses. We had grown up in the brave new days of the national health service and the development of mass consumer cultures in the 1950s, the contraceptive pill beckoned

---

[9] The italicised sections of the chapter.
[10] Nicola Lacey's account (1998: Introduction) of her own journey from liberal law student to feminist theorist is typically honest and eloquent.

us towards sexual freedom, abortion laws had just been reformed. Questions about instrumental versus symbolic effects of law, of structural inequalities, of critical legal studies had not begun to penetrate. Warwick University, where I did my undergraduate law degree, was regarded as at the vanguard of legal studies because it eschewed black letter, professional study for an explicitly social science, contextual approach. No women taught in the law school at that time.

> *I grew up in Oxford. My parents were not connected with the university though they certainly aspired to be and through their political activism crossed paths with many university people. When I was about six my father stood outside the gates of Lady Margaret Hall—a women's college in Oxford—and said, 'You'll go there one day'. I hadn't the faintest idea what he meant. When I graduated from Warwick in 1971 I won a prize. I do not recall anyone from my law school suggesting that I might consider becoming a law teacher. I don't know what led me to apply to do a Masters degree the following year other than that I was moving to London with my husband. It was then I encountered my first woman law teacher, Olive Stone at the London School of Economics. She encouraged me to apply for a post at Lady Margaret Hall. This was the first time I had entered an Oxford College building (although as children we often walked in the college grounds—at least those open to the public). I found the dining ritual very strange. At the interview I was asked a number of times whether I would be able to fit in as I'd taken my first degree at a provincial university. Would I possibly be able to adapt to the 'unique' tutorial system. Did I know anyone on the faculty? I couldn't see myself in the job at all. And nor could they.*
>
> *I then applied for a post at a polytechnic in London. I wasn't shortlisted until Olive Stone challenged them. I went for an interview and got the job. My explanation for not being considered in the first place is that my application made me sound too intellectual for the kind of enterprise they ran. My recollection is that the polytechnic employed more women than men law teachers. After a few weeks in the job one of the male lecturers took me into his office and asked me what I was going to do—it was really going very badly wasn't it?[11] Was it? I didn't know. I certainly thought it must be after that. I didn't think then that this was just a sad and frustrated bloke who found me threatening. Nor did I know then what I know now, that the giving of unsolicited 'advice' is a highly gendered activity.*
>
> *When I took up my next post, one of the professors said to me, 'You'll be a professor one day'. It didn't mean very much though I knew what a professor was. It was like saying I would go to the moon for all its relevance to me.*

The proportion of women professors in law schools is higher than the average across all disciplines. (McGlynn 1999:77) Rather than indicate an outbreak of gender awareness amongst lawyers, the explanations for this are almost certainly market led. The legal profession is an attractive and well-remunerated first choice career for (male) law graduates.[12] Secondly, law attracts large num-

---

[11] I met the same man 20 years later. He was still patronising, 'You have changed so much—you were such a funny little thing when you started.' Imagine that I say the same words to one of my younger male colleagues in 20 years—no, it can't be imagined.

[12] More than one of my interviewees said they decided not to enter the bar because they perceived it as the elite branch of the profession, by class as well as gender, and 'not for them'. 'The bar' denotes the barrister branch of the legal profession.

bers of students who are well-qualified and cheap to teach. Thus universities welcome large law departments and the total legal academic population numbers over two thousand. Women are unevenly distributed between them, replicating the common pattern of feminisation, concentrated in the lower status institutions and in the lower ranks within their departments. Three out of five UK law schools have no women professors, allowing prejudices to be reinforced and closing off the possibility of the world looking any different. As Chused (1988) argues, the presence of senior women influences appointment and promotion decisions; there is a tendency to select people like ourselves. (Wajcman 1998) It also seems that a high proportion (22 per cent) of senior women end up doing the unglamorous, semi bureaucratic, jobs such as dean of faculty, thus replicating findings about junior lecturers undertaking time-consuming and unrewarding administrative tasks.[13]

A number of different factors needs to be taken into account in examining current data, the most important of which is the major expansion in British higher education in the last decade. One in three secondary school leavers now goes to university. Only 25 years ago the proportion was one in 15 and, unlike now when the gender distribution is even, two thirds of those places went to men.[14] This meant that between 1970 and 1988 four times as many additional women entered university than men. (Halsey 1993) The move from elitism to mass participation has been accompanied (perhaps not surprisingly) by significant changes in mechanisms of accountability. Instead of few relatively rich and autonomous universities free to spend public money more or less as they wished (the cry of academic freedom worked for a long time in defence of this lack of accountability), funding increasingly reflects 'result budgeting', dependent on quality reviews, whether of teaching or research. This new accountability, where public funding comes to be directly affected by teaching and research performance, meant that discrimination began to be exposed in the more obvious cases. The very successful women who had not been promoted became suddenly valued by their own institutions or poached by others. It also brought in its wake a change in the nature of senior positions. Being a dean became onerous and paper driven. Resources were more scarce in general and distributed more selectively. This had a connected third, more subtle, effect which was the devaluing of the senior academic role.[15] Feminisation leads to the conclusion that if women can do a job, it can hardly be such a big deal. Was it a coincidence that women entered the academy and began to take senior roles in larger numbers at this point? In terms of resources and research reputation old universities

---

[13] However, generalisation is again difficult. In some new universities, dean is an appointed managerial position with salaries well above those of professors. In old universities, dean is often an administrative and largely bureaucratic position.

[14] Oxford and Cambridge were heavily dominated by men until the 1960s by a factor of 5:1 at Oxford and a staggering 10:1 at Cambridge. (Halsey 1993: 66).

[15] I am grateful to Katherine O'Donovan for this insight.

dominate; it should not surprise us that more women are found at all levels in new universities compared with the old. (McGlynn 1999: 82)

The reward and promotions system in UK universities takes some account of administration and teaching but it is primarily based on published research. In the words of one respondent in a study of UK female academics: 'Male academics do not treat women academics seriously in many cases, which since so much depends on opinions formed, personal appraisal, nominations to jobs etc is a discriminatory practice.' (Brooks 1997: 49) Examples such as allocation of administrative tasks and the prevalence of patronage were identified. (Brooks 1997: 47) Women may also attract a disproportionate share of pastoral work through being perceived to be more accessible, as well as absorbing administrative or pastoral work from less conscientious colleagues. Different standards may be applied to women who fail their obligations than to men. Women may be left with no time for or be perceived as uncommitted to research. Because research is higher order and intangible in the university value system, these 'failings' are not tolerated and at the same time the 'absent-minded' male intellectual is excused from the mundane work of administration. Kettle's in-depth interviews with eight successful women in universities revealed examples of patriarchal culture in the marginalisation of senior women; the deployment of promotion criteria more likely to be met by men; the prevalence of unfriendly working practices, and the existence of informal networks based on patronage.[16] (Kettle 1996: 54)

Five of the eight women in Kettle's study had no child care responsibilities, yet each believed that their university was deeply hierarchical and that promotion criteria were weighted towards men. This reinforces the argument that cultural explanations of the failure of women to succeed may be as powerful as structural and operational ones. (Kettle 1996: 63) Nonetheless both the realities of, and expectations associated with, parenting have a profound impact. Two thirds of the women law professors in my study had raised children during their careers. A fifth of the women reported that they had responsibility for looking after parents or elderly relatives.[17] One of the women in my study wrote:

> When I first became an academic . . . [XY] . . . operated a benign dictatorship. Meetings were only held to inform the troops of what had been done. . . . I remember a particularly revealing session with [XY] when an appraisal system was initiated. At that time I had been on leave . . . he asked why it was I had 'suddenly' decided to publish. I explained the impact of leave from teaching and remarked also that the children were a bit older which was a help. [He] asked what effect the children had on my job. It was absolutely apparent that he had no idea at all of the possible impact of either child or elderly relative care. To give him his due, when some of the problems were

---

[16] They spoke of top-down management, their universities seeming to be 'men's clubs', the invisibility of women at decision-making fora, and exclusion of women from informal networking.

[17] A recent survey of British academics found that only 5 per cent of men with dependent children had main responsibility for childcare compared with 55 per cent of women. (Blake and LaValle 2000)

explained he became active in supporting the careers of young women with children. I have a positive view of appraisal for this rather idiosyncratic reason.

In some respects, as one of the few professional areas of work where flexibility and self-determined workloads reign supreme, the academic career has been complicit in fudging issues affecting women such as child care responsibilities. This may explain why the debate about women in the academy has remained hidden for longer; the stresses in the system may well have shown earlier in institutional settings without this work-time flexibility. My study disclosed a number of examples of women who fitted child care around their work in a way that was undoubtedly draining but would have been impossible with a more rigid working day. It is possible but that does not mean that it is acceptable. Despite their ability to perform all the roles parenthood and their careers threw at them, their colleagues perceived them as not fully committed. The ghost of the seven day a week ivory tower intellectual survived only to haunt women academics. When men had rounded lives, were involved in sport or other leisure activities, or even took parenthood seriously, their professionalism was not doubted.

> When I had my first child it didn't occur to me that I should take maternity leave. I just thought that motherhood and work were incompatible even though my mother, whom I greatly admired, had always worked. I gave up my job. When I applied for a lectureship two years later I was asked at the informal interview, 'What is hubby going to do?' My answer should have been, 'Why are you asking?'. But it wasn't. I explained that he was a postgraduate student, so was flexible. Again it didn't occur to me that for them my answer legitimated my decision to work (no male breadwinner), and ensured that there wouldn't be a problem of his being tied to a job somewhere else in the country. One of the first things I received when I took up this post was an invitation to join the University Wives' Tea Club. One professor (the same one who predicted that I would be a professor one day) often commented- in a kindly way (he was a kind and decent man) 'It's a nice sunny day, you should be on the beach with [your son]'. He would not have said it to a male colleague and it was a pretty firm message that whatever place I had there was somehow compromised by the competing role as mother.

The ideology of care pervades women's experiences of work. The strongest theme in the interviews I conducted was the confirmation that women believe that they take on more pastoral work in universities. They think that students and colleagues believe that this is something women do better. Perceptions are of crucial significance in all of this; perceptions and expectations are insidious and unspoken; they are hard to prove and easy to refute. Women can be perceived as uncaring if they do not conform to these unspoken expectations. Ideologies of femininity and caring suggest that women are thought to be playing their natural role when they are good at teaching or with students, but more significantly are seen to be behaving unnaturally when they do not conform to these expectations. (Williams 2000)

As well as leading to exploitation through overburdening of women with undervalued administrative tasks, those same expectations can conversely be used to deprive women of opportunities to establish a record of departmental contributions to satisfy promotion criteria. The caring ideology often locks women into assumptions about their roles both in and out of work:

> *My children are pretty healthy. I am pretty healthy. The only time any of my children has been in hospital was for a few days in 1988. Yet I was told shortly afterwards that I could not be asked to do an administrative job because I might have to spend too much time looking after ill children. This should have been positive and meant that I had more time for other work. I later found this meant that however good your research—and this could be demonstrated by external refereeing—the teaching and administrative dimension allowed a subjective veto based very often on hearsay or on favouritism . . . At the first stage of the procedure, the head of department was asked to report on one's teaching. The first two times I applied for promotion pre-dated any system of student feedback or teaching evaluation. No-one had ever observed my teaching. At the informal feedback session to explain where I could improve my application I was told that I needed to improve my teaching!*

Teaching evaluation is of course just as gendered as everything else, and some would argue it is more so in law school because of the characteristics associated with good lawyering. Farley's analysis (1996) of student evaluations over a three-year period in one US law school confirmed what many of us have always suspected. Different language is used in commenting about women (men are 'accessible', women are 'approachable'); the same comments are interpreted differently and negatively (men are given to 'intellectual musing', women are confused; men speak fast because they are intelligent, women because they are nervous); and some comments are exclusively made about men (eg they are masters of their subject), or about women (comments on their appearance, use of their first name). It is my experience also that talking about the world in a way which includes women as well as men provokes the label 'rabid' or 'radical' feminist.

It is sometimes said that more women would be promoted if they only applied. This fails to take into account many things to do with choice, opportunity and self-perception, best summed up as the impostor syndrome. (Overall 1998) In my preliminary interviews comments such as 'the bar was not for me', and 'I felt an impostor' at university emerged.[18] This despite the fact that women admitted to university (and appointed to academic posts) may well be more qualified and motivated. (Epstein 1981) Successful women often do not perceive themselves as either powerful or influential. (Keller and Moglen 1987) And, in the UK at least, they have every reason to doubt their power. Stark evidence of the complacency characterising many involved in higher education was exposed when the new quality assurance agency appointed a panel to establish benchmarks for standard attainments in law degrees in 1998. By then, even the feeble excuse for ignoring women that there were fewer of them in law schools, and that 'time would tell', had lost any potency or legitimacy. Women had

---

[18] See also Susan Greenfield, a leading British scientist who reports that women scientists feel like impostors. (Times Higher Education Supplement 11 June 1999)

contributed more than half the students at law school for some years and there were 853 women law teachers, of whom 400 were in senior posts, and 43 were professors. Yet not one of these was asked to sit on the panel. This omission is even more extraordinary given the (gendered) emphasis on women as good teachers (rather than researchers) and given the evidence that students have different perceptions and apply different language in their assessments of women and men lecturers. (Farley 1996: 338–52)

Women's under-representation in senior positions is a complex product of many factors, including lack of mentoring and patronage, as well as vague promotion criteria, often subjectively applied. In universities and most of our social and political institutions power is held by men, and it is not surprising that the normative structures and rules within those institutions generally reflect and further the interests of those holding power in that system. One of my respondents puts it bluntly when she says, 'As with most universities the promotion appointments and pay systems are deeply suspect with opaque criteria and male dominated snobbery driving the systems.' It is within these broader cultural foundations that localised cultures and politics are played out and 'choices' are made. The very qualities of competence, compliance and social immobility which are taken to be natural in women may also make them ideal candidates for filling out the base of the pyramid, providing the teaching commitment that the expanding base of higher education demands. (Hagan and Kay 1995: 33) Hagan and Kay (writing of women lawyers in Canada) suggest that the increasing numbers of women, as well as being exploited in this way, may have thus unwittingly ensured the reinforcement of hierarchy rather than helped to dismantle it (see also Thornton 1998: 273). Examining and exposing the micropolitics of the academy, focusing on the ways in which power is relayed in everyday practices, reveals the subtext of organisational life. (Morley 1999) Seemingly trivial single instances acquire significance when located in a wider analysis of power relations. First of all women are made to feel slightly odd and out of the order of things if they are clever and assertive. Secondly, the combined effects of being patronised and dealt with differently, all the while being told that this is their imagination, lead to complex problems of lack of self-confidence and self-esteem. Vasil's research (1996) revealed that women are just as confident as men about social processes such as communication skills, speaking effectively in groups and assuming leadership roles. Where they feel less confident is in what Vasil calls 'playing the system' skills, self-promotion including developing strategies for promotion applications. Being in a minority also leads to whole sets of double thinking, especially once equal opportunities appear on the political agenda. Has merit or political correctness led to your success?

This section has introduced a range of considerations, structural as well as cultural, likely to impact on women's careers in law schools in the UK. There has as yet been no systematic analysis of the possible effects of the major changes of the last two decades which include the significant increase in university provision, the merging of the binary line between universities (the traditional elite) and polytechnics (more closely associated with community and life-long learning activities and under-funded for research), as well as the broader socio-economic transformations forged by women's wider participation in the labour market. Separately and in combination these factors have exerted powerful pressures on the shape and faces of law schools, particularly on the values attaching to teaching and research. (Bell and Gordon 1999: 646)

4 EQUAL AND DIFFERENT

I remember hearing Germaine Greer, who taught English at Warwick when I was a law student there, address the Students' Union (this was 1969—student revolution time) and attempt to shock us by talking about clitoral orgasms. We thought we were pretty radical.

In her most recent work, Greer suggests that in the process of 'women's lib' metamorphosing into feminism the essence of 'liberation' was allowed to slip away unnoticed. The liberation struggles of the 1960s and 1970s were not about 'assimilation but about asserting difference', but they became subsumed into a language of equality. (1999: 1) This is a useful way of conceptualising the eddying currents of radical political movements and their translation to the mainstream and then to law. It took another decade or more before feminists began to realise that asking to be treated like men was the wrong objective. While the dominant approach to gender equality in the legislation of the 1970s was 'equal treatment', the inherent difficulties with this liberal approach had been evident for some time. (Lacey 1998) Gradually, emphasis began to be placed on reducing barriers, such as the demands of child care and the expectations of domestic commitment, which were seen to prevent men and women achieving the same goals. It seems all too familiar now to see that this does not get us very much nearer to an answer either. We were still seeing the goals in male terms. Let us accept, Wajcman (1998: 26) argues, that men and women do not have single, gender-based identities.

Gender is not just a characteristic which divides people into two categories, 'men' and 'women'. We should concentrate on the fact that women workers are disadvantaged and accept that difference is used as the basis for unequal distribution of power and resources. Man is still the unmarked standard.

Most organisations, including universities, self-consciously declare that they are 'equal opportunities employers'. But this does not mean that proactive policies have replaced the reality of reactive and complacent practices. A useful typology of equal opportunities awareness in organisations distinguishes the following stages: from showing no awareness of the need for policies or practices; to paying lip-service to equal opportunities policies; to having a predisposition to equal opportunities; to having a commitment to equal opportunities; to the final stage where equal opportunities policies and practices are ingrained in the ethos of the institution. (CUCO 1994) Only one woman in my study believed that her institution had incorporated equal opportunities in all its decision-making while a further 10 thought their institution was committed. A third of the women law professors rated their universities as only at the predisposed stage while as many as a quarter thought they only paid lip-service to equal opportunities. If this last group accurately reflects their institution's record on equal opportunities, it confirms the view that the gap between policy and implementation is a serious problem in universities. (Farish, McPake *et al* 1995) Surveys indicate that, while nearly all universities claim to have an equal opportunities policy, only a third have accompanying action plans, only half train staff involved in recruitment and selection, and 20 per cent take no action on information derived from statistical monitoring. (CUCO 1997) In a recent survey I conducted on behalf of the Women Law Professors Network I found that only 40 per cent of heads of law school were required to undertake training in equal opportunities. They all believe sincerely and passionately that they understand and support equal opportunities.

I quoted earlier the woman who was cast in the role of educating her head of department in the realities of child care responsibilities. Her experiences following a career move to another university were better in some respects but not all:

> Generally, my experience at [University A] was one of exclusion from any decision-making process. . . . [When] I moved to [University Y] I found the experience delightfully different so far as the department was concerned . . . Once operating at the university level, however, a pattern similar to that at [university A] emerged with committees overwhelmingly composed of males blissfully unaware of EO concerns and yet believing the essential fairness and objectivity of their assessment and evaluations. A topic for discussion at the senior awayday was the reform of the University's mission statement to remove the concept of working towards EO because the University has got there! And they really believe it.

There are exceptions of course. But even the exceptions often provide evidence of women's progress being impeded. Here is the story of another woman who had many positive experiences as a young academic:

> I had a wonderful time as an academic in [university C]. The department had lots of women, including senior level and was a very social and intellectually stimulating environment in the late seventies and eighties. As a young academic I had plenty of time to work with my more experienced and senior colleagues. . . . In those days coffee time was a 'teaching and learning' experience. Senior colleagues debated with you legal issues prevalent in the newspapers, etc etc. . . .
>
> Even though it took longer in those days to get promoted to SL than now, my promotion was delayed. I did feel that 2 or 3 of my colleagues were promoted before me unreasonably. They included one woman. The official reason was that I had been away and therefore missed my 'turn'. I think if I had been male I would have ensured that although I was absent I did not miss my turn! That was perhaps the first time I felt that something unfair had happened related to gender.

It is increasingly recognised that procedures and policies are insufficient; cultural change is needed. Leadership from the top emerges in a number of studies, including this one, as a crucial factor in bringing equal opportunities compliance within the institution beyond mere lip-service. A vice-chancellor committed to the value of diversity in the university can be very effective. But without support from the senior officers, and they are overwhelmingly male, it is extremely hard for committed individuals to make much progress. The British government has recently begun to exert pressure on the university funding bodies to consider setting targets for the recruitment and retention of women, people from ethnic minorities and those with disabilities. (*Times Higher Education Supplement* 31 March 2000: 3) It is never too late to begin to analyse social and professional practices but it seems extraordinary that this suggestion has only just emerged 30 years after the establishment of the Equal Opportunities Commission. The issues are not, however, just about numbers. One of my objectives in this project is to explore the intersection between gender, management and university organisational structures.

5 WOMEN IN SENIOR MANAGEMENT

Management, like law, is an occupation that is historically and culturally associated with men. It is seen as intrinsically masculine, something only men (can) do. (Alvesson and Billing 1997: 135) 'The very language of management is resolutely masculine. Organisations are then a crucial site for the ordering of gender, and for the establishment and preservation of male power.' (Wajcman 1998: 7) Good managers are perceived as having masculine characteristics, and until recently adjectives such as 'competitive', 'aggressive', 'rational' and 'strategic' were associated with good organisations. (Belcher 1997: 60, 62) Yet all of these are seen as undesirable traits in women. In an ironic reversal 'female' characteristics have been adopted by management experts: 'emotional intelligence' is the new management catchphrase. Intuition, and the empathic qualities, are now to be nurtured. 'Women professors face essentially two criticisms. First, they are accused of not being "man" enough, and second, they are accused of not being "woman" enough.' (Farley 1996: 340) This is connected with the observation, supported by the stories of a number of women in this study, that women experience increasingly hostile receptions the more successful they become.

Women in management are either 'insufficiently authoritative (but therefore normal women) or too authoritarian (because this is abnormal for a woman)'. (Belcher, 1997: 62) A study of senior managers is a study of exceptional women in an atypical context. They are inevitably perceived as disruptive of the status quo. (Wajcman 1998:2) Too clever, too emotional, too female . . .

> *I have lost count of the number of times I have been told either that I am 'too' emotional or care 'too much'. But who wants to be an uncaring emotionless professor [I'd*

be called a hard careerist bitch] Apparently I am also intimidating because I am clever. Who wants to be an unclever professor? [I'd be criticised for not being much of a scholar] One of the questions referees are asked when candidates apply for a post at one UK university is to rate on a five-point scale the 'candidate's emotional maturity and stability'. Is open emotion good or bad? Is repressed emotion good or bad?

It is difficult for women to be themselves; indirectly this denies them the right to power. Those who acquire power are then subject to more criticism for it than are men who have always had it. (Heilbrun 1989) As Wajcman argues (1998: 30), if women are to succeed they have to deny aspects of themselves and become more like men. But this is an impossible task given the expectations placed on women in the domestic sphere and the sexualisation of their bodies.

I am reminded of the time I was interviewed for a post as professor at another university. I had applied for the job partly as a way of putting pressure on my own university to promote me beyond the senior lectureship they had finally given me the year before. I arrived at the law school and made my way to the departmental office as instructed in the invitation. I was dressed appropriately in a suit. 'Good morning', I said, 'I have an appointment with Professor X.' 'You can't have', the departmental secretary replied. I looked puzzled. She explained, 'He's seeing candidates for a chair this morning'. 'Yes I know', I said, 'I am a candidate for the job.' Later in the day I was taken to a buffet lunch. The Chair of the University Council commented, ' I see from your application that you live 40 miles away and are very involved in the community there. Would you want to leave that to move here?' I hadn't actually thought I would move but I wasn't sure whether to say, 'No problem, I'll just throw my home life, my involvement in my children's schools, and move because that is what you want,' or to say, 'Well actually I thought I would commute.' Then I was asked, 'I see you have three children, that must be very difficult to manage with a career'. Well, yes and no, nice of you to ask but I think you're really putting me firmly in my gender place again, relating to me only in my domestic role, and questioning whether I will be able to devote myself 100 per cent to my work.

Studies of women in senior management show that job segregation pervades all levels. In academic life women are often found in the interstices. (Morley 1999) A quick analysis of the subject specialisms of women law professors in the UK reveals that the most represented area is family law. It is closely followed by criminal law, public law and European law. With hardly any common lawyers, or property lawyers, there is a clear message from this about marginality and subject segregation. Socio-legal studies is another example where women are found in larger numbers. (Lacey 1998: ch. 7) It is often commented that women are 'attracted' to the 'soft' degrees such as arts, humanities and social studies. (Cree 1997) It seems that this process is replicated in their choices of options within subjects, and of their specialisms in practice. (Sommerlad and Sanderson 1998)

Women who assume roles and statuses traditionally filled by men find themselves in conflict with prevailing norms. Their presence makes the gendered content of jobs and workplace relations more visible, and their sex subjects them to a scrutiny that is absent when they occupy their 'natural' place in the gender hierarchy. (Wajcman 1998:51) Women have also denied the conflicts which they feel in relation to other women, their mothers, sisters, daughters and 'sisters' in work. (Keller and Moglen 1987) These two statements are not in opposition because the constructions placed upon women in authority cause inevitable ambivalence about their 'true' selves.

Margaret Thornton, a major theorist of the position of women in law schools, suggests a typology, a set of constructions into which women are placed. Their acceptance in the academy is contingent on their falling into one or other or a combination of these roles: the adoring acolyte, the body beautiful, the dutiful daughter, the Queen Bee. (Thornton 1996) Thornton's central argument is that the masculinist character of legal culture prevents the acceptance of women, and that while there may be little evidence of overt discrimination in pay and promotion,[19] subtle forms of discrimination, for example in the distribution of work, abound. (Thornton, 1998) It is not clear, however, that law is highly differentiated from other disciplines or other male-dominated professions. Thornton's efforts to analyse why the dismantling of formal barriers did not guarantee acceptance of women as authoritative practitioners of law should be seen as an example of a more general phenomenon. However, these signs may be exaggerated in law. I would suggest that many of Thornton's insights would apply in the hard sciences as well as in some areas of social science, arts and humanities. The dutiful daughter label is one with which many women, including those in this study, can all too readily identify (although I think I prefer the notion of 'willing wife'). Women are anxious to be seen to be good at their work, they are anxious to prove themselves competent and authoritative. The anxiety is there because there is an unspoken presumption that perhaps they are not competent and authoritative.(Carli and Eagly 1999) Displacing assumptions about the ordering of power and influence is not an overnight task.

Thornton's constructions express ideas about aspiration, behaviour, and hierarchy.

> People's desires can be in large part formed by the circumstances and options that they perceive as being open to them . . . In societies in which the options open to them are fewer than those open to men, it has always been a common adaptive strategy for women to adjust their desires to what they can realistically expect. (Annas 1993: 282)

Women are also adjusting in the face of constructions of their otherness. Although the women I have talked to do not readily recognise many queen bees, I believe that this is a difficult construction to avoid. It is critically connected with the argument that successful women are recruited as 'honorary males'. Meg Stacey puts it well when she writes that becoming a professor radicalised her more than anything. She had been embarrassed at being described as an

---

[19] Increasingly however there is, see Bett Report 1999.

exceptional woman before she was promoted. She had responded that she was just lucky. Once she was a professor, and was described as 'exceptional', she concluded that part of refusing to be an honorary male was refusing to be an exceptional woman. (1998: 99)

Flattering successful women into believing they are exceptional justifies their being kept as a minority, and that way the hierarchy is not threatened. However, the issue is not simple. In order to have achieved success women probably do combine some kind of exceptional attributes helped along with the usual measure of good fortune (including generally being white, upper middle class, often independent school educated and able-bodied) that takes men into successful positions. And of course they are exceptional in the sense of being atypical (because generally their male and female colleagues share those background characteristics). But ascending the hierarchy will often mean an inevitable, tacit acceptance of organisational ideology. Gaining access to power for women may often be at the cost of their sense of identity as women, or their solidarity with others. For example, one woman in my study seems to fear that identifying with women's issues may detract from her neutrality or authority:

> I remain opposed to gender studies for reasons I find hard to articulate (marginalisation, softness?); and I also think that the sexual harassment movement has gone much too far. . . . I am a follower of the small group of women who believe that sexual harassment codes do women no good, in that they represent them as sensitive, prudish, obsessed with protection, vengeful, humourless, and totally inept in dealing with men.

How women behave and are perceived as senior members of the faculty is a product of many different factors. Some women never seem to feel the chilly climate of universities while others are aware of it from the outset. (Chilly Collective 1995) Many women are inclined to internalise their feelings of inadequacy and lack of self-confidence rather than to look around for structural or external causes. For example, another woman in my study reported that gender had had no impact on her career at all, yet she also wrote that she 'experienced sexual harassment as a younger member of staff from a previous head of school. So did other young females in the law school.' Another was adamantly opposed to anything other than strictly equal treatment yet also added this piece of advice: 'If a woman looks too attractive, she is not taken seriously; if, on the other hand, she is not stylish at all, she will not be popular. The trick is to strike a happy medium between the two extremes.' In addition the practices are often localised and may be thought to be trivial when taken on their own. (Wylie 1995: 29) Stereotyping, devaluation and exclusion emerge as the three themes in women's experiences. Exclusion does not have to be obvious and tangible. Since we do not belong we are constantly fighting with contradictions and multiple consciousness. (Guinier 1994: 73) The question 'Do I belong here?' is raised the moment that the minority member enters a social setting. The further she moves up the hierarchy the more pronounced this effect.

I have received two formal invitations from the Vice-Chancellor in the last three months. This is progress since 12 months ago I do not think he knew who I was. Both invitations include the phrase: 'Dress—lounge suit'

Indirect discrimination and unconscious gender behaviour are more difficult to deal with than some of the more overt forms. As the next comment from the study suggests, it can be easier to deal with people who are up front patrician than with those who say the right things but continually do the wrong ones:

I worry that apparently changed attitudes have not made all that much substantive change to women's career opportunities. Twenty years ago the job itself was less demanding and allowed more flexibility. . . . Law schools (though few would admit it) are wary of women who are likely to have children. Quite apart from the need to take maternity leave, for all but superwomen the very early years of a child's life are likely to lead to lower productivity. Talking to my own female colleagues many say that they do not think that they could contemplate having a child yet. . . . I am increasingly concerned how far attitudes among some colleagues in law and the wider university, really have changed. . . . No-one would say, as was said to me, "you're no competition, you'll get married and go part-time" or "you ought to stay at home with that baby—children who are deprived of their mothers fail to thrive". Yet such overt attitudes have their benefits. You can hit back. Other colleagues hear what is said and rally round. Today expression of such attitudes is more insidious. Colleagues wonder if 'X is pulling her weight'.

Much feminist literature is premised on the assumption that gendering is a pervasive and on-going aspect of social constructions. Women have until recently been in a minority at all levels in higher education institutions. Over the last 20 years, however, as many women as men have entered the undergraduate stage; and while some disciplines still attract significantly more men, this is not the case for law. The law school is nonetheless highly gendered in many respects. Many of the women in this study were students and junior lecturers at a time when these disparities were even more marked than they are today. Yet a number of them appear to have negotiated their understanding of their role without the deployment of gender concepts, they do not believe gender has affected their relations with colleagues and students. This contrasts with those writers who assert the gendered subject in the class room. (Mossman 1998, Farley 1996) As I mentioned earlier, because law is associated with 'male' characteristics such as objectivity and rationality, some have argued that women lawyers are doubly problematised.

The main themes that emerge from this study of women law professors (for the full report, see Wells 2002) are the homogeneity of their backgrounds (education, class and ethnicity), the diversity of individual perceptions of gender effects and the significance of organisational cultures. Those who have worked in more than one law school (though a significant number have spent their career in the same one) often had quite different experiences in each of them. This did not seem particularly connected with passage of time—some went from (in their view) bad to good universities, others from good to bad. Many of

the women in the study either have children or responsibilities for other depend-
ants. A large number of them subscribe to the view that women either do, or are
perceived to, take on more pastoral work with students in their departments and
that this can have a negative effect on career progression. Those who thought
that gender had not had a perceptible effect on their own careers formed a very
small minority and an even smaller number said they thought it had no effect on
anyone else either. A number of those who had held managerial positions in the
department (head of school, for example) found relations within the department
or at the university level difficult and it was described more than once as the
worst period in their career in terms of workload and stress. Stress-related illness during their career was also reported by a considerable number. There is
some evidence that women professors are concentrated in the 'softer' areas of
family, public and criminal law. Did they go into those areas because the entry
points for publication were easier? Were they admitted to the professoriate
because they were not competing in the 'hard' areas? These are all questions for
further research.

It would seem that the majority of the women who were unaffected by gender nonetheless recognised that gender might be an issue in terms of representation or diversity, or that it might affect others. Many of the respondents entered
university at a time when the solutions were seen as less intractable and anti-
discrimination legislation was thought to provide the answers. It is not uncommon for people to be able to recognise gender disadvantage in others' lives but
fail to see that the culture in which they are immersed is itself masculinist.

Most of the women in this study are white, (very) middle-class and many of
them would not identify themselves as feminists. As Keller and Moglen (1987)
express it, we have 'achieved status in a world unlike [us] only to the extent that
it is predominantly male.' Gender is often submerged—there but not there.
Although their views on the impact of gender on their careers are diverse (and
often contradictory) the response rate to my study has been very high. This confirms my belief that most women appreciate that gender does matter despite
being unable to articulate the deep and complex depths of its effects. The major
changes we have witnessed and experienced in the higher education sector in the
last two decades have paradoxically both exposed and obscured previously hidden questions. Gender, ethnicity and disability are emerging more strongly in
education debates but are nonetheless still often seen as someone else's problem.
It seems that it is often difficult for people to reconcile the roles of structure and
agency in their achievements.

6 REFERENCES

Aisenberg, Nadya and Mona Harrington. 1988. *Women of Academe: Outsiders in the Sacred Grove*. Amherst, Mass: University of Massachusetts Press.
Alvesson, Mats and Yvonne Due Billing. 1997. *Understanding Gender and Organizations*. London: Sage.

Annas, Julia. 1993. Women and the Quality of Life: Two Norms or One? In *The Quality of Life*, edited by M Nussbaum and A Sen. Oxford: Clarendon Press.

Becher, Tony. 1989. *Academic Tribes and Territories: Intellectual Enquiry and the Cultures of Disciplines*. Milton Keynes: Open University Press.

Belcher, Alice. 1997. Gendered Company: Views of Corporate Governance at the Institute of Directors. *Feminist Legal Studies* V: 57–76.

Bell, Sandra, and Jane Gordon. 1999. Scholarship: the New Dimensions of Equity Issues for Academic Women. *Women's Studies International Forum* 22: 645–58.

Bett Report. 1999. *Independent Review of Higher Education Pay and Conditions*. London: Stationery Office.

Blake, Margaret and Ivana La Valle. 2000. *Who Applies for Research Funding?* Wellcome Trust.

Brooks, Ann. 1997. *Academic Women*. London: SRHE and Open University Press.

Cameron, Deborah. 1985. *Feminism and Linguistic Theory*. London: Macmillan.

Carli, Linda and A Eagly. 1999. Gender Effects on Social Influence and Emergent Leadership. In *Handbook of Gender and Work*, edited by G Powell. London: Sage.

Carter, Pam, Angela Everitt, and Annie Hudson. 1992. Malestream Training? Women, Feminism and Social Work Education. In *Women, Oppression and Social Work*, edited by M Langan and L Day. London: Routledge.

Chilly Collective, eds. 1995. *Breaking Anonymity: The Chilly Climate for Women Faculty*. Waterloo: Ontario: Wilfrid Laurier Press.

Chused, Richard. 1988. The Hiring and Retention of Minorities and Women in American Law School Faculties. *University of Pennsylvania Law Rev* 137: 537–69.

Collier, Richard. 1998. 'Nutty Professors', 'Men in Suits' and 'New Entrepreneurs': Corporeality, Subjectivity and Change in the Law School and Legal Practice. *Social and Legal Studies* 7: 27–53.

Commission on University Career Opportunity. 1994. *A Report on Universities' Policies and Practices on Equal Opportunities in Employment* London: CUCO.

Commission on University Career Opportunity. 1997. *A Report on Policies on Equal Opportunities in Employment in Universities and Colleges in Higher Education* London: CUCO.

Cownie, Fiona. 1998. Women Legal Academics—A New Research Agenda? *Journal of Law and Society*. 25: 102–5.

Cree, Viviene. 1997. Surviving on the Inside: Reflections on Being a Woman and a Feminist in a Male Academic Institution. *Social Work Education* 16: 37–60.

David, Miriam, and Diane Woodward. Eds. 1998. *Negotiating the Glass Ceiling: Careers of Senior Women in the Academic World*. London: Falmer Press.

Davies, Sue, Cathy Lubelska, and Jocey Quinn. 1994. *Changing the Subject: Women in Higher Education*. London: Taylor and Francis.

Equal Opportunities Commission. 1999. *Women in Senior Management in Wales*. Cardiff: EOC.

Epstein, Cynthia, and Rose Coser. Eds. 1981. *Access to Power: Cross-National Studies of Women and Elites*. London: Allen and Unwin.

Farish, Maureen, Joanna McPake, Janet Powney and Gaby Weiner. 1995. *Equal Opportunities in Colleges and Universities—Towards Better Practices*. Open University Press.

Farley, Christine Haight. 1996. Confronting Expectations: Women in the Legal Academy. *Yale Journal of Law and Feminism* 8: 333–58.

Greer, Germaine. 1999. *The Whole Woman*. London: Doubleday.

Guinier, Lani, Michelle Fine, Jane Balin, Ann Bartow, and Deborah Lee Stachel. 1994. Becoming Gentlemen: Women's Experiences at One Ivy League Law School. *University of Pennsylvania Law Review*. 143: 1–110.

Hagan, John, and Fiona Kay. 1995. *Gender in Practice: A Study of Lawyers' Lives*. New York: Oxford University Press.

Halsey, Albert. 1995. *Decline of Donnish Dominion: The British Academic Professions in the Twentieth Century*. Oxford: Clarendon Press.

Hearn, Jeff. 1999. Men, Managers and Management: the Case of Higher Education. In *Transforming Managers: Engendering Change in the Public Sector*, edited by S Whitehead and R Moodley. London: University College London Press.

Heilbrun, Carolyn. 1989. *Writing a Woman's Life*. London: The Women's Press.

Hull, Kathleen, and Robert Nelson. 1998. Gender Inequality in Law: Problems in Structure and Agency in Recent Studies of Gender in Anglo-American Legal Professions. *Law and Social Inquiry* 681–705.

Keller, Evelyn Fox and Helene Moglen. 1987. Competition and Feminism: Conflicts for Women. *Signs* 12: 493–511.

Kettle, Jane, 1996. Good Practices, Bad Attitudes: an Examination of the Factors Influencing Women's Academic Careers. In *Breaking Boundaries: Women in Higher Education*, edited by Louise Morley and V Walsh. London: Taylor & Francis.

Lacey, Nicola. 1998. *Unspeakable Subjects*. Oxford: Hart Publishing.

Lafferty, George and Jenny Fleming. 2000. The Restructuring of Academic Work in Australia: Power, Management and Gender. *Brit Jnl of Sociology of Education* 21: 257.

Lie, Suzanne Stiver, Lynda Malik, and Duncan Harris. 1994. *The World Yearbook of Education 1994: The Gender Gap in Higher Education*. London: Kogan Page.

McGlynn, Clare. 1999. Women, Representation and the Legal Academy. *Legal Studies* 19: 68–92.

McNabb, Robert, and Victoria Wass. 1997. Male-female Salary Differentials in British Universities. *Oxford Economic Papers* 49: 328–43.

Miller, Jody, and Barry Glassner. 1997. The 'Inside' and the 'Outside': Finding Realities in Interviews, in *Qualitative Research*, edited by D Silverman. London: Sage.

Monture-Okanee, Patricia 1995. Surviving the Contradictions: Personal Notes on Academia, edited by Chilly Collective, *Breaking Anonymity: the Chilly Climate for Women Faculty*. Toronto: Wilfrid Laurier University Press 15.

Morley, Louise. 1999. *Organising Feminisms: The Micropolitics of the Academy*. Basingstoke: MacMillan Press.

Morley, Louise, and Val Walsh. Eds. 1996. *Breaking Boundaries: Women in Higher Education*. London: Taylor and Francis.

Mossman, Mary-Jane. 1998. Gender Issues in Teaching Methods: Reflections on Shifting the Paradigm. *Legal Education Review*, 6:129–152.

Overall, Christine. 1998. *A Feminist I: Reflections from Academia*. Broadview Press.

Sandland, Ralph. 1995. Between 'Truth' and 'Difference': Poststructuralism, Law and the Power of Feminism. *Feminist Legal Studies* 3: 3–47.

Silverman, David, ed. 1997. *Qualitative Research*. London: Sage.

Smith, Lynn. 1999. Only Listen. . . . Some Reflections on Tony Parker's Methodology, in *Criminal Conversations,* edited by K Soothill. London: Routledge.

Sommerlad, Hilary, and Peter Sanderson. 1998. *Gender, Choice and Commitment: Women Solicitors in England and Wales and the Struggle for Equal Status*. Aldershot: Ashgate.

Soothill, Keith, ed. 1999. *Criminal Conversations*. London: Routledge.

Stacey, Meg. 1998. A Flying Start, in *Negotiating the Glass Ceiling: Careers of Senior Women in the Academic World*, edited by M David, and D Woodward. London: Falmer Press.

Thornton, Margaret. 1996. *Dissonance and Distrust: Women in the Legal Profession*. Australia: Oxford University Press.

Thornton, Margaret. 1998. Authority and Corporeality: The Conundrum for Women in Law. *Feminist Legal Studies* 6: 147–70.

Trow, Martin. 1994. *Managerialism and the Academic Profession: Quality and Control*. London: Quality Support Centre.

Vasil, Latika. 1996. Social Process Skills and Career Achievement among Male and Female Academics. *Journal of Higher Education*, 67: 103–14.

Wajcman, Judith. 1998. *Managing Like a Man: Women and Men in Corporate Management*. Cambridge: Polity Press.

Wells, Celia. 2001a. Working out Women in Law Schools. *Legal Studies*, 21. 116–136.

Wells, Celia. 2001b. Ladies in Waiting: The Women Law Professors' Story. *Sydney Law Review*, 23. 167–184.

Wells, Celia. 2002. Women law professors—negotiating and transcending gender identities at work. *Feminist Legal Studies*, 10. 1–45.

Williams, Joan. 2000. *Unbending Gender: Why Family and Work Conflict and What to Do About It*. Oxford: Oxford University Press.

Witz, Anne. 1995. *Professions and Patriarchy*. London: Routledge.

Wylie, Alison. 1995. The Contexts of Activism on 'Climate' Issues, edited by Chilly Collective, *Breaking Anonymity: the Chilly Climate for Women Faculty*. Toronto: Wilfrid Laurier University Press 29.

14

Lawyers in the Courtroom: Gender, Trials and Professional Performance in Israel*

BRYNA BOGOCH

Abstract

The effect of gender on the legal profession in Israel is discussed on three levels: the ascriptive level, the performance level and the evaluative level, with particular emphasis on the evaluative dimension. On the ascriptive level, it was found that although women comprise about one third of the legal professions in Israel, they comprise a majority of the State Attorney's Office where they have reached the peak of the professional pyramid, and comprise 40 per cent of the judiciary, including three of the 14 judges in the Supreme Court. Two criteria were used to measure the effect of gender on the performance level: the sentences imposed by men and women judges in serious criminal offences, and analyses of interaction in the courtroom. While some differences were found between the sentences imposed by men and women judges, these were not in accordance with theories of a different voice but were more successfully explained by the still tenuous position of women in the judiciary. In the analysis of courtroom interactions, it was found that women judges were more attuned to the face needs of lawyers, but that both men and women judges displayed less respect to women lawyers than to men. On the evaluative level, it was found that the comments of both witnesses and judges challenged the professional competence of women

* The research on which this paper is based is part of a larger study of gender bias in Israeli courts, directed by Bryna Bogoch and Rochelle Don-Yehiya and funded by the Ford Foundation Middle East Division under the academic auspices of the Jerusalem Institute of Israel Research. I would like to thank Prof Alice Shalvi and the Israel Women's Network for initiating the project and for their encouragement and support throughout. I am grateful to the staff of the Jerusalem Institute for Israel Research for their efficient professionalism and their unstinting efforts on behalf of the project. In addition, I am grateful to Mr Eitan Amram of the Statistics Department of the Israel Bar Publishing House for providing the early data on the gender composition of the bar and the judiciary, to Attorney Orna Lin, the head of the Israel Bar Association for permitting access to recent data, and to Ms Mical Liser-Albashan, the advisor to the Ministry of Justice on Women's Issues for data on the State Attorney's Office. I would also like to thank Ulrike Schultz for making it possible for me to attend the Workshop on Women in the Legal Profession at the Onati Institute for the Sociology of Law in July 1999.

*lawyers, and that similar strategies on the part of men and women attorneys
were assessed differently, to the detriment of the woman attorneys. In addition,
it was found that the sentences were higher for defendants represented by
women attorneys than those represented by men attorneys, while the reverse
was true for prosecutors. It was concluded that gender was the interpretative
framework within which the action of the lawyers was measured and the persuasiveness of their case was judged.*

1 INTRODUCTION

E VERYONE, IT NOW seems, is interested in studying women lawyers.
Indeed, the convergence of interest on women in the legal professions
from a variety of disciplines and theoretical positions has led to stimulat-
ing ideological debates and empirical research. The range of research topics is
extensive: from scholars of feminist jurisprudence who grapple with the law's
construction of gender and the difference women could make in the legal sphere
(eg Menkel-Meadow 1989; Williams 1989) to task forces that explored the experiences of lawyers, litigants and judges in and out of courtrooms (Gillis 1991;
Resnik 1996); from social psychologists interested in moral reasoning among
lawyers (Jack, Dana Crowley and Jack 1994) to sociologists of the professions
who have explored the structure of legal practice and the stratification of the
legal profession (Chambliss and Uggen 2000; Kay and Hagan 1998); from
historians who traced exclusionary practices in law and the construction of
lawyering roles (Drachman 1998; Sklar 1995) to socio-legal scholars who studied the relationship between gender and lawyering in current practice
(McGlynn 1998; Pierce 1995; Seron 1996; Thornton 1996); from criminologists
who explored issues of gender, legal practice and justice (Cain and Harrington
1994; MacCorquodale 1991; Martin and Jurik 1996) to researchers of the use of
language in legal settings who analysed microlevel expressions of power,
dominance, credibility and professional identity (Bogoch 1997; Conley and
O'Barr 1998). The diversity of research and depth of discussion has made the
study of women in the legal professions an important concern of the current academic agenda.

Carle (1999) has suggested that the question of how gender affects the legal
profession has been investigated on several levels: the ascriptive level, the role
level, and the evaluative level. Ascription refers to how gender can determine
who gets to perform what work. In this area, studies have shown that although
women comprise increasing proportions of the legal profession in many countries, there are still gender barriers that restrict professional practice, income
and advancement (Kay and Hagan 1995, 1998; MacCorquodale 1996;
Sommerlad and Sanderson 1998; Spencer and Podmore 1987). The role level
refers to how gender can influence the way in which work is performed. Many
studies on this level sought to determine whether women adopt a gender-specific

style of lawyering (Bogoch 1997; Carle 1999; Hotel and Brockman 1994; Jack, Rand and Jack 1989; MacCorquodale 1995; Thornton 1996). Empirical results are not clear-cut, and most rely on reports by lawyers (eg Pierce 1995) and responses to questionnaires (eg Hotel and Brockman 1994) rather than observations of lawyers in the office or the courtroom (but see Bogoch 1999). For example, Harrington (1994), Hotel and Brockman (1994), Jack and Jack (1989) and Pierce (1995) found some support for less adversarial behaviour by women, while Martin and Jurik (1996) and MacCorquodale and Jensen (1991) found that the difference was mainly in the greater sympathy and sensitivity of women lawyers to women's concerns. However, Bogoch (1997) found that there was almost no difference in the way men and women lawyers spoke to their clients, although clients were less deferential to the women lawyers, while Epstein (1991) concluded that there was no firm empirical basis for attributing a different style to women lawyers, and suggests a number of reasons for the persistence of this myth among academics. Still others (eg Thornton 1996; McGlynn 1998) have described the professional culture that defines lawyers' behaviour as aggressive and adversarial, but disapproves of women lawyers who conform to this ideal and undervalues women who do not.

These last results are associated with the third level of analysis, the evaluative level, which examines how work performances are judged. Here, the results are almost unanimous: from law students to lawyers, from academics to judges, women in the legal profession are held to different standards than those of men and are deemed less authoritative and less credible. Women students claimed they were not listened to in class and their comments were given less weight than those of men students (Guinier, 1994); women lawyers felt their authority was undermined by biased behaviour toward them by the opposing attorney (Riger, Foster-Fishman, Nelson-Kana, and Curran 1995); women academics felt they were isolated and marginalised by put-downs, snide remarks and lower ratings of their work no matter how well they performed (McGlynn 1998; Spencer and Podmore 1987); and even women judges did not escape the inferior evaluations that gender stereotypes imposed (Resnik 1996). It is within this framework that I will present the profile of women in the legal profession in Israel. Although I will present some basic data about the achievements (ascriptive level) and the performance (role level) of women in the legal profession in Israel, I will focus primarily on the evaluation of the performance of women lawyers in courtroom trials, through an analysis of the comments made to women by judges and witnesses, and of the results of decisions and sentences in criminal trials. Unlike previous empirical research on the evaluation of women in the legal profession, which was based on reported experiences and perceptions, this study is based on the systematic observation of actual courtroom interactions and on the analysis of judicial decisions. I will demonstrate how the public undermining of the professional competence of women lawyers may ultimately affect the judges' perception of their persuasiveness, and the final results of the trial.

2 ASCRIPTION: GENDER AND PROFESSIONAL PRACTICE

2.1 Women Lawyers

The history of women in the legal profession in Israel has yet to be charted. In fact, to date there has been no survey of the legal profession, and very limited demographic data are available in the official sources. From the information that is available, we know that until the 1990s, there was a steady increase in the number of women in the legal profession, which accelerated abruptly in the last five years as a growing number of colleges have begun offering diplomas in law in addition to the degrees granted by four established universities.[1]

Table 1: Proportion of women lawyers (active licenses) by decade

Decade	%Women	Total No
1950–1959	7	815
1960–1969	18	1563
1970–1979	28	3287
1980–1989	36	4135
1990–1999	36	12141

Table 1[2] charts the growth in the number of lawyers with active licenses in the first five decades of Israel's existence. As we can see, although the number of practising lawyers (at least, according to the number who renew their licenses) has risen dramatically, the proportion of women stabilised at about one third of the profession in the 1980s. At that time, the proportion was quite a bit higher than that of the United States, for example, where women comprised less than 25 per cent of the profession even in the early 1990s (Martin and Jurik 1996). These differences have narrowed and today[3] women comprise 36 per cent of the 22,513 practising lawyers in the country, which is similar to the proportion of women lawyers in other Western countries. In Israel as elsewhere it is expected that the proportion of women lawyers will increase in the near future, as half the law students in the country today are women.

The occupational segregation typical elsewhere (eg Sommerlad 1994) similarly characterises Israeli women lawyers. Few women are partners of the large prestigious commercial law firms[4] (Raday 1996), and most women work as

---

[1] In addition to the growth in the number of institutions providing legal education, it should be noted that the Jewish population of Israel doubled between the years 1964–1994.

[2] The data in Table 1 were collected from two different sources. The figures until 1992 were provided by the Statistics Department of the Israeli Bar Publishing Company and the later figures were provided by the Israeli Bar Association

[3] September 2000.

[4] The nature of legal practice has changed dramatically in Israel in the last few years. From a private bar composed mainly of solo practitioners and small-scale firms of up to a maximum of 15 lawyers, there are now a number of firms that employ more than 100 lawyers (Halperin-Kaddari, personal communication). We do not yet know the implications of these changes for women lawyers.

salaried employees, especially in the public sphere. Nevertheless, women have reached the peak of the profession in the public sphere. A woman is currently serving as Solicitor General[5] and as the Assistant State Attorney, the former State Comptroller was a woman, as are the legal advisers to important government ministries and public institutions (Raday 1996). Moreover, six of the nine Section Heads of the State Attorney's Office are women, and women comprise more than two thirds of the prosecutors and other legal personnel who work in the State Attorney's Office (Table 2).

Table 2: Men and women legal professionals in the State Attorney's office

	Men	Women	Total	% Women
Prosecutors	161	357	518	69
Other legal positions	52	84	156	54
District Head	3	6	9	67

The success of women in the State Attorney's office may be related to the relatively low salaries paid in that particular sector (Raday 1996). In fact, a young man working in the State Attorney's office told me there was a concentrated effort to hire men, in order to limit the feminisation of this sector and stem the perceived decline in its status.[6]

2.2 Women Judges

In the past, one place in the Supreme Court was traditionally reserved for a woman. Today there are three women out of 14 justices in the Supreme Court, more than one third of the District Court judges are women, and 44 per cent of the Magistrate's Court, with all its subsections (all of whom are professional judges with legal training) (see Table 3). The highest rank achieved by a woman so far in the judiciary has been Vice-President (Assistant Chief Justice) of the Supreme Court, and it remains to be seen whether the judge slated to become Chief Justice of the Supreme Court by virtue of her seniority will actually be nominated when the current incumbent retires.[7] Again, the pyramidic distribution of women judges in Israel mirrors that of other Western countries although the proportion of women judges at the higher levels in Israel is certainly higher than that in Britain, the United States, and many other countries (McGlynn 1998; Steffensmeier and Hebert 1999).

[5] Edna Arbel replaced another woman, Justice Dorit Beinish, who is now a judge in the Supreme Court and slated to replace Justice Aaron Barak, when he retires as President of the Supreme Court.

[6] In private conversations among feminist academics, it has been suggested that the unusually sharp criticism of the State Attorney's office in connection with the recent criminal investigation of public figures may be tinged with gender bias.

[7] Justice Ben Porat was the Vice-President, who then became State Comptroller. Justice Beinish made some controversial decisions when she was Solicitor General, and there has been some speculation that despite her seniority, her appointment is not certain.

Table 3: Women in the judiciary in Israeli courts (May 2000)

	Female	Male	Total	% Women
Supreme Court	3	11	14	21
District Court	36	63	99	36
Magistrate's Court*	141	178	319	44
Total	180	252	432	42

*Includes traffic, labour, family and juvenile courts

What makes the situation in Israel more difficult for equitable gender distribution is that there are no women judges in the Rabbinical courts which have jurisdiction over marriage and divorce, and are governed by religious law. The civil courts share jurisdiction[8] in some areas of family law although only the religious courts can grant the final decree. In 1995, the Family Courts Act established a new family law division within the magistrate courts, which became responsible for all family matters under the jurisdiction of the civil system. The establishment of the family courts system has not affected the jurisdictional split between the religious and the civil judiciaries, although it concentrates family issues in one forum, it employs judges who undergo special training in family problems and many of the courts maintain auxiliary units that provide mediation and counselling services. Nonetheless, the procedural changes introduced by these courts are seen as providing a more egalitarian forum for women than the Rabbinical courts partly because these family courts employ women judges. In addition, after a great deal of resistance and outright sabotage, women have been accepted to the professional ranks of Rabbinical court pleaders, a position that is comparable to that of legal representation in the civil courts (Shamir 1994). Although lawyers can also appear in Rabbinical courts, they often work in co-operation with pleaders who have special knowledge of religious law. Pleaders can also represent the client on their own. There were two institutions that trained women pleaders until this year, but the one at Bar Ilan University will be closed in the 2000–2001 academic year because of insufficient qualified registration. For religious women the position of pleader has become a new important avenue for professional achievement, and many see it as the first true entry of women into the realm of religious learning which is the most significant source of power and prestige in the Orthodox Jewish world.

---

[8] Couples tend to engage in a race to file a suit in the forum that is perceived to be favourable to their case, as this prevents the matter from being addressed in the competing arena. Civil courts are perceived as more favourable to women, while the religious courts are seen as more favourable to men (Halperin-Kaddari 1994).

3 ROLE: GENDER AND PROFESSIONAL STYLE

The question of whether women bring a particular style to the practice of law, or how gender is manifested in professional behaviour has hardly been studied in Israel. Part of the reason, suggests Raday (1996), is that:

> women's partnership with men in the legal profession has resulted in an integrated profession in which the female world view has recently gained a legitimate place, as expressed in the judgements of some male and some female judges, particularly in the Supreme Court (p 28).

She notes that although women judges have probably been more receptive to specific issues of discrimination against women, and some women lawyers have actively represented the claims of feminist groups, women judges and lawyers have generally not identified publicly as feminists nor have they been the flag bearers of equality for women.

In my own research which sought to discover whether women had a 'different voice' in the judging of criminal offences, I found that women judges alone on the bench were more lenient than men in the sentencing of offenders convicted of severe crimes against the person (Bogoch 1999b). However, when a panel of three contained at least one woman judge, the decision was more severe than the all-men panels.[9] While these results may partially support the association of women with a more caring, rehabilitative, non-punitive approach, the fact that women judges imposed lower sentences for sexual offences than for bodily harm offences indicated no special sympathy on the part of women judges for the victims of rape and sexual assault. Moreover, both men and women judges generally imposed higher sentences on those who harmed adults rather than children; only in all-male panels were sexual offences against minors treated more seriously than offences against adults. In fact, instead of a different voice, these differences between men and women judges are more successfully explained by the still tenuous position of women judges in the professional hierarchy that prevents the development of a separate collective voice (eg, see Sommerlad 1994).

The results of research on women lawyers are more ambiguous. While a small-scale study of women and men mediators found differences in negotiating style (Malach-Pines, Gat, and Tal 1999), the special voice of women lawyers in a legal aid office in Israel was more muted. Here it was found that contrary to the neutral, distant male professional paradigm, women lawyers were occasionally willing to give legitimacy to the client's emotional concerns, but did so by marking this behaviour as a departure from their professional role (Bogoch 1997).

---

[9] There were no all-women panels in our sample.

254   *Bryna Bogoch*

In the context of research on gender bias in Israeli courts, we also analysed courtroom interaction. The analysis of talk in the courtroom allowed us to determine whether there were differences in the behaviour of men and women lawyers in the public arena of the court, where legal professionals display their expertise before their colleagues, clients and the public at large. We observed 656 segments of testimony[10] in the District Courts in Israel and recorded language variables that had been of significance in studies of power and professional behaviour.

In general, more differences were observed in behaviour *toward* women and men lawyers in the courtroom (which is related to the evaluation of their conduct to be discussed below) than *by* the professionals themselves. Thus, there were few gender differences in the way lawyers addressed either witnesses, judges or the other lawyers, although all women were addressed and spoken to with less deference than were men in the same roles. Nevertheless, some interesting differences emerged.

Interruptions have been associated with power in talk, with gender and hierarchy often interacting to women's conversational disadvantage (James and Clarke 1993; West and Zimmerman 1987). In the courtroom interruptions may be used by lawyers as strategic ploys to channel the talk in the direction they desire or as an attempt to prevent the other side from challenging their own version (Jackson 1995; Matoesian 1993). Does the use of interruptions indicate a different style for women lawyers?

Table 4 shows that in three of the four sex and role combinations (male-female prosecutors and defence attorneys), women lawyers interrupted the opposing attorneys less frequently than men lawyers did. Thus, women prose-

Table 4: Lawyers and interruptions: mean number of interruptions by gender of participants

Gender of Interrupted Lawyers	Female*				Male			
	*Prosecutors		Defence Attorneys		*Prosecutors		Defence Attorneys	
Gender of Interrupter	Mean	N	Mean	N	Mean	N	Mean	N
Prosecutor								
Female	–	–	.90	29	–	–	1.58	262
Male	–	–	1.38	37	–	–	.87	293
Defence Attorney								
Female	1.55	29	–	–	.89	37	–	–
Male	1.86	262	–	–	.95	293	–	–

*Effect of gender of interrupted prosecutor significant, p<.05

[10] This unit of analysis refers to a new questionnaire that was filled out each time a lawyer examined a witness. The mean segment of testimony lasted 30 minutes, although there were some very long segments lasting almost 4 hours. See a full description of the procedure in Bogoch 1997.

cutors interrupted women less frequently than did their male counterparts (8.90 versus 1.38 average interruptions per segment of testimony), while women defence attorneys interrupted both women and men less frequently than men did (1.55 versus 1.86 interruptions of women, .89 versus .95 interruptions of men). The only exception was that women prosecutors interrupted men defence attorneys more frequently than the men prosecutors did. It seems that in general, women lawyers interrupted less frequently and were interrupted more frequently than their male colleagues. The exception of the prosecutors is interesting, because it is in the State Attorney's Office that women are in the majority and occupy powerful positions. Our data suggest that when women prosecutors face men opponents, they adopt the language behaviour associated with power and competition even more than men prosecutors do, whereas when they face women opponents, they seem to be less adversarial. Women defence attorneys, on the other hand, who are not as well situated in the professional structure as women prosecutors, appear to be adopting the male mode of interrupting women attorneys more frequently. It may be that only when women are secure in their professional position can they adopt their own style of lawyering.

Another aspect of language often attributed to women is that they are more attentive to the face needs of their conversational partner and thus are less forceful when they give them orders or make requests. (Mulac and Bradac 1995; Remlinger 1999; Ridgeway and Smith-Lovin 1996) Requests are controlling acts, in that they seek to determine the subsequent behaviour of the other person, and that is why various linguistic strategies are used to either mask or soften the imposition entailed by these acts and allow the conversational partner to 'save face'. In ordinary conversations conventionally indirect rather than direct forms, such as the performative or the imperative, are usually used to make requests, in order to obscure the control element[11] (Blum-Kulka 1989). Judges' requests in court are almost always in the direct imperative or performative form. However, the force of the direct form of the control act and the concomitant threats to face may be softened by the use of mitigating[12] devices, or intensified by the use of aggravating devices. The following examples will indicate the difference, the first showing the use of mitigators, and the next the use of aggravators.

(1) Segment 2208 (male judge to male prosecutor)
Mr. M, maybe it's possible not to lead the witness.
(2) Segment 7716 (female judge to female prosecutor)
Lady (*geveret*), if you stand up again I'll stop the session. I suggest you sit down.

[11] For example, instead of the direct imperative form 'pass the paper' or the performative 'I request that you pass the paper' we say 'could you pass the paper?' This allows the hearer to pretend that the request is a question of ability instead of an order, although the actual meaning is understood by both speaker and hearer because we conventionally use this indirect form.
[12] Blum-Kulka and House (1989) have called these upgraders and downgraders respectively.

We found a number of interesting differences in the behaviour of men and women judges. Not only were men judges more likely to give orders than women judges, but they gave more orders to women than to men attorneys. Six per cent of all men judges' comments were directives, compared to 4 per cent of the comments of women judges. However, men judges issued almost twice as many orders to women prosecutors as to men prosecutors (5 versus 3 per cent), and five times as many orders to women defence attorneys compared to men defence attorneys. In fact, a full 25 per cent of the comments made by men judges to women defence attorneys were directives to do something. Thus men judges are more aggressive than women judges, but especially to women lawyers.

Our results show that the addition of aggravating or mitigating elements to the requests are also in line with gender-specific expectations in the behaviour toward prosecutors, and in most behaviours to defence attorneys. Women judges were significantly more mitigated in their requests to prosecutors than were men judges. Women judges softened 15 per cent of their requests, whereas for men judges, mitigation accounted for 6 per cent. On the other hand, men judges aggravated 26 per cent of their requests to prosecutors, while women judges intensified only 19 per cent. The fewer instances of aggravation on the one hand, and the greater use of mitigation on the other, indicate that women judges apparently pay more attention to the face needs of their conversational partners than do men judges. This finding is in line with theories of a more co-operative and empathetic style adopted by women legal professionals (eg Menkel-Meadow, 1989) that have developed from Gilligan's (1982) thesis that women bring a special 'different voice' to interpersonal relationships. However, when we examined just which lawyers enjoyed the benefits of the face saving strategies by the judges and which lawyers bore the brunt of their harshness, we find that there were definite gender patterns. Women judges mitigated 11 per cent of their directives to women prosecutors, but 19 per cent to men prosecutors; men judges mitigated 5 per cent of their requests to women prosecutors but 7 per cent to men. In other words, both men and women judges were more considerate of the face needs of men lawyers. By contrast, women prosecutors as well as women defence attorneys were more likely to suffer the affront of aggravated requests made to them in the open arena of the courtroom than were their male counterparts. Here, both men and women judges were less considerate of women lawyers. For example, a full 43 per cent of directives addressed to women defence attorneys by women judges were aggravated, as compared to only 8 per cent to the men lawyers, while men judges aggravated 44 per cent of their directives to women and 14 per cent to men defence attorneys. On this measure there were no concessions by women judges to women lawyers, and their comments were frequently as brutal as those of men judges. Thus, while there may be evidence that women judges are more attuned to the face needs of lawyers, there does not appear to be a bond between women lawyers and judges. In fact, these results support the interpretation that women judges, like their male counterparts, display less respect to women legal professionals than to men.

The common metaphor of the courtroom as theatre emphasises the extent to which everyone who takes part in the courtroom 'drama' is 'on stage' and is constantly being evaluated by a variety of audiences. This is especially true for lawyers: their 'act' must impress their colleagues, their clients and the public at large, but most importantly their performance must impress the judges (and/or the juries, where it is relevant) who eventually decide whether their presentation has been persuasive. As Jackson (1996) has explained, the judges' decision about what happened outside the realm of the courtroom (the story *in* the trial) is determined by the events, behaviours and narratives presented within the courtroom (the story *of* the trial). It is only through the evaluation of the performances of all participants within the courtroom that judges can make final decisions about the events which led to the trial in the first place. These evaluations, however, are not made in a vacuum, but rather are structured according to cultural conceptions and schemata of knowledge (Jackson 1996). It is here that gender stereotypes can act as a filter through which the behaviours of the participants are understood and their credibility and persuasiveness evaluated.

4.1 Comments in the Courtroom

In a study of interaction in the District Courts in Israel (Bogoch 1999a), we found that comments made to women lawyers consistently challenged their abilities and undermined their professional status. These comments came from all courtroom participants, including even witnesses who are usually located on a lower rank in the courtroom hierarchy than the professional participants and whose discourse contributions are ostensibly limited to replying to questions. Certainly, they are not expected to remark on the lawyer's performance. However, our analysis of courtroom talk showed that neither discourse rules nor lower status applied to the witness when the lawyer was a woman. The following example demonstrates the refusal of the witness to accord the lawyer the authority that is usually taken for granted by professionals in the courtroom.

(3) Segment 5554 (male witness to female prosecutor)
    You are saying things that are not correct. If you ask me a question show me the source.

While lawyers may question the source of the witnesses' information, it is usually seen as part of the lawyers' prerogative to ask questions without any justification, even when they are seen as irrelevant by the witness (Bogoch and Danet

1984; Walker 1988). Thus, the fact that the witness demands the source of the lawyers' information reflects a kind of role reversal in which the professional status of the woman lawyer is challenged and undermined.

In the following example, the witness took the initiative and suggested lines of questioning to the lawyer:

> (4) Segment 4012 (male witness to female prosecutor)
> I see farther on something that is more interesting. Why don't you ask about that?

This suggestion not only implies that the lawyer was not doing her job very well and was not asking the really interesting questions, but that the witness was more knowledgeable than the woman prosecutor about what was important. The witness discounted the professional assessments of the lawyer and almost ridiculed her examination in the public forum of the courtroom.

However, there were even more direct challenges to the lawyer's competence by witnesses.

> (5) Segment 5530 (female prosecutor to male witness)
> Prosecutor: Mr D, I am telling you that it is preferable that you answer my questions.
> Witness: And I am telling you that you don't know what you are talking about.

This excerpt would be considered rude and insulting in almost any social context. The fact that it is made in open court by a witness to the examining attorney compounds both the gravity of the affront and its implications for the prestige of the lawyer. It should be noted that although witnesses complained to men attorneys about the tone or topic of the lawyer's questions, never did we find the type of challenges to the professional competence of the male lawyer that characterised the witnesses' comments to women attorneys.

However, if comments by the witness can have implications for the ways in which the professional performance of women lawyers is evaluated in court, the comments by the judges are most damaging. What judges say in court is imbued with authority: if the judge says so, it counts as correct, authoritative, decisive. Israeli judges are much more interventionist than their Anglo-Saxon counterparts, and the many comments addressed to the lawyers during the trial (but which are not recorded in the court transcripts) testify to the judges' constant scrutiny of their performance.[13]

While many comments are statements urging the lawyer to curtail the length of the examination or disputes about the relevance of the lawyers' questions, others more specifically challenge the way the lawyers are performing their role.

---

[13] Many reasons may be suggested for the greater activism of the Israeli judges. One of the reasons may be the less developed legal culture in Israel, so that judges feel they must socialise attorneys to the correct courtroom behaviour.

In general, we found a very different message addressed to women and men lawyers, and more often than not, the message was delivered in a more humiliating manner to the woman lawyer.

One of the most frequent complaints by judges was that lawyers ask the same question again and again.[14] In the following excerpts, a judge reprimanded first a male lawyer and then a female lawyer for repeating their questions. Note the difference in the tone and message of these comments.

(6) Segment 4047 (male judge to male defence attorney)[15]
Adoni assured me not to ask questions that came up already. That also came up twenty times already. *Adoni* will proceed.

(7) Segment 4053 (female judge to female prosecutor)
He said that at the beginning of his testimony, Madam. You are not paying attention.

Using the formal form of address, the judge reprimanded the male lawyer for asking a question that had been dealt with previously. The woman lawyer also asked a question on a topic that had arisen previously, and the judge addressed her using the address form that was parallel to the one used to the male lawyer. However, here the similarity between the comments made to the man and woman lawyer ends. From the judge's comment, it is clear that he regarded the repeated questions by the male lawyer as a deliberate violation of a previous promise, a strategic move in order to continue his aggressive examination. The judge chastised the lawyer, but used formal language, including the third person future as a remote imperative which reduces the threat to face implied in the request to proceed (Brown and Levinson 1987). The message to the woman lawyer who repeated the question was entirely different. The judge implied that the motive for the woman lawyer's repetition was not due to strategy but because she simply was not sufficiently attentive to the examination, and did not realise she was questioning on a topic that had already been discussed. The same behaviour by a man and a woman lawyer was interpreted very differently by the judges. Moreover, the comment to the woman was not formal or deferential, and the use of the pronoun 'you' rather than the third person, emphasises the blame implied in the comment to the woman lawyer as well as its lack of courtesy.

Similarly, in the following comments the judges reprimanded the lawyers for not presenting certain information to the opposing side before using it as a basis for their examination of the witnesses. The fact that the judge regarded the failure to provide the information as a strategy on the part of the male lawyer is obvious from the addition of 'you know that' to his statement 'you have to

---

[14] This is a known tactic of trial lawyers. In addition to holding the floor and demonstrating how combative they are, lawyers can hope that repeating the question will lead the witnesses to contradict themselves and thus damage their credibility (Danet and Bogoch 1980; Drew 1990).

[15] I really did not know what term to use here. This term, M'lord is not used in American courtrooms, although it is used in Britian, but the other possible translation, 'Sir' seems unnatural.

present it first to the other side'. The message is clear: the male lawyer knows that he has to present it to the other side, but is willing to try to get away with breaking the rules in order to maintain an advantage over the opposing side. He was doing what every good lawyer in the adversarial system should do. The woman lawyer, however, was treated as if she had forgotten or was remiss. She was not judged to be a fighting adversarial lawyer; rather, she was spoken to as if she was just not such a good or experienced attorney, because she did not know enough to give the document to the other side. Again, the interpretation of similar behaviour by men and women lawyers was made according to gender specific stereotypes.

(8) Segment 9003 (female judge, male defence attorney)
     You have to first present it to the other side. You know that.
(9) Segment 4095 (male judge, female prosecutor)
     It's clear that you are examining on the basis of a certain report. The defence should have received it.

In the final examples, it is the manner in which the judges criticise the lawyers' behaviour that demonstrates the difference in the ways in which women and men are evaluated in the courtroom.

(10) Segment 2226 (male judge, male defence attorney)
      I request that—Sir, that is not acceptable to me. Will *Adoni*[16] be so kind as to sit and wait patiently?
(11) Segment 7716 (female judge, female prosecutor)
      Lady (*geveret*), if you stand up again I'll stop the session. I suggest that you sit down. He is in cross examination and he can ask questions about his reliability.

Both men and women attorneys were standing up out of turn, while the opposing lawyer was conducting an examination.[17] The judges in both cases were patently upset by the lawyers' violations of courtroom rules of conduct. In example 10, the judge told the male lawyer that his behaviour was unacceptable to him. In other words, he phrased the lawyers' behaviour as contrary to *his* standards of courtroom decorum. The lawyers' behaviour was inappropriate rather than deficient or faulty. The judge's request is very formal and very polite: it uses the unusual third person form and the very formal politeness marker. It would be immediately identified as courtroom talk, in which the judge underscores his authority and his formal position in the courtroom but also gives deference to the professional position of the lawyer whom he addresses.

[16] The same address term, *adoni* was used in Hebrew for both address terms here, but I used what seemed most natural in English. The Hebrew version of the sentence is *hoil adoni lashevet vilikhakot bisavlanut*. The translation is not literal, but strives to render the very formal nature of the request and the addition of a formal politeness marker.
[17] Lawyers stand when they examine witnesses, when they object or when they otherwise address the court.

The comment to the woman lawyer was completely different. The judge addressed the lawyer as *geveret*, lady, a term that is not deferential at best, and probably rather derogatory (Bogoch 1999b). It is a market term rather than a term we expect to hear in a courtroom. Moreover, the judge threatened the lawyer that she would stop the hearing if she continued to stand up. Threats are brutal speech acts, and reflect great status disparity. They are rarely used in public institutional settings, because of the implications for the dignity of the recipient. In fact, in our data, they were used only three times to lawyers and two of these were against women lawyers.[18] The threat to a woman lawyer by the judge in open court that she would stop the hearing if she continued to 'misbehave' is demeaning to the lawyer, and undermines her professional authority and credibility. Finally, the addition by the judge of an explanation of courtroom procedure to justify her suggestion that the lawyer sit down also discredits the woman lawyer. The explanation implies that the lawyer did not know that during cross-examination, it is possible to test the veracity of the witness. In other words, contrary to the previous request to the male lawyer to sit because his behaviour was unacceptable to the particular judge, here the judge told the lawyer that her behaviour was unsuitable for a lawyer. This is the message that was repeated in the comments of judges to women lawyers in the courtroom.

4.2 The Outcomes of Criminal Trials

But over and above the humiliation inflicted on women lawyers, we must ask to what extent does this negative evaluation of their behaviour during the trial affect their success in the courtroom? McGlynn (1998) notes that although these snide remarks and put-downs may seem trivial, 'cumulatively they may undermine self-confidence and esteem, eventually isolating and marginalising women' (p 49). The women in her study maintained that the judges' badgering of the lawyers undermined their relationships with clients, and caused them to internalise the doubts others seemed to have. In our study, we wanted to see if the ramifications of the public challenges to women lawyers went beyond their own self-confidence or their integration in the profession. We wanted to determine whether there was a connection between the gender of the lawyer and the sentences handed out to the defendants in serious criminal trials.

The sample consisted of the 868 defendants in criminal cases, in which the judges' decision was handed down in 1988 and in 1993.[19] Only those defendants who were accused of offences against life (murder, attempted murder, manslaughter), sexual offences and bodily harm offences (assault and battery, grievous bodily harm) in which the maximum sentence was five years or more,

---

[18] They were also used on 5 occasions against witnesses, and again there were more women than men who were threatened, despite the rarer appearances of women on the witness stand.

[19] These years were chosen because of changes in the criminal code that occurred at the time.

were included in the sample. While most studies of sentencing have examined the relationship between various characteristics of the defendant and/or victim and the results of the trial, characteristics of judges have only recently been considered (Crowe 1998; Holmes, Hosch, Daudistel, and Perez 1993; Kutnjak 1995; Oswald and Drewniak 1996; Steffensmeier and Hebert 1999). The gender bias task force studies documented the claims of women lawyers that judges discriminated against them in their decision-making (eg Czapansky 1993). However, the relationship between the gender of lawyers and the results of trials has been examined mainly in experimental settings and mock trials (eg Hahn and Clayton 1996) and only rarely in the analysis of actual cases (eg MacCorquodale 1991).

One of the first things we discovered in our coding of the cases was that there was very little standardisation of the information in the court files, and thus, it was impossible to ascertain the gender of the prosecutor in 158 cases and of the defence attorney in 169 cases (ie either there was no name written, or the name was written with an initial so that it was impossible from either the name or any other information in the file to reveal the gender of the lawyer). For the 710 cases in which the gender of the prosecutor was known, 70 per cent were women, while of the 699 cases[20] with a defence attorney recorded, only 12 per cent were women.

We found no differences between men and women lawyers in the verdict of the trial, and about 88 per cent of all defendants were convicted no matter who the lawyer was. However, there were statistically significant differences between men and women lawyers in the length of time in prison[21] to which the defendants were sentenced. Table 5 presents the mean number of months to which convicted defendants were sentenced by the gender of the lawyers and the type of offence.

Looking first at the bottom row which shows the overall relationship between the gender of the lawyers and the sentence length, we can see that lower sentences were imposed when women were the prosecutors and higher sentences were imposed when women were the defence attorneys. Thus, when the prosecutor was a woman, the sentence was 37 months, compared to 40[22] months for the male prosecutor, while when the defence attorney was a woman, the sentence was 53 months, compared to 34 for men. Similar results were obtained when each offence was examined separately, with the exception of bodily harm offences. For example, defendants convicted of life offences when the prosecutor was a woman were sentenced to an average of 122 months, whereas with men prosecutors, the aver-

---

[20] In 45 cases, the defendants represented themselves. Israeli law at the time of this study required court-appointed lawyers for indigent defendants only in cases when the maximum sentence was 10 years or more. In other cases the judge had the discretion to appoint a lawyer, but was not required to do so.

[21] Only actual sentences were considered, not suspended sentences or any of the other punishments, such as fines or cancellation of driving licenses. Life sentences were coded as 300 months (25 years).

[22] The extremely low sentences given these offenders, when the maximum sentences ranged from 5 years to life in prison is another issue, which is discussed in Bogoch and Don-Yechiya (1999).

age was 209. Similarly, when the defence attorney was a woman, those convicted of life offences were sentenced to an average of 183 months, while when the defence attorney was a man, the sentence was 128 months. Thus, the woman prosecutor was less successful than the man prosecutor in attaining a more severe punishment for the offender, and the woman defence attorney was less successful in attaining a lower sentence for the defendant.

Table 5: Mean length of prison sentence (months) of convicted offenders by gender of lawyer and type of offence

Type of Offence	Prosecuting Attorney						Defence Attorney					
	Female			Male			Female			Male		
	Mean	SD	N	Mean	SD	N	Mean	SD	N	Mean	SD	N
Against Life	122	112	59	209	120	20	183	120	13	128	116	66
Sexual Offences	24	31	228	25	37	76	37	50	26	22	28	276
Bodily Harm Offences	23	29	159	16	21	95	19	27	37	21	29	221
All Offences Combined	37	60	446	40	75	191	53	84	76	34	59	563

Significance of effect of type of offence: p<.001
Significance of effect of gender of prosecutor: p<.001
Significance of effect of gender of defence attorney: p=.004

It might be claimed that, because within each offence category there are a variety of offences with a large range of maximum sentences,[23] perhaps the lower success rate of women lawyers can be explained by the different cases in which they were involved. In order to discount this possibility, we calculated the punishment actually imposed as a ratio of the maximum sentence for the most serious article of the criminal code of which the defendant was accused. This provided a method of standardising the offences and controlling for the effect of the seriousness of the crime. The results are presented in Table 6. Although results are less dramatic than those obtained for the number of months, again we found that, particularly in the case of defence attorneys, but also for prosecutors in some offences, female lawyers were significantly less successful than their male counterparts. For example, defendants who faced a male prosecutor in life offences were sentenced to three-quarters of the maximum term while defendants facing a woman were sentenced to only about half the maximum sentence. In sexual offences, a defendant represented by a woman was sentenced to 23 per cent of the maximum sentence, while when the defence attorney was a man, the defendant was sentenced to only 15 per cent of the maximum for the offence.

[23] For example, in the sexual offenses category, indecent acts under certain conditions could be punished by 5 years in prison, whereas the maximum sentence for aggravated rape is 20 years.

Table 6: Mean ratio of imposed sentence to maximum sentence for convicted offenders by gender of lawyer and type of offence

Type of Offence	Female			Male			Female			Male		
	Mean	SD	N	Mean	SD	N	Mean	SD	N	Mean	SD	N
Against Life	.46	.37	59	.74	.35	20	.63	.38	13	.48	.38	66
Sexual Offences	.17	.20	228	.16	.17	76	.23	.25	26	.15	.18	276
Bodily Harm Offences	.14	.17	159	.11	.17	95	.09	.08	37	.14	.18	221
All Offences Combined	.19	.25	446	.20	.27	191	.24	.29	76	.19	.24	563

Significance of effect of type of offence: $p < .001$
Significance of effect of gender of prosecutor: $p < .001$
Significance of effect of gender of defence attorney: $p = .07$

What can we conclude from these results? It might be claimed that women lawyers are just not as good as men in criminal cases, and that the traditional stereotyped image of women as peacemakers make them inappropriate for the more adversarial arenas of law (Harrington 1994). However, this claim is unacceptable, especially because women in Israel have reached the highest ranks in the State Attorney's office and have achieved widespread acclaim in the profession.[24] Instead, what seems to be happening is that judges are giving less credit to arguments made by women lawyers. We saw above how judges interpreted the same behaviour as a tactical manoeuvre on the part of the man lawyer, but as an error on the part of the woman. In this way, similar strategies on the part of men and women attorneys may be assessed and evaluated differently, to the detriment of the woman attorney. Gender is made salient through the challenges to the professionalism of women lawyers and the undermining of their competence throughout the trials. Gender thus becomes the interpretative framework within which the action of the lawyers are measured and the persuasiveness of their case is judged.

5 CONCLUSION

It is often claimed that women are oversensitive and that they attribute bias or patriarchal influences to remarks that are made in good faith and without derogatory intentions. Moreover, feminists are accused of 'making a mountain out of a molehill' and attributing too much significance to trivial slurs. We have shown that careful attention to the language of the interaction in the courtroom reveals that gender bias is just as pervasive as women have claimed, if not more so. Moreover, the analysis of the relationship between the gender of the lawyer

[24] In fact, the head of the Tel Aviv District Bar Association, the largest bar association in the country, is a woman.

and the outcomes of the trials demonstrates that these seemingly minor slights can have very significant consequences.

Carle (1999) among others has argued that 'gender is a pervasive social fact enforced at many levels' (p 269). Within the circumscribed structure of courtroom discourse, gender is played out in the talk of both lay and professional participants. However, it is not in the special different voice that women lawyers perform their professional roles in the courtroom, but rather in the gendered meanings attributed to their behaviour and in the evaluation by others about how they should (or perhaps more accurately, should not) carry out their professional duties. The combination of 'woman' and 'lawyer' still equals something less than the full claim to authority that 'lawyer' (which is taken to mean 'man' and 'lawyer') implies.

Nonetheless there are two results from our anlayses that allow some room for optimism that a separate women's voice may be developing. While women judges did not display special concern for women and children victims, and while they were just as harsh in their commands to women lawyers as men were, they still imposed lower sentences than their male counterparts and were more mitigated than men in their requests to lawyers in the courtroom. Women judges may then have a different style of judging, but ignore or contain it when dealing with other women because it is regarded as contrary to professional norms of behaviour. Thus, women judges may be wary of seeming to identify too strongly with women in order not to compromise their claims to professional neutrality, and thus they refuse to acknowledge any common bond with female victims or legal professionals. It may be that as their proportion of the judiciary increases, women will feel secure enough as professionals to acknowledge their gender ties and break free from the patriarchal norms of judicial behaviour. The voices of women judges have been heard recently in public on issues such as domestic violence, sexual offences and affirmative action.[25] It is possible that these new voices will be heard in the courtroom as well. Another indication of a different style of lawyering among women by women lawyers whose status in the profession is assured is our finding that women prosecutors were less intrusive of the examination of women defence attorneys. After all, it is in the State Attorney's Office that women have made their most impressive gains, and where their professional presence is most strongly felt. Perhaps we are now hearing the first whispers of the collective voice of women legal professionals in Israel.

6 REFERENCES

Blum-Kulka, Shoshana. 1989. Playing it safe: the role of conventionality in indirectness. In S Blum-Kulka, J House and G Kasper, eds, *Cross-cultural Pragmatics: Requests and Apologies*. Norwood: Ablex, 37–70.

[25] The numbers of judges who identify publically as feminists is still small, but even these voices have appeared only in the past few years.

Blum-Kulka, Shoshana and House, Julian. 1989. Cross-cultural and situational variation in requesting behaviour. In S Blum-Kulka, J House and G Kasper, eds, *Cross-cultural Pragmatics: Requests and Apologies*. Norwood: Aldex, 123–154.

Bogoch, Bryna. 1997. Gendered lawyering: difference and dominance in lawyer-client interaction. *Law and Society Review* 31, 4: 677–712.

Bogoch, Bryna. 1999a. Courtroom discourse and the gendered construction of professional identity. *Law and Social Inquiry* 24, 2: 601–647.

Bogoch, Bryna. 1999b. Judging in a different voice: gender and the sentencing of violent offences in Israel. *International Journal of the Sociology of Law*. 27, 51–78.

Bogoch, Bryna and Brenda Danet. 1984. Challenge and control in lawyer-client interactions: a case study in an Israeli legal aid office. *Text* 4, 1–3: 249–275.

Bogoch Bryna and Rochelle Don-Yechiya. 1999. *The Gender of Justice: Bias Against Women in Israeli Courts*. Jerusalem: Jerusalem Institute of Israel Studies. (Hebrew)

Brown, Penelope, and Stephen Levinson. 1987. *Politeness: Some Universals in Language Use*. Cambridge: Cambridge University Press.

Cain, Maureen, and Christine B Harrington, eds. 1994. *Lawyers in a Postmodern World: Translation and Transgression*. New York: New York University Press.

Carle, Susan D. 1999. Gender in the construction of the lawyer's persona. *Harvard Women's Law Journal* 22: 239–273.

Chambliss, Elizabeth, and Christopher Uggen. 2000. Men and women of elite law firms: re-evaluating Kanter's legacy. *Law and Social Inquiry* 25, 1: 41–68.

Conley, John M, and William M O'Barr. 1998. *Just Words: Law Language and Power*. Chicago: University of Chicago Press.

Crowe, Nancy. 1998. Diversity on the federal bench: the effect of judges' sex and race on judicial decision making. Paper presented at the Annual Meeting of the Law and Society Association, Snowmass Village, Aspen, Colorado, June 4–7.

Czapansky, Karen. 1993. Domestic violence, the family and the lawyering process: lessons from studies on gender bias in the courts. *Family Law Quarterly* 27: (2) 247–276.

Danet, Brenda, and Bryna Bogoch. 1980. 'Fixed fight or free-for-all'? An empirical study of combativeness in the adversary system of justice. *British Journal of Law and Society* 7: 36–60.

Drachman, Virginia G. 1998. *Sisters in Law: Women Lawyers in Modern American History*. Cambridge: Harvard University Press.

Drew, Paul. 1990. Strategies in the contest between lawyer and witness in cross-examination. In Judith N Levi and Ann G Walker, eds. *Language in the Judicial Process*. New York: Plenum Press, 39–64.

Epstein, Cynthia Fuchs. 1991. The difference model: enforcement and reinforcement of women's roles in law. In Judith R Blau and Norman Goodman, eds. *Social Roles and Social Institutions: Essays in Honor of Rose Laub Coser*. Boulder: Westview Press. 53–71.

Gilligan, Carol. 1982. *In A Different Voice: Psychological Theory and Women's Development*. Cambridge: Harvard University Press.

Gillis, Ann J. 1991. Great expectations: women in the legal profession. A commentary on the state studies. *Indiana Law Journal* 66: 941–975.

Guinier, Lani. 1994. Becoming gentlemen: women's experiences at one ivy league law school. *University of Pennsylvania Law Review* 143: 1–110.

Hahn, Peter W, and Susan D Clayton. 1996. The effects of attorney presentation style, attorney gender and juror gender on juror decisions. *Law and Human Behaviour* 20: (5) 533–554.

Halperin-Kaddari, Ruth, 1994. Family law and jurisdiction in Israel and the Bavli Case. *Justice*, 2: 37–40.

Harrington, Mona. 1994. *Women Lawyers: Rewriting the Rules*. New York: Alfred A Knopf.

Holmes, Malcolm D, Marmon M Hosch, Howard C Daudistel, and Dolores A Perez. 1993. Judges' ethnicity and minority sentencing: evidence concerning Hispanics. *Social Science Quarterly* 74: (3) 496–506.

Hotel, Carla, and Joan Brockman. 1994. The conciliatory-adversarial continuum in family law practice. *Canadian Journal of Family Law* 12: (1) 11–36.

Jack, Dana Crowley, and Rand Jack. 1994. Women lawyers: archetypes and alternatives. In C Gilligan, JV Ward and JM Taylor, eds. *Mapping the Moral Domain: A Contribution to Women's Thinking, to Psychological Theory and Education* Cambridge: Harvard University Graduate School of Education. pp 263–288.

Jack, Rand, and Dana Crawley Jack. 1989. *Moral Vision and Professional Decisions: The Changing Values of Women and Men Lawyers*. New York: Cambridge University Press.

Jackson, Bernard S. 1995. *Making Sense in Law: Linguistic, Psychological and Semiotic Perspectives*. Liverpool: Deborah Charles Publications.

Jackson, Bernard. 1996. Anchored narratives and the interface of law, psychology and semiotics. *Legal and Criminological Psychology* 1: 17–45.

James, Deborah, and Sandra Clarke. 1993. Women, men and interruptions: a critical review. In D Tannen ed, *Gender And Conversational Interaction* New York: Oxford University Press. 231–280.

Kay, Fiona, and John Hagan. 1995. The persistent glass ceiling: gendered inequalties in the earnings of lawyers. *British Journal of Sociology* 46: (2) 279–310.

Kay, Fiona M, and John Hagan. 1998. Raising the bar: the gender stratification of law firm capital. *American Sociological Review* 63: 728–743.

Kutnjak, Ivkovic. 1995. Does gender matter: the role of gender in legal decision making by Croatian mixed tribunals. *International Journal of the Sociology of Law* 23, 2: 131–156.

MacCorquodale, Patricia L. 1991. Criminal case outcomes: does gender make a difference? Paper presented at the Western Social Science Association meeting, Reno Nevada, April 1991.

MacCorquodale, Patricia. 1995. Gender, voice and values: the case of domestic violence. Paper presented at the American Sociological Association Annual Meeting, 1995.

MacCorquodale, Patricia. 1996. Gender, economics and opportunity: a comparison of attorneys in France and England. Paper presented at the Annual Meeting of the Law and Society Association, Glasgow, Scotland, July, 1996.

MacCorquodale, Patricia L, and Gary F Jensen. 1991. Female attorneys: in a different voice? Paper presented at the American Sociological Association Annual Meeting, 1991.

Malach-Pines, Ayala, Hamutal Gat, and Yael Tal. 1999. Gender differences in negotiation during mediation. *Sikhot* 13, 3: 231–238. (Hebrew).

Martin, Susan Ehrlich, and Nancy C Jurik. 1996. *Doing Justice, Doing Gender: Women in Law and Criminal Justice Occupations*. Thousand Oaks: Sage.

Matoesian, Gregory M. 1993. *Reproducing Rape: Domination through Talk in the Courtroom*. Chicago: University of Chicago Press.

McGlynn, Clare. 1998. *The Woman Lawyer: Making the Difference*. London: Butterworths.

Menkel-Meadow, Carrie. 1989. Exploring a research agenda of the feminization of the legal profession: theories of gender and social change. *Law and Social Inquiry* 3: 289–319.

Mulac, Anthony, and James J Bradac. 1995. Women's style in problem solving interaction: Powerless or simply feminine? In PJ Kalbfleisch, and MJ Cody, eds. *Gender, Power, and Communication in Human Relationships* Hillsdale: Elbaum. 83–104.

Oswald, Margit E, and Regine Drewniak. 1996. Attitude and behaviour of male and female judges concerning the punishment of offenders. In G. Davies, ed *Psychology, Law and Criminal Justice* NY: Walter de Gruyter. 296–304.

Pierce, Jennifer L. 1995. *Gender Trials: Emotional Lives in Contemporary Law Firms*. Berkeley: University of California Press.

Raday, Frances. 1996. Women in law in Israel: a study of the relationship between professional integration and feminism. *Georgia State University Law Review* 12: 525–552.

Remlinger, Kathryn. 1999. Widening the lens of language and gender research: Integrating critical discourse analysis and culural practice theory. http//www.viad rina.euv-frankfurt-o.de/~wjournal/199/remlinger.htm.

Resnik, Judith. 1996. Asking about gender in courts. *Signs: Journal of Women in Culture and Society* 21, 4: 952–990.

Ridgeway, Cecilia, and Linda Smith-Lovin. 1996. Gender and social interaction. *Social Psychology Quarterly* 59: 173–175.

Riger, Stephanie, Pennie Foster-Fishman, Julie Nelson-Kuna, and Barbara Curran. 1995. Gender bias in courtroom dynamics. *Law and Human Behavior* 19: (5) 465–480.

Seron, Carroll. 1996. *The Business of Practicing Law: The Work Lives of Solo and Small-Firm Attorneys*. Philadelphia: Temple University Press.

Shamir, Ronen 1994. Mission, feminism, and professionalism: rabbinical pleaders in Orthodox religious communities. *Megamot* 38 (3): 313–348. (Hebrew)

Sklar, Kathryn Kish. 1995. *Florence Kelley and the Nation's Work: The Rise of Women's Political Culture, 1830–1900*. New Haven: Yale University Press.

Sommerlad, Hilary. 1994. The myth of feminization: women and cultural change in the legal profession. *International Journal of the Legal Profession* 1: (1) 31–53.

Sommerlad, Hilary, and Peter Sanderson. 1998. *Gender, Choice and Commitment*. Aldershot: Ashgate.

Spencer, Anne, and David Podmore. 1987. *In a Man's World: Essays on Women in Male Dominated Professions*. London: Tavistock.

Steffensmeier, Darrell, and Chris Hebert. 1999. Women and men policymakers: does the judge's gender affect the sentencing of criminal defendants? *Social Forces* 77: (3) 1164–1196.

Thornton, Margaret. 1996. *Dissonance and Distrust: Women in the Legal Profession*. Oxford: Oxford University Press.

Walker, Ann Graffam. 1988. Linguistic manipulation, power and the legal setting. In L Kedar, ed. *Power through Discourse*. Norwood: Ablex. 57–79.

West, Candace, and Don Zimmerman. 1987. Doing gender. *Gender and Society* 1: (2) 125–151.

Williams, Joan C. 1989. Deconstructing gender. *Michigan Law Review* 87: 797–833.

PART 2

Women Lawyers in the Civil Law World

15

The Status of Women Lawyers in Germany

Abstract

In Germany it was particularly difficult for women to gain ground in the legal profession. During the Nazi regime they were expelled from all legal functions. Nor was there a great deal of change during the post-war period. It was only after reforms in the educational system in the 1970s that their numbers in the profession began to rise. While legal education has remained a male-dominated field, almost half of today's new recruits/entrants to the judiciary and the civil service are female due to women's advancement strategies and legal standing legislation. Although working conditions in the judiciary facilitate combining family and job, many women forego a career. However, as recruitment rates in these fields are currently low, quantitative change has been modest. The picture is different in the advocacy which absorbs the largest number of female law graduates and where the proportion of women continues to rise. Female practising lawyers' incomes are well below those of their male colleagues, especially in independent practice, and their influence in professional associations and representations is negligible. Women law graduates increasingly seek employment in jobs outside the classical legal professions, especially in industry. Future developments are difficult to predict at this stage.

1 OVERALL PROFESSIONAL PROFILE AND ETHOS

WOMEN LAWYERS IN Germany are not just practising lawyers. Unlike other countries, Germany subscribes to the notion of the 'unitary jurist' (*Einheitsjurist*), requiring identical academic qualifications—the passing of two legal state examinations—for all law graduates, irrespective of their future careers. Until very recently it was by no means uncommon for budding lawyers to take up to 10 years to complete this two-phase training, first at university then as state employees in legal practice in a number of fields. Successful candidates subsequently work as practising lawyers (*Rechtsanwalt/*

Rechtsanwältin), company lawyers (*Justitiar/in* or *Syndikus/Syndika*), judges (*Richter/in*), public prosecutors (*Staatsanwalt/Staatsanwältin*) or lawyers in the public service (*Jurist/in im öffentlichen Dienst*). Irrespective of their precise occupation, they all regard themselves as members of the same cast of 'jurists', the collective of trained lawyers. Intriguingly, German jurists tend to remain loyal to their career path once it has been chosen in spite of the uniformity of legal training for all branches of the profession. Switching from one career path to another only occurs during the first few years, particularly amongst women in search of the most agreeable working conditions.

Traditionally, the emphasis of legal training lay on practising judicial deci-sion-making as even in the 1970s, about one third of those who had completed their training were absorbed by the judiciary or the public service. With the expansion of higher education and the growth in the numbers of young jurists in the 1980s and 1990s, more and more of them were left with no choice but to apply for admission as practising lawyers. Not surprisingly, they felt ill-prepared for the job. Under the influence of growing criticism aimed at the rigidity of the legal education programme which, in turn, was reinforced by the impact of Europeanisation and globalisation, legal education was reduced to a maximum period of seven or eight years. Also, the syllabus has been renegoti-ated to take into account the need of future *Rechtsanwälte/Rechtsanwältinnen* for lawyering skills. There is a realistic expectation that this might be the first step towards the abolition of the notion of the *Einheitsjurist*, a notion that has long been seen as a hallmark of German society. However, so far German jurists have remained a very homogeneous group, sharing a common *corps d'esprit* characterised by liberal conservatism displaying strikingly patriarchal traits.

2 WOMEN LAWYERS IN GERMANY: A BRIEF AND SORRY STORY

As one of the earliest German female lawyers and contributor to a volume on lawyers in the world rightly observed, the road towards equality for women in the legal profession has often been called a road of suffering: no other profession has had to be conquered for women at such cost. (Erffa 1929: 471)

In Germany, as in many other countries, women were only admitted to uni-versity law schools at the beginning of the twentieth century, more precisely between 1900 and 1909. In 1912, the first women passed the first state examina-tion in law which to this very day is set by the appeal courts. However, unlike their male colleagues, these female law graduates were not allowed to call them-selves *Referendare*, ie candidates undertaking practical legal training required for anyone wishing to be a fully qualified jurist. It took the First World War and the abolition of the German monarchy for women to be admitted to this second phase of legal training, as the 1919 constitution of the Weimar Republic granted women equal status with men.[1] Yet an additional Statute on the Admission of Women to the Offices and Occupations of the Judiciary[2] had to be passed in 1922 before women were admitted to any of the legal professions.

In 1930, about two to three per cent of German law students and 74 of the 10,000 judges were women. In 1933, 252 of the 18,766 advocates were female. After the National Socialist seizure of power in 1933, women were systematically expelled from legal practice and barred from access to state-controlled practical training and to the judiciary. From 1935, no female applicants were admitted to the advocacy.[3] In 1936, Hitler signed a decree to the effect that women should no longer work in the judiciary or as advocates. (*Deutscher Juristinnenbund* 1984, appendix 26) Within the male power structure of Nazi ideology women constituted unwanted elements. Instead, they were expected to take care of the household and bear children for the *Führer*. By 1939, there remained a total of nine female advocates. Former female judges were moved into administrative functions, mainly child care and custody. During the war they were only reluctantly admitted to posts left vacant by men who fought on the battlefields, and whenever a male advocate returned from the front his female proxy was forced to withdraw.

The end of the Second World War brought no real change. Whenever men were available, women took second place. In 1950, the preliminary Statute on the Civil Service still contained a celibacy clause. Women could be discharged when they got married or they 'voluntarily' retired from public service in order not to cause social offence. Until the late 1960s/early 1970s it was considered inappropriate for married women to be gainfully employed, as this was seen as taking away jobs from breadwinners. Two earners in a family were looked upon with dismay or at least uncomprehendingly. Discussions on the question as to whether mothers should go out to work continued well into the 1980s, and still occasionally flare up today. Economic prosperity from the 1970s leading to a boom in education for men *and* women, the introduction of the pill as a safe method of birth control, and the accompanying change in notions of family life and women's roles within it have finally resulted in a substantial increase in the numbers of women in legal education and the legal professions.

3 INCREASE IN WOMEN LAWYERS IN THE PAST THREE DECADES

Tables 1 and 2 show the steady increase of the share of women in legal education and in the legal professions since the 1960s.

---

[1] Albeit not even then full equal rights (Art 108, 128 Weimar Constitution). It was only in 1949 that the famous pithy clause (Art 3 II), 'Men and women have equal rights', was included in the *Basic Law*, the constitution of the newly established Federal Republic of Germany.

[2] *Reichstagsdrucksache* Vol 346.

[3] In this as well as in subsequent contributions on lawyers in the civil law world (where there is no split between solicitors and barristers) the term 'advocacy' is used to refer to the totality of practising lawyers. For further detail cf. explanation in the introduction p xxxi.

Table 1: Proportion of Women in (Legal) Education

	At universities	In law faculties	*Referendare* (in practical training)
	%	%	%
early 1960s	27	c. 10–15	
1970	31	17	10
1975	36	25	
1980	38	32	28 (1982)
1985	40	39	
1987	40	40	33
1991	42	42	41
1995	44	43	43
1997	46	44	44 (1998)

SOURCES: Federal Ministry of Justice 1998/1999; Federal Statistical Office

Within three decades the number of women in legal education has quad-rupled. It is worth noting that until the mid-1980s the proportion of women in legal education was conspicuously lagging behind their share in the overall university student body. Until the mid-1960s legal education as a means of qual-ifying for leading positions in the state power structure had been an almost exclusively male domain. (Schultz 1990: 327) But in contrast to other 'typical' male subjects, in particular engineering, physics, mathematics and computer sci-ences, where women students continue to represent a minority, they have caught up with men in the field of law. There are a number of reasons for this disproportionate increase. Firstly, legal education acts as a stepping-stone towards many positions in the public sector, which in turn offers the most favourable working conditions for women wishing to combine family and work. This began to count particularly strongly when women's previous first choice in public service, ie school teaching, could no longer cope with the num-ber of applicants. Secondly, the study of law has traditionally been the prime choice of those who either are undecided or have been rejected by another fac-ulty, the latter possibly due to the operation of a *numerus clausus* applied there. Thirdly, more women have over the past 30 years developed an appetite for par-ticipation in the political process and for positions of power. These women are freeing themselves from the notion of a gender-based division of labour which relegates women to the private sphere of domestic life and family while the pub-lic sphere of profession and politics is perceived to be the natural preserve of men—a division which had brought with it a pronounced remoteness on the part of women from law and public institutions. (Schultz 1990: 329) Finally, the formerly dusty image of the judicial world as being dull and formalised has been undergoing a process of modernisation, possibly accelerated by a general shift away from contentious legal work to more creative modes of conflict resolution, such as consultation and mediation.

It took a long time before the increase in the number of women law students translated into an increase in their share in the legal professions (Table 2). By 1990, about 15 per cent of advocates and members of the judiciary were female. This percentage has continued to rise by around 1 per cent annually. Today, about a quarter of all practising lawyers are female. The actual number of women in the profession does, however, not tell the full story. If maternity and educational leave, part-time regulations and underemployment are taken into account, their overall share in the workload of the profession and their representation of the profession in public is still under 20 per cent.

Table 2: Proportion of Women in the Legal Professions

	Advocates (Anwältinnen) %	Judges (Richterinnen) %	Public prosecutors (Staatsanwältinnen) %
1960	>2.0	2.6	
1970	4.5	6.0	5.0
1980	8.0	13.0	11.0
1989	14.7	17.6	17.6
	= 7,960 of 54,108	= 3,109 of 17,627	= 661 of 3,759
1991	16.1	19.1	19.5
1993	17.5	22.0	25.9
1995	19.3	26.3	28.9
1997	21.2	25.5 *	27.9 *
1999	23.7	26.3	
	= 23,139 of 97,791	= 5,506 of 20,920	
2000	24.6		
	= 25,589 of 104,067		

Source: Federal Ministry of Justice (Judicial Statistics)

*Until 1995 the statistics for the judiciary only covered the old federal states. From 1997, data for the new federal states (the former communist part of Germany) have been included. This explains the slight decrease in the proportion of women judges and prosecutors in 1997. Generally speaking, the number of judges and public prosecutors in the Western part of Germany has remained stable in the past two decades. The increase by 3300 judges between 1989 and 2000 has been due to the additional judges required in the new federal states after reunification.

The proportion of women in the judiciary started to rise earlier and faster than that in the advocacy where the share of women only began to catch up over the last 10 years. On the other hand, in absolute numbers women advocates outnumber women judges and public prosecutors by far, in spite of the comparatively vast size of the German judiciary and its proportionately high female membership. In public prosecution the increase in women started later but has been more rapid and now exceeds that in the judiciary. One contributing factor might be the change in status of the prosecution service. While in the old German Empire prosecutors occupied highly respected positions, the reassessment of state institutions in the 1970s and 1980s resulted for them in a loss of reputation and has given the profession rather more the image of a necessary evil.

Traditionally, legal education in Germany has served as an entry ticket to most higher and top positions in public service and in industry, a situation rightly characterised as resulting in a lawyers' monopoly. (Dahrendorf 1965: 260) Although graduates from other disciplines have tried to compete, both sectors continue to offer a range of careers for law graduates, increasingly also for women. While women had been largely absent until the 1980s, their percentage share in areas outside the traditional fields of the judiciary and advocacy now exceeds that of men. (Bundesministerium für Bildung, Wissenschaft, Forschung und Technologie. 1995)

There are no specific data available on the proportion of women lawyers in particular fields in the civil service and industry though marked differences in gender-based distribution do exist. For example, large insurance companies and, in particular, their departments doing lower public profile work tend to employ women lawyers.

4 WOMEN IN LEGAL EDUCATION

4.1 Women Law Students' Academic Achievements

In spite of the overall increase in women lawyers, legal education has remained a more or less male reserve. Female law students in Germany tend to be discouraged and intimidated by the masculinist atmosphere in law schools, although things have improved over the years. But even if young women of today tend to regard themselves as immune to such threats, interviews with older women lawyers show that a certain degree of irritation and frustration is still inevitable,[4] be it only at a subconscious level. In spite of this the dropout rate amongst women is not much higher than that of men. Overall, just over 50 to 60 per cent of first-year students will eventually pass their second examination (Table 3).[5]

However, there is some evidence of women's failure rates in the first examination being slightly higher than men's.[6] This contrasts with the absence of any gender-based differences in second examination results as well as with women's superior performance in examinations in general.

German law examinations comprise anonymously marked written papers requiring an opinion on a complicated case (in some states in addition to a

---

[4] Cf my second contribution to this volume on 'Women Lawyers in Germany—Perception and Construction of Femininity'.

[5] For some 30 years the first examination on its own was not considered to offer an appropriate legal qualification. Current discussions regarding a restructuring along the lines of Bachelor and Master qualifications may change all this.

[6] Barbara Willenbacher (Hanover University) collected and evaluated examination statistics on a comparative basis.

Table 3: Failure Rates in Law Examinations

	First state examination		Second state examination	
	Total %	Women %	Total %	Women %
1985	28.4	32.5	10.9	11.1
1987	26.3	29.4	12.8	13.7
1991*	22.1	25.6	9.9	9.7
1995	27.2	29.8	11.0	10.7
1996	29.6	31.1	13.0	12.6

SOURCE: Federal Ministry of Justice (Judicial Statistics)

* In 1991, of 9635 candidates who passed the first examination 4115 were women (= 42.7 %). In the same year, of 7806 candidates who passed the second examination 2914 were women (= 37.3 %). The decline in the failure rate in 1991 may be explained by the need for additional lawyers in the five new states after reunification in 1990, which temporarily reduced bottlenecks in the legal labour market. Meanwhile the old complaint of a glut of lawyers has come back into its own, which in turn may account for the subsequently rising failure rates. Failure rates in the new federal states are disproportionately high.

thesis) and an oral examination. It is not unfair to suspect that women may be disadvantaged in the oral examinations of the first state examinations as assessment criteria are based on male notions and imply a test of conformity and an assessment of candidates' social capital.[7] Differences in the results of the first and the second examinations may be related to the fact that examiners in the former are law professors, while in the second panels are made up mainly of practitioners—an issue that merits closer analysis. It has to be added that either type of panel rarely includes female members.

During their practical training, candidates are subject to frequent assessments by their trainers, themselves judges, prosecutors, advocates or civil servants. These assessments include views on candidates' performance and overall personal suitability, offering ample scope for gendered notions and remarks—an area that still awaits systematic scrutiny.

4.2 Women Lawyers in Academia

The growth in the number of women students has had little effect on the number of university law teachers. Law professors occupy highly prestigious positions with good income prospects, both in terms of salary and additional income from activities such as writing expert opinions, work in arbitration and further

---

[7] As does, of course, any appointment process. In my own department, the good-looking, well behaved, upper middle class daughter did better than the bulky, gay, young man, although he had better marks in the written part. Anne Boigeol, in her contribution to this volume, records similar observations in the context of juridical oral examinations in France.

training, and lecturing in other institutions. The first female law professor[8] in Germany was awarded her chair in 1965, more than 50 years after law faculties had opened their doors to women.

The qualification process for a professorship is long and tedious. In addition to a doctoral thesis, a yet bigger theoretical work, the habilitation thesis, has to be produced. The average age of those who are fully qualified and are awarded a chair is over 40. Even if offered the chance of an academic career, women hesitate to subject themselves to these rites which are wholly at odds with the cycles of their lives (Table 4).

Table 4: Proportion of Women amongst those Gaining Doctorates or Habilitations

	Total		Law	
	Doctorates %	Habilitations %	Doctorates %	Habilitations %
1980	19.6		8.33 (32)	
1990	27.8	10.01 (110)	17.18 (134)	5.26 (1)
1992	28.9	12.89 (169)	18.12 (163)	23.33 (7)
1994	31.2	13.52 (200)	24.93 (257)	3.03 (1)
1996	31.1	12.93 (208)	23.97 (257)	0
1997	32.0	15.69 (273)	24.48 (308)	13.95 (4)

SOURCES: Federal Ministry of Education and Science and Federal Office for Statistics. From 1996 data on the new federal states have been included. In the eight years from 1990 to 1997 a total of 22 women obtained the habilitation qualification.

Women shrink from the profound assimilation process required for a successful academic career, which traditionally involves master-servant relations and male networks, and is steeped in a macho culture with strong homophobic mentoring elements. At present the percentage of women law professors is still below six per cent. Their numbers are particularly low at the top of the professorial scale (C 4) (Table 5). Until 1984 only one of the Federal Republic's 542 law professors on the C4 scale was female. By 1998 there were 34 women among 734 law professors at this level, equalling a share of 4.6 per cent. The overall increase in professorial posts has been due to events connected with German unification, in particular the creation of new law faculties at East German universities.

It is only during the last five years that the all-male club has shown the first signs of being infiltrated by women. However, it would be a legitimate question to ask whether the timing of this development at a point when public education generally is suffering a loss of prestige, can be attributed to mere chance or coincidence. It is noteworthy that the first two private law schools in Germany ever

[8] Anne-Eva Brauneck, Professor of Criminal Law and Criminology at the University of Gießen.

Table 5: Women Academics in Law Faculties

| | Professors (C3/C4 on salary scale) | Lecturers (*Hochschuldozenten*) and assistants* | Other academic staff (*Wissenschaftliche Mitarbeiter*)** |
	%	%	%
1982	1.1	15.4	18.5
1988	1.6	10.5	25.5
1990	2.1	14.4	27.4
1992	3.4	21.9	32.3
1995	4.5	22.2	32.1
1996	4.4	21.4	34.4
1998	5.6	21.0	38.5

SOURCES: *Statistical Yearbooks: 1985–1998*, and Federal Statistics Office. From 1992, data for the new federal states are included.

* *Hochschuldozenten* (whose numbers are small) and assistants are expected to allocate 50 per cent of their time to working for a qualification.

** *Wissenschaftliche Mitarbeiter* are contractually obliged to dedicate 100 per cent of their time to doing their job, although this may be interpreted differently in practice.

were established in the autumn of 2000. The share of women amongst their academic staff and students will need to be watched very closely.

5 WOMEN IN THE JUDICIARY

5.1 Entry into the Profession

Many women law graduates aim for a career in the judiciary. Their chances of success, however, are slim, as unlike the advocacy the judiciary cannot expand. On the contrary, current initiatives to cut public expenditure may lead to a reduction in the number of judicial posts. Although in past years about half of new entrants have been women (more than their fair share of newly qualified lawyers),[9] the gender composition in the judiciary in coming years will only change gradually.

Women keen to enter the judiciary suffer no gender-specific discrimination. Even before relevant statutory regulations had been passed, it had been a long established rule that pregnancy did not count as a reason for the rejection of a candidate.[10] As the judiciary, like any other public authority, requires

[9] Though varying from court to court. In Northrhine-Westfalia, in the district of the Hamm appeal court, 41 per cent of judges on probation were female; in Cologne the percentage was 55 per cent, in Düsseldorf 56 per cent.

[10] As early as the mid-1970s there were instances of highly pregnant women being taken on by the public service.

280   *Ulrike Schultz*

Table 6: Women in the Judiciary

	Law graduates %	Judges on probation %	Total number of judges %
1975		20.91	10.65
1981		23.97	13.59
1983		30.19	14.41
1989	35	36.64	17.63
1991	37	39.37	19.05 (51.82*)
1993	38	43.29	22.01 (39.92*)
1995		47.86	26.31
1997		50.08	25.51
1999		45.72	26.31

SOURCE: Federal Ministry of Justice (*Judicial Statistics*)

* Percentage of women judges in the five new federal states: the decrease from 1991 to 1993 is mainly due to the expansion of the judiciary in these states after reunification, when most newly created posts were taken by Western (male) lawyers. In East Germany as in all communist countries the judiciary was strongly feminised and of low prestige (cf contribution to this volume by Gisela Shaw). From 1997, statistics combine data from East and West.

members to adapt to the system, women seem well suited. They have been shown to be more conservative, from higher strata of society, more obedient, less competitive and more willing to adjust than men. (Heldrich/Schmidtchen 1982, Schultz 1990, Hassels/Hommerich 1993) The relatively high rate of female recruitment is also explained by the fact that of those with top examination results proportionately more women than men apply for posts in the judiciary, the latter generally giving preference to a career in the advocacy.[11] In Germany, examination results have always been of paramount importance for entry into the legal professions. However, in recent years judicial authorities have started to set up assessment centres. There is some evidence that these disadvantage women, as women tend to be less self-confident, less dominating and, in some instances, less versed in the communicative skills tested than their male competitors.[12]

[11] An uproar was caused when in 1985 Rudolf Wassermann, President of the appeal court in Braunschweig, demanded a quota for male applicants as more women with good examination results were applying.

[12] These, in any case, have been my experiences as a communication tutor for young lawyers. They match the gendered communication patterns recorded by Deborah Tannen in her book *You Just Don't Understand. Women and Men in Conversation* (1990). So far it seems no critical evaluation of the selection criteria used in assessment centres has taken place to establish how they relate to essential judicial competencies.

5.2 Working Conditions and Job Satisfaction

The judiciary offers ideal working conditions for women, particularly if they want to combine family and work: a reliably high income based on a fixed salary scale, a set workload, the usual paid maternity leave, the option of family breaks with a job guarantee over many years, and the possibility of working part-time with a corresponding reduction of the workload (an option now guaranteed by statutory regulation for virtually the duration of their professional lives). In addition, judges share all other benefits of the civil service, such as favourable pension and health insurance schemes, six weeks annual leave, regulations covering replacements etc. Overall, women's job satisfaction in the judiciary is high (Hassels/Hommerich 1993), which is partly explained by the fact that they hold an elevated position from the first day of their practice and are working in what can be described as a more or less competition-free zone.

In Northrhine Westphalia,[13] 17.3 per cent of female judges (154 out of a total of 889) work part-time, most of them for family reasons; seven men also work part-time, most of them not for family reasons. Judges working part-time tend to be less content with their work than those working full-time. They more frequently experience role conflicts, but do not strive to change their situation (as they have no real choice). (Mahnkopf 1987) A small proportion still take advantage of the possibility of a family break, which may last up to 12 years. Since the general option of a three-year educational leave for everybody in the workforce was introduced, the number of those opting to take a family break has gone down.[14] A survey carried out some ten years ago (Hassel/Hommerich 1993) showed that for 98 per cent of female judges and 92 per cent of female public prosecutors it was of great importance for their job satisfaction to be able to work in locations other than their office. Particularly women with young children made extensive use of this option. 78 per cent of female judges and 58 per cent of female prosecutors said that they tend to partly work at home.[15]

5.3 Horizontal Segmentation in the Judiciary

Women in the judiciary are concentrated in particular fields, such as family law. They like this work due to its routinised legal schedules and its richly 'human' features. As prosecutors, women prefer to work in general departments or with

---

[13] Since reunification the collection of federal statistics has been cut back and no federal data are available on these aspects. Data provided stem from Northrhine-Westfalia, my own federal state. With 18 million inhabitants it is the most populous of the German states. There, as in some other states, extensive gender statistics were produced following the Equal Standing Acts.

[14] In Germany, only some 1.5 per cent of the total number of employed persons on leave for family reasons are men.

[15] For an analogous phenomenon see the contribution by Eliane Botelho Junqueira on female judges in Brazil.

juvenile delinquents. (Reichling 1988) Of course, these are segments of the judiciary which men associate with women, which has a bearing on the kinds of posts offered to women by court directors and presidents. Self-selection and allocation thus operate in tandem.

Larger jurisdictions have a higher percentage of women than smaller, more 'exclusive' ones, though the latter are catching up. Also, branches of the judiciary that were created more recently and have expanded quite fast, such as social and labour courts, employ a particularly high percentage of women—an interesting piece of evidence to support the hypothesis that transformation encourages inclusion. (Hartmann 1999: 78 and 79) (Table 7)

Table 7: Distribution of Women in Different Jurisdictions

Jurisdictions	Total number	% Women
Ordinary courts	15,649	25.7
Administrative courts	2,406	22.1
Social courts	1,171	34.0
Labour courts	1,128	29.3
Constitutional courts	687	13.1
Tax courts	616	10.9
Disciplinary courts	107	13.2

SOURCE: Official statistics. Hartmann 1999, 80

Another factor to make for a high female share of posts seems to be the participation of lay judges, particularly if two lay judges sit with only one professional judge, as happens in some first-instance criminal and juvenile as well as social and labour courts.[16] Proportionately more women than men can be found in 'invisible' positions involving little outward representation, such as registry courts. On the other hand, positions involving high public profiles such as prosecutor for serious crimes are still male domains. Given the increasing participation of women, this may be a particular male professional project in order to preserve the male image of the profession associated with qualities such as competence, efficiency, objectivity, loyalty and toughness. (Böge 1995: 143, 148)[17]

5.4 Career Opportunities

Anyone aiming to attain a leading position in the judiciary has to negotiate the so-called third legal state examination, a six-month 'probationary' period at an appeal court, which also serves as 'conformity training'. This poses serious

[16] Cf. Mossman's report on women lawyers in Canadian law firms tending to work on 'pink' files, that is doing the invisible work in the back office, and men working on blue files with more client contacts.
[17] See also Anne Boigeol's chapter on similar developments in France.

problems for mothers of young children. The court may be at a considerable distance from their home, and they often have to work long hours. In theory, there is the option of working part-time, but this is hardly ever taken up, as male competitors suspect that these women might try to get better results by spending more time working on fewer cases.[18] The larger the court district, the fewer the women who attempt to acquire this additional qualification. The atmosphere in the higher courts is an additional demotivating factor.[19] Although it is not necessarily anti-feminist, it is nevertheless difficult to cope with for women. The higher the court in the hierarchy, the greater the number of elderly gents used to being looked after at home by selfless wives and harbouring corresponding views of the world. Some women lack self-confidence and for this reason decide against promotion, others take a conscious decision not even to try. In a sense, any judge occupies an elevated position from day one, and women often prefer the independence and flexibility of a first-instance solo-sitting judge to the constraints characteristic of working in a panel of judges. In the 1993 study (Hassels/Hommerich), a third of the female judges questioned (of whom only one third had children) said they would opt for a career; another third was undecided as they struggled to combine family and work; and one third openly renounced any career. Asked if they experienced discrimination or gender-based disadvantages, they were once again equally divided between those who replied in the affirmative, those who said no and those who were undecided.

Intriguingly, there are striking differences in the second step of the career ladder (R 2 compared to R 1) in the various districts. To take the districts in Northrhine Westphalia as an example: In Hamm, by far the largest district including rural areas and a more conservative population, only 12 per cent of female judges are at R 2 level, in Düsseldorf the figure is 17 per cent, and in Cologne it is 36 per cent. The distance women have to cover to get from their home court or their place of residence to Hamm may be one explanation for the low participation rate of women at this level, another may be the court climate and recruitment strategies. There are more women at R 2 level working as appeal court judges than there are working as presiding judges at district courts, the latter being considered to be the more senior. The overall percentage of women in career posts (R 2–R 6) ranges between 10 and 15 per cent.[20] Their curricula vitae show certain common characteristics: no career breaks, full-time work throughout, special functions, membership in professional associations and other networks and higher qualifications (eg better examination results, doctoral qualifications). More of them than those in R 1 are unmarried and fewer of them have children. (Hassels/Hommerich 1993: 247)

---

[18] An attempt has been made to offer women a chance to do this probationary period on a job-share basis at the Northrhine-Westfalian Ministry of Justice, but the take-up has been low. (I refrain here from speculating on how this might be explained.)

[19] This has frequently been mentioned in informal conversations with female judges and was confirmed by judges at administrative courts in Hesse, when I lectured at a meeting in October 1999.

[20] There are no up-to-date federal statistics available. Hartmann (1999: 89) collected data from Hesse, Lower-Saxony, Baden-Württemberg and Bavaria.

In recent years more women judges have been appointed to the highest federal courts than ever before, reflecting a genuine endeavour to demonstrate a commitment to gender equality. This is particularly true of those federal courts where judges are nominated on the basis of party political affiliation. Meanwhile five of the 16 judges at the Federal Constitutional Court (*Bundesverfassungsgericht, BVerfG*) are women, including the President of the court (Table 8).

Table 8: Women Judges at Federal Courts (the highest German courts) (1999)

	Federal Constitutional Court (BVerfG)	Federal Supreme Court (BGH)	Federal Administrative Court (BVerwG)	Federal Tax Court (BFH)	Federal Labour Court (BAG)	Federal Social Court (BSG)	Total
	5 out of 16	13 out of 123	5 out of 78	19 out of 133	11 out of 80	5 out of 67	
%	31.25	10.57	6.41	14.28	13.75	7.46	11.67

SOURCE: Official Court Records

Over the last 10 years, an extensive equality machinery has been set up for the entire German civil service. Having begun somewhat haltingly, this process has now gathered pace and is governed by very distinct regulations. In most federal states, equal standing legislation[21] requires the setting up of plans for the promotion of women. In fulfilment of this obligation the ministry of justice in Northrhine Westphalia[22] suggests the following staff development measures: regular individual interviews aiming to motivate women to plan their professional careers; greater participation in in-service training programmes; opportunities for short-term replacement and participation in training measures during family breaks; more frequent allocation of administrative roles of responsibility, which are an important factor in promotion and have traditionally rarely been offered to women; a higher share in the appeal court probationary period; more frequent assignments to special tasks; greater participation as examiners in legal education and examinations; equal opportunities for women working part-time. The aim is to achieve a 50 per cent share of women judges at courts of first instance and a 'trickle up' effect in terms of higher posts. The process is to be subject to regular monitoring by a specially appointed officer (*Gleichstellungsbeauftragte*).

In sum, then, a great deal has changed in recent years in public service and more seems to be about to change. The outcome, however, remains unpredictable.

---

[21] In Northrhine Westphalia the new *Gleichstellungsgesetz* came into force in November 1999.

[22] 1999, *Förderplan für die Gleichstellung von Richterinnen und Richtern im Geschäftsbereich des Justizministeriums NRW nach Ziffer 7 des Frauenförderungskonzeptes* (forerunner of the *Gleichstellungsgesetz*), Stuttgart: Boorberg.

6   WOMEN ADVOCATES

6.1 Overview

Since its creation in 1878, after the unification of the German Empire, the German advocacy has always been a homogeneous group sharing common values. Until 1991, 61 per cent were solo practitioners. Only 5.8 per cent practised in firms of ten and more partners, amounting to just 1.1 per cent of all partnerships. In the past 10 years the centrifugal forces have gained in strength. There is a rapid move towards internal differentiation, including a high degree of specialisation and stratification, with a tendency towards larger units and specialist groupings. A middle-class structure still prevails, but it is realistic to expect this to change over the next 10 years. Any assessment of the situation of women advocates can therefore claim only limited validity.

From 1993 to 2000 the number of advocates rose by 55 per cent.[23] Women have played their part in this development, and have, not entirely surprisingly, sometimes been accused of having brought it about. In recent years their share in admissions has ranged between 36 per cent (1996) and 42 per cent (1999).

Table 9: Women in the German Advocacy and Women Notaries

	Female advocates (Anwältinnen) %	Total increase in advocates (m & f) % and absolute figures	Increase in advocates (f) % and absolute figures	Advocate notaries (f) (Anwalts- notarinnen) %	Solo-notaries (f) (Nur-Notarinnen) %
1985	12.04			4.42	
1991	16.08			4.87	14.44
1996	20.03			7.41	18.95
1997	21.21	96–97* 7.97* (6283)	14.32 (2261)	7.85	18.65
1998	22.40	97–98: 7.53 (6411)	13.53 (2442)	8.03	18.36
1999	23.66	98–99: 6.86 (6275)	12.89 (2642)	8.24	18.40
2000	24.59	99–00: 6.42 (6276)	10.59 (2450)		

SOURCE: Official Statistics of the Federal Chamber of Advocates and the Federal Chamber of Notaries published annually in *BRAK-Mitteilungen*

* Highest increase since 1976 (8.7 per cent) when training periods were cut.

6.2 Fields of Practice and Income

As is the case in other countries, women advocates tend to occupy the less attractive, or at least the less well paid positions in the profession. More often than men

---

[23] 30–35% of first-year students (ie 60–70% of those taking their second legal examination) will be admitted to the advocacy.

women work as sole practitioners or in small firms. More women than men remain freelancers or in employment, the normal starting position for all young lawyers. In 1994, 7.5 per cent of German advocates were employed, 7 per cent worked as freelancers. 90 per cent of advocates were under 35 and 84 per cent of those under 40 belonged to these groups. However, while for men this represents a period of transition, this is not true for many women: 40 per cent of all employed and 32 per cent of all freelancers are women, irrespective of age. (Passenberger 1996b) Women are strongly under-represented in the larger, more affluent and supraregional firms (Hommerich 2001) and they are grossly under-represented in notarial functions, the latter guaranteeing a good income.[24] On the whole, women's incomes are significantly lower than those of men. (Table 10)

Table 10: Pre-Tax Incomes in the German Advocacy in 1994 (in DM 1000)

	Employed	Freelancers	Self-employed
Men	99	74	156
Women	81	64	62

SOURCE: Passenberger 1996 a

There is a part-time factor in these differences which has to be taken into account. In 1994, 10 per cent of advocates worked part-time. In the Western part of Germany these were almost exclusively women. (Passenberger 1996b) An age factor is relevant for the category of the self-employed, as women advocates are on average younger than their male colleagues and the average income doubles after eight years of practice. (Schmucker/Lechner 2000) Amongst employed advocates and freelancers the gender gap is greater than the data show, as here women tend to be older and with more years of practice behind them.

The most significant factor in explaining gender-based income differentiations is legal specialisation (Table 11). Women prefer 'social' and less prestigious fields, such as family, social welfare, immigration and asylum law. Men more often specialise in commercial, company and tax law. Since 1990 possibilities have been created to give formal proof of a specialisation and obtain 'specialist' titles other than the traditional one of 'specialist in tax law' (*Fachanwalt für Steuerrecht*). But even amongst those without specialist titles a comparable or possibly more marked gendered allocation of cases occurs. It is difficult to assess how far self-selection plays a part in creating this horizontal segregation.

Broken down into hourly rates the income differences are still more striking. (Table 12) This is the more remarkable as German advocates have to charge according to a fees-scale based on the value in dispute. Hourly rates are only common in consultancy and international work.

---

[24] Cf Gisela Shaw's contribution to this volume on the specific situation of women notaries in the new federal states.

Table 11: Proportion of Women Advocates with a Specialist Title

(01.01.)	Tax law %	Administrative law %	Criminal law %	Family law %	Labour law %	Social law %
1985	2.53	–	–	–	–	–
1990	2.89	3.28	–	–	6.57	16.31
1995	4.09	4.53	–	–	9.95	17.87
1998	5.65	7.31	7.22	47.76	13.31	21.03
1999	6.21	7.93	11.87	45.93	14.14	25.46

SOURCE: Official Statistics of the Federal Chamber of Advocates

Table 12: Average Pre-Tax Income Per Hour of Full-Time Advocates in the Old and New Federal States by Gender and Specialisation in 1996/97

		Men DM	Women DM
Generalist	Old	45	19
	New	32	28
Specialist	Old	64	35
	New	46	31
With specialist title/	Old	79	55
advocate notary*	New	57	43

* Also including advocates admitted as tax advisers and as chartered accountants
SOURCE: Schmucker/Lechner 2000

The table also shows up the differences between the new federal states in East Germany, the former communist part of Germany, and the old federal states in the West. In the new federal states advocates' fees are by law still pitched at 10 per cent below those in the West. Income differentiations between men and women are, however, less marked. This might be partly explained by the more egalitarian life style patterns of East Germans under the socialist regime, but it must be remembered that the majority of advocates in the East are, in fact, still Western imports.

6.3 Professional Choice and Entry to the Profession

For women their position in the advocacy is often of a transitional nature. They either want to practise in different settings or to give up practising altogether. Often they have no other choice than to open a practice of their own. In this case, they do best if they choose a small town or rural area.[25]

---

[25] I gained plenty of anecdotal evidence of this nature from working in further training for young female practising lawyers in 1997/98.

From interviews with women lawyers I have gained the impression that over time more women than men find their work too demanding, particularly in big international firms. In 1997 one woman lawyer gave a speech at a regional women lawyers' association meeting entitled 'Money or life? From international lawyer to first-instance judge.' After three years of slaving almost around the clock, she had applied to the judiciary which gave her more time to 'live' and more contact with life: real problems of real people and not intellectual sword-crossing for an anonymous rich firm for which losing or gaining a lawsuit made no financial difference. Nor had her having chosen life brought with it any significant financial sacrifice. The gain of time had meant a reduction in actual expenditure as the money she did have at her disposal could be used more prudently.

More women than men become advocates because they have no other choice. In a recent study on young lawyers, 31 per cent of women answered that they would have preferred to work in the judiciary, and 18 per cent in the civil service or as company lawyers. The corresponding figures for men were 13 and 8 per cent. A good income as a reason for their choice of the advocacy was quoted by 25 per cent of men and only 14 per cent of women. (Kääb 2000) In a 1985 study of young advocates with up to five years of practice behind them, more than 30 per cent of young female respondents compared to 17 per cent of men had only been taken on by a law firm because they agreed to work for substandard salaries. (Hommerich 1988) Given the growing pressures in the legal labour market, these figures will have risen for both sexes.

In the same study 70 per cent of women reported having been rejected for a position once or several times because of their sex. This may be a little different now, as during the last 15 years women have become a normal, albeit not always a fully accepted factor in the legal labour market. Blatant sex discrimination is disappearing, while hidden discrimination remains a reality. Women are less likely to be confronted with remarks such as: '*Nothing against women, but they are too gentle for this profession*', or: '*We are a commercial enterprise. Women simply are too worried about justice, that doesn't work.*' (Rülle-Hengesbach 1986: 63). But it is still common for women applicants to be asked about their family planning: '*We know it is against the rules and you need not answer the question, but . . .*' or: '*Where do you see yourself in ten years' time?*' The case of a young woman whose application for a position in a law firm had been disregarded and who had claimed damages on the basis of German anti-discrimination rules has just been decided in her favour. The decisive indicators for discrimination had been that the advertisement had been couched in terms of a male person (*junger Rechtsanwalt*), which was in breach of the rule of gender neutrality, and the firm was an all-male firm. This was the first case of this kind to be reported from the advocates' world.[26]

---

[26] Labour court in Düsseldorf (Az: 9 Ca 4209/99) on the basis of § 611a s 2 of the German Civil Code (*BGB*). This rule was inserted in 1980 in response to the first European Equal Opportunities Directive of 1976. As it had made little real impact, it has been reframed twice, in 1994 through the Second Equal Rights Act, and again in 1998. The burden of proof of non-discrimination is now on the employer.

6.4 Professional Representation

The professional structures are altogether male. Presidents of the Federal Chamber of Advocates (*Bundesrechtsanwaltskammer*) and presidents of the German Lawyers Association (*Deutscher Anwaltverein*) have always been men. The German Lawyers Association operates 31 legislative and expert committees and 14 working groups. Except for the committee on family law, all are chaired by men. The working groups have steering committees of up to 16 members. In 1999, of these, 219 were men, compared to 18 women (21 in 1996/97). There were no women in eg the committees of the groups on notarial functions, fees, commercial law, information media, insolvency, international lawyering, tax, partnership law, constitutional law, administrative law, ie the 'hard' topics. A token woman was included in 'softer' fields such as social law and labour law, two women each in dispute settlement, family law and non-legal personnel, three in marketing. In other words, the familiar picture! Of the 235 local and regional Lawyers' Associations 210 are headed by men, 25 by women. Even the visual appearance of gatherings at German lawyers' conferences re-enforces the impression of a traditionally male-dominated profession: such events are notorious for resembling gatherings of penguins with everyone—men as well as the few women present—wearing dark suits.

When in 1999 the new members for the Statutory Assembly (*Satzungsversammlung der Anwaltschaft*) were elected, it emerged that for one regional chamber, two out of four members were women. The women lawyers of that district had campaigned for their representatives. The male colleagues felt threatened and tried desperately to find ways of challenging the election outcome.

6.5 Equal Opportunities?

It is debatable whether women's progress and a women-friendly development can be attributed to the workings of the political equality machinery and the ongoing equality discourse in society. As advocates tend towards liberal conservativism, I see definite effects of another factor: the highly qualified daughters of formerly patriarchal lawyers make their way into the profession, and their fathers and consequently those around them go through a process of re-education. In one of the big international Frankfurt law offices the daughter of one of the seniors, mother of three children, is a partner. This firm was the first known in Germany to have introduced equal opportunities measures.[27]

---

[27] www.1999.puender.com/d_women.html.
   Another prominent example is Gerd Roellecke, law professor at the University of Mannheim. He wrote an expert opinion against double-income marriages in 1988: *Bewerberüberhang und 'Doppel-Verdiener-Ehen' im öffentlichen Dienst. Eine verfassungsrechtliche Anfrage* (de Gruyter, Berlin, Hamburg, New York). In reviewing Ute Gerhardt's book *Frauen in der Geschichte des Rechts* (1997), he writes: 'To promote women to leading positions is reasonable. . . . How unreasonable

Though the process has been long and tedious, progress has definitely been made. Even five years ago, a large well-known German law firm was reluctant to keep a junior partner in employment when it had become known that she was pregnant. Part-time work was out of the question. When she was expecting a second child she was told that this definitely was the moment to quit. In these circles, working as a lawyer, not only being a partner, is still considered to require total professional devotion and not an occupation that can possibly be combined with family obligations. The woman advocate referred to is now a part-time partner in a small highly specialised firm.

Meanwhile most of the bigger law firms working internationally have started to employ women advocates and to make them partners. This, in some sense, is a reaction to market expectations. Their clientele have a growing number of women in middle management and some, albeit not many, in top management and might judge an all-male setting as old-fashioned and backward. As a consequence a new class of tough business-orientated female lawyers is emerging. (Hommerich 2001) Generally accepted models for maternity and educational leave, for working contracts with a reduced workload, part-time partnerships etc. are still absent. So far no relevant article has been published on this subject by either of the two leading journals for the legal profession, ie _Mitteilungen der Bundesrechtsanwaltskammer_ to which every advocate subscribes, and the _Anwaltsblatt_ circulated to the 40 per cent of advocates who are members of the German Association of Lawyers (_Deutscher Anwaltverein_). No relevant regulation is contained in either the Reform Act 1994 for the Statute of Advocates or the new Order of the Profession regulating the ethics of the profession passed in 1996. Nor was the subject matter discussed at the meeting of the statutory assembly. (Schultz 1997: 72)

Efforts for change are made by women from within: the newly elected women members of the statutory assembly have submitted demands for: regulations to be included in the advocates pension scheme (which is comparable to that of the public service) relating to credit given for time spent on educational leave (_Erziehungszeiten_); the extension of qualification periods in case of child birth; modifications for requirements of in-service training during educational leave. This might just mark a beginning. But so far any indications of a breakthrough have been lacking.

7 REFERENCES

Bajohr, Stefan and Kathrin Rödiger-Bajohr. 1980. Die Diskriminierung der Juristin in Deutschland bis 1945. _Kritische Justiz_ 39.

nature is, every father can observe whose beloved and ambitious daughter gets a child. . . . That the daughter's ambition is not satisfied by child-rearing is due to individualism. . . . But individualism is part of the structure of society. That is why the daughter cannot escape it.' _Frankfurter Allgemeine Zeitung_, 14 October, p L 47.

Blankenburg, Erhard and Ulrike Schultz. 1988. German Advocates: A Highly Regulated Profession. In *Lawyers in Society*, ed by Abel, Richard L and Philip SC Lewis, Berkeley, Los Angeles, London: University of California Press, 124.

Böge, Sybille. 1992. *Weibliche Juristen? Eine historisch-soziologische Analyse des Zugangs von Frauen zu juristischen Professionen.* Unpublished Master's thesis. Kassel.

Böge, Sybille. 1994. Ungleiche Chancen, gleiches Recht zu vertreten: Zur beruflichen Situation von Frauen in der Juristenschaft. In *Studierende und studierte Frauen: Ein ost-westdeutscher Vergleich*, ed by Ruth Heide Stein and Angelika Wetterer. Kassel: Jenior und Pressler, 77.

Böge, Sybille. 1995. Geschlecht, Prestige und 'horizontale' Segmentierungen in der juristischen Profession. In *Die soziale Konstruktion von Geschlecht in Professionalisierungsprozessen*, ed by Angelika Wetterer. Frankfurt/M.: Campus, 139.

Böhm, Reglindis. 1986. Der Kampf um die Zulassung der Frauen als Rechtsanwältinnen und zum Richteramt. *Deutsche Richter Zeitung* 366.

Braun, Anton. 1993. Sozietäten. *BRAK-Mitt.* 185.

Bundesministerium für Bildung, Wissenschaft, Forschung und Technologie. 1995. *Absolventenreport Rechtswissenschaft. Ergebnisse einer Längsschnittuntersuchung zum Berufsübergang von Absolventinnen und Absolventen der Rechtswissenschaft.* Bonn.

Buschmann, Walter. 1989. Frauen in der Justiz. *Recht im Amt* 175.

Dahrendorf, Ralf. 1965. *Gesellschaft und Demokratie in Deutschland.* Munich: Pieper.

Deutscher Juristinnenbund. 1984. *Juristinnen in Deutschland. Eine Dokumentation (1900–1984).* Munich: Schweitzer .

Deutscher Juristinnenbund. 1998. *Juristinnen in Deutschland. Die Zeit von 1900–1998.* Baden-Baden: Nomos.

Erffa, Margarethe and Ingeborg Richarz-Simons. 1929. Der weibliche Rechtsanwalt. In *Die Rechtsanwaltschaft*, ed by Julius Magnus. Leipzig: W. Moeser, 471.

Gerhardt, Ute. 1997. *Frauen in der Geschichte des Rechts. Von der frühen Neuzeit bis zur Gegenwart.* Munich: Beck.

Graue, Eugen-Dietrich. 1993. Die rechtswissenschaftliche Promotion. In *Das Jura-Studium*, ed by Dagmar Coester-Waltjen *et al.* Berlin. New York: de Gruyter. 2nd edn.

Häntzschel, Hiltrud. 1997. Justitia—eine Frau? Bayerische Positionen einer Geschlechterdebatte. In *Bedrohlich gescheit. Ein Jahrhundert Frauen und Wissenschaft in Bayern*, ed by Häntzschel, Hiltrud and Hadumed Bußmann. Munich: Beck, 194.

Hartmann, Andrea. 1999. *Integration durch Marginalisierung? Eine empirische Analyse der beruflichen Situation von Richterinnen und Staatsanwältinnen im deutsch-französischen Vergleich.* Unpublished Master's thesis. Tübingen.

Hasseln, Sigrun von. 1984. Die Zulassung der Frau zum Richteramt—These des vierten Richtertages 1921. *Deutsche Richterzeitung*, 12.

Hassels, Angela. 1988. *'Frauen in der Justiz'—Vorstellung eines Forschungsprojektes.* Beitrag zur Tagung 'Juristische Berufsfelder im Wandel' der Friedrich-Naumann-Stiftung vom 04.–06.07.

Hassels, Angela and Christoph Hommerich, 1993. *Frauen in der Justiz.* Cologne: Bundesanzeiger.

Heldrich, Andreas and Gerhard Schmidtchen. 1982. *Gerechtigkeit als Beruf. Repräsentativumfrage unter jungen Juristen.* Munich: Beck.

Der Hessische Minister der Justiz. 1987. *Frauen in juristischen Berufen—ein Brevier für Referendare und Referendarinnen.* Wiesbaden.

Hommerich, Christoph. 1988. *Die Anwaltschaft unter Expansionsdruck. Eine Analyse der Berufssituation junger Rechtsanwältinnen und Rechtsanwälte.* Cologne, Essen: Bundesanzeiger, Verlagsges. and Deutscher Anwaltverlag.

Hommerich, Christoph. 2001. *Der Einstieg in den Anwaltsberuf. Eine empirische Untersuchung der beruflichen Situation von Rechtsanwältinnen und Rechtsanwälten.* Bonn: Deutscher Anwaltsverlag 2001.

Kääb, Ottheinz. 2000. Berufseinstieg und Berufserfolg junger Rechtsanwältinnen und Rechtsanwälte. *BRAK-Mitt.* 65.

Keuerleber, Gisela. 1987. Juristinnen. Jung und anmutig. Vor 65 Jahren wurden Frauen in der Justiz zugelassen. *Die Zeit*, 10 July 49.

Limbach, Jutta. 1986. Wie männlich ist die Rechtswissenschaft? In *Wie männlich ist die Wissenschaft?* ed by Hausen, Karin and Helga Nowotny. Frankfurt/M.: Suhrkamp, 87.

Mahnkopf, Ulrike. 1987. Möglichkeiten der Kombination von Familie und Beruf bei Teilzeitarbeit und halber Stelle aus der Sicht der Richterin. In *Frauen in juristischen Berufen*, ed by Der hessische Minister der Justiz, 57.

Meier-Scherling, Anne-Gudrun. 1975. Die Benachteiligung der Juristin zwischen 1933 und 1945. *Deutsche Richterzeitung* 10.

Oberlander, Willi and Alexandra Schmuck. 2000. STAR: Umsatz- und Einkommenentwicklung der Rechtsanwälte 1993 bis 1997. *BRAK-Mitt.* 16.

Passenberger, Jürgen. 1996 a. STAR. Berufliche und wirtschaftliche Situation von Rechtsanwältinnen. *BRAK-Mitt.* 50 .

Passenberger, Jürgen. 1996 b. STAR: Kennzeichen zur Berufssituation angestellter Anwälte und freier Mitarbeiter in Anwaltskanzleien in den alten Bundesländern 1994. *BRAK-Mitt.* 225.

Reichling, Ursula. 1988. Die berufliche Situation der Staatsanwältinnen. In *Frauen im Recht*, ed by Ulrike Schultz, Weiterbildungsprogramm der FernUniversität, Course 4, no. 3, 46.

Roten, Iris von. 1960. Die Juristin—ein weißer Rabe. In *Juristen-Spiegel*, ed by Martin, Hans. Cologne: Verlag Dr. Otto Schmidt, 2nd edn, 205.

Rülle-Hengesbach, Wiltrud. 1986. Das weibliche juristische Dasein im Vergleich zum männlichen Normalfall! In *Juristinnen. Berichte, Fakten, Interviews*, ed by Fabricius-Brand, Margarete, Sabine Berghahn, Kristine Sudhölter. Berlin: Elefanten-Press, 2nd edn, 63.

Schmucker, Alexandra and Birgit Lechner. 2000. STAR: Rechtsanwälte mit fachlichen Spezialisierungen und Zusatzqualifikationen im Einkommensvergleich. *BRAK-Mitt.* 118.

Schultz, Ulrike. 1990. Wie männlich ist die Juristenschaft? In *Frauen im Recht*, ed by Battis, Ulrich and Ulrike Schultz. Heidelberg: C.F. Müller, 319.

Schultz, Ulrike. 1997. Legal Ethics in Germany. *International Journal of the Legal Profession* 4: 55.

Tannen, Deborah. 1990. *You Just Don't Understand. Women and Men in Conversation.* New York: William Morrow and Co.

Wasilewski, Rainer, Alexandra Schmucker, Steffen Kaimer, Walter Funk. 1998. STAR: Umsatz- und Einkommensentwicklung der Rechtsanwälte 1992 bis 1996. *BRAK-Mitt.* 250.

Wetterer, Angelika, ed. 1992. *Profession und Geschlecht. Über die Marginalität von Frauen in hochqualifizierten Berufen.* Frankfurt, New York: Campus.

Wetterer, Angelika. 1993. *Professionalisierung und Geschlechterhierarchie. Vom kollektiven Frauenausschluß zur Integration mit beschränkten Möglichkeiten.* Kassel: Jenior und Preßler.

Wetterer, Angelika. 1995. *Die soziale Konstruktion von Geschlecht in Professionalisierungsprozessen.* Frankfurt, New York: Campus.

16

Women Lawyers in Germany—
Perception and Construction of
Femininity

ULRIKE SCHULTZ

Abstract

The idea of a married woman's place being at home and hence perceptions of gender difference are still deeply rooted in German social consciousness. This contrasts with political rhetoric as reflected in technocratically structured equal standing legislation and policies. This paper asks whether the legal profession changes women or whether women change the legal profession. Legal training in Germany aims to assimilate students to the image of a profession traditionally cast in a masculine mould. Professional legal practice confronts women lawyers with gendered expectations that are inherently contradictory, ie to conform with predetermined male norms while at the same time projecting a sufficiently feminine image to avoid being disadvantaged. The increase in the number of female lawyers has no doubt made its mark on legislation, and both male and female lawyers are aware of gendered differences in their respective habitus and behaviour. But it is difficult to detect any tangible difference between their own and their male colleagues' lawyering outcomes.

1 IDEALISM VS IDEOLOGY. THE CONTEXT FOR REFLECTIONS ON WOMEN IN THE LEGAL PROFESSION IN GERMANY

ALMOST 50 PER cent of newly appointed judges, public prosecutors and advocates in Germany are women. Already they make up about one quarter of all practising lawyers. Some 30 years ago they were still so marginal that in a study on the sociology of the legal profession in Germany, Kaupen wrote in 1969, 'A second point completely omitted here is the role of female lawyers who so far have not been of any significance in Germany.' (Kaupen 1971: 215) The increase in the proportion of women in the profession has sparked off the question what changes, if any, this has or may still cause, whether for instance in the way law is practised or in the image the profession projects to the world at large. Carrie Menkel-Meadow (1989), in the 1980s, was amongst the first to ask, 'Will women change the profession, or will the profession change women?'

In her opening speech at the 1995 German judges' biannual meeting Jutta Limbach, the President of the German Federal Constitutional Court, phrased it like this:

> Do women change the third power (i.e. the judiciary)? Are we witnessing in our administration of justice the emergence of a feminine element, articulated through empathy and leniency? Or is it that the judiciary and the study of law tend to have greater appeal for women who are structured similarly to men? (Limbach 1995: 425)

1.1 The Idealistic Element: the Image of the German Housewife

It is not surprising that the top German judge should wonder and worry about the effects of femininity. In Germany, particularly strong stereotypes of female roles and of the essence of femininity persist. For the German-speaking part of Europe, the classical description of women's role was provided by the poet Friedrich von Schiller (1759–1805) in his famous poem 'Das Lied von der Glocke' ('The Song of the Bell') of 1799.[1] Generations of schoolchildren had to learn it by heart. For Schiller, women's role is a domestic, not a public one. His notion of the indefatigable and hard-working housewife and mother is deeply ingrained in the German idea of womanliness. The classical age of German literature was succeeded by the so-called *Biedermeier* period, when this notion continued to be cherished as well as acquiring an added halo of idyllic domesticity. After World War I, economic issues tended to blur idealistic family models, but they also created a fertile soil for Nazi propaganda, the latter indulging in the glorification of the mother as the child-bearer and the heart and soul of the family. During the Second World War and the post-war period, many women had to be the breadwinners for the family, but a paradoxical continuity of the Dear-Mother–Image emerged in the Germany of the 1950s and 1960s. At that time it became a social status symbol for a man to be able to say that he could afford for his wife not to go out to work. Even today it is by no means uncommon to hear both men and women talk about the 'natural duties of the mother'.

It is worth stressing that this was and is broadly the model for what is a very homogeneous society, rather than a notion of relevance only to the bourgeoisie. German society has traditionally been very middle-class, and after the Second

---

[1] 'Der Mann muß hinaus/Ins feindliche Leben,/Muß wirken und streben/Und pflanzen und schaffen,/Erlisten, erraffen,/Muß wetten und wagen,/Das Glück zu erjagen./. . ./Und drinnen waltet die züchtige Hausfrau,/Die Mutter der Kinder,/Und herrschet weise/Im häuslichen Kreise,/Und lehret die Mädchen/Und wehret den Knaben,/Und reget ohn' Ende/Die fleißigen Hände,/Und mehrt den Gewinn/Mit ordnendem Sinn./. . ./Und füget zum Guten den Glanz und den Schimmer,/Und ruhet nimmer.'

World War a very egalitarian middle-class orientation prevailed. It is only during the past 10 years that there has been a growing trend towards stratification, brought about by an increase in the number of immigrants and a widening gap between high and low earners in the wake of Europeanisation and globalisation. Class structures are now becoming more marked and visible, but neither ethnic nor class problems have so far been able to impact on the legal profession or to give it cause for concern. The rise of women in the legal profession has to be seen and evaluated in this context.

1.2 The Pragmatic Element: Life Realities of German Women at the Turn of the Millennium

Given this attitude to family and working women, three almost equally sized tiers of women can be distinguished in Germany: those wholly dedicated to caring for their families, those struggling to combine family and job, and those concentrating entirely on their jobs. Women lawyers tend to be found in the second and third of these categories.[2] While three quarters of women in Germany have children, only half of women professionals do.

Bringing up children is a tall order for working mothers. Except for the big cities, there is an almost total lack of day care facilities for children under three; kindergarten hours are normally a nine to 12 affair; in the first two years at school children have two or three lessons in the morning and then return home; after that, school finishes at 1.15 pm for children up to the age of around 16 (with no school lunches provided). There is political pressure to change this state of affairs, but society is slow to accept the notion. Mothers with permanent jobs have to fend off the suspicion that they are neglecting their children, though today 47.7 per cent of women (compared to 68.6 per cent of men) are in gainful employment, albeit frequently in part-time jobs or with minor working contracts.[3] Couples in higher income groups make their own private child care arrangements. If there are no grandmothers available they tend to hire nannies. Except in large cities, public crèches and day care facilities for older children are considered a last resort for those who have no other choice.

In my own generation (born around 1950) women strove for a higher education in order to satisfy their husbands' conversational needs, to have a qualification if he should die or leave her (though in the latter case alimony payments could be expected), or to leave open the chance of making use of it once the children had left home (which hardly ever worked out that way). Almost all my

---

[2] However, ultimately there is little difference between the proportion of fully trained women lawyers in gainful employment and that of other women. Cf Bundesministerium für Bildung, Forschung und Technologie, 1995. *Absolventenreport Rechtswissenschaft*. Bonn.

[3] EUROSTAT (1997). *Statistik kurzgefaßt, Bevölkerung und soziale Bedingungen* No. 1/97: *Die Erwerbsbeteiligung der Frauen in der Europäischen Union*.

friends, now in their fifties, are housewives, possibly giving a hand to their doctor or lawyer husbands in their practices. Only those with posts in the civil service (*Beamte*) holding university degrees and professional qualifications, such as teachers and judges, do actually go out to work, albeit mostly on a part-time basis. Today, the proportion of highly qualified women is higher than it was in my day, but the labour market is less favourable than 25 years ago.

Annual surveys on time spent on housework and in the job have shown that men still consider domestic work as a woman's domain. Interestingly, the life concepts of men and women in what until 1990 was the German Democratic Republic and the old Federal Republic respectively differ dramatically. They differ particularly in terms of the level of acceptance of the notion of working mothers with young children. A representative study on equal opportunities for women and men carried out in 1994 and 1996, contained the question, 'Which of the following four possibilities is best for a mother'? (Table 1)

Table 1: 'Which of the following four possibilities is best for a mother'?

Best for a mother	Male East % 1994	1996	Male West % 1994	1996	Female East % 1994	1996	Female West % 1994	1996
Maternity leave (14 weeks)	21	10	7	6	19	14	7	7
Educational leave (up to 3 years)	62	63	36	32	70	63	42	42
Long break	13	20	42	46	9	20	43	43
Give up work	3	3	11	10	1	3	8	6

However, the table also shows that between 1994 and 1996 East German views moved slightly closer to those held by West Germans.

Attitudes in East and West also differ regarding public childcare. In the East 58 per cent (55 per cent of men, 61 per cent of women) believe that childcare outside the family is not harmful to children between the ages of three and six, while only 34 per cent in the West do. 47 per cent of Westerners even consider all-day public childcare to be damaging to a child's development, a view shared by only 14 per cent in the East. (Hempel 2000: 87)

1.3. The Political/Ideological Element: from Equal Rights and Equal Chances Towards Equal Standing

The traditional bourgeois housewife image in Germany was eventually eroded by social democratic ideas. These gained ground in the 1980s, when larger numbers of women went through universities and entered the labour market. At the same time, conservative women started to claim equal rights, although a strong essentialist undercurrent persisted. Even in 1987, women members of the Green Party passed a 'Mothers' Manifesto', demanding, 'Give us a chance to bring up our children!'

Nationwide women's agitation and cross-party initiatives which were aimed at bringing about change resulted in the drawing up of equal opportunities policies in federal states with social democratic governments. This, in turn, sparked off a rapid cleansing of statutes of any violations of the constitutional equal rights rule (Basic Law, Article 3 section 2),[4] a process which was accompanied by arduous and extensive public discussions. Meanwhile the bulk of the federal states have passed or are about to pass equal standing acts (*Gleichstellungsgesetze*), including quota regulations in favour of women—with the blessing of the European Court of Justice.[5] Any public agency with more than 20 employees (or 50 depending on the federal state) has to have an equal status ombudswoman with legally defined competences. Women's advancement plans and programmes have to be compiled everywhere in the public service. Some strong women have moved into leading positions, women's networks and mentoring programmes have been set up. And the author of the Mothers' Manifesto has since undergone two divorces and has embarked on a successful business career.

1.4 Epistemological and Methodological Issues

The question of whether women are essentially different from men or whether the gender difference is a social construct resulting in a distinct feminine form of legal practice is addressed in a number of contributions in this volume.[6] In what follows I want to add my own observations relating to the German experience. I have been particularly motivated by a personal need to explore and come to terms with my own past. I had always been aware of a dichotomy between the stereotypical demands made on women of my generation and my class, that is, on the one hand, to be attractive and a good wife and mother, and on the other hand to be a successful professional. I sometimes had a sense of schizophrenia in the face of having to live in two different and partly separate worlds. It was a heavy burden. I was faced with and had to meet divergent expectations. I was worried about my expectations of what was being expected of me. Over the years I tried (and I hope I learned) to question my own ideological position,

---

[4] Which does not mean that the rules are altogether adequate.

[5] EuGH, Urt v 17 10 1995 (Eckhard Kalanke) *Neue Juristische Wochenschrift (NJW)* 1995, 3109; v 11 11 1995 (Hellmut Marschall) *NJW* 1997, 3429; v 28 3 2000 (Georg Badeck *et al*) *NJW* 2000, 1549.

[6] Cf in particular contributions by Rhode, Mather, Felstiner, Sommerlad and Bogoch.

although I cannot yet be sure of that.[7] I did a lot of empirical research on the subject. I handed out questionnaires to students, young law graduates, practising lawyers, judges and public prosecutors, did a lot of interviews, always took notes whenever I overheard lawyers or lawyers-to-be talk of gendered experiences or notions. I analysed biographical and autobiographical accounts by women lawyers, and being a lawyer myself I was a participant observer. In this way I have built up a large stock of information, some of it entangled, partly unintelligible pieces of individual constructions of reality as well as my own perception of it.

I will not here enter into more detailed feminist theoretical debates about difference, sameness, deconstruction of gender and diversity. Gilligan's findings (1982) fascinated me at the time.[8] Later I adopted a more critical stance towards them as I realised the difficulties involved in isolating particular features, as personal qualities overlap and differ in intensity. Today I think that, of course, gender is at least partly socially constructed and therefore subject to change, as well as arising out of subjective notions and therefore difficult to grasp. But I have not ceased to be critical of the official women's advancement policies requiring women' quotas to be achieved within a set period of time, as I cannot see this doing justice to anyone.

Even discussing difference has today become almost politically incorrect in Germany.[9] This is associated with the old patriarchal dilemma that talking of difference as such implies a devaluation of women, a relapse into essentialism. But the gender discourse in Germany is contradictory within itself: on the one hand we are constantly warned of stereotyping. The 'organised' women's movement is keen to deconstruct any gendered notions and orientations, but takes for granted separate world experiences for girls and boys and women and men, as well as resorting to personnel management theories which highlight particular qualities distinguishing women from men.[10]

Currently new theoretical approaches are being developed advocating a reconciliation among the different strands of feminism. The desirability of allowing each of them a place while also relating them more specifically to concrete situations has been acknowledged in view of social transformations and the lessons learnt in evaluating social problems. (Knapp 1997: 1999) All this has

---

[7] I discuss my personal standpoint for reasons of openness and honesty, an approach which, in my experience, is adopted much more freely by women generally, while men tend to uphold the ideal of 'objectivity', keeping personal experience to themselves. But what, one may want to ask, does 'objectivity' stand for in this context?.

[8] Whenever I train young lawyers in rhetoric and negotiation skills, I am aware of the differences in spoken and body language. (compare the findings of Tannen (1990) to gendered patterns of communication).

[9] The discourse is dominated by sociologists who set the tone in attempts to deconstruct gender. They question the findings of developmental psychologists and communication theorists. (Nunner-Winkler 1991).

[10] 'They (women) are sensitive, intuitive, and emotion and performance are inseparably linked. Women are process-orientated, men target-orientated. Being a woman does not mean being better or worse than a man, rather it is an extra asset.' (From a 1997 trade union brochure).

filled me with curiosity and the desire to observe and critically record manifestations of gender in my own professional environment.

What follows are impressionistic recordings of my findings regarding the construction and living manifestation of gender in the field of law in Germany. My aim is to try and find answers to the question, 'Will the profession change women?', and/or 'Will women change the profession?'

2 WILL OR DOES THE PROFESSION CHANGE WOMEN?

The notion that women change on entering the legal profession presupposes that they are different from men and undergo change through working as lawyers in a legal environment. It also implies the expectation that such change makes them different from other women, whatever that difference may consist of.[11] A number of questions need to be asked: What does the profession expect from its male and female members? What are the expectations women have or are being faced with by others, and how do they respond to these expectations? Are they willing to adapt and assimilate, or are they resisting any such pressures?

To avoid any misunderstandings, I want to make it clear that I regard women as equally knowledgeable and competent as men, as shown by their examination results.[12] But there is ample evidence that in practice women are put under pressure to conform. In what follows I shall try to identify these pressures.

2.1 Assimilation Processes in Legal Education: Concepts and Construction of Femininity

The main purpose of legal education is the production and reproduction of a social structure. (Dezalay 1992) Legal education in Germany has been described as an initiation rite, a test in resilience (Kvale 1972), promoting arrogance as a typical feature of (male) lawyers.[13] Once one of the secret aims of legal education, ie to reserve the field of law for men and to keep women out, ceased to work, women had to fit in with these mechanisms of legal education. Exclusion and rejection were followed by assimilation, often accompanied by discouragement and subjection.

---

[11] Some attributes of professional women are fairly obvious. For instance, they tend to speak in lower-pitched voices than other women and apply a different dress code.

[12] Cf my other contribution in this volume, 4.1.

[13] The general public tends to perceive the field of law as specifically masculine, and women working within it as lacking in femininity. Thus, in a televised report from the Olympic Games in Sydney in September 2000, the German moderator Beckmann, a smart rather young man, interviewed the female bronze medal winner in high-diving: *You want to study law now, well, I wouldn't have thought that of you! That's totally unerotic!* (He had previously asked her whether she would—like her predecessors—pose for *Playboy* in the nude.).

2.1.1 Assimilation of Women Law Teachers

The strongest pressure to conform affects those who are supposed to help and assist in the process of professional socialisation, namely female university teachers in law faculties. As already mentioned there is a very male culture in law faculties. In my experience the few women law professors there are all try to fit in somehow; either the male way, 'I know I am called a man in a dress'; or: 'I learnt male language and behaviour like a foreign language',[14] or, more rarely, the female way (the sugar doll type). The latter group thereby comply with a stereotype held by (conservative) men. In return, they are rewarded by being graciously allowed to join the men, while also being undervalued. Intriguingly, being undervalued provides them with a strategic advantage, as they find it easier to get what they want. Otherwise the magical formula is to be inconspicuous, ready to conform and extremely competent, 'My asset is that I am not a beauty but not ugly either, just sufficiently good looking'.

Male law students form an alliance with male law teachers and expect women tutors to be tough (a female law professor of somewhat short stature and a house-wifely look was ridiculed as 'Miss Tiffy'). Women academics in law schools are generally under constant pressure to prove themselves and defend their positions. After a brilliant public lecture by a young female professor, one of her male colleagues rose to his feet and condescendingly declared in public, 'What you have said was not quite correct as such, but on the whole agreeably put.' (1997) In other words, the gatekeepers want to ensure that, even if tolerated amongst them, women contribute to the upholding of the gendered order.

2.1.2 Assimilation of Female Law Students

2.1.2.1 Expected Stereotypes

One way of ensuring the continuation of the old gendered order is to define gendered stereotypes. In earlier years when women law students were in a minority, they were the objects of critical observation and comment, whether in terms of the way they dressed or their more highly pitched voices (should they even dare to use them in public?). In the 1960s, a criminal law professor in Munich tested women's resilience in his lectures by telling dirty jokes, referring to drastic cases of sexual offences, and proclaiming, 'If you can't take it, please leave the hall immediately.' In 1970, when I had passed my first state examination and consulted a law professor about possible PhD work, he told me in all seriousness, 'Surely, you want to get married, and had better learn how to cook.' I also heard comments such as, 'Studying is bad for your looks. Don't read too much, your eyes look like paragraph symbols' (paragraph symbols being used in Germany to represent the sphere of law), and repeatedly the joke, 'If you haven't

---

[14] Prof Dr Ursula Nelles, Münster, in an interview for the journal *Stern*. Other sources need to remain anonymous.

found a doctor by the time you reach your fifth semester, you'll have to do it yourself.' When I started teaching at a university 10 years ago, I expected things to have changed. But that was not the case, neither in law nor in other subjects: *I welcome the young men in the audience who will move the frontiers of knowledge, and the young ladies who will beautify our lecture hall.* This is how first-year students of biology were received at Bochum university in the summer of 1993.[15] In the same year the President of Trier University was heard to say at the induction meeting for first-year students,

> You will face high demands and many of you will drop out, in particular those (women students) who studied crocheting and knitting for their final school examinations and whose only aim in enrolling at university is to find a suitable husband.[16]

In recent years I began questioning law students about their experiences, eg in Trier in 1996.[17] Most of them thought that law professors expected 'feminine behaviour' from women students, and masculine behaviour from men students, and half of them said that their fellow students expected the same. Here is a short list of some of the answers to some of my questions:

Feminine behaviour/qualities were defined as follows:

—nice, helpful
—tidy, tolerant, patient, with a sense of humour
—not over-ambitious, modest, self-conscious, insecure
—well mannered and groomed
—well behaved, self-effacing
—emotional, grateful for being allowed to study

In short, women were attributed with all the qualities traditionally (and often subconsciously) associated with femininity. Such stereotyped expectations were perceived to be very much alive in society. Only one student claimed never to have come across any of them.

Male behaviour/qualities were characterised as:

—self-assured, matter-of-fact, purposeful, resolute, competent
—putting up a show, combative
—conceited, above average intelligence
—career-orientated
—authoritative
—domineering in communicative situations
—expected by women to provide support

[15] Zielke, Andreas: 'Faux Pas Mehlhorn!', in *Bochumer Studentenzeitung* 417, 29 June 1993.

[16] Kirsten Pinkvoss, a third-year law student. She agreed to record in writing some of the discriminations she had experienced.

[17] I handed out a questionnaire to a group of 19 students (15 female, 4 male). As it was in connection with a lecture on women and law, the group was sensitised to gender questions. More details are given in the conference paper entitled 'Women Lawyers in Germany. Perception and Construction of Femininity', presented in 1996 at the Law and Society conference at Strathclyde University in Glasgow.

In answer to the question, 'Do law professors treat women students differently from men students?', women's responses reflected a sense of inferiority:

—at least partly by using sexist language;
—they undervalue women (perhaps unwittingly);
—depends on the professor, some disparage and humiliate women (Prof K: 'The passage from woman to whore is fluid.');
—they make antifeminist jokes eg relating to academic achievement, assessment results;
—only a few women students are taken seriously, but all men students are;
—more considerate, polite behaviour, sometimes errors/faults are more readily 'excused';
—they treat women with irony and condescending politeness;
—they display patronising attitudes towards women students, as for instance when praising them for something that would otherwise be taken for granted.

The question, '*Do men and women enjoy equal opportunities at university?*', met with the following responses from women:

—don't know; what gets assessed in the first instance is academic performance, and here all of us share the same starting conditions;
—women don't stand up and speak as often as men, there are no positive role models, there is conflict between ambition and the female role;
—in seminars and tutorials male students are more often asked and listened to, problems women have are less often given attention.

Men replied:

—if there is any personal contact between prof and student, informal male forms of communication may represent an advantage for male students

Answers to, '*Can sexist prejudices play a role in assessments?*' included:

—yes, in oral examinations (5x) (subconsciously);
—there is a prejudice that women work harder but are less intelligent;
—linguistic and social competence are expected from women as are intellectual ability and rationality from men.

Answers to, '*What other prejudices against women lawyers have you come across?*' were:

—women study law to find a well-heeled man (2x);
—women don't get to the point, they get ahead through their looks, not their ability;
—women are too emotional, not tough enough, not suited to 'male' work such as commercial law and capital crime cases, they have less understanding of economic issues;
—women will never be successful because of children and the housework;
—women judges pass severer sentences.

It is interesting to note that young lawyers during their practical training had obviously come across even more prejudices amongst their tutors (judges, public prosecutors, lawyers in public administration etc) than students had in dealing with university teachers. These stereotypes convey a message that is loud and clear, ie that women are inferior, less well suited to legal functions than men, and that they would be better advised to restrict themselves to their 'natural' duties; however, if they do want to hold their own as professionals, they will have to meet the standards set by men.

2.1.2.2 Textbook Stereotypes. Housewife Doing the Dusting, or: 'Diamonds are a Girl's Best Friend'

Another agent influencing socialisation in legal education are legal textbooks. In Germany law is taught and learnt on the basis of fictional cases. In 1977 two young women analysed the image of women in civil law cases. The result made many men smirk, but not the authors. (Papst/Slupik)[18] Almost 20 years later, between 1993 and 1996, I myself analysed legal textbooks then used by students. Not much had changed.[19]

Typical stereotypes of women are to be found in a much used textbook by Hans Brox on the general part of the German Civil Code[20] about which it has been said that 'there are few law students in Germany who did not study civil law with the help of Brox'.[21] Among the approximately 250 cases presented, only 20 contain a reference to women. Those that are mentioned feature in marginal roles of no significance to the legal construct. To mention just a few:

(1) The master instructs the maid not to open the door to anyone. His wife comes home having lost or forgotten her key. Question: is the maid going to be so stupid as to take her master's instructions literally, or is she capable of a supplementary interpretation and opens the door?

(2) The wife dusting her husband's desk finds a letter and posts it without making any attempt to establish the appropriateness of her action (mindlessness).

(3) The wife leaves everything in her will to her dog (emotional imbecility).

(4) Mrs A and Mrs B quarrel over an expensive designer dress (women's disposition towards squandering their husbands' money).

(5) On a 'coffee coach tour' (organised to tempt particularly women into buying excessively expensive and useless items) Mrs K has been talked into buying an electric blanket (commercial inexperience).

---

[18] Cf also Morgenthal 1983.

[19] I have never dared to publish the results in Germany. This would have been seen as an act of 'fouling one's own nest'.

[20] *Allgemeiner Teil des Bürgerlichen Gesetzbuches.* 18th edn. (Heymanns, Cologne, Berlin, Bonn, Munich, 1994) (1st edn. 1976), meanwhile in its 23rd edn. 1999.

[21] Rüthers, Bernd, Prof Dr Hans Brox zum 75. Geburtstag, in *Neue Juristische Wochenschrift* (*NJW*) 1995, 2086, 2087.

Other female characters are brides or a sweetheart who is given first place in her lover's will to compensate her for his adulterous liaison; there are girlfriends who get rings for their birthdays, a switchboard lady, widows, and finally a dead mother whose son is not allowed to visit her grave.

Admittedly, the repertoire of male roles is not wholly flattering either. Men tend to be drunkards, burglars, drug dealers, foreigners, ex-prisoners. Generally speaking, the clichés used are those to be found in illustrated magazines distributed by German bakers' and butchers' shops, or on the Saturday joke-page of provincial newspapers. The images of femininity are not only used in textbooks that go back to a first edition written decades earlier. Younger authors, out of sheer habit, also resort to them, thus ensuring their continued survival. A book first published in 1993[22] still presents maids, housewives who quarrel over the use of the wash-house, etc. And these are just a few examples of what is standard practice.

Nor can I make any more favourable claims on behalf of my own university, the (German distance-learning) FernUniversität Hagen. To quote from the summary of an evaluative report submitted to the equal opportunities committee in 1993: 'There is a striking absence in law study materials of independent, self-reliant women. All those represented are either housewives, brides, mothers, daughters or maids.'[23]

Materials used by tutors in German commercially run crammers (*Repetitorien*) attended at one time or another by the majority of law students and young lawyers, offer a particularly rich source of examples of antifeminist or gynophobic stereotypes. Their slippery language and drastic illustrations are supposed to act as light relief amidst otherwise dull dogmatic material.

What is irritating about these legal textbooks is that while changes in law regularly lead to revision—Brox's book has been regularly revised by a group of six co-authors[24]—social developments are ignored. This contradicts the high aspirations of law teaching as articulated in the anniversary address cited above:

> For Brox jurisprudence is not reduced to the technicalities of making and applying the law, but an ethical and responsible service for the common good. His law teaching was always geared towards firmly establishing in his students' minds the moral foundations of professional practice.[25]

2.1.2.3 The Use and Impact of These Stereotypes

Law students tend to deny any effect of these images on their minds: '*We just laughed about the cases.*' But that, indeed, is the crucial point. It is the laughter

---

[22] Klaus Schreiber, *Sachenrecht* 1st edn. 1993.
[23] Unpublished paper. Looking back at cases I myself made up years ago, I find more cases in which women were involved; I, too, used stereotypes, but my cases mainly reflected what I had heard, seen or experienced.
[24] Many of the books first appeared decades ago. They have since been kept up-to-date by whole chains of successive authors, each a kind of male heir.
[25] In a new project I analyse gender stereotypes in lawyers' obituaries and anniversary eulogies.

typical of the legal profession, signalling and ascertaining mastery, superiority and—what especially concerns women—patriarchy. (Kotthoff 1996) In my experience, the cases students are brought up with are engraved on their minds. They never cease to discuss and repeat them until the end of their professional lives.[26] This kind of socialisation patterned on an out-of-date as well as a chauvinist image of society not only works on the minds of male students but also on those of their female colleagues. They learn to think with a 'male' head. They are particularly tempted to do so as long as they are in a minority. They identify with the stereotype to an exaggerated extent in order to overcome a sense of insecurity. Only recently, debates on political correctness have begun in law faculties. This may be a stepping-stone towards change. But it will take an entire generation to create a new gender-neutral culture throughout the profession as a whole.

An explanation of why lawyers stick to and fancy the image of the good housewife can be found in a gendered view of the theory of the professions provided by Harriet Silius who wrote:

> The definition of profession implies that it is something extra, unique, a devotion demanding total commitment. . . . The conventional picture of professional work is decontextualized from other social practices . . . the absence of any reference to the social and emotional contexts of work reflects the existence of a pre-established support system available to men. . . . the line between work and private life is blurred. This means the incorporation of work demands into one's non-work relationships, premised on a private life which tolerates and supports immersion in work. . . . the professional career pattern requires either considerable sacrifice of social relationships or a source of inexpensive or free domestic labour. . . . It emphasises the exploitation of women's love and labour in order to enable male professional performance of work. (Silius 1994: 7)

Professional women are perceived as a threat to the traditional life model.

2.1.3 Preliminary Tentative Conclusion: Will the Profession Change Women?

The key question is how socialisation as outlined above impacts on women. Do they internalise the conservative value system, do they accept the global image of women as housewives in inferior roles, regarding themselves as mere exceptions? Do they agree that they are less efficient than their male colleagues? Or, alternatively, do they object to being stereotyped in this way and therefore make a point of getting as tough as men or—not unusual amongst members of minority groups—even tougher? After all, there is the assumption that they have the same competence, professional knowledge, efficiency and social capital as men,

---

[26] In a project on law-related education I observed that lawyers who teach law at school tend to fall back on the cases they themselves were taught on, even if the legal questions involved had lost their relevance.

if not more. But is this assumption really as widespread as we would like to think? And if women do live up to expectations normally associated with men only, are they being rewarded for it?

From biographical accounts we learn that in legal education women go through an alienation process. (Schultz 1993: 235) Many of them suffer for it. Are they really changed in the end? And what happens in legal practice? What about the pressure to conform there?

2.2 Subjection without Reward: Women Lawyers in Practice

2.2.1 *Female Judges with Male Qualities*

My sister who is a criminal judge has been referred to as the only male judge at the local court. Does this mean that the pressure to conform has worked on her and that she—who, in her age group, is in an extreme minority position—exaggerates this in order not to leave any room for doubting her competence? Most certainly, there is no evidence of her having come in for any rewards. Hers is a very typical case. As judges in Germany are career judges, they, as all other public servants in Germany, are subject to regular appraisal by their superiors. Having applied for promotion, my sister read in her appraisal report, 'She is a person of marked temperament and strong authority.' Had she been a man, at least the latter comment would have been a recommendation in the context of a promotion procedure. Not in her case, though. She was classified as 'well suited or very well suited' for this position, while a competing male with the same examination grades (crucial in this context) and no other advantages over her was classified as 'extremely well suited' and was awarded the position. The much vaunted anti-discrimination regulations were of no use to her. Affirmative action only works in cases where both candidates are equally qualified. In my sister's case, the same thing happened three times, and it was only after the intervention of the equal opportunities officer that she was finally promoted.

The key to the story is that she did not live up to the expectation that women have to be 'true' women: subordinate, meek and gentle. Therefore she could not be rewarded. But what do women have to be like in order to be successful? After all, 'true' women are seen to be of doubtful competence. These are conflicting, mutually contradictory demands.

Another example of how women lawyers (most likely the strong and able ones amongst them) are judged by men featured in an article by a prominent public lawyer who referred to female assistants (*Wissenschaftliche Mitarbeiterinnen*) to Federal Constitutional Court judges as 'the WiMins' or 'the out (of the) laws': 'WiMins have—as I have found through years of experience—an *exponential* sense of their own importance compared to their male colleagues.' (Zuck 1996)

2.2.2 Advocates' Problems

Two diverging patterns of behaviour and of expected behaviour are thus emerging. These can be further exemplified by reference to female advocates.

The good girl pattern: In the context of a further training course for recently admitted advocates in 1996, I asked young women about the prejudices they had experienced. They were reluctant to admit to any as that might have put into question their efficiency or professional competence. One woman working part-time said that she was regarded as a half-lawyer, a second-class advocate. Her partners and the staff in her office expected her to be 'small', a good girl, and to stay in the background. She referred to problems with (female) office staff. They were reluctant to accept work from her, even behaved offensively towards her. A client had asked her, '*Are you a real lawyer?*'

An old friend, advocate for 30 years, told me (in 2000) that in commercial arbitration proceedings the presiding judge had said to her in front of her client, 'Give my regards to the head of your firm and tell him that, once again, you have done a marvellous job.'

Tough guys in pin-stripe suits: In discussions I had with women lawyer groups,[27] women described themselves as becoming tough, hard, losing female qualities through their work in the profession.[28] In their study on Canadian lawyers Hagan and Kay (1995) report comments by many women in the profession which show that there is an enormous pressure to conform, that women either try to be males in skirts or run an enormous risk of dropping out. In Germany women lawyers have reported that when they appear in court their colleagues judge them according to their looks and behaviour. There seems to be an assumption, '*If she is too pretty she cannot be competent.*' A judge said in an open court hearing to a defending female counsel, '*A pretty woman like yourself should not be that aggressive.*' But what if a woman is ugly? In order to reduce the potential for being attacked, female advocates in particular attempt to adapt to the male norm at least in their dress code, giving preference to suits and trouser suits of inconspicuous cut and subdued colours.[29]

2.2.3 Further Conclusion

Women lawyers, therefore, find themselves in a catch-22 situation. On the one hand they are expected to 'remain feminine', on the other hand there is the pressure to assimilate to male behaviour. But if they comply they are considered to

---

[27] For instance at meetings of the German Women Jurists' Association.

[28] One woman quoted her grandmother's comment that she (the speaker) had changed through her legal education and professional work, 'but not for the better, child'.

[29] Photos accompanying an article in a managers' magazine on the future of the legal profession speak for themselves (Die Zukunft der Anwälte, *Managermagazin* 10/2000: 282).

be role breakers and thus run the risk of being sanctioned or at least of missing out on any rewards.

Of course there is no one unambiguous answer to the question, 'Does the profession change women?' As I have tried to show there is a general perception that women are different. Behavioural changes are expected, this is part of the professional socialisation process both men and women have to go through. Insofar as women are perceived to be different, a greater degree of change is expected, albeit not always applauded when it has occurred. To what extent women really undergo change over and above the normal professional socialisation process will depend on the individual. One thing is beyond dispute, that is, that women are under a constant and unacceptable pressure and strain.

One might therefore turn the question around and ask, 'Should women not strive to change the system?' Thus they might start by concerning themselves with the didactics of legal teaching, introducing issues of practical relevance into a context traditionally focusing on academic constructs and theoretical issues.

3   WILL WOMEN CHANGE THE PROFESSION? OR HOW DO WOMEN SEE THEMSELVES?

3.1 Changes in Legislation[30]

Among the most profound changes effected by women lawyers have been those to the profession's tools, ie the law. As long as male lawyers dominated the field, law was a male construct describing male life realities. Following the incorporation of the equal rights principle (Article 3, section 2) into the German constitution, the Basic Law, determined women advocates, over several decades, ensured its translation into individual items of legislation. Their most powerful tool has been the institution of the constitutional complaint filed with the Federal Constitutional Court. Step by step and ruling by ruling this court, which exerts extensive control over the law, legislation and jurisdiction, has assisted in the process of closing the gap between constitutional provision and actual legislation. (Jaeger 1996) Also, a growing number of female members of parliament have done their share in moving things on. Thus over the last 50 years family law has been rewritten and numerous amendments to labour law, social law, criminal law and tax law have been made. Given the remarkably dynamic interpretation of the equal rights clause, this process is anything but complete.

However, women's voice in law is still feeble. Only a very small proportion of relevant legal literature is written by women. Not one law textbook currently in use has a female author, and only one of the larger works used for reference and more detailed research has a female co-author (not entirely surprisingly the

---

[30] My analysis is based on a study I am currently conducting on the representation of women in individual statutory regulations, in the normative system as a whole, and in court judgments.

work is on family law).[31] Female authors of contributions published in the authoritative and most widely read German legal journal, *Neue Juristische Wochenschrift (NJW)*, are few and far between (Table 2):

Table 2: Authors of Legal Publications in Journals (by Gender)

NJW	Articles		Book reviews		Comments on judgments	
	m	f	m	f	m	f
1980	256	4	255	4	4	–
1985	270	8	190	7	12	–
1995	303	19	212	13	33	–
1998	335	27	208	7	53	–

Although this table shows a slight increase in contributions made by women over the years, their overall impact on the legal mainstream press remains negligible.[32]

One of the early demands of the women's movement had been to eliminate the male gender bias in the use of the German language. Women lawyers, particularly equal opportunities officers, and female politicians introduced this demand into the legal sphere. (Grabrucker 1993) Although the insertion of feminine forms alongside masculine ones occurs at the expense of succinctness and readability, the language of many statutes has been adapted and new statutes are expected to be gender-neutral or include reference to both sexes.[33]

3.2 Gender Difference in the Practice of Law: Habitus and Behaviour

3.2.1 How Female Advocates see Themselves

In autobiographical accounts women describe their professional selves as different from those of men: more flexible, more patient, devoting more time to clients, more attentive as listeners, not adhering to the classical separation of the case from the client, using less formal patterns of reasoning and thinking, not necessarily or only marginally adjusting their efforts to the expected fee.[34] (Fabricius-Brand 1986; Deutscher Juristinnenbund 1984)

---

[31] Gernhuber, Joachim and Coester-Waltjen, Dagmar, *Lehrbuch des Familienrechts* 4th edn. (Beck, Munich, 1994).

[32] An analysis of these articles would show that most of them are written in the established pattern of the male tradition.

[33] Though the language question has been ridiculed see, eg, Zuck (1994) and scorned by many men and women, considerable change has taken place. However, no systematic research on its effects has been done so far.

[34] Cf fn 14 and Deutscher Juristinnenbund 1984.

Similar impressions and ideas were put forward at the inaugural meeting for a network of women advocates in North Rhine-Westphalia in July 1999. One of the younger advocates said,

> My working style is completely different from that of my male colleagues. In the first instance, I look at the quality of my legal advice, only then do I think of the fee. After I had set up practice, I had to survive a long period of financial hardship. Meanwhile people have seen that I am a particularly dedicated worker. I now have a loyal clientele and a healthy bank account.

3.2.2 Client Relationships

In 1997 I also asked young women advocates taking part in my legal skills training about their perceptions of femininity—their own as well as that of their clients in professional relations.[35] Most of them were convinced that male lawyers treat clients differently. I got responses such as, '*Male advocates don't take female clients seriously. Female clients cry more easily in front of male advocates. Male colleagues take on the role of father, big brother.*'

Answers to the question, 'What perceptions of prejudices against against female clients have you come across?' were:

> Women have no talent for abstraction, don't understand legal regulations, are unstable, weak and naïve, that is why they are in trouble. They are emotional and unrealistic, poor witnesses, stupid girls. Women need the strong man to tell them what to do.

And also, '*Female clients are less interested in getting justice than in satisfying their financial interests.*'

Half of them thought that gendered behaviour is expected from women lawyers. Women lawyers are to display a high degree of '*patience, sensitivity, compassion, empathy, understanding, readiness to accept compromise and to give in, social skills, charm, perfection, trustworthiness, reliability.*' But one added, '*I am quoting a colleague: blond and stupid.*'

3.2.3 A Criminal Defence Lawyer's Experience

In November 1995, Barbara Sänger, a criminal defence lawyer from Cologne, spoke at a local meeting of the German Women Jurists' Association. She described in what way she saw her own approach to work as different from that of her male colleagues. Her account was a perfect illustration of the catalogue of gendered qualities and behaviour listed above. According to her, she is keen to create a *good atmosphere* in the courtroom (criticised by some as misplaced familiarity) and to come to the point. What matters to her is the case, nothing else, while her male colleagues' behaviour is characterised by showmanship. She tries *to be fair* to all involved, while male advocates do not hesitate to attack

---

[35] A total of some 100 questionnaires were sent out. The response rate was just under 50 per cent.

witnesses, which seems to her particularly mean in rape cases. She wants to offer a defence of high technical quality, to be an agent of justice, while her male colleagues are more interested in scoring points and making a name for themselves. They often provide press releases even where this is unethical. Her female socialisation has made her feel *responsible*, want to think and act on behalf of others and to cultivate loyalty in relationships with colleagues. She invests more time in her case work, acts whenever someone asks for her help, is *caring*, and is intent on giving personal assistance to her clients. If they are in prison, she goes to see them regularly, 'mothers' them. In contrast, she sees her colleagues' primary concern as getting things done.

She has a *moral aim*, strives to realise her ideals of justice and of helping delinquents to better themselves. To give them a chance to tell her the truth, she attempts to speak to them on their own before the trial, while her male colleagues conduct such meetings in the presence of parents (after all, the people paying the fees) and thereby risk being lied to.

3.2.4 Judges and Femininity

There is evidence that women's different habitus and social capital bring change to institutional climates. This includes the judiciary.[36]

A small, unpublished and rather informal study of women in the judiciary of the federal state of Hesse which was carried out in 1987, provides details on how these women see their position and work. For instance, women lawyers were asked whether they found themselves confronted with gender-related demands and behavioural expectations. Younger women undergoing their three-year probation tended to answer in the affirmative, older ones with more than 15 years of service behind them tended to say no, while views amongst those in-between were equally balanced. This is not atypical of generational groupings of women lawyers generally. Two thirds of the women said that they had met with prejudices against women lawyers, along the lines of, '*Women pass more lenient sentences*' or, '*Women lawyers are tougher than men*' etc. Yet most stated they they had no problems in coping with men's behaviour in court. Slightly over half of these women in the judiciary in Hesse thought that they themselves treated women in court proceedings differently from men, but that this had no bearing on the final outcome.

Their answers have allowed me to draw up a catalogue of female qualities and behaviour in professional work, which confirms and rounds off the findings from the autobiographical reports analysed above:

emotional climate   understanding, nurturing, patience, warmth, showing one's feelings

---

[36] Cf a report on a working group at the German Judges Day. 'Verändern Frauen die Justiz? Deutscher Richtertag in Mainz 1995', *Deutsche Richterzeitung* 1995, 449.

co-operativeness	less litigious attitudes, less aggressiveness, more mediation
non-authorian style	greater openness, less formality, no excessive self-esteem, readiness to admit to having made a mistake
less set on competition	less statute orientation, less keen on career planning, greater focus on job in hand and team work

Whether these are ideals, or whether or to what extent women actually live up to them remains a moot question.

In June 1994 I gave a lecture at the German national academy for judges on 'Women in Court'. My audience of 22 men and 5 women was asked to complete a questionnaire for me. They had already completed questionnaires about their experiences of gender-related demands and expectations vis-a-vis women lawyers (judges, public prosecutors, advocates), whether concerning themselves or others—colleagues, lawyers, clients, non-legal personnel etc. I had also asked them to list female qualities observed in their female colleagues, which could play a role in court proceedings. Their answers matched the catalogue of qualities I had compiled from the study on women in the Hessian judiciary, including emotiveness, sensitivity, empathy, greater ability or readiness to use emotional tools to help in the understanding of clients' problems, little inclination to restrict themselves to legal dogmatism, openness, willingness to discuss things, sympathy, ability to listen, co-operative behaviour, absence of aggressiveness.

I put forward this catalogue with some hesitation, anticipating protest, criticism and, at worst, hilarity. To my great amazement I found it being discussed as a catalogue of competencies that was seen as a tool to improve procedural practice. Is this re-evaluation of procedural values due to the impact of a female element on the administration of justice?[37]

3.3 Different Outcomes or: do Women Judge Differently?

The question remains whether women's sentencing practice differs from that of men. In 1993, an empirical study looked at attitudes of male and female judges to sentencing and compared those of criminal judges with those of judges in other branches of the judiciary. (Drewniak) The hypothesis was that women judges might be less interested in asserting their authority than in re-integrating offenders into society, that they might be less prone to resort to universal legal principles while displaying greater sensitivity to offenders' specific situations. However, no evidence of this kind of gendered orientations in conflict resolution emerged.[38] Women were more reluctant to punish offenders, but they did

---

[37] Afterwards I was however heavily criticised and blamed for dissipating absurd and noxious ideas—by two of the female judges.

[38] The study does not cover all gender aspects which may play a role in criminal proceedings. The author focused on male and female judges, she did not distinguish between male and female accused persons and did not look into differences in attitudes in the different 'generations' of female judges.

not show greater openness or willingness to take into account individual circumstances in apportioning punishment than did their male colleagues. On the other hand, attitudes towards sentencing amongst both male and female criminal judges differed from those amongst judges in other branches of the judiciary. Also, women judges generally preferred working in other jurisdictions, although statistically they were not under-represented in criminal courts compared with other courts. None of this, however, proves that gender is without significance in the context of sentencing practices.

Twenty years earlier the notorious German feminist Alice Schwarzer had studied sentences in cases of murder of male or female spouses (Schwarzer 1982, originally published 1977). She had concluded:

> The risk of a wife being killed by her husband is ten times higher than that of a husband being killed by his wife. Also, in court these women run a higher risk: the murderess almost always gets a life sentence or 10, 15 years, while the murderer may even be acquitted or get a suspended sentence. . . . In court, males are more or less amongst themselves.

A more recent study by Oberlies (1995) of verdicts for murder passed on men and women did not corroborate these results. However, she did find a correlation between the participation of female judges in the proceedings and greater chances for men to get away with a lenient sentence.

This matches results reported by Eliane Junqueira in this volume. Female judges in Brasil tend to be less generous than their male colleagues with respect to women demanding alimony. Similar impressions have been voiced in the context of German divorce proceedings. There is an obvious explanation, namely that professional women feel less sympathetic towards women who expect someone else to make a living for them. Cross-gender preferences have also been noted, ie women sentencing men more leniently and vice versa. (Women love men and men love women). Raab, in a study of attitudes and everyday theories of male judges vis-a-vis female offenders, found indications that in criminal proceedings behaviour conforming to gender roles is rewarded, while role breakers run the risk of less sympathetic treatment and stiffer sentences. She concluded that female offenders experience criminal proceedings as an investigation not merely into their legal conduct but also into their compliance with expectations regarding their role as women. (1993: 123)[39] Others (eg Frommel 1990, Bode 1991, Degen 1993) have described the workings of underlying male prejudice and preconceived notions in legal proceedings. It seems that women may differ in this respect. On the other hand, it is as yet unclear how far socialisation during legal education makes for a streamlining of lawyers' perspectives generally speaking.

We therefore need to acknowledge that the expectation of fundamental changes being brought about by the growing numbers of female judges is

---

[39] Dietlinde Gipser (1987) in a study on reactions of policemen to men and women respectively reached similar conclusions.

mistaken. Differences between male and female judges are in evidence as regards working styles, but hardly as far as outcomes are concerned. The *formation professionelle* serves its purpose leaving only marginal gender differences.[40] Many will find this a comfort. After all, one of the reasons why women were not admitted to legal studies and one of the objections against women practising as judges was that they might be unreliable and inconsistent in their judgments—on men. (Schultz 1990: 324) We now know that, on the contrary, male offenders might be better served by women judges. No doubt, more detailed research will give us greater insight into the effects of gendered prejudice of the kind described above, even if gender perceptions and constructions are basically (highly) individual and difficult to measure. It would also be interesting to establish whether women make a particular contribution to discussions on sentencing policies. One thing is beyond doubt, that is, that the rising proportion of women in the judiciary will not remain without consequences for sentencing practices.

The question whether and to what extent women may influence or even change styles and outcomes in the working of the advocacy will have to be left open as uncharted territory on the legal research map. It would be simplistic to interpret this question as, 'Do women draft contracts that are different from those drafted by men?' But given the differences in the two sexes communicative behaviours, it is more than likely that women will make their mark in one way or another.

4 A CHANGING IMAGE?

Persistent demands to make it easier for women to combine domestic and professional duties have resulted in lasting changes in the working conditions of the legal profession. Over the last 15 years equal opportunities policies coupled with strict anti-discrimination measures and provisions for the creation of equal standing have transformed traditional working conditions in the legal world. The image of the professional utterly devoted to and immersed in work for the common good has been called into question, more so in the judiciary than in private practice. The question is what impact this will have on public perceptions of and esteem for the legal professions. This is a general process affecting all occupational fields.

> The fact that a woman has become president of this highest court is a clear indication that this court is going downhill. Following patriarchal logic we have to state that the really important decisions are taken elsewhere.[41]

---

[40] Cf particularly the results presented by Felstiner *et al*, Mather, Bogoch, and Boigeol in this volume.
[41] Fronttheater der Macht, in *Loccumer Protokolle* 14/94: *Die Rolle der Richter und Richterinnen zwischen Rechtsprechung und Politik*.

Is state justice loosing in legitimation? And in prestige? It is a common assumption that the entry of women into a profession forces down that profession's prestige. (Costas 1995: 135) Is this really what is happening? (Schultz 1990: 350)

In postmodern Europe there is a strong tendency to devalue state institutions. Politics has suffered a loss of credibility. Hierarchies are abolished or levelled off, formal rules are weakened, authorities questioned. Is this due to female influence after all? In law hard and fast procedural rules are altered. In 1999, the new female Minister of Justice, Herta Däubler-Gmelin, submitted a bill to reduce to two the currently three tiers in civil courts.[42] The old Roman structures in the law of obligations are at stake. Mediation is gaining ground. The high female participation rate in mediation training shows that this communicative form of conflict settlement is particularly attractive to women. It remains to be seen to what extent it will eventually replace the traditional system of adjudication.

The image of the advocate has undergone obvious changes. There is a drift from the notion of advocates as 'organs of the administration of justice system'[43] towards a more business-oriented notion of the profession.

The image of the judge, too, has undergone change, albeit of a different kind. In a 1956 portrait of one of the first judges at the German Federal Constitutional Court, Karl Heck, we find an idealised description of a judge in Germany:

> a cross between a monk and an officer, characterized by selfless dedication but little creativity, creativity not being encouraged in legal education, and his profession—the way it is understood and lived—offering little opportunity to apply it. Judges, as seen here, are severe, precise, earnest and more or less identical looking beings wholly devoted to their duties and typically to be seen processing in court in military-style formation. (Hänlein 1996)

Forty years later, Jutta Limbach, the then female president of the Federal Constitutional Court, wrote in an article entitled 'In the Name of the People—Judicial Ethos in a Democracy' of 'the rule of detachment' (1995: 426):

> What is needed is a striving for objectivity. We all know that this is an ideal which cannot simply be prescribed. And it would amount to self-deception for someone to believe her- or himself to be wholly objective and able to let only the law speak. Both male and female judges are part and parcel of the history of their time.[44] They are women and men, not free-floating spirits.

What we have found, then, is a process of rapid change the effects of which are difficult to isolate, describe and evaluate. The impact of women on the legal professions has been identified as stronger in the judiciary than in the advocacy.

---

[42] Disputes relating to objects of only minor value are to be dealt with out of court by arbitration and mediation, conceivably on the basis of experiences gathered in other countries in Europe. This attempt at rationalisation for economic reasons represents an erosion of the German notion of providing maximum justice by means of comprehensive formal legal protection by the state.

[43] Cf. § 1 Federal Statute on Advocates: *The advocate is an independent organ of the administration of justice.*

[44] A reference to Simon 1975.

Feminists might wonder whether these are two hemispheres drifting apart. Or is it that individualisation remains the key concept after all? Whatever the answers may be, we are facing a dynamic process that needs to be closely watched and evaluated.

5 REFERENCES

Beck-Gernsheim, Elisabeth. 1980. *Das halbierte Leben. Männerwelt Beruf. Frauenwelt Familie.* Frankfurt: Fischer TB.

Becker-Schmidt, Regina and Gudrun-Axeli Knapp. 1998. Feministische Impulse zur Demokratisierung der Gesellschaft. In *Opposition als Triebkraft der Demokratie. Bilanz und Perspektiven der zweiten Republik,* ed by Buckmiller, Michael and Joachim Perels. Hannover: offizin.

Blankenburg, Erhard. 1988. Haben Frauen ein anderes Rechtsbewußtsein als Männer? In *Rechtsalltag von Frauen,* ed by Gerhard, Ute and Jutta Limbach. Frankfurt am Main, Suhrkamp, 143.

Bode, Malin. 1991. Arbeitsgericht—Ein Ort für Frauen?—Klägerinnen sind eigentlich nicht vorgesehen. *Streit* 107.

Bundesministerium für Familie, Senioren, Frauen und Jugend, and Statistisches Bundesamt eds. 1995. *Wo bleibt die Zeit? Die Zeitverwendung der Bevölkerung in Deutschland.* Wiesbaden: Statistisches Bundesamt.

Burgsmüller, Claudia. 1988. Vom Mythos einer feministischen Rechtsanwältin. In *Rechtsalltag von Frauen,* ed by Gerhard, Ute and Jutta Limbach. Frankfurt am Main: Suhrkamp, 159.

Costas, Ilse. 1995. Gesellschaftliche Umbrüche und das Verhältnis von Profession und Geschlecht: die juristische Profession im deutsch-französischen Vergleich. In *Die soziale Konstruktion von Geschlecht*, ed by Angelika Wetterer. Frankfurt, New York: Campus, 121.

Degen, Barbara. 1993. Die Frau als Aschenputtel im Erwerbsleben. In *Frauen im Recht,* ed by Ulrike Schultz. Weiterbildungsprogramm der FernUniversität, Course 4, no B1.

Deutscher Juristinnenbund, ed 1984. *Juristinnen in Deutschland. Eine Dokumentation (1900–1984).* Munich: Schweitzer 1984.

Dezalay, Yves. 1992. *Marchands de droit.* Paris: Feyard.

Drewniak, Regine. 1991. Sind Frauen die besseren Richter? *Kriminologisches Journal* 23, 112.

Drewniak, Regine. 1993. *Strafrichterinnen als Hoffnungsträgerinnen? Eine vergleichende Analyse strafrechtlicher Orientierungen von Richterinnen und Richtern.* Baden-Baden: Nomos 1994.

Fabricius-Brand, Margarete, Sabine Berghahn, Kristine Sudhölter. 1986. *Juristinnen. Berichte, Fakten, Interviews.* Berlin: Elefanten-Press, 2nd ed.

Field-Belenky, Mary, Blythe McVicker-Clinchy, Nancy Rule-Goldberger and Jill Mattuck-Tarulle. 1989. *Das andere Denken. Persönlichkeit, Moral und Intellekt der Frau.* Frankfurt: Campus.

Frommel, Monika. 1990. Gewalt gegen Frauen—Utopische, realistische und rhetorische Forderungen an eine Reform der sexuellen Gewaltdelikte. In *Frauen im Recht,* ed by Battis, Ulrich and Ulrike Schultz. Heidelberg: CF Müller, 258.

Frug, Mary Joe. 1987. *The Role of Difference Models in the Study of Women in Law*. Paper for Workshop on Women in Law, University of Wisconsin.

Gerhard, Ute. 1984. Warum Rechtsmeinungen und Unrechtserfahrungen von Frauen nicht zur Sprache kommen, *Zeitschrift für Rechtssoziologie* 220.

Gerhard-Teuscher, Ute. 1986. Die Frau als Rechtsperson. Über die Voreingenommenheit der Jurisprudenz als dogmatische Wissenschaft. In *Wie männlich ist die Wissenschaft?* ed by Hausen, Karin and Helga Nowotny. Frankfurt am Main: Suhrkamp.

Gerhard, Uta and Jutta Limbach. Eds. 1988. *Rechtsalltag von Frauen*. Frankfurt am Main: Suhrkamp.

Gerhardt, Ute. 1990. *Gleichheit ohne Angleichung. Frauen im Recht*. Munich: Beck.

Gernhuber, Joachim and Dagmar Coester-Waltjen. 1994. *Lehrbuch des Familienrechts*. Munich: Beck 4th ed.

Gilligan, Carol. 1982. *In a Different Voice*. Cambridge, Mass: Harvard University Press.

Gipser, Dietlinde. Ed. 1987. *Wenn Frauen aus der Rolle fallen: alltägliche Leiden und abweichendes Verhalten von Frauen*. Weinheim: Beltz 2nd ed.

Grabrucker, Marianne. 1993. *Vater Staat hat keine Muttersprache*. Frankfurt a.M.: Fischer TB.

Hänlein, Andreas. 1996. Richter des BVerfG a.D. Dr. Karl Heck. *Neue Juristische Wochenschrift* 3131.

Hagan, John and Fiona Kay. 1995. *Gender in Practice. A Study of Lawyers' Lives*. New York, Oxford: Oxford University Press.

Hempel, Marlies. 2000. 'Und eine Arbeit soll meine Frau haben und sie soll Chefin sein'. Lebensentwürfe von Mädchen und Jungen in Ost und West. In *Trend/Trennt-Wende? Eine Ost-West-Annäherung. Beiträge zur feministischen Praxis* 54, 87.

Jacobs, Alice D. 1972. Women in Law Schools: Structural Constraints and Personal Choice in the Formation of Professional Identity. *Journal of Legal Education* 24: 462.

Jaeger, Renate. 1996. Frauen verändern die Justiz—Verändern Frauen die Justiz? *Deutsche Richterzeitung* 121.

Karstedt-Henke, Susanne. 1985. Die Frau—das konservative Wesen. Einige Anmerkungen zu dem Beitrag von G. Smaus „Einstellungen von Frauen zum Strafrecht: Positives Rechtsbewußtsein?" *Zeitschrift für Rechtssoziologie* 299.

Kaupen,Wolfgang. 1971. *Die Hüter von Recht und Ordnung. Die soziale Herkunft, Erziehung und Ausbildung der deutschen Juristen. Eine soziologische Analyse*. Neuwied, Berlin: Luchterhand 2nd ed.

Klein-Schonnefeld, Sabine. 1978. Frauen und Recht. Zur Konstruktion des Rechtsbewußtseins von Frauen. *Kriminologisches Journal* 10: 248.

Knapp, Gudrun-Axeli. 1999. Gleichheit, Differenz und Dekonstruktion. Vom Nutzen theoretischer Ansätze der Frauenforschung für die gleichstellungspolitische Praxis. In *Chancengleichheit an Hochschulen—Vom „Sonderprogramm" zum Wettbewerbsvorteil*. Schriftenreihe der Landeskonferenz der Hochschulfrauenbeauftragten Schleswig-Holstein November 1999, 7.

Knapp, Gudrun-Axeli. 1997. Gleichheit, Differenz, Dekonstruktion: Vom Nutzen theoretischer Ansätze der Frauen- und Geschlechterforschung für die Praxis. In: Krell, Gertraude, ed: *Chancengleichheit durch Personalpolitik. Gleichstellung von Frauen und Männern in Unternehmen und Verwaltungen*. Gabler: Wiesbaden.

Kotthoff, Helga. Ed. 1996. *Das Gelächter der Geschlechter*. Konstanz: Universitätsverlag.

Kvale, Steiner. 1972. *Prüfung und Herrschaft: Hochschulprüfungen zwischen Ritual und Rationalisierung*. Weinheim: Beltz.

Lautmann, Rüdiger. 1980. Über Gesellschaftsdifferenzierungen in der juristischen Handlungsfähigkeit. *Zeitschrift für Rechtssoziologie* 165.

Limbach, Jutta. 1995. Im Namen des Volkes—Richterethos in der Demokratie. *Deutsche Richterzeitung* 425.

Lucke, Doris. 1984. Die Frauenforschung und ihre juristischen Abnehmer—zur rechtspraktischen Irrelevanz einer advokatorischen Wissenschaft. *Zeitschrift für Rechtssoziologie* 203.

Lucke, Doris. 1996. *Recht ohne Geschlecht? Zu einer Rechtssoziologie der Geschlechterverhältnisse.* Pfaffenweiler: Centaurus.

Mahnkopf, Ulrike. 1987. Möglichkeiten der Kombination von Familie und Beruf bei Teilzeitarbeit und halber Stelle aus der Sicht der Richterin. In *Frauen in juristischen Berufen*, ed by Der hessische Minister der Justiz, 57.

Menkel-Maedow, Carrie. 1989. Feminization of the Legal Profession: the Comparative Sociology of Women Lawyers. In *Lawyers in Society. Vol. 3 : Comparative Theories*, ed by Abel, Richard L and Philip SC Lewis. Berkeley, Los Angeles, London: University of California Press.

Morgenthal, Luise. 1983. August Geil und Frieda Lüstlein. Der Autor und sein Tätertyp. *Kritische Justiz* 65.

Münch, Ingo von. 2000. Juristen—„elitär und arrogant"? *Neue Juristische Wochenschrift* 1312.

Nunner-Winkler, Gertrud. 1991. *Weibliche Moral. Die Kontroversse um die geschlechtsspezifische Ethik.* Frankfurt, New York: Campus.

Oberlies, Dagmar. 1995. *Tötungsdelikte zwischen Männern und Frauen.* Pfaffenweiler: Zentaurus.

Papst, Franziska, and Vera Slupik. 1977. Das Frauenbild im zivilrechtlichen Schulfall. Eine empirische Untersuchung, zugleich ein Beitrag zur Kritik gegenwärtiger Rechtsdidaktik. *Kritische Justiz* 242.

Raab, Monika. 1993. *Männliche Richter—weibliche Angeklagte. Einstellungen und Alltagstheorien von Strafrichtern.* Bonn: Forum Verlag.

Reichling, Ursula. 1988. Die berufliche Situation der Staatsanwältinnen. In *Frauen im Recht* ed by Ulrike Schultz, Weiterbildungsprogramm der FernUniversität, Course 4, no 3, 46–49.

Rust, Ursula. Ed. 1997. *Juristinnen an den Hochschulen—Frauenrecht in Lehre und Forschung.* Nomos: Baden-Baden.

Schultz, Ulrike. 1990. Wie männlich ist die Juristenschaft? In *Frauen im Recht*, ed by Battis, Ulrich and Ulrike Schultz. Heidelberg: CF Müller, 319.

Schultz, Ulrike. 1993. Women in Law or the Masculinity of the Legal Profession in Germany. In *European Yearbook in the Sociology of Law*, edited by Febbrajo, Alberto and David Nelken. Milano: Giuffrè 1994, 229.

Schultz, Ulrike. 1994. Erwartungen und Erwartungs-Erwartungen von und an Juristinnen. Frauen mit Recht als Beruf. *Aktuelle Informationen des Juristinnenbundes* I–III.

Schultz, Ulrike. 1996. *Women Lawyers in Germany—Perception and Construction of Femininity.* Draft Paper.

Schwarzer, Alice. 1982. Männerjustiz. (from *Emma* 2/77) In *Mit Leidenschaft. Texte 1968–1982.* Hamburg: Rowohlt.

Silius, Harriet. 1992. *Gender Contract of Women Lawyers. The Case of Finland.* Paper presented at the Third European Conference of the Working Group on the Legal Profession. Aix-en-Provence.

Silius, Harriet. 1994. *Gendering the Theories of Professions.* Paper presented at the ISA conference Regulating Expertise: Professionalism in Comparative Perspective. Paris.

Silius. Harriet. 1996. *Why Do Women Lawyers Prefer to be Lawyers and to Forget that they are Women (Lawyers)?* Paper presented at the Fifth European Conference of the Working Group on the Legal Profession. Peyresq, France.

Simon, Dieter. 1975. *Die Unabhängigkeit des Richters.* Darmstadt: Deutsche Studiengemeinschaft.

Smaus, Gerlinda. 1984. Einstellungen von Frauen zum Strafrecht. 'Positives Rechtsbewusstsein?' *Zeitschrift für Rechtssoziologie* 296.

Stritt, Marie. 1898. *Das Bürgerliche Gesetzbuch und die Frauenfrage.* Frankenberg i.Sa.: Reisel.

Tannen, Deborah. 1990. *You Just Don't Understand. Women and Men in Conversation.* New York: William Morrow and Comp.

Zuck, Rüdiger. 1994. Die RechtsanwältIn: Genus oder Sexus? *Neue Juristische Wochenschrift* 2808.

Zuck, Rüdiger. 1996. WiMins—Die Gesetzlosen. *Neue Juristische Wochenschrift* 1656.

17

Women Lawyers in the New Federal States of Germany: from Quantity to Quality?

GISELA SHAW

Abstract

Socialist systems generally created a more benign environment for women's concerns than did Western capitalist societies. In conjunction with a determined downgrading of the social status of all branches of the legal profession, this made for a considerably larger proportion of women jurists in the German Democratic Republic (GDR) than in the (old) Federal Republic of Germany. German unification (1990) meant the abrupt and dramatic dissolution of the east German legal system. This produced a unique laboratory for legal historians and sociologists, one fascinating facet being the developments in the east German legal professions, including their substantial female membership. The paper traces the fate of women jurists from the creation of the German Democratic Republic (1949) to its disbanding and the setting up of five new federal states (1989/90) up until the end of the first decade of united Germany.[1]

1 WOMEN IN SOCIALISM: THE BUILT-IN DILEMMA

I T HAS BEEN argued that, structurally speaking, capitalism and communism are not at all far apart (Murphy 1988). And this for two reasons: not only are both built on the principle of exclusion, but exclusion in both cases is largely defined by ownership, albeit private ownership in capitalism and public ownership in socialism. Both ideologies profess the same substantive enlightened ideals of equality, liberty, fraternity and peace, only with different weightings. And

---

[1] A comparison with Malgorzata Fuszara's contribution on the legal profession in Poland will show a range of parallel developments due to the fact that under their Communist regimes both the German Democratic Republic and Poland broadly followed the Soviet model. However, a relatively gradual transition to Western-style capitalism in Poland strongly contrasted with the wholesale and abrupt collapse of the German Democratic Republic and its legal system. Developments since 1990 still display a number of parallel features but also significant differences.

both have allowed the process of formal rationalisation, the accumulation of power by the dominant class, to take place at the expense of the realisation of these ideals (244, 252). Within this structural framework, gender and other inequalities must be seen as derivative forms of exclusion cutting across the two opposing ideological blocks. However, historically the lack of equality for women in either camp occurred in different areas, to different degrees and for different reasons.

Nevertheless, as an ideology socialism certainly offered a more benign environment for women's concerns than Western capitalism in that in it equality, including gender equality, survived intact as the publicly proclaimed sociopolitical aim. But there was a snag: ever since August Bebel's and Friedrich Engels's pronouncements on the subject (Bebel 1988, Engels 1972), the overthrow of the rule of private property was assumed to be not only necessary but sufficient for women's liberation to occur. The German proletarian women's movement under its powerful leader Clara Zetkin never openly abandoned this main line of argument although Zetkin found herself increasingly hard pressed to sustain it, as reformist forces in the Social Democratic Party were driving her further to the left (Evans 1987). Indeed, by 1913, even she was calling for the creation of an independent socialist women's movement separate from the main party (a position she had to give up again later). The built-in dilemma never ceased to bug the socialist position. Again and again, Zetkin reaffirmed (a) her wholehearted opposition to having any truck with the bourgeois women's movement, and (b) her equally wholehearted support for the class struggle as the overarching goal (Zetkin 1971) while remaining deeply committed to the women's question, even when revolution in Russia was overtaken by the establishment of a centralist and patriarchal system and when the privileging of production as the sufficient condition for women's emancipation excluded other very tangible areas of inequalities from official party vision (Einhorn 1993: 20). Zetkin's dilemma has remained the key to the situation of women and their sense of identity in socialist countries, including the German Democratic Republic. It also and inevitably profoundly influenced the fate of women in that country's legal profession.

2 WOMEN LAWYERS IN GERMANY: UNPROPITIOUS BEGINNINGS

If in all Western countries the law is notorious for having held out longest as a male bastion, Germany has the dubious claim to one of the worst records in this context. Ironically, it was a Prussian lawyer and high-ranking civil servant, Theodor Gottlieb von Hippel, who in 1792 first suggested that there was absolutely no reason why women should not make good lawyers and be able actually to improve the judicial system (Hippel 1828). His argument was treated by his contemporaries as no more than a joke. After all, enlightened philosophers, including such thoroughly sensible and moderate men as von Hippel's deeply admired Königsberg contemporary and friend Immanuel Kant, took it as read that female sex and scholarship were mutually exclusive. In his memorable words,

> As concerns learned women: they use their books in about the same way as they use their watches, that is to wear them for people to see that they have one, although they are most likely not working or not set by the sun (Kant 1917: 307).

It took another century before the first German women put the Prussian prophet's theory to the test, although they had to go abroad, more precisely to Switzerland, to do so. In 1897, the young Anita Augspurg was the first German woman to be awarded a PhD in law by the University of Zurich. Professional qualifications entitling women actually to practise law in Germany were not available to them until 1922 (Berneike 1995; Geisel 1996; Gerhard 1988).

Only a very small number of women were able to take advantage of these newly gained opportunities before Hitler put a stop to it all. Along with racially and politically undesirable elements, in particular Jews and members of the political Left, all women were excluded from positions as judges and prosecutors, and no woman was newly admitted to the advocacy as a *Rechtsanwalt*. It therefore took until the end of World War Two before the history of women lawyers in Germany was ready to take off properly. To complicate matters, this history developed in two branches within two mutually hostile socio-political and economic environments on either side of the Iron Curtain: on the one hand, a democratically constituted state based on the separation of powers and operating a capitalist market economy; on the other hand, a state organised on the basis of socialist centralism and a centrally planned economy. The two systems operated very different strategies vis-a-vis (a) women and (b) the legal profession.[2]

3 WOMEN LAWYERS IN THE GERMAN DEMOCRATIC REPUBLIC (1949–1990)

State socialism in the GDR represented a patriarchy where the Party/state took over the role of the 'Father', simultaneously benevolent and all-providing on the one hand and disempowering citizens on the other (Henrich 1990; Dölling 1994). Power derived not from material wealth but from closeness to the sources of power. Members of the power hierarchy were selected primarily not on the basis of expertise and achievement but rather on the basis of loyalty to the rulers. Patriarchy and bureaucracy determined the position of law and lawyers in the GDR. There was no place for lawyers as an independent profession, but a great need for 'social workers' willing to guide and educate the public while themselves being guided and controlled by the Party. Where moral guidance failed, sanctions came in. Hence prosecutors became the pivot of the system.

---

[2] For a more detailed account of the history of women lawyers in Germany up to the end of World War II and the division of Germany see Ulrike Schultz's chapter on 'The Status of Women Lawyers in Germany'.

The general culture and working style were determined by lawyers' primary role as 'crisis managers', as one observer during the year of German unification put it (Markovits 1995), while private disputes and adversarial stances were of secondary importance. Male and female jurists, so she found to her amazement, spoke the same language, for better or for worse.

> At its best it is simple, concrete, pragmatic, focusing on results. At its worst it is unintellectual and imprecise. But I can never tell from the words alone whether they are spoken by a man or woman.

Both sexes seemed to talk not for effect but with the intention of listening and understanding (Markovits 1995: 44).

Within this patriarchal system women's emancipation was a declared state aim, albeit an emancipation imposed from above. The most important defining characteristic of this emancipation was women's equal involvement in the world of work. Work outside the home became just as important for women's sense of identity as for men's. Not entirely surprisingly, however, the low social profile of the legal professions was not unrelated to the relatively balanced gender distribution within them albeit still clearly staggered in line with the relative prestige and income attached to each. On the other hand, it would be misleading to interpret the relationship in terms of simple causality, as this would discount the effects of state-initiated large-scale positive discrimination in favour of women for ideological as well as economic reasons. What follows is a brief chronological outline of the history of women in the various branches of the profession during the 40 years of socialist rule.

The small number of women in Germany who, by the end of World War Two, were fully qualified jurists were generally well placed for a promising start, given the huge gaps within male ranks. This was particularly true of the Soviet occupied zone where, in contrast to the three Western zones, former Nazis within the judiciary (by definition all male), ie some 80 per cent of all judges and prosecutors, were removed from office (Feth 1994: 354). Amongst the first women jurists to be recruited by the Soviet Allies was Hilde Benjamin, from 1953 to 1967 the GDR's Minister of Justice, indeed, the first woman ever to hold that office (Feth 1997). Having qualified as a lawyer in 1929, Benjamin had entered the profession as one of only eight women amongst 3,000 male lawyers in the Berlin advocacy (Erffa 1931: 209). An active member of the young German Communist Party, she lost her right to practise in 1933. Her husband, Georg Benjamin, a Communist doctor of Jewish extraction, was murdered in a Nazi concentration camp in 1942. By the end of the war she had suffered many years of hardship and persecution and was more than ready to assist in the setting up of a system which she, like many of her contemporaries, believed to be the only possible counter-force to fascism. She became one of the small cohort of early women lawyers in the Soviet occupied sector of Germany which, in 1949, became the German Democratic Republic.

From 1945, the Soviet Military Administration (SMAD) took determined steps to bring about a wholesale personnel change in the judiciary of the Soviet occupied zone. In line with the post-1917 Soviet model new recruits were selected on the basis of criteria other than legal expertise, which were primarily ideological but also included a strategy of positive discrimination in favour of previously under-represented social groups, amongst them women. Hilde Benjamin soon became the key figure in this restructuring process. In her three-volume history of the German Democratic Republic's legal administration written in the 1970s and 1980s, she was able to report with some satisfaction that as early as 1949 around 14 per cent of judges and prosecutors were women (the Federal Republic took another 30 years to reach this figure) and that there was even evidence that women law graduates were beginning to be represented at the top of the career ladder. She paid special tribute to those amongst them who were mothers and possibly even single mothers while coping with their professional duties without the kind of support later generations of women were to receive (Benjamin *et al* 1980: 92–93).

In 1950/51 the first applicants were admitted to newly established two-year judicial training courses in a specially set up college in Potsdam-Babelsberg. Fifty-one, that is 24 per cent, of the first cohort of 200 were women (Benjamin *et al* 1980: 85), a previously unimaginably high proportion. At the same time university law courses, which were undergoing gradual restructuring to meet the needs of socialist centralism, also admitted increasingly larger numbers of women. The Party strategy to create a balanced gender distribution amongst law graduates continued with minor variations for the whole of the life of the GDR. As law graduates would also normally take up legal positions assigned to them, the balance was maintained across the system. In 1989, women occupied roughly half of the GDR's judicial positions (Shaw 1994a), and 37 per cent of career positions in the GDR judiciary (Deutscher Juristinnenbund 1998: 41) (Table 1).

Table 1: Judges in the GDR

	5.4.1970	%	31.12.1989	%
Judges at local courts	859		1,111	
Women judges at local courts	315	36.7	584	52.3
Judges at regional courts	313		301	
Women judges at regional courts	101	32.3	144	47.8

The advocacy proved to be the most resistant branch of the legal profession, both in terms of ideological malleability and in terms of opening their doors to women. During the early post-war years its membership had suffered considerable depletion through westward migration. But as the political line was to reduce rather than stabilise, let alone increase, the number of practising lawyers, new recruits remained few and far between, which also meant that women remained the exception. Hilde Benjamin quotes the example of the city of Halle where in 1953 some 46 per cent of *Rechtsanwälte* were over 65 years old (many of these by definition former Nazi members and, of course, almost exclusively male) and only three were younger than 40 (Benjamin *et al* 1980: 224–5). Until the early 1950s, the profession suffered relatively little Party interference and retained facets of self-government. This stopped when, in 1952, the last remnants of the country's federal structure were abolished and the legal administration reorganised along Soviet centralist lines.

In practice this meant that *Rechtsanwälte* were urged to give up private practice and join centrally controlled lawyers' collectives (Lorenz 1994). At the same time, their numbers were allowed to continue to shrink from 901 in 1951 to 562 in 1981, compared to some 41,000 in the Federal Republic of Germany (Brand 1985: 165–66). From then on they steadied around the 600 mark. The collectivisation process was a voluntary and hence a slow one, but by 1988 natural wastage, targeted replacement policies and financial incentives had left a mere 26 private practitioners (out of 580) (Lorenz 1994: 426). The profession's overall tiny size, but relatively wide margin of independence, high income levels and social prestige (Brand 1985: 160) made it the most sought after of the (five) branches of the legal profession. The number of women *Rechtsanwälte* gradually increased, but even then the advocacy's gender profile changed much more slowly and much less drastically than was the case in the judiciary. In how far this was due to slow turnover, deliberate chauvinist tactics on the part of collectives, central control and/or even women's lack of motivation and/or assertiveness would require further investigation. Anecdotal evidence certainly seems to suggest that women rarely even set their sights on achieving entry to the select club of *Rechtsanwälte*. In 1989 their share stood at around 26 per cent (Shaw 1994a: 196).

Restructuring the advocacy from an independent to a centrally controlled profession as part of the overall judicial reforms had brought about a change in its role. Its members' rights and functions were severely curtailed. This included the hiving off of the non-contentious jurisdiction from the courts in 1952 and a transfer of most of its functions to administrative agents, with the remainder going to a state-controlled notariat. For the advocacy this meant that those who had, in pre-GDR times, been lucky enough to gain a notarial appointment ('legal assistants of capitalists in the age of imperialism', as socialists saw it (Artzt 1952)) were now deprived of a significant source of additional income (Benjamin 1980: 137ff; Brand 1985: 147–153).

The notariat in eastern Germany underwent a radical transformation from a prosperous, independent and much sought-after profession to one tightly fitted into the state bureaucracy, with the lowest pay and lowest social status of all jurists. It also became the most strongly feminised branch. All this in stark contrast to the West, where notaries remained amongst the highest earners as well as the last bastion of a near-male monopoly—in 1994 the average women's share in the West German notariat was still only just over six per cent

(Bundesnotarkammer 1994). At the point of German unification, 67.8 per cent of all East German notaries were women, the spectrum ranging from 48.1 per cent in the district of Potsdam (the most desirable location) to 100 per cent in the district of Schwerin (the least appealing district) (Shaw 1997) (Table 2).

Table 2: Notaries in the GDR (1989)

	Total	Male	%	Female	%
Chemnitz	46	17	37	29	63
Cottbus	22	6	27.3	16	72.7
Dresden	36	10	27.8	26	72.2
Erfurt	30	14	46.7	16	53.3
Frankfurt/Oder	22	4	18.2	18	81.8
Gera	22	9	40.9	13	59
Halle	39	13	33.3	26	66.7
Leipzig	31	12	38.7	19	61.3
Magdeburg	28	13	46.4	15	53.6
Neubrandenburg	16	1	6.3	15	93.8
Potsdam	27	14	51.9	13	48.1
Rostock	22	2	9.1	20	90.9
Schwerin	17	–	0	17	100
Suhl	21	7	33.3	14	66.7
Total	379	122	32.2	257	67.8

At the time of merger with the West, the GDR legal profession as a whole displayed a relatively balanced gender distribution compared to that of any Western society. Yet, gender differentiations amongst the four classical branches of the profession matched relative levels of income and social prestige, with distinct female over-representation in the notariat, roughly a balance within the judiciary, and a remaining level of under-representation in the advocacy not significantly below that of the Federal Republic. State and Party control was considerable, not only in terms of recruitment, training, appointments, promotion, responsibilities and working methods, but also in terms of the actual conduct of individuals' professional duties.

4 EAST GERMAN WOMEN LAWYERS IN UNITED GERMANY: THE NUMBERS GAME

What changes has German unification brought to this overall picture? Legal unification meant that all legal personnel in the former GDR wishing to continue working in their professions had to relearn their trade as well as having to undergo personal ideological vetting. Significant shifts amongst the various branches of the profession had been set in motion as early as January 1990 when a law was passed by the East German parliament abolishing the strict barriers on admission to the Bar. The subsequent influx of newcomers to the advocacy was driven by four factors: the general appeal of the profession for those previously kept out by the centrally imposed *numerus clausus*; the realisation on the part of members of the judiciary who feared for their posts for ideological reasons that the advocacy, now a free profession and not (yet) threatened by ideological evaluations, would offer them a safe haven; the large number of commercial lawyers in state-owned companies facing redundancy; and, lastly, the rapidly growing overall demand for practising lawyers, as privatisation, restitution of property and rehabilitation began to absorb all available legal energies. The result was a steep increase in the number of *Rechtsanwälte* in the territory of the GDR even before its demise in October 1990. Given that in the GDR the profession had had a membership of no more than around 600 (as opposed to some 56,000 in the old Federal Republic), there was no reason to fear a shortage of clients, and law graduates generally, male or female, were spared the need to join the dole queues (Shaw 1994b).

For a variety of reasons, the situation for women in this general reshuffle continued to be broadly favourable. A brief look at each professional subgroup some four years after unification conveys the following picture. Women fared better than men in the ideological and professional evaluation which all members of the former GDR judiciary wishing to be taken over into the new system had to undergo from 1990/91. Women had been less closely embroiled in political crime (partly, but by no means exclusively, due to their lower age profile) and had been less well represented on the higher echelons of their profession from where post-holders were automatically removed. From among the 40 to 50 per cent of applicants who managed to pass the evaluation process and were taken over into the new system, women took a disproportionately high share. Berlin represented a particularly dramatic example, as amongst the tiny number of successful applicants (33 out of 371) over two thirds were (young) women (*Frankfurter Allgemeine Zeitung* 1993). In the state of Brandenburg, women accounted for 65.8 per cent of those being taken over (73 out of 111) (Brandenburg Ministry of Justice 1994). In the northerly state of Mecklenburg West Pomerania the figure was 51.2 per cent (63 out of a total of 123) (Mecklenburg West Pomerania Ministry of Justice 1994). In 1994, the overall gender picture for the total of 524 judges (excluding 12 male judges from West Germany brought back from retirement) in the state of Brandenburg was as follows (Brandenburg Ministry of Justice 1994) (Table 3).

In 1994, Brandenburg women judges therefore accounted for 40.7 per cent of this state's judges and just over half were products of East Germany, that is they had either been taken over into the new system or had at least graduated from an East German university. Amongst public prosecutors, too, women did better than men in the evaluation process. By 1994 the overall percentage of women prosecutors in the new federal states stood at 34 per cent (all-German average:

25.9 per cent). Of those who had graduated from GDR law schools, 45.3 per cent were women (*Deutsche Richterzeitung* 1994).

Table 3: Judges in the state of Brandenburg (1994)

	Former GDR judges (%)	Newly appointed East Germans (%)	Newly appointed West Germans (%)	Delegated from West Germany (%)	Transferred from West Germany (%)
M	38 (34.2)	15 (32.6)	109 (58.6)	83 (86.5)	61 (83.6)
F	73 (65.8)	31 (67.4)	77 (41.4)	13 (13.5)	12 (16.4)

Even the proportion of female *Rechtsanwälte* grew to a percentage higher than that in the GDR, not to mention the West. There is no obvious explanation for this, nor does the fact, as such, tell us very much about the success or otherwise of their career efforts. What we can conclude is that proportionately more East German women than men must have decided to set up or join a legal practice, as incoming lawyers from the West tended to be male rather than female. By 1994, 87.7 per cent of the total number of *Rechtsanwälte* in East Germany were newcomers from either East or West. The ideological scrutiny of practising lawyers belatedly instigated under political pressure in 1992 (Shaw 1994b) had little impact on numbers generally or on the gender balance in the profession. In January 1994, women made up 26.2 per cent of the profession, compared with an average in 1990 of 21.8 per cent in the GDR (March 1990) and 17.7 per cent in the old federal states. Across the individual states, the overall gender distribution in the advocacy in 1994 looked as follows (Tables 4 and 5):

Table 4: German advocacy (new federal states)

	Total number	Numbers of women	%
Brandenburg	703	160	22.8
Mecklenburg West Pomerania	640	163	25.5
Saxony	1,925	453	23.5
Saxony Anhalt	807	236	29.2
Thuringia	750	139*	18.5*
Total for new states	4,392	1,151*	26.2*

* Statistics available for Thuringia do not list the percentage of women. Figures for Thuringia are based on a different source (Berlin office of the *Deutscher Anwaltsverein*, figures for May 1994) and may not be wholly accurate.

Gisela Shaw

Table 5: German advocacy (old federal states by district)

	Total	Numbers of women	%
Bamberg	1,303	207	15.9
Braunschweig	557	89	16
Bremen	1,105	183	15.9
Celle	3,136	568	18.1
Düsseldorf	4,979	731	14.7
Frankfurt/M	7,038	1,387	19.7
Freiburg	1,851	335	18.1
Hamburg	4,428	943	21.3
Hamm	7,047	1,073	15.2
Karlsruhe	2,297	430	18.7
Kassel	916	157	17.1
Koblenz	1,611	243	15.1
Cologne	5,231	891	17
Munich	8,309	1,570	18.9
Nuremberg	2,062	406	19.7
Oldenburg	1,372	240	17.5
Saarbrücken	776	123	15.9
Schleswig	1,926	320	16.6
Stuttgart	3,209	530	16.5
Tübingen	1,120	187	16.7
Zweibrücken	855	126	14.7
Total for old states	61,128	10,739	17.7

By 1999 the overall share of women *Rechtsanwälte* in united Germany had crept up a little further, but more markedly in the old than in the new states (old FRG: to 22.5 per cent; former GDR: to 27.7 per cent) (*Anwaltsblatt* 1999).

For the notariat, unification was accompanied by events which were truly dramatic (Shaw 1997). A brief but fierce political battle was fought in the summer of 1990 within the West German notariat, which due to complex nineteenth-century developments under Prussian and Napoleonic influence was split into two main branches, ie full-time notaries with no legal practice and notaries who also worked as *Rechtsanwälte*. During the lifetime of the old Federal Republic, this split between full-time notaries (*Nurnotare*) and solicitor notaries (*Anwaltsnotare*) had not caused any serious problems. Both sides had had an interest in honouring an unwritten gentlemen's agreement to respect (region-based) existing demarcation lines and not rock the boat. However, this agreement failed to stand up to the challenges implicit in the prospect of German and, indeed, European unification. A golden opportunity had suddenly opened up for the two camps to reinforce their own territory and numbers as well as their influence in an expanding market by adding the notariat of the newly to be created five east German states.

In the context of German unification and the pending dissolution of the East German state notariat, the question arose which of the two historically available formats the notariat in the five newly to be created German states was to adopt. Each of the two West German groups was hoping to gain the upper hand. In the event, the very small but powerful and much better organised group of full-time notaries, led from Bavaria, Hamburg and the Rhineland, won the day by enlisting the trust and support of East German notaries, the majority of whom were women. Jointly they staged a street demonstration and practically blackmailed the outgoing GDR Minister of Justice (who had already reassured the solicitor-notaries camp of his support) into acceding to their demands. As a consequence, the full-time notariat was introduced in the five new states.

This confronted the existing East German notaries with the choice of either deciding almost overnight to continue their notarial work as independent professionals in a wholly unfamiliar legal and economic context, or accepting unemployment or retraining for a non-legal occupation, as they would not have stood a chance in trying to compete with experienced practising lawyers from West or East Germany. A large majority took the plunge into independence. In the new system, therefore, the much coveted state-allocated and strictly limited notarial appointments went primarily to former East German notaries. West Germans, mostly (male) former *Rechtsanwälte* or *Anwaltsnotare*, were recruited to make up the numbers, thus aligning the female-male divide with that between East and West. As Table 6 shows, the contrast between the gender distribution in the new and the old federal states could not have been starker (Shaw 1994a).

However, over the next five years (1994–1999), during which the East German state governments saw a need to increase the overall number of notarial posts by just under 50 per cent (from 556 to 819), East German women notaries rapidly lost ground as their share went down from just under half in 1994 (48.6 per cent) to just under a third in 1999 (31.9 per cent). This drop can largely be explained by significant numbers of men coming in from the West. During the same period, the male monopoly in the West German notariat suffered hardly a scratch (approximately 94 per cent) (Bundesnotarkammer 1999).

Table 6: Female notaries in the old and the new federal states of Germany (1.1.1994)

	Total	Number of women	%
Old federal states			
Anwaltsnotare	8,660	575	6.64
Nurnotare	1,053	32	3.04
New federal states			
Nurnotare	556	270	48.6

(These figures exclude Berlin.)

To conclude, in terms of sheer numbers, women jurists in East Germany during the first four years after unification held their own by maintaining a more or less strong presence in the four classical branches of the legal profession. Given the high level of mobility between East and West and, in particular, the steady influx of West German lawyers into the East, it is increasingly becoming less feasible or even meaningful to distinguish between East and West German lawyers except by reference to their places of work. What remains for the foreseeable future is a significantly higher percentage of women in the new than in the old federal states throughout the main branches of the legal profession.

5 WOMEN LAWYERS IN THE NEW FEDERAL STATES: FROM QUANTITY TO QUALITY?

A head count of female membership in professions tells only one part of the story and needs to be completed by an assessment of these women's professional standing and influence. Here the picture in relation to the new federal states of Germany is distinctly less rosy, indeed, painfully familiar.

Women judges and public prosecutors in the new states are generally still to be found at the bottom end of the judicial career ladder. There are at least two reasons for this. On the one hand, as is the case in the old states, the average age of women lawyers is significantly lower than that of men. However, more importantly, women members of the judiciary in the new states are much more likely to be graduates of GDR law faculties and therefore, by definition, had to start the post-unification period by completing a three- to four-year probationary period irrespective of their years of professional experience. For instance, just under half of women judges and over half of women prosecutors in the state of Brandenburg did their training in the GDR, while this applies to only just under one fifth of male judges and one third of male prosecutors. Consequently, most higher posts are occupied by men (from the West). By 15 November 1995, 92 per cent of all women judges and 95.7 per cent of all women prosecutors in the Brandenburg judiciary were to be found at the lowest point of the salary scale (male judges: 73 per cent; male prosecutors: 83.9 per cent). It will take many years before this state of affairs can be expected to change in any significant way.

Table 7: Qualitative gender profile of Brandenburg judiciary (November 1995)

	Male %	Female %
Level of entry		
Judges	73	92.3
Prosecutors	83.9	95.7
Career posts		
Judges	27	7.7
Prosecutors	16.1	4.3

Given that Brandenburg is the new federal state with the most clearly and consistently articulated equal opportunities policies, the gender distribution here is likely to be more favourable than in the other four East German states. The obvious gender imbalance in career posts can be mainly attributed to the fact that the percentage of East Germans is higher among women than among men.

The situation in the East German advocacy is much less clear-cut in terms of gendered structures, as East-West and gender differentiations are overlaid by further complicating factors rooted within the profession itself. *Rechtsanwälte* trained in the GDR have laboured under considerable handicaps, arguably greater even than those for members of the judiciary. Not only have they had to learn, largely from scratch, the law to be applied after unification and, in contrast to members of the judiciary, have had to pay for such retraining. They have also had to come to terms with working within the context of a market economy and in a climate of competition when market forces and competition had previously been totally alien concepts to them.

For East Germans, setting up a legal practice in united Germany required endless time, energy, commitment, entrepreneurial talent and a readiness to take risks, all of which came most easily to the generation under forty and those not hampered by family commitments. Today larger law firms, particularly those active in the international field, tend to be in West German hands. Specialisation, in as far as it was possible at all for East Germans, was largely determined by their previous area of work. While for lawyers who had worked in East German industry commercial law became a realistic option, former GDR practising lawyers, judges, prosecutors and administrators normally settled for family, criminal or labour law. Dealings with companies, especially West German companies, largely fell to lawyers from the old Federal Republic, while most East Germans, male and female alike, were still learning on the job and had some way to go before they could secure a substantial share in the more lucrative commercial market (Kirschner and Lienau 1994).

Traditionally, the German advocacy in general and women within it in particular have represented an under-researched field. German unification and the challenges associated with it have led to a first full survey conducted on the basis of data for 1993/94 by the German Institute for Independent Professions (*Institut für freie Berufe*) in Nuremberg on *Rechtsanwälte* in united Germany. This has brought to light a range of revealing comparative statistics. As far as women lawyers are concerned, it confirms clear-cut differences along the West-East divide on the one hand and along the male-female divide on the other.

Firstly, there are obvious structural differences between law firms in East and West generally (Passenberger 1995). Over 91 per cent of law firms in the East were set up in 1990 or later (West: 26 per cent), and 70 per cent were in the hands of sole practitioners (West: 56 per cent). Only 3 per cent of practioners in the East were able to offer specialist expertise (West: 16 per cent); the average working hours in the East were 62 (including several hours' retraining per week) compared to 50 hours for their Western colleagues, while income levels were significantly lower, with an average differential of between 30 to 40 per cent.

Within this spectrum, women lawyers in the new federal states (as those in the old states) were consistently to be found at the bottom end of the respective scales (Passenberger 1996). On average, they were younger, with fewer years of professional experience than their male colleagues (four years as compared to six years) and more inclined to set themselves up as sole practitioners. Their annual income as well as hourly rates hovered around two thirds of those in the West. They tended to be less able to offer specialist expertise, and where it existed this tended to focus on family, labour, rent and civil law (as opposed to labour, commercial and public law with men).

In sum, then, women legal practitioners in the East were suffering under a dual handicap, that of being East German and that of being female. What is interesting to note is that they seem to have retained a very different attitude to the role of gainful employment in their lives, as signalled by a number of factors. In contrast to their sisters in the West, East German women practitioners' working week was hardly shorter than that of their male colleagues (East: 58/60; West: 40/51). They hardly ever opted for part-time work, with 19 per cent of female practitioners in the East working fewer than 40 hours a week compared to 55 per cent in the West. Only 10 per cent worked on a salaried basis (15 per cent in the West).

The group of East German jurists for whom German unification brought a complete reversal of their professional status (one is tempted to say, from Cinderella to princess) are the notaries. Notaries in the West are drawn from amongst the brightest law graduates and are amongst the highest earners in the legal field, while, as we have seen, the opposite was true of GDR state notaries. Today both groups operate side by side in the new federal states. Data on notaries and their work are more than scarce, and the information contained in this paper is based largely on personal semi-structured interviews carried out in 1994. From these interviews it became clear that, in spite of the reversal of the fates of East German notaries, the East-West division overlays and reinforces the gender divide in the East German notariat and is reflected in income levels, types of specialisation and types of clients. This goes hand in hand with a marked difference in their respective style of work. East German notaries still tended to focus on individuals' needs rather than business efficiency, resulting in a less efficient use of their time. As former GDR notaries, a majority of whom are women, had hardly any specialist expertise in the commercial field, a good proportion of commercial business transactions, most notably with West German or international companies, was firmly in the hands of West Germans, most of whom were male. However, this did not seem to be causing any resentment or friction. The learning needs facing former GDR notaries were so immense, the supportive measures put in place by their West German colleagues so enormous, pressures of work in the context of privatisation and restitution of property so vast, and the reversal of their general professional fortunes so staggering that they seemed quite happy, at least for the time being, to accept this division of labour. Besides, as German notaries are state appointments based on need, competition between individuals was not a serious threat.

6 CONCLUSION

In summary then, different historical roots and a range of developments tied up with and deriving from German unification have produced, in the new federal states of Germany, a much more balanced gender distribution across the legal professions than has ever been seen in the old federal states. At least in the judiciary, the two sides will gradually approach each other in quantitative terms, as young entrants tend to be taken on in equal numbers from both sexes. On the other hand, unification has brought with it yet another, qualitative handicap for lawyers trained in the former GDR (and the majority of these are women), namely the degree of their absence from career posts which is even more pronounced than it is in the West. As the judicial age structure in the East is distinctly imbalanced compared with that in the old federal states, with those occupying higher posts having been appointed only recently and at a relatively young age, opportunities for promotion in the judiciary will remain generally modest and the share of women in career posts disproportionately low.

7 REFERENCES

Anwaltsblatt. 1999. Mitglieder der Rechtsanwaltskammern am 1. Januar 1999. 4, 216.

Artzt, Werner. 1952. Die Ausgliederung der freiwilligen Gerichtsbarkeit und die Errichtung des Staatlichen Notariats, in *Neue Justiz* no 12, vol 6, 517–521.

Bebel, August. 1988. *Woman in the Past, Present and Future*, introd by Moir Donald, London: Zwan; German original: *Die Frau und der Sozialismus*, first published Zurich 1879.

Benjamin, Hilde *et al* (eds). 1980. *Zur Geschichte der Rechtspflege der DDR 1949–1961*, vol II, Berlin: Staatsverlag der Deutschen Demokratischen Republik.

Berneike, Christiane. 1995. *Die Frauenfrage ist Rechtsfrage. Die Juristinnen der deutschen Frauenbewegung und das Bürgerliche Gesetzbuch*, Baden-Baden: Nomos.

Brand, Peter-Andreas. 1985. *Der Rechtsanwalt und der Anwaltsnotar in der DDR*, Cologne etc: Carl Heymanns.

Brandenburg Ministry of Justice. 1994. Personal communication.

Bundesnotarkammer. 1994. Personal communication.

Bundesnotarkammer. 1999. *Notarstatistik 1997–1999*. Personal communication.

Bundesrechtsanwaltskammer. 1994. Personal communication.

Deutscher Juristinnenbund e.V. (ed). 1998. *Juristinnen in Deutschland. Die Zeit von 1900 bis 1998*, 3rd completely revised edition, Baden-Baden: Nomos.

Deutsche Richterzeitung. 1994. Zahl der Richter, Staatsanwälte und Vertreter des öffentlichen Interesses in der Bundesrepublik Deutschland am 1. Januar 1993, January, 34.

Dölling, Irene. 1994. Identitäten von Ostfrauen im Transformationsprozeß: Probleme ostdeutscher Frauenforschung, in Elizabeth Boa and Janet Wharton (eds), *Women and the Wende: Social Effects and Cultural Reflections of the German Unification Process*, *GDR Monitor* No 31, Rodopi, Amsterdam: 95–106.

Einhorn, Barbara. 1993. *Cinderella Goes to Market. Citizenship, Gender and Women's Movements in East Central Europe*, London: Verso.

Engels, Friedrich. 1972. *The Origin of the Family. Private Property and the State*, Pathfinder Press. German original: *Der Ursprung der Familie, des Privateigentums und des Staats*, first published 1884.

Erffa, Margarethe Freiin von. 1931. Die Frau als Rechtsanwalt, in Ada Schmidt-Beil (ed), *Die Kultur der Frau. Eine Lebenssymphonie der Frau des XX. Jahrhunderts*, Berlin-Frohnau: Verlag für Kultur und Wissenschaft: 205–211.

Evans, Richard J. 1987. *Comrades and Sisters. Feminism, Socialism and Pacifism in Europe 1870–1945*, Sussex: Wheatsheaf.

Feth, Andrea. 1994. Die Volksrichter, in Hubert Rottleuthner (ed), *Steuerung der Justiz in der DDR*, Cologne: Bundesanzeiger: 351–377.

Feth, Andrea. 1997. *Hilde Benjamin—Eine Biographie*, Berlin: Berlin Verlag Arno Spitz GmbH.

Frankfurter Allgemeine Zeitung. 1993. Die Berliner Justiz im Schatten der Vergangenheit, 4 February.

Geisel, Beatrix. 1996. Alle Juristinnen haben ihre Stellung der Frauenbewegung zu verdanken!, in *Ariadne. Almanach des Archivs der deutschen Frauenbewegung* 30, 52–59.

Gerhard, Ute. 1988. Anita Augsburg (1857–1943). Juristin, Feministin, Pazifistin, in Kritische Justiz (ed), *Streitbare Juristen, eine andere Tradition*, Baden-Baden: Nomos: 92–103.

Henrich, Rolf. 1990. *Der vormundschaftliche Staat. Vom Versagen des real existierenden Sozialismus*, Reinbek: Rowohlt.

Hippel, Theodor Gottlieb von. 1828. *Über die bürgerliche Verbesserung der Weiber*, Berlin: G Reimer; first published 1792.

Kant, Immanuel. 1917. *Anthropologie in pragmatischer Hinsicht*, in *Kants Werke*, vol VII, Berlin: Georg Reimer; first published 1798.

Kirschner, Lutz and Marc Lienau. 1994. Rechtsanwälte im Übergang—Zur Situation des Berufsstandes in den neuen Bundesländern, in *Zeitschrift für Rechtssoziologie* 1, 66–81.

Lorenz, Thomas. 1994. Die 'Kollektivierung' der Rechtsanwaltschaft—als Methode zur systematischen Abschaffung der freien Advokatur, in Hubert Rottleuthner *et al* (eds), *Steuerung der Justiz in der DDR. Einflußnahme der Politik auf Richter, Staatsanwälte und Rechtsanwälte*, Cologne: Bundesanzeiger: 409–428.

Markovits, Inga. 1995. *Imperfect Justice: An East-West German Diary*, Oxford: Clarendon Press; German original: *Die Abwicklung. Ein Tagebuch zum Ende der DDR-Justiz*, Munich: C H Beck 1993.

Mecklenburg West Pomerania. 1994. Personal communication.

Murphy, Raymond. 1988. *Social Closure. The Theory of Monopolization and Exclusion*, Oxford: Clarendon Press.

Passenberger, Jürgen. 1995. STAR: Daten zur wirtschaftlichen Lage der Anwaltskanzleien den neuen Bundesländern, in *BRAK-Mitteilungen* 6, 230–232.

Passenberger, Jürgen. 1996. STAR: Berufliche und wirtschaftliche Situation von Rechtsanwältinnen, in *BRAK-Mitteilungen* 2, 50–52.

Shaw, Gisela. 1994a. Juristinnen in den neuen Bundesländern, in *Zeitschrift für Rechtssoziologie* 2, 191–207.

Shaw, Gisela. 1994b. *Rechtsanwälte* and German Unification, in *German Life and Letters* 2, 211–231.

Shaw, Gisela. 1997. Window of Opportunity or Flash in the Pan? Women Notaries in the New Federal States of Germany, in *German Life and Letters* 4, 557–573; also in Margaret Littler (ed), *Gendering German Studies. New Perspectives on German Literature and Culture*, Oxford: Blackwell 1997: 179–195.

Soden, Kristine von. 1997. Auf dem Weg in die Tempel der Wissenschaft. Zur Durchsetzung des Frauenstudiums im Wilhelminischen Deutschland, in Ute Gerhard (ed), *Frauen in der Geschichte des Rechts*, Munich: C H Beck: 617–632.

Zetkin, Clara. 1971. *Zur Geschichte der proletarischen Frauenbewegung Deutschlands*, Frankfurt/M: Roter Stern.

18

Women in the Dutch Legal Profession (1950–2000)

LENY E DE GROOT-VAN LEEUWEN

Abstract

This chapter focuses on two issues. The first is the quantitative distribution of women in the four classical legal professions in the Netherlands and at the various levels within each of these profession's internal hierarchy. It is shown that while the share of women in the legal professions is rising slowly but steadily, vertical segregation continues to persist. The second issue under investigation is the question whether women's approach to and conduct of their professional activities differ in any recognisable way from those of their male colleagues. It appears that although there is some evidence of minor gender-based differences (eg women appear to be capable of more accurate predictions of court rulings) there is no evidence as yet, at least in the Dutch context, to support the hypothesis of essential gender-based differences in women's and men's attitudes to and conduct of their professional activities as lawyers.

1 INTRODUCTION

T HIS CHAPTER CONSISTS of two parts: firstly an overview of the distribution of women within and across the various branches of the Dutch legal profession; secondly an exploration of issues surrounding the question whether any significant differences exist between the professional attitudes and performance of female lawyers as compared to male lawyers.

2 FEMALE PARTICIPATION IN THE DUTCH LEGAL PROFESSION

About one third of all jurists in the Netherlands work in the classical legal professions as practising lawyers, notaries, judges and public prosecutors. In 1994, of the 31,000 jurists in the Netherlands working a minimum of 12 hours a week, 8,500 were attorneys (*advocaten*), 1,196 were notaries, 2,500 worked as junior notaries (*kandidaat-notarissen*) and over 2,100 were members of the judiciary (including the prosecution service and trainee judges) (VSNU, report, January 1997). As in almost every country in Western Europe as well as in the United States (Sabbe and Huyse 1997(for Belgium), Soulez Larivière 1987 and Karpik 1999 (for France), Schultz 1990 (for Germany), Fuchs Epstein 1983 and Menkel-Meadow 1995 (for the USA)), the increased participation of women is one of the most visible changes among law students as well as within the advocacy and the judiciary in Holland (Table 1).

Table 1: Share of women amongst law students, judicial trainees (judges + public prosecutors), judges, public prosectors, attorneys, junior notaries and notaries

Year	Students %	Judicial trainees %	Judges %	Public prosecutors %	Attorneys %	Junior notaries %	Notaries %
1959–52	30		>1	0	6	3	>1
1960	26				8	5	1
1970	20	41	3	>1	11	3	1
1975	24	30	8	7	16	4	2
1980	33	32		18	18	6	2
1986	44	51	16	12	21	9	3
1990	48	59	20	16	26	16	3
1991			60			27	
1992		60			27	27	
1993		65			30		
1994		68				42	3
1995	51	68	34	33			

SOURCES: Roos 1981; *Jaarboek Emancipatie* 1997; De Groot-van Leeuwen 1991; Kester and Huls 1992; Klijn 1997

The first woman attorney was admitted in the Netherlands in 1903. From the 1950s, the percentage of female attorneys rose steadily to around one third today. The first woman judge and woman notary were appointed in 1947 (Sloot 1980: 169; Swaab 1990: 393). After a period of very slow growth, the percentage of female full-time judges rose above five per cent in the 1970s, and today stands at around one third of the profession. However, the situation is very different for the (Latin-type) Dutch notariat. Here, women make up almost half of the lower level notaries, but hold a mere three per cent of fully fledged notarial posts.

The frequently voiced suspicion of the existence of an inverse relation between the social status of an occupation and the proportion of women in that occupation, including the legal profession (interview with Mrs A van Es, Member of the Dutch Parliament, 1990; Hage 1990), has not been supported by hard evidence. However, not dissimilar to vertical segregation in university posts (one third of research assistants at Dutch universities are women, compared with a mere four per cent of full professors), the various branches of the legal profession have not done well in recruiting women to top positions.

Vertical segregation is particularly strong among notaries (Table 1).[1] But the judiciary does not reflect a balanced profile either. The first female president of a court was appointed as late as 1991. In 1995, of the 24 presiding judges in Dutch county and crown courts only two were women. There were no female chief public prosecutors at crown courts (attorney generals) at all. (Table 2)

There are two reasons for the fact that the share of posts held by women at the higher levels of the judiciary is so small. The first is linked to the fact that in the Netherlands there are two points of access to the judiciary: one directly after graduation from law school via a six-year judicial training programme, the other after at least six years' legal experience in a different branch of the profession, for example in a law firm. As the majority of those entering the judiciary from 'the outside' are men (97 per cent in 1986),[2] this makes for vertical segregation. The second reason concerns mobility after entering the judiciary. Research has shown that, everything else being equal, periods between career steps are longer for women than for men (De Groot-van Leeuwen 1991).

Table 2: Distribution of women throughout the Dutch court hierarchy

Level	1974		1986		1990		1995	
	No.	%	No.	%	No.	%	No.	%
High (supreme court judges, presidents and chief public prosecutors of all courts)	1	1.3	3	3.5	5	5.5	7	7.4
Middle (crown court judges middle level of judges and public prosecutors of county courts)	4	1.4	44	9.4	81	14.5	165	23.3
Low (county court judges and public prosecutors)	31	11.0	95	25.1	112	27.8	351	45.6

SOURCES: Groenendijk 1975 (for 1974); De Groot-van Leeuwen 1991, 1997a (for 1986, 1990, 1995)

---

[1] The striking imbalance in the gender composition of notariats has historical roots and is in evidence throughout the civil law world. The only exceptions are countries in central and eastern Europe that had been members of the Socialist Bloc (see Fuszara and Shaw in this volume).

[2] A similar trend has been noted for France. See Anne Boigeol's contribution to this volume.

Vertical segregation also exists within the Bar. In 1992, women made up less than 28 per cent in law firms with less than five employees, no more than 20 per cent in firms with 10 or more employees, and only a tiny minority of partners in large law firms.

Disproportionate under-representation of women jurists at higher levels of the profession is apparent in the composition of editorial boards and important legal committees. Thus, of the nine members of the executive board of the *Nederlandse Vereniging voor Rechtspraak* (Dutch Association for the Administration of Law) in 1996 only two were female. In the same year the editorial staff of the *Tijdschrift voor de Rechterlijke Macht* (Journal for the Judiciary) was made up of six men and two women. Of the nine members of the *Algemene Raad van de Nederlandse Orde van Advocaten* (Dutch National Bar) none was female in 1964, one in 1969, none in 1974, two in 1979, and one in 1995. Finally, the *Nederlands Juristenblad NJB* (Dutch Lawyer's Journal) has seven editors one of whom is female, while the *Weekblad voor Privaatrecht, Notariaat en Registratie* (weekly magazine on private law, notaryship and registration) has an all-male editorial board. It may not come entirely as a surprise that vertical segregation in the Dutch legal professions is part of a wider Dutch phenomenon. In a 1999 study of Eurostat, the Netherlands ranked near the bottom in a list of European countries in terms of the percentage of women in leading positions.

3 WHAT LINKS BETWEEN GENDER AND PROFESSIONAL ATTITUDES/PRACTICE?

Given the increasing participation of women in the legal professions the question arises whether will make a difference to these professions' performance. Four aspects are of particular interest.

3.1 Academic Achievement

'Women perform better', read the headline of an article in the Dutch *Sun* (1996) on the performance of women in education, stating, inter alia, that in the Netherlands girls achieve better academic results than boys both at secondary school and at university (Bakker 1996). A similar picture emerges with reference to the selection of trainee judges, which is based in particular on a psychological test. During the period from 1986 up to and including 1995 women consistently performed better than men, that is the percentage of women selected was disproportionately high in relation to the number of female candidates. Thus in 1986, 39 per cent of the total number of candidates, but 53 per cent of those selected were female.

There is no known answer to the question whether men and women differ in the quality of their judicial work. Malsch (1989) did, however, investigate the ability of male and female lawyers to predict judicial decisions in criminal law cases. She presented judges with criminal cases, asked them to predict the final outcome and assessed the predictions with a view to accuracy. Both men and women initially underestimated the severity of the verdict, but women proved slightly more realistic than men. This difference in realism increased when candidates were confronted with their incorrect predictions and were then presented with a new case. Women, so it appeared, were more inclined to learn from their mistakes, as their predictions now matched the final outcome much more closely than those of their male colleagues.

3.2 Career Ambitions

A survey among female junior notaries who had completed their traineeships eight or more years previously showed that more than half of the 30 respondents did indeed have the ambition to become fully-fledged notaries (Van Velzen and van Berge *et al* 1997). As this survey did not include men, no direct comparison is possible. What it does show, however, is that women notaries do have career ambitions.

In 1991, 130 members of the judiciary were interviewed, inter alia, on career expectations and ambitions (De Groot-van Leeuwen, 1991). Both women and men normally mentioned the next-highest level as their next career target. While men often made mention of even higher levels, such as membership of the Supreme Court, women only referred to such positions as examples of what they were not aiming to achieve. Furthermore, it appeared that for men promotion was much more a matter of course than for women. Both sexes mentioned family responsibilities in connection with career ambitions. But while men gave this as a reason for their desire to get promoted, women saw it as an argument in favour of not wanting promotion. For men, family responsibilities meant being the bread-winner, whereas for women it meant day-to-day care of the family. This tallies with results of studies of other professional groups. Thus research amongst academics on how they weighted factors determining their choice of career found that women's and men's answers diverged most strongly as regards the degree of importance attributed to financial rewards (Noordenbos 1989).

3.3 Reasons for Choice of Career and Legal Specialism

Male and female trainee judges, so it appears, choose their career for different reasons (De Groot-van Leeuwen *et al* 1996). In 1996, of the 170 trainee judges two thirds of the women amongst them opted for the judiciary because of its closeness to justice, whereas less than half of their male colleagues even mentioned this as a motive. What often mattered more to men than to women were challenge and variety. Flexible working hours and part-time employment were only listed by women.

A related issue is the choice of legal specialism, where there is some evidence of gender-based horizontal segregation. While women's participation in the two branches of the judiciary, ie judges and public prosecutors, reflects broadly equal participation (Table 1), gender does seem to make a difference to practising lawyers' choice of specialism. Significant differences have been shown to exist between female and male legal aid lawyers, with, for example, proportionately more women specialising in family law and more men than women in tax law (De Groot-Van Leeuwen *et al* 1996).

However, the mere fact that women lawyers tend to work in specific branches of the law does not necessarily imply that this is also where they would go if they could follow their own preferences. Although such preferences are, unfortunately, not known for the Bar, yearly surveys among members of the judiciary show that preferences for a specific area of law are not gender-linked to any significant degree (Josten and Van Tijn 1991) (Table 3).

Table 3: Preference for a specific area of law amongst judges and public prosecutors

	Women	Men
Total number questioned	328	673
Preferences amongst these	%	%
Criminal law	29	32
Civil law	43	41
Administrative law	15	16
Criminal and administrative law	0	1
Criminal and civil law	9	5
Civil and administrative law	2	2
No answer	2	3

3.4 Attitudes Towards Clients

When it became clear that women were about to break men's domination of the legal profession, many journalists, politicians and social scientists voiced fears that the quality of judicial work might suffer. For instance, women generally were supposed to be more reluctant to mete out punishment, except in the case of sexual crimes. But not only is there the question why this should present a problem, there is also a lack of evidence to support the claim. All we know is that penal sentences generally tended to become more severe in the Netherlands during the 1980s. For Germany, Drewniak (1991) has supplied data to show that there is nothing to warrant the assumption that men and women differ in their sentencing practices (Schultz 1990).

On the other hand, there is indeed evidence to show that there are gender-based differences in lawyers' attitudes towards clients. This was shown by a study on the number and the nature of complaints about attorneys brought before the disciplinary committees of the Bar in the Netherlands (Doornbos and De Groot-van Leeuwen 1997). The average frequency of male attorneys having to explain themselves before the committees was two and a half times higher than that for women. Moreover, sanctions of the committees were lighter for female attorneys. Interestingly, the nature of the complaints also differed; complaints about female lawyers more often concerned a lack of professionalism, while complaints about men were more likely to relate to their acting without clients' consent.

3.5 Patterns of Moral Reasoning

In the context of recent research on the ethics of attorneys (De Groot-van Leeuwen 1997, 1998) interviewees were presented with a number of pre-formulated ('hypothetical') cases and asked for their responses. One of these hypothetical cases was taken from Jack and Jack (1989). It concerns divorce proceedings and associated custody issues. The case was worded as follows:

> Supposing you are an attorney in a divorce proceeding and your client seeks custody of the two children of the marriage. In the course of your representation your client passes to you a bundle of documents that inadvertently contains a letter bearing on the fitness of your client to have custody of the children. The information in the letter is not known to anyone else and is not likely to become known to the other side. Without disclosure of the letter you believe your client will win the custody battle; you are equally confident that the other party will prevail if the content of the letter is revealed. In your own mind the information clearly makes your client a marginal parent and the other party a far superior parent.

Responses to this dilemma may be classified by reference to the concepts of 'ethics of rights' and 'ethics of care', the former being associated more strongly with men, the latter with women (Gilligan 1981; Gilligan 1982; Davis 1991). The choice to defend the client without any moral hesitations may be seen as matching the ethics of rights in its extreme, while a decision to deny one's client custody in order to do the best by the children may be regarded as an extreme application of the ethics of care. In my own sample of interviewees I found no marked differences in the responses of men and women respectively. Representatives of both sexes were more or less evenly divided between the two camps.

As a part of a course I taught at Utrecht University, five students were asked to include similar questions in a questionnaire to be filled in by 30 fellow students. Respondents had entered university between 1990 and 1995, their ages ranged between 19 and 26. Compared to the lawyers previously interviewed these students' choices veered much more towards giving priority to the protection of the children. Often the ethics of care perspective was articulated very clearly. A typical response was:

> I would never want to be instrumental in giving custody to a bad parent, even if that person were my client. . . . The crucial issue is to make sure that the children grow up in the best possible home.

Only six of the 30 students felt that priority should be given to their client. Responses included: 'I would continue backing my client. He hires me and trusts me to look after his interests. If you choose this profession, then you must do your best for your client.'

Another difference between the answers of students and practising lawyers concerned the action they planned to take to protect the children. Whereas the lawyers interviewed would have gone to great length to avoid disclosing the letter, 19 out of the 30 students declared that they would reveal the content of the letter without the slightest hesitation. Two of them added: 'I do ask myself whether a good lawyer should do this. But that is precisely the reason why I do not want to become an attorney.'

As was the case for practising lawyers, no marked difference was found between male and female respondents' answers. This led me to conclude that respondents' choices were determined more by professional formation than by gender.

4 CONCLUSIONS

Regarding female participation in the legal professions, the above allows us to draw four conclusions relating to women jurists in the Netherlands: (1) women are still a minority in the classical legal professions, but the situation is changing rapidly; (2) increased participation rates of women have not had any adverse effect on the prestige of the professions concerned; (3) female lawyers tend to work in areas of law that are different from those mainly occupied by their male colleagues; (4) women are under-represented at the higher echelons of the legal professions as well as tending to take longer to climb the career ladder.

In terms of any possible differences in the professional conduct of men and women jurists, studies carried out in the Netherlands have identified three areas where such differences have been found to exist: (1) female jurists are better at predicting court judgments; (2) women's ambitions overlap but do not wholly coincide with those of men; (3) fewer complaints are made by clients about female lawyers than about male lawyers. On the other hand, there were two areas where no significant differences could be found, ie neither women's preferences regarding legal specialisation nor their moral reasoning seemed to differ significantly from that of men.

Where differences have been found to exist, they are difficult to interpret, as cause and effect are not easily disentangled. For example, is the slightly slower career pace of women the effect of a tendency to be slightly less career-minded, or have women become less career-minded as a result of the lower career pace still determined by a culture of male domination? Furthermore, survey results may be affected by respondents having internalised ideologically determined roles for men and women in society. For example, when male trainee judges say more often than their female colleagues that they are attracted by the variety and the challenge of judicial work, while more female trainees than men claim that the appeal for them lies in working close to the locus of the dispensation of justice, this tallies with society's traditional expectations regarding the gender-based roles of men and women.

How do these findings relate to traditional views about the nature of the sexes in relation to each other, that is, the two main schools of thought of (1) the essential equality, and (2) the fundamental difference of the two sexes? Both views have profoundly informed the debate about the place of women within the judicial professions. Drabbe (1963: 533) claimed 'intellectual equality between men and women', but assumed it to be coupled with a 'different nature', the latter resulting in 'a different attitude to the same (ie judicial) work'. The author then goes on to distinguish between five opposing attributes in men and women, all of them said to affect their judicial work. According to Drabbe, men are more conventional, abstract, rational and active/decisive; women on the contrary are likely to be unconventional, concrete, intuitive and passive/hesitant. In more recent discussions, the view of women's essential difference has also been heard, as in the words of a judge who in 1986 wrote in a newspaper, 'It doesn't bear thinking about that there are only women sitting at that table. Not because they are better or worse, but because they are different'.

In a survey conducted in 1991 among members of the Dutch judiciary, supporters of the difference principle and those of the equality principle were both represented, but the latter by far outnumbered the former. Of those questioned, 12 per cent agreed with the idea that female members of the judiciary treated family matters differently, whilst 54 per cent did not agree. While 11 per cent were of the opinion that female members of the judiciary have a different approach to criminal trials, 63 per cent disagreed (Josten and Van Tijn 1991).

The data on the difference issue presented in this chapter, all of them collected from among 'mixed groups', do not lend support to the view that differences between men and women (which doubtlessly exist) significantly affect jurists' professional attitudes and work. This would suggest that the rise of female participation in the legal professions is not likely to result in significant changes in the professions' performance.[3]

---

[3] Other contributors to this volume have addressed this issue in a variety of different national contexts. See Bryna Bogoch (Israel), Eliane Botelho Junqueira (Brazil), Ulrike Schultz ('Women Lawyers in Germany: Perception and Construction of Feminity') and Malgorzata Fuszara (Poland).

5 REFERENCES

Bakker, Paulien. 1996. Vrouwen doen het beter, *Sun*, June: 38–40.

Davis, Katy. 1991. De rhetorica van het feminisme. Het Gilligan-debat opnieuw bekeken. *Amsterdams Sociologisch Tijdschrift* 4: 86–110.

Doornbos, Nienke and Leny E de Groot-van Leeuwen. 1997. *Klachten op Orde; de behandeling van klachten over advocaten.* Deventer: Kluwer.

Drabbe, LWMM. 1963. De vrouw in de rechterlijke macht. *Rechtsgeleerd magazijn Themis*: 532–548.

Drewniak, Regine. 1991. Sind Frauen die besseren Richter? *Kriminologisches Journal* 23, no 2. 112.

Eurostat. 1999. *NRC Handelsblad*, 3 July.

Fuchs Epstein, Cynthia 1983. *Women in Law.* New York: Ancor Press. Original edition, 1981.

Gilligan, Carol. 1981. In a Different Voice: Women's Conception of the Self and Morality. *Harvard Educational Review* 47: 481–517.

Gilligan, Carol. 1982. *In A Different Voice: Psychological Theory and Women's Development*, Harvard University Press.

Goede, de M and R Hoksbergen. 1975. Haalt de vrouw haar onderwijsachterstand in? *Intermediair* 30, 25 July: 15–23.

Groenendijk, Kees. 1975. De rechterlijke macht in Nederland; tussen balie en bureaucratie. *Beleid en Maatschappij* 6: 151–165.

Groot-van Leeuwen, Leny E de. 1991. *De rechterlijke macht in Nederland; samenstelling en opvattingen van de zittende en staande magistratuur.* Arnhem: Gouda Quint.

Groot-van Leeuwen, Leny E de, Sietske U van Rossum and Kees JM Schuyt. 1996. De aanloop tot de rechterlijke macht; verslag van een enquete onder raio's. *Trema*, no 5a, pp 107–124.

Groot-van Leeuwen, Leny E de. 1997a. De feminisering van de juridische beroepen; een overzicht van onderzoeksresultaten. *Justitiële Verkenningen* 9: 103–114.

Groot-van Leeuwen, Leny E de. 1997b. Polishing the Bar: the Legal Ethics Code and Disciplinary System of the Netherlands, and a Comparison with the United States, *The International Journal of the Legal Profession* 4: 9–23.

Groot-van Leeuwen, Leny E de. 1998. Lawyers' Moral Reasoning and Professional Conduct, in Practice and in Education. In *Ethical Challenges to Legal Education & Conduct*, edited by Kim Economides. Oxford: Hart Publishing.

Hage, Gert. 1990. Vrouwe Justitia. *Intermediair.* 11 mei.

Jaarboek Emancipatie. 1997. *Arbeid en Zorg.* 's-Gravenhage: Vuga.

Jack, Rand and Dana Crowley Jack. 1989. *Moral Vision and Professional Decisions. The Changing Values of Women and Men Lawyers.* Cambridge, Cambridge University Press.

Josten, Marc & Joop van Tijn 1991. De rechterlijke macht van Nederland; hoeders van recht en orde. *Vrij Nederland* 44, 2 November: 18–53.

Karpik, Lucien. 1999. *French Lawyers. A Study in Collective Action 1274–1994.* Translated by Nora Scott. Oxford: Clarendon Press.

Kester, John and Frits WM Huls. 1992. Veertig jaar advocatuur; veranderingen in de beroepsgroep, de bedrijfstak en de dienstverlening, 1952–1992. *CBS Kwartaalberichten rechtsbescherming en veiligheid* 5: 18–42.

Klijn, Albert. 1997. De notaris als rechtshulpverlener? *Justitiële Verkenningen* 2: 119–126.

Leeuwen, Silvia van, Albert Klijn and Gerard Paulides. 1996. *De toegevoegde kwaliteit, Een ex ante evaluatie van de werking van inschrijfvoorwaarden in de Wet op de Rechtsbijstand*, Arnhem: Gouda Quint.

Malsch, Marijke. 1989. *Lawyers' Predictions of Judicial Decisions; a Study on Calibration of Experts*. Leiden.

Menkel-Meadow, Carrie. 1995. Feminization of the Legal Profession: the Comparative Sociology of Women Lawyers. In *Lawyers in Society: an Overview*, edited by Richard L Abel and Philip SC Lewis. Original Edition, 1988–89. 221–280.

Molenaar. B. 1990. *Rechters de opkomst van de zwarte macht*. Bloemendaal: Aramith.

Noordenbos, Greta. 1989. *Are Careers of Women Academics Comparable?* Paper presented at the fourth Congress of the Society for Social Studies of Sciences, Irvine.

Roos, NHM. 1981. *Juristerij in Nederland; sociale ontwikkelingen in de opleiding en de beroepen van juristen*. Deventer: Kluwer.

Sabbe, Hilde and Luc Huyse. 1997. *De mensen van het recht*. Leuven: Halewyck.

Schultz, Ulrike. 1990. Wie männlich is die Juristenschaft? In *Frauen im Recht*, edited by Ulrich Battis and Ulrike Schultz, Heidelberg: CF Müller.

Sixma, Herman R and Wout C Ultee. 1983. Een berepsprestigeschaal voor Nederland in de jaren tachtig. *Mens en Maatschappij*: 360–382.

Sloot, Ben P. 1980. Officiële uitsluiting van vrouwen in juridische beroepen, *Nederlands Juristen Blad (NJB)* 45/46: 1186–1195.

Soulez Larivière, Daniel. 1987. *Les juges dans la balance*, Paris: Ramsey.

Swaab, Els. 1990. Vrouw in de maatschap. *Advocatenblad*, 15: 393–396.

Tazelaar, Frits. 1980. *Het beroepsprestige van 'hogere' beroepen en funkties in Nederland*. Utrecht: Rijksuniversiteit.

Van Velzen, CM and AA van Berge *et al* 1997. De vrouw als (kandidaat-)notaris, vroeger en nu. *WPNR (Weekblad voor Privaatrecht Notariaat en Registratie)* 6252: 25–30.

VSNU (Vereninging van Samenwerkende Nederlandse Universiteiten). 1997. *Onderwijsvisitatie Rechtsgeleerdheid*. 's-Gravenhage.

19

Choices in Context: Life Histories of Women Lawyers in the Netherlands

HELEEN FP IETSWAART

Abstract

This paper, embedded in the theoretical framework of career theory, presents qualitative empirical data gathered in the course of interviews with women lawyers in an attempt to find some answer to the question why women have still remained largely at the lower end or the margins of the legal career hierarchy. The life stories of these women, most of whom graduated in the late 1960s and early 1970s and became wives and mothers, allow us to glean a whole range of reasons that can bring about discontinuities in a woman's professional life, and even resignation and an end to her career. They also show the achievements, however limited these may seem in retrospect, of a group of women lawyers who were pioneers in their time.

1 INTRODUCTION

THIS PAPER SETS out to offer an explanation for the marginal position of women in the Dutch legal professions by looking at women lawyers' life histories.[1] The latter have proved to be a useful tool to a better understanding of the relative integration of women in the profession on the one hand, and of the stagnation of their actual impact on the profession on the other.

Careers may be described in terms of opportunities and choices. Both may simply present themselves, but may also be created by hard work, ingenuity and resorting to the help of others. Choices may be seen as individual, but they are always made in social contexts. These contexts may impose severe limitations on a person's chances of taking advantage of opportunities, of the availability of choices. The acceptance and rejection of choices is deeply gendered. It is in this sense that the life histories I collected can increase our understanding of the current role and place of women in the legal professions in the Netherlands.

---

[1] This chapter is based on several papers I prepared for conferences in recent years. Some of these contain more specific quantitative data (Ietswaart 1992, 1995a, 1995b, 1996). For statistical data relating to women in the Dutch legal professions see the contribution to this volume by Leny E de Groot-van Leeuwen.

2 WHERE ARE THE WOMEN LAWYERS?

For over 10 years now I have been wondering what happened to the capable women lawyers who, for many years, could (and should) have been in leading social positions in the Netherlands. After having spent 20 years abroad, I returned to Holland in 1989. I had been appointed as a full professor at the law faculty of the Erasmus University in Rotterdam. I soon discovered that, incredibly, I was the only full-time woman professor.[2] I asked the Vice-Chancellor whether the University had a positive action policy, and he answered, no, it had not, but he was very pleased I was a woman.

I looked around and found, for example, that there was no woman president of a district court at the time. The first woman was appointed to that position as late as 1991, followed by a second a few years later. As the first retired, there remained one, the equivalent of less than five per cent of the 19 district court presidents in the Netherlands. Upon further inquiry, I realised that women were generally under-represented in managerial and decision-making positions in all professional fields.

There were a number of questions I wanted to find answers to. Why was the first generation of women with access to higher education so little in evidence in public life? Why were women lawyers 25 to 30 years after graduating from law school participating so marginally in the decision-making processes on issues concerning not just the present but also the future of their society: in courts, in law practices, in law schools, in corporations, in government? Why the marginality in the public domain of intelligent women with a fair amount of professional experience, why the loss of professional talent, why the lack of input from women in shaping policy decisions affecting the world our children will live in?

The legal profession in the Netherlands is characterised by persistent segregation based on gender. (Sloot 1980; Schuyt 1988) About 30 per cent of all practising lawyers are women. The younger the generation, the higher the proportion of women amongst it. Few women, however, are partners in the larger, more established law firms. Many more women than men opt for being their own boss in a small law firm or as a sole practitioner. About 30 per cent of all in-house lawyers in banks and large companies are women. Among judges and prosecutors, the number of women is growing fastest. In recent cohorts of newly appointed judges, just over 50 per cent are women, while out of the total of approximately 1,500 judges about 28 per cent are women. As already mentioned, just one of the presidents of the 19 district courts is a woman, but none of the presidents of the courts of appeal are. As regards law teachers, only 5 per cent of the full professors in law schools and 7 per cent of associate professors are women.[3]

---

[2] There was one other professor, a Turkish woman, who had a part-time appointment, had her base in Scotland, and only flew in every once in a while.

[3] For further statistical data see Leny de Groot-van Leeuwen on 'Women in the Dutch Legal Profession (1950–2000)' in this volume.

3 ALTERNATIVES: WOMEN'S LIFE HISTORIES AND NEW PERSPECTIVES ON
CAREER THEORY

For my research, I have looked for inspiration to career theory. Judi Marshall
was among the first to emphasise two important facts: firstly, that the way in
which careers were normally conceptualised fitted the dominant life pattern of
men rather than women; secondly, that equally research on careers was almost
entirely focused on men. In her own work she shifted the emphasis to an investigation into the significance of careers for women as well as the nature of such
careers. (Marshall 1984, 1989, 1995).

A career, or rather the possibility of career development, is one aspect of the
position a person occupies in the labour market. A career may be defined as a
process of advancement on a professional path, frequently associated with
'progress' and 'success', with linear occupational advancement. A career is said
to be successful, if at more or less regular intervals desirable elements are added
to the individual's professional achievements, ie desirable in terms of traditional
career development. These desirable elements include money, status and prestige, power over people and resources (money), job offers in larger or more
important companies or professional environments. However, access to careers
is not available to women to the same extent as it is to men. Not only are women
less likely to have jobs offering the opportunity to develop a career in a traditional sense, they are also unlikely to have the same type of career as men within
specific sectors of the labour market, such as the legal field, where both sexes can
be expected to hold more or less identical qualifications.

Among scholars interested in women's careers, there is a growing awareness
that traditional career theory is not very helpful to them, as dominant notions such
as those of career and career development are based on descriptions of the careers,
experiences, ambitions, expectations and life choices of men (Diamond 1987). It is
true that until not so long ago relatively few women were present in professional
environments where issues of career and career planning were of relevance, thus
making it difficult to be aware of, let alone analyse, the gendered nature of descriptive and theoretical work on careers. Gutek and Larwood (1987: 8) write:

> Conveniently, employers offered women jobs that were easy to enter and that required
> relatively little training and afforded little potential for advancement. Thus there was
> little reason to study the career development of women. It was easily summarized:
> There was none.

It is also true that most male researchers were not interested in the question of
the cross-gender validity of their concepts and theories, having their intellectual
base in what I call the Kohlberg tradition, where men are implicitly the measure
of all evaluation and judgement. It was Kohlberg who wrote a number of influential books and articles on the development of moral judgement. The empirical base of his research and conclusions consisted exclusively of interviews and

experiments with (young) males (Kohlberg 1958, 1973). Carol Gilligan exposed this male biased method, and wrote her (later controversial) counter-analysis of moral development among youngsters (Gilligan 1982). She showed that all too frequently the mental and moral development of *men*, as well as their aspirations and ideas, are regarded as the norm, and any deviations from this norm are either ignored or defined as deficient, less developed and of lesser value.

When it comes to careers, we see that occasionally women's careers have also been studied, but mostly only to see in what ways they depart from the male standard (Gutek and Larwood 1987: 9). Not only has male behaviour in relation to professional choices and career planning been the basis of much existing career theory, male behaviour patterns and the value placed on them have also become the social norm at large. A 'real' career, 'real' commitment to professional work needs to be expressed in the male-type dominance of work over personal identity. Many women have internalised this norm as part of their strategy for professional survival. A woman who displays a different style in pursuing professional interests is easily considered deviant. And deviance has its price. Many researchers conclude that women are 'less motivated' and therefore ill-placed seriously to 'pursue careers' (Roberts and Newton 1986).

Alternative approaches to career theory are now being explored, as there is increasing empirical evidence (albeit limited as yet in volume) that women behave differently from men when taking decisions about their careers (Hennig and Jardim 1978; Abramson and Franklin 1986; Roberts and Newton 1986) and that existing theory is not sufficient to account for this.

Gallos (1989: 125) writes:

> Even in the infant stages of our exploration of women's development and lives, consistent messages about women and careers surface again and again. Women's dreams, in the Levinson (1978) sense, are more complex and compounded than the traditionally work-focused dreams of men. . . . Women have . . . images of work and relationships that create a preferred lifestyle rather than the concrete plans to play out a particular occupational role that Levinson (1978), Vaillant (1977) and others report about the men in their studies.

There is growing awareness that women's behaviour need not be thought of as an exception to the male norm but may be studied and appreciated in its own right. Recent literature has emphasised that women bring a different vision of reality to the world of paid work and career. Women's lives and their life choices are more complex than those of men. Many women face a different set of opportunities and a more compounded set of choices and problems than most men (Gallos 1989: 127; Marshall 1995). Women's lives are cyclical in nature, whereas men's lives tend to be more linear. Women tend to care about very different things besides professional work, all of which demand time and affection—intimate relationships, children, social life and friendships. They tend to attribute greater value to these factors and will sometimes, though not always, allow them to exercise a crucial influence on their life choices.

The question arises whether it is possible and/or useful to expand existing theory to accommodate the empirical data from studies on women's careers, or whether it is, at least temporarily, necessary to develop a separate theory on the careers of women. It is part of our socialisation to think of the social world as one. Although it comprises both 'men' and 'women', we have come to accept the view that men and women and their respective worlds are better understood if not regarded as separate (and not equal); that the best theory is the one that explains most, that is, the theory that best accommodates *all* phenomena of a particular type, such as for instance people's careers. However, we must ask ourselves whether the phenomena we are dealing with, that is careers and career development of men and women, are sufficiently comparable to be captured by one overarching theory.

4 LIFE HISTORIES OF WOMEN LAWYERS IN THE NETHERLANDS

My own research on women lawyers in the Netherlands focuses on the choices these professional women have made over a period of 25 years or more (sometimes less) in regard to their work: decisions to accept or refuse a job, to work part-time, to follow a male partner to another city, to take a career break in order to look after small children etc. I seek the answer (or answers) by means of an analysis of their life histories. I ask them for information about their professional choices, also in relation to other aspects of their lives, and about their reasons for these. I have, by now, collected a number of topical life histories of women,[4] which are fascinating in their diversity, richness and unexpectedness. They have also shown up the simplistic nature of my original approach, which was implicitly inspired by the notion of success in a traditional sense: why had women by and large remained at the margins, why had they not been more 'successful' in the male world they had been (officially) allowed to enter? The very terminology used in this question is rooted in traditional male ideas about paid work, career development, the importance of a social identity through paid work and the social rewards of a career. My own data clearly show the richness and complexity of women's lives and the intricacies of their decision-making regarding labour market participation and careers. In what follows I shall highlight a few of the patterns that have emerged.

4.1 The Pioneer Generation

As it turned out, I interviewed a generation of pioneers. I conducted open interviews with about 30 women, who told me their life stories in which options and

---

[4] The great value of the analysis of life histories as a method of research has been argued by Thompson (1981) and Berteaux (1981). A sub-dominant group of sociologists has been using the method for many years now.

choices, obstacles and professional advancement had a central place. These women worked or had worked in the different legal sectors—private legal practice, the judiciary, legal services, company legal departments. Many of them had graduated about 20 to 25 years earlier, but some were younger, thus allowing for a developmental dimension.

Virtually all the women who graduated in the late 1960s and early 1970s told me that they were the first of their kind in whatever they did. One woman had been the first married trainee in the judiciary (in 1971), several women had been the first woman lawyer in the town where they settled, many had been the first married woman lawyer in their firm. These women had ventured into new territory, they were frontier women, whether they were part of the women's liberation movement or not (most of them definitely were not, in an institutional sense). For one thing, they wanted to combine being a lawyer with having a family. For another, they wanted to be taken seriously as professionals. They had gone where no women in the Netherlands had gone before.

But these women were confronted with the fact that the new space they entered was only 'new' to them and was already occupied by others. As Rosemary Coombe states, 'We are always in spaces occupied by others, and by the historical specificities of their ways of being in the world' (Coombe 1995: 602). When women enter a profession, no new extra space is being created for them, nor is part of the territory left exclusively to them—they have to compete within the existing space. In particular, they encounter and have to fit into existing hierarchies, power structures and cultures.

> Dora graduated from law school in 1967. She wanted to be a commercial lawyer and was accepted as an apprentice in a large law firm in a major Dutch city. She was single at the time, and she worked very hard. In those years, her law firm would hire very few female law graduates, and Dora wanted to take full advantage of having this opportunity. She did well and liked the work. There were possibilities for her to become a partner at a later stage. Then she got married and wanted children. She quit her job, without even requesting part-time employment or some other way of continued activity in the legal practice while having a family. She was absolutely convinced it was impossible to combine working as a legal practitioner with family duties. So she became a judge. When her first baby was born, she started employing baby-sitters and housekeepers on a full-time basis, and she herself continued to work full-time. She would accept all assignments, including those which frequently took her out of town, and would hold hearings in distant places without ever allowing herself to voice any reservations because of family commitments. She has three children, and a self-employed, hard-working husband. She never really contemplated working part-time, because 'if you want to be somebody in your profession, you must work full-time'.

Dora anticipated hostile reactions in the law firm to her plans to have a family and adapted to the prevalent culture. Her presence in the law firm was only 'new' in that she worked in commercial law, with an emphasis on finance. For the rest, she was the 'normal' single woman lawyer whose presence was tolerated—as long as she was single.

4.2 Discrimination

How right Dora was to view as incompatible professional life as a practising lawyer in a large law firm with having a family, is shown by Saskia's story.

> I was a good student, I was a teaching assistant, and I graduated with honours. In 1970 I entered a small law firm in one of the major cities. I had got married shortly after I graduated from law school. For several years, I worked hard, including most Saturdays. I did my three-year apprenticeship with good results. As the firm was small, and we were a fine team, it was logical that I would become a partner in due time. I loved the work and I was good at it, I won prizes. My billable hours were in line with what my colleagues did, I had a good reputation among the clients.
>
> Then I got pregnant. I saw no problem, my husband said that he would love to care for the baby and the household, there was no practical problem. And I could work a little less. Shortly after I told people I was pregnant, the trouble began. All sorts of critical comments came my way. My billable hours were said to be below standard. As I had never bothered to keep track of them carefully, I could not prove the opposite, but then, why should I have to prove it? They said, there were complaints from clients that some files had been neglected, forgotten even. Nobody had ever told me that before, so how could it suddenly become an issue? Then I was told, it was unfortunate that I had not attracted a lot of new clients. I was shocked.
>
> A little later I was invited for lunch. It appeared there were three partners to talk to me. They made it clear they wanted me to resign, they would give me six months to find other work. They could not take the risk that it would not work out, a lawyer should be fully available, at odd hours sometimes, his full attention should be devoted to his work. I was flabbergasted, how could this happen to me, what had I done wrong? I did not have a lot to say. I had sort of a breakdown, but of course later on I found another job. But I have always resented that they took away from me the work I loved. I had to start my career all over again.

The same nonsensical arguments are still used today in law firms against young, pregnant women. In 1996, I interviewed a young woman who had just passed the bar exam (after the three-year apprenticeship in a small law firm). She, and indeed her elder sisters, had been fired the moment they made their pregnancy known. The same classic 'arguments' about the 24-hour availability for clients and the limitations that babies impose had been used on her. The strategies for making women lawyers resign, quietly, without any publicity, have remained the same over at least 30 years. And it seems they work. It is well known that victims of discrimination tend to blame themselves in the first instance for acts of discrimination. Women who experience the sort of discriminatory dismissal described above do not make a fuss, as they are convinced this will harm their career even more. They do not file lawsuits, they do not like to talk about these things. There is hardly any case law about it.

Another woman described how she was discriminated at the very outset of her professional life, as she applied for a job in one the most prestigious law firms at the time:

I was one of the best students in my class. I applied for a position at firm X because it was a high quality firm, it was known you got an excellent apprenticeship there, and it was not far from where my husband and I settled. There was a long selection process, and in the end two candidates remained, a young man and me. Although his CV was no better than mine, he got the job and I did not. I was told they had given preference to the man because they thought I was going to have a family, maybe not quite soon, but in due course, and a lot of productivity would be lost then after the investment made in me. As it happened, I worked nine years before I had kids, and the guy who got the job had an accident shortly after, was unfit for work on and off for a number of years, and ended up on disability. They never take into account that sort of risk, but the 'risk' of pregnancy and motherhood always looms large.

Discrimination in hiring, promotion etc. account for a fair share of the discrepancies found between legal careers of men and women. In the Netherlands, no specific study of legal professionals has been done to document gender discrimination, but it is clear that the relatively marginal position of women lawyers continues (Klijn 1981; Klijn *et al* 1992; De Groot-van Leeuwen, in this volume); and studies on other economic sectors document discrimination related to gender and motherhood (Veltman and Wittink 1990). Also, the cases brought before the Equal Rights Commission are largely about gender, and they are quite a few each year. However, not enough is known about the actual scope of this phenomenon, in pure quantitative terms.

4.3 Part-time Work: Progress and Obstacles

In the Netherlands, over 50 per cent of women in gainful employment work part-time. For women with a higher education, such as lawyers, the figure is slightly lower. The most important step forward that the pioneering generation helped to bring about was the opportunity of working part-time. At the same time, part-time work turned out to be one of the great obstacles to career advancement. This paradox is interesting. On the one hand, working part-time was, and is, precisely what many women want, so as to be able to combine a number of highly valued activities in life: having a profession, caring for children, spending time with the older generation, having a social life. And many women got what they wanted in that respect. Compared to the alternative of not being able to work professionally at all, it was progress. On the other hand, part-timers are excluded from upward mobility. Typically they have horizontal job patterns, that is, they either stay in the same job or move to different jobs of the same type, without improvement in salary or status. Until 1990, nobody working part-time could advance within the hierarchy of the judiciary and, in addition, there were fewer options in choosing a workplace, as one of my respondents explained to me. Yvonne graduated in 1980, her husband is a medical specialist.

At first, before I had children, I worked full-time in a legal aid office. I worked very hard, but I did not mind: we were very idealistic at the time, you know. After a number of years I had my first baby. I requested to work half-time, but my request was rejected. With one of my colleagues, I struggled for a half-time contract, but without success. All the other women in the office, mostly still without children, disagreed with me—they conformed to the (still) dominant view that 'it is impossible to work part-time in a legal practice', where clients 'have to be able to count on you day and night'. So I had to leave, very much against my will. I was offered a flexible contract, as a stand-by lawyer who would work when my colleagues were ill, absent etc. I am still bitter about this, because this was precisely the sort of 'contract' my colleagues and I were fighting in the context of private enterprises. Nevertheless, I did the part-time work for a while, but after a couple of years the problems with childcare became so complex, that I quit work altogether.

After recovering from this period full of stress and frustration, Yvonne took a job as a part-time teacher at a vocational school for social workers. That is where she still is.

Judy, by contrast, had things the way she wanted them most of the time.

After graduation in 1971, I did my apprenticeship in a nice small law firm. We did not have children very soon, I got a solid place in the firm before that. I had profit-sharing, but wasn't a partner. When my first child was born, they begged me to come back as soon as I could, on whatever conditions. From then on, I have worked three days a week. When the kids were in school full-time, I started putting in some work on my days off, if necessary. I very much like the balance I have now. As I do not work full-time, I have some spare time, for emergencies.

However, part-time employment in professional environments continues to be considered as being of secondary status. Judy never became a partner in her firm. Many men and women have heard comments like these from their superiors: 'If you really do that, your chances for advancement will be seriously reduced. You know that management functions cannot be entrusted to part-timers.' In constructing social hierarchies, part-time work is contrasted with full-time work. Working part-time is considered as an expression of limited commitment to a 'real' career, that is, if the time not spent on 'professional' work is spent on running a home with children. (Obviously, if the time is spent on part-time teaching at a university, there are no such adverse comments on 'commitment'). The sort of learning, the sort of experience one gets from care activities simply do not count as 'investment' in one's development and skills that can be recognised as valuable in a career.

4.4 Discontinuity

Women's professional lives show less linearity and more discontinuities than men's (Vogels 1995). Discontinuities come in different forms. Firstly, many women have at some point in their lives given up their job altogether by simply resigning—a highly unusual pattern of behaviour among men. Women resign from their jobs when several problems come together at one point in time. Typically, these include health problems, extreme fatigue as a result of the combination of paid work and the care for young children, the breakdown of childcare arrangements, illness of parents or parents-in-law.

> In the early 1970's I worked in the City, whereas we lived in Watertown, where my husband was a doctor in a hospital. I had to commute. When we did not have children, there was no problem. Later, I had lots of problems with childcare. Somehow it was always a mess. Either suddenly the child minder would not show up without notice, or she would unexpectedly leave after a couple of months, or she was off ill. I had asked to work part-time but my boss would not allow that. It was a drag. Sometimes my sister would help me out. Then my mother-in-law got very ill, we had to visit a lot, and take care of my father-in-law. I say we, but it was me who did it. I got very tired and upset by all that. And then the child minder quit. I just could not face the whole problem of looking for another one again, placing an ad, interviewing, selecting, explaining the domestic routine again. I just couldn't. And I resigned, almost without notice. I resolved the problem that way.

In the short run, the result of resigning is the loss of a place in the professional world and regressing in terms of career. But, as Glebbeek (1993) points out, much depends on what women do in the interim while not having a paid job. He compares the careers of women who continued professional employment all along, full-time or part-time (the 'stay-in-the-market' model) with those of women who had given up paid work while having young children (the 'quit' model). In addition, he compares within this latter group of women the achievements and satisfaction of those who invested in education and training while not having paid work, with those who had not done so. He concludes that staying in the labour market is not necessarily the best strategy. Women who do additional training during their 'time-out', have a fair chance of ending up with a more satisfactory career and greater diversity than women who stick to their jobs all along, thus having no time to explore new career paths, or invest in new skills and experiences. However, discontinuity can and does not infrequently result in downward mobility which, as a rule, is not just temporary.

Some women do not want to quit professional work altogether while having small children, but are not allowed to work part-time at their own job either. They may find an alternative in a much less demanding job, with fewer responsibilities and strictly controllable hours. This happens when women resign suddenly, for totally contingent reasons, but do not really want to be a full-time mother and housewife.

4.5 Sexual Harassment

Not infrequently, women are forced to leave their job because of sexual harassment. Many women volunteered to tell me what had happened to them. When

Jeanne had just finished her apprenticeship, she had to plead in a case out of town. She and a more senior male colleague who accompanied her were going to stay in a hotel. On arrival at the hotel, the colleague said, 'Oh well, you know, I booked just one room for us.' Jeanne protested and tried to get a separate room. None was available. She did not know what to do, and the colleague was quite amused by all this. In the end they shared the room, but nothing much happened as she insisted he should not touch her. Later on she heard that the man was boasting about his 'victory' to the other men in the office. Because of his action she had become the 'easy-to-get' woman. She felt very ill at ease and left the firm, but was unable to explain why she was looking for other work. Changing jobs because of sexual harassment is always a setback in a career, as the woman concerned has to start again, in a more junior position and on a lower salary, in a new environment. From interviews with numerous women in all sorts of professions, I have become convinced that sexual harassment is an important cause of discontinuity in women's careers generally. However, the scope of this problem is unknown as well as being hard to investigate, for the same reasons as it is hard to know how many women suffered discriminatory dismissal.

4.6 The Role of Partners

A remarkable fact about women of the older generation who entered professional life in the late 1960s and early 1970s is that they do not talk about their husbands. In their eyes, male partners have nothing (or very little) to do with their careers. Arranging for the continuity in her professional life is the woman's own business, not his. She has to run the household and take responsibility for its organisation. While his agreement is needed to hire a housekeeper and a babysitter, it is she who has to make appropriate arrangements. These women do not complain about their husbands, they consider it perfectly normal that they did what they had to do.

The generation that graduated from law school in the mid-1970s and later have tended to develop different strategies. Many of these younger women wanted to combine professional work, motherhood and other important aspects of life in a stable and satisfying manner. They also wanted to avoid the frustrations of their mothers, who had been dismissed from their jobs upon marriage and condemned to a life exclusively devoted to housework and child rearing. They wanted to work professionally, but on their own terms. These women were, on the whole, no longer prepared to behave in the world of paid employment in the same way as men did, that is with no reference to family life and responsibilities. They had domestic help and baby-sitters but no full-time housekeepers. One of the reasons for this was that from the early 1970s, full-time housekeepers became very expensive because of the steady increase in minimum wages. Wives expected their husbands to share more or less equally the care labour required by household and children. They also expected from their work environment a degree of recognition of their caring responsibilities, the most notable expression of which was the request to be allowed to work part-time. This generation gradually developed a new ideology of professional life. However, it was hard to move from ideology to practice. Many women ran up against obstacles. Many were profoundly frustrated, and in particular disappointed by their husbands' attitudes and behaviour. One of these disappointed women is Yvonne, whose job pattern was described above.

> Yvonne made specific demands on both her employer and her husband. She was quite clear that she wanted to work part-time temporarily, with the idea of working full-time again later. The employer did not want to be agree to this. Nor did the husband. Yvonne asked him explicitly to work less, accept more responsibilities at home. But he refused, he continued to pursue his career as a surgeon in his own way, saying to Yvonne, 'I could take up a job as a medical insurance officer, or something silly like that, but I would be very unhappy. I would have a nine-to-five job, but you would not want me to be that unhappy.'

Yvonne's husband earns quite a good salary. Most women lawyers I talked to were in the same position. They do not work for the money, they work because they want to do something useful with their education, because they love being a lawyer, because they do not want to be at home with children all the time. Husbands use the money argument to their own advantage. When the combination of paid work and caring for household and family becomes too much for a woman, in situations of crisis when two or three disasters occur at the same time (a child breaks a leg, the woman's mother-in-law falls ill etc), her husband may say, 'Why don't you quit for a while, it is getting too much, we don't really need your income.' Maureen's story fits this pattern. This is what she told me about her life in the late 1970s.

> At the time my husband was a lawyer who set up shop in the small provincial town A, along with two others. We went to live near A, although I worked in B. The kids were in school in A. Mostly I would be able to get the kids from school in the afternoon, but sometimes we arranged that Jim would do that. A few times he was really late, and the teacher had already taken the children to the neighbour's house when he finally got there. The children were very upset about having been left standing on the pavement. When children are involved you can't say, 'Let things get in a mess, he'll learn', as you may say about cooking dinner when friends come to visit. With kids, you just can't do that, they suffer. And I was considered a bad mother, while Jim did not think much of such incidents. We had a lot of fights about this. In the end, I quit my work in B, as it was too much commuting, and I was worrying a lot. This caused a real setback in my career, which took me a long time to repair.

Most women care about their image as mothers. They do not want their children to suffer from their own image as poor mothers, as for instance when children are sent home from school because they did not bring a proper Halloween outfit. Men do not feel guilty about such things, while women do. As the cost of feeling guilty is high, and as the norms for being a 'good mother' are being upgraded all the time, women are constantly busy doing a balancing-act, being good at work, being a good mother, and keeping a marriage together. This requires a lot of energy and frequent compromises as well. Often it will mean working part-time for a number of years, and lagging behind in professional experience compared to men of the same generation.

Women are particularly disappointed if their partners had indicated, in discussions about running the household after the birth of children, that they would co-operate. This is Jenny's story about the gap between what men may say and what they do:

> Rob wanted children more than I did. He very much liked the idea of having a 'real' family. I was hesitant because I liked my work so much, and I hate being a housewife. My work as a teacher gives me the best excuse for not being a housewife. Working I earn the money to pay the cleaning lady. In our discussions about having children, Rob said occasionally: 'If the worst comes to the worst, I can work less, I can work four days instead of five.' This reassured me at the time. In the end I got pregnant, and we had twins. This was more than I had bargained for. I had to take all the responsibility, make all the arrangements. Rob never worked part-time—if anything, he worked more after the kids were born. He never even remembered he had said a thing like, 'I could work part-time', he insists I made it up.

The professional advancement of women depends to a large extent on the attitude and behaviour of their partners. Women whose partners sincerely care about their wives' work and career opportunities and are supportive all the way, on the whole do better than women who have partners who, deep down, resent their wives' professional lives. Loyal partners will help out with household and children, and are prepared to forgo some career opportunities of their own, for the sake of a balanced relationship.

> Renata had been a judge in a district court for a number of years, when she was invited to apply for a position at the court of appeal in a town some forty miles from where she lived. She hesitated, thought she might not qualify. But her husband insisted that she should try. Reluctantly she made an appointment for an interview. Shortly before that she got a terrible attack of the flu, and she felt it was legitimate to cancel the interview, and forget about the whole thing. But her husband did not agree, he took the day off to drive her, stayed with her all day to encourage her, and everything worked out fine in the end. She has been an appeal court judge for many years now.

4.7 Anticipating Contingency

Women tend to anticipate contingencies. They are quite aware that other important things, besides professional demands and opportunities, are likely to happen (a relationship, a marriage, children, caring for elderly parents etc). They want to leave room to give these other things a proper place in their lives. But as it is uncertain how much time and energy may be required, they tend to play safe by avoiding heavy career commitments (Yeandle 1984; Marshall 1995). That is one of the reasons why women often take up, even today, part-time jobs from the very beginning after graduation, especially if they already have a steady relationship.

Dora's decision-making pattern is a good example. She did not even try to remain a practising lawyer when she was going to have children, she anticipated the complications and the eventual forced end to her career in the law firm. Another woman I interviewed, who wanted to take up legal work again when her children were well on their way in high school, only considered part-time work—and a few months later stopped looking for a job altogether as her parents-in-law fell seriously ill. Still another woman only wanted unpaid volunteer legal work (in this case with a refugee organisation) so that she could easily quit if and when her family needed more of her time and attention.

What women do not realise is that the course a professional life takes is determined at least as much by its starting-point and the degree of investment in training and courses during the period of professional life (Glebbeek 1993) as by possible discontinuities.

4.8 Finances: No Breadwinner Status

Women's decisions as to the course of their professional lives are in part determined by the fact that, most of the time, they are not, at least not in the strict sense of the word, the breadwinners in their households. I did not come across any single mothers. The professional women I interviewed tended to be married to professional men who earn a good salary. The professional men involved tend to emphasise that the household does not really need the income their wives earn, and that in any case most of it is used to pay for childcare and domestic help. There is a remarkable consensus that the husband's salary is used for payments on the mortgage, instalments to pay off the car and electricity bills, while the wife's salary is used for paying for childcare and the cleaning lady.

One aspect of this issue is that, for a multitude of reasons, women make career choices that men rarely make. They resign from a job because they do not like it very much without having another job, they work part-time for many years, they work below their educational levels while the children are small because that way they have fewer responsibilities at work and less stress. The limits of what women can choose and decide careerwise are very different from those facing men. Frequently, a woman's choice at a particular point in her life has two components: one, her own preference with regard to the mix of professional work and family life, and, two, the interests of her male partner in the slower career development of his wife and greater presence and care at home on her part.

One woman worked for many years as an employee in a small law firm, before setting up her own shop as a lone practitioner. She formulated the (financial) strategy in her professional life as follows:

After I had the children, I did not want to work full-time. I liked my work as a lawyer, and I wasn't going to give it up completely. But I also wanted to spend time with my children. I made sure I earned enough, after taxes, to pay for childcare and the cleaning woman their regular wages, before taxes. I never asked for more money than that. When I had to give my own employees a raise, I would ask my boss for a raise that was just enough to pay my additional expenses. I never asked for more.

This woman obviously did not think of her income as part of the household income. She did not feel responsible for the (continuity in the) family's financial standing. This is quite typical, yet almost paradoxical. Women who can most easily earn a good income because of the level of their education and skills and their capacity to pay for childcare, have the least (financial) incentive to do so. Women who are themselves responsible for the household income, now and in the long run (widows, divorced women), have also much more difficulty assuring the level and continuity of income they desire.

5 CONCLUSIONS

Although the participation of women in the legal profession has increased considerably over the last 30 years, their share in managerial, decision-making and prestigious functions has lagged far behind. Many women do legal work of one type or another, but few have the same power and influence as their male counterparts. The numbers of female partners in law firms, of associate and full professors in law schools, and of high-ranking officials in the judiciary remain very low and are in fact stagnating. These women remain tokens, and they do not have the power to make their own numbers grow—they are too few to represent a critical mass of any sort.

Women are well represented in the lower ranks of the judiciary, especially at trainee level, but their share in the total number of judges does not grow proportionately. This can only mean that there is a considerable turnover. Women constitute about 28 per cent of assistant professors in law schools and their numbers are not growing. Rising within that hierarchy is very difficult—at the next level the share of women is only about 7 per cent and stagnating. Women remain by and large at the margin of the legal professions.

How can we explain this limited development in the participation of women? I have argued that, firstly, the different sectors of the legal profession have to be studied separately. What constitutes an explanation in one sector, does not necessarily explain anything in another. Civil servants in the judiciary and the universities have for a long time suffered under restrictive legislation. Until 1957, women who married were dismissed from service. After 1957, the same was achieved by other means: wherever men in power decide about admission to the legal profession, they make marital status and/or motherhood a criterion, explicitly or implicitly. I have evidence that at least up to 1971, married women were barred from the judiciary. Among practising lawyers the same happened as motherhood approached. These habits are hard to change, and change is slow. The law barring married women from professional life had a strong radiating effect, in space and time, and caused much discontinuity in the careers of women.

Secondly, discontinuity was (and is) also produced by discrimination and sexual harassment. All discontinuity slows down careers and prevents women from arriving at functions of power and influence at a reasonable age. Many women I interviewed became discouraged in the process and turned their backs on the legal profession in order to do something else. Others resigned, lowered their level of aspirations, and contented themselves with horizontal career patterns. Continuing to desire something that is definitely out of reach is too frustrating in the long run. An apparent lack of ambition, and negative self-selection are the result, but it is institutions who are to blame for this, not the women concerned.

Thirdly, part-time work has played an ambiguous role in the process of increasing participation of women in the labour market. On the one hand, it facilitates participation wherever full-time work is out of the question. On the other hand, part-time work has kept women at the margins, as men in power have always managed to maintain that part-time work is incompatible with more prominent and responsible roles at management level. This norm has been institutionalised in the judiciary, where until 1989 no advancement was possible at all if someone worked part-time; in fact, this has been applied in all parts of the labour market. Only very recently has this rule been challenged,[5] with little success so far.

Finances have played a role as well. Most women I interviewed remained married over the whole period investigated. They did not need to fight for promotion and salary increases, which would also bring additional status and power, as the main family income was assured by their husbands. The few women who were breadwinners themselves demonstrated a different attitude— they could not afford to let themselves be marginalised. Obviously, these women typically worked full-time—the part-time status could not be held against them. Yet they, too, suffered structural drawbacks because they were being compared with women working part-time, ie those not 'wholly dedicated' to their profession.

Finally, at the micro level the role of the partners of professional women is important. If a woman has a really supportive partner who cares about her career (her happiness and his own image as a modern man) and shows this in words and behaviour, she is more likely to take advantage of career opportunities and move towards the centre of power.

A brief concluding word on childcare facilities. The relative lack of institutional childcare in the Netherlands affects all paid work outside the home. Childcare or rather the lack of it is both cause and effect in social development.

---

[5] In 1995, a woman civil servant was denied a managerial position because she worked four days a week; she won the law suit she initiated.

It is a cause of discontinuity in paid work and of additional stress and difficulty in balancing a woman's dual burden. It is also an effect, namely of a lack of real demand on the part of women. Apparently, Dutch women have not really wanted good childcare outside the home to develop. Generally, it is believed that exceptionally strong and strict conceptions of motherhood are at the root of this. It is, however, unclear how we are to explain this extraordinary notion of motherhood.[6]

The entry of women into the legal profession in the Netherlands began only about 30 years ago. This period is not only rather short to achieve structural change, it has also included several recessions, periods in which the weaker members of the labour force have tended to have a hard time and could hardly negotiate a better position. All in all, the pioneering generation has achieved a great deal in their own fashion, although not as much as younger generations think they did.

6   REFERENCES

Abramson, Jane and Barbara Franklin. 1986. *Where Are They Now?* New York: Doubleday.

Berteaux, Daniel. 1981. From the Life-history Approach to the Transformation of Sociological Practice, in: Berteaux (ed) *Biography and Society; the life-history approach and the social sciences*. London: Sage, 29–46.

Coombe, Rosemary. 1995. Finding and Losing One's Self in the *Topoi*: Placing and Displacing the Postmodern Subject in Law. In 29 *Law & Society Review*; 599–608.

Diamond, Esther. 1987. Theories of Career Development and the Reality of Women at Work, in Gutek and Larwood (eds), *Women's Career Development*. London: Sage.

Gallos, Joan V. 1989. Exploring Women's Development: Implications for Career Theory, Practice and Research. In *Handbook of Career Theory*, edited by Michael B Arthur *et al*, Cambridge: Cambridge University Press, Ch 6.

Gilligan, Carol. 1982. *In a Different Voice. Psychological Theory and Women's Development*; Cambridge: Harvard Univ. Press.

Glebbeek, Arie. 1993. *Perspectieven op loopbanen*. Tilburg: Tilburg University Press.

Groot-van Leeuwen, Lenie E de. 1991. *De rechterlijke macht in Nederland* (PhD thesis). Arnhem: Gouda Quint.

Gutek, Barbara A and Laurie Larwood. 1987. Women's Careers are Different. In *Women's Career Development*, edited by Barbara A Gutek and Laurie Larwood, London: Sage, 121–132.

Hennig, Margaret, and Anne Jardim. 1978. *The Managerial Woman*. New York: Pocket.

Ietswaart, Heleen FP. 1992. Labor Market Participation of Women in the Netherlands, 1960–1990; unpublished paper presented at the Law and Society Association annual meeting.

Ietswaart, Heleen FP. 1995a. Developments in Labor Market Participation of Dutch Women in Relation to Unpaid Work; unpublished paper presented at the Law and Society Association annual meeting.

---

[6] A not dissimilar state of affairs can be observed in Germany. Cf Ulrike Schultz,'Women Lawyers in Germany: Perception and Construction of Femininity', in this volume.

Ietswaart, Heleen FP. 1995b. Jobs and Careers of Women Lawyers in the Netherlands; unpublished paper presented at the Law and Society Assocation annual meeting .

Ietswaart, Heleen FP. 1996. Women in the Legal Profession: How Useful is Career Theory? unpublished paper presented at the Law and Society Assocation annual meeting.

Klijn, Albert. 1981. *De balie geschetst*; Den Haag: WODC.

Klijn, Albert, John Kester and Fred Huls. 1992. Advocatuur in Nederland, 1952–1992, in: 18 *Justitiële Verkenningen*, July.

Kohlberg, Lawrence. 1958. *The Development of Modes of Thinking and Choices in Years 10 to 16*; PhD diss, University of Chicago.

Kohlberg, Lawrence. 1973. Continuities and Discontinuities in Childhood and Adult Moral Development Revisited, in: *Collected Papers on Moral Development and Moral Education*, Moral Education Research Foundation, Harvard University, 1973, 56–65.

Levinson, Daniel Jacob. 1978. *The Seasons of a Man's Life*. New York: Knopf.

Marshall, Judi. 1984. *Women Managers—Travellers in a Male World*; Chichester: Wiley.

Marshall, Judi. 1989. Revisioning Career Concepts: A Feminist Invitation, in: Michael B Arthur *et al* (eds) *Handbook of Career Theory*; Cambridge University Press, ch 13.

Marshall, Judi. 1995. *Women Managers Moving On: Exploring Career and Life Choices*; London: Routledge.

Roberts, Paul and Paul Newton. 1986. Levinsonian Studies of Women's Adult Development; working paper, Berkeley: Wright Institute (unpublished).

Schuyt, Kees. 1988. The Rise of Lawyers in the Dutch Welfare State. In *Lawyers in Society*, vol 2, *The Civil Law World*, edited by Richard L Abel and Philip SC Lewis, Berkeley: University of California Press, 200–224.

Sloot, Ben P. 1980. Officiele uitsluiting van vrouwen en mannen in juridische beroepen. *Nederlands Juristenblad* 45/46; 1186–95.

Thompson, Paul. 1981. Life Histories and the Analysis of Social Change, in: Daniel Berteaux (ed), *Biography and Society*; London: Sage, 289–306.

Vaillant, George E. 1977. *Adaptation to Life*. Boston: Little, Brown.

Veltman, Albertine, and Roel Wittink. 1990. *De kans van slagen; invloeden van culturen en regels op de loopbanen van vrouwen*; Leiden: Stenfort Kroese.

Vogels, Hendrica MG. 1995. *Continuiteit en discontinuiteit in de loopbanen van vrouwen*. Doctoral dissertation, University of Tilburg: Tilburg University Press.

Yeandle, Susan. 1984. *Women's Working Lives; Patterns and Strategies*; London: Tavistock.

20

Women Lawyers in Poland under the Impact of Post-1989 Transformation

MAŁGORZATA FUSZARA

Abstract

This paper represents the first attempt to assess the effect on the situation of women lawyers in Poland of the socio-political and economic transformation process following the transition from socialism and a centrally planned economy to democracy and capitalism. Quantitative and qualitative data are presented and analysed in the wider context of changes affecting the profession as a whole. This is done in full awareness of the fact that a good deal more research is needed to provide a full assessment of these crucial developments in the history of the Polish legal profession in general and of its female members in particular.

1 INTRODUCTION

Some professions are and always will be reserved for men. A female medical doctor or lawyer is almost as abnormal as a female soldier or diplomat. (W Chomętowski, *Stanowisko praktyczne dawnych niewiast polskich (Polish Working Women's Practical Position in Poland in the Past)* Warszawa 1871, p 71).

I am appealing neither to conscious nor dignified feelings, I won't talk about grand principles of equality and justice, about importance or need for equality, or about the fact that these inevitably result in equal rights etc. for women. That should be obvious to anyone with a sufficiently developed and cultured mind. Whoever has not yet got to this point needs education, not proof. (L Petrażycki, *O prawa dla kobiet (For Women's Rights)* Wydawnictwo Polskie. Lwów 1919).

THE ABOVE STATEMENTS really require no commentary—both were made in times when female attorneys did not exist in Poland, but women were already trying to remove the barriers set for them in education and employment. However, society has moved on and with it the situation of women in Poland generally and of Polish women lawyers in particular. It was the communist regime's pro-equality rhetoric and low pay policy that helped to increase greatly the share of women in the Polish labour market between 1945 and 1989. In the case of lawyers two interesting questions arise, namely: has the presence of female lawyers influenced the resolution of cases, and has it meant a more favourable atmosphere in courtrooms, for example for female victims, such as mothers attempting to get maintenance payments? My research allows us to at least partially answer these questions.

The process of gaining access to the legal profession was no less protracted and laborious for women in Poland than for women elsewhere in the Western world. Once all legal obstacles had been removed, they still only very gradually gained ground in the various branches of the profession. It was during the communist period that, for a number of reasons, the legal professions all but ceased to be a domain of male predominance. However, women entered the period of transition on quite a good footing (albeit not on an equal footing with men) regarding positions in the traditional legal professions. After 1989 the profession itself underwent significant transformation due to economic and political changes. Were women able to hold their own in the new environment? Did they benefit or lose as a result of the transformations? Is the situation the same in all branches of the legal profession? These are some of the questions which now pose themselves.

This paper represents the first attempt to gauge the effect of this transformation process on the position of women lawyers in Poland. Following a brief historical overview of developments in the first half of the twentieth century, data are presented on quantitative as well as qualitative developments over the last three decades and a number of current trends are tentatively identified.

2 WOMEN LAWYERS IN POLAND: HISTORICAL OVERVIEW

2.1 Women Law Students and Academics

For a long time, opportunities for women in Poland to become lawyers were restricted not only by limitations imposed generally on their access to the legal profession, but also by educational constraints, that is, by university law faculties' resistance to admitting women applicants. For example, the oldest Polish university, the Jagiellonian University in Cracow, first admitted female students in 1894/1895, but the law faculty was the last to follow suit, with the first women law students being allowed in as late as 1919. For the first woman to join a law faculty as an assistant or to qualify as assistant professor took even longer. A key prerequisite for the latter was submission of a dissertation and the passing of an examination. Faculties that opposed the admission of women students (law, theology) as well as others where by that time women were already being enrolled (eg medicine) also opposed equal rights for women and men as university teachers.

At Warsaw University the issue of women studying law was a somewhat different one from Cracow. This university was only founded as a Polish university in 1915 after Poland had regained its independence after over one century of partition. Women were admitted to the law faculty from the very start, and this for mainly two reasons: firstly, the fact that universities in some other countries had already taken that step; secondly, because during the period of annexation, women had participated in the underground education process to the same extent as men (for instance in the work of the Scientific Training Association and the Flying University), and the statutes of these organisations provided for equal access to education 'regardless of gender'. Women had taken full advantage of these opportunities, for instance holding an 80 per cent share in the Arts Faculty organised by the Scientific Training Association in 1907–1915 (Halbesztadt 1996). Thus in Warsaw cultural barriers to co-education had already been broken down at an earlier stage.

In the first year of Warsaw University (1915) women made up 9 per cent of the student population. In 1918, their share had risen to 20 per cent, in 1923/24 to 35 per cent, and in 1932/33 to 41 per cent. This was followed by a slight decline in 1935/36 to 37 per cent, but there followed another rise to 40 per cent in 1937/38 (the last recorded figure before World War II). During the same period, the percentage of female students at the university's law faculty remained significantly lower, ie 3.6 per cent in 1915 and growing to between 15 and 20 per cent in the 1930s. In the academic year 1935/36, 17 per cent of graduates from the Warsaw Faculty of Law and Political Sciences were women (Halbesztadt 1996). Under the Communist regime, the law ceased to be a male-dominated discipline, and in the 1970s the proportion of women and men studying law in Poland began to equalise. In 1971/72, 45 per cent of law students were women, and by 1978/79, their share had risen to 47 per cent.

The collapse of the Socialist Bloc in 1989 represented a watershed in socio-political and economic life in Poland generally and in Polish higher education in particular. The state ceased to determine maximum student intakes for each university. While university education continued to be mainly free, certain fee-paying programmes were also set up within state-owned and private universities, bringing about a significant increase in student numbers generally. Many young people were keen to embark on studies of particular relevance to the newly evolving labour market, such as business, management, or indeed law. While in the academic year 1990/1991, the total university student population in Poland amounted to little over 19,000 (49 per cent women), by 1995/96 numbers had risen to 47,000 students (54 per cent women). In 1997/1998 the overall number of students reached almost 54,000 (53 per cent women). This dramatic rise in the student population affected law faculties in particular, as the transition from a socialist to a capitalist economy meant a shortage of lawyers in the Polish labour market as well as a steep rise in status and income for law graduates. Women fully participated in this process and female law students are now in a majority.

2.2 Women in the Legal Professions

Before women in Poland could begin to gain access to professions such as law, they needed to be granted full civic rights. The electoral law of 1918 (the first after Poland regained its independence) provided for voting rights for every citizen over 21, regardless of gender. The first constitutional Act of 1921, passed after the restoration of Polish independence, stipulated the equality of all citizens before the law.

Yet the legal professions remained closed to women for a little longer than others. Even after 1918, a decree on court articles dated 8 February 1919 restricted judicial functions to those of the male sex. Although this restriction had to be lifted after the introduction of the constitutional Act of 1921, the number of women in the legal profession remained minute for years to come. It took until 1929 for the first female judge, W Grabińska, to be appointed in Poland, and by 1937 there were just seven of them (Pietrzak 1994). The first appointment in Poland of a woman to the post of attorney at law had occurred a little earlier when H Wiewiórska, who had started her legal training in 1919, was registered on the lawyers' roll in Warsaw in 1925 (Burakowski 1976). As for the public prosecution service, it was virtually impossible to find women working there before the start of World War II. In the 1930s, there was only one woman who had achieved this (Pietrzak 1994).

3 WOMEN IN THE LEGAL PROFESSIONS: THE SITUATION TODAY

Today Polish law graduates of both sexes frequently take up administrative positions in government offices, banks and other public and private institutions. In this paper I will focus only on women working in the administration of justice, that is, judges, public prosecutors, practising lawyers and notaries. In particular, I am asking the question how their situation has been affected by the post-1989 socio-political and economic upheavals.

3.1 Women Judges

3.1.1 Statistical Data

As shown in Table 1, in the post-war period the share of female judges broadly increased in tandem with that of women studying law, with the proportion of male and female judges equalising around 1980. However, subsequent years have seen a disproportionate rise in the number of women judges, resulting in a situation where they now significantly outnumber their male colleagues. As will become clear below, this contrasts sharply with developments in other branches of the legal profession.

Table 1: Women Judges in Poland

Year	Women	Men	Total	% Women
1968	890	1791	2681	33,2
1970	952	1655	2607	36.5
1975	1272	1636	2908	42.4
1980	1489	1529	3018	49.3
1985	1971	1751	3722	52.9
1990	2850	1778	4628	61.6
1995	3745	2265	6010	62.3
1996	4016	2399	6415	62.6
1997	4207	2480	6687	62.9
1998	4436	2542	6978	63.6
1999	4586	2636	7222	63.5
2000	4594	2629	7223	63.6

Calculations based on information provided by the Polish Ministry of Justice

In the 1970s and in the first half of the 1980s, women's growing share in the total number of judges actually meant a decline in the number of male judicial appointments. In the 1990s, the situation changed in that the absolute number of judges of both sexes increased due to a shift of responsibilities to the courts of matters previously dealt with by an administrative procedure. Most of this increase was absorbed by the female sector of the profession. One explanation may be that the process of transformation resulted in an absolute increase but a relative decline in the financial rewards for judges compared to jurists choosing other career paths (especially in the advocacy), and this career therefore losing some of its attraction for men.

3.1.2 Careers

Yet, within the judicial profession, the participation of women was by no means evenly spread across all levels of the judicial hierarchy. Rather it was structured in the shape of a pyramid, with the highest numbers being found in the courts of lower instance. In 1975, for example, women judges constituted the majority (59 per cent) in district courts, whereas as little as a quarter (27.5 per cent) of judges were to be found in regional courts (the higher level). By 1990, women had come to form the majority in higher instance courts as well. But here, too, there were internal imbalances. While in district courts women represented 69.5 per cent of judges, in regional courts the figure was only 55.3 per cent. This overall profile had not changed significantly by the year 2000, when female judges held the undisputed majority of posts in district courts (66.2 per cent), a much slimmer majority in regional courts (58.4 per cent) and only a minority in the highest court (22 per cent in 1997).

A parallel phenomenon of uneven gender distribution within the judicial hierarchy is evident in the proportion of men and women holding the highest positions within courts. In 1990, women made up over 60 per cent of judges. However, they held only few executive positions (president/vice-president), especially in courts of higher instance. In regional courts, among 44 presidents only four were women (9 per cent), and among 62 vice-presidents only 13 were women (21 per cent), and proportions equalised at the level of courts of first instance (50 per cent). In 2001, the situation was similar in regional courts: out of 38 presidents four were women (11 per cent), and out of 59 vice-presidents 19 were women (32 per cent). In district courts women prevailed: women constituted 51 per cent of court presidents and 53 per cent of vice-presidents.

3.1.3 Female Adjudication

Contemporary socio-legal debates about women lawyers frequently home in on the question whether a gender shift in judicial personnel might affect the adjudication process and its outcomes. Given a positive slant, the question is: does the increase in the number and overall share of female judges reduce the risk of a gender bias affecting court decisions? A definitive answer would require thorough research. Interviews[1] I conducted in the early 1990s with parties claiming maintenance resulted in the voicing of occasional criticism (intriguingly by both men and women) of lack of impartiality on the part of female judges. Most notoriously, the Polish Association for the Protection of Fathers' Rights accused female judges of harbouring a bias in favour of women and of restricting fathers' rights to custody over their children. Although in Poland over 90 per cent of cases concerning custody for a child after a divorce are decided in favour of the mother, this is not a result of gender bias as the proportion of women who gain custody tallies with the number requested by the parties involved (Fuszara 1994).

Occasionally, critical comments directed at female judges are expressed by women in Poland, especially by those claiming maintenance (Fuszara 1994; Fuszara 1997).[2] The most common complaint against judges examining maintenance claims (including female judges) is that they take 'the men's side', burdening women with the whole problem of not only raising but also maintaining a child. This complaint is most often heard from women whose former husbands are alcoholics and/or unemployed. Here is a typical example:

> Alimony proceedings are a parody . . . the court thinks that the responsibility for maintaining a child rests exclusively with her . . . , the former husband is not responsible

---

[1] Research on maintenance cases was conducted in the family court in Warsaw in 1993. All court files from 1986 (140) and 1992 (97) were examined. 30 parties from 1986 and 30 from 1992 were interviewed. Parties were questioned on their economic situation, work, relations with their former spouse, their new family, their views on the court case etc.

[2] E Botelho Junqueira's contribution to this volume on Brazil makes for an interesting comparison.

for anything, he is a pensioner, and that's that. The fact that he is a notorious alcoholic seems to make no difference. The judge spreads her arms, saying, 'There is nothing more one can demand from him, as he simply doesn't have the money, while you have a job.' No one stands up for women's rights.

Another interviewee commented, 'Madame Judge was favourably inclined towards my husband. She said that if I had managed for the last ten years, then I would just have to carry on managing.' It is worth emphasising that the expression 'carry on managing' refers to a woman bringing up a child on unemployment benefit. 'No one takes into account that I do the child care. He (the former husband) is treated as the one who is lonely, poor and unhappy.' Charges of overindulgence towards men are frequently linked to situations where men are alcoholics. 'When the judge is a woman, it's even worse, as she takes pity on alcoholics.' And, 'Why does the court take the side of those with a drinking problem? We need money to live on, too.'

My findings indicate that the large proportion of women in the Polish judiciary, including family law courts where sometimes all judges are women, does not automatically imply a breaking up of gender stereotypes applied in the adjudication process. Divorce case studies in particular (Fuszara 1994) reveal that women judges tend to sustain stereotypes of male and female roles in the family. This leads us to conclude that in a patriarchal society the same traditional patterns of gender relationships are passed on to both sexes and are then applied by them in professional life, including judicial work.

It is worth noting that, although women judges are normally in the majority in Polish courts, some court departments (especially criminal departments) continue to be male-dominated. It is impossible to tell whether evidence of preferential treatment in sentences for rape and domestic violence (Zielińska 2000) is in any way connected with the under-representation of women in criminal departments. On the other hand, women bringing charges against prosecutors and police officers do claim that female victims of violent crime are often improperly treated by policemen or male prosecutors.

3.2 Women Public Prosecutors

The gender distribution in the Polish public prosecution service is not dissimilar to that amongst judges. As can be seen from Table 2, women's share among prosecutors has been steadily increasing over the last decade (albeit relatively more slowly than their share in the judiciary) and currently just exceeds 50 per cent. In the early 1990s, this was accompanied by a drop in the number of male prosecutors. As in the case of judges, the process of transformation included a relative decline in the financial rewards for prosecutors compared to jurists choosing careers in the advocacy, with the result that the prosecution service has lost some of its attraction for men.

Table 2: Women Public Prosecutors in Poland

Year	Territorial Prosecutor's Office			Prosecutor's Office of Appeal		
	Women	Men	% Women	Men	Women	% Women
1989	1316	2177	37.7	25	97	20.5
1992*	1816	2297	44.2	48	108	30.8
1994*	1969	2150	47.8	48	108	30.8
1996	2792	2732	50.2	63	118	34.8
1998	2537	2481	50.6	27	48	36.0
1999	2733	2639	50.9	27	48	36.0

*Data about the prosecutor's office of appeal refer to 1993. No data available from 1992 and 1994. Calculations are based on information from the Polish Ministry of Justice

As far as women's career structures are concerned, the pyramid profile applies here as it does among judges, as women are in the majority at the bottom of the hierarchy, whereas they are still in a minority at the higher levels of the prosecution service.

My studies in the early 1990s have shown that apart from accusing courts of gender bias, (female) respondents applying for an increase in maintenance payments complained that prosecutors and members of the police force (respondents spoke only of male prosecutors and policemen) just as judges, tended to take 'the side of the men'. One of the women talked about moral pressure put on her by a male prosecutor when she submitted a claim for an outstanding alimony payment. The prosecutor had asked her reproachfully whether she wanted to see her husband sent to jail. Other female respondents talked of the ineffectiveness of their claims against husbands, even if, as in one case, a husband had seriously beaten his daughter who suffered from epilepsy. Here the prosecutor refused any intervention due to a lack of other eye-witnesses. The same woman, whose former husband was a confirmed alcoholic, referred to the apathy of the police who, once called, refused to take any action and expressed their astonishment at the woman's inability to handle her own husband.

3.3 Women Attorneys, In-house Legal Advisers, and Notaries

3.3.1 The Situation Prior to 1989

The impact of the transition from a socialist and centrally planned system to a democracy and a free market economy was greatest in the advocacy (as well as being the most difficult to describe). During the communist period, Poland had two types of lawyers representing client interests, namely in-house legal advisers and attorneys. Generally speaking, the former were working for companies and represented these companies' interests. Their remuneration and working hours were fixed and their professional responsibilities related to the needs of the company that employed them.

Attorneys, on the other hand, were members of a profession more closely modelled on the classical profession of lawyers representing individuals' interests, and that mainly in court. Recruitment was subject to state planning and numbers were strictly limited. Between 1968 and 1980, they hovered around 5,700. Significant deviations from the classical model had been introduced to meet the needs of a centrally planned system. Most importantly, most attorneys worked within the organisational framework of so-called lawyers' co-operatives, while the number of those remaining in sole and/or private practice was very small.

After 1989, members of the profession have tended to describe these co-operatives as loose groupings of separate private practices, with each attorney being in charge of his/her own cases matching his/her specialism and preferences and conducting individual meetings with clients. (Kurczewski 1994; Kurczewski 2000). When asked how they used to come by their clients, attorneys who had practised under communism described the same universal mechanism of clients approaching a lawyer regardless of whether (s)he worked for a lawyers' co-operative or a private practice. They mainly owed their client-base, so they claimed, either to their 'good name' or friends' and former clients' recommendations rather than to their professional expertise in eg housing, divorce or crime. And all they shared with colleagues in the co-operative had been facilities and secretarial support.

However, it is important to point out that in spite of these claims on the part of attorneys to professional independence under communism (some of which certainly existed), there was also the significant fact that hardly any of them had had any choice whether to join a lawyers' co-operative or not, and that having joined, major restrictions were imposed on their professional activities. For example, lawyers could meet their clients only in their offices and were not allowed to see them in their homes. Key decisions relating to the lawyers' co-operative (such as the selection of the head) were taken at meetings of the membership as a whole that had to be held at least once a quarter. Lawyers' incomes were not based purely on their actual earnings. Firstly, there was a provision that 'an attorney's income cannot be less than the amount agreed upon by the district attorney'. As a result, every attorney had to get a minimum remuneration regardless of the volume of his/her 'contribution' to the lawyers' co-operative income. Secondly, the costs of the lawyers' co-operative, such as monthly rent, secretarial support and other office expenditure, were normally paid from a percentage taken off each attorney's 'turnover', which automatically meant that those with higher incomes were contributing a higher share.

Despite the profession's comparatively high degree of self-governance during the period preceding 1989 (compared, that is, with members of other branches of the legal profession), attorneys had no control over access to the profession. In addition to overall central state control of access to the profession, a survey among female attorneys carried out in 1981 (Szafraniec 1982) confirmed a suspicion that state authorities were setting up barriers to exclude certain individuals from the profession. These barriers were either political and imposed mainly during the Stalinist period (1947 to 1956); or they were social, for instance restrictions placed on access to legal training for children of an attorney, which happened in certain periods.

This survey, which has remained the only one that included female attorneys, can also give us some insight into certain aspects of their situation, although admittedly it cannot be treated as representative due to the relatively low response rate (of 640 questionnaires sent out, 131 were returned, but only 90 contained answers to all questions).

As in most countries at the time, women represented a minority in the advocacy in Poland (see Table 3 below). Among the reasons they gave for wanting to be a lawyer (apart from an academic interest) respondents listed professional independence, flexible working hours and family tradition. The answers relating to working hours indicate a strong linkage between family situation and female attorneys' work, as single women, those without children, or those with adult children were willing to work longer hours. According to the interviewees, the need to combine family life with working hours posed two kinds of problems. Firstly, women often emphasised difficulties with time allocated to each of their two roles and felt that they were 'snatching' working hours to cope with domestic duties, and vice-versa. Secondly, there was the nature of the profession itself which brought with it great emotional involvement and therefore added to women's burdens. Despite such difficulties, the majority of respondents (90 per cent) were satisfied with their profession. Their satisfaction was mainly based on their professional independence, a feeling of being able to help clients, the lack of routine work and, finally, a sense of achievement (Szafraniec 1982).[3]

Finally, notaries in pre-1989 Poland were a small group of specially trained legal personnel whose function in the legal system was neither highly regarded nor well paid.[4] By 1989, the share of women in the Polish notariat amounted to around two thirds of the total (see Table 5 below). Dramatic changes—arguably more dramatic than those affecting any other group of jurists—came about in the wake of the transformation process of 1989.

3.3.2 1989 and After

After 1989, compulsory membership of advocates in co-operatives was lifted and it became possible to open a private practice. To begin with, many continued to work for a group practice while also setting up a private practice or a

---

[3] Cf Ulrike Schultz's observations on German female judges' job satisfaction in her contribution to this volume on 'The Status of Women Lawyers in Germany'.

[4] Polish civil law during communism (eg the Civil Code of 1964) included few provisions as to when a notarial act was obligatory. Overall, notarial services were very rarely required, one example being some cases of donation. In some other cases, eg wills, a notarial act was only one option.

private firm. Some of the attorneys questioned[5] stressed that by staying with the group practice they were losing money, but that tradition, habit and perhaps some kind of need for security in case their private business went bankrupt made them stick to their old ways. At the same time they were keen to emphasise the continuities between their work in co-operatives and that in private practice, as both offered a sense of professional independence. As we saw above, this sense of professional independence, they claimed, had also been there prior to 1989. After all, their profession had always been functionally closer to market economy conditions than any other, operating 'in the market' with competitive rights, professional ethics and other mechanisms yet unknown to other professional groups, such as income tax payments, individual social security contributions, etc. All of this had contributed to their sense of identity as individual professionals unwilling to work in joint ventures or companies.

Attorneys also emphasise, however, that the attitude of younger people who graduated after 1989 is different from that of previous generations and that consequently they also practise differently. Upon completing their legal training, these younger people tend to prefer setting themselves up in small group practices of two or three or as a small law firm. Once successful, they start employing others, such as in-house legal advisers or other attorneys. These employees get their regular remuneration, but lose some of their professional independence. A new and different professional hierarchy of individuals and law firms has thus begun to evolve in the Polish legal market.

The main changes affecting practising lawyers have concerned the type of work they do. They now more often work on corporate and commercial cases and less with individual clients, thus straying from the classical model of the attorney's work being mainly about individual relationships with individual clients and offering individual assistance in complicated cases. The two main reasons for this change have been the lucrative nature of commercial legal services, and the growing impoverishment of large sections of Polish society. Attorneys themselves stress that after 1989 the most successful amongst them were those who were flexible and able to adjust to commercial and corporate requirements during a period of economic boom. Yet, some amongst them consider commercial activities as a sign of disloyalty to their original calling as guardians of individual client interests, especially in court.

Court work has been at the heart of a dispute between attorneys and in-house legal advisers regarding their respective area of operation. Such work has so far been the sole preserve of the advocacy, but legal advisers are more than keen to break into this monopoly and to be granted the same status as members of the advocacy, possibly by means of a merger of both branches of the profession. Given that attorneys are the smaller group by far (in 1991 there were approximately 7000 attorneys compared to 17,000 in-house legal advisers), an alignment of the two groups would have a huge impact on the open market for legal

---

[5] Ten interviews were conducted by the author in 1991. See also Kurczewski 1994 and 2000.

services traditionally dominated by attorneys. No wonder, attorneys oppose any plans of this kind.

The outcome has been that, on the one hand, attorneys have successfully defended their professional monopoly since legal advisers are not allowed to appear in court, except in commercial courts. It might be argued that changes in the type of cases handled by attorneys make the right to appear in court other than a commercial court increasingly less significant a factor in the dispute between attorneys and in-house legal advisers, as the key issue is a loss or gain in prestige. But attorneys still continue to oppose any merger with in-house legal advisers, arguing that the latter would be ill-prepared for independent practice as their legal training is shorter and the ground covered less comprehensive, and that the ethical and professional code governing attorneys would not apply to legal advisers, thus putting attorneys at a competitive disadvantage. These rules include, for instance, a general ban on advertising for attorneys and restrictions on the type of information they are allowed to publish about themselves. Such rules, attorneys argue, do not apply to other professionals who often provide costly legal services while lacking the expertise required.

3.3.3 Women Lawyers after 1989

3.3.3.1 Women Advocates

How are women lawyers faring amidst all these changes and upheavals? Under communism, when access to the advocacy was strictly limited, the share of women in the profession had increased steadily even when the numbers of men dropped, although overall it remained very modest (Table 3). The events of 1989 brought about a steep increase in total numbers (by approximately one quarter), which affected women much more powerfully than men (an 80 per cent increase for women, compared to a 13 per cent increase for men). In quantitative terms, therefore, the transformation process appears to have worked in women lawyers' favour. Today they represent just under one third of the total membership.

Obviously, these figures do not tell us anything about the impact of internal professional stratification on women lawyers. In the absence of any in-depth analyses, I have tried to get some tentative insights from data obtained from a District Chamber of Attorneys in Warsaw. The following picture has emerged.

Table 3: Women Attorneys in Poland

Year	Women	Men	Total	% Women
1968	732	4988	5722	12.8
1974	913	4853	5766	15.8
1980	1073	4567	5640	19.0
1992	1939	5146	7085	27.4
1998	2130	5086	7216	29.5

Calculations based on information from the roll of lawyers prepared by the Attorneys' Chamber.

Women's share among the attorneys in the Warsaw Chamber by far exceeds the average across Poland as a whole. In January 2000, there were 660 women and 1066 men on that Chamber's roll, giving women a share of 38 per cent. However, the roll comprises various categories of people, from retired members and those not actually practising, to part-time and full-time attorneys. Women are distributed unevenly across these groups. The biggest differences can be found among full-time attorneys where women make up only 30 per cent. Their share is higher amongst those practising part-time (40 per cent), higher still among those retired (42 per cent) and highest amongst those not practising or hardly practising (47 per cent), that is, authorised to work as attorneys but not using their qualification. (This does not mean that they do not work—they may, for instance, teach law at university—but that they do not appear in court and, for financial reasons (lower premiums), have decided not to be registered as active members.)

Another aspect worth looking into is the question how women attorneys are organised. The number of lawyers' co-operatives and the percentage of attorneys practising in such groupings has generally decreased. While in 1990 there were over 410 lawyers' co-operatives with 53 per cent of the country's attorneys, in 1994 there were only 121 with 12 per cent. The roll of the Warsaw Chamber for the year 2000 only comprises 86 attorneys working for lawyers' co-operatives (5 per cent), 40 per cent of whom are women. There are therefore no significant gender-based discrepancies apparent in this context.

The most significant difference shown up in the roll of the Warsaw Chamber occurs in the context of private law firms. On the roll, 53 law firms as well as the names of partners within them are listed. Of these firms, 34 (64 per cent) have no women partner at all. Only three law firms (6 per cent) list women's names only. The remaining 16 (30 per cent) list a combination of male and female partners, but in most of these (9) we are looking at firms set up by married couples. Generally speaking, in the Warsaw Chamber where the share of women is higher compared to their average share in Poland, 3 per cent of women (22 women) and 10 per cent of men (101) work in a firm which lists their names in its title.

The criterion applied here is obviously not perfect and leaves open the possibility of stratification within the profession of attorney, where women might be working mainly as employees or run small legal practices handling 'traditional' cases for individual clients rather than working for large corporations. The question whether women occupy leading positions in the biggest law firms requires a separate study. Informally, attorneys express doubt that it might be possible to find women in executive positions in the largest law firms.

3.3.3.2 Women In-house Legal Advisers

Amongst the legacies of the communist period in Poland is the large proportion of women in branches of the legal profession which were then neither very lucrative nor particularly prestigious, but whose status has changed significantly after 1989. They are in-house legal advisers and notaries. To begin with the former (Table 4):

Table 4: Women In-House Legal Advisers

Year	Women	Men	Total	% Women
1991	8631	9239	27880	48.3
1995	9352	9811	19163	48.8
1997	9731	10307	20038	48.6
1999	10030	10296	20326	49.3

Own calculations based on information from the Polish In-House Legal Advisers Council

As shown in Table 4, the traditionally high share of women amongst in-house legal advisers in Poland has remained high during the transformation processes which have occurred within the legal profession. Given the fact that in-house legal advisers by far outnumber attorneys and that during the second half of the 1990s women made up between 47 and 49 per cent of those training to be in-house legal advisers, a merger of the two branches of legal practitioners would result in an almost balanced gender distribution across the profession. Maybe this is an additional reason why the attorneys are strictly against a fusion. Even now, as described above, many activities and types of work can be carried out by members of either group.

3.3.3.3 Women Notaries

Finally, a word on women in the fourth of the classical legal professions in the Polish civil law system, that is the notariat (Table 5). Prior to 1989, notarial work in Poland (as was the case in the other Socialist Bloc countries), however worthy and interesting, was anything but profitable or prestigious and utterly unattractive to men. Hence the majority of notaries were women. The end of communism changed all that, as the introduction of a functioning market economy heavily depended on notarial certification and authentication of a whole range of public documents, and notarial fees became not inconsiderable. This has meant a wholesale reversal of the social and professional status of this female-dominated profession. Not entirely surprisingly, there has been a slight reduction of the share of women as the notariat has acquired considerable interest for men.[6] Future developments are awaited with some interest.

---

[6] This is the branch of the legal profession in Poland where similarities with developments in eastern Germany (see Gisela Shaw's contribution to this volume) are particularly striking. In both cases, the introduction of a market economy to replace a centrally planned socialist economy has dramatically reversed the fate of a profession formerly characterised by low income, low status and strong female domination.

Table 5: Women Notaries in Poland

Year	Women	Men	Total	% Women
1977	198	233	431	45.9
1980	250	212	436	51.4
1985	328	177	505	64.9
1990	470	240	710	66.2
1994	560	316	876	63.9
1999	753	436	1189	63.3

Calculations based on information from the Polish Ministry of Justice (figures up to 1990), and notarial registers published in the *Monitor Polski* magazine (figures from 1991).

4 CONCLUDING OBSERVATIONS

The wider changes that have affected the Polish legal professions have also had considerable impact on the situation of women within them, offering fertile ground for future research. In this first study we have been able tentatively to identify a number of trends in an overall still fairly fluid wider context. Our findings relate to both quantitative and qualitative developments. For instance, we have noted the equalisation of women's and men's quantitative share in a traditionally male dominated legal profession (public prosecution) and a greater than equal share of women in a profession which is prestigious but does not offer the same opportunities of high incomes as other branches of the legal profession (judges). In both professions, gender segregation continues to operate vertically, with women tending to occupy the lower levels of the pyramid while being much less in evidence at executive levels. In the traditionally most highly respected legal profession (advocacy) women are beginning to catch up numerically, but there is also now a new internal hierarchy emerging which tends to disadvantage women. Finally, the notariat, a legal profession which under communism was strongly feminised and suffered from a low profile and low income levels, has undergone a dramatic reversal of fate of particular interest to women who have so far managed to retain their overall strong position with only a slight reduction of their total share of posts in the latter part of the 1990s. In sum, then, we have a picture of the situation of women lawyers in Poland today that is neither wholly black nor wholly white, but full of new and unpredictable opportunities as well as threats.

I began the description of women's situation in the legal professions by presenting the history of women studying in schools of law. Not all law graduates work in the legal professions. It is interesting that after 1989, among women in the highest positions, we quite often find law graduates. At times, although relatively seldom, such an education is required for a given position. That was the case with the first ombudsperson in Poland. After its creation, the post was filled by a woman, law professor Ewa Łętowska. Nonetheless, female lawyers have held high positions not only when a legal education was a necessary condition for filling the post. Thus Poland's first female prime minister, Hanna Suchocka, has a PhD in law; the first female marshal of the Senate Alicja Grześkowiak is a professor of law; and the first female president of the Narodowy Bank Polski [*Polish National Bank*] Hanna Gronkiewicz-Waltz is also a law professor. What's more, nearly all of them (with the exception of Ewa Łętowska) are associated with the political right. We can thus assume that in their case their legal education has allowed them to overcome prejudices regarding 'women's appropriate role' and stereotypes which right-leaning politicians often associate with 'femininity.' 'Being a competent lawyer' turns out to be more important than 'being a woman' for an explanation of the political abilities of these particular women active in centre-right parties. It also turns out that after 1989 being a female lawyer in Poland has opened up a range of career paths previously not available.

5　REFERENCES

Burakowski, Tadeusz. 1976. Trudna droga kobiet do adwokatury. *Palestra* section edition *Szkice z dziejów adwokatury w Polsce* adw. dr Roman Łyczywek.

Fuszara, Małgorzata. 1997. The Activities of Family Courts in Poland in: *International Journal of Law, Policy and the Family*, No 11.

Fuszara, Małgorzata. 1994. *Rodzina w sądzie*. Warsaw: University of Warsaw.

Halbesztadt, Jerzy. 1996. Kobiety w murach Uniwersytetu Warszawskiego, in *Kobieta i kultura*, A Żarnowska and A. Szwarc (eds), Warsaw: DIG.

Kurczewski, Jacek. 1994. Legal Professions in Transformation in Poland. In: *International Journal of the Legal Profession*, vol 1 No 3.

Kurczewski, Jacek. 2000. Wojna i pokój dwóch profesji prawniczych w Polsce. in: *Prace ISNS*, Warsaw: Instytut Stosowanych Nauk Społecznych UW.

Pietrzak, Michał. 1994. *Sytuacja prawna kobiety w II Rzeczypospolitej*. Unpublished manuscript.

Szafraniec, Joanna. 1982. Kobieta w zawodzie adwokata, *Palestra*, No 2.

Zielińska, Eleonora. 2000. Women in the Criminal Justice System, in *Crime and Law Enforcement in Poland. On the Threshold of the 21st Century*, Warsaw: Oficyna Naukowa.

21

Women Jurists in Finland at the Turn of the Century: Breakthrough or Intermezzo?

HARRIET SILIUS

Abstract

This chapter analyses the labour market for women jurists in Finland in the light of developments in the 1990s. First, it sketches the history of gender relations in the Finnish legal profession with reference to women's entry into the profession in Scandinavia. Secondly, the article deconstructs the results of a comprehensive study of women in the legal profession in Finland, which the author conducted a decade ago. She now argues that some of her previous results need to be revisited in the light of new empirical data.

Drawing on feminist theory the author concludes that quantitative feminisation of the legal profession does not change the culture of law, the legal profession or legal work in the short term. Instead a complicated web of contextual circumstances must be taken into account in order to understand changes in the gendered relations of the legal profession.

1 INTRODUCTION

There is perfect equality [in the legal profession]. Also considering salaries. There is absolutely no discrimination.

Well, this kind of position is not what you would expect of a lawyer with my experience—at least it is not what is expected of men; but I'm quite happy with it.

If you don't act in a deviant way [compared to men], then you are not treated differently by other people either.

THE ABOVE QUOTATIONS were typical of Finnish women jurists whom I interviewed for a study on their work ten years ago[1] (Silius 1992). They tried hard to convince me that gender was an irrelevance in their

---

[1] I use the term *jurist* for all members of the legal profession. Finland is a civil law country, and jurists hold a Master's degree or higher degrees in law. No BA-level jurists (although they do exist) were included in the 1992 study.

professional context. At the same time, they provided me with many examples of gendered organisational culture and working practices. The study showed that women jurists did not reach higher positions, but hit a glass ceiling; that they were paid 20 to 40 per cent less than their male colleagues; that they were not fully recognised by their colleagues or superiors, had to work harder to be noticed, and were treated differently from men.

The aim of this article is to analyse the labour market for jurists in terms of shifting gender relations. I will first sketch the history of gender relations in the Finnish legal profession in the wider context of developments in Scandinavian countries generally. Secondly, I will revisit the results of the large study of women in the Finnish legal profession which I conducted a decade ago, looking at its main results and evaluating some of them in the light of developments in the 1990s. In accordance with a considerable body of related feminist work (eg Thornton 1996; several authors in this volume), my point of departure is that quantitative feminisation of the legal profession does not equate with feminisation in the sense of de-masculinisation, or a change in gendered practices of legal work, culture or the profession itself. I will argue that in assessing change in gender relations in the legal professions it is of utmost importance to take into account contextual circumstances that help to bring it about. I conclude by discussing the wider implications of the Finnish case.

2 WOMEN'S ENTRY INTO THE LEGAL PROFESSION IN THE NORDIC COUNTRIES

In Finland as in the other Nordic[2] or Scandinavian countries, the legal profession remained a male preserve longer than in many others. Yet, the first women's entry into university law schools occurred at around the same time as their entry into other faculties. The first Norwegian woman law student, Cathrine Dahl, graduated in 1890 (Støren 1984). The first Swedish woman jurist, Elsa Eschelsson, took her doctoral degree in law in 1897 having previously been awarded a Master's degree in philosophy (Källman 1981). She was also the first woman in Sweden to reach the highly valued position of *docent*[3] (Ohlander 1987). Her aim was to become a professor of law at Uppsala University, and she sat and passed all examinations required. The professors of Uppsala University, however, decided in 1911, after a long debate, that a woman

---

[2] The Nordic countries are Denmark, Finland, Iceland, Norway and Sweden. In English-speaking contexts they are often called the Scandinavian countries. They are all civil law countries with great similarities in legislation and societal conditions.

[3] Being appointed *docent* by peer review is evidence of potential suitability for a professorial post. At the time in question, *docents* were highly qualified part-time university teachers who lectured more or less regularly alongside the professor.

could not be appointed to a professorship.[4] When Elsa Eschelsson learned the decision, she took her own life (Ohlander 1987).

In Finland the first woman law graduate was Agnes Lundell in 1906.[5] Agnes Lundell began her career as the secretary of a senate[6] division. Amongst the problems she had to face was the question what her professional dress should be, given that her male colleagues wore a black dress suit. After lengthy disputes it was decided that Miss Lundell should don a specially designed silk gown. Another controversy was sparked off when, setting up her own law firm, Agnes Lundell was not allowed to use her female first name in the name of the firm, but had to replace 'Agnes' with the initial 'A' (Winter-Mäkinen 1995). In spite of having to conceal her gender, Agnes Lundell made a successful career as the first woman lawyer in Finland.

The first woman to enter the Finnish judiciary was Katri Hakkila in the 1930s. Male staff at the court found her such an odd phenomenon that at the start of her career they all, fellow judges as well as secretarial personnel, kept wandering into her room to stare at her. Between 1906 and 1948, only 100 women took a law degree in Finland (Winter-Mäkinen 1995). Compared to other professions or academic fields of study, remarkably few women entered the legal profession in Finland before the Second World War. In the first two decades of the postwar period, women still made up fewer than 10 per cent of the profession, which helps to explain why a female judge in my study undertaken in 1989 referred to experiences not dissimilar to those of the first woman in the judiciary: during her early years as a judge, a member of the jury in a rural court told his colleague after inspecting the court hall, 'The judge hasn't arrived yet. There are only the messenger and a woman in the hall'.

The dramatic expansion of the university system of the late 1960s affected legal education only later, ie in the late 1970s, with the impact on the labour market only appearing in the 1980s. From then on the share of women in the profession continued to grow (Table 1), rising from 28 per cent to 42 per cent in the course of the 1990s and reaching 43 per cent in the year 2000.

In 1989, the number of women amongst Finnish first-year law students for the first time exceeded that of men (Silius 1992), and in 1992 women law graduates for the first time outnumbered male law graduates (Pajuoja & Ervasti 1994). In spite of these developments, women still represent a minority in the profession in all Nordic countries. While Sweden headed the list of countries giving access to women into the profession, Finland appeared to be more hesitant. Table 2 shows the share of women in the Nordic legal profession in the mid 1990s:

---

[4] At the beginning of the century women in Sweden and Finland were not legally eligible to be appointed as civil servants. This legislation was changed in the 1920s.

[5] Women in Finland got the vote in parliamentary elections the same year.

[6] Since independence in 1917, the Finnish parliament has had only one chamber.

Table 1: The share of women in the Finnish legal profession 1928–2000

Year	Share of women jurists in %
1928	0.7
1940	1.7
1960	6.2
1975	13.6
1982	19.9
1985	24.0
1989	28.0
1999	42.0
2000	43.0

SOURCES: For 1928–1989: Silius 1992; for 1999 and 2000: data provided by the Association of Finnish Lawyers.

Table 2: The share of women in the legal profession in the Nordic countries in the mid-1990s

Country	Year	Number of jurists	Share of women jurists in %
Denmark	1994	25,418	31
Finland	1994	12,030	29
Norway	1995	10,556	31
Sweden	1995	12,388	37

SOURCE: Silius 1995

3 FINNISH WOMEN LAWYERS AT THE START OF THE 1990S

In the late 1980s, I conducted the first study on women in the legal profession in Finland (Silius 1992). The study had three aims: to analyse the labour market and working conditions of women jurists, to examine how women jurists managed to combine work and caring, and to study the type of work women jurists were engaged in. The study consisted of an extensive questionnaire survey (201 variables) directed at a large sample (one fifth of all women in the legal profession). The response rate was 69 per cent. The survey was followed up a few years later by targeted, qualitative interviews with 15 women jurists, all of whom had participated in the questionnaire study. The women selected represented a range of sectors of legal work, age groups, positions in working life and family situations. The results of the study were summarised in the form of three 'contracts' of women jurists: the work contract, the caring contract and the professional contract. From a labour market perspective the work contract was the most interesting one. It revealed the importance of gate-keeping, the segregation of the legal labour market, sexism in the legal profession, and the fact that male and female jurists followed very separate career paths (for details, see Silius 1992: 129–164).

At the time of the study, women made up between a quarter and a third of the legal profession in Scandinavia or the Nordic countries. In retrospect, the situation of the late 1980s and early 1990s made a study of this kind a very timely one, as it was then that, for the first time, the number of women in the legal profession was sufficiently large to be expected to begin to make an impact.

When analysing the results in the early 1990s, I concluded that two types of segregation affected the position of women jurists. The first and perhaps most important mode of segregation was a hierarchical one, with women jurists being allocated the position of 'the Other' by the established profession. The legal culture appeared to be unchanged by the entrance of women. The interviews created the profile of a profession with efficient gate-keeping mechanisms and important old boys' networks. The dominant culture of the legal profession seemed to foster masculine values. Women jurists had the choice between adopting these values and creating new spaces for themselves at the margins of or even outside traditional legal work, mainly in the public sector.

During the last 150 years, the public sector, in particular the state, has offered space for Finnish jurists to widen and shape their fields of work. Initially men, and later many women, too, were able to draw up new agendas by using their knowledge and skills creatively. In 1992, my conclusion based on interviews was that there existed a masculine professional contract, which most women in the profession had to accept. However, there were marginal sections of the profession which offered new arenas, such as legislative work, including setting up standards for the interpretation of laws and regulations in the fields of, for instance, the welfare state and human rights. I saw this as promising for the future. As the development of the welfare state was accelerating, there would be more space for women jurists, and in due course the law itself might become less masculine.

In addition to the existence of symbolic hierarchies, my 1992 study found evidence for the assumption of a second type of gender segregation, namely one concerning working and material conditions, resulting in the emergence of two separate occupational fields defined by gender. In the early 1990s, three quarters of all Finnish women jurists were employed by the public sector and less than one quarter worked in the private sector. Almost four out of 10 worked in the judiciary, while only one in 10 worked in a law firm. My conclusion was that the public sector was and would continue to be the main employer for women jurists. In the period from the 1960s up to the 1990s, public sector expansion showed no signs of slowing down. On the contrary the judiciary expanded, the state or the semi-state sector needed more jurists to develop citizens' rights, and even municipalities began to offer legal services, via a system of legal aid. As in all this Finland had started later and from a lower base, the country did its best to catch up fast with the other Nordic countries in creating a comprehensive Scandinavian-type welfare state.

Between 1928 and 1985 the share of the public sector as the main employer of jurists in Finland had ranged between 56 and 64 per cent (Silius 1992: 82–87). In

2000 the share was 58 per cent.[7] This implies that there had been no significant change over 70 years, a feature that is quite extraordinary in the context of a profession which has always been involved in both the private and the public sector. But the figure of 58 per cent might also signal redistribution over the two sectors following new patterns. In my analysis of 10 years ago, I predicted that women jurists would continue to opt for the public sector, and as their numbers were growing, the most dedicated ones would opt for judicial work. Given that scholars had already noticed an increasing feminisation of the judicial system in a number of countries (Bertilsson 1989 for Sweden, Boigeol 1993 for France), it seemed justified to conclude that the private sector would turn into a male stronghold, with large international law firms representing the top bastion.

This second type of gender-based segregation identified in the 1992 study went beyond the emergence of different career paths for women and men in that it was also reflected in income differentiation.[8] Women did not reach the top positions, even in the public sector where seniority was the key criterion for promotion. There was evidence of what, by Finnish standards, amounted to significant discrepancies in salaries and incomes of male and female jurists, which could not be explained away by reference to lack of years of experience, but, on the contrary, seemed to increase with individuals' years experience (Silius 1992: 145). In the public sector, where working longer hours had no influence on employees' salaries, the main reasons for salary differentials appeared to be either a women-dominated workplace or a low position in the hierarchy[9] (Silius 1992: 142). Surprisingly, the survey provided no evidence of any income differentials between women jurists in the public and in the private sectors. Three factors might help to explain this. Firstly, at that time there was little difference between salaries and incomes in the two sectors generally, with the private sector incomes being at a relatively low level; secondly, the average age of women jurists was relatively low; and thirdly, the total 1992 sample size was small.

4   DEVELOPMENTS IN THE 1990S: SECTORS AND SALARIES

The 1990s brought a number of changes to Finnish society, which also impacted on the legal profession. Firstly, there was the banking crisis of the early 1990s. As banks were restructured or even closed down, women jurists were perceived to be less costly than men. My 1992 study led me to expect that banking would be a future arena for women jurists. Generally, in the early 1990s, the Finnish economy was hit by a severe economic recession. Overall unemployment figures

---

[7] The share is calculated on the basis of data provided by the Association of Finnish Lawyers.

[8] The results are further elaborated in Silius (1995).

[9] From a European point of view, the Finnish labour market appears highly segregated into men's and women's work, and the two sectors are subject to two very different systems of financial rewards.

rose between 1992 and 1995 from around five per cent to around 20 per cent, making Finland the country with the second-highest level of unemployment in the European Union after Spain. The subsequent cuts in the public sector later in the 1990s did not, however, immediately affect legal personnel, but mainly those working in the areas of caring, health and education. What the recession did bring about was an end to the expansion of the welfare state, reductions in municipal legal aid and a contraction of the public sphere as an arena for experiments, alternative lawyering and new agendas.

In the last 10 years, dramatic changes have occurred within the labour market for women jurists. Recent figures provided in Table 3 indicate this very strikingly.

Table 3: Employment sectors of women jurists 1988, 1998 and 2000 (in %)

Sector	Employment	1988	1998	2000
Private (total)		23	37	36
	Law firms	9	10	10
	Industry	14	27	26
Public (total)		77	63	64
	Municipalities	7	5	5
	Courts	38	25	22
	State	32	33	37

SOURCES: For 1988: Silius 1992; for 1998 and 2000: data provided by the Association of Finnish Lawyers.

According to Table 3, women are leaving the public sector. As the public sector, as such, has not lost in significance as an employer for jurists (it still employs 58 per cent of the total), one can conclude that the anticipated sharp division between women in the public and men in the private sector has not materialised. On the contrary, women are now seen to be opting for the private sector. While in 1988 only 23 per cent of female jurists were working in the private sector, 10 years later this figure had risen to 37 per cent. At the same time, courts in 1998 were employing merely 25 per cent of Finnish women jurists, while the equivalent figure for 1988 had been 38 per cent. Contrary to my expectations, the small municipal sector (mainly legal aid) never did become an important niche for women, indeed, numbers here even shrank after 1988.

Looking at the situation in the private sector in greater detail, we find that in 1998 50 per cent of women were employed in insurance, commerce and business. The other 50 per cent were either working in private law firms (27 per cent) or in banking (23 per cent). Amongst the latter, 40 per cent were women and 60 per cent men.[10] A remarkable feature of women's employment in the private sector is that the share of women in law firms has remained unchanged during

---

[10] All new data in this article stem from raw data kindly provided by the Association of Finnish Lawyers.

the last decade. The data do not allow us to decide whether this is due to law firms avoiding to hire women or to a pull effect of expanding business firms.

All this invites the conclusion that the structure of the labour market for women jurists is gradually approaching that for men jurists. The hypothesis that there are two separate sectors for women and men has not been verified by statistics for the late 1990s. Yet, gendered differences do persist. In the late 1990s, 46 per cent of male jurists were working in the private sector, among them 19 per cent in law firms, compared to 37 per cent of women jurists of whom 10 per cent were working in law firms.[11] In other words, the Finnish advocacy continues to be male-dominated. Only 28 per cent of its members are women. This is also true for Sweden, where only one in eight practising lawyers is female. Yet the Chair of the Swedish Bar Association has, from 1999, been a woman (*Scanorama* 2000). Another area of legal work in Finland that continues to be male-dominated is the public prosecution service, where in 1998 only 27 per cent were women.

The most remarkable trend of recent years seems to me to be that judicial work has ceased to attract women to the same degree as it did in 1988. While then 38 per cent of women jurists worked as judges, this figure had dropped to 25 per cent 10 years later. By 2000 it had fallen to 22 per cent. As far as recruitment is concerned, mainstreaming in the judiciary by 1998 appeared to be almost perfect: 48 per cent of newly recruited judges were women. Two years later the share of men had grown from 52 to 54 per cent. These data fail to suggest that women are about to take over the courts in the new millennium. On the contrary, one might wish to hypothesise that courts in Finland are making sure that women do not take over.[12]

In 1988 the three main employment sectors for women jurists were, in order of priority: the judiciary, the state and the private sector. Today this order is reversed with the private sector having moved to first position, the state taking second place, and the judiciary having dropped to third place. Why should that be so? Without the benefit of careful analysis, we can only hypothesise. Firstly, if public sector legal work, as some researchers into Nordic legal work have argued (Alapuro 1988; Konttinen 1990; Burrage & Torstendahl 1990), is primarily welfare state work, Finnish women jurists may have become aware of the problems of the welfare state at an early stage and headed straight for a career in the private sector. While 10 years ago the judiciary was a dream career, this is probably no longer the case. Secondly, the relative expansion of the private sector brought about by the economic recession in Finland on the one hand and Finland's accession to the European Union and subsequently to the European Monetary Union on the other, may have increased its attraction for women jurists, as expanding new fields traditionally seem to open up spaces for women,

---

[11] In total, practising lawyers, or advocats, comprise only 15 per cent of Finnish jurists.
[12] Although courts are required to pay attention to equal opportunities, neither affirmative (positive) action nor any quotas are applied.

at least in the initial phase. Thirdly, the reorganisation of the court system, which accompanied the rationalisation of the public sector, brought with it a deterioration of working conditions and a reduction of chances of promotion. All this might suggest that the public sector, especially the judiciary, have lost their appeal as *the* career for women jurists. At the same time, the attraction of the private sector for them might be no more than a passing phase. Only time will tell whether what has been described here represents more than a mere blip in the employment patterns of Finnish women jurists.

If gender-based segregation in terms of areas of work does not seem to be increasing, how about income differences? After all, segregation might just be taking new forms. Women jurists might, for instance, be entering previously male-dominated fields but only to occupy the lower ranks, thus leaving income discrepancies intact. In 1988 women jurists' income in the private sector was only 65 per cent of that of their male colleagues, the highest gendered income gap among university graduates in Finland (Aitta 1988). The situation was more favourable for young jurists, where women's salaries amounted to at least 82 per cent of men's. As for the highest income levels, women managed to achieve a mere 57 per cent of what men were earning. Table 4 shows the situation in 1998 compared to 10 years earlier.

Table 4: Income of women lawyers in % of income of male lawyers in the private sector in Finland (1988, 1998)

	1988	1998	Change 1988–98
10th fractile[13]	82	89	+ 7
90th fractile	57	69	+ 12
Median	68	76	+ 8
Mean	65	73	+ 8

SOURCES: For 1988, Silius 1992; for 1998, Immeli 1999.

There is in these statistics clear evidence that the gender-based income gap that is between 7 and 12 per cent has narrowed considerably over the ten-year period. While the income differential in 1988 ranged between 43 and 18 per cent, it was only between 31 and 11 per cent a decade later. Were this trend to continue, the gap might close totally in the next 10 to 15 years.

Private sector incomes for lawyers are of particular interest not only because data are available to allow a study of developments over time, but also because they are on average around 25 per cent higher than those of jurists in the public sector (Immeli 1999). In addition, the private sector might reasonably be

---

[13] The 10th fractile shows that 90% earn *more* than this level, the 90th fractile that 10% earn *more* than this level.

Table 5: Salary differentials between female and male jurists in the public sector in Finland (women's salaries in % of men's) (1998).

	State	Differential	Municipal	Differential
10th fractile	81	−19	76	−24
90th fractile	85	−15	65	−35
Median	80	−20	73	−17
Mean	83	−17	77	−23

SOURCE: Based on data in Immeli 1999.

expected to be the one most sensitive to market mechanisms. A recent study by the Association of Finnish Lawyers allows us to complete the picture by showing salary differentials between men and women in the public sector (Table 5).

Comparing these figures with those for the private sector, we find that salary differentials between men and women lawyers are smallest in the state sector. On the other hand, in the lowest income group within the private sector, that is, among young jurists, these differentials are only 12 per cent, compared to 19 per cent in the state sector and 24 per cent in the municipal sector. In the top income group (90th fractile) women do best in the state (85 per cent), worse in the private sector (69 per cent), but worst of all in the municipal sector (65 per cent). All this might explain why women prefer the private sector to the municipal one. Figures for the latter suggest that the high degree of gender-based segregation may be due to women mainly working in legal aid, while men tend to occupy the top positions in municipal management. Because of the small number of jurists employed in this sector, this is, however, of no general importance to either female or male jurists. The reasons for women jurists' preference for the private compared to the state sector are obvious from Table 6.

Two fascinating developments in terms of women jurists' incomes have occurred during the last decade. Firstly, an income gap has come to separate women in the private from those in the public sector, a gap, which in the 1992 study had not yet been observable. By 1998 it had grown to between 15 and 38 per cent. There are several possible reasons for this: in the survey of 1992 women

Table 6: Women jurists' income/salary per month by employment sector in Finland (1998, in Euro)

	Private	State	Municipal
10th fractile	2271	1875	1904
90th fractile	4844	3868	3517
Median	4000	2691	2738
Mean	3360	2815	2753

SOURCE: based on Immeli 1999.

jurists were asked to tick the proper income level, while calculations in the 1998 study were based on absolute figures; also, in the earlier study, the number of private sector lawyers with top incomes may have been too low to affect the total results (this in turn may have been due to, for instance, high-income lawyers' lower response rate). Secondly, it is reasonable to assume that income differentials have increased for jurists generally in the two sectors.[14] As the share of women jurists in the private sector goes up, they also benefit from rising income levels there. In monetary terms, the two sectors seem to be moving in different directions.

5 CONCLUDING OBSERVATIONS

My 1992 study of women in the legal profession in Finland led me to draw up a number of hypotheses: that the Finnish legal profession would continue to be dominated by men and that a masculine culture would persist; that women jurists would flock to the public sector, preferably the judiciary, leaving men to monopolise the private sector; that the judiciary would therefore be subject to a gradual process of feminisation; that because of the distribution of female and male jurists over the various sectors and types work, income differentials would remain fairly stable; finally, that no major differentials amongst women jurists themselves would occur, as the majority of them would continue to opt for the public sector. However, at the start of the new millennium, this entire picture has changed.

Although today women jurists are no longer stared at or remain literally unseen (as was the case when they first entered the profession), they are still acting as pioneers when breaking into male occupational communities (Gherardi 1996). Examples of sexist behaviour can still be found in Finnish legal culture, while at the same time serious attempts to eradicate discrimination are being made. In gender terms, legal culture has become more heterogeneous. This is in line with feminist studies of organisational cultures (eg Korvajärvi 1998a and 1998b; Woodall, Edwards and Welchman 1997) indicating that as conditions change, gendering processes, too, are reshaped and become more complex.

This article suggests that women jurists in Finland are entering the private sector in growing numbers, where, however, they are more welcome in business than in law firms. The judiciary shows an exemplary gender balance in terms of mainstreaming, but there is nothing to suggest an increasingly feminised culture. And finally, as income differentials between female and male jurists are diminishing, growing discrepancies appear amongst incomes of women themselves, at least in the private sector where incomes generally are highest.

---

[14] It is difficult to provide specific evidence, as very few studies of jurists' salaries in the public sector exist. Besides, only the most recent statistics provide separate figures for the two sexes.

Comprehensive social changes have been identified as being at the root of these developments. I would suggest that the majority of these changes have been: firstly, the end of the expansion of the welfare state; secondly, the deregulation of markets; and, thirdly, the economic recession of the mid-1990s followed by the economic boom of the late 1990s. The contraction of the welfare state implied a relative drop in salary levels, tougher working conditions and a push away from what was traditionally the major employment market for women jurists, that is, the public sector. Deregulation in a number of markets has led to a pull to the private sector. The economic recession, including the banking crisis, has created new work opportunities for lawyers within the space of a few years. The present boom offers new jobs in private industry. As far as Finland is concerned, the special relation between the welfare state, the market, and the economic situation has been a crucial factor in changing working conditions for jurists. Apart from bringing about an increase in heterogeneity among women jurists, the new context might introduce a break-through in terms of fading segregation, diminishing income gaps, and a growing equal opportunities culture. As the legal profession is becoming more market-led, it will also become more sensitive to economic change. At the start of the third millennium, women lawyers working in business live in Nokia-Finland[15] in a fast growing economy. Any future recession is undoubtedly going to mean restructuring, downsizing and outsourcing in private companies. Such scenarios can affect the careers of women in management in a variety of ways. According to Woodall, Edwards and Welchman (1997) the experience of organisational restructuring is akin to participation in a lottery in which women are occasionally winners, but usually losers. This is why it is safe to assume that the situation at the turn of the century may be no more than an intermezzo in the history of Finnish women jurists.

Feminist theoretical discussions as well as the empirical results of this study underline the impossibility of assessing the past or, indeed, the future of women jurists in a unitary way. Women jurists no longer represent one homogeneous group.[16] Studying women in the legal profession requires targeting different groups of women in multiple societal contexts, using various methodological approaches as well as comparisons over time, while also drawing on feminist theory to facilitate an understanding and evaluation of empirical findings.

The Finnish case gives cause for pessimism as well as for hope. While, at the start of the new millennium, some Finnish women jurists burn themselves out under heavy workloads in state agencies, others in the private sector are doing better every day. On 1 March 2000, a woman jurist, Tarja Halonen, was inaugurated as the first woman President of the Finnish Republic. For women jurists in the public sector, this has been their greatest victory.

[15] Nokia, a company selling eg mobile phones, was in 2000 at the hub of the economic boom in Finland.

[16] Here I find myself in full agreement with other contributors to this volume (eg Rhode and Sommerlad).

6 REFERENCES

Aitta, Ulla. 1988. *Jämställdheten mellan kvinnor och män i de finländska akademikernas arbetsliv* [Equality between women and men in the working life of Finnish university graduates]. Helsinki: AKAVA.

Alapuro, Risto. 1988. *State and Revolution in Finland*. Berkeley: University of California Press.

Bertilsson, Margareta. 1989. Juristerna i välfärdsstaten [Jurists in the welfare state]. In *Kampen om yrkesutövning, status och kunskap* [The battle for profession, status and knowledge], Staffan Selander (ed). Lund: Studentlitteratur, 147–166.

Boigeol, Anne. 1993. La magistrature française au féminin: entre spécificité et banalisation. *Droit et Société* 25; 489–523.

Burrage, Michael & Torstendahl, Rolf (eds). 1990. *Professions in Theory and History*. London: Sage.

Gherardi, Sylvia. 1996. Gendered Organizational Cultures: Narratives of Women Travellers in a Male World. *Gender, Work and Organization* 3; 187–201.

Immeli, Pekka. 1999. *Lakimieskunnan palkkatutkimus* [Salary survey of the legal profession], Helsinki 16.5.1999 (manuscript).

Källman, Marianne. 1981.Våra förmödrar: Elsa Eschelsson [Our foremothers: Elsa Eschelsson]. *Kvinnovetenskaplig tidskrift* 2; 82–83.

Konttinen, Esa. 1990. *Traditional Power Groups and the Prominent Position of the Legal Profession in Nineteenth-Century Finland*. Paper presented at the XII. World Congress of Sociology, Madrid.

Korvajärvi, Päivi. 1998a. Reproducing Gendered Hierarchies in Everyday Work: Contradictions in an Employment Office. *Gender, Work and Organization* 5; 19–30.

Korvajärvi, Päivi. 1998b. *Gendering Dynamics in White-Collar Work Organizations*. Tampere: University of Tampere, Acta Universitatis Tamperensis 600.

Ohlander, Ann-Sofie. 1987. En utomordentlig balansakt. Kvinnliga forskarpionjärer i Norden [An extraordinary balancing act. Women pioneering scholars in the Nordic countries]. *Historisk tidskrift*, 1, 2–22.

Pajuoja, Jussi & Ervasti, Kaijus. 1994. *Suomen Lakimiesliiton historia* [History of the Finnish Legal Association]. Jyväskylä: Lakimiesliiton kustannus.

Scanorama. 2000. Woman at the Top. *Scanorama*, February, 2000. *The Specialist Lawyers' Supplement*.

Silius, Harriet. 1992. *Den kringgärdade kvinnligheten. Att vara kvinnlig jurist i Finland* [Contracted femininity. To be a woman lawyer in Finland]. Åbo: Åbo Akademis Förlag.

Silius, Harriet. 1995. Att vara kvinna och jurist [To be woman and a lawyer]. In *13 kvinnoperspektiv på rätten* [13 feminist perspectives on law]. Edited by Gudrun Nordborg. Uppsala: Iustus, 1–19.

Støren, Thordis. 1984. *Justitias døtre* [Daughters of Justitia]. Oslo: Universitetsforlaget.

Thornton, Margaret. 1996. *Dissonance and Distrust. Women in the Legal Profession*. Melbourne: Oxford University Press.

Winter-Mäkinen, Anneli. 1995. *Naisjuristien 1. vuosisata* [The first century of women jurists]. Helsinki: Lakimiesliiton kustannus.

Woodall, Jean, Edwards, Christine and Welchman, Rosemary. 1997. Organizational Restructuring and the Achievement of an Equal Opportunity Culture. *Gender, Work and Organization* 4; 2–11.

22

Male Strategies in the Face of the Feminisation of a Profession: the Case of the French Judiciary*

ANNE BOIGEOL

Abstract

In spite of considerable resistance on the part of their male colleagues, the share of women in the French judiciary has increased to such an extent that today parity of numbers has been achieved. This paper begins by tracing this process of feminisation. It then looks at male judges' responses to this threat to their traditional superior authority and shows that these have consisted, above all, in creating and recreating a differentiation of professional functions in order to maintain some form of male distinctiveness.

1 INTRODUCTION

SINCE THE END of the Second World War, all branches of the legal profession have been officially open to women.[1] But feminisation has not occurred at the same speed in all areas, with greatest inroads having been made into the judicial professions of judge and public prosecutor (*la magistrature*). In terms of pure numbers, parity has been achieved, as half of the *magistrats* are female. This feminisation, brought about by structural changes in society, has been instrumental in challenging the male domination of the judiciary. However, the process has been a protracted one, as male domination,

---

* Translated from the French by Gordon Hodgkin.
[1] In France, as in most civil law countries, there are several different branches of the legal profession, each one governed by its own code. There is the *magistrature*, which includes both judges and members of the public prosecution service. *Magistrats* have a status akin to that of civil servants. *Avocats*, on the other hand, are members of a liberal profession. In addition, there are professions such as notary, clerk of the court, *avoué* and official auctioneer, all of whom hold a *charge* and are at the same time members of a liberal profession and public officers. This inheritance from the *Ancien Régime*, further developed during the French Revolution, means that those holding a *charge* exercise delegated state power in the form of a lifelong monopoly in a certain area of professional activity. On retiring, they are entitled to present their successor for approval to the authorities.

albeit in gradual overall decline, has been constantly reinventing itself by means of ever-new processes of internal differentiation (Bourdieu 1998). This paper discusses the strategies developed by male French *magistrats* to modify the impact of the feminisation of their profession on their own positions. Following a brief historical overview of women's increasing access to judicial posts, the paper looks into the reasons for women's preference for the judiciary and the ways in which they are challenging male domination. Finally, men's responses to this process and their strategies to retain some form of domination are analysed and presented.

2   WOMEN'S ACCESS TO THE LEGAL PROFESSION

It has never been easy for women to enter any branch of the legal profession. Most of these were set up on an all-male model, and sometimes specific legislation has been required to create access for women. The first to open its doors to women members was the bar (*le barreau*), one hundred years ago. In 1900, a law was passed authorising women to become *avocats*. This followed a three-year battle led by a strong-willed aspiring *avocat* named Jeanne Chauvin who already held a doctorate in law and who undertook to fight the established professions, both *magistrature* and *barreau*, neither of which had any desire to relinquish their all-male monopoly.

In 1897, this young woman (her doctoral thesis had aptly been entitled 'A historical study of the professions open to women: the influence of semitism on the changing economic position of women in society') had presented herself to the Paris court of appeal in order to be sworn in as *avocat*. Although tradition required that the President of the Bar (*bâtonnier*) accompanied the candidate, Jeanne Chauvin had to make do with a mere *avoué*.[2] Her application was then turned down by the court, on the pretext that, according to old bar regulations reintroduced in 1810, 'the profession of *avocat* was considered to be *un office viril*'. Another argument put forward was that women lacked the civic right to hold a position in the legal administration, and that even *avocats* were occasionally called upon to stand in for judges. Glasson, a law professor, commented at the time that this represented a misinterpretation of the old notion of *office viril* and that, in any case, the notion had long since fallen into abeyance (Glasson 1898). When the law of 1900 was passed, it clearly stipulated that under no circumstances could a female *avocat* ever replace a judge.

Thus grand principles concerning women's lack of civic rights were invoked to prevent them from becoming judges, public prosecutors and *avocats*. These were, however, not invoked in the case of lay judges. Thus women were able to

---

[2] The *avoués* used to manage the procedure and represent people in courts; they drafted the written documents. The *avocats* did the pleading in court. In 1971 *avocats* and *avoués* merged under the name of *avocats*, except for courts of appeal where there are still *avoués*.

become judges in industrial tribunals as early as 1908, and in commercial courts, on identical terms with men, from 1931. The first legal *office* to admit women was that of official auctioneer (*commissaire-priseur*), possibly because it was indeed the least judicial of such *offices*.[3]

It was also in 1931 that a woman passed the *concours d'agrégation*, an academic competition, allowing her to become the first woman law professor in France,[4] as there was no need for new legislation to permit access by women to academia. In 1944, women were granted suffrage and could then also stand for parliamentary office. This, in turn, made it impossible not to allow them access to judicial office. In 1946 this was done, however grudgingly. Some of the other branches of the legal profession, that is notaries (*notaires*), *avoués* and bailiffs (*huissiers*), took a few more years before allowing women to join their ranks.

3 FEMINISING THE JUDICIARY

3.1 Feminisation of Law Studies and of the Legal Professions

Up to the beginning of the Second World War, law faculties in France had the largest number of students, but the lowest percentage of female students due to the lack of employment opportunities for female law graduates. In 1900, female students represented 3.2 per cent of the overall student body, but only 0.1 per cent of law students. In 1930, the figures were 25.5 per cent and 12.3 per cent respectively. By 1950, women made up 34 per cent of all students, but only 24.8 per cent of law students.

Feminisation increased from the mid-1960s with the arrival in the universities of the generations born after the war. This trend was much more pronounced amongst law students than in other disciplines, as for instance the sciences, the reason being, of course, the careers advice given in secondary schools in France. Empirical research into socialisation at school and subsequent relationships between the sexes has shown that, from a very early age, children discover at school that academic disciplines have sexual connotations. They then prefer to invest their academic energies and talents in those disciplines that reinforce their sexual identity and, in a more general sense, to develop the intellectual qualities associated with these (Duru-Bellat 1990). Thus there already exists a form of early channelling of students into certain career paths, which then takes on a more concrete form in their choice of *baccalauréat*. While boys are more heavily represented in the science-based *baccalauréat*, girls tend to sit the *baccalauréat* which leads, in particular, towards law studies, the so-called 'economics and social science' *baccalauréat* (Table 1).

---

[3] Law dated 20 April 1924. It was in 1928 that the first woman became an official auctioneer, by succeeding her husband.

[4] This lady, Madame Charlotte Lagarde-Béquignon, was not merely the first woman law professor in France. She also, in 1946, became the first appeal court judge, following her acceptance into the *magistrature*.

Table 1: The various types of *baccalauréat* showing total number of candidates and percentage of girls (1997)

'Science' (47.7%)		'Economics and social science' (27.2%)		'Arts' (25.1%)	
Number	% Girls	Number	% Girls	Number	% Girls
131302	43.2	74794	62.3	69017	82.2

SOURCE: French Ministry of Education DPD (BCP), 1999.

Table 2: Changes to the percentage of women amongst law graduates

Year	First degree		DEA*		DESS**		Doctorate	
	No	%W	No	%W	No	%W	No	%W
1997	15582	65.2	4454	60.1	4472	61.8	588	35.2
1988	8622	59.1	2359	51.8	2330	52.7	375	26.9
1977	6983	47.4	1890	34.6	900	36.9	349	18.9

SOURCE: French Ministry of Education . DPD, 1978, 1989, 1998 (*statistiques annuelles*).

* *Diplôme d'études approfondies* (graduate diploma after five years of study), which is the prerequisite for PhD registration.
** *Diplôme d'études supérieures spécialisées* (after five years of study), ie a diploma based on practical training preceding entry into employment.

From the early 1970s women began to outnumber men among first-year students in French law faculties. This trend then spread to all degree studies, the only exception being doctoral studies where male domination has persisted (Table 2).

As a result, there has been strong pressure from women on the legal employment market. But whereas all branches of the legal profession are subject to feminisation, there remain major discrepancies. This study is limited to the traditional branches of the legal profession, thus excluding in-house lawyers and those working in public administration.

A distinction can be drawn between, on the one hand, the judicial branches of the legal profession, that is, judges, public prosecutors, *avocats* and clerks of the court (*greffes*), which include high percentages of women, and, on the other hand, non-judicial branches, such as notary, bailiff, *avoué* and official auctioneer. The latter are all *charges* or *offices* in the tradition of the *Ancient Régime*, and their admission is subject to a *numerus clausus* (Table 3).

The distribution shown in Table 3 allows an analysis of the degree of feminisation of the various legal professions by mode of selection used.

Table 3: Degree of feminisation of the various legal professions

Profession	Number	% Women
Professors of Law (1998)*	1,261	13.6
Judges and public prosecutors (1999)	6,550	48.5
Avocats (1999)	33,545	45.0
Chief clerks of the court (1994)	1,015	67.0
Avoués (1997)	390	30.2
*Avocats aux conseils*** (1997)	87	14.6
Notaries (1997)	7,624	12.4
Bailiffs (1997)	3,247	17.7
Auctioneers (1997)	456	16.7

* These exclude *maîtres de conférences* (the lower grade, where the proportion of women is significantly higher, namely 33.3 per cent)
** *Avocats aux conseils* are a special category of *avocats*, who argue and conduct the cases in the *Conseil d'Etat* and *Cour de cassation* (supreme courts of administrative justice and of judicial justice). They hold offices whose number is limited, as are the numbers of offices of notaries, *avoués*, auctioneers or bailiffs.

SOURCE: Ministry of Education 1998 (personal communication) and Ministry of Justice (*Annuaire statistique de la justice* 1999)

3.2 Feminisation and Mode of Selection for the Various Legal Professions: Relevance of Selection by Examination Results

Women have found it easiest to enter those branches of the legal profession for which the selection process is based on academic merit.[5] Where recruitment is based on inherited property and requires other types of capital, especially economic capital, women are still under-represented. This applies to notaries, *avoués*, *avocats aux conseils*, bailiffs, or even official auctioneers, all of whom need to hold an *office* or *charge* to be able to practise. For a long time it was not essential to have a law degree in order to practise as, for instance, a notary; indeed, a degree counted for less than family relations or economic capital. An *office* needs to be either purchased or inherited. The *charge* is still generally left to one's son. Only when there are no sons is it left to daughters, as happens in the case of official auctioneers in accordance with the principle of the 'missing brother' ('*frère manquant*') or the 'ineligible brother' ('*frère défaillant*') (Quémin 1998).[6] When the incumbent wishes to retire, he presents his designated successor to the public authorities for approval.

[5] In England, it has been shown that co-opting of members of a profession via professional associations and on the basis of criteria other than purely academic ones has traditionally been detrimental to the interests of women (Crompton and Sanderson 1990). In this volume, Kate Malleson defines recruitment by consultation as essentially a system of self-reproduction.
[6] The theory of the 'missing son' was developed in Quebec by Isabelle Lavergnas, and used in France by Catherine Marry in connection with women engineers (Marry 1989); she then went on to add the category of 'missing brother' (Daune-Richard and Marry 1990).

In contrast, those branches of the profession where recruitment is based on an examination, whether this is competitive or not, are the ones which women have the greatest chance of entering. If they are well endowed with academic capital, they are well placed to succeed.[7] Couched in more general terms: it is the outsiders, those who have neither the personal contacts nor the capital traditionally needed to enter a particular profession, who have something to gain from this mode of recruitment. The competitive entrance examination for judges or public prosecutors dates from the beginning of the twentieth century. Up until that time social capital was required in order to be able to benefit from recommendations, especially political ones, if one wished to embark on a judicial career. One of the reasons for the introduction of the competitive examination was to include those 'candidates who had the knowledge but lacked contacts' (Rousselet 1947). It took another 40 years before women were able to benefit from this system.

3.3 Men's Lack of Interest in Judicial Careers

The waning interest of men in the judicial professions is not a new phenomenon; indeed, it even preceded the entry of women into the judiciary. First manifestations were a loss of social prestige followed by recruitment problems. Families with a legal tradition (judiciary, bar, notariat) that traditionally produced many future judges and public prosecutors, increasingly steered their sons towards other professions. The *avocats* who dominated access to positions in higher courts during the Third Republic almost ceased to turn to this profession.[8] This withdrawal of lawyers' families, especially the most powerful amongst them, opened access to the judiciary for middle-ranking civil servants and the provincial middle-classes with less capital, in particular less economic capital, at their disposal. But poor judicial salaries coupled with a lack of personal economic capital barred these new entrants from adopting the standard of living previous generations of judges and prosecutors had enjoyed. In the 1950s, the number of male applicants for judicial posts dropped tangibly, as rapid expansion in the public and semi-public sectors drove up the demand for public law specialists.

The arrival of the post-war generations on the job market had the effect of temporarily increasing the supply of male candidates. But by the 1980s, the lack of appeal of a judicial career became apparent, especially for young male lawyers, who preferred to turn to other legal fields, in particular that of the corporate lawyer (*barreau d'affaires*). Many young people began to see the

---

[7] According to a survey carried out at the French national judicial training establishment, women students were much more successful in their university studies than men students (Boigeol 1991).

[8] Alain Bancaud has noted that, between 1870 and 1940, 71 per cent of the most highly placed judges in the final court of appeal had either been conference secretary for the training course, or had been *avocats* for several years before joining the ranks of the judiciary (Bancaud 1993).

judiciary as a long and laborious career, where personal merit was rarely rewarded. Today selectivity is strong, candidates are numerous, but only one quarter of them are men (ENM 1999).

Intriguingly, women contribute to a certain slowing down of this loss of status of the profession of judge/public prosecutor. In the early 1950s, the chairman of the selection committee for the competitive entrance examination noted that, 'female candidates come from the social class from which all judges and public prosecutors were recruited in the old days.' Subsequent research has confirmed that successful female candidates tend to come from a slightly higher social class than male candidates (Bodiguel 1991; Boigeol 1991).

3.4 *Magistrature* and *Barreau*: Differing Patterns of Feminisation

If the various branches of the legal profession have opened their doors to women at different stages in history, patterns of feminisation have also varied. The comparison between bar and judiciary is revealing, as both include a high proportion of women. The feminisation of the French advocacy has been a gradual process and, even more significantly, has been going on for far longer, as women were given the right to become *avocats* as early as 1900. Before the Second World War, their share was 15 per cent, in 1950 it was 20 per cent, in 1970 it rose to 30 per cent and by the end of the 1980s it had reached around 40 per cent (Karpik 1995). Today it stands at 45 per cent (Ministry of Justice, DACS 1999). This trend is obviously accelerating a little, since in 1997 in the Paris bar women made up 34.5 per cent of registered *avocats*, but 58 per cent of trainee *avocats*. The degree of feminisation in judicial professions is even more spectacular, given that the first entry of women into the profession only goes back to 1946. After a slow start, feminisation accelerated from the 1970s onwards. Women represented 11.3 per cent of judges/public prosecutors in 1973, 28.5 per cent in 1982, 48.5 per cent in 1992, 48.5 per cent in 1999, and 49.8 per cent in January 2001 (Ministry of Justice, DSJ 2001).

Feminisation is more marked in all age groups in the judiciary than amongst the advocacy, although the difference is a little less pronounced in the higher age brackets (Table 4).

3.5 Choosing to Join the Judiciary

It is not only the method of selection which explains the very high proportion of women amongst judges and public prosecutors. Other factors also come into play in choosing a judicial career. A survey carried out in France's training college for judges and prosecutors (*Ecole de la magistrature*) in 1984/85 included a question regarding reasons for the choice of career. Half of the respondents gave as their main reason the wish for the exercise of power, whilst 40 per cent

Table 4: Age distribution and proportion of women amongst *avocats* and *magistrats* (1999)

Age	Avocats		Magistrats	
	Total	W.%	Total	W.%
20–24	59	67.8	–	–
25–29	4,892	64.2	218	78.9
30–34	6,617	55.1	618	66.5
35–39	5,452	49.0	961	58.7
40–44	4,677	45.3	1,136	55.2
45–49	4,750	36.6	1,386	47.5
50–54	3,744	27.0	1,284	36.1
55–59	1,526	22.7	527	31.7
60–64	846	21.4	290	27.9
65–69	514	21.4	137	27.7
70–74	327	13.8	1	
75+	232	13.8	–	–
Total	33,545	45.0	6,558	48.5

SOURCES: *Caisse nationale des barreaux français* and French Ministry of Justice

stated a taste for public service.[9] Only one in five gave security of employment as a reason. On the contrary, the prime reason given for not having chosen to become an *avocat* was the commercial aspect of the activities of the latter, which ties in with a wish to work in the public sector. Indeed, a number of judges, in particular women judges, who had passed the entrance examination for both the French advocacy and the judiciary ended up choosing the latter.[10]

Women are affected by all of these reasons. After having been excluded for so long from positions of real authority, they see a judicial career as an opportunity to wield major responsibilities from an early stage. In a speech given at the start of a new session of the Paris appeal court in 1984, one woman judge recalled:

> Let us not forget that for a woman, being a judge involves exercising power for the first time after an eternity of only ever being asked her opinion and advice, even if these were listened to with respect, and that she is still, in 1984, savouring the pleasure of having won the fight to exercise power under her own responsibility, her own name, her own signature and dignity.[11]

[9] Unfortunately, we do not have the figures for distribution by sex.

[10] At the end of the 1980s, 28 per cent of trainee judges/public prosecutors at the judicial college—a large majority of whom were women—had also sat the entrance examination for the French advocacy with a high success of 78 per cent. They obviously positively preferred a judicial career to that of an *avocat*.

[11] Speech given by Suzanne Martzloff (*Discours de l'entrée de la cour d'appel de Paris*, January 1984. *Gazette du Palais*, 12–14 February 1984).

Security of employment is appreciated by all, but is all the more important for a woman as it reduces the professional risk run by having children. Most importantly, judges and public prosecutor are offered a choice of careers which were previously an exclusively male preserve and some of which allow for very flexible working hours and make it easier to juggle the demands of career and family. As a female court president said in interview,

> The only difference between men and women is perhaps the latter's need to take greater account of working hours, which explains the fact that a married woman with young children will tend to choose a career where her actual presence at court is less imperative. Judges in France can work at home where they are not constantly disturbed by a string of barristers, as are public prosecutors or examining magistrates. ... This, no doubt, explains why so many qualified women opt for the judiciary. Their qualifications might well have enabled them to find a better paid career in the private sector, but the time available to them does not allow them, in a competitive situation, to win the day over equally qualified men.

However, the feminisation of the judicial professions has made it difficult for women to get the precise posts within this branch which would give them maximum flexibility in terms of working hours. As a result, there are more and more young women working as examining magistrates and members of a public prosecution team, both of which require regular court presence. There is no such thing as one female strategy, especially now that women represent nearly half of all judges. The media are rich in reports on high-profile court cases where the examining magistrate or the public prosecutor in a fraud case is a woman.

Faced with a massive 'invasion' of women into the judiciary, many of their male colleagues determined to retain some territory of their own.

4 OLD AND NEW FACES OF MALE DOMINATION IN THE JUDICIARY

4.1 Challenging the Old Masculine Model

The traditional model of the judicial professions has been a profoundly male one. Even if those who fought for women's access to these professions like appealing to history in order to demonstrate that even before Napoleon's rise to power women were not systematically excluded from exercising judicial functions,[12] modern-day judicial professions are clearly based on a masculine model. Authority within the family used to be paternal, before becoming parental. Just as the father embodied the 'paternal power' within the family, the judge was a figure embodying masculine authority. In a more general sense, the male sex was an integral part of the definition of functions of authority. The judge, after all,

---

[12] It is worth remembering, for example, that under the old laws female members of the nobility always had the same rights as men, in particular the right of suzerainty, allowing them to dispense justice. The same was true of abbesses within the jurisdiction of their abbeys.

had the possibility of pronouncing 'a fatherly and benevolent admonition'. Law and order, the existence of a 'law of the father' and the concept of sanctions[13] are notions which are associated with the male sex. This authority was embodied in men's bodies, voices and physical strength, which became the symbols of such authority.

The arrival of women on the scene has radically changed this professional and social order. It means that theoretically the professional model is no longer based solely on the male sex, as both men and women can exercise the same professions. Men have lost their monopoly. The current debate centres mainly on the notion of authority. Women are inevitably challenging a certain form of authority, as for instance this woman who was an examining magistrate in the 1970s. In an interview she denounced

> an extremely restrictive vision of authority, one which is linked to force, to physical presence, to the strength of someone's voice, linked to a host of masculine attributes, whereas authority can be something completely different . . . nowadays we can see that there is no need to shout, to hit the table with one's fist; efficacy can result from a complete mastery of the questions asked, from a very rigorous recording of oral proceedings, and can lead to the same result as the fear that someone inspires.

Moreover, it is not just the arrival of women on the scene which is at the heart of this challenge to the old model; it is also the professionalisation of the judiciary, and more precisely the fact that, from 1959, judges and public prosecutors have been trained in a dedicated college. As soon as judicial personnel were trained in a special establishment, with specific courses, educational categories and training in the exercise of authority, male predominance started to wane, at least to some degree. Women, just like men, became professionals who had mastered both a body of knowledge and the skills to apply it.

Faced with a father of North African origin who could not understand how a woman could take decisions concerning his child and his family, a woman judge specialising in cases involving minors emphasised her professionalism. In her own words, 'the more he treated me as a woman, the more I reacted to him as a professional'.

4.2 Processes of Differentiation

Male domination has considerably weakened, but it has not completely disappeared. Although on the retreat, it is constantly being recreated. The strength of this domination resides in the fact that it is supported by both men and women (Bourdieu 1998). However, as feminisation progresses, such differentiation becomes increasingly difficult to devise. We find within the profession the clas-

---

[13] There was the procedure of 'paternal punishment', inherited from the *Ancien Régime*, which allowed a father to have his son imprisoned if he gravely offended his father.

sic mechanisms of horizontal and vertical segregation structuring the participation of women in the employment market, but with certain nuances.

4.2.1 Differentiation by Function

The first stage of differentiation was the allocation to women of particular functions. Before 1946, it had already been proposed, in certain parliamentary bills, that women's access should be limited to positions of bench member and juvenile judge, because of women's 'inherent qualities'. This meant that men kept for themselves the functions of examining magistrate and public prosecutor, both of which were deemed incompatible with the nature of women. Even if the law eventually passed did not include such restrictions, they were still being demanded by a number of judges/public prosecutors at the end of 1946. At a meeting the judges/public prosecutors present vowed almost unanimously 'to try to restrict the access of women to the profession to the function of bench member or to juvenile courts'.[14]

Once they had entered the judiciary, women mainly gravitated towards the functions of bench member and juvenile judge, that is the very functions that had been envisaged for them. For a long time there were very few women public prosecutors or examining magistrates. This differentiation between women's jobs and men's jobs within the judiciary reflects a number of principles which have traditionally structured the division of labour along sexual lines. Men's work includes public prosecution, confrontation with the criminal 'milieu', liaising with the police, presence in court, visibility. Women are concerned with social functions, contact with families, social workers, but also purely judicial functions that are detached and noble and allow them to safeguard their roles in the family (Boigeol 1993).

As the number of women joining the judiciary grows year by year and women become more numerous than men amongst new recruits to the profession, the number of areas originally defined as 'male' has steadily decreased. Even if there are fewer women than men in the public prosecution service, their number is increasing. In January 1999, they represented 35 per cent of public prosecutors but 51 per cent of new recruits to public prosecution; as for examining magistrates, 49 per cent of these were women (Ministry of Justice, DSJ 1999).

4.2.2 Hierarchical Differentiation

The process of differentiation has now shifted to posts at the top of the hierarchy. To be sure, women have always been few in number in such posts, because not many of them rose sufficiently through the ranks to provide a seedbed of candidates for the highest posts. But the situation has changed; women have now moved up in the hierarchy, and many of them are in a position to be taken

---

[14] Report on the *Etats généraux de la magistrature, Le pouvoir judicaire*, 15 December 1946, p 6.

seriously as candidates for top posts; but very few of them apply. Thus, for medium-level courts, 51 per cent of judges eligible to become presidents of courts are women, but only 17 per cent of presidents are in fact women (Table 5). The public prosecution service, as is well known, is less feminised than the bench, and feminisation set in later. However, it appears that women working in the public prosecution service are less hesitant than their female colleagues working as judges to put themselves forward for promotion to top jobs. Perhaps the fact that they have already held down a job which has traditionally been considered as a male preserve allows them to go even further in that direction and to apply for positions of power.

Table 5: Women court presidents and heads of public prosecution services (January 2000)

Type of court	Presidents of courts			Chief public prosecutors		
	Total number	% Women	% Women eligible for nomination (est.)	Total number	% Women	% Women eligible for nomination (est.)
Courts of appeal	35	6.0	31.7	35	8.0	16.9
Highest courts	15	7.0		17	0	
Major courts	87	14.0	46.0	81	7.0	21.8
Medium-level courts	46	17.0	51.0	46	13.0	24.0
Minor courts	35	23.0	60.0	38	18.0	51.0

SOURCE: French Ministry of Justice. DSJ 2000

As a general rule, the share of women in top jobs, whether as president of a court or as head of the public prosecution service, drops the higher the level in the hierarchy. How is that to be explained?

Women tend to rule themselves out of the frame, either because they do not wish to occupy such posts, or because they consider their chances of getting promoted as too slim to make it worthwhile to apply. They prefer being an appeal judge to being president of a court. But is this really their preference, or rather a result of rationalisation based on the *de facto* situation? If women do not strive for top positions, this is often due to social *habitus* rather than natural inclination. This leaves the way clear for their male colleagues, who see progression to the top of the ladder as a natural part of their career plan.

In its last report, the *Conseil Supérieur de la Magistrature* (French Magistrates Council, known as CSM), which controls nominations for such posts, expressed regret that so few women were putting themselves forward for leadership positions. However, it is far from clear that the CSM has so far been particularly favourable to applications from women, particularly for the very highest posts, for example head of an appeal court. Recently it was the government, in the shape of the Justice Minister, which appointed two women to the post of head of the public prosecution service in two appeal courts. (The CSM merely gives its opinion in the case of heads of the public prosecution service). There is still a certain suspicion towards women with children who wish to take on managerial functions. Thus a woman candidate for the post of court president was asked by the CSM how she planned to cope with her family commitments as well as her professional responsibilities, a question one can hardly imagine being asked of a male candidate!

The top positions in the judiciary therefore represent the last bastion in which men are grossly over-represented, which proves yet again the existence of a glass ceiling for women. As the following table shows, the situation is not really improving. The pre-eminence of men in these top jobs is still very marked (Table 6).

Table 6: Recent changes in the proportion of women in judicial leadership positions

Year	Female presidents (%)	Female chief public prosecutors (%)	Overall (%)
1991	16.7	7.6	12.0
1992	19.2	10.6	15.0
1994	20.0	9.2	14.7
1995	16.4	8.9	12.6
1996	14.6	8.8	12.0
1997	13.2	8.8	11.0
1999	12.9	10.1	11.5
2000	14.6	10.1	12.2

Source: Ministry of Justice, DSJ, 1991–2000.

As the possibilities of implementing differentiation strategies diminish in the *magistrature*, male members either adapt to this new situation or seek new opportunities for differentiation.

4.2.3 Differentiation Via a Sideways Move

Within a profession which is rapidly being feminised, the last differentiation strategy, implemented mainly by male judges/public prosecutors (70 per cent), is to leave the judiciary, whether on a provisional or a permanent basis. This migration to professions outside the judiciary has developed for a few years now, but still only involves relatively small numbers. Judges and public prosecutors, like members of other public service groupings, can temporarily leave their posts in order to undertake other functions within society. They then either return to the judiciary with 'enhanced skills', or, alternatively, fail to return at all. This professional mobility allows the implementation of different strategies, all of which seek to enhance the person's career prospects, either by the acquisition of new resources, new skills which they can put to good use should they decide to return to the judiciary, or by offering their judicial skills to the market place outside. For instance, some members of the judiciary spend a few years in organisations like the French stock exchange regulatory body (COB), or in European organisations. They acquire highly sought after and extremely specialised skills, which—so they hope—will allow them to occupy interesting posts on their return to the judiciary.[15] Besides, members of the judiciary with special skills— usually those of examining magistrates or public prosecutors specialising in fraud cases—are much sought after by private industry where they are offered extremely well paid jobs. It is mainly men who follow this path, but there are also a few women (Boigeol 2000).

The ultimate differentiation strategy adopted by male lawyers is simply not to opt for a judicial career but to move into what is perceived to be the most prestigious and best paid area of law, in particular corporate law. The latter is a largely male-dominated field, even if the proportion of women partners in corporate law firms is increasing. Reliable statistics are not available, but an incomplete survey (Barszcz 1997) gives 16 per cent of women partners in 1996, 18 per cent in 1997.[16]

4.3 Male Domination and Feminisation as a 'Problem'

Within the judiciary, male domination has been eroded, even if it has clearly survived in terms of the gross over-representation of men in top positions. This is an area where no major change has occurred, as feminisation here continues to be regarded as a 'problem' by both men and women. Feminisation as such creates a feeling of unease, raises fears and uncertainty.

The arguments put forward have evolved a little, but the underlying message remains basically the same, namely that it is women that create the problems. Fifty years ago, it was considered that 'the presence of too many women is harmful to the prestige of the judicial system'.[17] Now it is claimed that feminisation 'is not healthy from the point of view of social equilibrium . . .'.[18] For a man to be faced in court with an all-female bench of judges, as well as a female public prosecutor, clerk of the court and barrister, is perceived to be unsettling. It is always women who, in one way or another, are seen to be responsible for a situation deemed unsatisfactory. This one-sided interpretation appears as yet

---

[15] In fact there is a strong distrust among *magistrats* in courts toward this kind of strategy.

[16] Despite this increase, corporate law still reflects the traditional division of labour: women represent 18 per cent of partners, 49 per cent of junior staff, and 90 to 100 per cent of administrative staff in law firms.

[17] Report from the deputy public prosecutor at the appeal court in Paris, training manager, addressed to the director of public prosecution, 17 November 1955.

[18] Report from the chairman of the panel dealing with the competitive entrance examination in 1992.

another sign of the tenacity of male domination which affects the way both men and women think.

4.4 A Feminine Model of Administering Justice?

What, then, has been the impact of the presence of women in the judiciary? Is there such a thing as a feminine model of administering justice? This question has hardly been addressed in France. Indeed, it has only begun to be addressed in other countries. With regard to the advocacy,[19] numerous studies have been conducted in the wake of Menkel-Meadow's work (1985), which in turn was an attempt to see whether Gilligan's theories on gender difference could be applied to findings on women in the legal profession (Gilligan 1982). On the other hand, little has been done in relation to the impact of feminisation on the way judges work. So far, there is little evidence to verify Menkel-Meadow's hypothesis that women lawyers have a distinctive voice of their own. Doubts are reinforced by a number of contributions to this volume (Felstiner, Mathers, Junquiera, Sommerlad).

In the first place, the very notion of a specific contribution from women is criticised in France as in other countries. To investigate the special qualities of women or the special contribution they can bring, it is argued, is surely to restrict them once more to one particular model, to an essentialist scenario which history has shown to be a dangerous one (Pisier 1997). After all, it is precisely in the name of these differences that women were excluded in the first place.

Secondly, the entry of women has been seen to challenge the fundamentally masculine nature of the professional model. Are we now going to replace this by a feminine model? We know that the first women tried desperately to conform, to be indistinguishable from men, and did their best to avoid doing anything that could be described as feminine (Boigeol 1993). The subsequent creation of a judicial training establishment, which contributed to the weakening of the masculine model, was hardly conducive to the emergence of a specifically feminine model.

Even if it is incontrovertible that men's and women's behaviour cannot completely escape the influence of the individual's social identity and experience, the assumption that there is a feminine model, in the light of research done so far, appears at least no more than hypothetical. It would imply that the way a woman arrives at a judgement is fundamentally different from that of a man. However, it seems increasingly less possible to talk about women as a homogeneous group. A study of sociological profiles has shown that women differ amongst themselves depending on their social origins, religious beliefs, marital

---

[19] In France, as in other civil law countries, all practising lawyers can today represent their clients in court, as from 1970 the division between *avoués* and *avocats* has ceased to exist. For further explanation see the Introduction to this volume.

status, etc (Bodiguel 1991). A number of contributions to this volume tend to confirm this.

The question of the specific contribution of women to the working of the judiciary is all the more difficult to address in France, as everything conspires to deny it. Indeed, judges are, in a way, constrained by their ideology of neutrality. In order to come to an impartial judgment, judges must undergo a process of disembodiment. It is essential for them to disregard their own sex, race, social origins, religion, political affiliations etc, in other words all the elements which constitute their social make-up, in order to be nothing but a judge. This process, even if symbolic in nature, nevertheless implies that the question of the judge's sex is irrelevant. The black robe symbolises the importance of the detachment between professional and private individual.[20] 'I defy you to find any difference between a judgment arrived at by a man and a judgment arrived at by a woman', say both men and women judges when questioned on the subject.

Whereas it seems difficult to identify a specific contribution of women to judicial practice, it nevertheless remains true that their presence changes the representation of the profession and the law by demolishing certain stereotypes, as noted by Clare McGlynn (1998) in respect of the situation in England. Users of the judicial system clearly see that the profession of judge/public prosecutor, like that of practising lawyer, is now open to both sexes, and that one is just as likely to be prosecuted and judged by a woman as by a man. This may well have repercussions beyond the confines of the judiciary. From now on, the situation of women is at least partially normalised. 'Partially', as the posts at the top of the hierarchical ladder are still largely monopolised by men. Even if change is only occurring slowly, there is pressure to bring it about. The judicial system is unlike any other, and its image could be affected if women continue to be largely denied access to leadership positions.

5 CONCLUSION

At a time when the French judiciary is emerging from a long history of submission to political power and is regaining some of its previous prestige, it is interesting to observe that this has not resulted in any slowing down of the process of feminisation within it. On the contrary, the proportion of women sitting and successfully passing the judicial entrance examination continues to be very high and is only slightly modified due to lateral recruitment, that is to jurists with previous professional experience in other more male-dominated sectors of the labour market being attracted to the judiciary. In this chapter the reasons for the

---

[20] Antoine Garapon analyses the wearing of the black gown as a stage on the path to the 'purification which marks a change of state for the wearer, and which reminds the latter of the duties the wearing of the gown implies. It puts a temporary stop to the human imperfections of the wearer, enabling the latter to rise above the merely mortal state'. Garapon also analyses the role of the black gown as a 'protective apron' (Garapon 1997: 83).

feminisation process and the differentiation strategies devised in order to maintain male dominance have been analysed. However, given the size of this process it no longer makes sense to treat women as a homogeneous group, which makes the search for specifically feminine patterns of judicial behaviour and practice even more difficult.

6 REFERENCES

Barszcz, Caura. 1997. *Radioscopie des cabinets d'avocats d'affaires*. Paris, Juristes associés. Rapport.

Bancaud, Alain. 1993. *La haute magistrature judiciaire. Entre politique et sacerdoce*. Paris: LGDJ.

Bodiguel, Jean-Luc. 1991. *La magistrature. Un corps sans âme*. Paris: PUF.

Boigeol, Anne. 1991. *Comment devient-on magistrat?* Vaucresson: CRIV.

Boigeol, Anne. 1993. La magistrature française au féminin: entre spécificité et banalisation. *Droit et Société*. No 25, pp 489–523.

Boigeol, Anne. 1996. Les femmes et les cours. La difficile mise en œuvre de l'égalité des sexes dans la magistature. *Genéses*. 22, pp 107–129.

Boigeol, Anne. 1997. Les magistrates de l'ordre judiciaire: des femmes d'autorité? *Les cahiers du MAGE*. No 1, pp 25–35.

Boigeol, Anne. 2000. Les magistrats 'hors les murs'. *Droit et Société*. No 44/45, pp 235–248.

Bourdieu, Pierre. 1998. *La domination masculine*. Paris: Seuil.

Crompton, Rosemary and Sanderson, Kay. 1990. *Gendered Jobs and Social Change*. London: Unwin Hyman.

Daune-Richard, Anne-Marie and Marry, Catherine. 1990. Autres histoires de transfuges? Le cas de jeunes filles inscrites dans des formations 'masculines' de BTS et de DUT industriels. *Formation et emploi*. No 29, pp 35–50.

Duru-Bellat, Marie. 1990. *L'école des filles*. Paris: L'Harmattan.

ENM (Ecole Nationale de la Magistrature). 1999. *Rapport du jury du concours d'entrée dans la magistrature*.

Garapon, Antoine. 1997. *Bien juger. Essai sur le rituel judiciaire*. Paris: Odile Jacob.

Gilligan, Carol. 1982 *In a Different Voice: Psychological Theory and Women's Development*. Cambridge: Harvard University Press.

Glasson, Ernest. 1898. Commentaire de l'arrêt du 30 novembre 1897 de la Cour d'appel de Paris. *Dalloz* 2, pp 185–195.

Karpik, Lucien. 1995. *Les avocats*. Paris: Gallimard.

Le Feuvre, Nikky and Walters, Patricia. 1993. Egales en droit? La féminisation des professions juridiques en France et en Grande-Bretagne. *Sociétés contemporaines*. No 16, pp 41–62.

Marry, Catherine. 1989. Femmes ingénieurs: une irrésistible ascension? *Informations sur les sciences sociales*, pp 291–344.

McGlynn, Clare. 1998. Will Women Judges Make a Difference? *New Law Journal*. May 29, pp 813–814.

Menkel-Meadow, Carrie. 1985. Portia in a Different Voice: Speculations on a Women's Lawyering Process, *Berkeley Women's Law Journal* 1; 39.

Ministry of Education (France), DPD. 1978, 1989, 1998. *Statistiques annuelles.*

Ministry of Education (France), DPD. 1999. *Tableaux statistiques.*

Ministry of Justice (France), DACS. 1999. *Statistiques sur la profession d'avocat.*

Ministry of Justice (France), DSJ. 1991–2001. *Statistiques sur la magistrature.*

Ministry of Justice (France). 1999. *Annuaire statistique de la justice 1994–1998.* Paris, La documentation française.

Pisier, Evelyne. 1997. Les femmes peuvent-elles exercer le pouvoir? *Cahiers du MAGE.* No 1, pp 51–53.

Quémin, Alain. 1998. Modalités d'entrée et d'insertion dans une profession d'élite: le cas des femmes commissaires-priseurs. *Sociétés contemporaines.* No 29, pp 87–106.

Rousselet, Maurice. 1947. *Histoire de la magistrature.* Paris: Plon.

23

Professional Body and Gender Difference in Court: the Case of the First (Failed) Woman Lawyer in Modern Italy*

VITTORIO OLGIATI

Abstract

This study is an attempt to go beyond traditional narratives about the history of women's access to the legal profession. The story that is told is the story of a failure and of its long-lasting multiple negative consequences. Looking at hermeneutical and factual operations of positive law within the context of the struggle for gendered professionaliation, the paper considers the first court case in Italy about a woman's admission to the professional body of lawyers. The leading hypothesis of the study is that the real issue at stake in court was not so much gender difference but gendered governance of politically relevant socio-institutional structures.

1 INTRODUCTION

WHILE THE FEMINISATION of legal professions has become a matter of fact in contemporary Western society—if by that we mean the rising proportion of women amongst law students and practitioners—one crucial question has lost none of its topicality since the first woman sought to be admitted as a lawyer: the question is, what impact gender and gendered professional strategies have had on the province of law (Sommerlad 1994), especially given that law itself has been increasingly trapped in its own contradictions as a hegemonic power structure (Poulantzas 1971).

This study approaches the question by looking at law within the context of the struggle for gendered professionalisation and vice versa. It does so by focusing on

* Paper presented at European Sociological Association—Network on Professions. First International Conference on 'The Social Scientific Reliability of Professions. Historical and Comparative Perspective', Fondazione Colocci, Jesi (Italy), 4–6 May 2000.

an emblematic case, namely the first court case in Italy about a woman's admission to the professional body of lawyers. This case is considered within an equally emblematic frame of reference, that is the hermeneutical and factual operations of positive state law, and within a historically determined Western European context, namely Italy in the 1880s. The case in point is that of the official enrolment of Dr Jur Lidia Poet in the *Ordine degli Avvocati e Procuratori* of Turin in 1883, the immediate action against her enrolment on the part of the local Court of Appeal, the final decision of the Court of Cassation, and the scholarly controversy which these events gave rise to.

The theoretical framework for the study will be outlined in brief, followed by a detailed discussion of the legal framework, with particular reference to state legal policy. A comparative review of both courts' decisions to prohibit women access to the legal profession will help to throw light on the legal issues raised by the case. A summary of the impact of the doctrinary debate within the legal profession both for and against the entry of women will complete the picture.

2 THEORETICAL APPROACHES

A study of a court case such as that of Lidia Poet is a way of putting to a historical test a general hypothesis currently on the agenda of gender-scientific debates, that is, the hypothesis that gender should not (only) be considered as an empirical indicator of differentiation in certain role plays, but can also be conceived of as an arena for cultural-political government projects. Interestingly, the hypothesis stems from the most advanced gender relation analysis of professionalism in formal organisations and bureaucratic settings (Davies 1996; Gherardi 1996), including legal practice (Sommerlad and Sanderson 1998). Focusing in particular on exclusionary and/or demarcatory professional strategies in such working environments, it throws light on two processes: firstly, the positioning of gender relations vis-a-vis gender identity within the field of activity under scrutiny; secondly, gendering practices as well as gendered policies, reinforced by relationships with dominant and/or subordinate social actors, within the respective space-time framework. Without underestimating the importance of gender as noun or datum signalling an essentialist attribute of personal difference, the hypothesis suggests that gender can be used as a verb also, to stress a process of genuine cultural-political disciplinary—'codifying' and 'codified'—modelling. This study will explore how and why this occurred in the particular case under consideration.

The study will also help to shed light on a neglected area of socio-legal research into the profession, that is the problematic subsumption of gender relations under the realm of positive law: ie the political neutralisation, through formal-legal technicalities, of the potential destabilising social consequences of the entry of an 'alien' or a formerly discriminated social actor into a particular sphere of action of a state whose constitution is based on the claim of universal citizenship.

A few observations on the particular features of the constitutional model of the legal profession will assist an understanding of the issue under discussion as well as its rationale. In Italy, as in other continental European nation states influenced, first, by institutional standards of the enlightenment and the French revolution, and subsequently by the legal architecture of the Napoleonic Code, access to and practice in the advocacy[1] as a fully qualified and licensed legal professional is by no means solely dependent on academic qualifications. Rather it is conditional on the practitioner being granted full legal civic membership within the political structure on the basis of socio-institutional *rites de passages* such as a state examination and an oath of allegiance. This explains why lawyers are provided not only with a professional monopoly, but also, and above all, with a veritable *status activae civitatis*, ie the power to deal with social and legal issues of constitutional relevance, such as legal disputes (Sarfatti Larson 1989).

Enlightenment standards, in Italy as elsewhere, had no room for women. Rousseau's social contract, which formed the very basis of modern constitutionalism allowing the shift from natural to civil society, was not concerned with women. Accordingly, civic rights in the nineteenth-century nation-state explicitly upheld gender-based formal legal exclusionary and discriminatory patterns (Pateman 1988). It was only towards the end of *La Belle Epoque* and the crisis of the liberal state, that this situation began to change and, in all Western countries, women began to gain civic rights and, gradually, access to membership in the legal professions. In this study, I shall analyse how and why in Italy such an inclusion was initially fiercely contested and subsequently graciously granted (civic rights being legal privileges both *de jure* and *de facto*) as a gendered government strategy.

3 EPISTEMOLOGICAL TOOLS

Some time ago Millerson, criticising unilinear and/or monocausal approaches to evolutionary traits of professionalisation processes, suggested that more attention was needed regarding their concrete historical location, and, in particular, the impact of time-lags and socio-institutional cleavages. In his view, it is only these variables, to the extent that they are recorded and signalled by concurrent processes of institutionalisation, that can provide evidence of the individual uniqueness of a profession, a uniqueness which is sharply constrained by unavoidable adaptation to the broader social and cultural milieu (Millerson 1964).

More recently, a number of scholars have stressed the importance of a full understanding of core patterns of professional models and special features of given processes of professionalisation, of structural intertwinement of short-term changes, fluctuations and conjunctures on the one hand, and revolutionary upheavals, long-term cycles and teleological time patterns on the other (Burrage 1989; Siegrist 1990).

---

[1] For the use of the term 'advocacy' in this context see footnote 3 in chapter 15.

In the Italian context, Farneti, a well-known Italian political scientist, studied the relationship between Italy's political system and civil society at the turn of the nineteenth century by looking at the leading technical-political role played by Italian lawyers. In his view, too, cleavages in the structuring of processes of professionalisation (ie changes in the type and duration of political issues relevant to the profession) and cleavages in the evolution of professional structures (ie changes in type and duration of professional issues relevant to society) are pivotal for plausible and socially adequate explanations of such a role (Farneti 1971). This paper focuses on a particular cleavage not investigated by Farneti, that is the rise of gender as a key factor in the evolution of both Italy's legal and social system and Italian legal professionalism.

4   WOMEN LAWYERS IN ITALY PRIOR TO ITALIAN UNIFICATION

Taking seriously the historical approach referred to above, we find that women acting as lawyers were anything but a total anomaly in the history of Italy. Of course, it is true that from ancient Rome up to recent times, women were forbidden to hold *virilia officia*, in accordance with the *Jus Commune* rule which said, 'foeminae ab omnibus officiis civilibus et publicis remotae sunt, et ideo nec judices esse possunt, nec magistratum gerere, nec postulare, nec pro alio intervenire, nec procuratores existere' ('women can have no part in any civic and public office, and therefore may neither be judges, nor act as magistrates, nor plead in court, nor intervene on behalf of others, nor be *procuratores*') (Gabba 1880). Yet it is true also that, like any rule, this one could not prevent repeated exceptions, particularly in periods of radical change (Addeo 1939). When these occurred, women did indeed seize the opportunity to appear as lawyers in court. Of course, they were members of an elite, either by class or by nature, as only intellectually gifted and well-educated women could play, afford or accomplish, such a public role/function. Yet, their presence cannot be explained merely by reference to individual attitudes and personal motivation, but also to a favourable socio-cultural climate and favourable political-institutional conditions.

Records show that in ancient Rome a number of women acted in court to defend either themselves or a client. As experts in ritual formulae and wordings, female priests ('vestals') could perform notarial functions as regards contracts and wills. In the Middle Ages, a number of women obtained a law degree and became eminent academic jurists in universities, such as Bologna, Padua and Pavia. During and after the Renaissance, women were allowed to act in court, either as lawyers or judges. Some of them held functions as diplomatic officers and even as legislators. A fictitious, but by no means atypical, specimen is Portia in Shakespeare's *The Merchant of Venice*. The fact that Prospera Porzia Malvezzi was a famous jurist in sixteenth-century Bologna, while Emilia Brembati in Bergamo was equally famous for having pleaded in court to save her brother, might raise the intriguing question whether the fusion in Shakespeare's character of the former's name and the latter's performance was entirely coincidental. From the seventeenth century to the Napoleonic campaigns, women could qualify in *utroque jure* (canonic and civil law), but were barred from appearing in court (Addeo 1939; Algardi 1949).

In fact, the first woman to obtain a law degree, not only in Italy, but in Europe and the entire western 'civilised' world—according to 'modern' (ie state-oriented university) standards was Marisa Pellegrina Amoretti, who gained a degree in *utroque jure* in 1777 at the University of Pavia. Shortly before this, a woman had obtained a degree in philosophy from the University of Bologna. However, the world's very first female university graduate was Elena Lucrezia Cornaro Piscopia who, having attempted in vain to be admitted to study theology, obtained a philosophy degree at the University of Padova in 1678. The historical event of the law degree conferred on Marisa Pellegrina Amoretti was—and still is—absolutely memorable for a number of reasons, not least political ones.

The ceremony took place in the Company of Jesus Church in Pavia, under the auspices of Maria Beatrice d'Este, Archduchess of Austria. Amoretti was accompanied by two noblewomen and surrounded by high-ranking imperial officers and members of the aristocracy. Before the defence of the dissertation, a renowned jurist and mentor of Amoretti delivered an oration to praise Empress Maria Theresia of Habsburg for her open-minded policy about women's education, quoting Plato on the opportunities opened up by the participation of women in the art of government. Then Amoretti, who had passed previous examinations by means of hundreds of theses in perfect Latin, discussed her doctoral thesis devoted—not by chance—to 'dowry law in ancient Rome'. Apart from being awarded a law degree, she also qualified for *cathedram magistralem*, ie as a law lecturer, and was rewarded with a laurel crown, a ring and the university's blazoned gold-embroidered band (Visintini 1998). The event was a highly formal one, unmarked by the 'university spirit'—the well-known Italian university students' *goliardia*. Rather the enlightenment legal policy of the Habsburg empire in Italy celebrated its own last glorious deeds.

A completely new cultural, political and institutional scenario emerged just after the *Risorgimento*, ie the unification of Italy in 1861. The various legal frameworks that had evolved in the regions over the centuries (Kingdom of Naples, Republic of Venice, Grand Duchy of Tuscany, etc), suddenly lost their rationale and soon disappeared. For the first time in the history of modern Italy, one could justifiably talk of Italian lawyers as a national body, unique in sociological as well as in legal terms. Indeed, the legal reform policy enforced by the new ruling elite brought about a re-organisation of the profession and provided the process of legal professionalisation with new strategic political goals (Olgiati 1987; Olgiati and Pocar 1988).

5 A NEW LEGAL SCENARIO

In the context of this study, two emblematic reforms deserve a special mention: the Legal Profession Act of 8 June 1874 imposing a university law degree as a prerequisite for access to the legal profession, and the Public Education Act of 13 November 1876 which explicitly allowed women to study law at university.

Both Acts served the purpose of creating the political means to allow learned agents to support and manage the constitutional change. There was little connection between them otherwise, as the two action systems—legal practice in court, and learning or teaching at the university—concerned two different institutions governed by opposite criteria: while the rationale of the Legal Profession Act implied a regulated selective closure in view of the political relevance of lawyers' role-function, the Public Education Act served to create a degree of 'democratic' openness in order to alleviate the shortage of educated people even among the power elite, and more broadly, to create greater social mobility and political legitimation.

Paradoxically, it was precisely the structural coupling of such mutually contradictory criteria that provided a potential legal key to re-open the door to the legal profession for women. To be sure, this had not been intended by the Italian parliament. Nor did members of parliament expect that sooner or later the system of the law itself—or its systematic logic—could raise a gender contradiction from within. In fact, it was structural pressure for legal and social modernisation and reform rather than a merely subjective interest on the part of women or a corporatist professional demand that forced the Italian parliament to give political priority to formal knowledge so as to speed up the process of nation-state building.

Yet, as soon as the first woman seized the opportunity to use her law degree as a stepping-stone to a legal career, the 'guardians of law-and-order' realised the seriousness of the issue. In fact, given the abstract nature and the universalistic pretensions of positive law, women's access to legal education could spark off general expectations well beyond the sphere of lawyering, and might well imply women's claim to full civic status in any socio-institutional sphere. In other words, it became clear that either the technicalities or the doctrinal assumptions of positive law could facilitate, sooner or later, a determined pursuit not merely of exceptional individual achievement but also of a collective mobility project in the form of a massive process of gender professionalisation of national dimensions, the first in Italian history.

The fact that an opportunity for such a process to be set in motion arose in 1883 just a few years after the promulgation of the two acts is highly symptomatic. It reveals a causal nexus between them and, more generally, throws light on the way in which ideological patterns of legal education may challenge the operation of the law.

6 LEGAL AND POLITICAL IMPLICATIONS OF THE NEW LEGAL FRAMEWORK

The co-existence of the Legal Profession Act of 1874 and the Public Education Act of 1876 was the unintended catalyst that opened up the gender potential of modern legal professionalism in Italy. A full understanding of the issue requires clarification of some aspects of the new legal framework.

The Public Education Act was not in any way intended to provide professionals with specialist knowledge. What it was to achieve was to enhance socio-institutional mobility through selection by acculturation rather than by membership of one particular social class. In fact, the Italian university system neither was nor is primarily concerned with vocational or professional training. Equally, an Italian university degree neither was nor is a vocational or professional credential. Yet, such university education and such a degree could constitute then and still does now, a statutory prerequisite for access to certain professions.

As regards the Profession Act, it stipulated that a university law degree was a prerequisite for an application to be allowed to enter the profession. However, this requirement served not so much to improve professionals' skills but to end the practice of conferring legal titles and status roles on members of the nobility and the bureaucracy simply on the strength of their privileged socio-institutional positions. It also abolished the route to the legal profession via local professional training schools.

The same law also required compulsory enrolment in the *Ordine* (the guild system) and registration in 'law lists', following completion of a two-year apprenticeship and the passing of a compulsory state examination. Again, such compulsory requirements were not a way to ascertain the level of competence, but were, as they are now, a way of raising candidates' awareness of key political issues of public order and of the priority of ideological 'harmonisation' over any form of professional commitment, as well as a way of making manifest the right/duty of successful candidates to provide professional services as a public function.

However, the Profession Act distinguished between the 'necessary and compulsory' function of legal representation and assistance, ie the status role and function of *procuratore*, and the 'free, additional and facilitatory' practice of consultation and pleading, ie the status role and function of *avvocato*. Hence, as a qualified practitioner could embody and perform both roles, only the *procuratore*'s status role and function could imply a full status of *activae civitatis* and of acting as a proper public officer. By contrast, the practice as a mere *avvocato* could not claim to be based on statutory public functions but merely on probity and ability (Bianchi 1886).

Further confusion arose from the fact that members of both professions had to register with a single type of guild, the *Ordine*, organised within the territorial disciplinary jurisdiction of the local court. This was to ensure substantial control over ideological, political and technical implications of lawyers' individual and collective roles as guardians of state-society boundaries, as well as directing individual and collective professional action towards national ideals and tasks rather than individual lawyer-client based self-interest or peer-group corporatist welfare.

Yet all the above notwithstanding, it turned out that it was not possible to neutralise politically the historically rooted Janus-headed position of Italian lawyers as boundary agents between state power and societal dynamics. Indeed, the *de jure* unclear division and the *de facto* overlapping and confusion between compulsory public office and free, ie private, legal practice, epitomised (and exacerbated) the fact that the same Profession Act was the result of a problematic political compromise based on the spurious conflation of two diverging professional projects, the one supported by the profession and the other by the government. The former was oriented towards overcoming the ancient corporatist models without losing traditional guarantees of autonomy and independence. The latter, while advocating the same ends, aimed also and above all at bringing the profession into line with the government's policy of the new ruling elite (Olgiati 1987; 1990).

As if this was not enough, political pressure to make Italian lawyers conform to the government's strategy was so deep-rooted and widespread that the Italian parliament failed to make the Profession Act tally with various existing norms of the civil and criminal codes concerning the supply of legal work and lawyers' position in court. Significantly, such pre-existing norms were not only relevant per se, as they did not fit the rationale of the new professional model. They were also integral components of the system of codification and of the official legal culture embedded in it; a culture and a system, it goes without saying, imbued with traditional male-oriented cultural and organisational values and beliefs, such as those about women's limited suitability for any legal issue. It is possible to argue that this technical mismatch was not the result of rational planning on the part of the legislator either. But it most certainly acquired key significance in Lidia Poet's court case.

7 THE LIDIA POET COURT CASE AND ITS SOCIO-LEGAL IMPACT

All this is essential for an understanding of the political and legal implications of a technical framework of which both Lidia Poet and the Turin courts were fully aware. Lidia Poet, having obtained brilliant results in her law examinations at the University of Turin, had no problem being enrolled as *praticante* in the *Ordine degli Avvocati e Procuratori* of Turin. Having fulfilled the requirement of a period of apprenticeship and passed the state examination, she applied to the same *Ordine* to be admitted as an *avvocato*. On 9 August 1883, after a heated debate, the council of the *Ordine* reached a positive decision, albeit not a unanimous one. To register their dissent, two eminent members of the professional governing body, who were also members of parliament, offered their resignation.

Of course, all the above could not go unnoticed in the courts. Provided with the power of control granted by the Profession Act, the *Pubblico Ministero* immediately opposed the *Ordine's* decision and requested the Attorney General at the Court of Appeal of Turin to put in an appeal against it in that same court. On 11 November 1883, the decision was indeed overturned. On 18 April 1884, the Court of Cassation of Turin confirmed this action.

An extraordinary outcry within and outside the courts followed. Yet, it was not only the media coverage or the debates in parliament that gave the case its great resonance. It was also the fact that, by rejecting Lidia Poet's claim, the courts demonstrated their ability to control the profession. This brought about the intense national and international attention that, paradoxically, led to condition any prospective gender-related developments in the profession as well as in Italian society at large.

Indeed, the failure of Lidia Poet's aspirations left a long-lasting mark not only in Italy, but also in Europe generally. So much so that a similar high-profile court case, concerning a Miss Popelin, took place in Belgium some 10 years later, as documented by critical comments about both the Italian and the Belgian court decisions in Ostrogorski's book *Die Frau im öffentlichen Recht* (Ostrogorski 1897).

In Italy, it took until 1905 for another woman to attempt to gain admission to the profession. That year, a young law graduate, Miss Pigorini from Ancona, applied to be enrolled in the *Praticanti Procuratori* law list. The *Ordine* rejected the application, arguing that such enrolment was designed to lead to training to become a *procuratore*, a public function that women were not legally permitted to perform. Pigorini's appeal against the *Ordine*, too, was rejected by the court. In her case, the court agreed with the *Ordine* about the lack of a specific law on the matter, by recalling—ironically—that, due to parliament's anticipated closure, a decree to allow women to enter the profession, just approved in a first-instance session, had unfortunately been aborted.

In 1909 another law graduate, Miss Dalmazzo from Turin, made an application similar to that of Pigorini. The *Ordine* enrolled the applicant in the *Praticanti* law list, stating however that such enrolment granted training but by no means implied a right to be enrolled in the *Procuratori* law list—a right whose validity had to be ascertained 'in the appropriate place' (Siotto-Pintor 1909). A few months later another law graduate, Miss Segre, was equally enrolled. Neither the former nor the latter ever became practising lawyers.

In 1912 Teresa Labriola, daughter of a well-known philosopher, successfully enrolled in the *Avvocati* law list of the *Ordine* of Rome, by appealing to an article in the Profession Act that provided for the enrolment of university law teachers. First the Court of Appeal of Rome, and then the Court of Cassation revoked the *Ordine's* decision and ordered that her name should be crossed off the list, stating that the equating of lawyering and university law teaching with public functions could not apply to women.

It was only in 1919 that the gates to the profession were opened. However, this was not the result of substantial professional development. Quite the contrary! The First World War was just over, and a completely new political, institutional and cultural scenario was emerging. New government projects had to be enforced, and the 'New Order' required all available human resources. The entry into the profession of the first Italian woman who actually practised in court, Elisa Comani Malintoppi from Ancona, was due to wider developments relatively unconnected to developments in the legal profession, that is a reform concerning citizenship rights that became law on 17 July 1919 (n 1176), which abolished the Italian husband's tutelage over his wife in the context of certain economic and contractual matters.

This law allowed women to take up 'all professions and forms of employment'. Within this categorisation it expressly included ('private') lawyering, while excluding professions 'implying juridical public powers' (Article 7) for which being of 'male sex' was a requirement (Article 8). In other words, women could enter the legal profession, but for the first time ever the Italian legal profession was grouped along with other (more or less professionalised) occupations and officially set apart from the judiciary, the police and the army, all three being perceived as core agents of state functions.

From then on the political disempowerment of the Italian legal profession vis-a-vis state-society interactions has continued. This does not imply that women's entry into the profession was the 'original sin' giving rise to this negative trend. The decline of lawyers' political influence, in Italy as in other European countries, has much more complex constitutional roots (including the rise of mass-party political systems as state-society boundary agents) (Olgiati 1987, 1996; Sarfatti Larson 1989; Szeleny and Martin 1989).

However, it is worth noting that women only gained access to the Italian judiciary in 1963 (Di Federico and Negrini 1989; Pocar 1991). Today, the police and the army are also open to women. Meanwhile a great number of changes have taken place in institutional settings. A striking example is the Catholic Church, an institution well known for its traditional reluctance to give up well established strict discriminatory rules. As late as 1967 pontifical universities finally liberalised access. In the 1970s, for the first time in its thousand-year old history, the Catholic Church allowed women to act either as lawyers or as notaries in its global legal system. In 1973 the first woman was entitled, by grace, to act as *defensor vinculi* and *promotor justitiae*, ie as a judge, at the Supreme Court of Apostolic Signature. In 1975 the first woman was enrolled in the Sacred Rota's law list after completion of a four-year course in canon law and the apprenticeship period at the Sacred Rotal Study, and entitled to act as a qualified lawyer at all levels of ecclesiastic courts (Zannoni Messina 1980). Given the above institutional history, one might reasonably ask the question: was the real issue at stake in Lidia Poet's court case a (manifest) gender difference or a (latent) gendered government policy?

8 THE ISSUE AT STAKE: GENDER DIFFERENCE OR GENDERED GOVERNANCE?

At first glance, there seems to be no doubt that the Lidia Poet court case was about gender difference. A young, brilliant, well-educated woman challenged at the same time a professional body, a judicial system, a legal system and a constitution, all deeply rooted in very male-dominated and male-centred cultural and organisational patterns.

The challenge was based on two ultimately unrelated law reforms that failed to tally properly with a number of statutory rules already in existence in Italy. Surely, therefore, Lidia Poet's claim was a typical example of a 'creative' interpretation of the law, that is, using gaps and loopholes in the law in order to achieve a socio-legal result. As such, it was also a political action exploiting legal technicalities—a typical function of lawyers' work. This might explain why the *Ordine* of Turin did not reject outright Lidia Poet's extraordinary individual claim.

Yet, the *Ordine*'s equally extraordinary decision was itself the very first relevant action taken by a professional body to test its own relative autonomy vis-a-vis the state, an autonomy formally granted by the Profession Act. As such, therefore, it was a substantial re-assessment of lawyers' (traditionally self-proclaimed) prerogatives of freedom and independence within the new constitutional framework.

Taken together, however, all this proved too much for the 'guardians' of the state-centred establishment. Hence Lidia Poet's appeals were, in turn, 'instrumentalised' from above, as they offered the courts the opportunity to kill no fewer than three birds with one stone: to maintain the control of the state over society, of the judiciary over the legal profession, and of the male sex over public offices. In sum, in both courts the issue at stake, that is the issue of strategic political relevance, was not so much the singularity of Lidia Poet's legal action, but rather the possibility of a long-term stabilisation, as indeed occurred, of a gendered system of governance which had no particular intention of granting women full citizenship.

9 A QUESTION OF LEGAL HERMENEUTICS: THE JANUS-HEADED NATURE OF THE LEGAL PROFESSION

Leafing through both the Court of Appeal and Court of Cassation decisions against Lidia Poet and the body of accumulated comments for and against, one is struck by the fact that the arguments, while claiming to discuss the existence or otherwise of a *positive* legal rule barring women from the legal profession, really concern quite another question, namely the question whether lawyers are public or private agents.

While both courts seem uneasy with the Janus-headed character of the profession, they do not hesitate to take a very firm stand. Although they cast doubt on the public nature of the profession, they eliminate the alternative of it being concerned with private matters only. Hence, their 'fair' solution to the problem is to affirm verbatim that although the Profession Act defines the law as a 'profession', it is nevertheless, in the final analysis, 'a sort of public office' or an agency performing 'public functions'. This leads them to conclude, on the basis of a systematic review of civil and criminal code rules concerning women's rights, that women cannot be granted access to the legal profession.

This same ambiguity, a main pillar of the Profession Act, became a veritable battlefield for jurists, who raised a range of exciting but politically devastating, doctrinal controversies. When the debate was finally concluded, this was not because of a *stare decisis* principle, but because the opposition between the respective supporters of the private and the public nature of the profession became so heated that it threatened to destroy the binary identity of the compromise model underlying the Profession Act. This was seen to be too serious a political issue to be resolved in the framework of a debate about the pros and cons of gender difference.

It is interesting to recall the way in which both courts justified their decisions. With reference to the alleged coupling of the Profession Act and the Public Education Act, they stressed the fact that state law favours citizens' equality before the law, but had no difficulty in linking this to a proviso that such equality was not only 'formal and abstract' but also 'relative and proportional', as certain social or natural inequalities were 'necessary and inevitable'. Consequently, while recognising that there was no rule that explicitly either prohibited or permitted women's access to the legal profession, they maintained that, given the silence of the Profession Act and the spirit of the whole positive legal system, there was no real inclination on the part of the law to grant women such access. To support their opinion, they recalled the long-lived tradition of Ulpianus' canon, which, in their view, was never abrogated (Bianchi 1886).

The reference to Ulpianus' canon, according to which women can have no part in any civic or public office (*foeminae ab omnibus officiis civilibus et publicis remotae sunt*), was far from being merely rhetorical in nature. It offered the courts the chance to identify a historical legal continuity from common law to positive law, and to relate this to the rationale of a number of civil and criminal code rules actually in force, which explicitly excluded women not only from certain public functions or certain public settings, but also from certain civic matters, such as business contracting (Gabba 1880).

Both courts avoided philosophical, sociological or moral arguments. Applying strictly positivist legal methods, they structured their discourse in such a way as to make any further attempts to query its validity seem pointless for the following four decades. Admittedly, from 1905 onwards a few did try again. But in these cases, the response of the *Ordini* was absolutely negative. The fact that each *Ordine* justified its own ordinance by explicit reference to technical details of court decisions is evidence that the Italian legal profession, as a body, tried to ensure that the matter should not be raised in court again and the profession's autonomy challenged. Indeed the courts' (ambiguous) formal recognition of the legal profession's Janus-headed nature turned out to be a double-edged sword, as it served as either a stick or a carrot. In other words, paradoxically the profession was compelled to rely on the same courts' decisions for a definition of its socio-institutional internal identity and for maintaining cohesion in the face of external pressures.

10 THE *INFIRMITAS SEXUS* IN POSITIVE LAW AND LEGAL THEORY

As has been noticed, a major strength of the courts' decisions was their reference to legal codes. This allowed providing positive, ie valid and certain, legal evidence of the logical impossibiliy of women entering a profession associated with the holding of 'a sort of public office'. Indeed, from a strictly technical point of view, Lidia Poet's claim was desperately weak and somewhat naive. So much so, that her attempt to exploit that system's gaps and loopholes turned into a real disaster.

It is perfectly true that Lidia Poet's claim arose from personal enthusiasm and an 'enlightened' faith in the progressive role of law in society. It is equally true that it helped a great deal to raise public awareness of women's fight for full citizenship. Yet, in technical terms, it was an 'irrational' claim at best. It blocked the entry of Italian women into the legal profession for 40 years and to other public offices for 80 years.

A look at a number of legal rules in force at the time and at the dominant legal doctrine about women's rights can help to explain this. As far as legal rules are concerned, let us consider the issue of women's legal capacity to act as lawyers. According to Article 268 cc a woman could not be a tutor or a curator. Article 10 cpc excluded women from acting as arbiters. Article 1743 cc stated that a married woman could not receive any legal mandate, even less a litigation mandate, without her husband's formal authorisation. How, then could a woman be a lawyer?

In dominant legal doctrine and jurisprudential debates of the time, references to women's gender-based weakness (*infirmitas sexus*) were a recurrent theme. In particular, most 'advanced' positivist scientific method stressed not only women's natural biological inferiority but also their 'weaker' rationality and 'unstable' nervous behaviour. Therefore, in spite of either Olympe de Gouges' 1791 *Declaration of Women's Rights*, which in Article 10 proclaims equal rights for men and women, or Gina Lombroso's (daughter of the famous Italian criminologist) demand to lower women's responsibility for criminal actions and the level of punishment for them, no one saw a discrepancy between the absolute denial of full (active and passive) political rights to women on the one hand and their full criminal responsibility on the other (Graziosi 1993). Again, how could women take on a public office, if gender difference in law was 'objectively' defined as based in a natural difference?

Needless to say, all the above gave a substantial 'competitive advantage' to eminent jurists, such as Gabba, Marghieri and Sacerdoti, who in their doctrinal commentaries resolutely attacked Lidia Poet's claim. Consequently, having in principle agreed with the courts, they devoted their main efforts as legal scholars to re-affirm the unquestionably public nature of the legal profession. The autonomy of the professional group vis-a-vis the state was thus almost denied and repressed.

On the other hand, jurists who like Mariani, Giuriati, Vidari, and Landolfi supported Lidia Poet's claim, could not but question this emphasis on the public nature of the profession and weaken the arguments relating to positive law and positivistic theorising. Thus, all their efforts were devoted to proving that the advocacy was a truly 'liberal' and private profession. After all, Lidia Poet had applied for enrolment in the *avvocato* law list only, a status role and a function defined by the Profession Act as 'subsidiary' and free, in contrast to that of the *procuratore* which is defined as 'statutory and necessary'.

Yet, taken to its final logical conclusion this form of argument ultimately denied the Janus-headed (public-private) nature of the profession. In fact, once the private nature of *avvocato* as opposed to the public one of *procuratore* was defined in technical legal terms, all that was left was a truly divided profession (Mariani 1884). Italian practitioners could not accept this result at all, either in theory or in practice, because it jeopardised the political compromise embedded in the Profession Act, as well as the cultural and social cohesion of the professional group in the face of state-society issues.

Hence, as soon as this argument was systematically advanced, it became apparent that the doctrinal debate had gone too far and had failed to bring about any substantial success for either side. What it had done was to fuel serious prejudices against the profession as a whole. Unexpectedly, however, the debate did not end here. Seemingly unconnected, but in fact nurtured by the legal climate, a more general theoretical discussion had started in the meanwhile at a higher academic level concerning the legal distinction between the notion of 'public' in the sense of a civic issue of a community, and the traditional notion of 'public' meaning a state-oriented attribute (Ranelletti 1905). Relying on this new academic distinction, those in favour of the entry of women into the profession claimed that a *procuratore* had to be conceived as a civic (private) agent also, and that the profession as a whole was indeed a truly 'liberal', private and professionalised body (Siotto-Pintor 1909).

The claim was technically questionable and politically risky for the vast majority of the profession. But it was one-dimensional enough to be recorded by the state establishment as a useful tool. So much so, that it was subsumed under the rationale of the above mentioned law on women's civic rights enforced in 1919, ie the law leading to a drastic legal disempowerment of and discrimination against Italian lawyers as key state agents. Hence the final outcome of the controversy actually was a long-lasting, general debacle for the profession, as the social perception of its socio-institutional credentialling system was also heavily implicated.

11 CONCLUDING OBSERVATIONS

In this study I have attempted to go beyond traditional and often apologetic narratives about the early history of women's access to the legal profession and, instead, entered the 'unpromised land' of professionalism. The story that has been told is the story of a failure and of its long-lasting multiple negative consequences. After all, social facts do not move towards and even less are unilinearly driven by happy endings only. Yet, the long-lasting positive legacy of this episode was that it set up gender difference and gendered governance as a litmus test for the socio-technical power structure of the Italian legal system. Certainly, this had not been Lidia Poet's aim. Miss Poet had acted individually to pursue an individual goal within the limits of the law of the time. By contrast, it is possible that the recognition of gender as a critical tool was precisely the aim of the *Ordine* of Turin.

As early as 1883, a professional body in Italy was prepared officially to recognise not only gender as an active component within its jurisdiction but also the gendered structuring of public offices and public institutional settings, such as the court system. On the one hand, this was an intuitive act of legal realism in the face of unrestrainable social pressure. On the other hand, it was also and above all a transgressive act of justice based on natural law (for natural law implies the possible need to violate positive law) vis-a-vis the increasingly questionable ideology and policy of the official establishment with regard to society's 'alien', legally discriminated against and culturally undervalued actors.

The price that the Italian legal profession as a whole had to pay for this dual socio-legal commitment has been extraordinarily high. However, equally extraordinary has been the historical merit of having perceived at an early stage the radical consequences of gender integration into a political-constitutional mainstream increasingly demanding the implementation of full citizenship for women as a precondition for legal modernisation and change.

The fact that gender integration was closely associated with the strengthening of professional autonomy vis-a-vis state-centered governance projects proves that this approach was not rooted in some political romanticism or occasional emotions, but rather in the complementary rationally grounded principle of connectedness and relational attachment to a wider social dynamics, requiring the admission that gender is socially constructed and thereby providing a stepping-stone towards future universal emancipation.

12 REFERENCES

Addeo, Piero. 1939. *Eva Togata*. Napoli: Editrice Rispoli.

Algardi, Zara. 1949. *La donna e la toga*. Milano: Giuffré.

Benvenuti, Bartolomeo. 1884. Lettera di Commento alla Sentenza 14 novembre 1883, Proc. Gen. Torino c. Lidia Poet, *Monitore dei Tribunali* 3, 59–63.

Bianchi, Antonio. 1886. Sull'esercizio della professione di avvocato e di procuratore. Testo e Commento della legge 8 giugno 1874 n. 1938, *Raccolta delle Leggi Speciali e Convenzioni Internazionali del Regno d'Italia*. Torino: Unione Tipografico-Editrice.

Burrage, Michael. 1989. Revolution as a Starting Point for the Comparative Analysis of the French, American and English Professions. In *Lawyers in Society. Comparative Theories*. Vol III, edited by R Abel and P Lewis. Berkeley: University of California Press, 322–374.

Costa, Pietro. 1974. *Il progetto giuridico. Per una storia del pensiero giuridico moderno*. Milano: Giuffré.

Davies, Celia. 1996. The Sociology of Professions and the Profession of Gender. *Sociology*, vol 30, no 4, 661–678.

D'Amico La Mantia, Marisa. 1980. *La donna nella professione forense. Atti del Convegno 'La donna e il diritto'*, Associazione Giuriste Italiane, Capri.

Di Federico, Giuseppe and Negrini, Anna. 1989. Le donne nella magistratura ordinaria, *Polis* 2: 179–224.

Farneti, Paolo. 1971. *Sistema politico e società civile. Saggi di teoria e ricerca politica*. Torino: Giappichelli.

Gabba, Carlo F. 1880. *Della condizione giuridica delle donne*. Torino: Utet.

Gabba, Carlo F. 1884. *Le donne non avvocate. Considerazioni di CF Gabba*. Pisa: Tipografia Nistri.

Gherardi, Silvia. 1996. *Il genere e le organizzazioni*. Milano: Cortina.

Giuriati, Domenico. 1884. Le donne avvocate. Lettera al direttore della Temi. *Temi Veneta—Eco dei Tribunali*, Anno IX, n 45: 29–30.

Graziosi, Marina. 1993. Infirmitas Sexus. La donna nell'immaginario penalistico, *Democrazia e diritto* 2: 99–143.

Le Feuvre, Nicky. 1998. Feminisation of Professional Groups in a Comparative Perspective: Some Theoretical Considerations. In *Professions, Identity and Order in a Comparative Perspective*, V Olgiati, L Orzack and M Saks (eds). IISL-Onati: *Onati Papers* 4/5, 233–253.

Mariani, Mariano. 1884. Ancora sull'ammissione delle donne all'esercizio dell'avvocatura, *Monitore dei Tribunali*, Anno XXV, n 10: 217–222.

Mariani, Mariano. 1884. Ancora le donne avvocate, *Monitore dei Tribunali*, Anno XXV, n 11: 451–454.

Millerson, Geoffrey. 1964. *The Qualifying Associations: a Study in Professionalization*. London: Routledge.

Monitore dei Tribunali. 1884. Commento editoriale alla Sentenza: Torino 14 novembre 1883—Proc. Gen. c. Lidia Poet, n 3: 59–63.

Monitore dei Tribunali. 1885. Commento editoriale alla Sentenza: Torino 18 aprile 1884—Publ. Min. e Proc. Gen. c. Poet Lidia, n 26: 404–407.

Monitore dei Tribunali. 1884. Editoriale. Gabba prof. CF—Le donne non avvocate, Anno XXV, n 17: 420–421.

Monitore dei Tribunali. 1885. Commento editoriale a: Istituto Lombardo di Scienze e Lettere—7 febbraio 1884: 'La donna può fare l'avvocato?' lettura di Ercole Vidari, n.26: 158–159.

Olgiati, Vittorio. 1987. Avvocati e notai tra professionalismo e mutamento sociale. In *Le libere professioni in Italia*, edited by W Tousjin. Bologna: Il Mulino, 87–128.

Olgiati, Vittorio and Pocar, Valerio. 1988. The Italian Legal Profession: An Institutional Dilemma, edited by R Abel and P Lewis, *Lawyers in Society. The Civil Law World*. Vol II, Berkeley: University of California Press, 336–368.

Olgiati, Vittorio. 1990. Diritto positivo e autoregolazione professionale nei Discorsi sull'Avvocatura di Giuseppe Zanardelli, *Saggi sull'Avvocatura*. Milano: Giuffré, 95–129.

Olgiati, Vittorio. 1996. Law as an Instrument of Organizational Totalitarianism. Fascist Rule over Italian Lawyers. In *Totalitarian and Post-totalitarian Law*, edited by A Podgorecki and V Olgiati. Aldershot: Darmouth, 123–167.

Ostrogorski, Mosei Yakovlevich. 1897. *Die Frau im öffentlichen Recht*, Leipzig: Otto Wigand.

Pateman, Carol. 1988. *The Sexual Contract*. Oxford: Blackwell-Polity Press.

Pocar, Valerio. 1991. Le donne magistrato. Una ricerca pilota. in *Sociologia del diritto*, XXVII, 3: 73–96.

Poulantzas, Nicos. 1971. *Potere politico e classi sociali*. Roma: Editori Riuniti.

Ranelletti, Oreste. 1905. Il concetto di 'pubblico' nel diritto, *Rivista italiana per le scienze giuridiche*, vol XXXIX.

Ronfani, Paola. 1994. Donne con la toga, *Donne nelle professioni degli uomini*, edited by P David and G Vicarelli, Milano: Angeli, 57–81.

Sarfatti Larson, Magali. 1989. The Changing Functions of Lawyers in the Liberal State: Reflections for Comparative Analysis. In *Lawyers in Society. Comparative Theories*, Vol III, edited by R Abel and P Lewis. Berkeley: University of California Press, 427–477.

Siegrist, Hannes. 1990. Professionalization as a Process: Patterns, Progression and Discontinuity. In *Professions in Theory and History. Rethinking the Study of the Professions*, edited by M Burrage and R Torstendahl. London: Sage, 177–202.

Siotto-Pintor, Manfredi. 1909. *Se la donna sia esclusa per legge dalla professione di procuratore e di avvocato*. Città di Castello: Tipografia Lapi.

Sommerlad, Hilary. 1994. The Myth of Femininisation: Women and Cultural Change in the Legal Profession, *International Journal of the Legal Profession*, vol 1, no 1, 31–53.

Sommerlad, Hilary and Sanderson, Peter. 1998. *Gender, Choice and Commitment*. Aldershot: Ashgate.

Szelenyi, Ivan and Martin, Bill. 1989. The Legal Profession and the Rise and Fall of the New Class. In *Lawyers in Society. Comparative Theories*. vol III, edited by R Abel and P Lewis. Berkeley: University of California Press, 256–288.

Visintini, Giovanna. 1998. La prima donna giurista in Italia. *Materiali per una una storia della cultura giuridica*, XXVII, n 2: 317–321.

Zannoni Messina, Adele. 1980. La donna nei tribunali ecclesiatici, *atti II Congresso Nazionale 'La donna nel diritto'*. Associazione Giuriste Italiane, Capri 17–21 sett. 1980.

24

Women in the Judiciary:
a Perspective from Brazil[1]

ELIANE BOTELHO JUNQUEIRA

Abstract

This chapter is based on original research examining the private and public lives of female judges in the state of Rio de Janeiro, Brazil. The primary goal has been to analyse the process of feminisation of the judiciary in Brazil, both in quantitative and qualitative terms by means of statistical data and in-depth interviews. In addition, the paper traces the impact of this process on individual female judges and their judicial decisions. How rapid has been the increase in the numbers of women within the Brazilian judiciary? Why do women choose to enter the judiciary in the first place, and what obstacles do they encounter on their way? What kind of discrimination, if any, do female judges experience? Does their involvement make a difference to the judicial process? These and other questions were put to respondents—judges and lawyers—in the context of a project which had the distinction of raising this issue for the first time in Brazil.

1 INTRODUCTION

WHAT CONSEQUENCES COULD the feminisation of the judiciary have for our understanding of the law and for the functioning of the legal system? Do female Brazilian judges think and resolve legal conflicts using a different logical process from that traditionally used by their male counterparts? Or does the changing gender composition of the judiciary have little bearing on the interpretation of the law, as social change in law faculties, legal professions and the judiciary itself might be more significant in this context than the gender variable? These and other questions were the subject of an empirical enquiry carried out by means of interviews with female judges from Rio de

---

[1] This is a new version of an article first published in Portuguese (Junqueira 1998). It is based on interviews conducted in 1996 with male and female state judges in Rio de Janeiro as well as with some practising lawyers. The research was supported by the Carlos Chagas Foundation. Fanny Tabak acted as consultant and Maria Matilde Alonso, Gisela Sapha Assumpção and Letícia Isnard helped as research assistants. English translation by Tom Bookless.

Janeiro[2] in order to establish the possible impact of gender on judicial decision-making processes in Brazilian courts.

American analyses remind us that the phrase 'feminisation of the legal professions' must be used with care, since it could refer both to the quantitative increase in the number of women and to the change of relationships within the judiciary (Menkel-Meadow 1986). Quantitative investigations attempt to understand the reasons for the increase in the presence of women in the profession, that is to say, how it is that the traditional obstacles to the entry of women are gradually being overcome (Cook 1978). The qualitative approach can be subdivided into two main aspects. The first stresses the importance of the influence of female characteristics on judicial decisions. The profession can only be feminised, therefore, if and when feminine characteristics—supposedly distinct from masculine ones—are acknowledged in the performance of professional activities (Davis *et al* 1993: 130; Allen & Wall 1993: 158; Gilligan 1982; Smith 1994). The second type of qualitative approach focuses on the presence of women on the Bench as an opportunity for them to liberate themselves from the state of submission in which they have traditionally found themselves.

In this article I combine quantitative and qualitative features, since I analyse both the reasons for the increase in the number of female judges in Rio de Janeiro and possible gender-based changes in the decision-making processes. I shall begin with an overview of the process of feminisation of the legal professions in Rio de Janeiro.[3]

Table 1: New enrolments in the Bar Association of Rio de Janeiro (1975–1995)

Year	Men		Women		Total	
	N	%	N	%	N	%
1975	1,416	65.7	738	34.3	2,154	100.0
1980	1,520	62.8	902	37.2	2,422	100.0
1985	1,943	56.7	1,481	43.3	3,424	100.0
1990	1,980	55.6	1,583	44.4	3,563	100.0
1995	2,353	45.4	2,835	54.6	5,188	100.0

SOURCE: Brazilian Bar Association, Rio de Janeiro

---

[2] It is often difficult in Brazil to find judges willing to be interviewed by researchers. I had to draw on my private network in Rio de Janeiro for interviewees, representing both criminal and civil law. It is acknowledged that the nature of the sample may have introduced a certain bias. Semi-structured interviews were conducted and recorded by myself, each lasting approximately one hour. I worked through a set list of questions, but the informality of the interviews permitted digression, and new topics were introduced by the judges themselves. The fact that this was the first ever research on this topic accounts for the absence of bibliographical references from Brazil.

[3] It must be remembered that Rio de Janeiro cannot be considered the norm for what happens in other Brazilian states. In the poorer and more traditional states the increase in the number of women in the legal profession has been very much slower.

Figures in Table 1 speak for themselves: in the course of 20 years the situation has been reversed and there are now more women joining the Bar Association than men. This does not, however, mean that women constitute a majority within the profession as a whole, as the gender composition of the total membership of the Bar Association of Rio de Janeiro during that same period still reflects a situation of male domination (Table 2).

Looking at the judiciary we find that as in other countries the presence of women is less in evidence. Even so there has been a significant increase (Table 3).

Table 2: Male and female lawyers in the Bar Association of Rio de Janeiro (1975–1995)

Year	Men		Women		Total	
	N	%	N	%	N	%
1975	20,256	81.7	4,546	18.3	24,802	100.0
1980	27,875	74.8	9,415	25.2	37,290	100.0
1985	37,546	69.9	16,170	30.1	53,716	100.0
1990	46,243	66.3	23,512	33.7	69,755	100.0
1995	56,272	62.2	34,233	37.8	90,505	100.0

Table 3: Male and female judges in the judiciary of the state of Rio de Janeiro

	Men		Women		Total	
	N	%	N	%	N	%
1985	395	86.8	60	13.2	455	100.0
1990	320	79.4	83	20.7	403	100.0
1995	443	71.9	173	28.1	616	100.0

SOURCE: Rio de Janeiro State Courts

At the time this investigation was carried out there were 173 female judges in Rio de Janeiro, representing 28.1 per cent of the total. How did they see their profession? Why did they decide to become judges? What professional discrimination had they encountered? How did they reach their judicial decisions? These were a few of the questions put to our interviewees.

2 CHOICE OF CAREER

How can we explain the gradual increase in the number of female judges in Brazil? Is there a lessening of interest in judicial work among men for financial reasons, as recorded in France from the 1950s (Boigeol 1993) and more recently in the USA (Berger & Robinson 1992–93)? Or are there other phenomena that might help to explain the feminisation of the Brazilian judiciary?

The increase in the number of female judges is obviously related to the growing number of women entering the labour market in general. As one interviewee said, 'the phenomenon is widespread'. There is today a greater female presence not only in the legal professions but also in other occupations traditionally regarded as typically masculine. ('Nowadays I can see many female taxi drivers and bus drivers, something that was not seen until recently.') In relation to the higher status professions the respondents recalled their own personal experiences. While their female colleagues at university were mainly interested in marriage, today's law students are already beginning to prepare for their professional examinations while still at university. The fact that most female students were already married at the start of their studies and others married while at university had reinforced the myth circulating in Brazilian society that women followed university courses (especially in certain subjects) looking for a husband.

According to one respondent, however, this gradual increase in the number of women in the labour market should not be seen simply as a feminine success story. Talk of women 'occupying' space in the labour market in fact attempts to disguise the fact that, as a result of currently low salaries, men are unable to provide for their families single-handed. This respondent implied that women represent a reserve workforce to be used by the labour market at times of expansion while keeping wages and salaries of both men and women at a low level.

Women are increasingly present on the Bench. And not just women but young people generally, since problems on the labour market and the strong competition for jobs in private law firms mean that the public examinations for the judiciary represent the main professional opportunity for young law graduates. As a result the professional profile of the judiciary has been changing substantially over recent years. Also, due to the power vested in it, the judiciary is considered by both men and women as the 'apex of the profession'. ('It is always an advantage, you have a certain power. I think that power attracts people. People look at you in a different way.') The judiciary does indeed wield greater power than any other profession not only in the legal system but also in the state apparatus generally, since it is the judge, not the mayor or legislator, who decides directly on questions of freedom, property and even interpersonal relations (family issues etc). This power, which can be seductive, is seen as one of the attractions of the profession: the judge is treated and viewed differently from other people and is spoken to with particular respect. Not surprisingly, the judiciary ranks high amongst young people's career ambitions.

Apart from offering a position of prestige, the judiciary like other public functions offers financial and professional stability. At a time when the labour market as a whole is shrinking, especially with regard to the higher status professions, the fact that the public legal professions are still holding entrance examinations makes law studies an attractive proposition. Becoming a judge represents, therefore, one of the few opportunities on offer in the current labour market for a stable job and a reasonable salary. ('Both men and women look for stability in life, which is difficult to achieve.')

If both sexes are attracted by the salary which allows them to achieve a 'reasonable status', financial stability seems to be especially important for women, as it guarantees 'peace of mind'. ('Women go for the entrance examination more for financial stability than for self-esteem and pride in what they are doing...'). Moreover, although in the long term work as a private legal practitioner may offer greater financial rewards, achieving success as an independent professional in a highly competitive market is much more difficult, especially for women:

> Being a lawyer is much more demanding. In fact you have to work very hard, because otherwise you don't get your money. Being a judge represents stability. You may not earn as much as a good lawyer, but. . . .

Apart from discrimination by professional colleagues women in law firms also encounter discrimination by clients who often prefer being defended by a male lawyer, as if women lawyers were technically less competent. As one male lawyer admitted, Brazilian society is still very male oriented:

> It would be very difficult to convince clients that a woman would look after them competently, that she was a responsible person. It would be quite hopeless. It would be something very complicated to do.

Not only is there a lack of trust in a woman's professional ability, problems for women in law firms also derive from other factors, such as the need to dedicate more time to their private lives, which makes them more vulnerable in their careers. Women also find it harder, particularly in private law firms, to engage in the strategies and networking used by men to attract clients ('rainmaking', as it is called in the United States). This produces a professional stratification, with certain legal areas (such as corporate and contractual law) being reserved for men, while women tend to end up working in areas of lesser prestige in the legal hierarchy, such as family law.

The judiciary seems to offer greater opportunities to combine domestic and professional activities, a feature which attracts women far more than men. ('Women have many jobs, many commitments. Women have marriages, children, households . . .') Although all respondents complained about the volume of work, in one way or another they did acknowledge that the judiciary allowed them a flexible schedule to reconcile their professional duties with their roles as mothers, wives and housewives. The volume of individual Brazilian judges' work may be high, but they are free partly to work from home, one reason being the poor infrastructure in their chambers where they have to receive lawyers. They therefore tend to work on their most complex cases and rulings at home and to go to their chambers only for part of the afternoon four times a week (it has become almost a rule that Brazilian judges do not conduct hearings on Fridays). For women with children, this means that they can devote mornings to their children, helping them with their schoolwork or taking them to the innumerable extra-curricular courses which middle-class Brazilian children attend. Mornings, as well as Fridays, might also be dedicated to shopping in the supermarket, visiting the doctor etc. ('There are judges who do not work on Fridays. There are judges who work from one o'clock to six o'clock. This gives you time to spend on your house and family.') In case of a domestic emergency (illness of a child, absence of the maid/nanny, for example), the worst that could happen to the female judge would be having to cancel all her hearings, a solution not open to the female practising lawyer.

A career in the public sector therefore solves the most fundamental problem for female lawyers, that is how to reconcile their private and public lives. Research in the United States has confirmed that the only way women can achieve professional success as lawyers is by downgrading the importance of their private lives and dedicating themselves full-time to their careers (Hagan and Kay 1995: 82). Or, in the words of one of the male lawyers interviewed, the judiciary allows women to make their profession compatible with the 'natural desire to be a good mother'.

> Being a judge has a special characteristic. It allows a full professional activity within the family environment. This is true for both men and women. The male judge can work at home, just as a female judge can work at home. It is much more compatible with the natural desire to be a good mother than is possible in the case of lawyers.

Yet, women see considerable disadvantages in a judicial career, namely the sheer volume of work and the stress involved. As one of the female respondents stated in answer to the question whether this career would be attractive for women, 'I don't think so. On the contrary, the judiciary seems designed to put women off.' Struggling with human problems, conflicts of interest and disputes makes a career on the Bench very stressful. However much they try to separate work from home, judges cannot cut themselves off completely from the problems which they have to deal with at work. Hence the predominantly negative associations with the profession on the part of both men and women: stressful, difficult, causing suffering etc.

> If you take on this job, you are going to be extremely unhappy (. . .) You are constantly subjected to criticism, you live with stress, you live with stomach pains, you live with ulcers, resolving conflicts of interest. In the courts, nobody lives in peace; everyone fights.

There is something else, though. The need to maintain one's independence and to respect the privacy of the parties involved makes a judge a solitary being. In principle, judges are not allowed to comment on their cases or on their decisions. Decisions are essentially reached in isolation. The professional isolation is particularly strong for those working in a small town. Despite being physically separated from their families for most of the week, judges are obliged to maintain a certain social distance from the community in which they work, in order to preserve their image of authority. On the other hand, the community itself, as a mark of respect, observes its distance relative to judges. The hardship this causes particularly affects female judges, since Brazilian society in general, and especially in small towns, imposes stricter norms of behaviour on women. If male judges must, in principle, maintain a reserved attitude, in the case of female judges this need becomes even more pressing, since the community is permanently watching their behaviour.

The reciprocal process of self-imposed and community-imposed isolation not only affects their daily lives but also the possibility of establishing new emotional relationships. The comments below initially deny that this problem is specific to judges (since in all professions 'you have to know how to choose . . . so that you don't get involved with certain people') and indicate that this problem is greater in small towns. Suitable behaviour is required from all judges because they are figures of authority ('They expect that such figures will lead a life which conforms to the norms considered appropriate for the authority they represent'), but in small Brazilian towns different moral and behavioural norms are applied to men and women—and, therefore, to male and female judges. While it is accepted that men, even married men, have lovers in their districts (this can even confer 'prestige' on them as it is regarded as 'natural'), women are required to lead a celibate life.

> Women are observed more closely. What for the man is a natural thing, let's say, he even has a certain, let's say, I don't mean prestige, I don't know, a certain, I can't find the right word to explain . . . For the woman it is a terrible thing. For example, the man can be a Don Juan . . . Women can't afford this luxury.

However, the main complaint of female judges with regard to their profession relates to the volume of work they have to undertake. This is higher than that of other public legal professions and counterbalances the high social and professional prestige they enjoy. Other public legal professions demand less dedication, knowledge and responsibility, offer a better work structure, do not involve postings to small towns and allow one to pursue a legal career. Sacrifices made by judges are greater for women because of the need to reconcile professional and domestic duties. All are faced with a double day's work, with little or no help from their spouses. The idea that female judges can also be successful as mothers, wives and women seems, therefore, to be more of a dream than a reality:

> As a judge you lose a lot. You lose a lot of time from your life. Dedication is almost exclusive. You don't have time to go to the gymnasium, to the supermarket, you don't have time to go to the hairdresser's, you don't have time to dye your hair . . . You don't have time to do a whole range of things that you want to do. You don't have time for any of this and you know about it when you become a judge. . . . Those who become judges begin to say, 'But I can't put aside my feminine side . . .'. Then what do you do? You keep trying, trying, trying . . .

3 RELATIONSHIPS WITH MALE 'EQUALS'

To what extent does becoming a judge effectively mean entry into a profession offering equal opportunities? Or is it the case that in practice women judges face discriminatory situations? In spite of the apparent contradiction in a body charged with upholding legal principles, including that of equality between men and women, such discrimination does seem to exist. In fact, all respondents, whether from personal experience or not, mentioned instances of discrimination female judges suffered from male colleagues purely because of their sex. These comments arose in the context of either selection or promotion procedures.

Many referred to discriminatory processes in the initial selection of women judges as something that no longer applies.

> It may be that the first female judges felt a lot of discrimination. Today this is no longer the case. . . . In the past, women commented that men turned women down . . . The High Court judges did not want women colleagues but could not say that women couldn't become judges. So what did they do? They turned them down.

In fact, this was the experience of one of the respondents who, not content with studying law at a time when there were few women lawyers in Rio de Janeiro, dared to apply to be a state judge.

> The High Court judges when they talked with us used to say, 'We don't have anything against you, but this is not a job for a woman, it is too heavy a burden, you will be faced with very difficult situations, and women are more fragile'. And we used to say, 'No, we want to be judges and we shall be able to cope'. This reached the point where, when I took my oral exam, the judge said, 'Look, we have nothing against you personally, but I shall do all I can to make sure you fail'. And I jokingly said to him, 'You are wasting your time, I'm going to pass'. And in fact I passed. I came out sixth out of twenty-five who passed. . . . They couldn't understand. At that time it was thought that women couldn't cope with a job full of serious problems.

However, the problem continues to be around in parts of the country. If the rejection of application requests seems improbable, since this would be against the Constitution, it is certainly still the case that more subtle mechanisms are being used to prevent an increase in the number of women judges. In São Paulo, for example, where women were not allowed to be judges until 1981, the public examinations are not anonymous. Therefore, my respondents represented the acceptance of women for judicial office as a victory, not so much because of the constitutional demands of sexual equality or because of the changes in social life, but because male judges had, in a way, been 'forced to acknowledge' the intellectual ability of women.

> The way male judges regard female judges has changed a lot. It has changed mainly in the intellectual area, since women take the first places in the exams. The men have been forced to acknowledge that they are good, that the women are good.

Although discrimination in the selection process has been overcome, women judges still face discrimination in the promotion process: at the time of the investigation there were only two female High Court judges in Rio de Janeiro, a fact pointed out by all the respondents.

> The Court is a men's club. Perhaps this works against women when it comes to promotion. I think women have more difficulty because of this. In future when women are the majority there and it becomes a women's club, the men will start to suffer. . . .

4 IMPACT OF GENDER ON DECISION-MAKING PROCESSES[4]

What might be the specifically feminine characteristics to differentiate the performance of a female from that of a male judge? Do women make decisions in a different way from men? And if so, in what areas and for what reasons? What specific contribution, if any, can women make to the process of adjudication and thereby bring about change?

Respondents felt that the simple fact of being both a woman and a judge has important social consequences, as it makes the female judge a point of reference for other women, especially in less developed districts where problems of feminine submissiveness are more prevalent.

> If you are the district judge in a small community, you are going to be at least a point of reference, and even serve as an example for other women who want one day to achieve an active social position of some standing. It is important from this point of view.

In other words the woman judge represents a model of professional success. She proves that women can achieve important positions in Brazilian society. These include key positions of power monopolised until recently by men. Consequently, she is able to advance the feminist cause as a whole (although this respondent did not make use of feminist language, of which she had a 'horror'). She continued,

> The importance? It is important that women reach the apex of the social pyramid, whether as a judge or in other spheres. It is extremely important because women need to achieve these posts, simply because of the number of women in society, to achieve a balance, and a fair distribution of labour and wealth.

Now, if the increase in the number of female judges is important, in what way, more specifically, can women be expected to contribute? To what extent can a woman be in touch with her feminine side while carrying out the functions of a judge? Is it the case that female judges see their legal practices, their decision

---

[4] Readers might find it interesting to compare this section with thoughts on the same subject in two other contributions to this volume, namely Malgorzata Fuszara's analysis of the Polish situation, and Ulrike Schultz on 'Women Lawyers in Germany—Perceptions and Constructions of Femininity'.

procedures, as different from those of their male colleagues? Also, is it the case that others in the legal profession, including male judges, perceive women making decisions in a gender-specific way? Can it be that there is a female/feminist way of deciding certain legal matters? Opinions on this subject are varied, ranging from those that deny that there is any such difference to those that acknowledge that, in certain areas, male and female judges assume gender-specific positions.

Responses drawing on the myth of judicial impartiality saw the judge as equidistant from both parties and, therefore, necessarily asexual. In consequence, gender would remain outside in the decision-making process.

> No, I never take this into account. The only thing I consider is whether in a given case I am doing my job as a judge. Whether it is a man or a woman is irrelevant. I don't even consider it. In this way, I would say that I am asexual. There is no change in my judgment in either case.

This type of response can have two roots that are not mutually exclusive. On one hand, there is the belief that dispensing justice implies neutrality, that a judge can at any given moment become an asexual being. On the other hand, thinking like an asexual is associated with thinking more like a man and denying one's feminine identity, since it would mean thinking in accordance with the dominant decision-making processes which are, following a feminist point of view, necessarily masculine. In other words, if the law is being quoted and applied under a male dominated system, claiming to be asexual is synonymous with male definitions of justice.

Another attempt to deny gender differences tries to attribute the differences in the decision-making processes to the life experiences of each judge (Tacha 1995).

> No. What really matters is one's life experience. Life experience is something fundamental if a judge is going to be a good judge. For example, if I have to award to a woman the custody of a child, I am not going to take into account that she is the mother. I am going to take into account whether she is a good mother, whether she is in a position to provide for her children economically and emotionally. I am also going to take into account what is best for the children. Nowadays, the legal code expressly states that the judge must also listen to the children, and must not make a decision without taking their views into consideration. The children have a preference, although this may not be a decisive factor. In these situations one makes a decision according to one's experience.

However, personal experience derives, logically—or, at least, also—from family life (being single or married, for example) and from the role played by the judge in relation to children. This supposes that male and female judges with children perform their roles as fathers/mothers differently, according to the custom of Brazilian society.

> The experience that women bring as mothers and housewives also helps. It helps because in fact you're going to find here women, housewives with those problems that

are involved in legal situations. This baggage—the experience of dealing with work and home—really helps the female judge.

The differences in the decision-making processes are not related to sex but to gender as determined by the current structure of conjugal society, the family arrangements and the division of domestic chores. In spite of being married and having children, male judges, as is the case with men in general, do not see certain problems related to their marriages and children as their concern.

One of the male lawyers interviewed stated that the differences in the decision-making processes are not related to gender but are the result of differences in the personalities of individual judges or, more precisely, in their view of the world. Taking the criminal area as an example, some judges appear more sympathetic in the context of crimes carried out by marginalised sectors of society, while adopting stricter positions when judging crimes perpetrated by agents of the state. Others are liberal with regard to crimes committed by the police involved in imposing public order and strict with regard to crimes committed by marginalised sectors, arguing that poverty is no justification for criminality.

Another group of responses, in spite of denying gender differences in the interpretation of the law, refers to possible differences in the decision procedures adopted by male and female judges. This relates not so much to substantive questions of law but to the impact of gender on the way decisions are reached. Women, as opposed to men, were said to be particularly concerned with detail and with producing a more substantial justification for their decisions.

> Their ability is the same. But the way they decide is definitely different. I can sense in women's decisions rather more detail. Women concern themselves with certain details. Their decisions are more elaborate in this sense. They try to justify their decisions with the opinions of legal experts.

According to this respondent, the underlying reason for women's concern with detail may not merely be the different 'temperaments' of men and women but also a strategy employed by women to safeguard their position on the Bench by attempting to prove that they are 'as capable as men'. Attention to detail and meticulous argumentation, always backing up decisions with reference to case history, then represents a conscious female strategy, in contrast to greater self-confidence among male judges that allows them to make decisions more independently. It is intriguing to think that, while attempting to be seen 'as capable as men', female judges are, in fact, using methods not used by their male colleagues. In other words, in their attempt to be equal, they end up becoming different.

Although responses denied gender differences or reduced these to procedural matters, several interviewees did concede that men and women, at least in two legal areas, do make gender-specific decisions. One such area is criminal law. Especially in the traditional case of murder in legitimate defence of honour, a crime (nearly always perpetrated by men) was justified by the behaviour of the victim (almost always a woman). However, the main area where decision-making processes were seen to allow for gender-specific features were family disputes. Almost all respondents acknowledged that women decide family problems differently from men. But what does this mean in practice? Could it be that female judges adopt a more protective attitude towards the female party, granting requests for maintenance, while men (who may be financially exploited by ex-wives) choose a stricter approach out of a sense of solidarity with the men against whom the claims are being made? Quite on the contrary, respondents agreed that female judges are much 'tougher' in cases of requests for alimony made by women, while male judges are more generous and decide in favour of the claimant. ('I think that men are more generous with women claimants in matters of maintenance. We are the tougher ones.')

Again, one needs to look for reasons. In the first place, the objective attitude taken by female judges was seen by them as helping women who request a financial contribution from their ex-husbands to better develop and fulfil their potential as human beings. As one of the female judges commented, 'the more people protect women, the more they are going to be discriminated against'. In other words, advancing the position of women means helping them to break away from the economic dependency to which they have been subjected by encouraging them to take up their place in society. This stance was defended with the argument that it is the one most in tune with the constitutional principle of equality of men and women—granting a woman maintenance could be considered unconstitutional, since it would presuppose that women are less self-sufficient than men.

> When there is a problem of feeding a family I try to open the eyes and the mind of the woman. The 1988 Constitution makes it absolutely clear that there should be equality between men and women, absolutely clear. It is a constitutional principle. The thing is that Brazilian women were not prepared for it. They still aren't. But they have to assume this premise, this obligation to themselves and society.

This type of attitude does not mean, however, that female judges are insensitive to women's problems. Quite the opposite, they are aware of the difficulties posed by a young and limited labour market, in which people of more than 35 years of age are considered 'too old' for entry into a profession. Therefore, female judges may grant a woman temporary maintenance to prevent her having difficulties finding a job (because of her age or lack of experience or professional qualifications). ('If she is young, and can work, I sometimes grant alimony until she finishes a course or until she finds a job.')

However, alongside these nobler concerns, one could also sense a more negative attitude towards women seemingly shunning work and wanting to remain dependent on their husbands, as well as towards women who want to 'make a killing' through marriage and divorce.

> I don't know whether this behaviour is just or unjust. But when a young woman comes in requesting maintenance, you feel a certain, I wouldn't say, antipathy, but you don't

look favourably on that situation. You ask yourself, 'Why isn't she working? She is young and healthy'.

In short, these female judges were holding themselves up as role models, as women who have faced up to the challenges of the labour market and have enjoyed professional success while coping with domestic responsibilities— women who are permanently trying to reconcile conflicting roles. ('There is this considerable tendency for the female judge to justify herself. If she works so hard and struggles so much, why should others depend for food on their ex-husbands?')

5 CONCLUSION

If judges are responsible for resolving conflicts in accordance with Brazilian law, it is ultimately their function to safeguard observance of the constitutional norms and principles. Judges (naturally including female judges) are responsible, for example, for ensuring that, in accordance with the 1988 Federal Constitution, 'men and women are equal with regard to rights and obligations'. Judges (including female judges, it is important to stress) must uphold the new constitutional norms that have restructured family relationships, especially Article 226, according to which 'the rights and duties within conjugal relationships are exercised equally by men and women'.

The ambiguity of the experiences of women judges derives, therefore, from their exercising a public function that transforms them into guardians of these principles, while at the same time having to uphold a sexual division of domestic roles in which women must serve and men must be served. But the effort made by female judges to not see themselves and to not be seen by others as different from their male colleagues raises some questions. If in reality there are no gender-based differences in the decision-making process, one needs to ask whether this homogeneity is due to the fact that men and women simply make decisions in exactly the same way (with the question of alimony remaining the great exception that proves the rule). Or might the process of socialisation in the legal world, which derives from the fact that male and female judges have studied in the same law schools, be sufficient to remove gender differences when it comes to interpreting the most substantive judicial questions? To what extent does court work reinforce this process of assimilation? Might it be that women receive more or less explicit messages that their entry into the profession presupposes a renunciation of 'feminine'/'feminist' positions that would challenge the dominantly 'masculine' jurisprudence? Or is it that female judges in their competition with male judges use the strategy to conceal (or even eliminate) all gender differences, in the search for a more equal relationship?

All we have to go by are responses that deny gender-based differences in judicial decision-making processes, while at the same time referring to procedural differences in areas where women's behaviour tallies with what is often described as archetypically female (and denying differences that in the light of this archetypal model would be unfavourable to women). The strategy seems quite clear, that is, to deny any difference in the professional behaviour of male and female judges on the grounds that women's decisions are no different from those of men. Just as judges from lower social classes develop strategies to distance themselves from their origins in order to fit in with their new 'elite' status, women try to deny both their sexuality (by dressing austerely, for example) and gender difference by conforming to the decision-making processes dominant in court. In short, they become 'asexual' beings.

6 REFERENCES

Allen, David & Wall, Diane. 1993. Role Orientations and Women State Supreme Courts Justices. 126 *Judicature* 156.

Berger, Marylin & Robinson, Kari. 1992–93. Woman's Ghetto Within the Legal Profession. 8 *Wisconsin Women's Law Journal* 71.

Boigeol, Anne. 1993. La magistrature française au féminin: entre spécificité et banalisation. 25 *Droit et Société* 489.

Cook, Beverly. 1978. Women Judges: The End of Tokenism. *Women in the Courts*. Virginia, National Center for the State Courts.

Davis, Sue *et al*. 1993. Voting Behavior and Gender on the US Courts of Appeal. 126 *Judicature* 129.

Gilligan, Carol. 1982. *In a Different Voice*. Cambridge: Harvard University Press.

Hagan, John and Kay, Fiona. 1995. *Gender in Practice*. New York: Oxford University Press.

Junqueira, Eliane Botelho. 1998. A mulher juíza e a juíza mulher. In Bruschini, Cristina and Hollanda, Heloísa Buarque. *Horizontes Plurais*. São Paulo: Editora 34.

Menkel-Meadow, Carrie. 1986. The Comparative Sociology of Women Lawyers: The 'Feminization' of the Legal Profession. 24 *Osgoode Hall Law Journal* 89.

Smith, Susan. 1994. Diversifying the Judiciary: The Influence of Gender and Race on Judging. *University of Richmond Law Review* 28

Tacha, Deanell. 1995. W Stories: Women in Leadership Positions in the Judiciary. 97 *West Virginia Law Review* 683.

25

Lee Tai-Young (1914–1998): The Pioneer Woman Lawyer of South Korea

HAESOOK KIM

Abstract

The Korean legal profession remained exclusively male until 1952, when Lee Tai-Young passed the judicial examination, the sole gateway to the elite Korean legal profession. How was she able to imagine the previously unimaginable? How was Lee Tai-Young able to chart a career that no woman had travelled before? To answer these questions, this article focuses on Lee Tai-Young's formative years. Her childhood, education and marriage, most of which took place during the Japanese colonial period (1910–1945), can be seen as important factors that influenced her unique career. The paper concludes with an account of how she was able to become the first woman to pass the judicial examination. Her life history serves as a case study of a woman who struggled between feminist and feminine identities in the process of achieving her goal in a modernising society.

1 INTRODUCTION

IN THIS ARTICLE, I analyse the life history of Lee Tai-Young, the pioneer woman lawyer of South Korea. The primary source of information is interviews with Lee Tai-Young, which I conducted in Korea in 1990 and 1991. All quotations without references are from these interviews (translated from Korean).

Lee Tai-Young was 38 years old when, in 1952, she became the first Korean woman lawyer. Although she was the wife of a prominent politician, she achieved this honour not through his influence, but by passing the extremely prestigious and competitive National Judicial examination,[1] a distinction traditionally reserved for only a few privileged sons of prominent families.

---

[1] All Korean jurists—judges, prosecutors and practising lawyers—have to pass the state-administered judicial examination. The Ministry of General Administration, an agency of the executive branch, sets the quota for the number of candidates who may pass, thus effectively functioning as a gatekeeper to the legal profession in Korea.

At that moment, Lee Tai-Young became a 'modern subject' (Hegel 1967; Giddens 1990; Habermas 1984; Ferguson 1991), that is, a person who is the product of the processes of modernisation and, with modernity, acquires a new consciousness. Instead of tradition governing her thought processes, social practices 'were constantly examined and reformed in the light of information about those very practices, thus constitutively altering . . . [her] character.' (Giddens 1990: 38) This radical reconsideration of convention, which applies to all aspects of modern life, presupposes the knowing or reasoning self. It is premised on the 'speaking subject' and the subject's own accounts of her experiences. Lee Tai-Young's life history became a complex terrain, where old habits of being a woman in a patrilineal family setting—she was the mother of three children and a daughter-in-law taking care of her husband's widowed mother—were contrasted with the Christian/modern view of human beings and the world, a view she had learned at school. Old understandings had to be renegotiated, as her ambitions grew and educational and professional opportunities opened up to her.

Structural constraints and cultural reproduction, through socialisation and educational processes interacted in her decision-making regarding family and work, reflexively monitored by herself. In Lee Tai-Young's life history, and in those of the women jurists who followed her, the co-existence of the female (socially constructed) identity and the feminist (politically aware) identity is apparent. In what follows, I analyse the role Lee Tai-Young played in constructing her life, working both within the framework of and against patriarchy, as the pioneer woman lawyer in Korea.

2 PARENTAL FAMILY

Research has shown that there is a strong relationship between a woman's professional achievement and her parents' class status. In the United States, pioneer women lawyers often had fathers or husbands who were lawyers (Drachman 1998: 9–36). In fact, studies of American women lawyers in the 1960s and 1970s found that their parents had a higher occupational status, educational attainment, and income than did male lawyers' parents (Epstein 1991: 24–26). However, in Korea the situation was different. None of the elected members of the South Korea parliament came from upper class families in Seoul, whereas over 90 per cent of male members came from above upper middle class families (Soh 1991: 26–27). Lee Tai-Young's father lost his parents when he was young, migrated to Pukjin and became a gold-miner. He married Kim Heng-Won, the daughter of a notable family in the area, whose grandfather had been a man of knowledge of Chinese classics and was said to have been a local government official (Strawn 1988: 3). As Lee Tai-Young recalled, her father 'worked and died in the gold-mine, three thousand *chok* below the ground, where men were working half naked due to the intense heat.' This story of the daughter of a miner can be understood only in the context of the fundamental social changes that were occurring during Korea's modernisation period that began at the end of the nineteenth century.

At that time, East Asia was opened up to Western imperialism. It was in 1876 that the 'hermit kingdom' of the Choson dynasty was forced to accept Japan's imposition of a Western-style unequal treaty. China, in an effort to reassert its traditional hegemony over Korea, played the Western imperial powers off against each other and, in 1882, arranged more unequal treaties between Korea and the United States, Britain and Germany. The three Western nations were given extraterritorial rights for their citizens in Korea, consular representation, fixed tariffs, port concessions and other benefits. In Korea, this included the United States' access to a gold-mine in Pukjin, Lee Tai-Young's birth place, in the northwestern corner of the Korean peninsula. Though described by Lee Tai-Young as a 'remote mountain village where villagers lived on corn and potatoes rather than on rice,' Pukjin had an unusually international flavour. Only four years after Japan had, in 1910, annexed Korea as a colony, the young Lee Tai-Young grew up seeing 'Americans, who managed the mining business, Chinese, who grew and sold vegetables, Japanese, who were in charge of the administration of the village, and Koreans, who worked in the mine.' She herself would take advantage of these social changes to combine a traditional with a modern woman's role.

In Korea, the death or absence of the father has often been associated with women who entered the male-dominated arena of Korean politics (Soh 1991: 26–27). When Lee Tai-Young's father died in 1915, he left behind a widow and three children—two sons of 13 and four, and Tai-Young, who was just one year old. He himself had lost his parents as a child. Thus, in the absence of patrilinear relatives, it became Lee Tai-Young's mother who had to provide financial support for the family. This went against the traditional gender role. Lee Tai-Young's mother opened a little store patronised by the villagers, did sewing on consignment, and raised pigs. Lee Tai-Young recalled her mother as 'the hardest working person I have ever known.' At the same time, the eldest son became the symbolic head of the household and the substitute father figure for Lee Tai-Young.

Korean tradition held that a husband's family took responsibility for his widow. If he had no relatives, it was likely that the widow herself, not her family, assumed responsibility for her children.[2] Luckily, Lee Tai-Young's mother was assisted by her family who were financially able to help her. Moreover, she understood the importance of education for success.

For her family as for many others in Korea, especially during the time of drastic social transformation that characterised the transition from the premodern to the modern period, education became the key to upward social

[2] Strawn mentions in her biography Lee Tai-Young's family's brief stay with the maternal family after her father's death. Her mother's decision to move out of her family's home is attributed to Mrs Lee's desire for independence (1988, 4).

mobility (Ableman 1997: 871–93). Lee Tai-Young's mother received sufficient financial support from her family for her eldest son's education. After having completed local elementary school and middle school, he was sent to a high school in Seoul, which was 'harder than sending a child to the U.S.A. to study abroad today.' He eventually went to study in Japan.

Lee Tai-Young's mother also pushed the idea of education for her little ones, the second son and the daughter. Lee Tai-Young recalled her mother's 'revolutionary' attitude toward girls' education. Although she herself was uneducated and most families in the village did not send girls to school, she placed a high premium on schooling. She said to Tai-Young and her second brother, who was three years older, 'Considering our poor family's financial situation, I am not sure whether I can send both of you to high school. I will send to high school whichever of you does better in school.' Lee Tai-Young recalled that from that time

> I was in constant competition with my elder brother. As a girl, in addition to other chores, I had to take care of my eldest brother's child. So after school, when I came home, I carried the baby on my back and, finding a cool place under a tree, I read and read and read. At night, I used up candles for reading, even after my brother went to sleep.

Later in life, Lee Tai-Young, remembering her mother's promise, was puzzled that her 'unenlightened [uneducated]' mother came up with the idea of equal education regardless of gender. 'Was she trying to motivate us to study hard? That is one question I would like to ask, if only she were alive today.'

Lee Tai-Young's mother provided a complex image of a woman's role for her daughter. On the one hand, she fulfilled the traditional role of 'good wife and wise mother', taking excellent care of her children and advising neighbours with marital problems to work harder to maintain family harmony. Lee Tai-Young also recalled her own perplexity that her mother should have allowed her daughter-in-law to play a traditional female role. When the eldest brother got married and brought his wife home, young Tai-Young noticed, 'Instead of my sister-in-law becoming a sister to me, all she did was work, work, and work, without many words.' In this sense, the Lee household was not very different from others of that time. A married woman, physically and symbolically, belonged to the husband's household and his lineage. On the other hand, Lee Tai-Young's mother was the breadwinner who, unlike others, believed in equal education regardless of gender.

Religion is often cited as another variable that affects women's professional achievement. Lee Tai-Young's emergence as a 'modern subject' is closely related to her religious heritage. Lee Tai-Young's maternal grandfather was the founder of the Methodist Church in Pukjin. As an infant, she was baptised in the church. She grew up spending much time in the church sitting next to her mother and grandmother. Though Protestantism was only introduced into Korea in the late nineteenth century, by the early twentieth century Lee Tai-Young was already a third-generation Christian.

The northwestern area, including Pukjin, was one of the first in Korea where Christianity was received and prospered. Before the first king of the Choson Dynasty moved the capital to Seoul at the end of the fourteenth century, the area around Pyongyang had been the seat of government. During the Choson dynasty, the people of that region suffered discrimination, which became one of the reasons suggested for the rapid spread of Christianity there. The existence of a gold-mine under American management was another reason for missionaries to settle in Pukjin.

Before Lee Tai-Young started her schooling in Pukjin's Kwang Dong Primary School in 1918, she had been attending Sunday school. She also studied the Bible, memorising verses and listening to the preacher's sermons. She often spoke on special religious days and thus became a speaking subject in a public space at a time when the ordinary lot of a girl in Korea was obedience, silence, patience, and endurance at home.

Lee Tai-Young was five years old when a public speech contest was held at her school in the context of a national competition for children between the ages of 12 and 14 years.

> When I found out I was not going to speak [at the contest], I was angry. So I told the teacher I wanted to make a speech. His reply was that I was too young. I countered that, if I was so young, why had people made me speak at the church all the time? He finally agreed to let me participate in the contest.

When the teacher asked her what she wanted to talk about, Lee Tai-Young answered, 'I have something which bothers me: why people cry when a girl is born, sighing and clicking their tongues with much regret, whereas people celebrate when a boy is born, making rice cakes and giving gifts to the family.' The title of the speech was, 'I Am a Girl'. In her speech, Lee Tai-Young took note that a girl's birth carried less social significance than a boy's. In that very act, she emerged as a speaking subject criticising the Neo-Confucian gender practice of male preference in Korea.

Another factor that aided her was male sponsorship. Her eldest brother 'acted as my father, the "enlightened" [modern educated] person. His growth was the basis from which I became the person of today.' He became the man of the house at the age of 13, when their father died at the mine. He also became the first member of the Lee family to get a modern education. It was education that enabled him to become a member of the intellectual elite that collectively would carry out the modernisation of Korea, especially after liberation from Japan in 1945.

When Lee Tai-Young was six years old, her eldest brother asked her if she would like to be a lawyer. She replied, 'What is a lawyer?' Her brother said she would not understand, but that he would explain it to her when she grew up. 'The idea of becoming a lawyer was the seed planted in me by my big brother. Of course, I had no idea what it was,' recalled Lee Tai-Young. This sometimes caused embarrassment. Villagers at Pukjin, not quite accustomed to seeing a girl attending school, used to stop Lee Tai-Young and ask, 'Little girl, what are you going to do with your education when you grow up?' Without hesitation, Lee Tai-Young would answer, 'I want to become a lawyer.' They asked, 'What is that?' She would answer, 'I don't know.' From that time on, villagers fondly called her *mengkongee*, a fool. It was then that she began to cross the boundary to the modern world, which admittedly she still only partly understood.

Her eldest brother was sent to study in Japan by the missionaries. Even then he continued to act in his paternal role, sending letters and books to Tai-Young and reminding her not to lose sight of her dream to become a lawyer. In a letter he wrote, 'Tai-Young, when you grow up you will become either a lawyer or a legislator.' He also sent copies of *Youngnokhoe*, an intellectual periodical for university students. She told him that she could not understand it. He replied, 'Just read it repeatedly and look at the pictures also. At least try to read the titles of articles.' However, the crucial moment of understanding came later.

3 EDUCATION

As has been widely noted, education plays a key role in women's professional achievement. In Korea, Christianity was one of the forces behind the spread of modern education, together with certain Korean state policies of modernisation. Lee Tai-Young's education closely fits this pattern. In 1915, the year when Lee Tai-Young started kindergarten and first grade at Kwang Dong Primary School in Pukjin, there were 56,253 elementary school boys and 5,976 elementary school girls nationwide (Kim 1979: 233). At the secondary level, numbers drastically decreased, ie 822 boys and 250 girls. This is the overall context within which Lee Tai-Young's educational opportunities need to be interpreted. She was one of those fewer-than-6,000 girls who were enrolled at primary school and whose prospects of being able to move on to university studies were extremely slim.

At Kwang Dong Primary School, Lee Tai-Young excelled academically. As she herself said, she was always in competition with her second brother in the hope that she could, like her eldest brother, continue her education to the high school in the city. Her determination and anxiety are well illustrated by an episode that happened after the family moved from Pukjin to Yongbyon. After finishing high school in Seoul, her eldest brother became a secretary to American missionaries in Yongbyon. This marked an important moment for Lee Tai-Young's family. Yongbyon, less remote than Pukjin, was the county seat with a population of over 8000. It was an area of active missionary work, with a public elementary school and two private schools, the Methodist Soong Dok Boys' School and the Soong Dok Girls' School, all of which reinforced Lee Tai-Young's academic ambitions, as well as her concern that her mother might not keep her promise regarding her daughter's education.

When Lee Tai-Young was 10, there was another public speech contest. This time, both children of the Lee family were selected by the school to enter. Lee

Tai-Young's topic was, 'Please Educate Both Girls and Boys Equally'. In her speech, she used the metaphor of an ox cart with two wheels: 'If two wheels are not equal, the ox cart is of no use. Since we, boys and girls, were created equally by God, why not educate us equally, so that we can serve all humanity.' When asked about her motive for selecting this topic, Lee Tai-Young replied, 'Even though Mother repeatedly promised to educate the ablest child regardless of gender, I must have worried. I chose the topic partly to reinforce Mother's promise.'

When Lee Tai-Young was 16, she graduated from her local high school (freshman and sophomore years) and passed the examination to enter a missionary high school in Pyongyang. Accompanied by her eldest brother, she took the train for the first time to the city of Pyongyang. On their way to Chung Eui Girls' High School, she saw a big sign saying 'Law Office of Park Tae-Sung'. She still did not know what a lawyer was and was shocked. She pulled her brother's sleeve and said, 'Somebody already became the lawyer. Why did you tell me to become the lawyer when someone else is already a lawyer? I bet you did not know that!' He reminded her that in their home town there were two medical doctors, both of whom were there to cure people's illnesses. 'Lawyers are those who cure *han* [a sense of suffering due to injustice]. Lawyers are those who study law and with words cure people who suffer from injustice,' explained her brother. This made her even more determined to become a lawyer, even though she did not have any idea of how to realise her dream.

At Chung Eui Girls' High School, Tai-Young began her junior and senior high school years. After graduation, she returned to the elementary school she had attended in Pukjin as a teacher. During her time there she applied to Ewha Womans College and was accepted.

When Lee Tai-Young arrived at Ewha Womans College, it offered three majors: liberal arts, music, and home economics (last one added in 1927). 'In retrospect what I really wanted to study was "women's studies"', she recalled later. 'Of course, there was no such thing as "women's studies" then.' In the end, Lee Tai-Young majored in home economics. An important influence was Miss Morris, who taught a Western-style home economics class, in which she emphasised that 'if women want to be liberated from this yoke [of household labour], you need to be creative.' According to Tai-Young, 'that statement alone made it worthwhile to study home economics. That was it. It was more than studying law.' Another professor's comment also helped to crystallise her view on women's traditional labour:

> When Professor Chang said, 'The night-long pounding sound of wooden sticks which iron out clothes folded on a stone slate, is the sound of wooden sticks beating on Korean women's heads,' it woke me up. I wanted to liberate women. I wanted to liberate women from Kimchee jars, beanpaste jars. That was why I chose to major in home economics.

Without much effort, she was able to remain the top student in home economics and thus receive a scholarship from Ewha.

In her sophomore year, there arose an opportunity to study law. She met Professor Chung Kwang-Hyun, who became and remained a mentor for Lee Tai-Young throughout her legal career:

> One of the electives offered at that time was law and economics. It was my subject— law! I had almost buried it in my heart as hopeless when I started to get engaged in the new subject [home economics]. After the mid-term, Professor Chung Kwang-Hyun called me and asked whether I wanted to study law. I replied: 'I have been longing for it.' He asked what I meant, 'longing' to study law. So I explained how I had heard about studying law from my brother and, finding it impossible, I had almost given up the idea and instead was studying home economics at Ewha. Upon hearing this Professor Chung repeated his question, 'Do you want to study law?' I asked him, 'Could I do it?' 'From now on, I will teach you,' was his reply. Now the dream had been re-awakened.

This meeting resulted in the formation of the first academic society at Ewha, the Society for the Study of Law and Economics. In the first year, 14 students signed up to study law under the tutelage of Professor Chung, a visiting professor from the neighbouring Yonhui College [later Yonsei University]. After a year, half of the students had dropped out. In the second year, more dropped out. In her senior year, Lee Tai-Young was the only one continuing, spending countless hours copying Professor Chung's manuscripts, proofreading them, or just reading them. 'Professor Chung believed that I would learn something about law by doing such jobs,' said Lee Tai-Young. Her encounter with Professor Chung was a turning-point in her life and he continued to mentor her throughout her career.

At Ewha Womans College Lee Tai-Young's feminist consciousness was maturing. During her junior year, she entered a third public speech contest. The title of her speech was, 'Korean Women, Second-Generation Noras.'

> I had read Ibsen's *A Doll's House* numerous times. I told the audience that Nora did not just exist in the novel of Ibsen. 'All of us in Korea, all women are Noras, second-generation Noras. The original Nora had lived at the beginning of the nineteenth century, while we, the second generation Noras, live in the twentieth century. Oppression still exists, our ignorance still exists. But Nora was a fool. We, unlike Nora who lived thirty to forty years ago, are not going to leave home. We will kick our husbands out,' said I. When I said that there was an uproar. The audience— mostly men—rose up from their seats and started shouting and pointing their fingers at me. I could not continue the speech. My speech was stopped by the Japanese police who were there in order to suppress any signs of anti-colonial statements by speakers. After the audience became calm, I continued. By this time I was seething with fury and words poured out forcefully without any hesitation. I continued, 'That's the problem. Why should she leave? She raised children, did all the work. It was she who saved his life. She did all the right things. The house was hers. Then the husband turned around and threw Nora out of the house. The rotten bastard betrayer! It is the husband who should have been thrown out of the house.' I repeated my curse words against him [Nora's husband]. I was not aware of what I was saying. At this, the audience responded. 'We will not keep such a woman as you

at home. We will kick you out! A woman deserving a divorce!'³ Anyway, I won the first prize.

In her senior year at Ewha, one of the required courses was 'Women and Work', taught by Dr Helen Kim, one of the first graduates of Ewha College. Dr Kim had remained single to devote herself to the education of women. She had been convinced that for a woman to participate in society on an equal footing with men, she needed to give up family life. Throughout the course, Dr Kim emphasised the impossibility of combining work and family. Her pet phrase was, 'Choose one: marriage or work.' On the last day of the class, she asked her students the following question, 'Who [among women] do you respect most?' Lee Tai-Young recalled the following:

> When it came to my turn to answer, I said, 'Curie *pu-in*'.⁴ Dr Kim asked me back in surprise, '*Madame* Curie?' I said, 'Yes. Curie *pu-in*.' Dr Kim seemed a bit offended at my answer, as all her teaching throughout the semester seemed to have been in vain. But I purposefully answered, 'Curie *pu-in*'. Curie *pu-in* did research together with her husband, then went home to have meals together, had children and continued her work. I liked her style. I wanted to do both, work and family.

4 MARRIAGE

After graduating from Ewha Womans College, Lee Tai-Young got a job as a faculty member at Pyongyang Women's Bible College, teaching home economics and the Bible, as well as directing the choir. Lee Tai-Young's family was concerned for their only daughter's marriage prospects. However, Lee Tai-Young herself was not much interested in any initial approaches from other families, even though they included some quite prominent suitors. Instead, she thought that she would have a 'special marriage'. While traditionally Korean families arranged marriages for their children, Lee Tai-Young, a graduate and teacher, was able to express her own wishes.

Through church functions, Lee Tai-Young had become acquainted with Dr Chyung Yil-Hyung, a Christian minister who had recently returned home from the United States after getting his PhD from Drew University. He was well known for serving the poor, an unusual activity for one with a doctoral degree from abroad. In the 1930s, only a handful of Koreans had obtained doctorates abroad, and those few easily obtained good teaching positions in Seoul. Instead, Dr Chyung decided to start a church on the outskirts of Pyongyang serving factory workers.

Lee's family did not think that Dr Chyung was a good marriage prospect because of his poor financial standing and the fact that he was the only son of a widow. Her family worried that she would not only be financially badly off but

---

³ This is one of the worst curses against a Korean woman.
⁴ This is the Korean way of addressing a married woman, equivalent to 'Mrs' in English.

would also have sole responsibility for the household as well as having to fit in with her mother-in-law's wishes, as was required of a filial daughter-in-law.[5] As time went by, Dr Chyung Yil-Hyung won her family's favour and, by the end of 1936, when he proposed to her, her family consented. The marriage ceremony was held on 26 December 1936, at the Chung Eui High School auditorium. Lee Tai-Young had a Christian Western-style wedding ceremony with a Christmas tree lit nearby. Not only was the form of the wedding modern, but also the way the parties—parent and daughter—negotiated the marriage. However, Lee Tai-Young acted on traditional principles by moving into Dr Chyung's house where he lived with his mother who managed the everyday life of the household. Lee Tai-Young kept her job at the bible school out of financial necessity, since her husband's income as a pastor for the urban poor was low and unreliable. When she brought her monthly salary home, she agreed to her husband's request to give all the money to her mother-in-law, who then dispensed it as she saw fit. This created a symbolic balance of power between the mother-in-law, as the producer and guardian of the patrilineage, and the modern daughter-in-law, who was in gainful employment.

The period of national crisis and the resulting social upheaval allowed a gender role reversal in Lee Tai-Young's family. The Japanese, who had colonised Korea in 1910, were becoming suspicious of young intellectual Koreans, including some of those who had studied abroad. The Japanese colonial police suspected that Chyung Yil-Hyung's urban industrial mission work was a disguised form of anti-Japanese nationalist resistance. On the morning after the wedding, when Lee Tai-Young, according to custom, made a deep bow to her mother-in-law, the first statement from her mother-in-law was, 'Are you aware that your husband has been detained by the Japanese police fourteen times in connection with his activities in the Korean Independence Movement and his urban labour mission?' (Strawn 1988: 33–52). From that time on, she knew that she had to make a living for the family, including her mother-in-law. Her husband was often jailed and the food and medicine he required forced her to look for a way to earn more money.

One day, a home economics teacher told her about the quilt business. Even though she had no background in business and she knew nothing about quilts, she had no other choice. 'I started to learn how to make quilts. After making quilted bed-spreads, I carried them on my head hawking them in the streets. I had turned into a quilt-peddler. I did not do well,' recalled Lee Tai-Young. On one of those wretched days of poverty, Lee Tai-Young came across Professor Chung, her mentor. He just looked with great sympathy at his former student, now carrying a huge pile of quilts on her head and a baby on her back. 'As he turned away from me, he muttered, "All the work in law, what a waste it was!"

---

[5] The power struggle between a mother-in-law and a daughter-in-law is intensified if there is an only son. Even among contemporary Koreans, the only son of a widow is the least desirable partner for marriage.

This became one of the most hurtful things anyone has said to me in my life,' said Lee Tai-Young.

5 NEW OPPORTUNITIES

In 1945, national liberation from Japan brought changes in Lee Tai-Young's family. Upon hearing the news in Pukjin, where the family had moved after her husband's release from jail, her husband organised the town's celebration. She herself made a big Korean flag, the possession or display of which had been forbidden during the colonial period. Afterwards, in a quiet moment, her husband asked her what she wanted most, now that the nation was liberated. Lee Tai-Young declared, 'I will never work for money again.'[6] Overwhelmed by the hardship she had endured as the breadwinner during the colonial period and sensing the opening up of new possibilities at the birth of a new nation, Lee Tai-Young determined that from now on she would work for social causes, irrespective of economic considerations. This was made possible because of her resumption of a traditional gender role and her marital status. Soon afterwards, Lee Tai-Young's husband was called to Seoul to join a group of leaders who were involved in rebuilding the nation after the liberation.

From Seoul, Lee Tai-Young's husband wrote to her: 'From now on I will carry the burden [of taking care of the family] on my shoulders and you can fulfil your dream of studying law. There is a rumour that soon Seoul National University is going to become co-educational and open its doors to women.' Thus for Lee Tai-Young the opportunity to study law came from her supportive husband as a reward for her hard work, not only as breadwinner, but also as producer and protector of his lineage.

It was in March of 1946 that an official announcement was made about Seoul National University becoming co-educational. The chance to take the entrance examination was coming. But how could Lee Tai-Young prepare for it?

> The next day I dusted off the law books that I had brought from Seoul. When I left Seoul, I had left most of the household things behind, but I brought an apple- crate full of law books. The very next day after I got that letter, I opened *Introduction to Law*. I read those few books a couple of times. But I read them with my soul. How else could I have prepared for the entrance examination for the law department of Seoul National University in the next spring?

After she passed the entrance examination, another issue arose. 'This time it was about my educational background [academic qualifications],' she said.

---

6 Lee Tai-Young stated, 'Since then, during my entire career as a lawyer, for 37 years, I have not made a penny. At that time . . . I did not know I would end up founding the first free legal aid centre. I just made a resolution to devote my work to the public without any compensation.'

> Those who applied to the law department had been former students at Tokyo Imperial University, Keijo Imperial University [later Seoul National University], or other colleges before liberation. I was the only woman applicant, and I had graduated from the Home Economics Department of Ewha Womans College. The deans of national universities held a meeting to discuss my case and decided to give me a chance, the first woman applicant to the department of law in Korean history.

After Lee Tai-Young enrolled in the law department, she combined all of the responsibilities of a traditional wife with those of a full-time law student. It was not easy for her to become a student again at the age of 34, with a politically prominent husband who had countless guests visiting him daily at home. She also had three children to raise and an elderly mother-in-law to take care of. And in her second year of law college she gave birth to a daughter, her fourth child, whom she breast-fed daily while attending law college.

In taking the very demanding judicial examination, Lee Tai-Young faced even more acute gender role problems. All the male students would take two to three years, and sometimes up to 10 years, to prepare for the judicial examination (West 1991, Murphy 1967). During this period students acquire the status of 'koshisang'.[7] A koshisang typically spends most of his waking hours (12 to 18 hours) in isolation, studying for the examination. He does this in a secluded place, such as an isolated room in a Buddhist monastery in a remote area, or later a quiet cubicle in a commercial study hall especially designed for those who are preparing for koshi examinations. During this preparatory period, a koshisang is supported by the family, so that he can devote his time and energy totally to prepare for the examination. Being a woman, however, Lee Tai-Young found herself in a totally different situation:

> When the time came for me to take the koshi, I needed to study a lot more. But I could not mention that to my mother-in-law. It was already too much for me to ask for her understanding when I was absent so much from home and domestic duties to study law. Taking time off from home to go to college was already beyond the norm for a married woman. On top of that, requesting additional time off from home just to prepare for the examination seemed inexcusable.

Eventually she chose the strategy of prolonging her student status, which she had already negotiated with her mother-in-law as an undergraduate, by entering the graduate programme in law. Though she took only a couple of graduate courses, she pretended that she had to attend classes every day as she had done as an undergraduate. In this way she was able to find some time away from home to go to the college library and prepare for the examination. Unfortunately, Lee Tai-Young failed the Judicial examination at her first attempt. 'Only five out of thousands passed the first judicial examination held in 1950. . . . Those who passed had been studying law in Japan before liberation,' she said. This she saw as one of the explanations for her failure.

[7] Literally it means students preparing for the higher civil service examination [later the judicial examination].

Undaunted, Lee Tai-Young made up her mind to try one more time. While she was preparing for the next examination, the Korean War (1950–53) broke out. Like many others, the Lee family left Seoul and resettled in Pusan, crammed together with many relatives and friends. Living conditions were not at all favourable for Lee Tai-Young to prepare for the examination. Her solution was to live by herself in a quiet place, where she could concentrate on studying, far from household duties and war events. When Lee Tai-Young made her intention known to retake the Judicial examination, the family accepted it without much resistance. She felt a certain desperation though. 'I made up my mind that I would commit suicide if I failed this time. Why? How could I face my family after living by myself and leaving my children behind at home? It was unutterable [for a married woman].'

In 1952, Lee passed the judicial examination. The celebrations that followed illustrate the social significance of her success, which became the cover story of the major newspapers. The Lee-Chyung family celebrated the occasion. Public celebrations were announced. The first of these was organised by Dr Helen Kim, President of Ewha Womans College from which Lee Tai-Young graduated. Dr Kim set up a huge white tent and invited three hundred guests. Considering that this happened during the Korean War and among refugees in Pusan, this festivity was on a grand scale. The second celebration was organised by the Director of the Research Center for Women's Problems on a ship in Pusan Harbor. At this second celebration, her husband, Dr Chyung, also received an award for being a supportive husband throughout Lee Tai-Young's ordeal.

6 CONCLUSION

The concept of 'modern subject', that is, a modern person as a rational and autonomous agent, originated during the Enlightenment. Many feminist writers have noted how Western ideas equated maleness with humanness (see Bordo 1986, Pitkin 1984, Di Stefano 1991, Irigaray 1985). For women, the process of acquiring modern structures of consciousness involved moving between what Linda Gordon has called female experiences and feminist identity (Gordon 1986: 14). This is precisely what we find in the life history of Lee Tai-Young.

Lee Tai-Young's emergence as a modern subject became possible due to structural factors, in particular on the one hand the expansion of educational opportunities, especially at a missionary women's college, and national liberation on the other. It also depended on cultural processes mediated by family and marriage, such as a 'revolutionary' and supportive mother and a triangle of male sponsorship, composed of her brother/substitute father, her mentor and her husband.

Lee Tai-Young's public speeches reveal her own important contribution to the development of her self-awareness as a feminist in modern Korea. In the first 'I Am a Girl' speech, she emerged as a speaking subject whose everyday view/practical consciousness turned into discursive consciousness. In her second speech, 'Please Educate Us Regardless of Gender', she not only recognised the gap between ideal and reality, but also articulated the means by which to overcome it, namely additional education and the creation of gender equality. In her college years, her position became definitely feminist and 'controversial'. Thus in her third speech, 'Korean Women, Second Generation Noras', she advocated an active fight for justice and against women's domestic oppression.

As a woman in a society undergoing colonial modernisation while retaining many Confucian traits, she found that there were limits to her feminist goals. She tactfully opted to negotiate her role as an economically productive member of the family, handing control of the household budget to her mother-in-law and deciding to forego gainful employment, once national liberation made normalisation of the patriarchal family possible. Her emerging feminist vision combined women's liberation from domestic labour with an unquestioned acceptance of the traditional gender division of labour. Female experiences and feminist identity thus co-existed uneasily in Lee Tai-Young as a modern gendered subject. Yet, Lee Tai-Young, the first woman to pass the national judicial examination, reached the pinnacle of Korean society, which until then had been reserved for a few men from prominent families. In doing so, she not only extended the traditional honour to her own family, but also to half of Korea's population—women.

7 REFERENCES

Ableman, Nancy. 1997. Women's Class Mobility and Identities in South Korea: A Gendered, Transnational, and Narrative Approach. *Journal of Asian Studies* 56 no 2: 398–420.

Bordo, Susan. 1986. The Cartesian Masculinization of Thought. *Signs* 11: 439–56.

Bourdieu, Pierre. 1990 (1980). *The Logic of Practice*. Stanford: Stanford University Press.

Bourdieu, Pierre. 1977. *Outline of a Theory of Practice*. Cambridge: Cambridge University Press.

de Lauretis, Teresa, ed. 1987. *Feminist Studies/Critical Studies*. Bloomington: Indiana University Press.

Di Stefano, Christine. 1991. *Configurations of Masculinity: A Feminist Perspective on Modern Political Theory*. Ithaca, NY: Cornell University Press.

Drachman, Virginia G. 1998. *Sisters in Law: Women Lawyers in Modern American History*. Cambridge: Harvard University Press.

Epstein, Cynthia F. 1991 (1981). *Women in Law*. New York: Basic Books.

Ferguson, Kathy E. 1991. *The Man Question: Visions of Subjectivity in Feminist Theory*. Berkeley: University of California Press.

Giddens, Anthony. 1990. *Consequences of Modernity*. Stanford: Stanford University Press.

Gordon, Linda. 1986. What's New in Women's History. In *Feminist Studies/Critical Studies*, edited by Teresa de Lauretis. Bloomington: Indiana University Press.

Habermas, Jürgen. 1984. *The Theory of Communicative Action.* Vol 1. *Reason and the Rationalization.* Boston: Beacon Press.

Hegel, GWF. 1967. *The Phenomenology of Mind.* Trans. JB Baillie. New York: Harper and Row.

Irigaray, Luce. 1985. *Speculum of the Other Woman.* Trans. Gillian C Gill. Ithaca, NY: Cornell University Press.

Kim, Yung-chyung. 1979. *Women of Korea: A History from Ancient Times to 1945.* Seoul: Ewha Womans University Press.

Murphy, J. 1967. *Legal Education in a Developing Nation: The Korean Experience.* Dobbs Ferry, NY: Oceana Publications.

Pitkin, Hannah. 1984. *Fortune Is a Woman.* Berkeley: University of California Press.

Soh, Chunghee Sarah. 1991. *Women in Korean Politics.* Boulder: Westview Press.

Strawn, Sonia. 1988. *Where There Is No Path: Lee Tai-Young, Korean Pioneer for Women's Rights—Her Story.* Seoul, Korea: Legal Aid Center for Family Relations.

West, James. 1991. *Education of the Legal Profession in Korea.* Seoul: International Legal Studies.

26

Women Lawyers in Japan:
Contradictory Factors in Status

YURIKO KAMINAGA, JÖRN WESTHOFF

Abstract

This article discusses Japanese women lawyers as a distinctly élite group in Japanese society. Our historical overview shows that, in contrast to women in Japanese society as a whole, their membership of the legal profession conveys on them special social acceptance. However, empirical data from a 1991 survey also indicate that they do not remain unaffected by being associated with the low status of Japanese women in general. Their professional situation and their own views on women's rights are researched and analysed using two key factors, ie Factor E referring to their élite condition as professionals, and Factor L referring to their low status as women.

1 INTRODUCTION

1.1 General Observations

WOMEN IN LAW constitute a distinctly élite social stratum among Japanese women. At the same time their activities are constrained, reflecting Japanese women's low status in the labour market and in society at large. For the purposes of this paper, the former will be referred to as Factor E (or Elite Factor), the latter as Factor L (or Low Status Factor). Following introductory observations regarding Factor L (Section 1.3), the main part of this paper will be devoted to an analysis of the élite condition of women lawyers deriving from their professional status. Basic statistics on numbers, typical types of work and clients of women lawyers will be followed by an assessment of their attitudes toward their own job, and their role and position in the profession and in Japanese society at large.

1.2 Methodology

The data on which this paper is based are partly the outcome of a survey conducted in February and March 1991, broadly confirmed by a follow-up in 1997—the first research ever on the working conditions of women lawyers in Japan. Because of their small numbers, women lawyers had previously not been counted as an independent category even in such a large survey as that carried out on behalf of the Japanese Federation of Bar Assocations in 1986, entitled *Nichibenren Gyomu Chosa* (hereafter *Gyomu Chosa*). In 1991, questionnaires were sent to a random sample of 199 female lawyers working in the Tokyo area. As the response rate was fairly low (22 per cent), the findings cannot be regarded as conclusive.[1]

1.3 Women in Japan

At first glance, women in Japan today appear to make use of their equal rights to the same extent as women in other industrialised countries. Neither the share of women among the overall work force (40 per cent in 1990) nor the total percentage of women in gainful employment (50 per cent in 1991) display any significant difference (Weber 1997: 5). However, there are indications of the continuing impact of certain semi-traditional ideas, forms of behaviour and social expectations on women's working biography, some of which are rooted in more recent history.

In post-war Japan, Japanese women were still expected to give up their jobs at the time of marriage. Most firms would dismiss women upon their marriage (*kekkon taishoku*), in the expectation that their productivity, in any case lower than that of male workers, would decrease further after marriage because of their duties as mothers and housewives (Upham 1987: 131f.). This tradition is rooted in and had contributed to Japan's economic rise after the Meiji Restauration in 1868, when young unmarried women started working in the export-oriented textile industry and earning the country foreign currency, which enabled Japan to build up its heavy industry on which its economic rise was based. In line with the expectations young women had in a rural society, women industrial workers fortunate enough to have survived the unhygenic working and living conditions in factories and living quarters, returned to their former lives, which sooner or later meant marriage, children and working in the primary industries or in small, usually family-based enterprises.

---

[1] The low response rate itself poses a question regarding their status in terms of Factor E and Factor L. The reasons for non-participation in such a survey could be: (1) business/work overload; (2) indifference to or avoidance of women's issues. Also, it is well known that research into the professions, especially the legal profession, poses particular problems as they tend to be flooded with questionnaires of all kinds.

Although due to a shortage of male workers during the war, young women in post-war Japan were already employed in white- and grey-collar work, full-time work continued to be reserved exclusively for young unmarried women. As late as the early 1960s, only some eight per cent of the female labour force were married (Post-Kobayashi 1994: 315). With the rapid growth of the Japanese economy from 1959, the increasing demand for workers led to a mobilisation of older and married women. Nevertheless, in most cases they were not hired as regular workers, but only on a part-time basis or with temporary contracts (Weber 1997: 7).

In 1975, Japan signed the UN Convention on the Abolition of Discrimination against Women. However, the Convention was not ratified by the Japanese Diet for another 10 years. It was due to international pressure and the government's intention to present Japan as a modern nation, that the idea of equal rights for men and women, which the strong conservative camp especially in the governing Liberal-Democratic party (LDP) regarded as un-Japanese, finally made its way through the Diet and led to the passing of the Equal Employment Opportunities Act (*Danjo Kôyô Kikai Kintôhô*) of 1985.

The Equal Employment Opportunities Act expressly prohibits unequal treatment of men and women with respect to dismissal, in-firm training and company welfare programmes. The Equal Employment Opportunities Act merely recommends equal treatment and requests that the employer 'make every effort' to introduce equal opportunities into the assignment of work and into promotion procedures. The political parties in power hold the view that this obligation, although legally unenforceable, will work in favour of women, because 'administrative guidance' (*gyôsei shidô*) can exert a certain pressure (Marutschke 1999: 216). While in other fields (eg pollution control) *gyôsei shidô* has produced good results, it is unlikely to work in the field of equal opportunities. The 'recommendations' contained in the Act already represent a compromise between government and employers' organisations, the latter having argued for a 'reform', ie the elimination of certain rules from the Labour Standards Act meant to protect women from, for instance, night shifts.

Factor L is alive not only in labour relations but also in society in general (Lebra 1976; Hielscher 1980; Herold 1980; Braw and Gunnarson 1982; Gô 1983; Ishikawa 1989; Hirowatari 1993). Women continue to be regarded and treated as inferior to men in terms not only of physical but also of mental capacities. On the other hand, a heavy burden is placed upon them as families and society expect the traditional, harmony-oriented, sacrificing mother and daughter to be solely responsible for child-rearing and care for elderly parents (typically parents-in-law, especially if the husband is the eldest son and thus traditionally the future head of the family). Although today one rarely sees in Japanese streets women tying up their husbands' shoelaces, wives are still expected to serve and be considerate of men's needs.

Strong and powerful women who are successful in their careers are rare in public and political life, with the exception of Takako Doi, the charismatic leader of the Japanese Social Democratic Party. The influence of women in policy- and law-making remains small. Though formal equality of men and women is provided for in the Japanese constitution, eg in Article 14 and Article 24 which deals with equal treatment in family law, traditional thoughts and patterns of behaviour, such as the concept of *ie-seido*, the feudal 'family system', work against a common awareness of women's equal rights even today, and even in the understanding and interpretation of the law (Westhoff 1999—especially for matters concerning family law).

2 WOMEN'S RIGHTS COMMITTEE OF THE JAPANESE BAR

In 1976, the Japanese Federation of Bar Associations responded to this situation by organising a special committee on women's right (hereafter Women's Rights Committee). The committee's objective was: (1) to conduct research into women's legal status and rights; (2) to investigate existing laws and recommend any changes; (3) to explore and resolve cases of serious infringement of women's rights; (4) to negotiate and make recommendations to governmental bodies. The first year of the committee's work can be taken to have had a certain symbolic interest. While working on a large-scale inquiry into the 'national action plan' drawn up by the Prime Minister's Office to accommodate the 1975 UN Mexico Resolution in the context of the International Women's Year, the committee also had to investigate and settle the problem of sexual harassment committed by instructors in the national Legal Training and Research Institute (Japan Federation of Bar Associations 1977: 59).

In its annual report in 1980, the Committee deplored the scarcity of women in the legal profession (a total of 417, equating to some 3.6 per cent of the lawyer population) (Japan Federation of Bar Associations 1980: 63). Since its inception, the committee has been actively involved in investigating a whole range of aspects of women's right, such as the Equal Employment Opportunities Act, the treatment of gender stratification in textbooks for schools, existing laws on children's rights, the sexual division of labour, part-time workers' rights and so forth.

In 1991 their agenda comprised a recommendation on the partial amendment of the Equal Employment Opportunities Act, including the following: (1) prohibition of all sex discrimination in hiring procedures and in the work place; (2) employers' obligations to prevent/correct sexual harassment; (3) affirmative action in specific occupational categories and/or ranks and positions; (4) the establishment of an Equal Opportunities Commission to replace the Equal Opportunities Mediation Commission; (5) the shortening of legal working hours; and (6) maternity regulations and social security measures to support men and women in employment. Other issues on their agenda were the drafting of a law on child care leave, the organisation of a symposium on child care and nursing leave, the promotion of equality in education and the drafting of a recommendation on a proposed law on child support payment (Japan Federation of Bar Associations 1991: 92–4).

The committee has also begun an investigation into women's participation in decision-making processes within governmental bodies and commissions. At the same time, it has insisted that the bar itself should undergo similar investigations to be seen to be setting a good example. The following will show how great the need for such investigations still is.

3 THE 1991 SURVEY

3.1 Demographic Factors

Reflecting the fact that before 1980 fewer than 10 per cent of the successful candidates for the national bar were women, the respondents of the 1991 survey tended to be young: 21 per cent were in their twenties and 36 per cent in their thirties, compared to only 24 per cent, 19 per cent and 17 per cent in their forties, fifties and in older age groups respectively. This situation, though slightly skewed in favour of the youngest group, is mirrored by the respondents' years of experience. More than half had one to 10 years (with 48 per cent having fewer than five years and 10 per cent five to nine years), 22 per cent had 10 to 19 years, 14 per cent 20 to 29 years, and only 4 per cent had more than 30 years (for a general picture of women in the legal profession in Japan, see Tables 1–3).

As to marital status, a little over half of the respondents were married, but fewer than half had children under 20, ie minors as defined by Japanese civil law. Their income level was apparently above the general average income of Japanese

Table 1: Women Lawyers in Japan after World War II

	1949	1955	1960	1965	1970	1975	1980	1985	1991
Lawyers	3	11	46	79	191	320	437	622	845
Judges	2	0	0	0	0	56	75	93	141
Prosecutors	1	2	4	7	7	19	30	25	49

Table 2: Women Lawyers in Japan in 1991

	Total	Number of Women (%)
Lawyers	14,433	845 (5.9)
Judges	2,823	141 (5.0)
Prosecutors	1,173	49 (4.2)
Total	18,429	1,035 (5.6)

Table 3: Years of Experience of Lawyers in Tokyo Area and Women Lawyers in the Survey

	Tokyo Area (%)	Survey Sample (%)
< 5 years	98 (22.6)	19 (48.7)
5–8 years	73 (16.9)	3 (7.7)
> 9 years	262 (60.5)	16 (43.6)

men—not to mention the general average income level of women, which was 50.3 per cent of that of men (1989) (Japan Federation of Bar Association 1991: 92). Half of them took less than 50 per cent responsibility for household chores—in striking contrast to the average Japanese working woman in non-professional jobs who, as a norm, shoulders 100 per cent of all domestic duties.

The reason for this disparity may be that these women lawyers were either unmarried and/or childless, or that their professional duties prevented them from taking a full part in domestic work. Other explanations are conceivable for married women lawyers, such as: (1) their marital relationship may be more democratic, that is, less divided along gender lines and reflecting the legal ideal they are meant to be committed to; (2) their high income may allow them to buy in domestic help or to eat out etc.; (3) various combinations of (1) and (2). All that the data suggest is that women lawyers are relatively privileged compared to women in Japan generally. Here we see Factor E in operation with respect to social status.

3.2 Legal Work

The biggest group among the 1991 respondents were employed by law firms (52 per cent), which might have been due to their relatively young age and modest level of experience. In contrast, only 21 per cent of all private practitioners in Tokyo were associates, ie had employee status (Committee on Legal Practice 1988: 32). (Table 4) With 26 per cent, women were also under-represented in partnerships, as 39 per cent of all lawyers in the Tokyo area had partnership status. The largest number (26 per cent of female lawyers) worked for only two-lawyer law firms. Work in firms with over 11 lawyers was as rare for female lawyers as for men.

The next largest group of female lawyers were sole practitioners (21 per cent). This may mean that women lawyers tend to be young and have not yet established themselves professionally, possibly experiencing difficulties in respect of office management or client recruitment. Compared to an overall 41 per cent in the *Gyomu Chosa* by the Japanese Federation of Bar Associations, women lawyers were under-represented in sole practice (*ibid*). They were over-represented in small firms with two to five lawyers (52 per cent), compared to the per-

Table 4: Number of Lawyers in Law Firms in Tokyo Area

	Nichibenren Gyomu Chosa (men and women combined) (%)	Survey (women only) (%)
Sole Practitioners	304 (40.5)	9 (21)
2 Lawyers	171 (22.8)	11 (26)
3 Lawyers	89 (11.8)	2 (4)
4 Lawyers	54 (7.3)	4 (10)
5 Lawyers	31 (4.1)	1 (2)
6–10 Lawyers	81 (10.8)	5 (12)
More than 11 Lawyers	23 (3.1)	8 (19)

centage for all lawyers (46 per cent) given in the *Gyomu Chosa*. This is an indicator of the presence of Factor L. Unlike the situation in other countries, women lawyers in Japan usually cannot rely on fathers or husbands as partners in law firms. In this respect, therefore, women lawyers in Japan do not differ from women working in other fields, thus Factor L remains the main factor for their over-representation in small law firms. (These results derived from the 1991 survey were confirmed by a follow-up survey of 1997, the latter showing only minor deviations.)

A serious controversy over the policy for hiring women in law firms is worth mentioning here. On the occasion of the graduation from the national Legal Training and Research Institute, where all candidates for legal careers, having passed the national bar examination, have to enrol for further professional training, women students as a group submitted a complaint to the Japanese Federation of Bar Associations about firms' discriminatory hiring practices (Japan Federation of Bar Associations 1976). They had found not only that women were facing various kinds of discrimination, such as low initial salaries, discouragement by interviewers, or priority being given to male candidates, but that one third of the recruiting firms had advertised posts as for 'men only'. (This practice is to be prohibited by the Equal Opportunities Act of 1999.)

In 1987, a leading young woman lawyer wrote an article in *Liberty and Justice*, the official periodical of the Japanese Federation of Bar Associations, criticising the employment situation for women in the field of law even after the enactment of the Equal Employment Opportunities Act in 1985 (Fukushima 1987). She referred to the results of the questionnaire that her voluntary group had sent to new graduates from the Institute. Various forms of gender-based discrimination were revealed in their responses: (1) blatant statements along the lines of 'We don't want women'; (2) discouraging remarks to candidates, such as 'In the legal profession women are still disadvantaged'; (3) men being given preference over women in the same interviewing round; (4) failure even to respond to applications from women; (5) telling the candidate that the office had a woman already and that that was enough, and so on. Firms' reluctance to hire women was reflected in their taking longer to reach a decision and keeping women candidates waiting. Female interviewees had been asked discriminatory questions concerning their private lives, such as their prospects of marriage, their intention to have children, the identity, characteristics and religious beliefs of their partners etc.

The surveys which form the basis of this paper did not include any questions about this kind of discrimination at the level of entry into the profession, but the 1991 survey did ask two related questions, one general and one more specifically personal, about women lawyers' feelings regarding discrimination in their everyday working lives (Table 5). At a general level, 43 per cent saw women as mildly discriminated against at work, while 7 per cent registered evidence of 'severe discrimination'. Only three lawyers thought that being a woman worked in their favour, while 16 (38 per cent) were undecided. Referring to personal experience, 35 per cent admitted having been 'mildly discriminated against', and four per cent felt 'severely discriminated against'.

The difference between these two sets of figures may be explained by the fact that many of the respondents tended to be young women in their twenties and being discriminated against for them was a problem of relevance only to older women. Alternatively, women lawyers might like to see themselves as more successful and better placed than the average woman in their age groups. It seems that Factor E is working specifically for the youngest group.

Women lawyers have difficulty gathering information about the situation and working conditions of female colleagues.[2] One reason is that three quarters of female lawyers are the only representatives of their sex in the office. This situation not only isolates women lawyers in the workplace but also strengthens Factor E. Each of them is a pioneer ('the first') in the legal workforce and likely to remain so for some considerable time, if not forever. They are the chosen ones, the stars of their firms as well as of the entire legal profession. They are there to demonstrate that the profession abides by the ideal of gender equality in Japan.

Table 5: How Being a Woman Affects Legal Practice

	−2 (%)	−1 (%)	No Effect (%)	+1 (%)	+2 (%)
In general	3 (9)	13 (42)	11 (36)	3 (10)	0
Own cases	2 (7)	11 (36)	13 (42)	4 (13)	1 (3)

[2] Some all-women law firms have been set up in Japan. Details regarding their practice remain to be studied. A brief report 'Fujin nomi niyoru Kyodo Jimusho' ('All-Women Law Firms') can be found in *Liberty and Justice*, Vol 27, No 5, May 1976, pp 44–45.

3.3 Type of Work

Just like their male colleagues, most respondents in the 1991 survey were generalists, and 40 per cent of their working hours were devoted to court work. However, one quarter of respondents had no court work, and about one fifth spent less than 20 per cent of their time handling law suits. The majority of cases dealt with by women were inheritance cases (43 per cent), followed by landlord-tenant cases (41 per cent). 35 per cent mentioned family law, and 31 per cent miscellaneous civil matters. Just under 24 per cent dealt with company law, only 21 per cent with tort cases (Table 6).

Table 6: Type of Work and Women's Cases

	Inheritance (%)	Tenancy (%)	Family (%)	Civil (%)	Company (%)	Tort (%)
General	18 (43)	17 (41)	15 (35)	13 (31)	10 (24)	9 (21)
Women	24 (28)	12 (33)	16 (44)	4 (11)	0	4 (11)

No comparable data are available for lawyers in the Tokyo area generally, but some interesting statistics are to be found in *Gyomu Chosa* (Committee on Legal Practice 1988: 64). It lists debt collection cases as most common, making up over 20 per cent of lawyers' civil work. These are followed by landlord-tenant cases (11 per cent). Other major areas of civil work are property transactions, executions of titles to a debt, tort, credit collections and inheritance. These figures indicate that women lawyers are engaged in, or assigned to, very specific areas of law, mainly family law or cases involving the middle or lower class. They are excluded from the mainstream or lucrative legal practices. This type of case distribution is likely to contribute to the low status of women in the profession, or to Factor L. Considering that male lawyers in Japan do not engage in particularly lucrative cases either, the effect is relative. But, when examined in the light of sex discrimination in hiring practices and male domination in handling court cases, Factor L is conspicuous (Japan Federation of Bar Associations 1976: 73).

3.4 Clientele

But did women lawyers think that they should represent women clients and work for the upgrading of women's status in Japan? Their actual female clientele varied. Apart from five who had no women clients, the rest were divided into four groups. One quarter had more than 50 per cent, another quarter had between 30 and 49 per cent; a little over a quarter had 10 to 29 per cent, and the last quarter had fewer than 10 per cent. Female clients bring in mostly inheritance, family and divorce cases (Table 6). Among these female client cases, 74 per cent did not involve women's rights issues. Even where such issues were of relevance, the cases tended to be family and divorce cases. Labour law or sexual harassment at work were each mentioned only once.

3.5 Views on Japanese Law

When asked whether, in their legal practice, they had found problematic laws and/or cases in terms of women's rights today, women lawyers' responses were split. While 41 per cent answered 'yes' (ie conscious of women's rights issues), 43 per cent replied 'no'. The degree of consciousness rose with age: 71 per cent of women older than 50, 50 per cent of those in their forties, 43 per cent of respondents in their thirties, and 33 per cent under 29 (Table 7). Another relevant factor was the nature of their legal practice; those dealing with women's rights cases more often saw problems in existing laws (89 per cent). By contrast, 65 per cent of those who do not deal with women's rights cases saw no problems.

About 36 per cent were concerned that overall the Japanese legal system did not sufficiently protect women's rights, but a little more than that percentage (40 per cent) were undecided. Only a small portion of respondents (14 per cent) praised the Japanese legal system for being responsive to women's rights issues. Age proved to be a weak correlation, but a strong correlation was evident with respect to women's rights consciousness: 65 per cent of those who were conscious regarded women's rights as insufficiently protected by Japanese law, with 24 per cent undecided; corresponding figures for those classified as 'not conscious' were only 24 per cent and 65 per cent respectively (Table 8).

Table 7: Cross-Tabulation of Age and Rights Consciousness

	20s	30s	40s	50s and over	Total
Conscious	3	6	3	5	17 (49%)
Not conscious	6	6	4	2	18 (51%)
Total	9 (26%)	12 (34%)	7 (20%)	7 (20%)	35 (100%)

Table 8: Cross-Tabulation of Rights Consciousness and Views on Japanese Law

	The law protects women's rights	The law does not protect women's rights	Total
Conscious	11	6	17 (50%)
Not conscious	4	13	17 (50%)
Total	15 (44%)	19 (56%)	34 (100%)

Almost half of the women lawyers stated that there were, indeed, laws which specifically helped to protect women. Age was especially correlated to this positive view (71 per cent in their fifties and over, 63 per cent in their forties, 60 per cent in their thirties). The youngest lawyers in their twenties stood apart as a very distinct group, with 57 per cent denying the existence of any laws supportive of women's rights (Table 9).

Table 9: Cross-Tabulation of Age and Views on 'Helpfulness' of Japanese Law

	20s	30s	40s	50s and over	
Yes	3	6	5	5	19 (58%)
No	4	4	3	0	13 (39%)
	7 (21%)	11 (33%)	8 (24%)	7 (21%)	33 (100%)

(One person in her thirties had an idiosyncratic answer.)

Experience also proved to be significant in terms of women lawyers being able to identify such laws. All women's rights lawyers (defined as lawyers who handle women's rights cases) took a positive view, while those with no such cases were unable to think of any. Among those who thought that women's rights were not protected by the existing legal system, 79 per cent nevertheless took a positive view with regard to individual items of legislation.

However, when asked about the Equal Employment Opportunities Act of 1985, more than half of those taking a positive view were critical of its effectiveness. Moreover, 78 per cent agreed with the following statement: 'Given the established custom of sex discrimination, the Equal Employment Opportunities Act is not sufficiently forceful to challenge reality.' Some 20 per cent also thought that the law had an adverse effect, in that it tied women to traditionally low-status employment and widened the gap between male and female positions (Table 10). These responses contrast with the finding that women lawyers who did not criticise the law as ineffective were those who believed in the existing legal system as a protector of women's rights.

Table 10: Cross-Analysis of Views on the 'Helpfulness' of Japanese Law and 'EOA'

	EOA does not work	Not forceful enough to challenge custom	Total
Yes	8	10	18 (58%)
No	8	5	13 (42%)
Total	16 (52%)	15 (48%)	31 (100%)

3.6 Sexual Harassment

Further questions about current women's rights issues were couched in the form
of multiple-choice questions. One of these concerned sexual harassment, a topic
which was beginning to gain attention from the mass media in Japan. Three
quarters of respondents agreed that sexual harassment was a real and serious
problem. 63 per cent also agreed with the statement that it was a serious invasion of women's rights and dignity. But 32 per cent thought that 'the claim of
sexual harassment is an over-reaction on the part of the women involved'.

65 per cent of lawyers who were conscious of women's rights problems in
Japan, compared to 35 per cent of those who were not, considered sexual
harassment to be a 'real and serious' problem for women. Of those who felt that
women's rights were not sufficiently protected by the existing system, 80 per
cent thought that sexual harassment was 'real and serious'.

Women's rights-consciousness also affected responses to the statement,
'Sexual harassment is a serious invasion of women's rights and dignity.' 70 per
cent of those who were conscious of problems and 44 per cent of those not conscious agreed to it. This might mean that in order to be able to conceptualise a
behaviour such as sexual harassment at a period when the concept itself is still
unclear and in a society which has customarily been tolerant of this form of
behaviour, one needs to be conscious of women's rights.

3.7 Affirmative Action Policy

The final set of questions on current issues concerned affirmative action policy
in favour of women of the kind to be found, for instance, in the United States of
America. Over half of respondents regarded such a policy as instrumental to an
improvement in women's position in society. However, 35 per cent said:
'Affirmative action should be taken in favour of socially disadvantaged minorities, but not in favour of women.' The same percentage was of the view that
affirmative action would provide further incentives to companies and schools to
be indulgent towards discrimination, once they had attained a certain proportion of women in their workforce. One fifth also agreed with the statement,
'Affirmative action is based on the underestimation of women's ability, treating
women as being incompetent in competition with men.'

One interesting finding concerns the relationship between respondents' views
of the Equal Employment Opportunities Act on the one hand and of an affirmative action policy on the other. Most of those (three quarters) critical of the
law's effectiveness recommended 'affirmative action' to promote women's status in society.

Affirmative action was supported as a measure to improve women's status by
76.5 per cent of those who are conscious of women's rights in Japan, in contrast

to 47 per cent of those who are not. But their assessment of the existing legal system in terms of protection for women bore no relation to their support of affirmative action. 60 per cent of both those viewing it positively as well as of those critical of it believed that affirmative action would improve women's status in society. This might suggest that an affirmative action measure could gain support from different ideological positions and be regarded as a neutral instrument. It might also insinuate that women's status in Japan is so low that women lawyers feel that some concrete steps to ameliorate the situation should be taken immediately.

However, the majority of those who felt discriminated against in their legal work did not support affirmative action (only 31 per cent thought that it might work). By contrast, 68 per cent of those who themselves did not feel discriminated against supported affirmative action, as did the four respondents who saw being a woman as beneficial to their professional activities. These findings allow for two interpretations: either respondents concluded from their own experience that the reality of infringement of women's right was so severe in Japan that no governmental policy would work, and that they therefore became pessimistic; or an affirmative action policy appealed to unconcerned lawyers as a substitute for fundamental legal and value changes in Japanese society.

The other side of an affirmative action was represented by support for the statement, 'Affirmative action measures should be taken for other socially disadvantaged people, not for women.' Over half (56 per cent) of very young women lawyers under 30 agreed with this, while agreement from representatives of older generations declined in inverse proportion to their age: 40 per cent of those in their thirties; 33 per cent of those in their forties; and none of those in their fifties and older. These data once again raise the issue of the special characteristics of very young women lawyers in terms of Factor E. The very young may not have encountered any discriminatory treatment against themselves or other women because of either their inexperience or their élite status. We will return to this issue in our concluding remarks.

Encountering cases of discrimination is relevant to the realisation that discrimination exists. There were some women's rights lawyers (defined as lawyers who handle women's rights cases) who agreed with 'affirmative action in favour of other socially disadvantaged groups but not in favour of women', while 43 per cent of those without such cases were supportive. There was also a relation with women lawyers' concern for women's legal rights. None of those in support of women lawyers' duty to work on behalf of women agreed with the statement, compared to almost half of those opposed to it.

3.8 Supporting the Women's Cause

In response to the question, 'There is a view that women lawyers should work on behalf of women, do you agree or disagree?' 31 per cent of respondents in this survey strongly disagreed and 26 per cent disagreed (overall level of disagreement: 57 per cent). Only six respondents (14 per cent) agreed, and 29 per cent were undecided.

Responses to this question by women lawyers who were conscious of women's rights fell into three categories. While 29 per cent agreed, those who disagreed and those who were undecided were divided equally. Of those who saw the existing legal system as not conducive to protecting women's rights, 20 per cent agreed, 33 per cent were undecided, and 47 per cent disagreed. Of those who were of the opposite view regarding the legal system, 17 per cent agreed and 67 per cent disagreed.

A problem becomes visible when cross-tabulated, namely the existence of a group of women lawyers who refused to be associated with women's rights issues. Among those who were unable to identify a law designed for the protection of women, 69 per cent could not decide whether the legal system was protecting women's rights (ie indifferent); 69 per cent of the same respondents expressed disagreement with the proposition that female lawyers should work on behalf of women (ie insensitive). Even those who had themselves experienced discrimination did not think that women lawyers should work on behalf of women.

These findings are perplexing and discouraging for those who would regard women lawyers as the proper representatives and protectors of women's rights. They are expected to be understanding and concerned because of their marginal and contradictory situation, torn between Factor E, ie their élite position as lawyers compared to other Japanese women, and Factor L, that is their low social status due to their sex.

4 CONCLUSION AND FUTURE OUTLOOK

The survey findings reflect the fact that Factor L continues to be in operation within the legal profession itself. Women lawyers are not exempt from the low status allocated to women in Japanese society generally. An example of the low social acceptance of women lawyers as competent legal professionals emerged in the context of a survey amongst students in a class at Toho Gakuen Junior College. It turned out that students' readiness to rely on women lawyers as their legal representatives was limited to certain areas of law, such as divorce and family law. Hardly any of them would have wanted a female lawyer in cases concerning, for instance, negotiations with a construction company over faulty work (Table 11). This reflects, firstly, limited acceptance by clients, including women clients, and, secondly, an assumption on the part of society at large that using a woman lawyer in negotiations is likely to entail some form of disadvantage.

The dissociation on the part of women lawyers from a female clientele found in the study could be the reflection of this prejudice. At the same time, the low

Table 11: Preference for Sex of Lawyer on the Part of Young Women

Case Type	I %	II %	III %	IV %	V %
Criminal Arrest	14.5	31.6	43.4	9.2	1.3
Divorce	7.9	3.9	22.4	39.5	26.3
Negotiation	47.4	14.5	36.8	1.3	0

I   'I absolutely want a male lawyer'
II   no preference for sex
III   'I would rather have a male lawyer'
IV   'I would rather want a female lawyer'
V   'I absolutely want a female lawyer'

status of women in society does not make women look particularly promising as future clients: their financial resources are limited, as most of them are dependent on their husbands or, if they work full time, they earn about 60 per cent of men's incomes; their subservient attitudes prevent them from taking their grievances to the courts; and their low status in business makes for narrowly defined legal needs. All of which reduces their attraction as legal clients.

Besides, the legal logic of equal treatment and legal ethics of indiscriminatory representation and a ban of solicitation provide women lawyers with legal grounds to offer their services to anyone, regardless of sex. As long as they do not have women clients and women's right issues in their legal practice, women lawyers may remain as uninformed, indifferent and insensitive as some of the respondents in the study.

Factor E in their own status also prevents women lawyers from recognising other women's problems. The youngest group under 30 is a good example. Along with all other young women in Japan after the liberation movement and the governmental surrender to international pressure to implement women's right, they are, at least nominally, protected from blatant discrimination. In a society where women in professions and management are still pioneers (the 'first'), they are treated with respect, if not curiosity.[3] Before they realise that this is the result of the magic of youth and beauty, which Japanese men most appreciate in young women, and before they face the burden of family responsibilities, factor E may continue to play a major role in their self-perception.

Factor E outweighs Factor L in the legal profession for yet another reason. As recent feminist studies have revealed, the law has been a men's arena, dominated by male logic and male language (West 1988). Those who successfully master its logic and language as well as its mentality, are able to survive within it.

---

[3] This type of treatment by men in the office is prevalent in Japan, especially after the Equal Employment Opportunities Act came into force in 1986. Major reasons for this phenomenon are: (1) in the male-dominated society men become confused. Most of the time they treat women as a joke or try to patronise them as their 'mascot'. (2) Or they use women's presence as 'remission of a sin' vis-a-vis governmental supervision.

This may explain why women in the legal profession in Japan prefer equality to feminism. To reach the élite position of male lawyers, women lawyers may wish to dissociate themselves from women in society generally and from Factor L.

5 REFERENCES

Braw, Monica and Gunnarson, Hiroe, 1982. *Frauen in Japan. Zwischen Tradition und Aufbruch*, Frankfurt a. M.
Committee on Legal Practice, Japan Federation of Bar Associations, 1988. *Nihon no Hôritsu Jimusho* (Law Offices in Japan), Tokyo: Gyosei.
Fukushima, Mizuho, 1987. Sex Discrimination Shown in Recruitment of Associates by Law Firms, *Liberty and Justice* 38, No 12.
Gô, Daigoro, 1983. *The Family Relations in Japan*, London 1983.
Hayashi, Yoko, 1991. Josei hôritsuka no hanseiki (A Half-Century of Women in the Legal Profession), *Shosai no Mado*, No 405, pp 7–12.
Herold, Renate, 1980. *Die Blume am Arbeitsplatz. Japans Frauen im Beruf*, Tübingen 1980.
Hirowatari, Seigo, 1993. Die Förderung der Gleichberechtigung von Mann und Frau in Japan, in *Recht in Japan* 8, pp 39–63.
Hielscher, Gebhard (ed), 1980. *Die Frau* (= OAG-Reihe *Japan modern*, Vol 1), Berlin 1980.
Ishikawa, Eikichi (ed), 1989. *Ie to jôsei (House and Woman)*, Tokyo 1989.
Japan Federation of Bar Associations, 1976. Problems in the Recruitment of Law Firms, *Liberty and Justice* 27, No 5, pp 73–5.
Japan Federation of Bar Associations, 1977. Annual Report of Committees. *Liberty and Justice* 28, No 3, pp 59–60.
Japan Federation of Bar Associations, 1980, Annual Report of Committees, *Liberty and Justice* 31, No 3, pp 62–5.
Japan Federation of Bar Associations, 1991, Annual Report of Committees, *Liberty and Justice* 42, No 3, pp 92–4.
Linhart, Ruth, 1991. *Onna da kara. Weil ich eine Frau bin. Liebe, Ehe und Sexualität in Japan*, Wien 1991.
Lebra, Joyce *et al.* 1976. *Women in Changing Japan*, Boulder 1976.
Marutschke, Hans-Peter, 1999. *Einführung in das japanische Recht*, München 1999.
Post-Kobayashi, Bettina, 1994. Geschlechtliche Egalität in der Arbeitswelt. In: Ölschleger, Hans-Dieter *et al* (eds), *Individualität und Egalität im gegenwärtigen Japan*. Tokyo, 309–337.
Upham, Frank K., 1987. *Law and Social Change in Postwar Japan*, Cambridge (Mass.).
Weber, Claudia, 1997. *Frauenförderung auf Japanisch*, Frauenvorträge an der FernUniversität 12, FernUniversität—Gesamthochschule in Hagen.
West, Robin, 1988, Jurisprudence and Gender, *The University of Chicago Law Review* 55, No. 1, 1988.
Westhoff, Jörn, 1999, *Das Echo des ie: Nachwirkungen des Haussystems im modernen japanischen Familienrecht*, Munich.